Fictions of Masculinity

Fictions of Masculinity

Crossing Cultures, Crossing Sexualities

Edited by Peter F. Murphy

NEW YORK UNIVERSITY PRESS
New York and London

NEW YORK UNIVERSITY PRESS
New York and London

Library of Congress Cataloging-in-Publication Data
Fictions of masculinity : crossing cultures, crossing sexualities /
edited by Peter F. Murphy.
p. cm.
Includes bibliographical references and index.
ISBN 0-8147-5497-X—ISBN 0-8147-5498-8 (pbk.)
1. Masculinity (Psychology) in literature. 2. Literature,
Modern—20th century—History and criticism. I. Murphy, Peter
Francis.
PN56.M316F53 1994 93-44104
809′.9352041—dc20

New York University Press books are printed on
acid-free paper, and their binding materials are chosen for
strength and durability.

Manufactured in the United States of America

10 9 8 7 6 5 4 3 2 1

For

Paul Richmond,
David Brown, and Victor Chaltain.

Dear friends
who have tried,
over the past twenty years,
to keep me honest.

Man turns a little bit of soft, delicate and highly sensitive flesh into the factor which bestows power on him; he is blind to the warmth, the fragility and the hypersensitivity of his penis. . . . He does not see the softness of his glans, the fragility and extreme excitability of the frenum, the sensitivity of the shaft along the urethra, the rough tenderness of his scrotum. He tries, on the contrary, to desensitise the whole organ as best he can to give it the coldness and the hardness of metal. What he loses in enjoyment he hopes to compensate for in power; but if he gains an undeniable power symbol, what pleasure can he really feel with a weapon between his legs?

—EMMANUEL REYNAUD
Holy Virility: The Social Construction of Masculinity

Contents

Acknowledgments

In many ways this book represents more than just another collection of literary criticism. Feminism, as the guiding principle behind all of these chapters, provides a radically new way to understand the dynamics of interpersonal relationships. As a political theory and as a personal practice, feminism requires us to examine the way we think, the way we work, the way we love.

Since the late sixties and early seventies, when feminism began to have a profound effect on my life and on my politics, many people have contributed to my ability to bring a feminist perspective into my scholarship. Whereas not all of the people who have contributed something to the production of this anthology may see themselves as feminists, many do. Of these, I want to thank in particular, Claire Kahane and Ellen DuBois: teachers, colleagues, critics, and friends. Without their continued demand of me to be more rigorous in my thinking, to write more precisely, and to look beyond what appears to be obvious, my work in the field of feminism and masculinity would have remained much less sophisticated. They are not, of course, responsible for any remaining short-sightedness on my part.

Other colleagues who have made invaluable contributions to the editing and overall production of this book are Neil Schmitz, Bruce Jackson, and Carole Southwood. Neil has been a close friend, an invaluable mentor, and a fellow traveler throughout my many years in Buffalo. For this book he was always available to help me determine which essays to give serious consideration and which to eliminate; he was also there when the job seemed too daunting or the tough decisions imponderable. Bruce Jackson, an extraordinary critic in his own right, helped me to hone my writing skills and to understand more fully the job of an editor. Carole Southwood encouraged me to believe in the project even when the evidence seemed clearly in opposition to such optimism. Her ability as an editor was unsurpassed; her continual insights and suggestions improved the overall quality of this anthology.

For their support both of my scholarship and of my struggle to make feminism relevant to a critique of masculinity I want to thank Michael Kimmel and Thaïs Morgan. Michael has been a staunch supporter of this project since its inception several years ago, and Thaïs has been "the writer over my shoulder" since I began working with her on another project five years ago. Indeed, Thaïs has taught me more about writing than anyone else with whom I have worked over the course of my twenty-five years in the academy. Without both of their continued belief in this project I am not sure I would have made it to the end.

Over the past two decades I have been fortunate to have many close friends, male and female, who have struggled to make feminism a significant, even determining, factor in their lives. These friends, friends for whom personal and political change has remained central, are important to me in many ways, and it is with great pleasure that I acknowledge them here: Mike Boughn, Billy Burton, Diane Christian, Art Efron, Gladys Fox, Charles Haynie, Peter Hirshman, Paul Hogan, Bob Keesey, Jennifer Lehmann, Yvonne Price, and Jon Welch.

Two scholarly institutions in Buffalo, one old and one new, have assisted in the production of this book, and I want to thank them both: Talking Leaves Bookstore and Shuffaloff Press. And, although she will no doubt castigate me for mentioning her name in such a secondhand place as the acknowledgments, I will take the risk of thanking Susan Pearles whose support, love, and radical insights have contributed more to this work and to my life than any other singular experience.

At a time when political correctness may tend to encourage an uncritical embrace of feminism, multiculturalism, and any number of other "isms," friends who are either not influenced by these theories or even opposed to them are difficult to find. Two of my male friends, neither of whom are in the academy, have, through their unwillingness to accept many of the academy's assumptions, contributed immeasurably to my own critical engagement with a feminist perspective. Firsthand experience of masculinity in the North Country of New York State provides challenges and insights that any number of graduate seminars may never begin to approach. I want to acknowledge the difficult questions and the relentless disbelief of two of my most important critics (and friends)—Richard Chaltain and Steven Bowman.

As academics, many of us know how difficult the completion of any published work can be even with the encouragement of the Chair or of the Dean. Here, too, I was fortunate to have the unparalleled support of my Dean, Thomas Rocco and my Associate Dean, Anne Bertholf. For their interest in and commitment to the completion of this book I owe many thanks. Without their understanding of the problems one faces when trying to write the last paragraph or the last word (or even the first paragraph, for that matter), the completion of this anthology would certainly have been that much more formidable.

Others at Empire State College contributed to the successful completion of this book, but I want to mention, in particular, Rosemary Ruper and Emily Riley. I am grateful also for the scholarly examples set by two historians, Nick Cushner and Bob MacCameron. And for her computer wizardry, I thank Frieda Mendelsohn. For its financial contribution, which allowed me some much needed time off to complete the manuscript, I wish to acknowledge the SUNY Empire State College Foundation.

My graduate students at the Universidade Federal do Rio Grande do Sul in Porto Alegre, Brazil, where I was a Teaching Fulbright, forced me to clarify many of the ideas that inspired this collection. Even though we were involved in a seminar on "The Politics of Love," issues of male heterosexuality remained central to our discussions. Unwilling to accept my tendency toward generalization, these students solicited more lucid thinking and unambiguous characterization. Their contributions to this book, while subtle and indirect, have made it a better anthology.

I would be remiss if I did not thank Niko Pfund, my editor at New York University Press. Niko brings together a kindness and a rigor that is rare. Without his suggestions and observations this anthology would not have reached its present level of professionalism. In addition, some anonymous readers provided clear direction about strengths and weaknesses, and although I did not agree with all of their comments, their contributions were extremely helpful.

Most of the chapters in this collection are published here for the first time, but some have appeared previously. For permission to reprint the chapters by Habegger, Radavich, Murphy, Leverenz, and Dellamora I want to thank, respectively: G. K. Hall, *American Drama, Twentieth Century Literature, American Literary History* (Oxford University Press), and *Victorian Literature and Culture* (AMS Press). For permission to quote from individual works by authors examined in this collection I wish to acknowledge: Maxine Groffsky for quotes from Edmund White's unpublished essay, "Straight Woman, Gay Men"; John Hawkes for quotes from *The Passion Artist*; Penguin USA and The Provost and Scholars of King's College, Cambridge, for quotes from E. M. Forster's "Albergo Empedocle," in E. M. Forster, *The Life to Come and Other Stories*, ed. Oliver Stallybrass; Penguin USA for quotes from Richard Rodriguez, *Days of Obligation;* David R. Godine Publisher for quotes from Richard Rodriguez, *Hunger of Memory*; Random House for quotes from James Cain's *The Postman Always Rings Twice;* the author's Estate and their agents, Scott Meredith Literary Agency, for quotes from David Goodis, *Cassidy's Girl;* Grove/Atlantic Monthly Press for quotes from John Rechy, *The Sexual Outlaw,* copyright © 1977, by John Rechy; and John Burgee, Architects, for permission to reprint the photograph of the model of the AT&T Building.

Fictions of Masculinity

Introduction: Literature and Masculinity

Peter F. Murphy

This collection is inspired by the realization that masculinity, like femininity, is a fictional construction. Myths of masculinity have been perpetuated in literature, art, popular culture, and the politics of our daily lives. This anthology focuses on the role literature has played in reinforcing the assumptions about masculinity and, at times, helping to establish the norm of manhood. These chapters also attempt to identify other images, other roles, other options for men and masculinity.

Women writing about women dominate contemporary work on gender. Men have been far more willing to discuss female sexuality than their own; at the same time, many of the more radical and challenging analyses of male sexuality have come from women.[1] When men consider the issue of female sexuality they often speak from assumptions of security about their own unexamined masculinity. In the introduction to *Speaking of Gender* (1989), Elaine Showalter maintains that "for men to discuss masculinity [is] already to diminish or threaten their own manliness" (7). One idea behind the chapters in this book rests on the belief that men have to interrogate their own sexuality if there is to be a revision of masculinity.

As a set of rhetorical constructions (fictions), masculinity involves diverse and continually changing sexualities. This anthology examines the deep structure of masculine codes in fiction and asks the question "Who are the men in modern literature?"

Studying the tropes of Western masculinity and the force of the dominant values, the authors synthesize insights from feminism, psychoanalysis, poststructuralism, and new historicism to explain how male sexuality is influenced by and reflected in fictional representations.

By examining images of masculinity in modern literature, the chapters explore traditional and nontraditional roles of men in society and in personal relationships. The authors inspect the representation of men in literature—the fiction of manhood—and they attempt to unravel the assumptions behind this imagination. And they speculate on possibilities for creating a new image of masculinity by identifying what literature has to say about changing these social roles.

Much feminist literary criticism suggests that misogynist literature benefits men. This book seeks to identify ways in which literature victimizes men as well as women. An analysis of the misandric[2] nature of literature is long overdue.

The recent proliferation of books on men and feminism suggests that a multitude of voices is beginning to chip away at men's traditional silences about their sexuality. Writings by men on masculinity go back at least fifteen years and, in the case of literary criticism, over three decades to the publication of Leslie Fiedler's *Love and Death in the American Novel* (1960). Fiedler's focus on the ways in which masculinity was constituted over two hundred years of American literature informed much critical thinking about men's roles in fiction and resonates throughout several of the chapters in this anthology.

For Fiedler, several recurrent themes dominate the literary construction of manhood. From the novels of Charles Brockden Brown to those of William Faulkner and, more recently, John Updike, men's struggle to avoid women has been a dominant theme. Escape and flight, manifest in bachelorhood and male camaraderie, represent appropriate means to eschew women.

At the same time, though, physical impotence and spiritual failure characterize many men in American fiction. Men as cowards with a lack of moral firmness, stupid men and alcoholics, and men who die when most needed are the men who victimize women in American literature. Such are the roles American literature provides. What remains most baffling is "why men, too, should have accepted this travesty on their nature and role in life; but they did, in fact, accept it, even repeating [it] in their own books" (Fiedler 1960, 90). How this complicity on the part of male authors manifests itself in negative constructions of masculinity in literature informs several of the chapters here.

More recent material on masculinity, especially that published in the United States, emerges out of pop psychology and relies on, at best, a liberal analysis of men's social and sexual roles. Robert Bly's best-seller, *Iron John* (1990), exemplifies this perspective, although his hostility to women and his reliance on such classic primitivist metaphors for masculinity as king, soldier, and warrior presents a more poignantly reactionary position than did his precursors.

Beginning with the early classics of the American men's movement[3] the focus has been on "the psychological hang ups of an apparently timeless hyper-competitive and dominance-seeking masculinity [which urges] men to get their heads straight" (Hoch 1979, 30). An exception to this approach is Jon Snodgrass's pioneering anthology, *For Men against Sexism* (1977), which established an early forum to discuss the relationship between feminism and masculinity. Focusing on patriarchy as the system of male power and privilege, the essays in Snodgrass's collection document and analyze men's opposition to sexism. Even today, though, many activists in the American men's movement ignore the effects of large social systems on men and male personality. British and French writers, on the other hand, have presented a radical, even socialist, perspective.[4]

Over the past fifteen years several British publications have focused on the social and historical construction of masculinity, culminating recently in the publication of two major book series.[5] From a review of the theoretical debates and political forces that have worked to define sexuality during the past two centuries to a concern with issues of identity, desire, and choice, these works have argued for a historical and cultural understanding of sexuality.[6] Sexuality, then, must be viewed in the context of the structures of language and culture. This insight provides a broad framework out of which can emerge a deconstruction of literary representations of masculinity.

By tracing dominant Western conceptions of masculinity from the Bible to the present, a radical psychoanalytic reading might focus on men's internalization of masculinity. Paul Hoch (1979), for example, argues that the distorted social roles allotted to women and men in our society have similar social and cultural causes. Hoch claims culture has taught us that just as women are supposed to be both innocent and sexy, men are supposed to be both "white hero" and "black beast."

Myths about male sexuality have informed men's lives over the past two centuries and focus, frequently, on the relationship between a man and his body. Man's obsession with his penis as a symbol of power, an instrument of appropriation, and a weapon, exemplifies this relationship,[7] a relationship that resonates throughout modern literature.[8] But, as Reynaud's (1983) epigraph to this book makes clear, if a man gains "an undeniable power symbol, what pleasure can he really feel with a weapon between his legs?" (42).

Because many men are forced to comply with macho standards of performance, standards frequently reinforced in modern literature, they experience their power and sexuality as heavy burdens. By adopting a model of sexuality and social relations that is neither hierarchical nor exploitative, men can begin to construct alternative relationships among themselves as well as with women. Though men still have many more risks to take and much more to say about male sexuality, these chapters provide a forum in which literature becomes the basis for a close scrutiny of male sexuality. The chapters try to address ways in which literature provides insights or models for what these relationships might be like.

Except for Fiedler (and a few others) men have just begun to articulate a critical analysis of masculinity in contemporary culture and in modern literature.[9] More recent, and sometimes more radical, books have been written by sociologists, psychologists, and historians, not literary or cultural critics. Sociologists have focused on the relationship between power and masculinity with particular emphasis on the relations of power within which men's domination and women's oppression exist. They look at the worlds of men at work and at play, in politics and in science, and they examine the changing roles of men in American history and society. John Stoltenberg's *Refusing to Be a Man* (1989), for example, probes the social fiction of manhood and identifies a political and ethical construction based on sexual injustice.[10]

In the United States gay studies dominate much of the work on masculinity. Here too, though, critical analyses have been done by historians, sociologists, and psychologists, not literary critics. With the exception of James Levin's *The Gay Novel* (1983) and David Bergman's *Gaiety Transfigured* (1991), some of the most important work on homosexuality has been written by historians.[11] British sociologists have analyzed the resistance to dominant heterosexual assumptions about sexuality in the context of political organization and the possibility of alternative moralities and life-styles.[12]

As with the American men's movement in general, pop psychology has dominated writings on homosexuality, though a radical psychological perspective has informed some of the more important works in gay studies. Guy Hocquenghem, for example, develops a critique of psychoanalysis relying on Lacan, Deleuze, and Guattari and centers on the debate over "the transhistoricity of the Phallus" (31).[13]

Only recently, with David Bergman's ground-breaking book, *Gaiety Transfigured: Gay Self-Representation in American Literature* (1991), has a long overdue contribution to gay literary criticism arrived.[14] Bergman makes clear that his book should not be seen as a history of gay American literature, a history that he believes will not be written for quite some time. Even while acknowledging the difficulty of compiling such a critical history, Bergman maintains that for many gay people "homosexuality . . . is a literary construction. Gay men learned to speak about their sexuality in a rhetoric of despair and degradation" (6–7). This reliance on literary representation for a gay identity had a particularly profound effect on gay youth.

As the chapters in this anthology demonstrate, masculinity in general and male sexuality in particular cannot be understood as static, ahistorical, or essential. Literary representations of manhood have both relied on dominant cultural assumptions about masculinity and exposed the untenability of those assumptions. Whereas several of the chapters contribute to the critical work being done in gay studies of literature (e.g., David Bergman, Rafael Pérez-Torres, Jim Elledge, and Richard Dellamora), others confront the seeming one-dimensionality of male heterosexual behavior (e.g., David Radavich, David Leverenz, Christopher Metress, and Peter Murphy). The subtitles under which they are organized should make clear the fluidity of any gender categories; many of the chapters that cross cultures also cross sexualities, and vice versa. Crossing sexualities cannot include only those chapters about homosexuality; Radavich on Mamet and Murphy on Hawkes, for example, examine the complexity of male heterosexuality. Crossing cultures may not rely only on chapters examining nonwhite societies. Dellamora and Bergman on British men, and Leonard Duroche and Peter Schwenger on aspects of the German and/or Eastern European experience explore the dynamics of male sexuality, not just gay or straight, Western or nonwestern. Any differentiation remains problematic. The distinctions used here have relied primarily on an attempt to establish useful categories, not to create comprehensive or ineradicable classifications.

Leverenz's effort to link, rhetorically, the construction of masculinity to the stages of U.S. capitalism provides a broad historical context in which to read and interpret the many and varied works of literature examined in the other chapters. Radavich's chapter on David Mamet, whose plays realistically portray normative straight male society, gives a focal point for many of the other chapters as well. Each approaches that core from eccentric and even radical viewpoints (e.g., Nazi Germany, phenomenology, prostitution, male violence, homosexuality, and transvestism).

Leverenz reads the cultural poetics of manhood in texts by Cooper, Norris, London, Wister and Burroughs. In this way, the chapter traces the motif of a beast-man hero, from Cooper's "Hawkeye" and Frederick Jackson Turner's Andrew Jackson at the end of the "Frontier" essay, to the increasingly patrician male (Teddy Roosevelt, Tarzan, Bruce Wayne) who descends into the animal/underworld/underclass to redeem powerless middle-class capitalist civilization from its unmanliness. His historical framing of various narratives that depict the fantasmatic incorporation by men of both a primal violence and a cultivated code of honor or civility suggests some reasons for the peculiarly American obsession with powerlessness and manliness, despite an obviously empowered and dominant middle class.

Radavich analyzes Mamet's single-minded quest for lasting, fulfilling male friendship protected from the threats of women and masculine vulnerability on the one hand and the destabilizing pursuit of power and domination on the other. Mamet's concerns about masculinity take on a particularly intense resonance in the latter part of the twentieth century, as the traditional bastions of male companionship have increasingly been called into question. A desire for dominance, usually between men of unequal rank or age, battles with an equally strong desire for loyalty and acceptance, resulting in hard-won, intense, fundamentally unstable intimacy established in the absence of women. The duality of this conception results in a darkly comic artistic vision suited to a society in transition, moving from the comfortable economies of empire to the new, less stable realities of shared power and enterprise.

Murphy's chapter on *The Passion Artist* pursues the darkly comic vision of John Hawkes. Focusing on the impact feminism has had on this important postmodern male novelist, Murphy resists much Hawkes criticism that sees his fiction as just more misogynist male pornography. The novel explores the sexual awakening of Konrad Vost by examining the relationship between masculinity and femininity. By elucidating the fantasies, doubts, manifestations, and transformations of male heterosexuality in the context of a world besieged by hatred, fear, and shame, the novel conveys the male protagonist's sexual awakening from the artist of dead passion to an "artist . . . of the willed erotic union" (Hawkes 1978, 181). This long and brutal voyage culminates in Vost's acceptance of his role as a man, due in no small part to his experience of what it is like to be a woman.

In a similar fashion, Metress counters the more traditional reading of hard-boiled detective fiction, which sees the male characters as complete and heroic men at successful play in the fields of male desire. By focusing on the American *roman noir* of Woolrich, Thompson, and Goodis, Metress examines a genre that offers a chilling contrast to the sometimes unsteady but ultimately reassuring images of honorable masculinity inscribed in the worlds of Hammet, Chandler, Spillane, and MacDonald. The novelists of this suggestively deviant strain, according to Metress, give us "complete men untarnished by and unafraid of physical and sexual challenges to their masculinity. . . . Such writers people their novels with fragmented men stained by an absurdly tragic past and tormented by emasculating landscapes of frustration and paranoia." Goodis, for example, not only gives us images of men without power but men without desire for power. Working out of a hard-boiled tradition that encourages above all else an assertive phallocentric poetics of masculine integrity, Goodis gives us instead a world where self-erasure offers the only hope of survival in a rude and absurdly antagonistic universe.

Transition, change, and emergence characterize the fictional masculinities examined throughout this book. A close weaving of text and context allows Dellamora to make important points about Forster's position at a moment of emergence, at a moment when possibilities for a discourse about masculinity are being redefined. He concentrates on the ways the successful prosecution of Oscar Wilde affected male homosexuals of that period and, in particular, the severity of this impact on Forster. Examining "Albergo Empedocle" (1903), Forster's first published short story, Dellamora focuses on the "heterosexual contract" and identifies ways in which this story "conveys the tone-deafness of its young men to the possibility of female alterity." For Dellamora, this deafness "may owe not so much to Forster's personal blindness . . . but rather to the structure of heterosexual interchange that defines woman."

Extending the work initiated in his previous essay on "The Masculine Mode" (1989) and in his book-long study, *Phallic Critiques* (1984), Schwenger examines how men write and, in particular, how they write in relation to the father. Beginning with the looming figure of Kafka's father, Schwenger's chapter moves to the larger figure of the Father in Freud's *Totem and Taboo*—the father whose murder is supposed to have originated the forms of culture as expiation. Schwenger then turns to Donald Barthelme's *The Dead Father,* which uses both these predecessors in a novel whose parodic postmodern strategies undermine the father's power and indicate the possibility of a culture beyond patriarchy.

In a chapter concerned also with discourse and writing, Alfred Habegger analyzes the soldiers' language in Stephen Crane's *The Red Badge of Courage* and explicates the relationship between the idea of loose talk and the representations of spoken language. Habegger examines ways in which "this inarticulateness, so pervasive and obvious in Crane's narrative, has to do with much more than an illusory realism of speech. Crane is also saying something about the social and moral constraints on expression." Crane's dialogue frequently "shows that unrestrained speech brings a risk of combat and inadvertent self-ostracism." Commenting on the frequency with which soldiers are wounded in the head in Crane's novel, and how often these injuries are linked to the capacity to speak, his reading draws out an insight into the larger cultural compulsions that render the process of masculine maturation one that is cognate with a heightening of discursive incapacity.

Duroche examines the conflicting male narrators that come to bear on an adolescent during the period of National Socialism—what it was like to grow up as a man in Nazi Germany. Duroche's analysis of *Katz und Maus* fits nicely beside Habegger's reading because it too tries to gain a purchase on the logic of modern masculinity by seeing it as inducing a necessary disturbance of communication. Indeed, Duroche's chapter is invaluable for its effort to think about the questions of masculinity raised in Grass's text in terms of the ways in which patriarchal language itself implies a compulsory narrative of "masculinity."

In his chapter on J. R. Ackerley's memoirs and autobiographical fiction, Bergman continues his examination of the power of gay literature to structure identity, complementing Schwenger's piece on the importance of the father. In Ackerley's works the recurring figure of the Ideal Friend epitomizes a tradition of gay literary representation going back at least to Homer. As Ackerley envisions the Ideal Friend, he is ostensibly heterosexual, but reserves a place in his affections and sexual responses for a single homosexual man—Ackerley himself. He is rough, lower class, and without intellectual or artistic pretensions—in short, Ackerley's seeming opposite. Yet a closer examination of Ackerley's work, particularly *My Father and Myself,* indicates that the Ideal Friend, like Ackerley himself, is modeled after his father and constitutes the working out of a reverse Oedipal relationship.

Pérez-Torres's piece on Rechy contributes to the discourse on homosexuality discussed by Dellamora and Bergman. He argues that the construction of a rebellious sexual other in *The Sexual Outlaw* reproduces many of the same repressive heterosexual social attitudes against which Rechy's novel speaks. Bringing Bakhtin and Guattari to bear on this text, Pérez-Torres offers insights into the effects of de- and reterritorialization. By rendering some of the complications of Rechy's gendered position in relation to his politics, the chapter exposes some of the contradictions and conflicts evident in notions of critical alterity.

Frank O'Hara's unwillingness to make explicit his homosexuality, coupled with an apolitical (though, at times, seemingly conservative) attitude toward the rapidly changing American society of the 1950s and 1960s, introduces another complex gay experience. Frank O'Hara's forty-four love poems chronicling his relationship with Vincent Warren must be understood, Elledge argues, as more than simply love poems. O'Hara's tendency to disguise, obscure, and even ignore the genders of the poems' lovers is examined in the broader context of O'Hara's selective openness about his homosexuality. The significance of O'Hara's "fear of reprisal by a homophobic society, a disinterest in homosexuality as theme or content in poetry, and a disregard for politics in general" informs Elledge's reading of the "Warren series." Seeing this sequence of poems as examples of how the lack of gender identification in love poetry strengthens the poetry, Elledge argues that the reader's attention becomes focused on matters that transcend gender: "Specifically, O'Hara investigates love, its intricacies, ironies and paradoxes."

Suzanne Kehde, Miriam Cooke, and Martin Danahay analyze some examples of the representation of masculinity in non-Western literature. Kehde's chapter draws together ideas from postcolonial theory and some of the current work being done around the questions of sexuality. Recognizing the importance of the imaginary in femininity and in the construction of masculine subjectivity, she emphasizes the political implication of gender construction. For Kehde, Hwang's play debunks traditional Western ideas of masculinity, femininity, and the rationale for the colonial enterprise by showing how these imbricated notions underlie the male fantasy most completely projected in Puccini's famous opera. *M. Butterfly* deconstructs not only *Madame Butterfly,* but also Lacan's theory of the totalitarian domination of the phallus by showing how belief in masculinist mythology can so cloud the judgment that a man may live for twenty years without noticing that his lover isn't a woman, with disastrous consequences for his material practice. *The Quiet American* exposes, also, the discourses of gender and colonialism. Unlike Hwang's play, though, Greene's novel provides no critique of gender stereotypes and little of imperialist assumptions. Indeed, Greene fails to acknowledge that there might be some connection between them.

By examining the early novels of Naguib Mahfouz, the Egyptian Nobel Laureate, Cooke uncovers the dynamics of gender construction in his treatment of Arab "neopatriarchy." She focuses particularly on the relationship between male protagonists and prostitutes in a neopatriarchal society. Like Kehde's chapter, this one keeps femininity in the discussion of masculinity (in the figure of the female prostitute), and also recognizes a broad political context. Danahay examines ways in which Rodriguez's poetics reflect and respond to the predominant white male construction of masculinity; Rodriguez both incorporates this culturally dominant representation and transcends it. Danahay complexifies the solidity of the public/private split that Rodriguez seems to want to repress and reads Richard Rodriguez's autobiography as a bildungsroman attentive to the processes of acquiring the social status of masculinity. His reading explores these processes in terms of the distinctive ways they are affected by the cultural marginality of those who choose between a "macho" masculinity that is resistant to competence in English as the language of the dominant social order, and a "feminization" through education that gains one access to a degree of power within that social order.

Individually and collectively, the chapters included here contribute to what Elaine Showalter refers to as "the genuine addition of gender as a 'central problem in every text' read and taught, 'whatever the era and whoever the author' " (1989, 11). In this way, the authors and I hope to problematize masculinity in ways not unlike the early impact of feminist theory on literary constructions of femininity.

Notes

1. Indeed, even in the emerging field of "feminism and literary constructions of manhood" women have edited two of the more important books. See Laura Claridge and Elizabeth Langland, *Out of Bounds: Male Writers and Gender(ed) Criticism* (1990); and Thaïs Morgan, *Men Writing the Feminine: Literature, Theory, and the Question of Gender* (1994).
2. Misandric is used here as an antonym for misogynist, meaning not so much a hatred of men as a negative representation of masculinity. Needless to say, though, the misogynist and misandric representations of gender are not necessarily mutually exclusive. Literature frequently incorporates negative representations of both women and men.
3. See, for example, Warren Farrell (1974), Marc Fasteau (1975), and Jack Nichols (1975).
4. For a more detailed review of how much more radical British men's studies work is than American, see Peter F. Murphy (1989).
5. Three works stand out as central to a radical examination of masculinity: Jeffrey Weeks's *Sexuality and Its Discontents* (1985); Paul Hoch's *White Hero Black Beast: Racism, Sexism and the Mask of Masculinity* (1979); and Emmanuel Reynaud's *Holy Virility: The Social Construction of Masculinity* (1983). Weeks has published several studies of sexuality ranging from an overview of gay politics from the nineteenth century to the present (*Coming Out,* 1977) to a chronicling of the regulation of sexuality since 1800 (*Sex, Politics and Society,* 1981). Both book series are being published by Routledge and Chapman: Jeff Hearn's Critical Studies on Men and Masculinities, and Victor Seidler's Male Orders. See also the books by Rowena Chapman and Jonathan Rutherford, eds. (1988); Andy Metcalf and Martin Humphries (1985); David Morgan (1992); David Porter, ed. (1992); Michael Roper and John Tosh, eds. (1991); Jonathan Rutherford (1992); and Victor Seidler (1989, 1991a, 1991b).
6. See, in particular, Jeffrey Weeks's *Sexuality and Its Discontents* (1985).

7. See Emmanuel Reynaud (1983).
8. Fiedler (1960) points out that Faulkner tended to portray "the hysterical masculine protest of his time in the image of the maimed male, revenging himself on woman who has maimed him with the first instrument that comes to hand, a weapon in place of the phallus" (346–47). Gilbert and Gubar (1988), in the first volume of their projected three-volume study, *No Man's Land,* comment on how literary representations of the penis frequently present it as "a therapeutic instrument in the domestication of desire, [which] was always on the verge of turning into the penis as pistol" (48); "not only has the penis now been redefined as a weapon, it has been defined as a weapon whose aggressive onslaughts women ought to want" (113–14).
9. *Men in Feminism* (1987), edited by Alice Jardine and Paul Smith, represents an early example of this effort. A provocative anthology of contemporary feminist thinkers, this collection provides a major contribution to the articulation of a male feminist theory. The ideas presented in this book should help men who are involved with feminism to apply that critical theory to their own lives as men and as teachers, especially teachers of literature. By calling for men to assume "the responsibility of speaking their own bodies" with the realization that men "still have everything to say 'about' [their] sexuality" (37), Paul Smith begins to counter the concern of many feminist critics who "worried that male critics would appropriate, penetrate, or exploit feminist discourse for professional advantage without accepting the risks and challenges of investigating masculinity, or analyzing their own critical practice" (Showalter 1989, 7).

   Though a relative dearth of books on men's roles in fiction still exists, at least a half-dozen new texts have been published over the past decade. Alfred Habegger's *Gender, Fantasy, and Realism in American Literature* (1982) focuses on the novels of Henry James and William Dean Howells. Peter Schwenger's *Phallic Critiques* (1984) looks at masculinity in twentieth-century literature (e.g., Mailer, Hemingway, Mishima). Three relatively new and important books include: Wayne Koestenbaum's *Double Talk: The Erotics of Male Literary Collaboration* (1989), David Leverenz's *Manhood and the American Renaissance* (1989), and Richard Dellamora's *Masculine Desire: The Sexual Politics of Victorian Aestheticism* (1990). Koestenbaum examines literary collaboration between male authors, Leverenz focuses on nineteenth-century American literature, and Dellamora analyzes the cultural construction of masculinity in nineteenth-century British literature. Joseph A. Boone and Michael Cadden's *Engendering Men: The Question of Male Feminist Criticism* (1990), examines literature spanning the past four hundred years. As the title suggests, this is a collection of essays by male critics that attempts to begin the task of retheorizing the male position in our culture. The essays examine poetry, fiction, the Broadway stage, film and television, and broader cultural and psychoanalytic texts.

10. For a sociological perspective see Arthur Brittan (1989) and Michael Kaufman (1987). For a historian's view see Mark Gerzon (1982), E. Anthony Rotundo (1993), and Peter N. Stearns (1979). At least three other publications on men and masculinity should be mentioned. Mark Carnes and Clyde Griffen's new anthology *Meanings for Manhood: Constructions of Masculinity in Victorian America* (1990), is a collection of essays by historians that includes "Middle-Class Men and the Solace of Fraternal Ritual," "Suburban Men and Masculine Domesticity, 1870–1915," and "On Men's History and Women's History." Harry Brod's anthology, *The Making of Masculinities: The New Men's Studies* (1987) exemplifies the recent development of men's studies programs. Including essays from diverse disciplines, this collection assumes the relevance and desirability of men's studies programs, rather than posing such academic alternatives as a critical consideration. And, Arthur and Marilouise Kroker's new anthology, *The Hysterical Male: New Feminist Theory* (1991), "traces out the logic of imminent reversibility in received patriarchal discourses in psychoanalysis, art, theory and culture. . . . What results is an intense, provocative and creative theorization of feminism under the failing sign of the unitary male subject" (xiv). These three books add an important dimension to historical, social, and cultural considerations of masculinity.
11. See Jonathan Katz's (1976) documentary history of lesbians and gay men in the United States, John D'Emilio's (1983) historical overview of the political struggles and social movements instrumental in the emergence of contemporary American gay culture, and John Boswell's (1980) comprehensive study of attitudes toward homosexuality from the beginning of the Christian era to the fourteenth century, which represent some of the more important works in gay history published during the past twenty years.
12. See the Gay Left Collective's *Homosexuality, Power, and Politics* (1980), for a collection of essays examining "the ways in which power has shaped . . . notions of homosexuality and resulted in a sustained sexual oppression" (7).
13. See Guy Hocquenghem's examination of *Homosexual Desire* (1978), which emerges from a major concern with language, psychoanalysis, and Marxism.
14. See also James Levin's *The Gay Novel* (1983), in which he used "the characters in the novels [he examines] as models of what attitudes were towards homosexuality and how this affected the lives of those who were homosexually oriented" (2). Limiting his field to those

novels in which the character is aware of his homosexuality, Levin's book is as much a social history of homosexuality as it is a work of literary criticism. Mark Lilly's *Gay Men's Literature in the Twentieth Century* (1993) is also of relevance here.

Works Cited

Bergman, David. *Gaiety Transfigured: Gay Self-Representation in American Literature.* Madison, WI: University of Wisconsin Press, 1991.

Bly, Robert. *Iron John.* New York: Addison-Wesley, 1990.

Boone, Joseph A., and Michael Cadden, eds. *Engendering Men: The Question of Male Feminist Criticism.* New York: Routledge, 1990.

Boswell, John. *Christianity, Social Tolerance and Homosexuality.* Chicago: University of Chicago Press, 1980.

Brittan, Arthur. *Masculinity and Power.* London: Basil Blackwell, 1989.

Brod, Harry, ed. *The Making of Masculinities: The New Men's Studies.* London: Allen and Unwin, 1987.

Carnes, Mark C., and Clyde Griffen, eds. *Meanings for Manhood: Constructions of Masculinity in Victorian America.* Chicago: University of Chicago Press, 1990.

Chapman, Rowena, and Jonathan Rutherford, eds. *Male Order: Unwrapping Masculinity.* New York: Routledge, 1988.

Claridge, Laura, and Elizabeth Langland, eds. *Out of Bounds: Male Writers and Gender(ed) Criticism.* Amherst, MA: University of Massachusetts Press, 1990.

Dellamora, Richard. *Masculine Desire: The Sexual Politics of Victorian Aestheticism.* Chapel Hill, NC: North Carolina Univ. Press, 1990.

D'Emilio, John. *Sexual Politics, Sexual Communities: The Making of a Homosexual Minority in the United States, 1940–1970.* Chicago: University of Chicago Press, 1983.

Farrell, Warren. *The Liberated Man: Beyond Masculinity: Freeing Men and Their Relationships with Women.* New York: Random House, 1974.

Fasteau, Marc. *The Male Machine.* New York: Dell, 1975.

Fiedler, Leslie. *Love and Death in the American Novel.* New York: Stein and Day, 1960.

Gay Left Collective, ed. *Homosexuality, Power, and Politics.* London: Allison and Busby, 1980.

Gerzon, Mark. *A Choice of Heroes: The Changing Face of American Manhood.* New York: Houghton Mifflin, 1982.

Gilbert, Sandra M., and Susan Gubar. *No Man's Land: The Place of the Woman Writer in the Twentieth Century, vol. 1, The War of the Words.* New Haven, CT: Yale Univ. Press, 1988.

Habegger, Alfred. *Gender, Fantasy, and Realism in American Literature.* New York: Columbia Univ. Press, 1982.

Hawkes, John. *The Passion Artist.* New York: Harper and Row, 1978.

Hoch, Paul. *White Hero Black Beast: Racism, Sexism and the Mask of Masculinity.* London: Pluto Press, 1979.

Hocquenghem, Guy. *Homosexual Desire.* London: Allison and Busby, 1978.

Jardine, Alice, and Paul Smith, eds. *Men in Feminism.* New York: Methuen, 1987.

Katz, Jonathan. *Gay American History: Lesbians and Gay Men in the U.S.A.* New York: Avon Books, 1976.

Kaufman, Michael, ed. *Beyond Patriarchy: Essays by Men on Pleasure, Power and Change.* New York: Oxford Univ. Press, 1987.

Koestenbaum, Wayne. *Double Talk: The Erotics of Male Literary Collaboration.* New York: Routledge, 1989.

Kroker, Arthur, and Marilouise Kroker, eds. *The Hysterical Male: New Feminist Theory.* New York: St. Martin's Press, 1991.

Leverenz, David. *Manhood and the American Renaissance.* Ithaca, NY: Cornell Univ. Press, 1989.

Levin, James. *The Gay Novel: The Male Homosexual Image in America.* New York: Irvington Publishers, 1983.

Lilly, Mark. *Gay Men's Literature in the Twentieth Century.* New York: New York University Press, 1993.

Metcalf, Andy, and Martin Humphries, eds. *The Sexuality of Men.* London: Pluto Press, 1985.

Morgan, David. H. J. *Discovering Men.* New York: Routledge, 1992.

Morgan, Thaïs, ed. *Men Writing the Feminine: Literature, Theory, and the Question of Gender.* Albany, NY: SUNY Press, 1994.

Murphy, Peter F. "Toward a Feminist Masculinity." *Feminist Studies* 15, no. 2 (Summer 1989): 351–61.

Nichols, Jack. *Men's Liberation: A New Definition of Masculinity.* New York: Penguin, 1975.

Porter, David. ed. *Between Men and Feminism.* New York: Routledge, 1992.

Reynaud, Emmanuel. *Holy Virility: The Social Construction of Masculinity.* London: Pluto Press, 1983.

Roper, Michael, and John Tosh, eds. *Manful Assertions: Masculinities in Britain since 1800.* New York: Routledge, 1991.

Rotundo, E. Anthony. *American Manhood: Transformations in Masculinity from the Revolution to the Modern Era.* New York: Basic Books, 1993.

Rutherford, Jonathan. *Men's Silences: Predicaments in Masculinity.* New York: Routledge, 1992.

Schwenger, Peter. "The Masculine Mode." In *Speaking of Gender,* edited by Elaine Showalter. New York: Routledge, 1989.

———. *Phallic Critiques: Masculinity and Twentieth Century Literature.* New York: Routledge and Kegan Paul, 1984.

Seidler, Victor J. *Recreating Sexual Politics: Men, Feminism and Politics.* London: Routledge, 1991a.

———. *Rediscovering Masculinity: Reason, Language and Sexuality.* New York: Routledge, 1989.

———, ed. *The Achilles Heel Reader.* London: Routledge, 1991b.

Showalter, Elaine. "Introduction: The Rise of Gender." In *Speaking of Gender,* 1–13. New York: Routledge, 1989.

Snodgrass, Jon, ed. *For Men against Sexism.* Albion, CA: Times Change Press, 1977.

Stearns, Peter N. *Be a Man! Males in Modern Society.* New York: Holmes and Meier, 1979.

Stoltenberg, John. *Refusing to Be a Man: Essays on Sex and Justice.* Portland, OR: Breintenbush Books, 1989.

Weeks, Jeffrey. *Coming Out: Homosexual Politics in Britain from the Nineteenth Century to the Present.* London: Quartet Books, 1977.

———. *Sex, Politics, and Society: The Regulation of Sexuality since 1800.* London: Longman, 1981.

———. *Sexuality and Its Discontents: Meanings, Myths and Modern Sexualities.* London: Routledge, 1985.

I

Fictions of (American) Masculinities: A Historical Overview

1

The Last Real Man in America: From Natty Bumppo to Batman

David Leverenz

In the summer of 1989, one of the glossiest men's magazines appeared with a picture of Sean Connery on the cover. Dressed in a creamy ivory tuxedo, standing with arms folded against a beige background, visible only to the waist, he embodied elegance, sensuality, and virility. The caption proclaimed him "The Last Real Man in America."

Why should the Last Real Man in America be a British actor? The taunting ambiguity implies that no American can claim true manliness anymore; to see it at all is to see it vanishing. Only a working-class Scotsman who secured his international image as James Bond, an Englishman equally skilled in civility and violence, can temporarily import virility to American shores. Yet the pleasurable visual framing of his face as white on white on beige seems curiously reassuring. Connery represents the last, best hope, the master of everything not quite seen, dark, and below the belt. He can protect a civilized, yet effete Us from a barbaric though enviably violent Them.

The July cover of *Gentleman's Quarterly* slipped from my mind until late August, when I was standing in a check-out line at a Florida supermarket and noticed the September cover of *Celebrity Plus,* a decidedly downscale fan magazine. This cover featured Harrison Ford in a woodsy setting, with a yellow blurb announcing, "Rare Interview! The 'Last' Real Man."[1] Faced with such a flagrant intertextual rip-off, I began wondering: In what other country could variations on that come-on sell magazines? To ask the question exposes the strange mixture of bravado, anxiety, and nostalgia in the motif. Male readers in more traditionally patriarchal cultures might well feel insulted. Why did I feel a bit wistful, even teased? The motif has a beleaguered quality to it, as if urban, yuppie, corporate, feminist America had become intrinsically emasculating.

It was the summer of 1989 when Batman, the Last Real Man in Gotham City, galvanized the highest short-term gross in movie history by dramatizing a double myth of man-making. To save hapless bourgeois cosmopolitans from their high-tech powerlessness, Bruce Wayne becomes half beast and descends into the underclass, a downward mobility that also gives steel and grit to his aristocratic boyishness. The year before, another sweetly bumbling Bruce Wayne patrician had managed to step into Ronald Reagan's manly image and position by banishing what a *Newsweek* cover story had labelled "The Wimp Factor" with two brilliantly chosen counterimages. Willie Horton, the underclass rapist, evoked the powerlessness of middle-class voters as well as the spinelessness of liberal officials. With a more subliminal audacity, George Bush secured his mythic transformation into an electable manly image by choosing Robin as his running mate. The war with Iraq confirmed that new image so completely that cartoonist Pat Oliphant "temporarily retired" George Bush's purse.[2] Collectively, the war enacted a drama of national remasculinization in which "humiliating" Saddam Hussein avenged the still festering humiliation of Vietnam.

From spring through summer 1991, the number one best-seller was *Iron John: A Book about Men.* Robert Bly's book speaks to many midlife American men who look into themselves and find mostly rubbery adaptations. The movement Bly has inspired depends less on a recoil against feminists than on a widespread need to struggle beyond workplace-generated norms for fathering and male friendships. Many men want to feel both "wild" and strong yet emotionally open and vulnerable with other men, beyond the capitalist constraints enforcing competitiveness, mobility, and self-control. Astutely repackaging psychoanalytic confessions in Native American patriarchal trappings, Bly's movement offers Indian tribal ceremonies as initiation rites and mentoring support groups for remasculinization, in ways quite continuous with turn-of-the-century middle-class lodge rituals. Under this patriarchal cover, as Mark Carnes has argued for Masonic ceremonies, men can express their hidden nurturing side as well as their anger and grief about inadequate fathering, without feeling feminized or weak.[3]

The first Last Real Man in America, Cooper's Natty Bumppo, dramatizes a similar white flight from civilized unmanliness to Native American traditions of patriarchal comradeship. Especially in *The Last of the Mohicans* (1826), the novel-romance that established Natty's image as heroic frontiersman, an elegiac nostalgia suffuses Cooper's portraits of red and white heroes alike. As a variety of critics have demonstrated, Cooper simultaneously replicates and displaces expansionist conflicts by subsuming a collective story of manifest destiny in an elegy for primitive manly character.[4] Fleeing civilization and progress, "Hawkeye" or "La Longue Carabine"—almost his only names here—finds his soulmate in Chingachgook, the first "gook" to inhabit the enduring white myth of the self-subordinating man of color. When the reader meets Natty and Chingachgook, however, the two characters are vehemently arguing over why white people have any right to take the Indians' land.

At first Natty claims that the whites are just doing what the Indians used to do to each other. But it does seem unfair, he acknowledges to himself, that white men have bullets. Worse, modern white men no longer publicly shame the "cowardly" and acclaim the brave; they "write in books" instead of telling their deeds in their villages, Natty says in disbelief, and they spend their "days among the women, in learning the names of black marks," instead of hearing the deeds of the fathers and feeling "a pride in striving to outdo them" (35). Eventually the two friends agree to blame the whole problem on the Dutch, who gave the Indians firewater (37). But the solution seems patently inadequate to the tensions raised by the protracted argument. Or rather, the solution allows them to feel that their friendship can evade history, much as Natty frequently proclaims his uncontaminated white identity, "a man without a cross," while plunging further and further into crossover liminal realms of mixture.[5] At the end, when Chingachgook's son Uncas dies and the father himself ironically becomes the Last of the Mohicans, the "self-command" of both grieving friends gives way to bowed heads and "scalding tears" (414). Childless, facing death, and bonded with natural manly feeling, the two embody a double elegy for a vanishing patriarchal simplicity inexorably giving way to the settlements. Why would Cooper write a book to mourn the passing of a manliness that scorns the womanish writing of books? Because he and his civilized male readers could condescend to this "Natural Bumpkin" yet long for the manliness that Natty Bumppo represents.

Ostensibly devising a paternalistic narration to harmonize civilized and savage life with principles of moral conduct, as the 1850 preface to the *Leatherstocking Tales* sententiously claims, Cooper fortunately brings stress-points and contradictions out into the open. He reserves his most pointed mockery for the maladapted transplant from high civilization, David Gamut, the musician in the wilderness. On the frontier, where traditional class status seemingly yields to a hierarchy of natural manliness, psalm-singing David Gamut begins at the bottom. He can't even manage his mare. The hapless male musician has been a contrasting foil in various Real Man myths since the time of Hercules, who as a boy knocked his music teacher dead with his lyre. It was an accident, as the Greek myth tells it; the little lad just didn't know his own strength. Benvenuto Cellini begins his swaggering autobiography by recounting how he pleaded, fought, and fled from his doting father, who so desperately wanted Benvenuto to play the flute. The most recent American version of this myth comes from *Trump: The Art of the Deal:*

> Even in elementary school, I was a very assertive, aggressive kid. In the second grade I actually gave a teacher a black eye—I punched my music teacher because I didn't think he knew anything about music and I almost got expelled. I'm not proud of that, but [!] it's clear evidence that even early on I had a tendency to stand up and make my opinions known in a

very forceful way. The difference now is that I like to use my brain instead of my fists.[6]

At least Cooper presents David Gamut with amused respect for his civilized "gifts." Moreover, by the end of *Last of the Mohicans* David Gamut has ascended the scale of manliness. He demonstrates fortitude and integrity where other men display villainy and cowardice. He also helps to harmonize their beleaguered group, much as Cooper's narrative seeks to blend civilized and savage virtues through a traditionally patriarchal rhetoric of mutual respect and honor.

Like any conception of manhood, an emphasis on honor functions ideologically, which is to say, as a social fiction constructed by empowered constituencies to extend their power, yet felt as a natural and universal law. It shames individual deviance to protect the group, making men more fearful of losing the respect of other men than of losing their lives in battle. Cooper vividly dramatizes a ritual of public, tribal shaming in contrasting the stoic self-command of Uncas with the abject behavior of Reed-that-bends, both captured by the Hurons. Soon the Huron chief acknowledges the unflinching, manly stranger as someone who has "proved yourself a man" (286). Shortly thereafter, the father of Reed-that-bends publicly disowns his son, in the "bitter triumph" of a lonely "stoicism" over a father's "anguish" (293). If Chingachgook, Colonel Munro, and the aged Tamenund cannot protect their children or their people from kidnapping and carnage, they take solace in their rigid adherence to a traditional manly code of honor and shame.

If manhood is not forever, its seemingly ageless durability has less to do with testosterone than with social constructions of male shaming to protect the social unit.[7] In that respect, capitalism's great change has been to destabilize small-scale patriarchy, in which rituals of honoring and shaming depend on a long-term, knowable audience for their effectiveness. Natty Bumppo's characterization preserves traditions of patriarchal honor yet exposes their flimsiness by presenting him as a man of fixed integrity who is always on the move, forever estranged from stable community. Writing for an audience of strangers in an emerging mass market,

Cooper depicts Natty as an embodiment of patriarchal honor without the patriarchy, entrepreneurial mobility without the entrepreneur. An incipient clash between two social constructions of identity yields to an idealization of cross-color male chumship in an ahistorical mode. Yet Cooper taunts civilized readers with a vague sense of the shamefulness inherent in the white march westward—not, paradoxically, the guilt from exercising oppressive power but the shame from accommodating to a large-scale nation-state. There domestic intimacy and career advancement have superseded a manliness that already starts to take on the status of a compensatory simplification—a myth of mourning the fathers, not of emulating them.

Baffled by what he hears of the settlements, Natty wonders if it could be true that these new ways of living offer something "which binds man to woman closer than the father is tied to the son" (315). Urbane readers could indulge his naïveté yet feel the twinge of loss. How silly: Natty feels neither sexual desire nor delight in home companionship. How sad: no civilized white man feels the fabric of father-son bonds as Natty does. Once again Cooper forces his readers into contradictions evaded by Natty's portable manliness. His hero seems unnaturally asexual, yet more natural than men of the settlements, many of whom found their homes defined by their women and the marketplace defined by their competitive aloneness, without communal or paternal anchors.

That rhetoric, too, bespeaks a sentimental mystification. The instant success of *Last of the Mohicans* depended in part on Cooper's ability to recast emerging power relations as elegiac nostalgia. Fatherly yet childish, the Indians are vanishing to the cultural museum of literature by their own choice and accord. Besides, according to the implicit fantasy, so long as lower-class vagrants like Natty help to dispossess the Red Men for the better sort, some of his best friends can be Indians, and he can call his readers women or bookish or even married. Cooper's double elegy for patriarchal manhood, red and white, veils a postpatriarchal set of power relations based initially on class and racial dominance, and driven ultimately by capitalist modes of circulation that unsettle all modes of collective, stable identity except those based on the nuclear family and specialized skills in the corporate workplace.[8]

In Shakespeare's day, "pioneer" meant the basest manual laborers in the army, the men who dug trenches and mines. At the onset of his frenzy, Othello tells Iago,

> I had been happy if the general camp,
> Pioneers and all, had tasted her sweet body,
> So I had nothing known.
>
> (III, iii, 342–44)

Something of that baseness carries over to Cooper's portrait of his garrulous, illiterate hero. Yet a new myth of manly heroism also begins to emerge in Natty, situated as he is midway between preindustrial hierarchies of the honorable versus the base and a new, more diffusely fluid circulation of entrepreneurial middle-class energies.

As Kenneth Cmiel's *Democratic Eloquence* emphasizes, traditions of "character" could not hold against a democratization that blurred the boundaries separating genteel from vulgar, high from low. A new "middling culture" mixed formal and folksy speech to redefine proper public language and self-presentation. Along with a pervasive push for upward mobility came a premodernist sense of role-playing, offering "numerous identities . . . a multitude of expressive choices." Other historians, notably Stuart M. Blumin, analyze the paradox of a new middle class whose male members experience identity as competitive individualism, with class consciousness applied only to those at the top and bottom.[9]

If middle-class male constructions of "self" become linked to roles and competitive upward mobility in an increasingly professionalized workplace, "class" becomes either a genteel self-refashioning or a depth into which no capitalist climber must fall. Horatio Alger's most successful novel, *Ragged Dick* (1868), presents a Bowery urchin who rises to middle-class respectability not simply by pluck, luck, and entrepreneurial industry but also by continually telling tall tales about himself. He extravagantly fictionalizes his classy connections to play linguistic dress-up. Ragged Dick knows he will be capitalized by his genteel mentors only as he embraces both the speculative mobility of voice and the Protestant work ethic produced by capitalism.

In that context, a new myth of manly heroism takes on the self-divisions and psychic mobility fostered by a marketplace beyond small-scale ideological controls. An avenging hero, half animal and half human, fusing beast and patrician, descends into an evil underclass to save a helpless bourgeois civilization. From Tarzan to Batman, the mass-market myth expresses the paradox of a collectively empowered middle class in which men feel personally powerless, unmanly, or unreal except as they compete in the workplace. Simultaneously, the mass-market myth appeals to a fantasy of working-class remasculinization through often sadistic violence, diffusely directed against black men, gay men, and women.

The paradox has its contradictory sources in the Jacksonian era, when both Cooper's works and the Davy Crockett tales begin to exploit the beast-man motif, though without the later patrician incorporation. In Carroll Smith-Rosenberg's analysis, the Davy Crockett stories voice a widespread sense of being "powerless in the face of massive and unremitting social transformation." Challenging but not overthrowing the bourgeois struggle for legitimacy, Crockett's adventures represent several kinds of liminality: male and female adolescence, a society in transition from patriarchal communities to industrial capitalism, and crossovers between dominant and marginal groups. The tall tales of young, violent males taking on the bestiality of their animal or subhuman opponents celebrate individual freedom and personal control while dehistoricizing capitalist forces of change and inverting bourgeois heterosexuality.[10] Dramas of incessant personal dominance and humiliation seek to recast these dynamics in the preindustrial interpretive framework of honor and shaming.

In *The Last of the Mohicans*, Cooper edges Natty toward beast-man status, especially in the last third of the story, where Natty infiltrates an Indian village by dressing up as a bear. There, however, Cooper does almost nothing with the tensions latent in such a crossover. Fifteen years later, in *The Deerslayer* (1841), Cooper at last plunges toward the new myth, as readers learn for the first time how Natty got that strange animal name of "Hawkeye."[11]

In Chapter 7, Natty becomes a man by killing his first Indian. Instead of taking a scalp, Natty takes a new name as his trophy, a name bestowed on him by his victim. Behaving with traditional honor, Natty had refrained from shooting the Indian unfairly. But honor can't protect him against a "savage" whose body betrays his sneaky bestiality: his eyes rage like a "volcano," his nostrils dilate "like those of some wild beast" (108). Fortunately, just as the Indian crouches like a "tiger" in the bushes to shoot, Natty senses danger, whirls, cocks his rifle, aims, and fires, all before the Indian's tightening finger quite pulls the trigger. This is the kind of woodsmanship that Mark Twain so gloriously debunks in "Fenimore Cooper's Literary Offenses."

The mythic transformation begins after the shooting. Prone though still conscious, the victim watches Natty "as the fallen bird regards the fowler," while the lad feels "melancholy" as he stands over the "black" eyes of the "riptyle" (110–11). Then the Indian dies like a man. With "stoicism," "firmness," and "high innate courtesy," the Indian raises his hand to "tap the young man on his breast." The red man's dying words rechristen the white man: "eye sartain—finger lightning—aim, death—great warrior soon. No Deerslayer—Hawkeye—Hawkeye—Hawkeye. Shake hand" (113–14).

One could argue that this mutual mythic transformation relieves white readers of guilt for the pleasures of Indian killing. While a red man threatens, the narrative depicts him as a snaky beast. After he ceases to be dangerous, he becomes a man so that he can bless the suitably depressed killer with a new identity: Deerslayer becomes Manslayer. But the naming goes the other way, from Deerslayer to Hawkeye. A bird's soaring, predatory quickness dignifies and sharpens Natty's rightful yet brutal dominance. Here is a new myth of American manhood in the making: to be civilized and savage in one composite, self-divided transformation. The myth dramatizes a potential for downward mobility on the liminal frontier, to save the manhood of upwardly mobile men in the settlements.[12]

By the turn of the century, the new myth shapes a multitude of texts, from Turner's frontier thesis (1893) to Frank Norris's *McTeague* (1899) and Jack London's *Call of the Wild* (1903). Norris's tale of brute-man's downward mobility from petty bourgeois aspirations to theft and murder has grotesque violence to women at the center of McTeague's descent. If the dentist's hapless ambitions can be blamed on his mother and his wife, who goad him out of his natural niche as a miner to compete in a profession requiring intelligence and dexterity, McTeague takes his "apelike" revenge by killing his wife after nearly biting her fingers off. Throughout, Norris's patronizingly self-conscious genteel narration simultaneously relishes McTeague's brutality while exposing McTeague as a figure of urban powerlessness, helpless against complexity, rivals, or his own desires. Lashing out whenever he is made to "feel small," this Last Real Man in America ends his life as a comic butt, handcuffed to a pursuer's corpse in the desert, where he stares stupidly at a bird cage. Incapable of the self-transformations and poses by which "the Other Dentist" achieves success, McTeague represents a cautionary tale of the brute inherent in all real men, and the monstrous desires that have to be masked in the upward march to genteel decorum.[13]

For Jack London, the Last Real Man in America is a dog who turns into a wolf. London's *Call of the Wild* mocks the silliness of self-absorbed, hysterical Mercedes, the only woman who ventures onto the arctic tundra, especially when she tries to talk about theater and art. As she vanishes into an ice hole, the narrative all but says good riddance. Buck's allegorical manliness also survives his chumship with John Thornton, who saves and cherishes Buck with a "genuine passionate love" (74) climaxing in an ecstasy of penetration and talking dirty, from which the onlookers discreetly withdraw.[14] But Thornton, too, is only human, with a capitalist lust for gold, and therefore powerless when confronted by the arctic underclass, the subhuman Yeehats. In avenging Thornton's death and tasting human blood for the first time, Buck enacts Deerslayer's rite of initiation with a hint of comic reversal: the dog "had killed man, the noblest game of all" (98). Now he can fulfill the "pride" of his downwardly mobile call of the wild by taking over the leadership of a wolf pack.[15]

In human society, however, Buck too is powerless. As the first sentence declares, "Buck did not read the newspapers." He cannot understand why he is being bought and sold. The arbitrary buying and selling of Buck, which structures the plot, takes on meanings beyond his comprehension, yet obvious to those who can read:

Men need to carry the news, men want to find gold. Unlike Norris, London unambivalently contrasts Buck's natural leadership with the degeneracy of such men. Nevertheless, ideal manliness thrives in Buck only because he becomes less and less human, more and more wild, while his admiring narrator—like Cooper—writes a "wild" book about him for boy-men readers who feel trapped in their maturation and long for exotic virility.

Like tales of musician-bashing, the beast-man myth is as old as the dawn of story-telling. Its transformation into late nineteenth-century myths of vanishing American manhood also draws on age-old myths of a hero's descent into the underworld and on the cross-cultural bourgeois myth of an aristocratic hero who makes himself inhuman in order to become superhuman (e.g., the Count of Monte Cristo). Ultimately, as Victoria Kahn suggests for Machiavelli's rhetorical finale in *The Prince,* where manly *virtù* beats womanly Fortuna into submission, all myths of manliness may seek allegorical stabilization to ward off the perception that "the individual is not at all in control of his behavior."[16]

The special American quality lies in the new myth's exaggerated emphasis on frontier liminality, in the contradictory class mobilities, and in the incipient note of mourning. Why would upwardly mobile readers relish downwardly mobile heroes? The answer may lie in the narrative voices so divided between class loyalty and gender urgency. Those tensions bespeak a world in which both class and gender were starting to feel like nostalgic props.

To read Frederick Jackson Turner's "The Significance of the Frontier in American History" in the context I'm sketching here exposes his fascination with redemptive manly savagery and belligerence. For Turner, the frontier is "the meeting point between savagery and civilization," and therefore a crucible for "rapid and effective Americanization." Stripping a man of his European manners, the frontier "takes him from the railroad car and puts him in the birch canoe. . . . Before long he has gone to planting Indian corn and plowing with a sharp stick; he shouts the war cry and takes the scalp in orthodox Indian fashion. In short, at the frontier the environment is at first too strong for the man." Unlike Cooper, Turner relishes the prospect of such assimilation. The strong man "transforms the wilderness" only after the wilderness has transformed him. A hybrid, both savage and civilized, he is no longer ridden by class-linked, European manners; "here is a new product that is American" (463).[17]

Not until 1920, when Turner at last expanded his brief essay into a book, do the gender issues become flamboyantly manifest. Climaxing his vision of the frontier as a natural factory for manufacturing American manhood, Turner all but lets out a war whoop when the New World produces Andrew Jackson. Outrageously casting Thomas Jefferson as a frontier prophet, "the John the Baptist of democracy," Turner presents Jackson as democracy's incarnation, explicitly "Moses" and implicitly Christ. Above all, Jackson stands forth as the First Real Man in America. Why? Because when Jackson tried to speak on the floor of the Senate, his rage blocked his words. Turner exultingly quotes Jefferson, without a hint of Jefferson's patrician recoil: "When I was President of the Senate he was a Senator, and he could never speak on account of the rashness of his feelings. I have seen him attempt it repeatedly and as often choke with rage" (471).

What Ishmael finds both appalling and fascinating in Ahab, Turner celebrates in Jackson without reservation.

> At last the frontier in the person of its typical man had found a place in the Government. This six-foot backwoodsman, with blue eyes that could blaze on occasion, this choleric, impetuous, self-willed Scotch-Irish leader of men, this expert duelist, and ready fighter, this embodiment of the tenacious, vehement, personal West, was in politics to stay. . . . The men of the Western World turned their backs upon the Atlantic Ocean, and with a grim energy and self-reliance began to build up a society free from the dominance of ancient forms. (471–72)

To be aggressive, rebellious, enraged, uncivilized: this is what the frontier could do for the European clones on the East Coast, still in thrall to a foreign tyranny of manners.

If Turner's bull-in-the-china-shop image of manliness empowered his own assault on an overbearing Eastern establishment, it also empowered the emerging profession of American history.[18] Just as with Norris and London, however, a diffuse sense of civilized powerlessness lurks at the margins of his text. He reemphasizes at the end that the frontier is closed now; the days of democratic man-making seem to be over. Now, to challenge the new "manufacturing aristocracy," he finds not frontier fire-eaters but only inequality, poverty, and labor unions. Turner's muted ending evokes a baffled Lone Ranger surrounded by Marxists and plutocrats. As he concludes, the frontier has been a safety valve, postponing the conflict between capital and labor: "But the sanative influences of the free spaces of the West were destined to ameliorate labor's condition, to afford new hopes and new faith to pioneer democracy, and to postpone the problem" (473).

As if waiting in the wings to seize the image of bully-boy patrician leading the nation away from class conflicts toward a renewal of collective virility on international frontiers, the man who most successfully exploited the emerging myth of the cross-class beast-man was Theodore Roosevelt, not Eugene V. Debs.[19] Roosevelt epitomized manly zest for the new imperial nation in part because of his jaunty energy, but also because his image brought together both aspects of the new myth: the top rung of the ladder of social aspiration and the gladiatorial animal arena sensed at the bottom. In what other advanced industrial country could a former president, an asthmatic child of old money, make a serious run for his country's top office under the banner of "The Bull Moose Party"?[20] Later in 1912, after Roosevelt's quixotic drive for national leadership failed, he accepted the solace of another presidency, from the American Historical Association, as fitting reward for his various books about manliness on the Western frontier.

Like Turner, Roosevelt both celebrates and mourns the frontier as a crucible of man-making whose time has passed. *Ranch Life and the Hunting-Trail* (1888), for instance, begins with an epigraph from Browning: "Oh, our manhood's prime vigor! . . ." The book depicts the "daring and adventurousness" of stockmen (7) and the reckless, "defiant self-confidence" of cowboys (9) in Cooper-like terms, as "a primitive stage of existence," which is now "doomed, and can hardly outlast the century" (24).[21] Here "civilization seems as remote as if we were living in an age long past. The whole existence is patriarchal in character: it is the life of men who live in the open, . . . who call no man master" (6). Written self-consciously to Easterners, the book carefully differentiates among the exotic frontier types while warning that the West "is no place for men who lack the ruder, coarser virtues and physical qualities, no matter how intellectual or how refined and delicate their sensibilities" (10). For those who can take it, the frontier brings out mutual honor and self-respect—not "the emasculated, milk-and-water moralities" but "the stern, manly qualities that are invaluable to a nation" (56). Cowboys are "much better fellows and pleasanter companions" than men on small farms, Roosevelt declares, "nor are the mechanics and workmen of a great city to be mentioned in the same breath" (10).

Roosevelt had an immense personal impact on the two writers who inaugurated the most enduring twentieth-century myths of American manliness. In Owen Wister's *The Virginian* (1902), dedicated to Roosevelt, an urbane Eastern narrator quickly discovers that the ungrammatical but self-possessed hero from old Virginia (never named) embodies the essence of true gentlemanliness and bravery. Wister had been a David Gamut in the making. A *summa cum laude* graduate in music from Harvard who had played privately for Franz Liszt on the European tour preparing him as an opera composer, he suffered his first nervous breakdown in 1884, and went to Wyoming at the suggestion of his doctor, the ubiquitous S. Weir Mitchell. Over the next two decades, Wister and his friend Frederic Remington together created the myth of the cowboy, at the moment of the cowboy's obsolescence. Both men cherished Roosevelt's example and friendship.[22] In the second edition of *The Virginian* (1911), Wister's "Rededication" hails Roosevelt as an inspiring "benefactor" who brought "sincerity" back to public men after "nigh half-a-century of shirking and evasion." Earlier, as president, Roosevelt had specifically praised exactly what Wister had intended in crafting his cowboy myth: *The Virginian* fused frontier democracy with chivalric aristocracy, joining gentlemanly ideals of honor and rhetorical wit with frontier ideals of manliness.[23]

As Wister's first preface acknowledges, however, his book is an elegy for a rough nobility that must inevitably fade, in the transition to what has become "a shapeless state . . . of men and manners" (xi). Beyond the domestic comedy, in which the hero's "rhetorical aplomb" brings schoolteacher Molly Stark Wood to accept his patriarchal dominance despite his lower social status, Wister's enduring contribution has been the genre of the American western, where the plot culminates in a face-to-face shoot-out between good and evil. That drama has shaped and simplified national self-perceptions from the Virginian versus Trampas to General Schwarzkopf versus Saddam Hussein. Giving closure to the recurrent saga of triumph and humiliation, a man of honor who is also a man of violence stands tall and alone against the darkening sky, as elegiac counterpoint to the sunset of self-reliance and the rise of the corporate state.

Perhaps not surprisingly, the writer who codified the Last Real Man myth by fusing beast with patrician had been rejected by Roosevelt's Rough Riders. Published in 1912, the year of the Bull Moose Party, Edgar Rice Burroughs's *Tarzan of the Apes* presents a benignly self-divided hero.[24] Tarzan, or Lord Greystoke, an orphan child of British aristocrats who is raised by African apes, enacts the age-old drive of dominance over other males—but only as an ape. When his equally age-old gentlemanly instincts are aroused, he turns chivalric, especially with Jane, who shares his double self. In the novel's most mythic moment, having saved Jane from Terkoz, an ape-ravisher, Tarzan first "did what no red-blooded man needs lessons in doing. He took his woman in his arms and smothered her upturned, panting lips with kisses." Jane's primal self responds; her civilized self recoils. So "Tarzan of the Apes did just what his first ancestor would have done. He took his woman in his arms and carried her into the jungle" (156–57).

As Marianna Torgovnick emphasizes, however, Tarzan immediately feels great confusion about what a man ought to do. Should he rape, as Terkoz would? Yet he is a man, not an ape; how should a Real Man act?[25] Having carried her off against her (civilized) will, Tarzan resolves to "act as he imagined the men in the books would have acted" (166). These are the books in his parents' cabin that he is teaching himself to read, though as yet he can speak not a word. Giving Jane a locket, "like some courtier of old . . . the hall-mark of his aristocratic birth" (168), he sleeps outside her bower to make her feel protected from him as well as by him. By the end of the book, when Tarzan first speaks to her, he is bilingual and can drive a car.[26]

Burroughs's myth transforms Cooper's Hawkeye to a Rooseveltian pince-nez strong man. Tarzan the aristocrat lets another man claim Jane in marriage, because no gentleman would think of asking a lady to break a promise, while Tarzan the ape posts this terse warning on his parents' cabin door:

THIS IS THE HOUSE OF TARZAN, THE
KILLER OF BEASTS AND MANY BLACK MEN.
DO NOT HARM THE THINGS WHICH ARE
TARZAN'S. TARZAN WATCHES.
TARZAN OF THE APES. (103)

No one notices Tarzan's casual equation of beasts and blacks, or his presumption of property rights, Eric Cheyfitz comments. What everybody wants to know is his name, which means "White Skin." Only mother-love is exempted from the novel's pervasive racism. African blacks represent an evil worse than apes, except perhaps on the generically male side. Equally brutish are the ship's low-class mutineers.[27] If Tarzan's character divides Natty Bumppo's harmony of civilized and savage gifts, the plot fulfills almost every civilized white fantasy of class and race domination.

So, more desperately, does *Batman*'s plot, which begins with Batman fighting urban muggers and ends with the hero on a tower fighting first a black man and then the Joker, his trickster double, the "artist of homicide." In *Batman,* human powerlessness is everywhere. Cooper's patriarchal controls vanish in the first scene, as Daddy takes his family down the wrong street toward urban danger, much as Tarzan's father led his family into African violence. Neither these fathers nor the city fathers can stop the seeping evil represented by "Axis Chemicals" and the Joker. "Axis," of course, brings to mind the World War incipient in these depressionlike scenes. Anton Furst's sets not only evoke the awed helplessness induced by Nazi architecture but also call attention to themselves *as* sets, making moviegoers half aware of their own presence as dwarfed spectators. Everyone sits in the dark, watching the flickering lights, wondering where the sun went, and passively awaiting the next random spectacle of mutilation.

Only a superhero could save this civilization of victims. After the Joker challenges Batman via the TV screen to a "mano-a-mano" combat, he dispenses money and poison gas to the greedy, faceless, depression era masses, along with cynical words about the uselessness of their ordinary lives. Enacting again and again the only drama he knows, he exposes everyone's loss of face. He disfigures the women he dominates, he turns underworld rivals into skulls, and he defaces himself with his ceaselessly inhuman smile, the inverse of the Batman symbol. Nor can Lord Greystoke's aristocratic instincts serve Bruce Wayne as a source of chivalric power. Stripped of his dress-up costume, the hero seems all too human and adolescent, to the initial disgust of Batman fans who expected a version of the *Dark Knight* comic book.

Here, in fact, the moviemakers may have been more attuned to their mass-market audience than sophisticated reviewers have allowed. If "Me Tarzan, you Jane" is Tarzan of the movies, simplifying Lord Greystoke's double self into a Noble Savage primitivism, Burroughs's novel voices a contradictory fusion of savage violence with a comedy of manners. This double drama of man-making mixes brutal dominance and humiliation with civilized self-control. From a very different perspective, the postmodernist uses of psychoanalytic doubling and gender crossover in Frank Miller's *Batman: The Dark Knight Returns* and Alan Moore's *Batman: The Killing Joke* (both of which influenced the movie) jettison the contradictory myth, replacing it with a Noble Deconstructionist.

In the adult comics, a battered, aging Bruce Wayne desperately tries to ward off the contemporary chameleonism, cynicism, and even psychosis that the Joker gleefully welcomes. "You had a Bad Day once, am I right?"[28] says Joker to Batman. "Why else would you dress up like a flying rat?" Everyone has been driven crazy; it's even crazier to pretend that it makes sense to keep on struggling. Where these comic books dramatize the story of an agonized, midlife consciousness on the verge of self-deconstruction in a world unravelling toward relentless urban violence and moral nihilism, the movie draws on similar images of futility while telling the story of a young near-Fauntleroy, whose salvational mission redeems the world, assuages his pain, and makes him a man.

Like Sherman McCoy in Tom Wolfe's *Bonfire of the Vanities* (1987), another rich boy-man who yearns to be "King of the Jungle" and "Master of the Universe," Bruce Wayne seems to have it all yet doesn't even know how to manage his first date with Vicki Vale. Their comic awkwardness at opposite ends of his enormous dining room table resolves into speedy downward mobility to the butler's kitchen, where they can get to know each other like kids on a sleepover. Wolfe's cynical narration has no such endearing touches. Readers meet Sherman McCoy on his knees, trying to put a leash on his dachshund before walking to his mistress's apartment. Over 600 pages later, unleashing the Bernhard Goetz inside himself, the real McCoy feels a climactic rush that comes not from sex, not from money, but only from punching a tall black man in the solar plexus. "You cold-cocked him!" a friend says, astonished (651–52). Vitalized at last, McCoy wants to do it "*again*" and "*again*" (656). While the people around him wonder if he has become a "lunatic," he shows his teeth and "let out a short harsh red laugh" as the band of demonstrators retreats "down the marble halls."[29] With that bestial surge, the book ends. This is the urban context for *Batman*'s more cross-class appeal. Both plots offer what Richard Slotkin has called the frontier fantasy of "regeneration through violence" as a restoration of manliness, overcoming diffuse fears of urban powerlessness and depersonalization lurking below the ostensible fears of random muggings.[30]

Bruce Wayne's double drama of man-making occurs at the level of cosmopolitan gender stereotypes as well as beast-man myth. The Gatsbylike boy-man becomes a Real Man, in human terms, when he visits Vicki Vale to tell her his half-human identity. Angry because she thinks he has stood her up on a date, she starts to voice her outrage. "Shut up," he explains, and pushes her down on the couch. Accepting that move without a murmur, the Pulitzer Prize-winning photographer waits expectantly. Ahhhh, viewers should feel; we can relax. He *is* a real man after all. He *can* carry her off into the jungle, or the Bat Cave. Besides, it is a typically feminine trivialization to reduce all the horrors of what the Joker tried to do to Vicki in the Museum to being stood up on a date. Part of the scene's comedy, as Bruce reverts to inarticulate stumbling in his attempt to tell her about himself, is Vicki's immediate inference that he must be gay. But viewers now know better: the anxious rich kid will be a gentleman of force, the last one, not another lost or vicious urbanite, of whatever sexual persuasion.

Thereafter, despite Vicki Vale's fast-track city career, their dialogue updates *Tarzan*'s traditionally gendered comedy of manners while the plot enacts sadistic fantasies of man-making and humiliation. In Vicki's apartment as in the Bat Cave, it is much more important for a man to talk about his work than for a woman to talk about her feelings. When Vicki at last insists on bringing up Love, Bruce-Batman responds with an almost parodic imitation of the credo, "Later—a man's got to do what a man's got to do." From then on, Vicki becomes a marginal inconvenience and support for Batman's work identity. She never seems annoyed that he stole her potentially prize-winning photographs of him. Instead, she plays the traditional helpmeet, who lies a little about her weight and shows courage to aid his career. At the very end, Vicki does the ultimate, self-degrading sacrifice to help her man triumph. She goes down on the Joker, slowly and unmistakably sliding down his body and off the screen, to divert his attention.

As beast-patrician and fair young damsel are chauffeured away into their snug seclusion, one could imagine a feminist ending. Vicki Vale will return to her career with exclusive Batman photos, win a second Pulitzer Prize, and move on up to become the first female anchor of a prime time news show. Meanwhile, Bruce Wayne will have retired from his dangerous, adventurist, and unpaying job to become a contented house husband, managing the friendly servants who do the child care, the laundry, and the dishes.

On balance, however, it seems more likely that Vicki Vale's voluptuous presence as faithful sidekick functions primarily to remove the threat of homosexuality from the Batman myth, not to awaken hopes of a feminist swerve.[31] Several years before the movie was made, Batman fans responded to a poll by vigorously demanding that Robin be dumped. He seemed too wimpy and twerpy; some used gay-baiting terms. Yet much of the movie's power comes from its playing with the adolescent ambiguities in Michael Keaton's role. He *could* have become a Robin, or a homosexual, or an effete impotent snob, or a faceless husband to a strong career woman. Instead, he resolutely masculinizes himself in a world that seems hell bent on robbing every man of a father and virility. The fact of Kim Basinger's casting looms larger than her stereotypic gendering to empower the hero as yet another Last Real Man in America.

I draw six conclusions from this sketch of a changing myth. First, ideologies of manhood have functioned primarily in relation to the gaze of male peers and male authority. By suppressing complex feelings often involving women, such ideologies produce good workers, competitors, and fighters in the public sphere. Here several of Eve Kosofsky Sedgwick's arguments are to the point. In *Between Men* and *Epistemology of the Closet* she argues that "homosocial desire" builds on homophobia and misogyny to perpetuate patriarchal oppressions. Ultimately, the construction of public maleness as a privileged category to serve the social unit fosters a male preoccupation with measuring self-worth in the eyes of one's workplace peers. What Sedgwick takes to be the generating issue, an increasingly phobic and paranoid (hetero)sexual self-construction of maleness in the last century, seems to me a prime consequence of capitalism's early construction of the workplace as the exclusively gendered site for public rewards.

In theory, the workplace could be gender neutral. In practice, as Daniel Gilmore concludes in *Manhood in the Making,* a society's preoccupation with manhood "directly correlates with male-role stress," especially "when men are conditioned to fight." Gilmore intriguingly suggests that both male codes of combative or stoic assertiveness and female codes of self-sacrifice have to be learned, but that men need ritual and ideological socialization because they are more "atomistic," whereas women are "normally under the control of men," especially in precapitalist societies.[32] In capitalism, too, fathering and competition play roles at least as central in male self-construction as any forms of sexual desire or ambivalence about mothering, in large part because competitiveness drives the energy of any market economy.

What changes is how the respect of one's peers and authority is constituted. In preindustrial, small-scale societies, whether in Native American villages or Greek and Italian city-states, manhood connotes honor, fatherhood, citizenship, sexual prowess, and bravery in battle as well as pride of craftsmanship and primacy as family provider. In modern economies—especially in the United States where, as Alfred Chandler argues, capitalism has taken an exceptionally competitive form—patriarchy has given way to a more amorphous mixture of collaboration, rivalry, and role-playing to give upward mobility in the professionalized marketplace.[33] The evolving beast-patrician myth of man-making incorporates a mid-nineteenth-century image of entrepreneurial individualism with turn-of-the-century class extremes to stabilize a violent yet hypercivilized compensatory fantasy.

Second, the myth has become both more homophobic and more ambiguously playful about sexual identity. Not one of Cooper's contemporary readers would have dreamed of calling for a Kim Basinger to replace Chingachgook, though it's fun to imagine what Natty would do. Cooper half tried once, and egregiously failed, in *The Pathfinder* (1840). On the other hand, *Batman*'s social comedy flirts with Bruce Wayne's potential gayness, while his animal cross-dressing evokes Mark Seltzer's label for Jack London's heroes, "Men in Furs."[34] *Batman*'s disappointing sequel comfortably incorporates a strong, daring, and angry animal-woman (Catwoman), while erasing the more dangerous homoerotic energies playing at the margins of Batman's self-construction. What's missing is any disruptive, doubled charge between Batman and the Penguin. Taken together, the two movies confirm Sedgwick's basic insight about violent homosocial bonding across the body of a woman, perhaps with the additional covert pleasure of aristocratic and brute males coupling inside one heroic, isolated, guarded yet vulnerable male body.

Third, the myth continues to idealize, marginalize, and mutilate women. Though Jane and Vicki Vale are a good deal more respectably sexy than shrinking Alice Dunham or intrepid Judith Hutter in *The Deerslayer,* women continue to function in these narratives as adjuncts to a man's remasculinization, providing emotional supports and physical targets.

Fourth, the incipient theme of effete, feminized urbanity in Cooper becomes an explicit rejection of high society manners in Turner and Jack London, an attempt at amalgamation in Wister and Burroughs, then a cross-class dramatization of civilized powerlessness in *Batman.* In that sense, "woman" may be a token signifier for a larger, stranger issue, present also in *Tarzan* and *McTeague,* where spirited modern heroines become helpless victims: Why should the power of bourgeois civilization breed such fantasies of middle-class male powerlessness?

In *Epistemology of the Closet,* Sedgwick provocatively emphasizes "the production and deployment, especially in contemporary U.S. society, of an extraordinarily high level of self-pity in nongay men." She attributes this to an incipient panic about the "incoherences implicit in modern male *hetero*sexuality." More diffusely, pervasive fantasies of abusing and victimizing women can be legitimated by male fantasies of "maudlin" self-pity, as if to scapegoat one's own sense of victimization.[35] Here again, however, gender panic may be more symptom than source. A middle-class man's sense of being powerless or unreal, or incoherent at the edges of his gender construction, can be produced by a workplace-fostered obsessionality in which the safest way to feel embodied desire is to hyperventilate about homosocial achievement or dominance.

Fifth, I see three stages in the progression of the new myth. In the "Hawkeye" stage, Natty's lateral mobility and chumship with Chingachgook complement a nostalgic mourning for precapitalist patriarchy and a covert fantasy that frontier bumpkins can rid the civilized world of Indians. In the turn-of-the-century stage, McTeague, Buck, and Turner's Andrew Jackson dramatize a downward mobility from lower-class status into savagery to redeem and/or shock effete Eastern gentility. Norris seems to have written *McTeague* as a manly riposte to the feminized tea-party "realism" of Howells's *The Rise of Silas Lapham* (1885).[36] A relish for violence to women surfaces in Norris, London, and Burroughs, becoming a fascination with grotesque mutilations in *Batman.* In the third, post-Teddy Roosevelt stage, the hero seems comfortably (Tarzan) or uncomfortably (Bruce Wayne) divided between an old-money class identity and a role as bestial avenger, while urban civilization seems faceless and impotent. Here upper-class status seems stereotypically inadequate to empower masculine privilege.

Sixth, and finally, an ambivalence about the powers of the female body saps the strength yet girds up the loins of these Last Real Men. As he leads his pack after a rabbit, Buck feels "an ecstasy" of blood-lust, "a complete forgetfulness that one is alive," like an inspired "artist" or a "war-mad" soldier, "sounding the deeps of his nature, . . . going back into the womb of Time. He was mastered by the sheer surging of life, the tidal wave of being" (*Call of the Wild,* 49). Ape-man McTeague feels insensibly reborn in his manliness as he reaches the mountains, where Mother Nature is not "cozy, intimate, small, and homelike, like a good-natured housewife"—or the woman he has murdered—but "a vast, unconquered brute of the Pliocene epoch, savage, sullen, and magnificently indifferent to man" (212–13). With a simpler dichotomizing, Batman becomes invulnerable in his womblike Batmobile and Bat Cave, though instantly vulnerable in his all-too-fragile and phallic Batplane, shot down by a single blast from Joker's ridiculously long toy gun.

Here manliness seems regenerated not by violence but by umbilical connection. Perhaps, to apply Mark Carnes's argument about overtly patriarchal lodge rituals again, the macho masks hide and license a male maternalism: Tarzan feeds, shelters, and holds Jane just as Kala mothered him.[37] Or perhaps the womb-surge is even more basic. If Tarzan makes inarticulate sounds and howls in ecstasy while his blood pounds like a tidal wave, if Batman feels like sleeping upside down before careening toward the moon, it's not that a nice young gentleman has suddenly got rape and murder on his mind. The Last Real Man in America is just having his period.

Such fantasies empower women only tangentially and metaphorically. They legitimate male violence with a traditional sex role polarity: Within every animal-man hides a Good Mother. The claim belies the ugliness always latent in the Real Man myth. For me that darkness became most visible in a $10 batman shirt, a spin-off from the first movie: Not the Michael Keaton boy-man who plays protective urban terrorist, but Batman for the skinhead market. Under the blood-orange moon, his teeth gleam over dark, random corpses. By his left foot lies a prone, sallow body whose spiked Mohawk haircut clearly brands him as a dying Indian or street gang member, with a gun pointing aimlessly upward behind his shoulder. By his right foot, with a manacled arm reaching up Batman's cloak in a curious gesture—a prisoner? a slave? a homoerotic invitation?—lies a burr-head black man. Other scattered bodies and a litter of guns, knives, chains, and eerily disconnected limbs sprawl about his feet, evoking an American landscape filled with skulls and crossbones, urban muggers, and frontier violence. Above it all, collapsing American history into an image of the beast-man, stands Batman-Dracula, Master of the Universe and vampire bat, about to drink their blood. Here is the psychic landscape lurking below Sean Connery's white-on-white cover of *Gentleman's Quarterly*.

The skinhead Batman glories in the racist violence on which the myth of the Last Real Man in America has fed, from Cooper's Indian wars to Buck's killing of the Yeehats to Tarzan's killings of African blacks. Part of the myth's pleasure lies in what James Bond called the hero's "license to kill," a license helping to make the myth so serviceable in the international arena. A more basic pleasure lies in the ritualistic arena of mano-a-mano rivalry, where women and other complex states of being are out of sight and out of mind.

The myth of a Last Real Man depends on its equal and opposite myth, that of a subhuman underclass, to generate ceaseless dramas of dominance and humiliation. These ahistorical dramas of self-empowering express and evade both the felt facelessness of upwardly mobile men in the settlements and the diffuse resentments of the immobilized. So long as corporate capitalism structures male identity primarily through role-playing and workplace competition, the craving for Real Man myths will continue despite the entry of women into management positions. In a world where Sherman McCoys at the top and their fast-lane counterparts at the bottom measure worth only as supremacy in the cash flow game, the men at the top will talk of "hemorrhaging money" (*Bonfire,* 330) whereas the men at the bottom hemorrhage violence. Batman embodies an intimate circulation of old money and new blood.

But capitalism's opening beyond small-scale patriarchal stabilizings to diversified international markets, like academia's opening to multicultural constituencies, encourages the circulation and exchange of more heterogeneous energies. A currently intractable impasse between capitalism's production of material abundance and its production of a useless urban underclass fosters much of the anxious urgency invested in the ideology of upward mobility. If you are not rising, as a person or a corporation, you must be powerless, or falling—into what? An unemployable underclass remains the bourgeois bogeyman and cautionary tale, the demonized other for middle-class resentments and fears. Yet the competitive pluralism intrinsic to any large-scale market checks and challenges anyone's will to power, whereas marketing itself enforces a continuous reassessment of otherness and difference among potential buyers. Equally to the point, the corporate workplace encourages collaborative as well as competitive energies, often beyond the imagination of academic artisans and entrepreneurs. An edgy tolerance for diversity has been one of capitalism's more unacknowledged cultural achievements.

Ideologies die operatic deaths, and individualism's deflection of capitalism's various contradictions into manliness has led to an exceptionally long aria–165 years and counting. From the beginning, the myth of the Last Real Man in America fuses idealizations of high civility with increasingly brutalized representations of lower-class violence. From the beginning, too, the myth has subsumed an elegiac simplification of history, grieving for the passing of frontier self-reliance and patriarchal dominance. In the cosmopolitan perspectives of another 160 years or so, the myth may well be set beside the grandfather clock and the Model T Ford as another example of persistent yokelism.

On the other hand, the myth's tenacity signals the vitality of capitalist paradoxes. Perhaps on a multinational stage, Real Man myths will even expand their market: the Last Real Man in Czechoslovakia, the Last Real Man in Argentina. Eventually there may well be more gender-neutral stories to tell. Yet myths of self-empowering will still mix elegance with violence to tease people away from thinking about what makes them feel unreal.

Notes

1. The *Celebrity Plus* cover presents Harrison Ford as, in smaller print, a "Crusader" who "Shoots from the hip in This Candid Talk." The story simply depicts him as a man at ease with himself, living in

Wyoming with his family, remembering his hard knocks, and fishing instead of playing Hollywood games. The *Gentleman's Quarterly* essay, by Diane K. Shah, entitled "All Together Now: Sean Connery Is an Icon," bears a similarly tangential relation to the "Last Real Man" packaging on the cover.

2. Barbara Gamarekian, "The Cartoonists' Art: Nothing Is Too Sacred," *New York Times*, Tuesday, 19 March 1991, B2.
3. Mark C. Carnes, *Secret Ritual and Manhood in Victorian America* (New Haven, CT: Yale University Press, 1989). See also Susan Jeffords, *The Remasculinization of America: Gender and the Vietnam War* (Bloomington, IN: Indiana University Press, 1989). As Walter Benn Michaels has pointed out for D. H. Lawrence's forays into New Mexico and classic American literature, such remasculinization through wildness depends on the previous extinction of the Indians to transform them from a social threat into an assimilable culture resource. See "The Vanishing American," *American Literary History* 2 (Summer 1990): 220–41. T. J. Jackson Lears, in *No Place of Grace: Antimodernism and the Transformation of American Culture 1880–1920* (New York: Pantheon Books, 1981), and many others emphasize connections between turn-of-the century feelings of powerlessness and fantasies of hypermasculinity.
4. Amy Kaplan, "Romancing the Empire: The Embodiment of American Masculinity in the Popular Historical Novel of the 1890s," *American Literary History* 2 (Winter 1990): 659–90. Kaplan applies this argument to turn-of-the-century chivalric romances of imperialism. See also Lora Romero, "Vanishing Americans: Gender, Empire, and New Historicism," *American Literature* 63 (September 1991): 385–404. My discussion of manliness on the frontier also builds on well-known studies by Leslie Fiedler and Richard Slotkin. Page references to Cooper's *The Last of the Mohicans: A Narrative of 1757* (1826; reprint, New York: Signet, 1980), are incorporated in the text.
5. In "No Apologies for the Iroquois," chap. 4 of *Sensational Designs: The Cultural Work of American Fiction 1790–1860* (New York: Oxford University Press, 1985), Jane Tompkins emphasizes the crossover liminalities throughout Cooper's narrative.
6. Donald J. Trump, with Tony Schwartz, *Trump: The Art of the Deal* (New York: Warner Books, 1987), 71–72. Trump goes on to talk with pride about stealing his younger brother's blocks and going to military school, where he found teachers he could admire, particularly a former marine drill sergeant who was "the kind of guy who could slam into a goalpost wearing a football helmet and break the post rather than his head." This Real Man would "go for the jugular if he smelled weakness," but he would treat you "like a man" if you "finessed" him with respect (72–74). Trump's autobiography shares

several characteristics with Cellini's: both seem to have been dictated, both celebrate competitive prowess, and both show considerable relish for outstripping their fathers, though each pays ostentatious respect to his father as well.

7. David G. Gilmore, *Manhood in the Making: Cultural Concepts of Masculinity* (New Haven, CT: Yale University Press, 1989), takes a cross-cultural approach to the social construction of masculinities, arguing that traditional manly codes of stoicism, physical strength, sexual prowess, and bravery function to protect the social unit. Gilmore's useful and unpretentious survey concludes that the "Ubiquitous Male" criteria of "Man-the-Impregnator-Protector-Provider" function in "either dangerous or highly competitive" social situations to force men beyond their longing to retreat to "childish narcissism" (222–24), a state repeatedly linked to Melville's Bartleby (109, 174–75). My own book, *Manhood and the American Renaissance* (Ithaca, NY: Cornell University Press, 1989), chap. 3, argues that all ideologies of manhood draw on male fears of being humiliated, and more diffusely of being seen by other men as weak and vulnerable (72–73). Pericles' Funeral Oration to the Athenians is the most eloquent summation of precapitalist manliness I have run across; he explicitly links honor in battle to a man's fear of humiliation and the desire to have the respect of one's fellow men.
8. See Stephen Greenblatt, *Shakespearean Negotiations: The Circulation of Social Energy in Renaissance England* (Berkeley: University of California Press, 1988), 75–76, on individual identity as a "way station on the road to a firm and decisive identification with normative structures," structures that he elsewhere discusses as masks and mobile improvisations whose instabilities themselves are part of power's circulations. Compare also a fine review-essay by Thomas K. McGraw, "In Retrospect: Berle and Means," *Reviews in American History* 18 (December 1990): 578–96, which reassesses the Berle-Means thesis about American capitalism's tendency toward industrial concentration and the separation of ownership from control. McGraw speaks of the sociology of executives: their "submergence in a corporate culture obsessed with competitive market performance, their keen identification of self with company" (586). Alfred Chandler's recent book, *Scale and Scope: The Dynamics of Industrial Capitalism* (Cambridge: Harvard University Press, 1990), contrasts American competitive corporate capitalism with England's more family-based capitalism and Germany's more collaborative capitalism.
9. Kenneth Cmiel, *Democratic Eloquence: The Fight over Popular Speech in Nineteenth-Century America* (New York: William Morrow, 1990), 92, also 58; Stuart M. Blumin, *The Emergence of the Middle Class:*

Social Experience in the American City, 1760–1900 (Cambridge: Cambridge University Press, 1989), esp. 269–92. As Blumin notes, the middle class' "individualistic, competitive values . . . were those most at odds with sustained, explicitly class-based organization" (257), despite "the increasingly distinctive three-class structure of daily social life" (288), especially in the cities, where "class segregation" increased (284) and an accelerating suburbanization of the middle class exacerbated class divisions. Blumin also suggests that middle-class values gained such ideological hegemony because the preindustrial upper class gave way to "more specialized celebrities" at the top (296), whereas manual workers had enough money to define themselves as middle-class consumers. Mary P. Ryan, *Cradle of the Middle Class: The Family in Oneida County, New York, 1790–1865* (Cambridge: Cambridge University Press, 1981) recurrently discusses the new middle class' fear of falling into the new working class—a more fundamental motive for upward mobility, in her view, than the drive for competitive success (184, 210, 238). See my notes to chap. 3 of *Manhood and the American Renaissance*; also Cmiel, *Democratic Eloquence,* on the "polysemic" diversity of language and self that accompanied the triumph of "middling" oratory over elite traditions of refined language and character. Cmiel notes the paradox that, after the Civil War, class divisions hardened while elite symbols diffused into mass culture (145–47).

10. Carroll Smith-Rosenberg, *Disorderly Conduct: Visions of Gender in Victorian America* (New York: Oxford University Press, 1985), 90, also 100–107. *Meanings for Manhood: Constructions of Masculinity in Victorian America* (Chicago: University of Chicago Press, 1990), a recent anthology of essays edited by Mark C. Carnes and Clyde Griffen, historicizes masculine gender constructions more complexly than I can do here. See esp. Anthony Rotundo's essay, "Boy Culture" (15–36) and Griffen's speculative overview (183–204). Filene's *Him/Her/Self: Sex Roles in Modern America,* 2nd ed. (Baltimore: Johns Hopkins University Press, 1986), 69–93, surveys late nineteenth-century American male anxieties, esp. in relation to women and domestic roles.
11. Page references to *The Deerslayer or the First War-Path* (1841; reprint, Garden City: Dolphin-Doubleday, n.d.), are incorporated in the text.
12. Compare Richard Slotkin, *Regeneration Through Violence: The Mythology of the American Frontier, 1600–1860* (Middletown, CT: Wesleyan University Press, 1973); my emphasis on the inversions of upward/downward mobility differs here from Slotkin's quasi-Jungian sense of the frontier beast-man myth as a mythic initiation into soul-archetypes, where manhood becomes a sacred marriage through violence with the anima and natural fertility goddesses (156, 539, 543).

In *The Fatal Environment: The Myth of the Frontier in the Age of Industrialization 1800–1890* (New York: Atheneum, 1985), esp. discussing General Custer, Slotkin's more sociological focus for myths of manhood could complement Cmiel's and my own sense of entrepreneurial role-playing. Slotkin argues (377) that the masculine imperatives of self-assertion and stern command, with their feminine inversions, lead to a double bind: self-reliant, yet subordinate to authority, a subordination that Custer split as masculine and feminine. Slotkin also emphasizes Custer's resolution of this split through role-playing and self-dramatization (378, 383).

13. Walter Benn Michaels, *The Gold Standard and the Logic of Naturalism: American Literature at the Turn of the Century* (Berkeley: University of California Press, 1987), situates McTeague's desire in relation to American anxiety about money circulation (148–54) and more profound insatiabilities of desire generated by capitalism. June Howard, in *Form and History in American Literary Naturalism* (Chapel Hill: University of North Carolina Press, 1985), comes closer to my view in framing Norris's contradictions about masculinity as part of "inconsistent fears" ranging from genteel class nervousness about proletarianization to petty-bourgeois feelings of entrapment "between the working class and the corporation" (95–96). The issues resolve into a sense of powerlessness diffusely projected on a monstrously empowered Other, which Howard links to manly brutality in both Norris and Jack London (51–63, 117–25, 140).
14. Jack London, *The Call of the Wild and White Fang* (Toronto: Bantam Books, 1981), 85–86: "Thornton fell on his knees beside Buck. Head was against head, and he was shaking him back and forth. Those who hurried up heard him cursing Buck, and he cursed him long and fervently, and softly and lovingly. . . . Buck seized Thornton's hand in his teeth. Thornton shook him back and forth. As though animated by a common impulse, the onlookers drew back to a respectful distance, nor were they again indiscreet enough to interrupt." Quotations from *The Call of the Wild* are incorporated in the text.
15. Christopher P. Wilson, *The Labor of Words: Literary Professionalism in the Progressive Era* (Athens, GA: University of Georgia Press, 1985), 155–56. Wilson notes the subtle undertone of "satire" created by adopting Buck's limited point of view concerning human desires (102–4). Wilson is also astute on the links between professionalism and narcissistic masculinity emerging at the turn of the century (xiv, 197–99). Like D. H. Lawrence's, London's emphasis on virility enables both a half-veiled homoeroticism and what Wilson calls a "rediscovery of threatened craft ideals" (104). Mark Seltzer's "the Love Masters" uses London's *Sea-Wolf* to culminate his complex argument about the machinelike disciplining of men's bodies as represented

in various texts—"an erotics of discipline" yet a promiscuous transgression of boundaries, including the natural and the unnatural. See Seltzer, *Bodies and Machines* (New York: Routledge, 1992), 149–72.

16. Victoria Kahn, "*Virtù* and the Example of Agathocles in Machiavelli's *The Prince*," *Representations* 13 (Winter 1986): 63–83. I am indebted here to discussions with Brandy Kershner. Kahn's essay brilliantly teases out the differences between princelike and subjectlike readings of the Agathocles-Borgia contrast—if we're taken in by humanistic morality, we're unreflective subjects—before exposing "the essential emptiness of the concept of *virtù*" (77).
17. Turner's "The Significance of the Frontier in American History" (1893) is reprinted in *Frontier and Section: Selected Essays of Frederick Jackson Turner*, ed. Ray Allen Billington (Englewood Cliffs, NJ: Prentice-Hall, 1961), 37–62. An expanded version, "The Frontier in American History" (1920), is reprinted in *The Historians' History of the United States*, vol. 1, ed. Andrew S. Berky and James P. Shenton (New York: Capricorn, 1966), 462–73, quotations incorporated in text.
18. A great many studies in the last fifteen years have emphasized the rise of the professions after the Civil War. Robert H. Wiebe, *The Search for Order 1877–1920* (New York: Hill and Wang, 1967), esp. chap. 5 on "A New Middle Class" (111–32), deftly sketches the complex tensions empowering an emphasis on class and a resolution through the professions. In "Revisiting the Vanishing Frontier: The Legacy of Frederick Jackson Turner," *Western Historical Quarterly* 18 (April 1987): 157–76, William Cronon notes Turner's fear that without the frontier, immigrants could not escape class conflicts (167). Cronon argues that "almost in spite of himself," Turner "gave American history its central and most persistent story" (176), initially man on the frontier but finally humans interacting with landscape, or environmental history that began as western history (171). This sympathetic approach minimizes or misses Turner's insistence on manmaking as the goal of environmental interaction.
19. Compare Wiebe, *Search for Order*, 132; also Nick Salvatore, *Eugene V. Debs: Citizen and Socialist* (Urbana: University of Illinois Press, 1982), on Debs's appeal to native artisan traditions of American manliness rather than to European traditions of socialism.
20. David McCullough's biography of Roosevelt's childhood, *Mornings on Horseback* (New York: Simon and Schuster, 1981), esp. 90–108, speculates that Roosevelt unconsciously used his asthma attacks to gain days alone with his father: "father and the out of doors meant salvation" (108). Roosevelt's National Progressive party, formed in June 1912 after he had been humiliated at the Republican convention, was given its nickname by the newspapers because he told

reporters he felt as fit as a bull moose. The manly response to wounding caught the nation's fancy.

21. Theodore Roosevelt, *Ranch Life and the Hunting-Trail* (1888; reprint, Ann Arbor, MI: University Microfilms, 1966), quotations incorporated in text.
22. Grant C. Knight, *The Strenuous Age in American Literature* (Chapel Hill: University of North Carolina Press, 1954), 55, also 72 on Roosevelt the literary critic (as President!), esp. a 1907 essay criticizing London's *White Fang* for depicting a fight between dog and wolf that is "the very sublimity of absurdity." Knight situates Roosevelt's image and impact in the context of American imperialism (50–59, also 6–12). I am indebted here and elsewhere to Gordon Hutner.
23. Owen Wister, *The Virginian* (1902; reprint, New York: Grosset and Dunlap, 1929), quotations incorporated in text. On rhetorical play in *The Virginian* and its uses for dominating the independent, equality-minded heroine, see Lee Clark Mitchell, " 'When You Call Me That . . .' : Tall Talk and Male Hegemony in *The Virginian*," *PMLA* 102 (January 1987): 66–77. On the sometimes vexed Wister-Remington friendship, see Ben Merchant Vorpahl, *My dear Wister—: The Frederic Remington–Owen Wister Letters* (Palo Alto, TX: American West Publishing, 1972), which also thoughtfully sketches their lives and works. Wister had three serious breakdowns, a second in 1895 (171) and the last in 1909 (323), which he cured with another trip to Wyoming. On Wister's music background, see 9–10. Remington was a Yale football player whose drawings for Roosevelt's *Ranch Life* helped to establish his journalistic career (26), while his famous painting of Roosevelt's Rough Riders charging up San Juan Hill (a fiction) helped to launch his friend into national politics. Remington's letters to Wister about the Cuban invasion are flagrantly racist in their indiscriminate contempt for "a lot of d— niggers" (221), "the Dagoes or the Yaps" (225, also 233). Remington's burly macho postures contrast with Wister's more guarded gentility throughout, for example in asking about Wister's recent marriage, fresh from the success of the Spanish-American war: "How do you get on with your wife—who is boss? or haven't you had time to settle that yet. I believe that sometimes takes several campaigns. Annexation is attended with difficulties" (279). I am indebted for this reference to Carl Bredahl.
24. Edgar Rice Burroughs published *Tarzan of the Apes* as a magazine serial in 1912, then as a book in 1914. Quotations from the reprinted novel (New York: Ballantine, 1983) incorporated in text.
25. Marianna Torgovnick, *Gone Primitive: Savage Intellect, Modern Lives* (Chicago: University of Chicago Press, 1990), 52. Torgovnick's chapter, "Taking Tarzan Seriously" (42–72), teases out the tensions in various Tarzan books between the doubt-filled Tarzan, who can fleet-

ingly imitate maternal modes and learn from blacks, and the macho Tarzan required by the nearly all-male audience, gradually suppressing the character who dares ask, "What does a man do?" (70, also 68–71). See Gail Bederman's " 'The Women Have Had Charge of the Church Work Long Enough': The Men and Religion Forward Movement of 1911–1912 and the Masculinization of Middle-Class Protestantism," *American Quarterly* 41 (September 1989); 432–65, on the gender struggle in churches at this time.

26. Speaking French and (haltingly) English, Tarzan drives Jane away from a forest fire in Wisconsin, before he relinquishes her to her fiancé, the presumed Lord Greystoke.
27. Eric Cheyfitz, in "*Tarzan of the Apes:* U.S. Foreign Policy in the Twentieth Century," *American Literary History* 1 (Summer 1989): 339–60.
28. Alan Moore, *Batman: The Killing Joke* (New York: DC Comics, 1988), n.p. See also Frank Miller, with Klaus Janson and Lynn Varley, *Batman: The Dark Knight Returns* (New York: DC Comics, 1986).
29. Tom Wolfe, *The Bonfire of the Vanities* (New York: Farrar, Strauss & Giroux, 1987); quotations incorporated in text. Torgovnick, in *Gone Primitive,* 259, also links *Bonfire* with Tarzan's jungle.
30. Richard Slotkin, *Regeneration Through Violence*; cf. also Martin Green, *The Great American Adventure: Action Stories from Cooper to Mailer and What They Reveal About American Manhood* (Boston: Beacon Press, 1984), which argues rather simply that the American tradition of manly adventures is imperialist, while also claiming that it constitutes the finest aspect of American literature.
31. See Frederic Wertham, *The Seduction of the Innocent* (New York: Rhinehart, 1954), for a 1950s psychoanalytic (and homophobic) assault on Robin. Frank Miller's *Batman: The Dark Knight Returns* plays with Robin as a crossover gender figure.
32. Gilmore, *Manhood in the Making,* 221.
33. On traditional societies, see Gilmore, *Manhood in the Making,* though he implies the codes and ideologies have not changed much. On capitalism, see Chandler, *Scale and Scope*; Cmiel, *Democratic Eloquence.* Lears's *No Place of Grace* voices a hesitant admiration for religious and masculinist stances in opposition to inchoate modernization, for example, 138, on the "eloquent" and "admirable" manly stoicism of combat, regretfully assimilable to modern nihilism, or 258–59, on the "softened" quality of '"male"' and '"female"' ideals through therapeutic secularism rather than transcendent religion, yet the potential "heroism" of religious-based protest and dissent (181, 260). Lears's conscious ambivalence about the loss of manly strength and religious transcendence gives his book its own complex eloquence. An earlier essay by David Brion Davis, "Stress-seeking and the Self-Made Man in American Literature, 1894–1914," in *From*

Homicide to Slavery: Studies in American Culture (New York: Oxford University Press, 1986), 52–72, links the turn-of-the-century fascination with the "strenuous life" to the breakdown of traditional Protestant bonds between material success and spiritual salvation; stress-seeking man "became an embodiment of sheer vitality in a limitless void" (72).

34. Seltzer, *Bodies and Machines,* 166–72.
35. Eve Kosofsky Sedgwick, *Epistemology of the Closet* (Berkeley: University of California Press, 1990), 145. Sedgwick's extensive analysis of homosexual panic and gender incoherences in Melville's *Billy Budd* and James's "The Beast in the Jungle" locates the 1890s as a crucial moment for the binary construction of sexualities to opposed categories of homosexual and heterosexual.
36. Frank Norris, *McTeague: A Story of San Francisco* ed. Donald Pizer (1899; reprint, New York: Norton Critical Edition, 1977). See Norris, "A Plea for Romantic Fiction" (1901): "Realism is minute, it is the drama of a broken teacup, . . . the adventure of an invitation to dinner" (in *McTeague,* 314). Next quotation from Norris incorporated in text.
37. I am indebted here to discussions of *Tarzan* with a freshman honors class at the University of Florida, as I am indebted to Barry Qualls and Wendy Wall for discussions about *Batman.* See Carnes, *Secret Ritual and Manhood,* esp. 139–50, and Torgovnick, *Gone Primitive* 69, on maternal imitation, also 64–69 on ambivalence about matriarchy in other Tarzan books.

II

Crossing Cultures

2

Barthelme, Freud, and the Killing of Kafka's Father

Peter Schwenger

In 1919, when he was thirty-six, Kafka wrote a letter to his father—forty-five typewritten pages long, with three additional handwritten pages—which is a prime example of Derrida's wry observation that a letter can always not arrive at its destination (Derrida 1987, 444). In the case of Kafka's letter this assertion is true on a number of levels, and first of all the literal. Kafka's mother was given the hefty document to deliver to his father; she never did so. After keeping it for a while she gave it back, perhaps feeling that the estrangement between father and son was so great that attempts to explain it could never repair the damage, and might possibly make it worse. If we read the letter today, feeling rather like eavesdroppers, we ask ourselves about its destination in a figurative sense: Where is this letter going? What is the end point of its argument? The answer is again "the father." But we may now read, beyond Kafka's father, that which he may be said to represent: a certain element of writing—indeed of culture itself—which a number of theorists have called by the father's name. The problem posed by this element moves through the letter and beyond it to raise the question of how we can write to free ourselves from the patriarchal elements of writing. In this chapter I will use Kafka and Freud to explicate the problem. Then I will turn to Donald Barthelme and, briefly, the architect Philip

Johnson to suggest a process for resolving the problem—a process, I should stress, which is not to be taken as a destination, the destination of Kafka's letter. Yet all of these men, in their own ways, are addressing Kafka's father.

At one point in the letter Kafka (1966) confesses to his father that "my writing was all about you." He gives only one example, quoting the last line of *The Trial*—"He is afraid the shame will outlive him, even"—and connecting it to the sense of boundless guilt that Kafka had developed in relation to his father (73). The pressure of Hermann Kafka's domineering personality had invaded the child's very thoughts: "All these thoughts, seemingly independent of you, were from the beginning burdened with your belittling judgments; it was almost impossible to endure this and still work out a thought with any measure of completeness and permanence" (23). Still, completeness and permanence of some sort might have been available if the father's own behavior had these characteristics—but it was riddled with contradictions of which the father himself was unaware and that consequently did not diminish his confidence and authority in the slightest. Kafka draws his examples from the dinner hour, the obligatory family communion that often becomes the family battleground. Eating in the Kafka family was governed by innumerable edicts issued by the father and blithely disregarded by him, the one constant exception to the rule. For instance: "At table one wasn't allowed to do anything but eat, but you cleaned and cut your fingernails, sharpened pencils, cleaned your ears with a toothpick" (27). Kafka admits that these lapses were in themselves unimportant:

> They only became depressing for me because you, so tremendously the authoritative man, did not keep the commandments you imposed upon me. Hence the world was for me divided into three parts: one in which I, the slave, lived under laws that had been invented only for me and which I could, I did not know why, never completely comply with; then a second world, which was infinitely remote from mine, in which you lived, concerned with government, with the issuing of orders and with the annoyance about their not being obeyed; and finally a third world where everybody else lived happily and free from orders and from having to obey. (27, 29)

We may as well disregard this last world, which we—the "everybody else" of whom he speaks—know to be a wistful illusion. We then have two worlds whose tension makes up much of Kafka's fiction: the remote, inaccessible world of authority, and the world of the bewildered paranoiac. Kafka's situation resembles that of many of his protagonists, and can be summed up in these words from the letter: "Nothing was in my very own, undoubted, sole possession, determined unequivocally only by me—in sober truth a disinherited son" (89, 91).

Yet Kafka, while bemoaning these problems, is in a sense attached to them. He pictures the resolution of his problems that would ensue if he were to marry and thus escape the old patterns, shifting the relationship with his father. "Then," Kafka says, "I could be a free, grateful, guiltless, upright son, and you could be an untroubled, untyrannical, sympathetic, contented father. But," he goes on, "to this end everything that ever happened would have to be undone, that is, we ourselves should have to be cancelled out" (115). Here Kafka verges on admitting that his father is necessary to his sense of self, a self, however unsatisfactory, to which he cannot help but be attached. At the very end of his letter he goes past that verge and allows his father to make essentially the same accusation in an imagined rebuttal of the whole letter. Here, in part, is what his father says to him:

> You are unfit for life; to make life comfortable for yourself, without worries and self-reproaches, you prove that I have taken your fitness away from you and put it in my own pocket. Why should it bother you that you are unfit for life, since I have the responsibility for it, while you calmly stretch out and let yourself be hauled through life, physically and mentally, by me. . . . You have only proved to me that all my reproaches were justified, and that one especially justified charge was still missing: namely the charge of insincerity, obsequiousness, and parasitism. If I am not very much mistaken, you are preying on me even with this letter itself. (123, 125)

So Kafka, assuming the voice of his father, argues against himself; and there is powerful evidence to support that argument in Kafka's reluctance to marry and thus achieve the adulthood and freedom described before. Among Kafka's many explanations for that reluctance, the most significant one has to do with his writing—the writing that, we recall, is always about Kafka's father. He asserts quite simply that marriage will endanger his writing.

He does not specify *how* his writing will be endangered. He has indicated clearly enough, though, that tying the nuptial knot would immediately *un*tie the Gordian knot of Kafka's relations with his father. And this he cannot afford to do, even if he were psychologically capable of it. For this relationship with his father is the ultimate source of his writing, of his art. The moment it is resolved, his writing must cease. In this sense, the father's imagined accusation of parasitism is fully justified.

Up to this point in the letter, the logic of Kafka's psychoanalysis has been crystalline, if complex; and he has been rigorously fair, even to the point of adopting his father's voice and arguing compellingly against himself. If it is possible at all for people to be clear and fair about such things, Kafka has been so. But at this point he is cutting down to the bone. And the scrupulous logic to which he has aspired throughout the letter is now completely overthrown. Continuing to speak of marriage and what it could offer him, Kafka has this to say:

> The simile of the bird in the hand and the two in the bush has only a very remote application here. In my hand I have nothing, in the bush is everything, and yet—so it is decided by the conditions of battle and the necessity of life—I must choose the nothing. (117, 119)

The choice is an astonishing one, but it is by no means the most astonishing aspect of this passage. The *reason* for the choice intrigues me: "so it is decided by the conditions of battle and the necessity of life." Really, Kafka gives no reason. He neatly sidesteps responsibility for what is after all *his* choice, *his* decision. He does so first through a passive construction: "it is decided." And to answer the natural question of who or what decides, Kafka brings in only a couple of dimly perceived abstractions straight out of bourgeois parlor art: "the conditions of battle"—and we see, perhaps, a helmeted, heroic figure fighting "the battle of life"—and *lebensnot,* the necessity of life—the Greek *ananka* or fate, perhaps, complete with classical drapery. This moment is a flicker of bad faith, a retreat into foggy cliches at the very moment when Kafka owes an explanation (at least to himself) of the reasons for his choice.

That explanation can be found in Kafka's letter, but it must be assembled and extrapolated from scattered hints. Near the beginning of the letter, for instance, he speaks of the nothing that he is to choose at the letter's end. "This sense of nothingness that often dominates me (a feeling that is in another respect, admittedly, also a noble and fruitful one) comes largely from your influence," he tells his father (17). He does not pursue the parenthetical aside, despite its significant admission that the father's influence is in some way a fruitful one. Its fruits must be those previously mentioned products of the father's influence, Kafka's writings. We begin to realize that if his father had not actually existed, it would have been necessary for Kafka to have invented him.

In these circuitous ways we have arrived once more at that destination in Kafka's letter that is also an origin, the idea of the father. But really it is the origin only of another stage in the process: we may now move through the fissures of Kafka's letter and into Derrida's *Dissemination* (1981). In that work Derrida asserts bluntly that "writing is parricidal" (164). This assertion is justified in the context of Derrida's distinction between writing and the spoken word:

> One could say . . . that the "speaking subject" is the *father* of the speech. . . . *Logos* is a son, then, a son that would be destroyed in his very *presence* without the present *attendance* of his father. His father who answers. His father who speaks for him and answers for him. Without his father, he would be nothing but, in fact, writing. At least that is what is said by the one who says; it is the father's thesis. The specificity of writing would thus be intimately bound to the absence of the father. (79)

Moving from the father's thesis to the situation of the son, Derrida gives this description:

> Writing is the miserable son. *Le misérable* . . . . His impotence is truly that of an orphan as much as that of a justly or unjustly persecuted patricide . . . . Writing can thus be attacked, bombarded with unjust reproaches . . . that only the father could dissipate—thus assisting his son—if the son had not, precisely, killed him. (145)

These are figures of speech, of course, not real figures; nevertheless the two may sometimes be interchanged. So it is with Kafka's father. In all his blocky bourgeois solidity he is made to evaporate:

he becomes not so much a presence in Kafka's work as a pervasive absence, a nonexistent authority like that of *The Trial* and *The Castle.* Thus the son ensures that "the dead father, first victim and ultimate resource, not be there" (145).

These words of Derrida echo the terms of yet another text on the father, one that has plainly influenced him and may have influenced Kafka: Freud's *Totem and Taboo* (1961). The theory it advances can be applied to Kafka's fiction, to all fiction, and perhaps to all culture. In this book, Freud uses psychology in an attempt to resolve a problem in anthropology, that of the totem. Every member of a primitive tribe belongs to one or another totem, usually an animal. The people of the totem have a special relationship to the totem animal: it is sacred and may not be killed. Moreover, people may not marry within their own totem. Freud first notes some clinical cases showing that children often displace feelings for their father onto an animal. Then he points out that the two prohibitions of totemism—against killing the totem and against marrying within it—coincide with the two crimes of Oedipus. Finally, he lingers on certain ritualized exceptions to the rule, in which the tribe kills the totem animal and devours it. The animal is duly mourned in a clear attempt to disclaim responsibility for the killing; a festivity follows at which every sort of license is permitted. Freud now substitutes the real father for the symbolical animal, and suggests that all these tribal institutions are ways of coming to terms with one crucial event in the tribe's evolution. The earliest form of the tribe was probably, like that of many animal hordes, one in which a powerful male drives out all rivals, including his own sons, in order to keep all the females for himself. Freud suggests a scenario where the exiled sons learn to cooperate, with results that he bluntly puts in a single sentence: "One day the brothers who had been driven out came together, killed and devoured their father and so made an end of the patriarchal horde" (141). He then argues that the guilt for this act is handed down through the generations, in a kind of collective unconscious. The prohibitions of totemism appease that guilt; the debt to the dead father is paid and made fruitful through cultural forms—legal, religious, artistic.

This "fruitful moment of debt," as Freud has called it, is echoed in Kafka's words. A "fruitful" feeling of nothingness, he says to his father, "comes largely from your influence." And elsewhere he says "on every side I was to blame, I was in your debt"—*Von alle seiten her kam ich in deine Schuld,* where *Schuld* has the force of both "guilt" and "debt" (47). Kafka owed a debt not only to his father, but to Freud. He had broken through into his true voice with "The Judgement," a story he said had "come out of me like a birth" in one night's sitting in 1912; and he had thought of Freud while writing it. The Oedipal content of that story, as well as its relation to dream, could have been derived from Freud's writings before 1912. But it is significant that the first part of *Totem and Taboo* was published in that year.

Freud's theory may be applied to itself, because his problematic relations with his own father provided the impetus for explaining human failings, as well as the shape of that explanation. As much as Kafka, Freud could have confessed to his father "my writing was all about you." Marie Balmary and Marianne Krull have both published studies of Freud's relationship with his father. The more fully articulated of the two is Balmary's *Psychoanalyzing Psychoanalysis: Freud and the Hidden Fault of the Father* (1982). She begins with a couple of facts about Freud's father that have only recently come to light: His supposedly second marriage was preceded by another one completely covered over in the family history; and Sigmund was born not nine months after his parents' marriage but seven months. The possible Don Juanism of his father is the "hidden fault" that returns, like any repressed, in a multitude of unconscious betrayals throughout Freud's life, and may have played its part in Freud's renunciation of the seduction theory. In *Freud and His Father* (1986), on the other hand, Marianne Krull argues that Freud's renunciation of the seduction theory was a result of compromising evidence arising from his own self-analysis. Recognizing in himself the classic symptoms of the hysteric, Freud could not pursue the possibility that his father could, in any form, be guilty of originating those symptoms. Removing the Oedipal to the realm of fantasy allowed him to take all the guilt upon himself, as the son does in "The Judgement."

But guilt is also debt, and moreover fruitful debt, engendering perhaps the whole body of Freud's work, the payment of the parricide.

The cases of Freud and Kafka seem to validate the view that the father underlies all culture. Culture, in this view, is fundamentally patriarchal, and we are bound to it irrevocably by guilt even while we attempt to free ourselves from its bonds. Can we disentangle those bonds only by disentangling the fabric of culture itself? In Freud there is no disentangling; we must accommodate ourselves to the patriarchal pattern. But that problematic pattern, whose guilt-laden dynamics are said to have originated art, may be resolved by art and perhaps fundamentally altered by it. The suggestion comes from Freud (1961) himself:

> In only a single field of our civilization has the omnipotence of thoughts been retained, and that is in the field of art. Only in art does it still happen that a man who is consumed by desires performs something resembling the accomplishment of those desires and that what he does in play produces emotional effects—thanks to aesthetic illusion—just as though it were something real. (90)

The "real" effect of art is probably due less to aesthetic illusion (a vague term in any case) than to the fact that the unconscious recognizes no illusion. The unconscious, Freud argued in renouncing his seduction theory, does not distinguish between real events and those of fantasy. To the degree that art partakes of fantasy, then, it becomes part of the unconscious and can work its changes there.

But, to get more particular, what *kind* of art can work best, that is, work its changes on the patriarchal inheritance of our unconscious? What artistic strategies are adequate to this deep-seated complexity? One answer is provided by a work that owes a considerable debt to both Kafka and Freud, and moreover deals explicitly with the patriarchal problem: Donald Barthelme's *The Dead Father* (1975).

Barthelme's book opens with this description, worth quoting in full for the tone it sets:

> The Dead Father's head. The main thing is, his eyes are open. Staring up into the sky. The eyes a two-valued blue, the blues of the Gitanes cigarette

pack. The head never moves. Decades of staring. The brow is noble, good Christ, what else? Broad and noble. And serene, of course, he's dead, what else if not serene? From the tip of his finely shaped delicately nostriled nose to the ground, fall of five and one half meters, figure obtained by triangulation. The hair is gray but a young gray. Full, almost to the shoulder, it is possible to admire the hair for a long time, many do, on a Sunday or other holiday or in those sandwich hours neatly placed between fattish slices of work. Jawline compares favorably to a rock formation. Imposing, rugged, all that. The great jaw contains thirty-two teeth, twenty-eight of the whiteness of standard bathroom fixtures and four stained, the latter a consequence of addiction to tobacco, according to legend, this beige quartet to be found in the center of the lower jaw. He is not perfect, thank God for that. The full red lips drawn back in a slight rictus, slight but not unpleasant rictus, disclosing a bit of mackerel salad lodged between two of the stained four. We think it is mackerel salad. It appears to be mackerel salad. In the sagas, it is mackerel salad.

Dead, but still with us, still with us, but dead. (3)

In what follows there are echoes at first of Gulliver among the Lilliputians: the gigantic figure is chained down, tiny arrows are sometimes found in its right leg. Its left leg, however, is artificial, and contains facilities for confession. "The confessions are taped, scrambled, dramatized, and then appear in the city's theatres, a new feature-length film every Friday" (4). This strikes the Freudian note: It is a clear though comical example of guilt giving rise to culture. Further flickers of Freud occur throughout the novel. "What is your totem?" a character asks (150); there is a briefly entertained proposal to eat the father (74); reference is made to "this little band of brothers." The band in question is made up of nineteen by and large faceless men, led by Thomas, the son figure. There are also Julie, his mistress, and the buxom Emma, who joins the party for no discernable reason. And of course there is the Dead Father.

Barthelme's novel is the story of a journey, a quest. Straining at a cable, the group drags the great figure of the Dead Father down the road, a transported colossus. At lunch break the Dead Father joins the group, makes passes at Julie, demands his rights and privileges, has tantrums, slays assorted fauna in the vicinity. Though "we *want* the Dead Father to be dead," as stated near the novel's beginning (5), he is not, exactly. This too is in keeping with Freud's theories in *Totem and Taboo.* The whole totem system, according to Freud, is a form of deferred obedience to the Dead Father, undertaken out of guilt. The prohibitions so rigidly enforced by the culture are a version of those enforced by the father to ensure his power, especially his sexual power, within the tribe. Thus the father whose death is celebrated in certain ritual killings of the totemic animal is in another sense not dead at all, but lives in the culture that continues to dominate his offspring. As "A Manual for Sons" interpolated in Barthelme's book has it:

> Fatherless now, you must deal with the memory of a father. Often that memory is more potent than the living presence of a father, is an inner voice commanding, haranguing, yes-ing and no-ing—a binary code, yes no yes no yes no yes no, governing your every, your slightest movement, mental or physical. At what point do you become yourself? Never, wholly, you are always partly him. That privileged position in your inner ear is his last "perk" and no father has ever passed it by. (144)

The goal of the journey is definitively to bury the Dead Father, who is far too alive. That is to say, the son Thomas, like the son Franz, is trying to purge himself of guilt and the patriarchal control that is its consequence. For instance, a story Thomas tells the Dead Father opens with the bewildering paranoia of so many of Kafka's tales:

> One day in a wild place far from the city four men in dark suits with shirts and ties and attaché cases containing Uzi submachine guns seized me, saying that I was wrong and would always be wrong and that they were not going to hurt me. Then they hurt me. (40)

And later Thomas tells the Father "when I explain myself I tend to stutter" (56)—a problem he shares with Kafka, who explains it as the product of his father's influence. But explaining this, and everything else, in his letter has ultimately failed to serve Kafka's purpose. Likewise, Thomas does not achieve his purpose by explanation, and does not even attempt to do so. Nor does he achieve that purpose through the symbolic act of the journey, or of the burial that concludes it. Thomas, or rather Barthelme, or rather the reader, achieves the work's purpose through its *tone.*

The concept of tone fascinates Derrida, perhaps because it is the most elusive element in literature, and yet often the one that conveys the most. In *The Post Card* (1987), he calls tone "the final index, the identity of some addressee who, lacking anything else, still dictates dictating" (145). But because identity, in Derrida's view, does not exist, neither does a stable tone; it "confuses itself and explodes all by itself, nothing to be done, unity of tone does not exist." He speculates, without quite believing himself, on possible techniques for underscoring this: "By mixing genres? By exploding the tone from tone to tone? By passing very quickly from one tone to another?" These are precisely the techniques that Barthelme adopts.

Barthelme's *The Dead Father* (1975) uses dozens, perhaps hundreds, of literary tones, genres, modes: snippets of larger systems that then play off one another. If culture, as Freud suggests, is a form of deferred obedience to a patriarchal law, it would seem to be impossible for any cultural artifact to break free of that law. For the law is not any *particular* order, but the very concept of ordering itself; and there is no such thing as a cultural artifact without an ordering principle, a law harking back to aspirations for control that are rooted in patriarchy, in the father. But Barthelme sees that the ordering principles differ, if only by a tone, in different artifacts. "Culture" is not a monolithic entity but an enormous heap of variegated systems of order. Culture is a scrapheap, like that described by the Dead Father in the novel as the product of his liaison with an attractive young lady:

> We spent many nights together all roaratorious and filled with furious joy. I fathered upon her in those nights the poker chip, the cash register, the juice extractor, the kazoo, the rubber pretzel, the cuckoo clock, the key chain, the dime bank, the pantograph, the bubble pipe, the punching bag both light and heavy, the inkblot, the nose drop, the midget Bible, the slot-machine slug, and many other useful and humane artifacts, as well as some thousands of children of the ordinary sort. I fathered as well upon her various institutions useful and humane such as the credit union, the dog pound, and parapsychology . . . . I overdid it but I was madly, madly in love, that is all I can say in my own defense. (36)

The venerable myth of the male god who begets culture, such as Prometheus or Thoth, provides a major structuring principle behind this passage. But a counterprinciple arises from the broadening of the idea of culture to take in pop culture, including inventions of considerably less mythic dignity than fire or the alphabet.

There is a satiric edge to this passage, but it is difficult to decide which way it cuts. The mythic world and the modern world are rendered equally absurd. One's allegiance is to neither system of order: the reader is poised in the space between.

Juxtaposition creates this effect, and creates a similar effect in the catalog of objects. In admittedly minor ways, each of these objects represents a principle of order. But when all these principles are juxtaposed and jumbled, the effect becomes ludicrous. There is nothing innately amusing about credit unions, or about dog pounds, or about parapsychology. Through listing them all in one breath in this context, however, the disparate nature of their systems of order becomes apparent; and the chuckle, when it comes, is at the expense not of any one of these systems but at the expense of the idea of order itself. Lewis Carroll uses a similar technique for a similar subversive purpose when he speaks of "shoes and ships and sealing wax, / Of cabbages and kings."

The nonsensical disparities in Carroll's catalog are played against the linkages of its smoothly alliterative sound. In Barthelme's novel, too, sound is a major element. For not only does the ordering principle of culture wax and multiply; it becomes diluted to a mere sound, a tone, or rather a series of tones: the mythic, the pop, the epic, the lyric—but above all in Barthelme the innumerable versions of contemporary banality.

Of this last, the most extreme and the most intriguing versions are the conversations between Emma and Julie. In the following example, one or the other of them speaks each sentence or fragment; it is unclear *which* one, and it probably doesn't matter. Perhaps it begins with some jealousy between the two women over Thomas:

> Wake up one dark night with a puckle in your eye.
> We chat.
> About what?
> That's my business.
> Then perhaps he regards you kindly.
> Series of failed experiments.
> You have performed well under difficult conditions.
> Animals in which the brain strangles the esophagus.
> Years not unmarked by hideous strains.

Willfully avoided gathering to myself the knowledge aforementioned.
And when not surly, pert.
The letter a failure but I mailed it nevertheless.
It's wonderful and reduces the prison population too.
I was surprised to see him in this particular bar.
Very young he's.
Parts of hero all over.
Many of them connected by legal or emotional ties.
Stares calmly at something a great distance away.

(153–54)

This is a good deal more far out than the first passage I quoted, a good deal further removed from an underlying sense of order. Though the conversation baffles our attempts to trace a coherent sequence in the whole, it also teases us with the feeling that each of its elements is a fragment from some perfectly familiar, even banal context. To restore one of these to its probable context: " 'You have performed well under difficult conditions,' he said to the slim young lieutenant standing at attention before him." This might be from one of those old-fashioned Henty novels for boys, which is pretty banal stuff. It's tempting to think, then, that the whole passage comments on the banality of communication between people—an idea that is itself banal. Something else is going on here, and it has to do with the fact that these are two women in conversation. Feminist linguists like Robin Lakoff have determined that women, far more than men, are capable of holding a conversation that is made up of indirections, obliquities, and unspoken understandings. Whereas men feel that they have communicated only when they have fully articulated their points, pinned them down to logic and fact, women know they are communicating even when the words themselves don't seem to be saying much. Such is the case here. The sense that each fragment is drawn from a familiar context only intensifies the opposing sense of soft ruptures and ricochets in the sequence. The conversation proceeds in a series of tangents rather than in a straightforward ("manly") way. All this suggests that these conversations between the two women represent the furthest remove from the principles of order that still govern other parts of Barthelme's patriarchal text. Exaggerating the technique that Barthelme uses—the juxtaposition of tones in order to undermine the principles of order they represent—these conversations are the strongest challenge to the presence and principle of the dead father in the text. A while ago I spoke of Emma being introduced into the story for no apparent reason. Perhaps Barthelme introduces her only so that these conversations between women can take place.

In extreme or less extreme versions, Barthelme is always writing about texts and contexts, and arranging delicately surreal battles between them. The effect is to undermine the authority of all texts, including his own. That authority is of course the authority of the father. The Dead Father, Julie says, is obnoxious, but "still he has something" (67). What he has, she decides, is "authority." Kafka describes his father as quintessentially "the authoritative man," and for Freud "the father is the oldest, first, and for children the only authority." In her book *Thinking about Women* (1968), Mary Ellman speculates about what might be the underlying characteristic of a "masculine" writing style: "authority," she concludes. If she is right, Barthelme's novel represents an interesting paradox: a male author authoritatively undermining male authority, both explicitly through his subject matter and implicitly through the strategies of his writing. And beyond the figure of the Dead Father, Barthelme's story undermines the Freudian authority that canonized this larger-than-life-size figure in the first place by telling a story.

Barthelme represents only one version of this kind of strategy, which I would argue is a basic strategy of postmodernism. By now, of course, any talk of a "basic strategy" of postmodernism is a kind of dancing through the minefield. This will be a short dance. In the sense in which I am choosing to see it (and choice is an important element of interpretation as it is of politics), postmodernism is characterized by a playing of "the Law" against itself in structures of irony. Often this is done by combining elements from various laws, and systems of order, in surreal juxtaposition. The clearest and most vigorous demonstrations of this postmodern aesthetic are found in contemporary architecture. As an example, take the building that has been said to have started it all, the AT & T building in New York, designed by Philip Johnson. A huge skyscraper is incongruously crowned with a classical pediment. The architect's model is especially surreal (fig. 1), charged with a curious power that is dreamlike, indeed Kafkan—this might be the castle keep to which Joseph K aspires. An "official" architecture, which usually represses a culture's unconscious, here expresses it. It's as if the commercial world of Kafka's big business father had been assimilated to the vision of the son. Yet this is not a simple case of Oedipal overthrow of the father, where the patterns of the unconscious are obeyed without even being recognized as such. Work like that of Philip Johnson brings that unconscious to the surface, conceivably helping to prevent a blind repetition of the Oedipal pattern.

The anxieties of the individual, then, and perhaps of the culture, are literally brought into the daylight in a building like this. But in stressing the anxiety related to this architecture I wouldn't want to overlook its wit and its playfulness. For these too are elements in the postmodern, as they are in Barthelme—and indeed in Kafka, who when first reading aloud *The Trial* to his friends repeatedly broke into laughter. Such playfulness is a form of release from both unconscious tensions and constricting patterns of authority. It provides a subversion of patriarchal authority that is not a rebellious challenge: that would only repeat the Oedipal cycle, as it is repeated in the dreary cycles of Greek mythology. Rather, authorities are turned against themselves, working to subvert the idea of authority. This allows one the freedom not to meet the force of the father but to *sidestep*.

I do not want to argue that the postmodern aesthetic, in architecture or literature, will instantly unravel knots in which the psyche has been tied for centuries. But I would argue that culture, far from being the passive child of an originary father, may be the means by which we come to a consciousness of the father's stature as something we have conferred on him, and that we can demystify. Rather than again burying the father in our unconscious and that of our culture, we must unearth him from the fictions created by our psyche. When we do so, the gigantic figure of the father dwindles down to the size of us. Daughters and sons alike, we have the promise of finally coming of age.

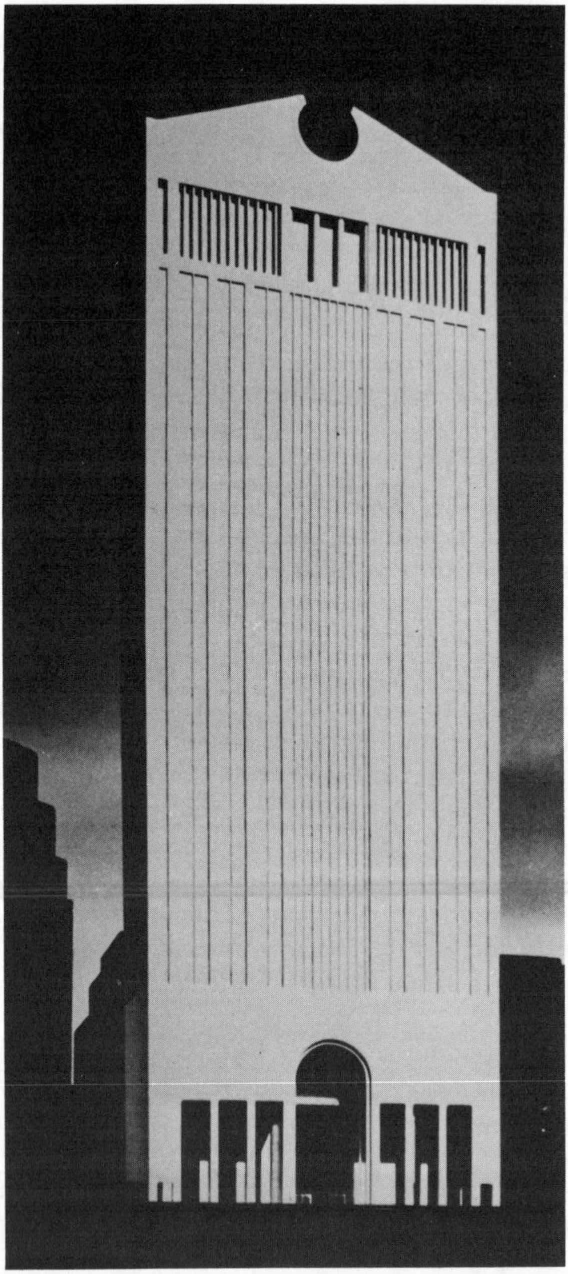

Figure 1. Architect's model of the AT&T Building. Photograph reprinted by permission of John Burgee, Architects.

Works Cited

Balmary, Marie. *Psychoanalyzing Psychoanalysis: Freud and the Hidden Fault of the Father.* Baltimore: Johns Hopkins University Press, 1982.

Barthelme, Donald. *The Dead Father.* New York: Farrar, Straus & Giroux, 1975.

Derrida, Jacques. *Dissemination.* Trans. Barbara Johnson. Chicago: University of Chicago Press, 1981.

———. *The Post Card: From Socrates to Freud and Beyond.* Trans. Alan Bass. Chicago: University of Chicago Press, 1987.

Ellman, Mary. *Thinking about Women.* New York: Harcourt Brace Jovanovich, 1968.

Freud, Sigmund. *Totem and Taboo.* Trans. James Strachey. London: Routledge, Kegan & Paul, 1961.

Kafka, Franz. *Letter to His Father/Brief an Den Vater.* Trans. Ernst Kaiser and Eithne Wilkins. New York: Schocken, 1966.

Krull, Marianne. *Freud and His Father.* Trans. Arnold J. Pomerans. New York: Norton, 1986.

3

Günter Grass's *Cat and Mouse* and the Phenomenology of Masculinity

Leonard Duroche

Homines, mihi crede, non nascuntur, sed finguntur.
—Erasmus

This chapter addresses what has been a puzzling lack in Grass scholarship to date. Although a great deal of attention has been given to Grass's social criticism, no critic has examined his critique specifically as one of the male system and no one has considered the significance of gender position in the construction and reception of Grass's narrative figures and narrative situations. When *Cat and Mouse* (*Katz und Maus* 1963) was written, gender consciousness, certainly *male* gender consciousness, had not been raised to a level where it was problematized by critics.[1] To my knowledge no one has yet explicitly thematized a number of pertinent questions: (1) To what extent does *Cat and Mouse* examine the masculinity models available in the specific historical context of National Socialism? (2) How do gender position and specifically the psychological and physical factors of male pubescence within the patriarchal system, particularly under the confused social psychological conditions of Nazism, determine the multiple narratives of the novella? After the appearance of *The Flounder* (1978; *Der Butt* 1977), which mythologized the battle between the sexes and created a minor uproar among feminist critics (see Erickson 1988, vol. 1, chap. 1), it is particularly puzzling that anyone could ignore the issues of gender in the earlier works, especially in *Cat and Mouse.* Among all Grass's narratives, *Cat and Mouse* focuses almost exclusively on the male lifeworld.[2] (3) Does it make sense to view Mahlke, like his predecessor Oskar in the previous volume of the Danzig trilogy, *The Tin Drum,* as singular in his deformity and abnormal, which is how the majority of critics has seen him? Or is it more likely that he is representative of male experience precisely because of his dysfunctionalism?[3]

In an attempt to address these concerns, I focus very much on the surface of the narrative rather than try to gather the narrative under larger overarching categories. Nor do I hunt for master metaphors or structural features to provide the key for unlocking the meaning *behind* the text. *Cat and Mouse* is an initiation story that, very much like *The Adventures of Huckleberry Finn,* deals with a boy growing up in troubled times, a dystopic German version of the theme. Like Huck, Mahlke, the protagonist, is a half-orphan. Unlike Pap, Mahlke's father is a positive father figure, a train engineer, who died heroically in a train accident while trying to save lives. Local geography, Danzig's position on the Baltic Sea, provides the physical setting, and Grass invests the sea with a complex symbolic significance that equals Twain's treatment of the Mississippi. The action in the first part of the novella takes place largely on the deck of a partially submerged Polish minesweeper. Like Huck's raft, the minesweeper is an adolescent male refuge from the adult world and the site of adolescent male rituals, including what Grass calls at one point the "masturbation olympics."

Narrated time in *Cat and Mouse* covers but a portion of Mahlke's life, from the onset of puberty to shortly before the end of World War II, and coincides with the rise and fall of the Third Reich. Two events mark puberty for Mahlke. The first is an achievement: learning to swim, becoming an expert diver. Grass calls it *freischwimmen,* which means earning a swimming proficiency certificate, but within the context of the novel takes on broader connotations of liberation (literally, freeing oneself through swimming). Only Mahlke can reach the furthest recesses of the submerged Polish minesweeper. The second event is biological, with challenging psychological consequences: Mahlke develops a very large Adam's apple which embarrasses him as it bobs up and down conspicuously, and that he tries to cover up with all manner of things.

When a former graduate of his school, decorated with the Knight's Cross, Germany's highest military honor, visits to give patriotic speeches about his experiences, Mahlke discovers what one critic has called "an appropriate fig leaf to cover his physical—and psychological—nakedness" (Thomas 1982, 98f.). When a second "hero" visits the school, Mahlke steals the medal. He later confesses, is expelled from school, finishes at an inferior school, and eventually winds up as a gunner in the tank corps. Mahlke finally gains the Knight's Cross legitimately by knocking out an impressive number of enemy tanks. Aided by the Virgin, his aim is unerring: Before a hit the Virgin appears marking the critical site—with her belly. She holds there not the Christ child, but a paternal icon, the picture of Mahlke's father. When he returns to his original school to give his long-planned hero's speech, he is turned down because he had earlier disgraced the school. He goes AWOL, takes flight finally to the minesweeper—at the suggestion of Pilenz, supposedly his only friend. The weather is cold and Mahlke has eaten himself sick on wild gooseberries. Pilenz, who goes with him, hides the can opener Mahlke needs in order to use his supplies. Then, Pilenz does not return at the time he had promised and when he finally does, there is no sign of Mahlke, who has apparently drowned. Pilenz writes the history of "the Great Mahlke" partly out of guilt, partly out of his own misguided hero worship.

Grass's narrative functions as a phenomenology of male adolescent experience, a rich description of the struggles and pain involved in the transition from childhood to youth and young adulthood.[4] That this struggle takes place in almost the very worst of circumstances, within a morally corrupt and finally collapsing social structure, does not restrict the significance of the novella to its own time frame. Much of what the novella explores has to do with the accumulated inheritance and consequences of the historical development of patriarchal culture within bourgeois capitalism. That is what justifies calling Mahlke's story a "male narrative." It typifies one possible path of an adolescent struggling to grow up. Largely unaware, Mahlke acts out specific narratives that history, time, and place have fabricated for him. Yet he believes his choices are his own. As Max Horkheimer reputedly said, "You can't talk about fascism without talking about capitalism."[5] National Socialism was only one, though a particularly horrible, result of the inheritance of patriarchy under bourgeois capitalism. Only partly and ineffectively dismantled following World War II in Germany and Japan and, despite the emergence of the women's and later the men's movements, left more or less intact elsewhere, modern hegemonic masculinity is still perpetuating social narratives that control men's lives, fabricating or reconfirming notions of the hero and constructing in young men malleable subjects to play the parts.

What are the issues or the questions that one asks of a male narrative? They are not unlike the kinds of questions that more traditional scholarship has already asked of texts, but they are framed from a conscious gender perspective and place at the center of investigating male experience, understood not as ungendered, "universal," human experience but as a construct of sociohistorical conditions. For the time period of Grass's novella and its current reception these are questions about father-son relations, including the problem of "die vaterlose Generation" (the generation without fathers) or, as Michael Schneider has more recently labelled it (1981, 9; 1984a, 4), "die vatergeschädigte Generation" (the generation damaged by its fathers). Since the 1980s, American men, and more recently European men, have intensified a search for the father, sometimes expressed more intensely as "father hunger," sometimes more mythically as the "Telemachos theme." That search has carried over into literature and intellectual life. It includes the theme of the dead (or the undead) father (see Rickels 1988).

A related theme is male expressiveness and particularly the inability of men to mourn for fathers or for brothers. Inexpressiveness suggests the machinelike nature of males as they have been socialized, particularly in wartime, thus the theme of the male body and men and machines. Also inevitable are the issues of male intimacy and friendship, and their flipside, male isolation and loneliness. More generally, a scholarship informed by a gender perspective asks what kinds of masculinity models exist or existed? Does a society provide meaningful rites of passage for male children through puberty and adolescence toward the production of positive adult males? Three of these issues touch on most of the others and are dealt with here. They are the themes of male intimacy and friendship, male writing/being written as male, and the relation of father and son.

Perhaps the best place to begin is with male friendship, because to address this issue is to take a stand on one of the "problems" to which earlier scholarship has devoted a good deal of attention: Is Mahlke "the" main figure or is Pilenz, his biographer and the first-person narrator of the story, equally important? What is the nature of their "friendship?" Croft (1987, 119) argues that "Pilenz as narrator proves to be as significant in the novel as its hero Joachim Mahlke"; Hollington (1980, 53) agrees. Keele (1988, 66) contends that Pilenz is the real subject of the book, whereas Cunfliffe (1969, 87) argues he is "not himself an important figure." Hayman (1985, 51) claims that "Grass has never since filtered so much of his message through a personal relationship." Reddick (1988, 109) asserts that "all this ambivalence and private psychology . . . are certainly not of central importance." And so on and so forth. I shall argue that *Cat and Mouse* is specifically an exploration of male relation.

If we focus on the gender issue, the appropriate questions are not whether Pilenz is a real friend or a traitor, but what are male relationships like, in general? How is gender scripted? How can narration, the act of writing or telling, examine varieties of male experience? One must consider *both* Pilenz and Mahlke. They are representative adolescent males caught *in* and, to a greater or lesser degree, compromising *with* the hegemonic male system. That is an overarching system offering to men as well as to women prefabricated scripts and limited choices that they may elect or reject. To look at both young men as situated within the context of the patriarchal system broadens the focus to encompass *all* social relations, self-self, self-other, self and society.

It is useful, I believe, to consider what feminist theorists have written concerning the impact of patriarchy on friendship among women and to consider why it should affect men differently. Dale M. Bauer opens her recent book, *Feminist Dialogics: A Theory of Failed Community* (1988), with a discussion of the threats to female friendship. The argument of the book, she says, has to do with "women's misreadings of the patriarchal ground of all of their relations: with each other, with their daughters, with their husbands and lovers, with their own histories." Using a short story by Edith Wharton as an example, Bauer argues "that the patriarchy, far from being the natural or originary foundation of human culture, in fact, functions to reduce experience . . . to some manageable minimum, to erase heterogeneity and Otherness" (ixf.). The effect of this is to make women "essentially ignorant of each other as women." What she says of women applies to men as well. To rephrase Bauer, *all* human beings caught up within the male system are "essentially ignorant of each other [as human beings], thereby allowing the displaced anger they feel to be vented on the other rather than on the cultural system by which they have been defined" (x).

One may draw two conclusions from Bauer's argument. The first helps explain Grass's title. The novella opens with teenage boredom and aggression. It is summer vacation. Boys wait for a ball field to be freed up so they may play. One of them, most likely Pilenz, sees Mahlke lying on the ground, his huge Adam's apple bobbing, and sets a cat loose on the "mouse." The first conclusion is that the game of cat and mouse is already inherent in the system, the role of the outsider and the persecution impulse are already parts of an inherited script. Kaiser makes this point when he reminds us that neither Pilenz nor Mahlke can remember who set the cat on Mahlke: "That indicates the degree to which in this moment Pilenz acts out of an impulse of the entire group, which forms Mahlke's environment, the extent to which the act is embedded in the situation, and actually flows from it" (Kaiser 1971, 13; see also Croft 1987, 119). *Cat and Mouse* is about the tension between conformity and heterogeneity in males' relation to one another and to the group. The novella revolves around the desire to establish one's own identity and the impulse to erase Otherness, as if erasure—of Self or of the Other—were the only path to identity. Pilenz's seemingly self-contradictory identification with and aggressivity toward Mahlke may make somewhat more sense if we remember the features of the Lacanian Imaginary before it relates to the Symbolic Order. Fredric Jameson (1977) writes that

> this is the type of relationship . . . which we have seen to result from that indistinct rivalry between self and other in a period that precedes the very elaboration of a self or the construct of an ego. As with the axis of Imaginary space, we must again try to imagine something deeply sedimented in our own experience, but buried under the adult rationality of everyday life (and under the exercise of the Symbolic): a kind of situational experience of otherness as pure relationship, as struggle, violence, and antagonism, in which the child can occupy either term indifferently, or indeed, as in transitivism, both at one *[sic]*. (356)

A second conclusion, if one applies Bauer's position to men, is that the isolation of and alienation between men is of a particular kind. The human gaze, so Sartre taught us, can be a loving gaze establishing connection between Self and Other. But it can also objectify and hold the Other from a distance, thus reinforcing the separation between Self and Other. The latter stance, as contemporary film criticism so frequently reminds us, characterizes male behavior. In *Cat and Mouse* the male gaze dominates. A strong visual quality characterizes the writing. Exteriors are lovingly and enviously depicted, suggesting at times a voyeurist narrator. Yet there is an almost total lack of access to the Other. Grass reminds the reader often enough of Mahlke's taciturnity and inability to open himself. As Hollington has said: "The emphasis . . . is on external and visible behavior" (Hollington 1980, 53). Pilenz almost never has access to the interiors, physical or psychological, where Mahlke dwells. His ignorance of his friend's inner life, for which critics often excoriate him, reflects a sad but true aspect of male friendship:

> And as for his soul, it was never introduced to me. I never heard what he thought. In the end, all I really have to go by are his neck and its numerous counterweights. (40)
>
> (Und seine Seele wurde mir nie vorgestellt. Nie hörte ich, was er dachte. Am Ende bleiben sein Hals und dessen Gegengewichte. [545])

Pilenz's very act of writing, besides being a penance and an act of mourning, is also a futile attempt to write the Self by writing the Other. The exploration of narration as a cognitive tool in men's attempts to understand who they are is by now a fixed feature in male consciousness-raising and in male gender studies. Grass's attempt to show both the power and the pitfalls of narration—uncovering fictions, inventing fictions—anticipates and parallels other literary descriptions of male rites of passage. The way in which the structure and events of *Cat and Mouse* resonate with other texts suggests that Grass has seized upon deep truths about the pain and struggle of adolescent male behavior. Thematic similarities are striking, for example, in Stephen King's (1983) novella "The Body," the text on which the film *Stand By Me* is based, which incidentally also thematizes male writing. King depicts the loss of intimacy and growing alienation from other males that begins with puberty: As boys approach that threshold, the acceptance and intimacy of childhood become mixed with aggression, separateness, and finally indifference. The narrator, very much like Pilenz, is writing the history of one particular summer's experiences with his then-teenage friends, most of whom are now dead. At one point he says something about language that also sheds light on Grass's text: "The word is the harm. Love isn't what these asshole poets like McKuen want you to think it is. Love has teeth; they bite; the wounds never close" (423). Pilenz may be treacherous and ultimately on the side of the cat, but he has also been bitten. He loves and he hurts; that is, he wounds and he is wounded. He writes about the great Mahlke to separate from Mahlke, but he is perpetually drawn back to him. He writes to discover who he is, but cannot separate from the Other. The complexity of male friendship in *Cat and Mouse* demands that one say something more about "love's bite." Grass portrays the strong homosocial desire that is possible between men. As in Twain's *Huckleberry Finn* or more recently in King's short story, there is in Grass's novella a deep sense of male intimacy. Though it is this very intimacy that may finally make treachery possible, there are undeniably strong homoerotic overtones in the narrative. It is disturbing—though in a homophobic culture not surprising—that so many critics have confused male intimacy with homosexuality. Croft (1987, 119) implies it and Thomas (1982, 109) takes it more or less for granted, to name just two examples. Croft, in fact, applies the terms "sterility and therefore deadness" to Mahlke's supposed homosexuality, reflecting an implicit (hetero)sexist and probably bourgeois capitalist attitude toward sexual economy, which is unable to see any relation as productive, that is, nonsterile, unless it is reproductive (119f.).

My point here is not to pick on fellow critics, but simply to suggest that our biases, when "reading" men's lives and relationships, are very deeply ingrained. Whereas men are socialized in ways that lead them (us) to confuse intimacy and sex, Grass seems to know the difference between the two. In *Cat and Mouse* he portrays young men discovering sexuality, still not fully aware whether they are male or female (548/47). Girls may begin to appear on the horizon, but boys are still also interested in, or have not yet been frightened away from, developing male relations to other males. Grass has Pilenz make the point that if Mahlke was more interested in men than in women, it was certainly not because he was *verkehrt* ("queer").

As for Pilenz's own homoerotic relation to Mahlke, there are other explanations. A good deal of it is envious admiration, identification with the human sublime, with *der große Mahlke* ("the great Mahlke"). Keele calls Pilenz's *fictional* attendance and search for Mahlke at the 1959 Regensburg reunion of former Knight's Cross recipients, an event that actually happened (supported by the West German army), "a bitter indictment by Grass of postwar militarism, a powerful statement that there are those in the Bundeswehr [other 'survivors' like Pilenz] seeking a resurrection of the old, messianic glory of the Nazi era. These sexual duds, Grass implies, seek in the mysticism of phallic gun barrels the fulfillment they cannot attain in normal life" (Keele 1988, 73). Rickels, in an altogether different context, speaking of what he calls "mourning sickness," says that "what is threatened with extinction during mourning is heterosexual libido itself: he who cannot stop mourning becomes the widow of his heterosexuality" (1988, 5).

Grass's graphic descriptions of emergent male sexuality are further ways in which he satirizes dysfunctional male narratives. Earlier criticism has made much of Mahlke's sexual exploits while tending to overlook what motivates him. That is not so much a sense of competition with other men, but with his own father. The male relation that ultimately is most important for him is that between father and son. As for the supposed grotesqueness of his Adam's apple and its sexual symbolism, the novella makes it clear that it is not objective size, but the self-perception and the self-conscious perception of one's peers—in this case young men uncomfortable in their own bodies—that is important. Mahlke's uncontrollable Adam's apple, like Pinocchio's suddenly elongating nose, stands for the awkward male teenage body, which seemingly has a life of its own. Mahlke ultimately comes to terms with his body changes and body image and even admits that perhaps his "mouse" was not all that much bigger after all. Though one of his friends gives his "article" the qualities of a disease, a goiter (555/59), the real disease is his masculinity, or hypermasculinity. In the figure of Mahlke and through the legends his admiring buddies tell about him, Grass satirizes a genitally organized sexuality and the fantasy that bigger is better. The point is not whether Mahlke's potential is productive or sterile (Croft 1987, 119), but rather that it is *over*productive. Overproductivity and overcompensation have their own liabilities, whatever the nature of the economy, and represent imbalances. Leonard reminds us that Mahlke's "deformation" is not only involuntary, in fact, something nearly every currently living male has inherited; she also points up the double edge of male strength: "What starts off as a promising act of emancipation, turns into an act of self-annihilation" (Leonard 1974, 29f.). Though Pilenz attempts to describe through his narrative what the "hero" should be, it is interesting that at the same time he doubts the very concept of "hero." There is something simultaneously attractive and grotesque about the ideal. Thus he is simultaneously awed and repelled. He admires and envies the status of the hero and offers his narrative as a memorial. But he also kills the hero, and his own nonbelief foils all resurrection scenarios. For these reasons, it is worth paying more attention to the act of writing—and of being written, both of which Grass thematizes through the novella.

Gerhard Kaiser's (1971) compact little book on Grass offers essentially a phenomenology of narrative consciousness in its first few pages. As his point of departure, he compares the function of narrative in Grass's tale with that of a nineteenth-century author, C. F. Meyer. Meyer's *Die Hochzeit des Mönchs (The Monk's Wedding)* is a story within a story in which the interior story, the defrocking of a monk, is not so much the theme as is its telling. Kaiser contrasts this kind of reflection on the narrative process with that of *Cat and Mouse,* which is yet a degree higher: Pilenz is not only a narrated narrator, he knows he is being narrated, or as he says, invented (*erfunden*; 527/8).

Kaiser contends the awareness of being the product of another consciousness is part of a modern development of narrative that shifts from thematizing consciousness to thematizing language, in which consciousness is already constructed. I contend that this development is not strictly "literary," but is reflected in male experience in the "real world" as well, in what Husserl called the Lebenswelt ("lifeworld"), that complex structure of consciousness that emerging from our "being-in-the-world." Being gendered is one part of "being-in-the-world." The male lifeworld originates in the gendered encounter with a world already structured before our own advent, from our unique perceptual relation to that world, and from the attempt to construct our own meanings against the background of the preexisting meanings of the world into which we are born.

Narration does not construct a fictional world of social relations with the aid of language; rather those relationships already exist in language itself. Grass seems unusually aware of that. *Cat and Mouse* exemplifies how that plays out in male experience. Pilenz, or more accurately, the fictional consciousness speaking, recognizes itself as linguistically constructed and is aware that the only possibility of elevating itself to the status of linguistic subject is by recognizing and negating its object character. That, Kaiser contends, can no longer be done by attempting to break out of the constraints of language, by creating a new language, but only by seeing through language. To the extent that the concept of the individual as an entelechy within society has been placed in question, *historia (die Geschichte)* has become a dubious category, whether understood as the history of collectives or the story of individual persons. Thus in the place of a world *mediated* through history and stories there is now only consciousness, a consciousness that understands—or misunderstands—itself and the world only as histories and stories. It takes the "world" as "tellable," without coming to any positive conclusions about the nature of "tellability." Which "stories" are liberating? Which stories are imprisoning, confirming the status quo? As Kaiser points out, even Pilenz, the invented narrator of *Cat and Mouse*, who knows he is invented, at first passes himself off as a sovereign master of the tale, who plans it in ad lib fashion.[6] Kaiser draws one set of conclusions from these observations, dealing with the problematization of narration in a narrow sense. I would like to draw attention to a second set of implications, namely the way in which both the contents of the text and the reflection on the writing of the text are suggestive for an understanding of narrative in a broader nonliterary sense and thematize the notion of male as invention.

Pilenz, far less innocent than Mahlke, seems very much aware that he as male is "invented." He is not terribly bothered by that. Several times he repeats the notion, expressed in the first chapter: "Over and over again the fellow who invented us because it's his business to invent people obliges me to take your Adam's apple in my hand and carry it to every spot that saw it win or lose" (8; "Der uns erfand, von berufswegen, zwingt mich, wieder und wieder deinen Adamsapfel in die Hand zu nehmen, ihn an jeden Ort zu führen, der ihn siegen oder verlieren sah" [527]). At one point he asks: "If only I knew who made the story up, he or I, or the one who is writing this in the first place!" (131; "wenn ich nur wüßte, wer die Mär erfunden hat, er oder ich oder wer schreibt hier?" [593]). And at another point: "Who will supply me with a good ending?" (188; "Wer schreibt mir einen guten Schluß?" [623]).

Mahlke's naivete contrasts almost grotesquely with Pilenz's self-knowledge. Leonard (1974) writes that no other character in Grass is as completely a victim as Mahlke: "Not only does the system exploit his physical courage and extraordinary will-power, but in the end it refuses to grant him the recognition for which he has fought so tenaciously. Mahlke is unaware of this exploitation"

(32f.). His unawareness is sad but, again, representative. With his unraised consciousness Mahlke believes he has played by the rules and has done what "real men" are supposed to do.

Kaiser (1971, 8) postulates a difference between the narrated narrator and the narrator's narrator, arguing that the author as ultimate narrator, in a final ironic continuation of the topos of *deus artifex,* manifests a freedom that is absolute and unconditional. I wish to argue that all the narrators, *including* the author as *apparent* last narrator, are caught in a wilderness of mirrors behind which there is always another force "inventing" the narration and the narrator. Such a view posits the fictionality of the subject both in art *and* in reality. That is not to argue, however, for a *mise en abîme,* a Romantic infinite regress. There is an original inventor: the "wilderness of mirrors" has its ultimate source in the real relations of production in bourgeois capitalist patriarchy.[7] Given the sociohistorical setting of *Cat and Mouse,* the theme of male as fiction, the fictionality of our masculinity, is particularly apt. One entire generation of males and much of the following, although in one sense "invented" by their society, were also forced to attempt to invent themselves in the absence of fathers. And that leads me to the significance of the father in the fatherless generation.

Without wanting to be as Freudian, or post-Freudian, as Laurence Rickels, I am going to attempt to approach the problem of the father in *Cat and Mouse* via ideas and implications found in Rickels's recent book, *Aberrations of Mourning* (1988). It, like *The Fictional Father* of Robert Con Davis (1981), is another attempt to deal with the power of the dead father, that figure who, be it in our critical practice, the tales we tell, or the lives we lead, is said to haunt us all. Rickels explores "a phantasmatic *Geistesgeschichte* not addressed within the traditional framework of theories and histories that emphasize only Oedipal structures." I find the search for other than Oedipal models of father-son relationships particularly appealing. Rickels tries to provide "a reading of both reading and writing that would go beyond notions of patricidal writing," beyond killing the father (1988, 1).

To apply Rickels' ideas to *Cat and Mouse* is to read the novella as an attempt to bury the dead, or—as Rickels would argue—the undead father. That attempt connects with the inability to deal with the dead, with the important themes of "the homeless dead," "the missing grave," "the imitation corpse" (8), and with the enormous difficulty or impossibility of the survivors to mourn and thus "detach [their] memories and hopes from the dead" (7). These are themes that have not only prevailed in West German literature, including Grass, but that have taken on new urgency with the attempts of those students who came to intellectual maturity during the Student Revolution of 1968 to come to terms with their own fathers, many of whom had been Nazis. Michael Schneider, perhaps the most widely read commentator on the student generation's preoccupation with the father, speaks of a "Hamlet complex" (Schneider 1984a), of an entire generation haunted by the father, and entitles one of his essays "Not all those who are buried are dead" (Schneider 1984b). *Cat and Mouse* clearly has its Oedipal aspects, but embedded in it, too, are scenes that, following Rickels, we might call "Oresteian," scenes manifesting drives within the son that center "on the urge to retrieve a lost father" (Rickels 1988, 174). In the introduction to his daring psychohistory, which the dust jacket calls "a Nietzschean challenge to and within the Freudian system," Rickels speaks of a primal identification with the father and alludes to Freud's rendering of "the death-wish bond with the father [as] the model of all mourning sickness," a task that can be done "only by keeping the mother in the shadow—as the shadow—of the moving target" (12). Here it is perhaps appropriate to remind readers that Pilenz names three motives driving Mahlke's ambition: (1) the Virgin Mary, the only woman in his life; (2) the urge to distract attention from his Adam's apple; (3) the wish to be recognized by an all-male institution, symbolized by "*unser Gymnasium*" (our high school). I identify this third motive force as the desire for male, particularly adult male—that is, symbolically—paternal approval. As Miles (1975) has said, "It is the applause of the school which he covets above almost any other" (90). While the tendency has been to focus on the first two motives, I shall argue for the greater importance of the third.

Much of what Mahlke does seems aimed at a "return or reanimation of the missing father" (Rickels 1988, 177). In his long-planned hero's speech he wants to speak not so much of himself, but of his father. A shot in the wrong direction, his attempt to become a hero on a par with the father fails. Those who dwell on the Christian imagery and ironic parallels between the life of Mahlke and the life of Christ can borrow an alternative reading from Rickels, in his etymological play with *Versöhnung:* "Reconciliation—*Versöhnung*—remains the implicit aim of both sign and son: to become son (*Ver-söhnung* [a play on the words *Sohn* = son and the German for reconciliation]) means to become the acknowledged second person, sign, likeness—and ultimately, the original image—of the father" (Rickels 1988, 181). Mahlke not only literally walks in his father's footsteps (he wears his father's shoes and many of his clothes), he assumes the role of the adult male in his house and his mother and aunt defer to him as if he were the father. Rickels speaks of a "substitutive economy of symbolic positions organized around the father, who . . . is already his own shadow when alive and then, once dead, is broadcast live" (3). Such a description applies quite literally to Mahlke's father. Mahlke's postpubescent life seems dedicated to finding a position from which he can relate to and vie with his hero father, the only positive male model in the entire narrative. He at first seems to find that place when he discovers the radio room, which, though it is above water, can be reached only from below. One must dive deep into the belly of the boat and swim a long way underwater. Only Mahlke can do so. He constructs there a shrine suggestive of ancestor worship, complete with sacred relics. His descent into the belly of the sunken minesweeper represents an "Orphean journey," dedicated to penetrating "the underworld only to excavate and commemorate the father, and never to the point of bringing back a lost object—an object which, since capable of being lost, would not be paternal" (3).

When Mahlke forsakes the boat in his *Flucht nach vorne* ("retreat forward," his attempt to overcome the system by joining it), he leaves the realm of positive sacrificial heroes to attempt the passage into manhood on his own. As Reddick (1988) and others have argued, it is "precisely his phenomenal 'Flucht nach vorne' that first exposes his 'mouse' to the gaze of 'one cat and all cats,' and that makes him even more exposed and vulnerable in direct proportion as his seeming successes become ever more brilliant" (115f.). But that does not establish Mahlke's singularity, rather just the opposite. If we transfer Mahlke's *Flucht nach vorne* from Nazi Germany to the offices and washrooms of the corporate world, the mouse as a symbol of a distorted, aggressive, achievement-oriented supermasculinity remains just as meaningful, and the implication that this is a masculinity that necessarily self-destructs strikes us not at all as odd but as quite familiar.

The turning point for the novella comes when Mahlke returns to his school to receive his reward, his recognition in giving his hero's speech, and is rejected by the false father, Klohse, the school director and Nazi party leader. At this point *Cat and Mouse* becomes a story of failed initiation. Mahlke's *Untergang,* his descent into the underworld at the end of the novella, is a retreat from awareness won on the threshold of manhood, an awareness that Reddick (1988, 115) calls "disastrously partial," or—in the words of a colleague—"disastrously insightful." Mahlke discovers an obscene and duplicitous world. His retreat is not unlike the retreat of other male protagonists unable to cope with their first confrontation with the complexity of the world and with death, as for example, in Hemingway's "Indian Camp." The difference, adding to the profound pathos of Grass's initiation story, is rooted in the historical context, in the inevitable absence of a wise adult male to bring the boy safely through the initiation experience. There is neither an adult male, a loving father, in whose arms he may nestle, safe as though a little boy again, nor a trusting peer to support and stand by him. There is only an age-old male isolation. At the very end Mahlke attempts to join the father, but his entry into the father's realm is prevented by the envious and abandoned son/brother who hides the key, the *Büchsenöffner* (can opener).[8]

But *Cat and Mouse* is not only about burying the dead father. It is also about burying the dead brother, whether one reads that as applying to either Pilenz's biological brother or to Mahlke or to both. Pilenz must deal with dead fathers and sons in different ways. He too has a "dead" dad who is nightly "killed" by the replacements in his mother's bed, who wear the slippers of the usurped husband without realizing the significance of that in the eyes of the son. (Once again this is the "Hamlet motif.") The death of Pilenz's biological brother also elevates the latter to a revered status, one that Pilenz envies and hates him for. His blood brother is beyond his reach, but not Mahlke. Ultimately the choices offered to the men in Grass's dystopic world seem to be between choosing or "refusing to survive the [death of the heroic] father"[9] or attempting to placate the haunting ghost of the murdered, but unburied brother.

One of the conundrums of Grass criticism has been the inability to reconcile the social optimism of his political writings with the apparent pessimism of his literary texts. A possible solution lies perhaps in recognizing—and then liberating oneself from—the essentialist tendencies implicit in much current scholarship, not just on Grass. Many critics have invested Grass's literary phenomenology with normative character and positive ontological status, that is, they seem to have understood his narratives not as descriptions of the way things (including men and women) have been and are sociohistorically, but the way they necessarily are and have to be. Though one should not always trust authorial commentary, we can take at face value, I believe, the statement Grass made in his *Text und Kritik* interview: "In my Novelle *Cat and Mouse* . . . I have undertaken the attempt at portraying the fabrication of a military hero by society" (cited by Hollington 1980, 64; his translation).

Gerhard Kaiser's (1971) distinction between the unfreedom of the invented narrator and the freedom of the author figured earlier in discussing masculinity models as fictions. That distinction can also help resolve the seeming contradiction between Grass's literary and political writings. Kaiser argues very convincingly for the logical necessity of differentiating between the inevitability of events in Grass's (or any other author's) narratives and the possibility of change in the real world. He reminds us that the rules governing scientific experimentation also apply to narrative "possible worlds" (my term, not Kaiser's). Though verisimilitude may hold sway so that fictional events "appear under the guise of the real," the represented world "is defined once and for all as invention, play, intellectual experiment, and its proximity to reality thus has the simulation character of experiment."[10] Even if the fictional world, as a phenomenological-psychological reduction of modes of lived experience, necessarily looks very much like the "real world" as we perceive it in the natural attitude, there is nothing that guarantees the ontological necessity of the fictional world. This is a point well worth remembering when reading male fictional narratives, particularly when we can discern more than a single voice (see Duroche 1987). As Kaiser (1971) says:

> Even experiments simulating natural conditions do not in fact take themselves to be nature nor wish to be confused with it. They differentiate themselves from the latter by the fact that no matter how the experiment is set up, the inevitability in the running of the experiment is always subordinated to the premise of the free choice of experimental conditions [the narrative premises of the narrator]. Thus this tale [*Cat and Mouse*] operates inevitably and inexorably under the conditions postulated. It does not produce however an inevitable and unchangeable world, does not inflate artistic consequences into metaphysical necessity, but rather presupposes that with conditions set differently different consequences would necessarily ensue. The unchangeability within the story manifesting its own inventedness implicitly points to the changeability of the world. Its changeability does not enter into the narrative's formation because it precedes it. (9f.)

Following from the previous position, Kaiser then presents his argument that both the story and its narrator thematize their production *by* and groundedness *in* another consciousness. Kaiser points to the radicalization of social problematics that began with classicism and reaches into our own time. One result of that development has been to narrow the arena in which subjects can act, as subjects. He speaks of a narrowing of the stage of human self-realization "with the reality of action and consciousness [of the subject] shrinking to simply the reality of consciousness alone." In this process "the figures of the linguistically constructed fictional world of literature have increasingly been allowed to [compelled to] change from subjects into the objects of their life circumstances." To understand this state of affairs is to understand how we are "written," as men and as women. The awareness that we do not think, feel, and act as subjects but as objects calls forth in us a loud "No!", a refusal to accept that state of affairs. The consequence is to produce a critical consciousness-raising by seeing through language. To understand our inventedness is to understand the possibility of other possible worlds. In Grass, so

Kaiser contends, "the possibility of action is still present in the narrative, though relativized as the consciousness of the narrator's narrator." Consciousness becomes the new "place of action." It is ultimately the consciousness of the reader, that is the dynamics between the reader and the text, between enunciation and the enounced, that grounds the political potential of narration and brings forth the impetus to change.

To read Grass in the way I have suggested is to discover the political potential of narration as a possible cognitive tool for the examination and reconstruction of masculinity. There is more than one story to tell. It is difficult to think of a single contribution to recent Grass commentary that excels Helen Croft's 1973 study. But as in so many critical encounters with Grass's text, she becomes victimized by her methodology, by Jungian essentialism and the freezing of the future by the patterns of the past. It is logical that she should reach the conclusion that Grass's "ultimate vision is that of a *humanity* unable to cope, and without any real hope of rejuvenation" (Croft 1987, 121; my emphasis). That would certainly seem to be the case for the conception of masculinity that Grass describes in *Cat and Mouse.* But is that the one readers are stuck with? New possibilities open up if the reader understands that conception as a social construct and Grass's narrative as satirical critique of that construct. A social construct has a history and an ability to change, even if *very* slowly. If critiquing the inherited male past is a first step toward change, then Grass has made in *Cat and Mouse* a major contribution to the process of reconstructing masculinity.

Does Grass ever offer more than a critique and a horror story? Not in *Cat and Mouse.* At the level of story it offers essentially aversion therapy. Only at the level of discourse, in thematizing narration, does it suggest to the attentive reader the possibility of alternative masculinities. Are there any glimmers of hope elsewhere in Grass's work? The answer is a cautious "yes." *Very* faint glimmers are seen not only in *The Flounder,* but even as early as *The Tin Drum.* The last lines of *The Flounder* offer a note of hope in describing the male narrator's determination to catch up with Ilsebill, mythic representation of woman, so that perhaps the seesaw domination of one sex over the other can finally end (see

Erickson 1988, vol. 1, chap. 4). In the final scene of *The Tin Drum,* Oskar, another damaged male who is misshapen but finally growing, ascends the escalator, slowly resolving to confront *die schwarze Köchin* (the Black Cook: "Black Witch" in the English translation), what one might call Oskar's "shadow self." But as Pilenz is fond of saying, that is another "dismal complicated story, which deserves to be written, but somewhere else, not by me and certainly not in connection with Mahlke" (551/53).

Notes

1. I have tried to provide English translations for all German quotes. I have quoted the German only in the case of Grass's own texts and have used the standard Manheim translations with the first number referring to the German, the second to the English text. Unless otherwise noted, all other translations are my own.
2. For the brevity of her discussion Irène Leonard offers some of the most incisive commentary and comes closest to seeing Mahlke as *male* victim of a *male* system. (See Leonard 1974, 32f). Miles (1975) is one of the few to recognize explicitly that the novella deals with what it meant to be a young male under Nazism. Thomas (1982) focuses somewhat more than many others, though only implicitly, on exclusively male issues. Behrendt (1976, 132) is typical in speaking of Mahlke's oversize Adam's apple as "the symbol of *human* striving."
3. I have also explored this thesis, male pathology as norm, elsewhere. See Duroche (1986–87).
4. Kaiser (1971), to my knowledge, is the first and only other writer to suggest this way of looking at the novella:

   > The point of this narrative stance [Pilenz's repetitive, unending, unendable, self-correcting narration, which forces him not only to speak *about* but also *to* Mahlke] consists in preventing the reader from reading Mahlke's story as that of an exceptional pathological case which is being presented here objectively, as a clinical example, so to speak. The reader is forced to read the story as something else: not the pathology of an individual, but the pathology of a society, the history of a social relation, of which the presentation is part of that relation." (19)

   I shall return to the idea of the last sentence when discussing the implications of writing as a male.
5. A statement attributed by Michael Schneider to Max Horkheimer (Schneider 1981, 12f; Schneider 1984a, 7). The most brilliant, though chilling, exposition of the connections between patriarchy and fascist

mentality is Klaus Theweleit's *Männerphantasien* (1980; *Male Fantasies,* 1987, 1989), which provides part of the theoretical background for this chapter. Theweleit presents a very comprehensive study of the psychosocial circumstances out of which the Freikorps, and from them, fascist mentality arose, and of the connections between bourgeois patriarchy and fascism. The book is indispensable for any study of twentieth-century Western patriarchy, images of the body, connections between man, machine, technology, and male-dominated culture.

6. This paragraph paraphrases the argument of Kaiser (1971, 10–12 passim).
7. I am indebted to my colleague Russell Christensen for this and several other formulations within this chapter.
8. Interpreting Gottfried Keller's death bed dream, Rickels (1988, 184) speaks of the appearance of the knightly, armored dead father as "death's delegate in a conserving can."
9. Rickels (1988, 259) in reference to Kafka.
10. Much of what follows in this and the next paragraph is either direct translation (quoted material), or close paraphrase of Kaiser (1971, 9ff.).

References

Bauer, Dale M. *Feminist Dialogics: A Theory of Failed Community.* Albany, NY: State University of New York Press, 1988.

Behrendt, Johanna. "Die Ausweglosigkeit der menschlichen Natur: Eine Interpretation von Günter Grass' *Katz und Maus.*" In *Günter Grass: Ein Materialenbuch,* edited by Rolf Geiβler. Darmstadt: Luchterhand, 1976, 115–35.

Croft, Helen. "Günter Grass's *Katz und Maus.*" *Seminar* 9 (1973): 253–64. Reprinted in *Critical Essays on Günter Grass,* edited by Patrick O'Neill. Boston: G. K. Hall and Co., 1987.

Cunliffe, William Gordon. *Günter Grass.* New York: Twayne, 1969.

Davis, Robert Con. *The Fictional Father: Lacanian Readings of the Text.* Amherst, MA: University of Massachusetts Press, 1981.

Duroche, Leonard L. "Alternative Senses of Male Narratives: Other Voices/Other Choices." *Men's Studies Review* 4, no. 4 (1987): 6–7.

———. "On Reading Kafka's 'Metamorphosis' as a Masculine Narrative." *The University of Dayton Review* 18, no. 2 (Winter–Spring 1986–87): 35–40.

Erickson, Nancy. "A Contextual Analysis of Cooking Vocabulary in Günter Grass's *Der Butt* with Concordance." (2 vols. Ph. D. diss. University of Minnesota, 1988).

Grass, Günter. *Cat and Mouse.* 1963. Reprint. New York: Harcourt, Brace and World, 1987.

———. *Danziger Trilogie: Die Blechtrommel. Katz und Maus. Hundejahre.* Darmstadt: Luchterhand, 1980.

———. *Der Butt.* Darmstadt: Luchterhand, 1977.

———. *The Flounder.* New York: Harcourt Brace Jovanovich, 1978.

Hayman, Ronald. *Günter Grass.* London: Methuen, 1985.

Hollington, Michael. *Günter Grass: The Writer in a Pluralist Society.* London: Marion Boyars, 1980.

Jameson, Fredric. "Imaginary and Symbolic in Lacan: Marxism, Psychoanalytic Criticism, and the Problem of the Subject." *Yale French Studies* 55/56 (1977): 338–95.

Kaiser, Gerhard. *Günter Grass: Katz und Maus.* Munich: Wilhelm Fink, 1971.

Keele, Alan Frank. *Understanding Günter Grass.* Columbia, SC: University of South Carolina Press, 1988.

King, Stephen. "The Body." In *Different Seasons,* 289–433. New York: Signet, 1983.

Leonard, Irène. *Günter Grass.* New York: Barnes and Noble Books, 1974.

Meyer, Conrad Ferdinand. *Sämtliche Werke: Historisch-kritische Ausgabe.* Edited by Hans Zeller and Alfred Zach. Vol. 12, 7–98. 1883. Bern: Benteli, 1958–1991.

Miles, Keith. *Günter Grass.* New York: Barnes and Noble Books, 1975.

O'Neill, Patrick, ed. *Critical Essays on Günter Grass.* Boston: G. K. Hall and Co., 1987.

Reddick, John. *The "Danzig Trilogy" of Günter Grass. A Study of the Tin Drum, Cat and Mouse and Dog Years.* New York: Harcourt Brace Jovanovich, 1988.

Rickels, Laurence A. *Aberrations of Mourning: Writing on German Crypts.* Detroit: Wayne State University Press, 1988.

Schneider, Michael. "Fathers and Sons, Retrospectively: The Damaged Relationship between Two Generations." *New German Critique* 31 (1984a): 3–51.

———. "Nicht alle sind tot, die begraben sind." In *Nur tote Fische schwimmen mit dem Strom* . Cologne: Kiepenheuer and Witsch, 1984.

———. "Väter und Söhne, posthum. Das beschädigte Verhältnis zweier Generationen." *Den Kopf verkehrt aufgesetzt.* Darmstadt: Luchterhand, 1981.

Theweleit, Klaus. *Male Fantasies.* 2 vols. Minneapolis: University of Minnesota Press, 1987, 1989.

———. *Männerphantasien.* 2 vols. Frankfurt: Verlag Roter Stern, 1979. Reprint. Hamburg: Rowohlt, 1980.

Thomas, Noel. *The Narrative Works of Günter Grass: A Critical Interpretation.* Amsterdam: John Benjamin, 1982.

4

Naguib Mahfouz, Men, and the Egyptian Underworld

Miriam Cooke

If you would like to know what men are, then you should be a woman. If you would like to know what women are, then you should ask God.

—Jacob Lorenz

Any discourse which fails to take account of the problem of sexual difference in its own enunciation and address will be, within a patriarchal order, precisely indifferent, a reflection of male dominance.

—Steven Heath
"Difference," *Screen* 19, no. 4 (1978–79): 53.

At any given moment, gender will reflect the material interests of those who have power and those who do not. Masculinity, therefore, does not exist in isolation from femininity—it will always be an expression of the current image that men have of themselves in relation to women. . . . Those people who speak of masculinity as an essence, as an inborn characteristic, are confusing masculinity with masculinism, the masculine ideology. Masculinism is the ideology that justifies and naturalizes male domination. As such, it is the ideology of patriarchy. . . . It gives primacy to the belief that gender is not negotiable—it does not accept evidence from feminist and other sources that the relationships between men and women are political and constructed.

—Arthur Brittan
Masculinity and Power (London: Basil Blackwell, 1989), 3–4.

In this chapter I shall be examining some of the early novels of Naguib Mahfouz in an attempt to uncover the dynamics of gender construction. As Brittan writes, masculinity and femininity are never givens but power-based constructions that are in a state of perpetual negotiation in everyday life as well as in literature.

At a time when metanarratives are coming under scrutiny and criticism, it is appropriate to examine those of modern Arabic literature as well, neopatriarchy for example. In his innovative theorization of modern Arab (read, any neocolonial) society, Hisham Sharabi[1] has described the dichotomization of emergent classes as neopatriarchy. At the top is the newly empowered, traditionally patriarchal, yet spiritually bankrupt bourgeois man schooled in the ways of the European ex-potentate; at the bottom is the ever poorer and weaker subaltern. Naguib Mahfouz's novels and short stories may be considered to be multiple, Egyptian elaborations of such a totalizing discourse[2]: His men are either obsessed by the empty striving for advancement within a circumscribed, deified[3] bureaucracy, or, they are alienated, disillusioned revolutionary intellectuals who search—often aided by drugs and drink—for the meaning of existence in a modernizing, amoral, and Godless world. A subplot of this master narrative is the psychological and sexual victimization of women by selfish, greedy men. In her full-length study of Mahfouz's women, Fawzia al Ashmawi-Abouzeid describes Mahfouz's oeuvre as yet another kind of metanarrative: "the struggle between tradition and modernity as well as the evolution of customs and relations between men and women in contemporary Egyptian society."[4]

To read Mahfouz's fiction as metanarrative is to approach his work from only one of many possible directions. Perhaps part of the problem, for a Western reader at least, is that literature from the Arab world as well as literature from all parts of Asia and Africa, those dark continents of which we know little, is read as allegory. Allegory is one of a text's subtexts for which the protagonists are vehicles. For the literary detective, these novels wear their plots as coats. Once this coat has been peeled off, all are relieved to find the reassuring meaning; whatever does not fit the broad strokes of the allegory is artifice that should not interfere with the social or political message. The sleuth work has been accomplished and the reader can proclaim the coat to have been well tailored or cut with an axe.

In this chapter, I shall try to read Mahfouz without expectations of allegory derived from mandates for sociopolitical commitment. Liberating the text from its immediate subtext opens up semiological depths that would otherwise remain masked by that seemingly impermeable level. The text is now susceptible to different readings that uncover new facts and foci. Protagonists can be read as not merely carrying messages, but as being textual constructions that construct the text. If they are not credible, nothing else will be.

Mahfouz has pluralized the actors on his urban Egyptian stage to portray men and women from the rich, the petit bourgeois and the destitute classes. Heterosexual relations are paradigmatic of relationships of power pertaining throughout Egyptian society. Male characters are constructed out of their relationships with others according to the binary model of master/slave. Men who cannot control their own lives, or those of insubordinate men, turn to women as objects over which they can have dominion. The relationships of Mahfouz's men with women are always explicitly grounded in asymmetric power. Women's insubordination, in other words any hint of autonomy, threatens these men's fragile identities and represents the final stage in their alienation. They cannot confront and therefore they escape women's challenge, thereby stunting any possibility of growth. Their conception of masculinity is too rigid to accommodate interaction with women on the basis of equality. The women, however, enter into relationships for a variety of reasons. Because they are less programmed in their needs and desires, they are more difficult to fathom. Women's lack of clear definition, despite apparently self-evident categorization, emblematizes the incomprehensibility of forces confronting Mahfouz's men.

Yet, Mahfouz seems to be saying something else. He told Salwa el-Naimi: "Our world is 'masculine' and one cannot imagine it otherwise. . . . Women continue to struggle to become part of social life. But I could not describe a world in which women play the same roles as men."[5] But is this the point? For a world in which women play the same roles as men does not yet exist, nor is it perhaps desirable that it should. Sameness implies mimicry and therefore a replication of a system of asymmetric power. Therefore, because domination is inherent to these same roles, a world in which women played the same roles as men would look the same and would be as unjust and patriarchal as one in which men were the sole players. What matters is equal access to power, defined as audibility and effectiveness of voice. Reading with the protocols of the text, even though apparently against the author's intention, I argue that Mahfouz's fiction echoes with women's voices as they act out their lives in society, whether it be in the home or with the men in the "public sphere." Yet, I am not claiming that he has concentrated on them at the expense of delineating male protagonists. His fiction often betrays the delicate balance of power maintained in real life relations among men, among women,[6] and between the genders.

Mahfouz's women are not images, flat symbols of good or evil in Egyptian society. Yet this is precisely what most critics have asserted. Fawzia al Ashmawi-Abouzeid concludes her study of Mahfouz's women with a taxonomy of what female protagonists represent: (1) social situations; (2) a whole class; (3) a type of daily life; (4) the evolution of customs over three generations. She adds, "The role of the female character consists in making this social evolution more concrete and to clarify the nature of male/female relations in contemporary society" (161). Her study focuses on three protagonists: Nafisa of *The Beginning and the End (Bidaya wa nihaya)* is the "[incarnation of the] middle class Egyptian woman of the between-wars period who is living through a harsh economic crisis and of a struggle between tradition and modernity." Her quest is "passive" (161). Nur of *The Thief and the Dogs (Al-liss wa al-kilab)* is another incarnation, this time of the "proletarian woman *[fatat al-tabaqa al-sha'biyya]* whom misery and social ill-fortune have turned into a prostitute" (162). Finally, Zahra of *Miramar* is the "[incarnation of] the Egyptian fallaha [peasant] after the 1952 Revolution. . . . [she] is a symbol of the myth of Woman/Egypt" (163–65).

In *Ramziyat al-mar'a fi al-riwaya al-'arabiya wa dirasat ukhra* (Symbolism of women in the Arabic Novel and other studies,

Beirut, 1981), Jurj Tarabishi has analyzed the portrayal of women in *Respected Sir* and *Miramar.* He is more interested in Uthman Bayyumi's mystical quest as well as in the development of the four male characters in *Miramar*[7] than he is in Mahfouz's women, the avowed subject of his inquiry. He calls Uthman's struggle with women "not so much a struggle between the sacred and the profane as between depravity and life, between selfishness and life. . . . Uthman escapes women because they are the mirror in which he sees reflected the barrenness of his soul. . . . His relationship with Qadriyya is not with her but with himself" (91–92). This is also true for the four men in *Miramar* who use Zahra as a reflection of themselves (120). It seems that Zahra is a symbol, but a "living symbol" who is skillfully drawn despite her symbolic role. Tarabishi concludes that Zahra's future is in her hands (124), but he does not consider that fact significant enough to warrant revision of the mirror/symbol role.

In the interests of uncovering political allegory, Menahem Milson has reduced characters to symbols to further his detective work:

> Naima in *Fear (Al-Khawf)* and Saniyya in *Hanzal and the Policeman (Hanzal wa al-askari)* represent the idea of Egypt, the motherland and the people. This is a most important icon which appears in quite a number of allegorical stories of Mahfouz: Zahra in *Miramar,* the young women in *The Lord Giveth Death and Life (Yumit wa yuhyi),* the woman in labor in *The Child of Pain (Walid al-ana),* Qaranfula in *al-Karnak,* Saniyya al-Mahdi in *Only One Hour Left (al-Baqi min al-zaman saa),* Randa in *The Day the Leader was Killed (Yawm qutila al-za'im).* . . . The outstanding qualities of . . . secondary female characters are charm, endurance, fortitude in adversity and hope.[8]

For Mona Mikhail, Mahfouz's women are symbols who "tend to embody ideas and ideals. . . . Mahfouz's classical 'putain respectueuse' of *The Beginning and the End (Bidaya wa nihaya)* or that of *Miramar* represents an always illusory truth."[9]

It may be that the persistent symbolization of Mahfouz's women is due to the fact that until recently the study of women's roles in men's literature has been confined to the discussion of images in isolation from their impact on the evolution of the male characters. If a woman made only brief appearances, critics did not feel she warranted much of their discursive space. I shall argue that Mahfouz's women are much more than symbols. They are as critical to the development of plot as are male protagonists. What is more, they are often critical to the development of male characters. While Mahfouz's men need women, his women would like to—and quite often do—escape their need for men. Female protagonists are much more than Luce Irigaray's masquerading woman whose desire exists only as a mirror to masculine desire. On the contrary, Mahfouz's women have ambitions and desires that propel the narrative in ways that masquerade would not allow.

To understand the significance of Mahfouz's women, we must strip away the sexist bias that has informed canonical readings and view his works through a feminist optic. Such a reading will resemble the first visit of a Western tourist to the Arab world. This tourist, filled with prejudices and stereotypes, ventures into the streets of Casablanca, Tunis, Cairo, and Baghdad and suddenly realizes that the women are not all veiled. When we read Mahfouz's novels we are like that tourist, conditioned by the oft-repeated and apparently axiomatic commentary that his female protagonists are flat symbols of this and that. When we come across a woman with a complex personality who is motivated by individual goals that have nothing to do with men except as instruments of her advancement, we label her amoral. We gloss over the intricacies of her evolution in the plot, all the while commending Mahfouz for having drawn a credible woman among the panoply of paper dolls.

Because of the profusion of characters in a majority of Mahfouz's novels and short stories, it is not always possible, or indeed desirable, for each character to be rounded. Mahfouz himself has said that "from a minor real detail, I manage to create a whole life."[10] The reader should then be sensitive to the fact that this is just as true for the men as it is for the women. Yet, when critics have described sketchiness, or flatness, in Mahfouz's character portrayal, it has often been the women who have been singled out for attention.

Mahfouz has provided us with a wide tapestry in which women's experience is elaborated and valorized. Mahfouz does not allow the reader to get away with any one image, because for him no group, however apparently homogeneous, behaves in uniform fashion. It is important to read Mahfouz's oeuvre as a whole so that the resonance from one novel to the next can be felt and echoes of a simply delineated woman in one story can be read in the thoughts and actions of a woman in another story. Fully aware of the sexist preoccupations and prejudices of his fellow men, Mahfouz has depicted among the vast caste of women strong moral individuals who have been able to survive despite male opprobrium at trespassing on their turf. But he has also given us the weaker women who have not been able to overcome the obstacles. He has satirized men who respond in stereotypical fashion to women's new and unexpected roles. He has painted the canvas of Egyptian society, always striving to get the whole picture, either by proliferating characters or by embedding a single character in a vivid social context. Mahfouz's women do not live in a world apart where they suffer independently; his men and women are part of the same universe, they are locked into mutually dependent relationships so that what one does influences the other.

In fact, Mahfouz's men are often flatter than his women. The women cannot be reduced to a few types. What draws many of the women characters together is terminology: beautiful or ugly daughters, piously self-sacrificing or assertive mothers, virtuous or adulterous wives, fading or alluring spinsters, and above all prostitutes. The simplicity of these designations is deceptive, for Mahfouz creates memorable women whom readers grow to love or hate as though they knew them personally. Some are educated, some illiterate, some kind and some mean, some chaste and some loose. Vivacity is achieved by the introduction of the unexpected into a mundane character. For example, in *The Beginning and the End,* the reader learns that the tender-hearted, recently bereaved widow has never kissed her children (203). This piece of information explains previous and later behavior not only of the widow but of all who come into contact with her. And then, as though he were wont to stereotype, Mahfouz writes of this same woman that "unlike many of her sex, Samira was not a chatterbox" (231). Samira has been eased out of any possible pigeonhole, and although she is only a secondary character, we feel that we know her as an individual distinct from the others we have and will meet in Mahfouz's literature.

However, the most interesting and creative women are the "prostitutes," those literary figures whom Simone de Beauvoir has described as projections of male fantasy.[11] What does this word prostitute mean to Mahfouz? In his 1946 novel *Khan al-Khalili,* he wrote that "the real woman is the prostitute who has rejected the mask of hypocrisy and who does not have to pretend to love and to be modest and loyal" (39–40). Twenty seven years later, he takes this definition further. In *Love in the Rain (Al-hubb taht al-matar),* Mahfouz has Husni Hijazi say: "But 'prostitute' no longer means anything" (87). Does this mean that throughout this considerable oeuvre, Mahfouz is using a signifier whose signified is other than expected? I would suggest that this is indeed the case, and that this is why so many have misread Mahfouz's women: They have viewed them from a single vantage point that, like the assessment of plot in relation to allegory noted earlier, allows only for praise or regret of in-depth characterization.

The *Concise Oxford Dictionary* defines a prostitute as one "who offers her body to promiscuous sexual intercourse esp. for payment or as religious rite." Does this exchange adequately express the motivations and actions of Hamida of *Midaqq Alley* (*Zuqaq al-Midaqq,* 1947), Nafisa of *The Beginning and the End* (1949), Yasmin of *Children of Gebelawi* (*Awlad haratina,* 1959), Nur of *The Thief and the Dogs* (1961), Riri of *Autumn Quail* (*Al-summan wa al-kharif,* 1962), Basima in *The Search* (*Al-tariq,* 1964), Warda of *The Beggar* (*Al-shahhadh,* 1965), and Qadriya of *Respected Sir* (1975)? If we deconstruct this word in the context of all of Mahfouz's works that contain prostitutes as main or subsidiary characters, we will see that what they have in common is not so much a commodification of body for survival, but rather an urge for independence.

This subsuming of Mahfouz's prostitutes under a single rubric of revolt is not meant to essentialize but rather to open new possibilities of analysis. Through the lens of revolt the behavior of Mahfouz's prostitutes acquires a level of activism absent from the creation of prostitutes in conventional male writing.[12] Reading the behavior of Mahfouz's prostitutes as acts of revolt allows us to understand their literary roles also.

Mahfouz's depiction of prostitutes makes explicit what remains implicit in his other women: men reify all women so as to avoid dealing with the reality of their lives and experiences. This objectification protects men against their own weakness and allows them to weave fragile delusions of power and control. One of the best known examples can be found in the first volume of the Trilogy, *Palace Walk* (*Bayn al-Qasrayn,* 1956). Sayyid Ahmad Abd al-Jawwad is the stern patriarch who rules his household with unrelenting rigidity. During one of his very rare absences, his secluded wife Amina is urged by her children to visit the Husayn Mosque. While she is out, a car knocks her over and injures her slightly. The affair comes out into the open. To her surprise, the stern patriarch does not punish her at once: he waits until she has recovered from her accident and then throws her out. This moment of independence that she stole forces him briefly to view her as an individual and one whom he loves. His love frightens him because it makes him vulnerable, and so he has to close her out. Mahfouz's men are safe only as long as the women with whom they consort are subsumed in their roles. A measure of Mahfouz's control in characterization is that it remains allusive.[13] Amina is not unrealistically transformed by her experience, she is merely shown to have become wiser. The Amina of *Sukkariyya,* the third volume of the *Trilogy,* is a gloomy, inflexible woman, a far cry from the bright innocent of *Bayn al-Qasrayn.* Abd al-Jawwad's Achilles heel has been glimpsed. Time takes care of the rest.

Mahfouz's prostitutes are self-willed, strong individuals who for the space of the novel, or part of the novel, find themselves linked to a man—as client, lover, wife, or mother—whose need for her is greater than is hers for him. In *Children of Gebelawi* (1959), Rifaa tries to save Yasmin from her pimp, the alley strongman. He marries her. Yasmin is disappointed that Rifaa is more interested in her soul than in her body, more interested in what she represents than in who she is. She rejects this spiritual commodification and returns to her pimp. Her indignation is such that she becomes instrumental in Rifaa's execution. In contrast with this Judaslike figure, Mahfouz two years later in *The Thief and the Dogs* (1961) creates a completely different prostitute. Nur, meaning "light," is the only enlightenment that the alienated protagonist can find. She is more honest, more patriotic, and closer to God than is the God-fearing shaikh.[14] Yet, like many other women in Mahfouz's fiction, Nur is a resource Said Mahran is unable to tap because all he wants is to control her.

Prostitutes are often portrayed as stronger and more intelligent than the generality of womankind. Basima in *The Search* tells her son: "Your mother is far more honorable than their mothers. I mean it. They don't know it, but if it weren't for their mothers my business would have floundered" (5). Sabriyya al-Hishma, whose name means the Patience of Modesty,[15] uses her profession to achieve the kind of respectability and security of which she had always dreamed: she collects enough money to be able to leave her brothel, and at the age of fifty she marries a young man and lives happily ever after. These women are aware of the social opprobrium attached to their label, but it does not stand in the way of the accomplishment of their goals. For them it is not a problem; it is for the men who choose to interact with them.

Here is the crux of the matter. The men who choose to interact with these prostitutes do so with the understanding that they are quite simply prostitutes, women who sell their bodies and who in that transaction temporarily lose possession of those same bodies. Mahfouz demonstrates again and again that this is not the case. The woman who sells her body not only retains control of that body, but also of its surplus value. She is doubly empowered: she is in control of the illusion that she is surrendering just as she is in control of the man's desire and burgeoning need for her body and not that of any other woman.

Mahfouz uses prostitutes to demonstrate men's inability to deal with women except as masks and symbols. In *Respected Sir,* Uthman Bayyumi is the son of a cart driver who is promoted up and up until he becomes director-general. Throughout his journey to the top, Uthman feels he might be aided by marriages to daughters of influential superiors, yet the time never seems quite right. This is particularly the case because the eligible woman he fancies when he is at a particular civil service grade is no longer a social superior and therefore helpful when he has moved up.

While he waits, this respected civil servant virtually lives with Qadriyya, the somewhat unattractive "half black" prostitute he has frequented since youth. From time to time, he resorts to the local matchmaker, only to be disgusted with her suggestions. One candidate is an aging, though attractive, never-married headmistress whom he finally manages to seduce and in whom he then promptly loses interest. At another time, he courts one of his office personnel. But, as always, when the woman seems to want marriage, Uthman escapes. He is afraid that marriage, at least with someone of her station, will hinder his plans (85). Marriage must bring advantages, not responsibilities. He can think of only one escape from this fear that connection with women who need him engender: marry a prostitute, the emblem of passivity and of masculine power. Surely Qadriyya will not threaten his control of his own life and affairs.

However, marriage is not for the autistic; it compels recognition of another as a human being. Uthman comes to realize that Qadriyya the prostitute is above all a woman with a will and a way of life of her own that she is not willing to sacrifice because of a change in her institutional status. When she had earlier spoken to him of her political concerns and commitments, he had dismissed them as irrelevant (42). He had never felt the need to keep himself politically informed, much less to sympathize with the political activities of a prostitute. Anything she had done that did not relate directly to the pleasure he gained from her body was of no interest, and it presented no threat. But then he marries her, this unattractive woman with her political passions and her drink and drug addictions. Marriage makes them both miserable: Qadriyya because she has to contend with a man who has never taken women seriously as individuals; Uthman because he has never taken women seriously as individuals lest they threaten his smug sense of self.[16]

Respected Sir exemplifies the problematic relations all Mahfouz's men have with women. Middle- and upper-class women represent their class and nothing more. They are prizes to be coveted because of what association with them promises. Prostitutes are symbols of pleasure. Men cannot imagine that the function masks an individual, and that once they have stripped away the function, by marriage for example, what is left is the individual. As long as Uthman keeps Qadriyya on the side and does not have to deal with her on a level of equality, he does not have to try to understand who she is. He continues to preoccupy himself with other women, but as always at the level of function: Who are their parents? Will they help him fulfil his grandiose ambitions? Would they make attractive wives? These are flat questions, and because our viewpoint is Uthman's we get flat answers going little beyond yes or no. Whenever these women start to encroach on his life, start to make demands however undemanding, he immediately backs away, afraid of losing part of himself in a relationship where he will not always be in charge. Losing his life's companion, the "half black" fat prostitute, to his wife deprives him of the only kind of relationship it was possible for him to have with anyone—that of taker. The novel ends with Uthman ruminating the only satisfaction he can wrest out of life: a splendid tomb.

Many of Mahfouz's male protagonists are torn between attraction to and fear of women. Umar in *The Beggar* and Isa in *Autumn Quail* hope to reconcile desire and disgust through association with a prostitute. Umar cannot keep away from women, yet rejects all who need him; the greater the need, the more violent the rejection. First, he abandons his pregnant wife who had cut all ties with her Christian family by marrying a Muslim. He turns to the prostitute Warda assuming that she will demand nothing beyond financial recompense. But Warda has feelings and Umar turns from her at the moment that she begins to love and, he fears, need him. He grows to hate women, which is exemplified by his relentless chasing after anonymous women. Warda perspicaciously observes: "Men don't believe in love unless we disbelieve in it" (85). Isa, a high ranking civil servant in the pre-1952 government, loses his position as well as his hope for an advantageous marriage after the Revolution. Like others of Mahfouz's men who have despaired of life, Isa takes up with a prostitute called Riri. His relationship with her is not human but symbolic; it concretizes for him his own degradation. She was "a symbol of the utter humiliation into which he had sunk" (80). Yet even at his most abject, Isa clutches at the shabby remains of his masculinity in an attempt to protect himself against any weakness. When Riri announces that she is pregnant—in other words that she is establishing herself in a relationship of wife and therefore of possible demand—he rejects her summarily. He even ignores her when they run into each other in a cafe. Years later, he sees her in her husband's cafe with "his" daughter. By that time he has come to need her and the stability she offers in the new role she has assumed. She, on the other hand, no longer needs him. This is one of the topoi of Mahfouz's writings: incongruence of needs in time and kind.

But what is the motivation for these women into whose minds we are not allowed to enter? How did Qadriyya, Warda, and Riri become prostitutes? Were they victims of terrible circumstances? That is the usual literary explanation proffered for the fall to prostitution, often with the added flourish that this victim's virtue exceeds that of those whose business is virtue. Yet, if we turn to two earlier novels we will read of prostitutes—Hamida in *Midaqq Alley* and Nafisa of *The Beginning and the End*—whose destinies elaborate another story. These are not so much stories of a fall, but of a rebellion couched in terms of a fall.

It is in *Midaqq Alley,* his best known novel in the West because of its early translation into English, that Mahfouz creates one of his most convincing women. Hamida, the beautiful orphan adopted by the alley matchmaker, is the evil product of socialization by vicious women. In fact, she is so strong and determined that Mahfouz can ironically describe her as "most unfeminine" (21). Here he sets up the norm of femininity: weakness, passivity, and vacillation. Hamida knows this, and she eschews the feminine condition. She has to break out of a world that expects her to be other than she wants to be, a world that condones older women's oppression of young women. She will only break that particular cycle if she can escape the constrictions of her space. We get to know Hamida through her conversations with the alley inhabitants. We sympathize with her claustrophobia, and are ultimately relieved to escape its stranglehold even though the agent of this release is a pimp, ironically named Ibrahim Faraj, or Abraham the Liberator.

Hamida becomes one of the few women characters in Arab men's literature to make a real choice. She makes her decision as an individual with complex interests and goals. Although it is true that she may have chosen prostitution because her choices were limited, she did not choose it because she was forced. Mahfouz does not present society as uncomplicatedly oppressive. Hamida has rejected her destiny as a traditional Egyptian woman for whom marriage is the sine qua non for social acceptability. She is not condemned by her circumstances to sell her body—she is engaged to a respectable young man and has a secure, if poor and unexciting, future in the alley. She chooses to emulate the Jewish factory girls whose economic freedom gives them the means to dress well and to seem to be in control of their lives and their bodies. This is what Hamida craves, despite the pain she inflicts on all who care for her. Freedom from the alley means more, much more, than security in an oppressive world.

Hamida has thought carefully of her options and has chosen outside what was offered. Certainly, Hamida's fate can be explained as an allegory for the invasiveness and corruption of western values leading to the fragmentation of traditional society. And the use of a female protagonist as the vehicle for this allegory indicates how this form of imperialism is perpetrated through women, the vessels of honor and culture. Moreover, the fact that her decision mirrors and participates in a stage of Egyptian feminism does not mean that we should reduce Hamida to yet another kind of symbol.[17] This symbol would be of the morally reprehensible influence of Western notions of equality and women's rights at the expense of community. For Hamida emerges out of a milieu in which there is almost as little freedom for men as there is for women to act out a new pattern. Had she been upper class such a decision might have led to an exemplary path like that trod by Huda Sha'rawi, the pioneer of Arab feminist activism. Under such social and economic circumstances, her courage and anger at her limited horizons as a woman could have helped others, as did Sha'rawi's. But Hamida is not upper class. She is from the lowest echelons of society, and, what is worse, she is an orphan. She has no status and no resources other than her beauty and intelligence. She uses the one to exploit the other so that she can effect the break. Mahfouz does not indicate whether Hamida is happy. Here we have an example of his intuition of a twentieth-century Egyptian woman's dilemma: rejection of socially sanctioned norms of behavior had become for some women an imperative for which the cost could not be counted.

Why does Hamida not choose to work in the factory like the Jewish girls instead of opting for the most compromising of all women's occupations? Is it because the rewards are more immediate and less strenuous? Or is it that working in a factory or even only as a seamstress, as does Nafisa in *The Beginning and the End,* was no more valued, no less shameful than earning an honest wage as a prostitute? As always, the issue is the woman's independence. This independence is at the core of men's fear of women, disguised as indignation at the threat directed at family honor.

In *The Beginning and the End,* Mahfouz traces the "fall" of another woman. In this case, however, the woman is from the petite bourgeoisie and far from being beautiful, she is plagued by her ugliness. More than most of his women, Nafisa demonstrates Mahfouz's ability to create not only a woman but a prostitute from within. Nafisa is not universal woman but a unique individual. Nafisa and her three brothers are introduced just after their father has died suddenly without leaving provision for his family. There is general consternation because none of them has a skill or training. However, Nafisa has been sewing for friends and neighbors gratis, and the family realizes that her dressmaking skills are their only immediate resource. Although her three brothers—a drug addict and two schoolboys—are at first shocked that they have sunk so low as to have a seamstress in the family, their attitude does not outweigh their satisfaction with her earnings. Very soon none can imagine life without the fruits of Nafisa's labors.

Mahfouz allows the reader to enter Nafisa's confusion as the certainties of class and status are undermined. What was previously inconceivable is now possible. This is particularly true as far as her relations with people outside the family are concerned. She no longer has to play the game by the rules of the class into which she was born. No man of her class has ever expressed the slightest interest in her. The only one to have paid her attention is the grocer's ugly son. Whereas she is securely fixed in the ranks of the lower middle classes, Sulayman is beneath contempt, a worm whose lechery she shunned with horror. Yet, with the destabilizing of her social situation, she begins to humanize the worm. She sees in him the possibility to rebel against the limitations of her physical handicap. She can break out of the prison of her petit bourgeois upbringing and of her ugliness; she can initiate contact with a man. She seeks rather than tries to escape Sulayman's admiration.

Sulayman is delighted with this turn in events. Before her father's death, Nafisa had been a social superior and therefore his hope for improvement in status. He has dared to hope because she was so ugly that she repelled peer suitors. However, now that she has become one of the lower classes, she represents something else: satisfaction of lust. He is soon able to make this desperate woman do what she knows she should not do or what she would never have done before: walk hand in hand with him in a disreputable part of town. He finally lures her into his family apartment while everyone is out. This is not a scene of easy seduction presented from the male or the outsider's perspective. Mahfouz articulates Nafisa's experience as though seen through her eyes. Nafisa's monologues that combine admonitions to herself as well as desperate justifications lead the reader through each tiny decision that leads to her submission. When Sulayman has his way, the moment is evoked in her mood: "a mixture of anxiety, pleasure and despair" (104). She knows that she is losing control, but the hope of realizing her goal as a woman, which was to attract a man and to get married, makes her act in ways she would never have anticipated.

But Sulayman is a man like all the others; women will always be one-dimensional, reducible to icons and epithets such as respectable or shameful. He has had his pleasure and now despises this shameful creature. The courting pretense is over, he has proven his virility at no cost at all—he even asks her to lend him money she knows he will not return. Another monologue takes the reader into Nafisa's confusion: "How can I squander money like this . . . when our home needs every millieme I earn. . . . He is not a man. . . . But I love and want him. . . . I have no one else in the world" (116). He has not acted as he should have and therefore Nafisa declares him not to be a man. Yet, much to her dismay and confusion, she thinks she loves and needs him. For him, this is a victory. For her, this is a shock because she realizes that she has no one else to care for her. Moreover, she has now become a particular kind of woman, without the assurance that she is indeed such a woman, for the usual exchange has not happened, or at least it has happened in reverse.

Confirmation of her ignominy and doom comes soon with the announcement of Sulayman's engagement. Ironically, she is asked to sew the bridal gown. Betrayal gives Nafisa the courage to confront the scoundrel, to mock his unmanly subjugation to his father—the ultimate insult—and finally, in a farcical scene, to beat him in public. Sulayman begs her to stop, and when she will not he threatens to call the police. Although he acts like a woman, he can paradoxically invoke male prerogative, saying "You have no claims on me" (131). As a man he has socially sanctioned rights that allow him to escape what a woman could not escape: answerability for amoral behavior. Even at her bravest and most rebellious, Nafisa's actions serve only to consolidate an unmanly man's manliness.

Nafisa has encouraged the advances of a social inferior whom she despises but has come to need because he is her only hope for affection. Here Mahfouz indicts the family that uses Nafisa, in fact needs her, but whose members condemn her because of what they have driven her to do: earn her living and theirs as a seamstress. Her brothers, despite their radically different characters, are chips off the same block. Their equivalence is nominally marked: Hasan, Hasanayn, and Husayn. Each name is derived from the same root HSN, which means good. Hasan is good, Hasanayn is in the dual form and means doubly good, and Husayn is in the diminutive form and means quite good.

Husayn is the most virtuous in his manner and therefore the most sinister and hypocritical. Nafisa gives him the money that allows him to start his career as a teacher in Tanta. Piously mouthing concern at the need to take dirty money, he starts his new life full of good intentions toward his family. Now he is going to be the breadwinner and this bread will be clean. For the first few months he sends home a substantial share of his salary. With time, however, he is less happy to part with so much and one month he determines to tell them that he is sick. He keeps the money to buy himself a suit. His mother is worried and comes to Tanta to make sure her son can cope. He lies without flinching. His defense of this purchase out of the allowance he should have sent to his family is heinous: he has acted against the interests of his family, yet he has convinced himself that he has done no wrong. He continues to bemoan his misfortune at having the siblings he has and longs for the return of the soul to the family when it has been cured of its evil ways (200). Mahfouz's intertextual reference to Tawfiq al-Hakim's patriotic novel *Awdat al-ruh* (*Return of the Soul,* 1933), which extols the woman as a symbol of purity and Egypt, is ironic. Nafisa is a symbol of shame; all know that their honorable and successful futures depend on Nafisa's dishonorable employment. Without her dishonor there can be no honor for them.

Hasanayn represents lust: lust for his chaste fiancée prefigures his lust for power and social standing that allows him to betray his family. He sees in Bahiyya, the daughter of the esteemed Ahmad Bey Yusri, the hope for social advancement: "Mount her and you'll mount a whole class" (246; cf. 276, 287), as well as the satisfaction of carnal desire. Throughout his three-year engagement, he can only talk to Bahiyya of his desire, knowing that her honorability mandates modesty. Yet, as soon as Bahiyya is pronounced by his illustrious colleagues at the War College to be unsophisticated, he loses interest. His disinterest grows with her growing interest and reaches crisis when she offers herself to him (298, 315–16). In the meantime he is fashioning a respectable facade. He moves the family out of their neighborhood and tries to keep Nafisa at home and out of the sight of their new neighbors. Like Husayn, he hopes that papering over the past will assure another future. Yet, like Husayn he continues to use the money that Nafisa earns from her prostitution and that Hasan earns from pimping to establish his highly respectable career.[18]

Hasan does not have the pretensions of his brothers. He knows he has failed, and in some ways his marginality mirrors that of Nafisa. Yet he, too, despises and ignores Nafisa. Before establishing himself as a pimp and alley bully, he tries singing for a living. When he hears of Sulayman's wedding, he offers his services. No one is more surprised or gratified than Sulayman, who had expected the brother's visit to be one of revenge for his sister's disgrace. The offer to sing at his wedding implied condonement—even if only through ignorance—of his dishonorable behavior and of her betrayal. Subconsciously, patriarchal forces regroup to close out space for women, except in their routinized roles. As her world collapses, Nafisa turns against her mother (126). This turn is as powerful as it is unexpected. With the death of the father, her mother has become the primary authority figure. In some ways, she has assumed the male role and in the mimicry had become male. This female father figure incarnates Nafisa's shame.

Shame is incurred when Nafisa leaves the home to earn her family's living. The transition from seamstress to prostitute is easy and almost irrelevant. After rejecting the lewd advances of a mechanic, she gives in. She is hurt at his roughness after he has had his way, yet she eventually picks up the ten-piaster piece that he has thrown at her. She knows that the decision to take the money is part of a continuum that began with her family launching her into the outside world to sell her services on their behalf and will end with her determination to sell her body on her own behalf. In this connection, it is worthy of note that Mahfouz repeats throughout that Nafisa gained pleasure from her sexual encounters. This is not to say that Nafisa is happy, but that through this vocation she finds a level of satisfaction of which she would otherwise have been deprived. In a society that values women for their physical charms, an ugly woman has no place, no right to happiness, and certainly no right to physical pleasure. With the loss of Sulayman, Nafisa knows that she has no hope of marriage. By offering her body, she can attract the attention of men who would be repelled by her face.[19] Unlike the beautiful Hamida, who became Titi so as to gain autonomy and independence, the ugly Nafisa used her body to glean seconds of pleasure and tenderness even if they were then turned into the coldness of cash and cruelty.

For her two younger brothers her work as seamstress as well as her unmarriageability epitomize the family's degradation. The irony underlying the novel is the anxiety that all feel about Nafisa's job and status simultaneous with their ignorance not only of her prostitution but above all of her independence of them and of social convention. The family's blindness to the reality of their sister's and daughter's life reflects Mahfouz's awareness of the shallowness, selfishness, and insensitivity of men and their surrogates with respect to women.

It is Nafisa's suicide that reveals the chasm dividing the world of men from that of women. When the ruthlessly ambitious young officer is summoned to the police station to identify his sister, who has been caught with a man, he is horrified. He does not, nor ever will, know that this is not the first incident. His outrage is such that he feels honor-bound to kill her to safeguard the family reputation. But he cannot do the deed. Nafisa senses his anguish and offers to kill herself—the ideal solution. He has been instrumental, yet he does not have to compromise his situation further by soiling his hands with shameful blood and will not have to render an account to the world of the reasons for this murder. When Nafisa throws herself into the Nile, Hasanayn feels a slight twinge. Yet when the body is dragged out on to the bank he is just one of the curious onlookers. His decision in the last lines of the novel to throw himself into the Nile from the same spot Nafisa had chosen does not mitigate his crime, but only suggests at best that he has been inspired by his sister's courage, and at worst that he cannot face a life his family has so tarnished for him and that he can no longer patch over. This depiction of blindness, terminal selfishness, and cowardice parodies patriarchal obsessions with honor as vehicled through women who are perceived to be without subjectivity. There is no act that Nafisa can commit, however depraved or noble, that will make her real to the men with whom she deals. To them, she is as flat as a mirror. Yet, as a mirror she reflects and thereby creates their image.

This chapter has examined a few of Mahfouz's novels that revolve around the relationships men have with prostitutes. I have sought to demonstrate that Mahfouz's prostitutes are not fallen women but rather modern women who have been exposed to new options and values and who have rebelled against traditional social expectations. They are forging a different future during a period of transition. Despite the gravity of this challenge, men continue to be preoccupied with themselves and with existential issues. They are blind to reality, particularly that of the women with whom they absentmindedly consort. When these women assert themselves, the men withdraw.[20] This inability to relate to women except as fantasy or stereotype replicates or perhaps constitutes their alienation.[21] Mahfouz mocks his men whose delusions of power and knowledge women expose.

From his first publication, a collection of short stories entitled *Whisper of Madness* (*Hams al-junun,* 1938), to the most recent classically intertextual novels like *The Nights of the Thousand Nights* (*Layali alf laila,* 1982) and *The Travels of Ibn Fattuma* (*Rihlat Ibn Fattuma,* 1985), Mahfouz has created a caste of men and women whose actions and beliefs affect each other. In the longer works, Mahfouz explores heterosexual relationships in depth. In the shorter fiction there is more allusion. It is the intensity of women's relationships with men rather than their symbolization of larger forces that makes Mahfouz's portrayal of women exceptional.

In considering his vast and varied oeuvre, can we argue that Mahfouz writes as a feminist? If the criterion is attention to the multiplicity and evolving nature of urban Egyptian women's experience, then perhaps. Mahfouz has opened up the deprived and angry lives of women in the poor and not so poor areas of Cairo. He has written of the first women students at the Egyptian university where he was matriculated only two years after women were first admitted. He has written of the changing reaction to women's education over half a century. He has focused on changing marriage customs; he proceeds from a time when neither men nor women could see their prospective partners to a time when they were introduced through the photograph,[22] to a still more recent time when women proposition men.[23] He has concentrated on the workplace and shown how time has changed men's attitudes.[24] He recognizes at the same time that this new economic freedom also entails emotional freedom: women have earned the right to choose whom to love and especially whom not to love.[25] He has written of powerful women who were part of what he calls the women's renaissance or who were members of the Women's Wafdist Committee,[26] and who did not have to bow to society's conventions. Above all, he has entered the Cairene and Alexandrian underworlds and has fully fleshed out the lives of prostitutes who are not merely symbols or projections of fantasy but often complex personalities who use their humiliation against their humiliators.

But is he a feminist? Mahfouz's depiction of women has changed over the past fifty years. In his sociorealist novels of the 1940s and 1950s, he displayed a sensitivity to women's issues and particularly to prostitution as a form of rebellion that may be dubbed feminist. However, in the existential novels of the 1960s that revolve around a single male, many of the women seem flat and transparent. Young women during this period represent the extremes of emotion latent in the men who are so self-absorbed they can only see and interact with these women as aspects of themselves. In the 1970s, his attitude changes once again. By constantly proffering the male perspective and reiterating the strangeness of women's new visibility, Mahfouz emphasizes the importance of caution. Like Camelia Zahran, these women had to "bear in mind the eastern complexes which their male colleagues inherited from their forefathers at home" (*Al-maraya,* 282). If women did not remain constantly on their guard men would be vindicated in their fearful preconceptions.

During the latter half of Mahfouz's career, we read of men's fear of phallic mothers, "the real killers" (*The Search,* 78). In *Wedding Song,* Sabir says, "She is my foremost enemy: father is insane, an addict, but mother is the engineer of all the evil in the world" (80). The man who is intoxicated with one woman will be like the son under the control of his mother; he will lose his reason because he will need the object of his obsession no matter how vicious and adulterous she may be. The only solution beyond numbers is to control this woman with an iron fist, to not allow her any freedom or to allow oneself feelings. The woman who is not controlled will surely control. Mahfouz attempts to overcome the negative attitude toward women prevalent in twentieth-century Egypt but he is increasingly trapped in a web of prevailing notions and fears.

When he wrote *Midaqq Alley, The Beginning and the End* and the Trilogy over thirty years ago, Mahfouz must have felt free to create specific, complex women who gradually attained a measure of autonomy. Subsequently, his women have become flatter, more sketchily delineated. We can only surmise about the reasons, but it could be that as women have attained greater acceptance in society they have become more threatening. It is not so easy to be a male feminist in a world full of women.

Notes

1. Hisham Sharabi, *Neopatriarchy* (London: Oxford University Press, 1989).
2. In his introduction to the English translation of Elias Khoury's *Little Mountain* (Minneapolis: University of Minnesota Press, 1989), Edward Said has written, "Mahfouz's precedence assures [later generations of Egyptian writers] a point of departure . . . discursive patterns of a narrative structure that was not merely a passive reflection of an evolving society, but an organic part of it. . . . Mahfouz's novels, his characters and concerns have been the privileged, if not always emulated, norm for most other Arab novelists" (xiii).
3. "The State is an exhalation of the spirit of God, incarnate on earth" (*Respected Sir,* Questet, 1986, 143–44; originally published as *Hadrat al-muhtaram,* 1975).
4. Fawzia al Ashmawi-Abouzeid, *La Femme et l'Egypte Moderne dans l'Oeuvre de Naguib Mahfuz 1939–1967* (Geneva: Labor et Fides, 1985), 160.
5. Interview with Salwa el-Naimi, "Notre Père Mahfouz," *Magazine Littéraire* 251 (March 1988): 28.
6. "The Visit" from the *Black Cat Tavern* collection (in Arabic, 1967) explores the terrors and anxieties of the faded beauty who never married and who has no support system. She is physically and psychologically dependent on her callous servant who is economically dependent on her.

   In *Wedding Song* (Cairo, 1984; originally published as *Afrah al-qubba,* 1981), we read of two prostitutes who confront the same circumstances with different outcomes: one is killed; the other becomes a brothel madam. Tahiyya, the murdered actress, is never given a voice. Her story is recounted by four protagonists, none of whom has ever seen her as a person. The reader glimpses a woman whose only function has been to fulfil men's dreams and desires. On the other hand, there is Halima al-Kabsh, the mother-in-law who, despite the resentment she feels toward her, understands Tahiyya as no man ever had or could. She is able to learn from a woman's experience.

7. In fact, he writes after eighteen pages on the men: "Is it not time for us to talk about Zahra herself?" (120) and he does so for just over four pages.
8. Menahem Milson, "Najib Mahfuz and Jamal Abd al-Nasir: The Writer as Political Critic," *Asian and African Studies* 23, no. 1 (March 1989): 10.
9. Mona Mikhail, *Images of Arab Women: Fact and Fiction* (Washington, D.C.: Three Continents Press, 1978), 92. In a more recent work entitled *Brides at the Feast: Studies on Arab Women* (*Ara'is fi al-mawlid dirasat hawla al-mar'a al-'arabiyya* [Cairo: Dar al-'Arabi, 1987]), Mikhail discusses Hamida as a fallen virtuous woman (saqita fadila) and as a victim (78). However, she does insist that Hamida is a strong woman who is rebelling against society.
10. Salwa el-Naimi, "Notre père Mahfouz," 28.
11. Simone de Beauvoir, *The Second Sex* (New York: Vintage, 1974), 157–223.
12. "Even among male writers who are sympathetic toward prostitutes, the tendency is to create the character from without, to rely on the role of 'prostitute' in defining the character, rather than to single out the individual in that role. . . . [Their men] see the women's actions in terms of themselves and are blind to their meaning for [the women]." Amy Katz Kaminsky, "Women Writing about Prostitutes," in Pierre L. Horn and Mary Beth Pringle, eds., *The Image of the Prostitute in Modern Literature* (New York: Frederick Ungar, 1984), 120, 125.
13. She is quite unlike the mother in the Moroccan novel by Driss Chraibi, *La Civilisation, Ma Mère!* (Rabat, 1972), whose exposure to the world after protracted seclusion leads to violent self-consciousness and political activism.
14. Compare also the shaykh and the prostitute in "The Mosque in the Alley" (*Dunya Allah,* Cairo, 1963).
15. *Al-maraya* (Cairo: Maktabat Misr, 1974), 174-77.
16. Men's fear of women is a topos in modern Arabic literature. Fiction writers have often described dangers imagined to be inherent in beautiful women, cf. Yusuf Idris, "Affair of Honor" (Hadithat al-sharaf), in which the merest suspicion of illicit relations was enough for the innocent woman to be punished; Yahya Haqqi, "The Empty Bed" (Al-firash al-shaghir), in which a young man is so disturbed by women's sexual responsiveness that he finally resorts to necrophilia.
17. "One can easily tell that Mahfuz gives great importance to his female characters and that he uses them as a mirror in which the evolution of customs is reflected. Through his paper characters, he elaborates

the stages in the emancipation of the flesh and blood contemporary woman" (al Ashmawi-Abouzeid, *La femme et l'Egypte,* 160).

18. Like Nafisa, Hasan has a perspective from his marginal position and he is amused by the irony. When Hasanayn highhandedly demands that Hasan return to the straight and narrow, Hasan retorts: "If you really want me to abandon my tainted life, then you, too, must abandon yours" (294).
19. "How delicious is flirtation even if it is a lie. She was in a shameful situation but this restored the self-esteem and dignity of a woman whose wings had been broken" (165). Note the use of the broken wings image so common in feminist literature.
20. In *Chatter on the Nile* (*Tharthara fauq al-Nil,* Cairo, 1966), the mostly male occupants of the houseboat reject Sammara Bahjat when she confronts them with the emptiness of their lives and their social irresponsibility.
21. In *The Beggar* (*Al-shehhadh,* Cairo, 1965), Umar's daughter Buthayna writes teleological poetry as had her father when he was young. Yet he cannot understand her spiritual yearnings, assuming that women write only about love. The woman who is his mirror hides behind his reflection whether she wants to or not.
22. See, for example, *Hikayat haratina* (Cairo, 1982), 30.
23. See, for example, *Al-maraya,* 27, 82, 320.
24. "We had become as accustomed to having girls in our midst as to the rumors flying around during the difficult period before marriage" (*Al-maraya,* 282).
25. See, for example, *Al-maraya,* 112.
26. See, for example, *Al-maraya,* 9, 55, 87.

III

Crossing Sexualities

5

Man among Men: David Mamet's Homosocial Order

David Radavich

Apart from C. W. E. Bigsby's booklength study (1985), curiously little scholarly attention has been paid to the insistent masculinity of David Mamet's plays. Published in editions frequently bedecked by the author's tauntingly phallic photo-portrait with cigar, the major plays either totally exclude or marginalize women, concentrating instead on myriad variations of homosocial male order. Mamet's dramatic world is both self-consciously and half-consciously male, with references to homosexuality, fear of violation by other men, insistent desire for male friendship, and pursuit of domination and acceptance operating at the core of the dramatic conflict. In one interview, Mamet admitted, "I don't know anything about women. . . . I'm more around men; I listen to more men being candid than women being candid" (Fraser 1976). Only two of his more successful plays, *Sexual Perversity in Chicago* (1978) and *Speed-the-Plow* (1987), include female characters at all, who, in both instances, are experienced by the male characters and by the audience as essential disturbers of the natural male order. The central body of Mamet's work concentrates on a single-minded quest for lasting, fulfilling male friendship protected from the threats of women and masculine vulnerability on the one hand and the destabilizing pursuit of power and domination on the other.

Mamet's concerns about masculinity take on a particularly intense resonance in the latter part of the twentieth century, as the traditional bastions of male companionship have increasingly been called into question. Eve Kosofsky Sedgwick (1985) has described homosocial desire in a "pattern of male friendship, mentorship, entitlement, rivalry, and hetero- and homosexuality . . . in an intimate and shifting relation to class" (1). This reference to class may be expanded to include age, rank, and other social factors creating a functional inequality. Chapter 1 of her pathbreaking *Between Men: English Literature and Male Homosocial Desire* details "male homosocial desire within the structural context of triangular, heterosexual desire" (16). Mamet's *Sexual Perversity* and *Speed-the-Plow* highlight this triangular configuration, whereas other of his plays deal with the struggle to form and define exclusively male bonds. A desire for dominance, usually between men of unequal rank or age, battles with an equally strong desire for loyalty and acceptance, resulting in a hard-won, intense, fundamentally unstable intimacy established in the absence of women.

From the outset, Mamet's plays have asserted the primacy of male friendship: "A man needs a friend in this life. . . . Without a friend, life is not. . . . It's lonely. . . . It's good to have a friend. . . . To help a friend in need is the most that any man can want to do" (97–98). This excerpt from the Seventh Variation of *The Duck Variations* (1978) represents a paean to such friendship, as two men in their sixties engage in "Spectator Sports" together, in this case observing ducks (not "chicks"), as a means of solidifying their bond. The men of Mamet's later plays bond through frequenting bars (*Sexual Perversity,* 1978), performing together (*A Life in the Theater,* 1977), or driving business deals (*Glengarry Glen Ross,* 1983; and *Speed-the-Plow,* 1987), but in each case the primacy of close male friendship is asserted in the face of intruders, either rival men or, more seriously, women.

Sexual Perversity presents the challenge in the form of Deborah, erstwhile lesbian, who becomes involved with Dan, the steady buddy of Bernie. In the course of the play, many sexual perversions are trotted out for verbal display, as the title suggests, but most involve the degradation of women: "The Way to Get Laid Is to Treat 'Em [Women] Like Shit" (22). In an early extended narrative, Bernie describes his encounter with a "chick" who dresses for sex in a Flak Suit, asks him to make war noises, then douses them both with gasoline and sets all on fire. A later narrative centers on King Farouk, who arranges to have "his men run a locomotive right through the broad's bedroom" and later "whacks her on the forehead with a ballpeen hammer" (34–35). Bernie acts as spokesman for most of these "perversities," though Deborah and Joan act out some of the vicissitudes of lesbian affections and jealousy. The one "perversion" omitted in the play—probably the most common variation from heterosexuality in our culture—is adult male homosexuality. Its absence appears all the more striking as Bernie successfully undermines and fights off the challenge Deborah presents to his relationship to Dan, so that at the end the two men reunite in a friendship that, although nominally situated in a heterosexual context of "casing chicks," nonetheless posits a male bond of superior endurance.

Although lacking some of the intellectual trappings of traditional comedy, Mamet's plays embody many of its major elements, including the disruptive intrusion by an outsider followed by chaos and the final reunion of the happy couple (in this case male). In *Sexual Perversity,* Dan's sexual interest in Deborah threatens to shatter the male bond, forcing Bernie to counterattack with measures that one usually associates with heterosexual dating: outings to the movie house, evenings in Bernie's apartment, and sojourns to the beach. After this concerted effort on Bernie's part, Dan succumbs to his eventual partner's way of thinking, explaining to another co-worker, "And *he* [Bernie], he puts his arm around my shoulder and he calms me down and he says, 'Dan, Dan . . . don't go looking for affection from inanimate objects' " (53). The subtextual reference to women as "inanimate objects" brings the supremacy of male bonding full circle by play's end.

In the absence of a clear cause for Dan's break-up with Deborah, the bonding activities with Bernie that negate or exclude women serve to reassert the primacy of their same-sex friendship. Both men find it difficult to appreciate the otherness of female experience, which they consider either frivolous or irrelevant.

While in bed with Deborah, Dan cannot imagine "having tits": "That is the stupidest question I ever heard. What man in his right mind would want tits?" (40). When Deborah confesses to having fantasized about other women the last time they made love, Danny responds, "The last time I masturbated I kept thinking about my left hand" (40). The solipsistic impulse, albeit in a comic context, serves to isolate both men from a deeper experience of the feminine. The fear of the female, and of female sexuality in particular, dominates Mamet's early plays, as males jostle for position and affection among themselves apart from women.

American Buffalo ([1975], 1981), one of Mamet's most successful plays, features an all-male cast in a Chicago pawnshop where homosocial desire finds its decadent arena. Unlike *Duck Variations,* with its placid contemplations, this play foregrounds homosocial pursuit and defense and introduces the cuckolding and rape imagery important to Mamet's portrayal of American capitalism. In an interview Mamet reiterates the important link: "Look at Delorean. He completely raped everybody in Northern Ireland with that scheme" (Roudané 1986, 74–75). Although in *Sexual Perversity* Bernie and Dan work together in a faceless contemporary office, the underworld of second-rate business functions in *American Buffalo* as a more symbolic setting for Mamet's portrait of capitalism gone awry.

At the outset of *Buffalo,* Dan chastises Bob for incompetence, exerting his dominance in a pattern that clearly establishes Mamet's concern with the man "above" and the man "below." In *Sexual Perversity,* Bernie functions as Dan's superior in experience, offering fatuous advice and controlling much of the subsequent action. Don maintains supremacy in *American Buffalo* more clearly through financial control of Bob, and through his rôle as teacher/mentor and status male. The allusion to education embodied in Joan is transferred here to both Teach and Don, who continually moralize, philosophize, and pontificate about the nature of life, people, and business. The "knowledge" actually taught, however, is both corrupt and clumsy, so that by the end, the traditional mentoring of males in the world of business has collapsed into mutual incompetence.

American Buffalo differs from other Mamet works in the intense triangular relationship among the men, where Teach clearly poses a threat to the central if unequal bond between Don and Bob. Their friendship is only haltingly acknowledged—at the end, after injuries and humiliation/threat bring them together—but Teach recognizes it and hopes to establish his own relationship with Don by replacing Bob and ousting Fletcher. The men jockey for one-on-one friendship within whose boundaries emotional loyalty can be assumed and women can be regarded with mutual distrust. Denigrations of women abound: "Only . . . from the mouth of a Southern bulldyke asshole ingrate of a vicious nowhere cunt can this trash come" (803–4). And whenever Teach seeks to vent frustration with himself or his fellows, he resorts to homosexual slander ("you fruit") or images of impotence/emasculation ("dick on the chopping block") (884, 893). Clearly, insults that homosexualize or womanize men negate their potency, thereby diminishing their status and value.

Anxiety about manhood pervades these plays, at least partly the result of "improperly construed [masculine] initiations" (Raphael 1989, 144). "Makeshift" males struggle with "the deep-seated fear that [they] might never become 'men'" (145, 190). In *American Buffalo,* Teach responds to Don in anger, "I am not your wife. . . . I am not your nigger," where, presumably, the secondary status of both doubles the rhetorical effect of his outburst (888). Later, feeling rejected, he laments, "There is no friendship," and "I look like a sissy" (895). The threat of being emasculated, either by women (Grace and Ruthie, a lesbian couple) or by men, is ever-present, only to be allayed through a strong male bond that empowers each male in it. Hence the "honor among thieves" element in *American Buffalo* maximizes potency through a supposed pooling of expertise (in this case, a shared incompetence) (Roudané 1986, 76). At the end of the play, Don, through a clever Mametesque pun, tacitly acknowledges the intimate connection between sex and business: "It's all fucked up. . . . You fucked my shop up" (894). The twisted initiation ritual embodied in their struggle results in closer male bonds but leaves in its wake both physical wounds and the destruction of the locus of their enterprise.

Supplementing the central, all-male triangle in *American Buf-*

falo is a recurring motif of cuckoldry, whereby coins function as the battleground for sexual revenge on the successful man ("fucking fruit") as well as on the wife ("dyke cocksucker"): "Guys like that, I like to fuck their wives" (847, 820). For the first time, Mamet ties business practices to the sexual/power act of rape in a singularly evocative metaphor of masculine revenge for perceived inadequacy. Indeed, rape and prostitution, primarily of men by men, becomes the central metaphor for American capitalism in Mamet's later plays. The desire for an enduring male bond is inextricably linked to a mutually conceived crime for the dual purpose of perpetration and profit. Beneath the comic surface, the dramatic structure reveals the swirling, conflicted emotions of men for and against other men.

A Life in the Theater (1977) contains the most penetrating stage metaphor of homosexual interconnection in all of Mamet's work. The older actor, Robert, discovers that his zipper is broken and reluctantly agrees to allow his younger colleague, John, to pin his fly for him. As Robert stands up on the chair, he urges John in the endeavor:

ROBERT: Come on, come on. *[JOHN puts his face up against ROBERT's crotch.]* Put it in. . . . Come on, for God's sake. . . . Will you stick it in?
JOHN: Hold still. There. *[Pins fly awkwardly.]*
ROBERT: Thanks a lot. (144–45)

This arresting metaphor captures the latent homosexual desires and fears implicit in the playwright's characterization of male friendship. Robert, symbolically emasculated by a broken zipper, stands physically above John on the chair and metaphorically above him by age and experience, while the young man attempts to "pin" him—a clever pun on sexual penetration and domination. At no point in the entire scene, clearly intended as a stage ruse for the audience's titillation, do the two males acknowledge either the humor or the sexual implications of their actions; subsequent interactions reflect no awareness of this sequence of events. The symbolic failure of the pinning suggests a taunting almost-consummation that results instead in collapse and lack of connection.

The sexual triangle implicit in several Mamet plays receives up-front treatment in *A Life in the Theater,* although the shared woman never appears. John accuses Robert of impregnating his wife, Gillian, but in a consummately comic scene, does not seem overwhelmingly shattered by the revelation: "What are we going to do about this?" (31). Elsewhere, the two men assert the primacy of their bond as Robert denigrates his female co-star, "When we're on stage she isn't there for me," and John responds by acknowledging his desire for substitution: "I wanted to be up there with you" (14–15). Later, John wipes the makeup off Robert's face, and they go out to dinner together, an occasion reported subsequently by John in a telephone conversation as "going out with . . . an Actor" (24). At the end of the play, Robert cries, complaining that John makes him "feel small" (49). The transaction becomes complete when the older man gives the younger one money, solidifying the reversal in power and the insistent connection between (unconsummated) sex and lucre.

In contrast to *A Life in the Theater, Glengarry Glen Ross* (1983) showcases the sexopolitical battle of the male "pack," with one-on-one friendships relegated to somewhat lesser status. In yet another all-male play of characters now middle-aged, the focus shifts to male rape ("fucking up the ass") and enslavement (18). And the "screwing" is not merely verbal. The audience watches Moss "screw" Aaronow by forcing him into a criminal plot, one of many attempts by the men to emasculate other men, either psychologically or financially. In a moment of frustration, Roma declares, "We're all queers," and Levene accuses Williamson of "not having balls," establishing a figurative equivalence between homosexuality and castration (27,49). As Leverenz (1989) has pointed out, such cut-throat sexual dueling among males "has to do with manhood: a way of empowering oneself through someone else's humiliation" (245).

The sexual images in this play therefore turn correspondingly negative. Moss insults the police investigator by referring to him as a "cop without a dick" (41). Roma turns later to Williamson: "You stupid fucking cunt. . . . I don't care . . . whose dick you're sucking on" (65). Here, the eunuch, the homosexual, and the female become equally debased versions of the male, as gender slurs are used to harass, insult, and blackmail other males. Such language of bravado, domination, and humiliation is immediately understood and never questioned by any of the characters. When Levene thinks he has made a legitimate blockbuster sale, he announces his triumph in genital terms: "And now . . . I got my balls back" (70). The phallus thus valuates the currency not only in business but also in society at large. In the ethos of Mamet's plays, a man symbolically deprived of his penis through personal insecurity or deprecation by other males becomes, by definition, a faggot or a cunt, debased both sexually and professionally.

What's curious about *Glengarry,* and about most of Mamet's better-known works, is the marginalizing of any real sex. Gould and Karen spend a night together (on a male wager) in *Speed-the-Plow* but say virtually nothing about the love-making itself afterward. In *Sexual Perversity,* Dan and Deborah lounge together in bed, discussing the apartment, Deborah's lesbian experiences, and the virtues of "come" and penises. The noticeably tentative affection disappears altogether later in the play, for reasons unknown. In *Glengarry Glen Ross,* Roma declares sex essentially meaningless: "The great fucks that you may have had. What do you remember about them?" (28). In the masculine world of Mamet's early plays, men primarily pursue not sex but position ("above" or "below"), power, and male loyalty.

Somewhat later, in *The Woods* and *Edmond* (1987), what Sedgwick (1985) calls "homosexual panic" emerges as a central theme (89). In the latter play, Edmond and Glenna discuss their hatred of "faggots":

EDMOND: Yes. I hate them, too. And you know why? . . . . They suck cock. (Pause.) And that's the truest thing you'll ever hear. (266)

The context here, decidedly tongue-in-cheek, provides a stark contrast with Nick's confessions to Ruth in *The Woods*. Having invited Ruth to share a vacation by the lake, Rick makes clear his disinterest in making love: "Why don't you leave me alone?" (86). Finally, Nick confesses to a homosexual past:

NICK: I have to tell you something. . . . I have to tell you we would come up here as children. *[Pause.]* Although some things would happen . . . . Although we were frightened. . . . And many times we'd come up with a friend. With friends. We'd ask them here. *[Pause.]* Because we wanted to

be with them. *[Pause.]* Because . . . . *[Pause.]* Wait. Because we loved them.
RUTH: I know.
NICK: Oh, my God. *[Pause. He starts to cry.]* I love you, Ruth. (115–16)

Ruth's knowledge and acceptance in this passage provide the essential absolution, allowing Nick to break down and purge his anxieties. If the play ends inconclusively, Nick nonetheless moves tentatively beyond what Ruth calls "this manly stuff" he has "made up" (102).

Speed-the-Plow (1987) seems to move beyond the homophobia articulated in Mamet's earlier plays. Here, the homosexual imagery is noticeably positive and comic, accepted without reservation by the two main characters. Rather than hurling gay-bashing insults at each other, as in earlier plays, Fox and Gould refer to themselves as "two Old Whores" and the "*Fair*-haired boys" (23, 31–32). References to "*your* boy" and "*my* boy" turn males into commodities, and other gay references flow freely in the assumedly more tolerant atmosphere of the Hollywood movie set. Fox proposes filming a "*Buddy* picture" featuring black guys who "want to get him [the protagonist] . . . going to rape his ass" (12). The intimate link between rape and business is reiterated: "It's 'up the ass with gun and camera' " (27). As studiously as Mamet's earlier male characters refused to acknowledge homosexual elements in their behavior, Gould and Fox trade gay one-liners with a new-found freedom of expression: "They'll *french* that jolly jolly hem"; "Just let me turn one more trick" (33).

Like *Sexual Perversity* and *American Buffalo, Speed-the-Plow* again features a tight male bond threatened by an intruder and eventually reestablished after a threat of dissolution. Karen's rôle emerges more fully than in *Sexual Perversity,* partly because Joan and Deborah have become fused into one voice, offering a direct frontal attack on the bastion of male unity. Again, the relationship between Gould and Fox is noticeably unequal (Gould has been "bumped up" above Fox), and sexual references link directly to business:

GOULD: You put as much energy in your job as you put into kissing my ass . . .
FOX: My job is kissing your ass. (39)

Their relationship dates back some eleven years, with Gould, in his new position, functioning as Fox's protector. As archetypal woman, however, Karen represents a severe threat to this male harmony, advocating the "moral high ground" that both Gould and Fox have abdicated in their pursuit of success in the world of men.

Karen is a secretary, symbolically temporary both professionally and sexually, with no surname, rendering her several stages inferior to either man, so that Fox, with obvious impunity, can threaten to have her killed if she does not leave. Unlike Gould, Karen exhibits a complete awareness of the sexual implications of their appointment to discuss the merits of the radiation screenplay, offering to palliate their mutual loneliness in a night together. Gould, the same man Fox wagered could not bed Karen, seems caught off guard by the straightforwardness of her proposition. Karen's probing dialogue reduces Gould to monosyllabic questions: "You came to? . . . I asked you here to sleep with me? . . . *I'm* frightened. . . . Why did you say you would come here anyway . . ." (76–77; final ellipsis in original).

Fox counterattacks by calling Gould a "wimp," a "coward," a "whore," and a "ballerina" (92–94). In one of his most extreme insults, Fox claims, "You squat to pee" (92). The womanizing deprecations, noticeably lacking homosexual equivalents in this play, finally collapse as Fox utters his two quintessential claims on Gould's attention: "I love this guy, too" and, more poignantly, "Bob: I need you" (102, 104). In all of Mamet, this is the baldest statement of homosocial desire for intense male friendship, forceful enough to overrule any female objection. When Karen later admits that she probably would not have slept with Gould had he not favored the "radiation script," their night together crumbles into a sham of (self-)deception and strategy, with whatever affection they might have exchanged evaporating into silence. Gould decides in favor of the "*Buddy* play," and the work ends suitably with the male "couple" reunited, albeit without any overt sexual interaction.

In *Speed-the-Plow,* the perception of women as sexual "weakeners" or "corruptors" of men receives its most direct expression. Karen's influence on Gould diverts his attention and attitudes from what works in the male world (the "*Buddy* play") to what works in the world of higher, more humane values traditionally associated with women (the "radiation play"). More cogent than Deborah's in *Sexual Perversity,* her point of view nearly persuades Gould to take the "high road" he has abdicated in a long climb up the professional ladder. But Fox's claim proves the stronger, and Gould succumbs to the pressures of male bonding implicit in the world of business. Once again in Mamet, male friendship emerges as more powerful, more significant, and, ultimately, more enduring. As Roland Barthes (1978) described the potential threat of women in another context, "A man is not feminized because he is inverted but because he is in love" (14).

The male characters in Mamet's plays inhabit a homosocial milieu where male bonds offer the primary reality, where women threaten the tightly stretched, fragile if enduring fabric, and where sexuality is largely expressed in words and distorted transactions rather than in mutually satisfying love-making. The Mamet males, with the possible exception of Fox and Gould, fear the sexual intimacy their bond implies, turning that fear outward instead into a denigration of females and of other males as homosexuals and *castrati.* Sedgwick (1985) sees this "homosexual panic" as a central motivating force in the maintenance of the capitalist patriarchy (89). Not surprisingly, Mamet's plays wed male bonding to the often corrupt practices of business. The instability of the bonding, the fierce competitiveness with which his characters struggle to escape the dichotomy of their announced desires for women and their more enduring preference for the company of other men, suggests both the decay of the relatively comfortable old professional order and the panic of being forced to acknowledge the needs such relationships imply.

As Leslie Fiedler so provocatively pointed out in his *Love and Death in the American Novel* (1966), the masculine desire for an innocent, intimate bond transcending sex and operating outside the perceived strictures of female society has remained an enduring theme in American literature: "In our native mythology, the tie between male and male is not only considered innocent, it is taken for the very symbol of innocence itself; for it is imagined as the only institutional bond in a paradisal world in which there are no (heterosexual) marriages or giving in marriage (350)." Mamet's characterizations of male friendship establish him firmly within this tradition, evoking images of latter-day Huck and Jim attempting to negotiate the shoals of modern life on a raft. But the contemporary playwright's interpretation of this theme differs considerably from earlier manifestations by foregrounding the tensions inherent in such relationships and by deconstructing their self-willed innocence. The agitated "casing" of Dan and Bernie, the hard-won, unstable intimacy of Don and Bob or Gould and Fox, ranges far from the stylized boyhood innocence of Twain's Huck and Tom. More than any other American playwright, Mamet enacts a searching, multivalent drama of homosocial desire questioning and assessing itself.

As strategist, Mamet is essentially a comic satirist, with an underlying sense of anxiety and pain. On the one hand, his plays can be savagely funny in attacking the predatory instincts of Western enterprise capitalism. And his exploitation of sexual taboos for ridiculous effect places him squarely in the comic mainstream of verbal dexterity and social "tweaking." On the other hand, the central quest for satisfying male friendship underlies all his works, adding a more serious element that encourages audience sympathy for men seeking to find loyalty and acceptance in a world disturbingly competitive, hostile, and transitory. The duality of this conception results in a darkly comic artistic vision suited to a society in transition, moving from the comfortable economies of empire to the new, less stable realities of shared power and enterprise.

The structure of Mamet's major plays typically revolves around fortifying and defending besieged male friendships that nonetheless cannot be fully acknowledged or relied on. This sets up an inherently ironic perspective. Although most of Mamet's work results in a united male "couple," the dénouement cannot assure much equilibrium, given the professed heterosexual imperatives and inherent competitiveness of males as the playwright portrays them. Male friendships in Mamet are also destabilized by inequalities of age, rank, or experience, as well as by the men's inability to weave male friendships into their relations with women. The men in the later plays seem more comfortable with the terms of their bond, but without successful integration into the larger world of dual-gender interactions, such friendships must remain fragile, isolated, and defensive.

Yet the troubling, contradictory elements of Mamet's view of masculine reality provide much of the taut intensity of his dramatic view of decadent, wounded patriarchy. The old loyalties have broken down or become corrupt, and the formerly comfortable structures of male interactions have given way to confusion and dissatisfied longing (Robert Bly's, 1990, "grief for the absent father"). Pervading the major plays is a spirit of melancholy for something lost, a kind of lamentation for male friendship that seems ever-volatile and subject to unpredictable dissolution. Mamet's contribution has been to articulate the intimate connection between sexual and business practices and to underscore the homosocial desire driving relations among men. His characters seem caught in a shifting social pattern they do not comprehend, locked into what Rich (1984) calls "archaic sexual attitudes" (B4). Yet whatever faults they may have, whatever incompetence, stupidity, or dishonesty, they are driven by the extremity of their situations to admit a need and affection for each other that hitherto remained unvoiced. Mamet's searching, half-articulated stage vision of contemporary masculinity dramatizes the struggle of American males to accept and affirm one another in a shifting climate of gender expectations and identities.

Bibliography

Barthes, Roland. *A Lover's Discourse: Fragments.* Trans. Richard Howard. New York: Hill and Wang, 1978.

Bigsby, C. W. E. *David Mamet.* Contemporary Writers Series. New York: Methuen, 1985.

Bly, Robert. *A Gathering of Men with Bill Moyers.* PBS Interview. WILL-TV, Champaign-Urbana. January 8, 1990.

Fiedler, Leslie. *Love and Death in the American Novel.* New York: Stein and Day, 1966.

Fraser, C. Gerald. "Mamet Plays Shed Masculinity Myth." *New York Times,* 5 July 1976, A7.

Leverenz, David. *Manhood and the American Renaissance.* Ithaca, NY: Cornell University Press, 1989.

Mamet, David. *American Buffalo.* 1975. In *Nine Plays of the Modern Theater.* Ed. Harold Clurman. New York: Grove, 1981.
———. *The Duck Variations.* In *Sexual Perversity in Chicago and The Duck Variations.* New York: Grove, 1978.
———. *Glengarry Glen Ross.* New York: Grove, 1983.
———. *A Life in the Theater.* New York: Samuel French, 1977.
———. *Sexual Perversity in Chicago and The Duck Variations.* New York: Grove, 1978.
———. *Speed-the-Plow.* New York: Grove, 1987.
———. *The Woods; Lakeboat; and Edmond.* New York: Grove, 1987.
Raphael, Ray. *The Men from the Boys: Rites of Passage in Male America.* Lincoln: University of Nebraska Press, 1989.
Rich, Frank. "Theater's Gender Gap Is a Chasm." *New York Times,* 30 September 1984, B1,4.
Roudané, Matthew C. "An Interview with David Mamet." *Studies in American Drama, 1945–Present* 1 (1986): 72–81.
Sedgwick, Eve Kosofsky. *Between Men: English Literature and Male Homosocial Desire.* New York: Columbia University Press, 1985.

6

Male Heterosexuality in John Hawkes's *The Passion Artist*

Peter F. Murphy

A critical sequence in John Hawkes's fiction: *The Blood Oranges* (1970) to *Virginie: Her Two Lives* (1981), presents a radical theory of male heterosexuality. During this ten-year span Hawkes also published *Death, Sleep and the Traveler* (1974), *Travesty* (1976), and *The Passion Artist* (1978).[1] The first three of these novels make up what Hawkes came to call "the sex triad."

As one of the few contemporary male authors affected directly by the feminist movement, Hawkes is at the forefront of the male response. His fiction examines such issues as: domination/submission, father-daughter incest, pornography, the "Lolita" complex, men's relationship with their mothers, jealousy, and power. With the recent conflict within feminism over erotica versus pornography, Hawkes gives an honest and vivid portrayal of one man's involvement; often his vision resembles that of many men.

The Blood Oranges introduces an important theme for a critical engagement with male heterosexuality. Cyril, the male antagonist, articulates an explicit theory of nonmonogamous marriage. His theory diverges quite dramatically, though, from the typical double standard of most male writers. In *Death, Sleep and the Traveler* and *Travesty* Cyril's theory unravels in the specific behavior of the male characters. Cyril's suggestion that husbands and wives should make love with whom they please and that each should help the other in accomplishing their seductions becomes problematic in *Death, Sleep and the Traveler.* Allert, the husband, is quite unhappy with the knowledge that his wife has a boyfriend. As if to retaliate, Allert falls in love with Ariane, whom, it seems, he murders. A lovely young woman who believes in free love, Ariane seduces Allert by playing her flute in the nude. She represents another recurrent male fantasy in Hawkes's novels: small, diminutive women. The Lolita complex informs this novel as it does many of his other works of fiction.

In *Travesty,* the theory of nonmonogamous marriage explodes and claims for its victims not only Papa, the male protagonist, but his daughter, Chantel, and his wife's lover, Henri. Both *Death, Sleep and the Traveler* and *Travesty* demonstrate the difficulty men, not women, have with open relationships. They provide the basis to begin rethinking the recurrent male obsession with nonmonogamy and free love. It is, after all, Papa who kills himself and two others, not his wife, who sleeps comfortably at home.

In *Virginie: Her Two Lives,* Hawkes relies on a female narrator for the first time in his fiction. Formalistically similar to Virginia Woolf's *Orlando* (1928), the story describes a young girl's life during two different historical periods: 1740 aristocratic France and 1945 post-World War II Paris. In 1740, Virginie helps Seigneur operate a school for women and in 1945 she and Bocage run a surrealist bordello. As a parody of de Sade, Seigneur represents the full spectrum of male heterosexuality. An ironic perversion of a Sadeian discourse, *Virginie* can be read as a feminist text.

The Passion Artist commands a central position for a critical appreciation of Hawkes's ideas about male heterosexuality. Exploring the sexual awakening of one man, Konrad Vost, the novel focuses on the relationship between masculinity and femininity. More than any other of Hawkes's novels, *The Passion Artist* "lays bare the horrors of the masculine mind" (O'Donnell 1983, 116). Vost's sexual development occurs in the surrealist context of a riot-torn women's prison and a stark and desolate marshland. His own life is desolate, as well. Claire, his wife, died several years earlier, but he cannot accept her death. His young daughter has become a prostitute. His mother, Eva, has been imprisoned for the murder of his father. In this novel, as in much of his fiction,

Hawkes combines "dislocation of cause and effect, distortion of rational processes, insistence on the psychic truth beneath the recognized surfaces" (Greiner 1985, 12). In an anti-real, Kafka-esque setting, Hawkes explores relentlessly the contradictions as well as the possibilities of male heterosexuality.

Vost's transformation begins when he volunteers to help put down a riot in La Violaine, the local women's prison in which his mother is incarcerated. His experience inside the prison battering the prisoners and eventually as the captive of his mother and her bestfriend, Hania, provide valuable insights into Vost's sexuality in particular and male heterosexuality in general. While hunting escaped prisoners, Vost fantasizes about some of the women escapees and learns firsthand the intimidating power of masculinity. These encounters force Vost to confront the ordeal of women's lives and become a better man. In this context, innocence and purity are illuminated against the setting of male violence against women, submission and domination, marriage, bestiality, and pornography.

The Passion Artist explores the fantasies, manifestations, doubts and transformations of male heterosexuality in the context of a world besieged by hatred, fear, and shame. The novel conveys Vost's sexual awakening from the artist of dead passion (as was Papa in *Travesty*) to "an artist . . . of the willed erotic union" (TPA, 181). Vost evolves from being a man who hates his body and denies his sexual longings to one who finally feels comfortable with his sexuality. This long and brutal voyage culminates in Vost's acceptance of his role as a man, due in no small part to his experience of what it is like to be a woman. As he endures the life of a woman, Vost learns about the potential for men's liberation.

His participation (along with many other men) in squelching a violent rebellion by the women inmates focuses many of the issues raised in this novel. What transpires between the men and the women, as well as among the men, explains much of what it means to be a man in contemporary society. Through the image of the riot, Hawkes examines male fantasies about and male bonding around violation in its various manifestations and the relationship between power and sexuality.

The volunteers represent the complete gamut of males in our society. They are "husbands, fathers, bachelors" (TPA, 46), "workers, shop owners, professional men" (TPA, 53). They come from all classes of society and represent every relationship men have with women, except friendship. If they were friends they wouldn't be in the prison trying to squelch the riot; they would empathize with the women and defend their right to rebel. The possibility that such men exist is given explicit consideration.

Initially, the men seem to feel ashamed about their participation in putting down the women's rebellion; even though Vost knows two of the men, they don't speak or even acknowledge each other's presence. Most of the men are relatively innocent of inflicting pain on anyone and prefer to stand far apart from each other. At the same time, however, they are "fully or partially aware of the fact that the blows [they were] about to strike would fall on the flesh and bones of a woman" (TPA, 47). They felt either guilty about their actions or eager to begin. These husbands, fathers, bachelors (brothers) want to beat their wives, daughters, mothers, sisters.

The extent to which Vost becomes involved with the suppression of the women and the extent to which he enjoys his brutality against them emerge as crucial points in the novel. He "prepared to drive the stick into the face of the disbelieving woman. . . . He swung his arm with all the strength he could manage and brought the stick crashing against the side of the woman's head. . . . And for a moment he wished that the rioting all around him would never cease" (TPA, 54–55). Vost's obsession provides a perceptive portrayal of a male fantasy and in this way enlists the reader directly into the novel's prose. The issues of power, sadomasochism, bondage, and pornography are engaged powerfully, allowing readers to confront their own complicity in such violence. At first, the reader might feel horrified. Almost immediately, though, he feels compelled to consider the accuracy of the fictional portrayal. If violation were sanctioned, especially against women, many men would find it difficult to control themselves. More than half of the men surveyed in a recent poll said that they would rape a woman if they were absolutely sure they would get away with it (Sidran 1981, 30). In light of this, Vost's behavior in the woman's prison is not incredible at all. In a society in which such violation is an everyday occurrence, Vost represents Everyman.

In the context of this "sanctioned violation" (TPA, 53) Vost "found himself wanting nothing more than to beat the woman first to surrender and then to unconsciousness. He was not given to physical exertion. . . . Yet he was determined that he himself would administer the blows that would fell this woman who had become victorious in a man's clothing" (TPA, 51). Vost's outrage is exacerbated by the women's attire; they transgress gender boundaries when they put on men's clothes. Vost's trial, later in the novel, reveals the possibility that women have a similar confused and antagonistic response to men attired in women's clothing. Here, as elsewhere in the novel, Hawkes seems to be suggesting a similarity between the sexes. Opposition to rebellion against gender boundaries may not be innate to the male condition but rather a socially learned, culturally reinforced stereotype that neither men nor women can transcend easily.

While the riot continues, the voice of a young woman, a "young invisible victim" (TPA, 55), can be heard in the background. The vividness with which Hawkes describes Vost's attack on his victim, combined with the description of the young woman sighing in the background, accentuates the issue of violence against women. Invisible victims remain a major problem in contemporary society: as long as they remain invisible no one has to act. If we are neither victims nor perpetrators, we are innocent. But, as Hawkes makes clear throughout this novel, no one is innocent; we are all culpable and share similar fantasies of domination and submission. For Hawkes, "if we don't know our destructive potential we can't very well assume genuine responsibility for the world around us. . . . I'm just writing about the things that are most deeply embedded in the human psyche" (Fielding 1976, 45). Expanding on these ideas, Hawkes explains that his "work is an effort to expose the worst in us all, to cause us to face up to the enormities of our terrible potential for betrayal, disgrace and criminal behavior" (LeClair 1979, 27).

Vost is stimulated erotically by the stark and unbridled violence against women. Later, he changes and evolves. For now though, through the medium of the unbreakable length of wood the young woman's pain leapt to his clenched hands; in his hands and arms he could feel the small perfect body losing its form. . . . And, as the childlike woman took random useless steps, cowering and dangling her arms, the dress fell and exposed one shoulder while on the oval face the lips began to glisten with a wetness rising from deep within that miniature anatomy. (TPA, 56)

Even while he is battering this woman to death, her exposed shoulder remains a point of interest, of sexual excitation. Vost becomes even more titillated as her lips begin to glisten. The small, childlike woman resounds throughout Hawkes's fiction and in *The Passion Artist* it reaches new significance. Eventually, and despite her large size, Vost learns to love Hania.

One scene in particular explores the issue of submission/domination and the relationship between power and the erotic. Following the riot, Vost dreams he has been taken captive by the women in the prison. He stands trial for the crimes he has committed against these women and against one woman in particular. His accuser, a young woman, is "as small as a child yet clothed in a tight gown of a sparkling mauve material which exposed the diminutive anatomy that could belong only to an adult woman" (TPA, 63). This small and childlike woman, attired in a sensually colored gown, has complete power over Vost. She charges him with not knowing anything about women explaining that all he ever did was comment on her size without ever touching her. Despite the fact that he is condemned and powerless, a victim of her every whim, Vost finds his accuser sexually arousing. Even in his discomfort and humiliation he feels a growing rapture. Though accused of sexual impotence and complete ignorance of women he realizes

that all the agreeableness of her mannerisms concealed a petulance even more desirable than the legs, the hips, the musical voice . . . [and that] now, against his will, in the darkness of a condition that could not have been more contrary to that of erotic excitation, now he was overcome with the knowledge that in his locked and inaccessible loins the army of mice was beginning to run through the forest that was filled with snow. (TPA, 65–66)

In contrast to the assumption that men must dominate to obtain sexual pleasure, Vost finds himself sexually aroused to the point of orgasm, an orgasm he prefers not to have. The suggestion that men may also obtain pleasure from being submissive counters the assertion that pornography manifests an inherently male need to be the dominator. Current feminist arguments against pornography (e.g., Brownmiller 1975; Dworkin 1981; and Griffin 1981)[2] are confronted throughout the novel; Vost's journey examines the question of sexual difference.

Vost awakens from his dream to find himself in the hospital. He arrived there after having fallen in the ranks of the victims of La Violaine. The women had managed to rout the voluntary male militia and now control the prison. Vost leaves the hospital, decides to join the hunt for the women prisoners, and goes into the marsh after them. Here, Vost encounters the young woman in his dream. The bruises he had inflicted upon her body during the riot contribute to Vost's erotic sensations and enhance his vision of her beauty. Vost begins to fall in love with this young woman whom he had beaten unconscious and now spies upon. She brings out feelings in Konrad Vost that had always been fleeting and uncomfortable.

Vost's ambivalence about his sexual passion compels him to leave the scene immediately. As he leaves, he is threatened by one of the armed guards hunting for the escaped women. Vost betrays the young woman in an effort to save his own life: "The brute maleness of the man and dog [and] the stench of their intimidation" (TPA, 97), remind Vost that, confronted by the savage power of masculinity, one cowers. This firsthand experience of the fear and intimidation that male sexuality presents to women every day of their lives furthers Vost's sexual awareness.

From this immediate encounter with the malignant potential of masculinity, Vost confronts yet one more component of the female sexual experience: their assumed role as the means to men's sexual satisfaction. Lost in the fog that has covered the marsh, Vost stumbles upon an old abandoned barn in which he decides to spend the night. Unknown to him, he shares it with two women who have escaped from the prison. When these women giggle, Vost assumes, as would many men, that their giggling was intended for him. He believes they are flirting with him. He couldn't be more wrong, for these escaped women convicts proceed to "rape" Vost. They force him to fondle their breasts and vaginas so that they can have an orgasm but every time he tries to get them to reciprocate they abuse him. They maintain complete control of this sexual encounter and force Vost to satisfy them without any concern at all for his pleasure. One of the women "began squeezing rapidly the front of his trousers as if to arouse and crush desire in a single gesture" (TPA, 107).

Vost's "rape" parodies the sexual experience many women have at the hands of impatient, selfish men socialized to believe that women were created to satisfy their sexual needs. At the same time, however, it explicates, vividly, the experience of rape. "Submission, revolt, attack, submission; so the darkness was consumed in revolt, attack, submission" (TPA, 109–10), describes much female experience of sex at the hands of husbands, lovers, rapists.

Later, Vost is relieved upon awakening to discover himself a captive in La Violaine. He "found himself exactly where he had always wanted to be without knowing it: in the world of women and in the world of the prison . . . where he would receive the punishment he deserved and desired. [Here he would] suffer at will the presence of the women he had spent his life avoiding" (TPA, 120). This direct confrontation with women, and in particular the environment of the prison within which it will occur, contributes much to Vost's awakening. Here he will "be brought to [a] rudimentary knowledge of submission, domination, the question of woman" (TPA, 121). Within the walls of this woman's prison and at the hands of Hania, his mother's bestfriend, Vost will learn the experience of women and will become a more sexually liberated male.

One of the first and certainly most important lessons he learns derives from his original characterizations of the two women who play such a significant role in his liberation: his mother and Hania. These women, who replace his wife, Claire, "promised him not sentimentality but flesh and light" (TPA, 122). They will give him not tender feelings of loss or regret but sexuality and the knowledge that accompanies it. Vost becomes aware that the stereotypical view of women as virgin/whore does not work. As Eva becomes the "notorious woman revealed," she can no longer be characterized as a whore. And Hania is "identified . . . no longer as the nun [virgin] she had once been" (TPA, 121). Vost begins to see beyond the socially accepted characterization of women as either evil and dangerous or pure and sensitive.

In his prison cell strewn with articles of women's clothing, in this "splendor of depravation," Vost recognizes for the first time "the trespasser inside himself" (TPA, 125). Here, in confinement and at the hands of his female captors, Vost begins to comprehend his identity as a man. In La Violaine, which derives from the French viol, violteur, violenter, or violer—meaning to rape, to violate, to transgress—Vost becomes aware of his sexually prescribed role as a man—a violator and a rapist. At the same time, though, he realizes his own vulnerability. When Eva and Hania enter his cell, Vost struggles to "retain some semblance of pride in the midst of submission" (TPA, 128). Simultaneously, he realizes that for Hania indignity does not exist. Through years of submission and brutality at the hands of the prison guards and men in general, "there could be no indignity, nothing repugnant" for Hania (TPA, 130).

At this point, Eva shares her ideas about marriage with Vost. She explains the difficulty a woman has being a wife because most women find themselves not only married to a child but bearing children. She concludes with some radical insights into motherhood and female identity, insights echoing Simone de Beauvoir (1974) and Shulamith Firestone (1970): "We who spend our lives in prison know three things: that the family is the first prison; that among prisons the actual is preferable to the metaphorical; and that the woman is not a mother until she leaves her child" (TPA, 129). With this knowledge Vost becomes educated, even politicized. He realizes that he no longer grieves for Claire and that his marriage is over. Finally, he severs his ties with his dead wife, Claire. This contributes significantly to Vost's awareness. The more exposure to the female social experience Vost encounters, the more he appreciates their plight at the hands of men and patriarchy.

Eva amplifies her ideas of motherhood and of being a good wife when she relates her own experience giving birth to Vost. The ultimate moment of his recognition provides insights about himself that he needed to know, but of which he believed he would never be made aware. Eva was informed by a village doctor, who resented her small size and beauty, that her baby was dead inside her. The doctor prescribed abhorrent things for her to do to expel the fetus.[3] After much excruciating pain and violence to herself, she almost succeeds in aborting the baby. It lives, however, albeit extremely premature. Eva maintains that her son, Konrad Vost, holds the responsibility for the destruction of an otherwise beautiful experience by making it into something extremely painful and grotesque. Stressing that she had been married for a while before becoming pregnant, Eva seems to suggest that childbirth destroys innocence; but motherhood, not sex, makes a woman into a victim.

Vost is astonished by the graffiti on the walls when he awakens at dawn of his first full day at La Violaine. He reads the slogans and aphorisms written by the women inmates and is surprised by "the humorous or violent jottings of women whose vulgar cravings were the equal of the vulgar cravings of any man" (TPA, 155). Two inscriptions in particular impress him more than the others:

> "In memory of a Sunday in summer" [made him wonder whether it was possible] that a woman, especially in this place, had been capable of such generosity. After all, the nostalgia and resignation captured in the expression were as shockingly appropriate to the mind of a man as were the obscenities that made him flush with embarrassment. (TPA, 155)

The second inscription, " 'Love is not an honest feeling,' [made him ponder] who but a man could have written these words? . . . Yet the authors of these sayings had in fact been women" (TPA, 155). The novel reiterates the point that women have sexual fantasies and sexual cravings similar to those of men. Hawkes seems well aware that one man can be embarrassed by the sexual longings of a woman just as a woman can be disconcerted by the sexual cravings of a man. This revelation resists the radical feminist position maintaining that pornography describes only male fantasies. According to one feminist perspective, pornography, written by men and for men, is evil and oppressive. This notion oversimplifies sexuality in general and distorts male sexuality in particular. As Ellen Willis (1981) points out in her response to the feminist opposition to pornography:

> the view of sex that most often emerges from talk about "erotica" is as sentimental and euphemistic as the word itself; lovemaking should be beautiful, romantic, soft, nice and devoid of messiness, vulgarity, impulses to power, or indeed aggression of any sort. Above all the emphasis should be on relationship not (yuck) organs. This goody-goody concept of eroticism is not feminist, it is feminine (224).

One aphorism in particular stands out for Vost: " 'Between my legs I do not have a bunch of violets.' " This statement "excluded him forever; it was the clue to the object of his desperate quest; it could not have been written by a man" (TPA, 156). Here, as elsewhere in the novel, Vost searches for the difference between men and women. For Vost, learning that the vagina is not a bunch of violets helps move him beyond his previous characterization of a vagina as "the nostril of a dead bird" (TPA, 67) or as "a small face beaten unrecognizable by the blows of a cruel fist" (TPA, 151). Soon, with Hania, Vost will come to realize the beauty and desirability of women's sexual anatomy.

First, however, Eva Laubenstein introduces the theories of Dr. Slovotkin, the prison doctor. Slovotkin's obsession with the difference, if any, between the man and the woman seems to echo the object of Vost's own desperate quest. Unlike Slovotkin, though, Vost is less a theorist than a simple man confused about his own sexuality as much as he is by women's. Slovotkin, on the other hand, parodies the contemporary "feminist" man. Obsessed with his theory of androgyny, Slovotkin tries to have sex with every woman in La Violaine. That "he never tired of taking his victims or stating his theories" (TPA, 157), sounds a little like the radical man at the cocktail party who mouths feminist theories for the sake of getting laid.

Slovotkin has a theory though, and an important one for the overall meaning of this novel. Eva explains it at length:

> Slovotkin proposed, first, that the person is essentially a barren island and that for each of us life's only pleasure is the exploration of other barren islands: in this way being a man or woman merely enhances the interesting differences of people who are in fact the same. He proposed, secondly, that in the souls of their bones the man and woman are opposites: as extreme as that. Finally he proposed that the man and woman are both the same and opposite. (TPA, 157)

Slovotkin's opportunistic use of feminism confirms Eva's point that his "dedication to his single question was no more than a ruse to feed his insatiable craving for the bodies of women" (TPA, 159). Slovotkin insisted, even in the face of death, that his first and third theories were correct. He asserted that, setting aside reproduction, men and women have the same capabilities. Simultaneously, he claimed that men and women are both the same and opposite. He concluded by explaining the impossibility of being the one without knowing the experience of the other.

This substantiates Eva's assertion of the similarity between Slovotkin and Vost. Vost seems to have known Slovotkin's theory, though without the premeditated opportunism of Slovotkin's work. In the woman's prison, which is a metaphor for women's experience in contemporary society, Vost has encountered a woman's life: the fear of male sexuality and the tendency to cringe before it. Like many women today, he has been used as a vehicle for sexual satisfaction without having the partner concerned with his satisfaction. He has experienced the submissive role of the woman and has been dominated in the sexual encounters he has had since joining the men in their efforts to squelch the women's riot.

Slovotkin's theory remains only superficial, however, as it becomes obvious that only women are qualified to speak about androgyny or the relative equality of the sexes: they have experienced the servitude of the female at the hands of the male. In taking Slovotkin's theory one step further, Eva points to a crucial truth: "The woman is not naturally a martyr; the man is not naturally a beast" (TPA, 160). This important addition to Slovotkin's theory highlights Eva's disagreement with the radical feminists' belief that men represent the enemy: naturally evil, inherently aggressive, and prone to violence against women. Eva maintains that women are no more naturally passive and gentle then men are naturally brutal; Vost demonstrates this insight throughout his entire experience at the women's prison.

As if remembering an important addition to any theory of sexual politics, Eva reminds Hania that only the childless woman retains her youth. Echoing her previous assertion that for women "the family is the first prison . . . [and] that the woman is not a mother until she leaves her child" (TPA, 129), Eva stresses the importance for women not to become mothers, or at least not to remain mothers. Motherhood as a woman's sole occupation destroys women's individuality and self-worth.

The culmination of Vost's sexual awakening occurs with Hania while he is a prisoner at La Violaine. As Hania undresses, Vost finds himself confronted once again with the issue of the difference or similarity between men and women. He sees in Hania "the presence of the hidden thighs that were as large as a man's and yet of the soft line belonging only to a woman" (TPA, 178). Parts of Hania's body, like many women's, resemble a man's just as many men resemble women. Here, as elsewhere in the novel, Hawkes seems to be pointing out the problematics of biology as destiny, especially when that argument suggests women are not physically capable of doing the same things men do.

Vost continues en route to his liberation. He has not arrived there yet. Upon seeing Hania naked he ponders, "why was it that when a man of his age saw for the first time hair and light glistening between a woman's legs he felt both agitation and absurdity? And yet was he even now beginning to learn that what he had thought of as the lust of his middle age was in fact the clearest reflection of the generosity implicit in the nudity of the tall woman?" (TPA, 178). Vost's middle-age crisis, or his insecurity as a man, is eclipsed by Hania's appeal as a caring, giving woman; these qualities make her attractive to him. He falls in love with Hania and, though this love has very little hope for the future, he begins to feel comfortable with his feelings. A significant moment in Vost's awakening emerges when he realizes his ability to feel comfortable with himself, to trust his emotions, and to be able to love someone.

Vost is a man in the social, cultural, and political sense of that identity. Unlike the women surrounding him in the prison, he has never learned certain things about himself as a sexual being or, like so many men, he has not learned how to express his emotions. He does not know how to sing and in particular he does not know the language of song, the discourse of celebration. And, Vost does not know how to dance. He is appalled to realize that even though he had been both a husband and a father he had never learned to dance. His male armor has not allowed him to relax and feel comfortable with himself. Like many men, Vost's sexual repression makes him afraid of his body, his emotions, and his feelings. Hawkes seems to suggest that whereas society may very well be patriarchal, men too are excluded from the discourse that supposedly belongs to them alone. They have to struggle against all the armor society has foisted upon them in the process of making them men. In order to do that men need to scrutinize male discourse in the same way feminists today seek a new language.

Vost's experience with Hania moves him closer to his liberation. While making love to him, Hania tells Vost to watch her as she performs fellatio on him. She points out that "passionate sensation depends on sight" (TPA, 179). Hania confronts another stereotypical distinction between men and women: for men, sexual experience is thought to be a more visible encounter than it is for women. Hania maintains, however, that the visual experience enhances sexual pleasure for both men and women.

Vost is amazed that even while continuing to take his penis in her mouth, Hania does not change her facial expression in the slightest. His confusion is exacerbated by his feelings of arousal. Vost has not recovered completely from his distress over his body and his fear of being repulsive to a woman. He still harbors feelings of doubt and apprehension about his sexuality and his attractiveness. Though on his way to a quasi-liberation he still has not arrived. Overcoming the socialization of manhood in this society necessitates a long, difficult struggle. Hawkes does not pretend that it is easy. Eventually, though, Vost becomes more comfortable with himself and his passions. As Hania takes his penis in her mouth his penis has become "that part of his anatomy that he could no longer deny" (TPA, 180). Finally, Vost accepts his sexuality. An important moment for his awakening, this newly found ability to acknowledge his passion moves Vost much closer to at least a semblance of sexual liberation.

Hania provides Vost with additional knowledge about the difference between men and women as sexual beings. She tells him that " 'in no other way, . . . can a woman so reveal her eroticism as by an act of the will. . . . As for you,' she said, 'the force of amorous passion is respect. You are now aware of your own respect and mine' " (TPA, 180). This respect is crucial for Vost, for throughout his life self-respect has been something he lacked. His love for Hania and his appreciation of himself and his body have allowed him to respect someone else as well as himself. When Hania asks Vost to perform cunnilingus on her, he discovered that her dilation was such that

> the exterior of her body could no longer be distinguished from its interior; when she encouraged him to discover that the discolorations of the blown rose are not confined to the hidden flesh of youth, it was then that in the midst of his gasping he realized that the distinction between the girl who is still a child and the woman who is more than mature lies only in the instinct of the one and the depth of consciousness of the other. (TPA, 180–81)

These important insights do not help him discover the "small face beaten unrecognizable" or the "nostril of a dead bird," but a woman's sexuality: not just one isolated part, one organ, but rather a component of a much larger form, a part of a whole all intricately and intimately connected. Vost realizes that the difference between the young schoolgirl he was seduced by earlier in his life and the woman he has in front of him has nothing to do with physiology or age but rather experience. Hania's "depth of consciousness" makes her a desirable and satisfying woman.

As the night draws to a close, Vost finds himself "in the arms of the tall handsome woman who had loved him and seduced him as well" (TPA, 183–84). The possibility that a woman, and in this case maybe a wife, would be able to love and seduce someone at the same time provides a telling conclusion to the relationship between Vost and Hania. None of Vost's previous experiences with women had demonstrated both of these possibilities simultaneously. Most of the women he had encountered were interested primarily in seducing him. There was certainly not much love exchanged. Claire, Vost's wife, seemed capable of love toward Vost but not seduction. Hania emerges as all these women and more as she becomes the woman capable of both seduction and love. For Hania, women have vital, aggressive sexual needs upon which they are quite capable of acting.

Male sexuality, on the other hand, remains confused and uncertain. Though Vost has made progress toward sexual liberation he can share this accomplishment with very few men. His continued existence is problematic in a sexually oppressive society. As he leaves the prison early the next morning his old friend, Gagnon, shoots him down. As he dies, Vost knows "that the hole torn in his abdomen by Gagnon's shot was precisely the same as would have been opened in his flesh by the dog in the marsh" (TPA, 184). Men's omnipotence, coupled with a fear of their sexuality and a hatred of "the woman within" (Hoch 1979, 68) manifests itself in domination and control.[4] Gagnon's response represents the pathetic desperation of threatened male power.

Vost dies because the liberated man in contemporary society is a contradiction in terms. In the first place, there cannot be a fully, completely liberated man (or woman, for that matter). In the second place, as one moves closer to becoming a liberated man, he moves further away from being socially acceptable as a man. The liberated man, like the gay man, both of whom have had the female experience of male power, cannot be countenanced in a homophobic and sexist society that fears and hates female sexuality, especially when embodied in a man.

Notes

1. All quotations from the novel in the text are cited parenthetically in the text as TPA.
2. Andrea Dworkin highlights this position when she maintains, for example, that "the major theme of pornography as a genre is male power, its nature, its magnitude, its use, its meaning" (1981, 24). Later in this same book, Dworkin states that "male sexual aggression is the unifying thematic and behavioral reality of male sexuality" (57). Susan Griffin (1981) points out that "the world of pornography is a world of male gesture and male language and a male ethos" (52). This kind of reductionism posits a male essence and a male nature that are as damaging and reductionist as many reactionary ideas about women; for example that biology is destiny.
3. Contemporary American feminism has spent much time examining the history of women as victims of the medical profession. For example, see Ehrenreich and English (1979), and Drefus (1977).
4. For a more extensive examination of "the feminine other within the male unconscious" and how it informs current literature on men and masculinity, see Murphy (1989).

Works Cited

Brownmiller, Susan. *Against Our Will: Men, Women and Rape.* New York: Bantam, 1975.

Beauvoir, Simone de. *The Second Sex.* New York: Vintage, 1974.

Drefus, Claudia. *Seizing Our Bodies: The Politics of Women's Health.* New York: Vintage, 1977.

Dworkin, Andrea. *Pornography: Men Possessing Women.* New York: G. P. Putnam's Sons, 1981.

Ehrenreich, Barbara, and Deirdre English. *For Her Own Good: 150 Years of the Experts' Advice to Women.* New York: Doubleday, 1979.

Fielding, Andrew. "John Hawkes Is a Very Nice Guy and a Novelist of Sex and Death." *Village Voice* 24 (May 1976): 45–47.

Firestone, Shulamith. *The Dialectic of Sex: The Case for Feminist Revolution.* New York: Bantam, 1970.

Greiner, Donald. *Understanding John Hawkes.* Columbia, SC: University of South Carolina Press, 1985.

Griffin, Susan. *Pornography and Silence: Culture's Revenge Against Nature.* New York: Harper and Row, 1981.

Hawkes, John. *The Blood Oranges.* New York: New Directions, 1970.

———. *Death, Sleep and the Traveler.* New York: New Directions, 1974.

———. *The Passion Artist.* New York: Harper and Row, 1978.

———. *Travesty.* New York: New Directions, 1976.

———. *Virginie: Her Two Lives.* New York: Harper and Row, 1981.

Hoch, Paul. *White Hero Black Beast: Racism, Sexism and the Mask of Masculinity.* London: Pluto Press, 1979.

LeClair, Thomas. "The Novelists: John Hawkes." *New Republic* 10 (November 1979): 26–29.

Murphy, Peter F. "Toward a Feminist Masculinity: A Review Essay." *Feminist Studies* (Summer 1989): 351–61.

O'Donnell, Patrick. "Life and Art: An Interview with John Hawkes." *Review of Contemporary Fiction* (Fall 1983): 107–26.

Sidran, Maxine. "The Hating Game: Men's Response to Women's Independence: Don't Get Even, Get Mad." *Quest* (October 1981): 16–23.

Willis, Ellen. "Feminism, Moralism, and Pornography." In *Beginning to See the Light: Pieces of a Decade,* 219–27. New York: Knopf, 1981.

Woolf, Virginia. *Orlando.* New York: Harcourt Brace and Jovanovich, 1928.

7

Living Degree Zero: Masculinity and the Threat of Desire in the *Roman Noir*

Christopher Metress

I.

In "The Simple Art of Murder," his seminal manifesto on the poetics of that most masculine and most American of literary creations, the hardboiled detective novel, Raymond Chandler praises his gender-specific hero with a hard and handsome rhetoric:

> In everything that can be called art there is a quality of redemption. It may be pure tragedy, if it is high tragedy, and it may be pity and irony, and it may be the raucous laughter of the strong man. But down these mean streets a man must go who is not himself mean, who is neither tarnished nor afraid. The detective in this kind of story must be such a man. He is the hero; he is everything. He must be a complete man and a common man and yet an unusual man. He must be, to use a rather weathered phrase, a man of honor.[1]

Chandler's chivalric musings have long encouraged us to see the hardboiled novel as a redemptive arena of honorable masculinity in which complete and untarnished men seek to fulfill their desire for justice in a world gone mean with sin and depravity. For instance, George Grella links the hardboiled detective to the earliest American prototypes of heroic masculinity: "His characteristic toughness and redeeming moral strength conflict with the values of his civilization and cause him, like Natty Bumppo or Huck Finn, to flee the society which menaces his personal integrity and spiritual freedom."[2] John G. Cawelti concurs, saluting the hardboiled hero as "an instinctive protector of the weak, a defender of the innocent, an avenger of the wronged, the one loyal, honest, truly moral man in a corrupt and ambiguous world."[3]

Hardboiled fiction, however, is a "corrupt" and "ambiguous" genre and, as such, it contains within it contentious images of masculinity. As David Madden notes, "Just as one must distinguish between the formal detective story invented by Poe and the private-eye thriller initiated by Hammett, one must also distinguish between the latter and the 'pure' tough-guy novel, though they developed concurrently and cross-fertilized each other."[4] Thus, although Geoffrey O'Brien is right to assert that the "hardboiled novel was born complete in [Hammett's] *Red Harvest* in 1929,"[5] we need to realize that since its inception the hardboiled novel has developed along two distinctly different paths. The first path is the one pursued by the likes of Hammett, Chandler, Ross Macdonald, and John D. MacDonald, and it is readily known to us as the hardboiled detective novel (or, in Madden's words, "the private-eye thriller"). The heroes of this line are just that—heroes. They may be, as O'Brien says of Chandler's Marlowe, "disillusioned and increasingly bitter," but they are, nonetheless, "unmistakably chivalrous."[6] According to Cawelti, the hardboiled detective novel encourages us to identify with "important characteristics of the detective, his masculinity and courage, his integrity and sense of honor." Ultimately, such a work will reflect "common fantasies," fantasies, we must note, which fulfill distinctly masculine appetites: "the desire to escape from the anxious tension between conformity and resentment; the desire to replace the sense of inner corruption and insecurity and to avenge oneself upon the successful by physical force; the desire to completely dominate women and thereby overcome their sexual and social challenge."[7] However, if we understand hardboiled fiction as containing nothing more than the hardboiled detective novel, then we overlook a distinctive path within the genre, one that offers us a chilling contrast to the sometimes unsteady but ultimately redemptive images of loyal, honest, and moral masculinity inscribed in the world of the hardboiled detective novel. Among the poets of this other, richly suggestive path are such neglected writers as James M. Cain, Horace McCoy, Cornell Woolrich, Jim Thompson, and David Goodis. Rather than giving us complete men untarnished by and unafraid of the physical, social, and sexual challenges to their masculinity, these writers offer us fragmented men stained by absurdly tragic pasts and tormented by emasculating landscapes of frustration and paranoia. This alternative route within the genre has acquired many different names, such as Madden's "tough-guy novel," but despite its distinctly American origins it is best known by its French designation—the *roman noir*.

As concurrent and cross-fertilizing fictions, the hardboiled detective novel and the *roman noir* do share many of the same preoccupations, and there is perhaps none more revealing and fundamental than their preoccupation with the relationship between masculinity and desire. In the hardboiled detective novel, the hero is a common man, and as a common man he is necessarily faced with that most common of choices—that is, what will he desire and how will he secure that desire? The potential objects of desire for the hero are many, but these desires usually fall within the scope of four categories: power, money, sex, and/or justice. The men and women encountered by the detective are more often than not corrupted by an uncontrollable obsession for some combination of these first three categories of desire. Only the detective seeks the fourth desire—justice. His quest for this justice, however, is repeatedly threatened by the temptations of power, money, and sex. The detective succeeds as the hardboiled and masculine hero of his narrative because he is able to control his passion for these first three temptations and keep them subordinate to his more noble desire for justice.

We need only turn to the ending of Hammett's *The Maltese Falcon* to see this kind of struggle and subordination at work. After his swift and violent search for the Maltese Falcon fails, Sam Spade faces Brigid O'Shaughnessey, the deceptive seductress who is both his lover and the murderer of his one-time partner, Miles Archer. Spade tells Brigid that, despite his affection for her, he is going to turn her over to the police. Shocked, Brigid cannot believe that Archer means as much to Spade as she does; Spade offers Brigid eight reasons for turning her in. The first three reasons, worth quoting in full, reveal Spade's hierarchy of values, a hierarchy in which his passion for Brigid is subordinate to his desire for justice:

When a man's partner is killed he's supposed to do something about it. It doesn't make a difference what you thought of him. He was your partner and you're supposed to do something about it. Then it happens we were in the detective business. Well, when one of your organization gets killed it's bad business to let the killer get away with it. It's bad all around—bad for that one organization, bad for every detective everywhere. Third, I'm a detective and expecting me to run criminals down and then let them go free is like asking a dog to catch a rabbit and let it go. It can be done, all right, and sometimes it is done, but it's not natural.[8]

Spade enumerates four more reasons for his decision, but his eighth and final reason is perhaps the most revealing: "If [these first seven reasons] mean nothing to you forget it and we'll make it this: I won't [let you escape] because all of me wants to—wants to say to hell with the consequences and do it" (439). Remember, Spade is not without his lesser desires for money, power, and sex. At different moments in *The Maltese Falcon,* he indulges each of these passions. At the conclusion of the novel, however, Spade turns his back on them—on all those things that "all of [him] wants"—and seeks instead to do the right thing, to pursue and serve justice. It is this ability to contain—and ultimately reject—his improper desires and act upon the proper ones that makes Sam Spade the hero of his narrative; it is an ability that makes him both a common man—because he possesses desires—*and* an unusual man—because he can govern them.

What Chandler says of Marlowe is also true of Spade, for Hammett's hero is indeed "the best man in his world and a good enough man for any world."[9] He is "the best man" not because he is without desire for money, power, and women, but because he possesses a sense of justice and honor that can master those desires. We must note, as Chandler does in "The Simple Art of Murder," that the detective is very much a creature of passions. According to Chandler, however, the detective must strike a heroic balance between an emasculating rejection of desire and an inhuman surrender to desire, and, not surprisingly, it is his honor that helps him strike that manly balance: "I do not care much about [the detective's] private life," Chandler says of Marlowe, "[for] he is *neither a eunuch nor a satyr;* I think he might seduce a duchess and I am quite sure he would not spoil a virgin; if he is a man of honor in one thing, he is that in all things. . . . If there were enough of him, the world would be a very safe place to live in" (emphasis added).[10]

Chandler's detective, via his honorable masculinity, makes the world safe, if not for democracy, then at least for virgins. We cannot say this of the *roman noir,* however, for a world filled with the heroes of Cain and McCoy, of Thompson and Goodis, would be a very unsafe place indeed for both duchesses and virgins. The detective's code of honor, which demands that he fashion the scope and direction of his desires, is absent from the *roman noir* because desire (any desire, whether it be for love, for money, for justice, or for revenge) is the foundation for self-annihilation in these narratives. Whereas in the hardboiled detective novel the hero must learn, and can learn, to gain control of his passions, to fashion an honorable hierarchy of desire, in the *roman noir* such appetites cannot be so readily controlled and manipulated. Instead, the *roman noir* questions and negates the mastery of desire that is so fundamental to the masculine heroics of the hardboiled detective novel. If, as Chandler suggests, the masculinity of the detective hero is defined by his response to desire, then, as the novels of Cain, Thompson, and Goodis suggest, the masculinity of the *roman noir* hero is threatened by—not defined by—his response to desire. In the *roman noir* then, the problem for the hero is not how to order desire, how to subordinate and pursue passions in a manly and honorable way (avoiding the "unmanly" fates of both the eunuch and the satyr), but whether or not he can desire at all without initiating a swift process of self-destruction.

In this chapter, I want to pay particular attention to three novelists of the *roman noir*—Cain, Thompson, and Goodis—and how each of them explores the process of self-destruction engendered by the presence of desire. In his first novel, *The Postman Always Rings Twice* (1934), Cain establishes desire as the central problem of the *roman noir,* a problem that is also at the heart of his next two novels, *Double Indemnity* (1935) and *Serenade* (1937). While these first three novels form a unified trilogy of desire, *The Postman Always Rings Twice* stands by itself as the ur-text of the *roman noir,* for in it Cain successfully images a fragmented masculinity that is at the mercy of—that is, does not have mastery over—destructive and disobedient desires. Building upon Cain's vision of desires unmastered, Thompson and Goodis offer us heroes who know that desire leads to self-annihilation and who thus fight, above all else, to erase their desires. For Thompson's characters, however, the fight to erase desire is never successful for very long and, ultimately, Thompson's novels explode with desires gone wild, with men who destroy themselves (and, quite literally, the narratives they inhabit) because of their inability to master their obsessions. Whereas few of Thompson's heroes ever escape the self-destruction that eventually attends the pursuit of desire in the *roman noir,* Goodis's heroes do survive, but their survival is qualified because it depends upon being "a soft-mouthed nobody whose ambitions and goals aimed at exactly zero, . . . [at being a man whose] presence . . . meant nothing."[11] This kind of "living degree zero," living without desire, is Goodis's grim and bitter solution to the problem of desire raised by Cain in the earliest *romans noir,* a solution Chandler would have found profoundly distasteful (for Chandler, recall, the hero "is everything"; for Goodis, however, the hero is "nothing," "exactly zero"). Thus, if Cawelti is correct in claiming that the hardboiled detective novel reflects the "common fantasies" of masculinity—fantasies in which male desire for escape, security, vengeance, and domination are reassuringly fulfilled—then the *roman noir* reflects the "common nightmares" of masculinity—nightmares in which desire imprisons, fragments, dislocates, and overpowers any man foolish enough to possess and pursue it.

II.

In a particularly resonant passage in *Notes from Underground,* Dostoyevsky, speaking through his nameless protagonist, sums up Cain's vision of desire as well as any critic can or has: "I will admit that reason is a good thing. No argument about that. But reason is only reason, and it only satisfies man's rational requirements. Desire is the manifestation of life—of all of life—and it encompasses everything from reason down to scratching oneself. And although, when we're guided by our desires, life may often turn into a messy affair, it's still life and not a series of extractions of square roots."[12]

While Frank Chambers, the hero of *The Postman Always Rings Twice,* is not able to recognize and articulate his vision of desire as eloquently as Dostoyevsky's underground philosopher, his first-person narrative is, at its very core, a narrative of a life turned messy by the affairs of desire. Much the same could be said for the first-person narratives of *Double Indemnity* and *Serenade.* Appropriately, then, many critics have been quick to note that in Cain's fiction desire "encompasses everything." According to O'Brien, the matter is quite simple: "In Cain's books, desire is all there is."[13] For Joyce Carol Oates, the great lesson of Cain's fiction is that "the world extends no farther than the radius of one's desires."[14] Madden concurs, describing Cain's protagonists in such a way that we cannot help but note how desire defines everything they do: "High on sex, often apotheosized into home-brew mysticism, drugged on orgasmic optimism, and gorged on food, they set off from their caves, make the kill, and consummate the ritual with another orgy of sex and food."[15] Finally, Frank Krutnick is even more direct in his assertion that desire—a specifically sexual, but ultimately disruptive desire—is central to Cain's fiction. According to Krutnick, Cain's early tales "begin with the eruption of desire at the sight of the woman, an eruption that displaces the hero and locks him within a trajectory leading to transgression—most often through the crimes of adultery and murder, the murder of the woman's husband—and ultimately, to catastrophe." For Krutnick, Cain's novels provide us with a perfectly "frantic 'imaging' of male desire."[16]

When Frank Chambers is tossed off the back of a hay truck at the beginning of *The Postman Always Rings Twice,* he seems anything but frantic. As a lawyer will later say of Frank, he is the kind of guy who is always "knocking around . . . never doing any work, or even trying to do any."[17] However, despite his surface serenity, what Paul Skenazy calls his "aimless peace,"[18] Frank is a creature of passions, a man with a voracious appetite. When he wanders into the roadside cafe owned by Cora and her husband, Nick Papadakis, Frank orders "orange juice, corn flakes, fried eggs and bacon, enchilada, flapjacks, and coffee" (1) for breakfast. Unfortunately, Frank's appetites do not end here, for when he first spies Cora he desires to devour her as readily as he devours his breakfast: "Then I saw her. She had been out back, in the kitchen, but she came in to gather up my dishes. Except for the shape, she really wasn't any raving beauty, but she had a sulky look to her, and her lips stuck out in a way that made me want to mash them in for her" (2). It takes less than twenty-four hours for Frank to satisfy his hunger for Cora. When Nick leaves for Los Angeles the morning after Frank first lays eyes on Cora, the two of them are left alone for the first time. "I took her in my arms," Frank tells us, "and mashed my mouth up against her . . . 'Bite me! Bite me!' [she said]." Frank, of course, obliges: "I bit her. I sunk my teeth into her lips so deep I could feel the blood spurt into my mouth. It was running down her neck when I carried her upstairs" (9).

In this swiftly paced narrative, sexual desire quickly engenders a desire for violence (a desire, albeit, which is already implicit in the brutal sexual relationship between Frank and Cora). The lovers' first attempt to kill Nick Papadakis fails. Their second attempt, however, is successful. Frank and Cora stage a car accident, making it look as if they and Nick have inadvertently driven off the road and dropped fifty feet into a ravine. Of course, Nick is dead before Frank pushes the car into the ravine. In order to make it look as if they too plummeted down the ravine with Nick, Frank rips Cora's blouse, leaving her "wide open, from her throat to her belly" (46). To heighten even further the realism, Frank hits Cora in the eye as hard as he can. Both acts, however, generate sexual excitement. Quickly, desire gets the best of them. This desire literally "un-mans" Frank, for he describes himself as "some kind of animal" (46), and in the famous passage that ends the chapter, Cain makes a resonant connection between desire and self-destruction, a connection that is at the very heart of the *roman noir:*

> Next thing I knew, I was down there with her, and we were staring in each other's eyes, and locked in each other's arms, and straining to get closer. Hell could have opened for me then, and it wouldn't have made any difference. I had to have her, if I hung for it.
>
> I had her. (46)

After Frank has Cora, the local district attorney wants to have her as well, that is, have her tried for Nick's murder. He manages to coerce Frank into accusing Cora of the crime. When Cora discovers this, she in turn accuses Frank. The two look as if they are indeed going to hang for pursuing their desires until an unprincipled lawyer, playing one insurance company off of the other, manages to free them. Cora gets probation and $10,000 from her husband's insurance, and she and Frank try to return to the lives they have made for themselves.

With Nick dead, however, Cora and Frank no longer share the same desires. Nick wants to wait out Cora's six-month probation, sell the tavern, and leave town. At first, so does Cora, but after six months of solid business—people flock to the tavern to catch a glimpse of the woman who may have killed her husband—Cora wants to buy a beer license and expand the restaurant. Frank, however, wants no part of this scheme, and when Cora is away at her mother's funeral in Iowa, he closes up the business and heads to Mexico with another woman. Frank returns from Mexico before Cora herself returns from Iowa, but it is not long before Cora discovers that Frank has once again betrayed her.

Earlier in the novel, just after she receives her probation, Cora tells Frank, "We were up on a mountain [the night we killed Nick]. We were up so high, Frank. We had it all, out there, that night. . . . We had more than any two people in the world. And then we fell down. . . . Our mountain is gone" (87). The mountain, for Cora, is a space of fulfillment; it is both the place where she and Frank kill Nick and the place where she and Frank engage in their most passionate sex. For Cora, these two acts of desire are transcendent moments—they lift her "up so high"—and the mountain, her place of consummate desire, represents the moment when they "had it all," when they were the masters of themselves and their destinies (as she later tells Frank, "God kissed us on the brow that night," 88).

Now, however, after Cora learns of his betrayal in Mexico, Frank reinscribes her mountain in terms focusing not on the redeeming or transcendent qualities of their consummated passion but on its destructive and imprisoning dimensions. As the following passage suggests, Frank realizes that it is not they who master desire but desire that masters them: "We can kid ourself *[sic]* all we want to, and laugh about the money, and whoop about what a swell guy the devil is to be in bed with, but that's just where we are. . . . We're chained to each other, Cora. We thought we were on top of a mountain. That wasn't it. It's on top of us, and that's where it's been ever since that night" (111).

Chained to each other by their appetites for violence and sex, Frank and Cora now spend their evenings together in silence, plotting out in their minds how to kill each other. But they are offered one last chance for happiness, one last chance to get rid of the fear that has turned their love into hate. When Cora tells Nick that she is pregnant, Frank wants to marry her. Cora agrees, but she also wants Frank to make a deeper, more profound choice. She suggests that tomorrow, after they get married, they go to the beach. "You can kill me swimming," she tells Frank. "We'll go way out . . . and if you don't want me to come back, you don't have to let me" (113).

Frank doesn't kill her. As he swims out into the water with his bride, his desires change. He is no longer a man who needs to devour everything around him. As he swims back to shore, we see a different man, one who, while still possessing passion, now seems free of every destructive appetite and urge:

> We started back, and on the way in I swam down. I went down nine feet. . . . I whipped my legs together and shot down further. . . . And with my ears ringing and that weight on my back and chest, it seemed to me that all the devilment, and meanness, and shiftlessness, and no-account stuff in my life had been pressed out and washed off, and I was already to start out with her again clean, and do like she said, have a new life. (114-15)

At this moment, as he surfaces from the water, Frank becomes an almost Chandleresque hero. In a world full of meanness, Frank, for the moment at least, is not himself mean. Like Chandler's Marlowe, Frank is not purged of all desire—he has not become a "eunuch." Rather, his desires are purified; he has come away "clean," thus avoiding the fate of the satyr as well as the eunuch. With his desires refashioned into a more acceptable hierarchy (he leaves all the "meanness" down in the water, bringing back to the surface only those desires that are "clean") Frank, like the baby in Cora's womb, is about to be born into a "new life," with, one senses, a new chance to pursue his desire for family and assume the honorable and exclusively masculine roles of husband and father.

But Cain's universe is one in which the pursuit of desire disables rather than enables an honorable masculinity. When Frank surfaces from his purifying dive, with all the devilment and meanness pressed out of him, Cora, treading water nearby, tells Frank that she feels "funny inside" (115). Both of them fear that she is miscarrying. As she fatigues, Frank must tow her to shore. Now, instead of desiring her death, he desires only to save the life of his wife and child. After getting her to the car, he speeds toward the nearest hospital. Caught behind a truck, Frank tries to pass it on the right. In his frantic pursuit to save that which he most desires, he does not see the culvert wall in time, and, as he tells us, "There was a crash, and everything went black" (115).

While in the water, Frank purifies his desires, becoming a seeker not of death but of a "new life" of love and family. But this new world, this "clean" world, quickly turns "black." In a further, equally cruel twist of fate, Frank is sentenced to hang for Cora's death. As Frank puts it, the district attorney "had it all figured out. We murdered the Greek to get the money, and then I married her, and murdered her so I could have it all" (117). Frank insists, however, that "I never really wanted anything, but her" (119). If this is true, then Frank's narrative represents his successful struggle to move beyond his earlier, less noble desires for power, money, and sex. At the end of the novel, so it seems, Frank has indeed cleansed himself and has indeed subordinated and mastered his base desires so that he might pursue the more noble desire of love.

But as he awaits his execution, Frank can no longer be certain that he is the master of his desires, and as he protests his mastery, we think that he does protest too much:

> There's a guy in No. 7 that murdered his brother, and says he didn't really do it, his subconscious did it. I asked him what that meant, and he says you got two selves, one that you know about and the other that you don't know about, because it's subconscious. It shook me up. Did I really [kill Cora on purpose], and not know it? God Almighty, I can't believe that! I didn't do it! I loved her so, then, I tell you, that I would have died

> for her! To hell with the subconscious. I don't believe it. . . . You know what you're doing, and you do it. I didn't do it, I know that. That's what I'm going to tell her, if I ever see her again. (119)

At the end of *The Maltese Falcon,* Sam Spade knows what he is doing and why he is doing it. The same is not true for Frank Chambers, and it is this ambivalence over the mastery of desire that marks a key difference between the hardboiled detective novel and the *roman noir.* In the end, neither we nor Frank are certain of his desires, and Frank, without the certainty he needs, cannot, like Spade, construct an honorable hierarchy of motivations.

Ultimately, it matters not what Frank desired as he tried to pass the truck on the highway that afternoon. If, on the one hand, Frank was indeed trying to kill Cora, then he was unchanged and was once again pursuing an impure and insatiable desire, a desire he had to fulfill even if he had to hang for it. On the other hand, if Frank was no longer a mean man, if he was seeking to fulfill a set of purified desires, what then? The outcome is the same. In either case, Frank hangs for his desires. The fault, Cain seems to be telling us, lies not in the direction of Frank's desires, but in the fact that he desires at all. Whether acting out of meanness or out of love, out of his old devilment or out of baptismal newness, Frank is destroyed by his pursuit of desire. When, after his conviction, Frank claims "I never really wanted anything, but her," he may be wrong, but he has articulated the problem of desire at the very heart of the *roman noir.* The profound despair of this novel, the despair that Camus exploited so well in *The Stranger,* rests upon the unspoken assumption that even a single, simple desire—represented in a single, simple syntactical construction, "but her"—can have the most catastrophic implications for the construction of the self. Ultimately, Frank Chambers would have been better off if he could have just said "I never really wanted anything." His life, of course, would not have amounted to much, but then again his life would also not have destroyed so much. Such renunciation, although it would have allowed him to survive, would have also, on the other hand, deprived him of a more "complete" masculinity. Without desire, to be sure, he could never have assumed the honorable masculinity that attends a man's devotion to his wife and child, but at least he would not have been responsible for the death of that very same wife and child.

Operating as the generative text of the *roman noir*, *The Postman Always Rings Twice* gives articulation to the despair of masculine desire, a despair out of which a generation of popular novelists would fashion their frustrated and disturbing visions of fragmented and ineffectual masculinity. For Jim Thompson, this despair of desire leads his heroes into a violent and often psychopathic engagement with the world, toward a sense that if one possesses desire and desire engenders self-destruction, then one might as well get on with the business at hand, might as well play out the self-annihilation as swiftly and as violently as possible. For David Goodis, however, the self-destruction of masculine desire leads in the other direction. Instead of giving into the pull of desire and thus initiating the inevitable, Goodis's men try more diligently to erase that pull, exchanging, as it were, the despair of desire for the despair of nothingness. They seek the degree zero implicit in the revision of "I never really wanted anything, but her" to "I never really wanted anything," seeking as they do a place where "nothing could bother them, nothing at all."[19]

III.

When Jim Thompson died in 1977 at the age of seventy, all twenty-nine of his novels were out of print. Thus, in 1981, Geoffrey O'Brien was certainly justified in conferring upon Thompson the dubious title of "Most Neglected Hardboiled Writer."[20] Over the past decade, however, Thompson has swiftly arisen from the ashes of this neglect. In a 1990 issue of *Vanity Fair*, for instance, James Wolcott noted that with "three movie adaptations (with more being prepped), two forthcoming biographies, a series of paperback reissues—Jim Thompson is due to become the coolest dead writer in rotation."[21] Writing at the same time, crime-novelist Lawrence Block agreed: "Jim Thompson is a hot ticket these days. . . . Suddenly, he seems to be everybody's favorite writer."[22]

If, as Luc Sante argues, "Cain spawned a genre. The ingredients of compulsion, self-destruction, revenge, and blind chance awakened a kind of poetry in pulp writing,"[23] then, as Cain's offspring, Thompson took the poetry of pulp writing and pushed it to the discordant edges of madness and nightmare. According to Max Allan Collins, "Thompson is to Cain as Spillane is to Chandler: stronger, darker medicine, the violence and sex starkly, unapologetically depicted, the protagonist's mental state constantly verging on and often into psychosis. . . . Certainly anyone who finds Jim Cain unpleasant will, upon encountering Jim Thompson, rush for the exits immediately."[24]

Despite the differences in intensity between Thompson and Cain, the hero of almost any Thompson novel would benefit from the renunciation of desire encouraged by Cain in the closing pages of *The Postman Always Rings Twice.* In fact, several of Thompson's heroes believe they have indeed renounced desire, have indeed "never really wanted anything." Sheriff Nick Corey of *Pop. 1280* (1964) characterizes himself as "just a nothing doing nothing."[25] The only problem, however, is that the citizens of Pottsville, Texas, population 1,280, want Corey to do a better job of "sheriffin' " the county; they want him to do more than "just grinning and joking and looking the other way" (9). Because they want him to "do a little something" (9) instead of "doing nothing," Corey is forced to act, and he decides that whatever he wants to do he can do. So, when the town's two pimps, who have for a long time been causing Corey "a powerful sight of trouble" (9), continue to bother him, Corey concludes "something plumb drastic" (10) needs to be done. When he next meets the pimps they end up "in the river, each with a bullet spang between his eyes" (40). After this, Corey continues to kill whomever he pleases. The way he murders his lover's husband shows us that Pottsville would have been better off if it had just allowed Corey to continue on as "a nothing doing nothing," to continue living degree zero:

> "The second thing I'm gonna do," I said, "is somethin' I should have done long ago. I'm gonna give you both barrels of this shotgun right in your stupid stinking guts." And I did it.
>
> It didn't quite kill him, although he was dying fast. I wanted him to stay alive for a few seconds, so that he could appreciate the three or four good swift kicks I gave him. You might think it wasn't real nice to kick a

dying man, and maybe it wasn't. But I'd been wanting to kick him for along time, and it just never had seemed safe until now. (68)

Nick Corey, like so many of Thompson's protagonists, is better off being a man without desire. Otherwise, given the opportunity to pursue some need or want, and in every novel they are presented with abundant opportunities, Thompson's protagonists cannot control themselves. Some of his heroes are, at heart, full of what Sheriff Lou Ford of *The Killer Inside Me* (1952) calls simply "*the sickness.*"[26] Others, like Toddy Kent of *The Golden Gizmo* (1954), are "peaceful [men who] don't ask much but to be left alone and leave others alone," except that circumstances (usually in the form of a woman) keep them from following that "basic pattern."[27] Most of Thompson's heroes, however, experience the "two-way pull" of Clinton Brown, the emasculated war veteran of *The Nothing Man* (1954), a pull in which violent and often self-destructive desires compete with and win out over the impulse to leave well enough alone:

I was experiencing that peculiar two-way pull that had manifested itself with increasing frequency and intensity in recent months. It was a mixture of calm and disquiet, of resignation and frantically furious rejection. *Simultaneously I wanted to lash out at everything and do nothing about anything.* The logical result of the conflict should have been a stalemate, yet somehow it was not working out that way. The positive emotions, the impulse to act, were outgrowing the others. The negative ones, the calm and resignation, were exercising their restraining force not directly but at a tangent. (emphasis added)[28]

Nick Corey, strangely enough, is one of Thompson's luckiest heroes, for despite the fact that he gives in to his most psychopathic desires, gives into the "frantically furious" pull "to lash out at everything," he survives.[29] Other protagonists are not so fortunate and, for the most part, they meet brutal fates as a result of their pursuit of desire. When Ford, the easygoing but deeply disturbed sheriff of Central City, for the first time meets Joyce Lakeland, Central City's newest prostitute, he too, like Clinton Brown, is being pulled by disquieting desires. After she calls him a "son-of-a-bitch" for impersonating a client just to gain access to her trailer home, Ford experiences a welling of uncontrollable anger: "I had to get out of there. I knew what was going to happen if I didn't get out, and I knew I couldn't let it happen. I might kill her. It might bring *the sickness* back" (13). But Lou Ford cannot get out of there, and soon he is smacking her around her bedroom and tearing her clothes off. "I don't know how long it was before I stopped, before I came to my senses," Ford tells us afterward. "All I know is that my arm ached like hell and her rear end was one big bruise, and I was scared crazy—as scared as a man can get and go on living" (14).

Ford, however, does not go on living for long. His afternoon with Joyce Lakeland has indeed brought back *the sickness*. With his sickness tapped, Lou Ford, like Nick Corey, begins to stack up bodies, beating and killing whomever he pleases. Soon, of course, he leaves too many bodies behind and the police are on his trail. At the end of the novel he is alone in his kitchen, asking himself how come his "life doesn't depend on anything that makes sense" and wondering "where in the hell [he] got the idea it did" (184). Unable to find an answer, and unable to master his sickness, he methodically plans his own suicide. He goes into his basement with a "gallon bottle of alcohol and [a] box of tall candles" (185) and returns to his kitchen without them. As the basement beneath him slowly burns, he sips on coffee and smokes a cigarette, waiting for Joyce Lakeland and her police escort to show up at his house. Soon, his house is surrounded by police and, sitting at his kitchen table, playing with the knife he will use on Joyce when she shows up at his door, Lou Ford reveals his belief that his life has been nothing but one long drama of self-annihilation: "You wonder if you've done things right [in setting up your own suicide], so's there'll be nothing left of something that shouldn't ever have been, and you know everything has been done right. You know, because you planned this moment before eternity way back yonder someplace" (185). When he leaps out of his front door, sticking a blade between Joyce's ribs, the house suddenly bursts into timely flames and, Ford tells us, the "room exploded with shouts and yells, and I seemed to explode with it, yelling and laughing and . . . and . . ." (185).

Such apocalyptic endings are standard Thompson fare. No matter how much they want to fight the two-way pull that finally demands they pursue desire rather than remain as calm and resigned "nothing men," Thompson's heroes are driven by passions that explode their very being. Such passions turn Nick Corey into a deluded psychopath, one who thinks that he is the second coming of Christ, put on this earth to grant and take life as he pleases. For Lou Ford, desire, which can only be described as a sickness, leads to his self-destruction. He knows desire to be his enemy, but he cannot master it no matter how hard he tries. It is almost as if Thompson's heroes subconsciously desire their own deaths, which they see as the only way out of the two-way pull: If they cannot return to being "a nothing doing nothing," then at least they can welcome the "nothingness" of death.

This is true of Kid Collins in *After Dark, My Sweet* (1955). Collins, an ex-boxer and recent escapee from a mental hospital, seems to know little of what he wants, but he, unlike most Thompson protagonists, has a vague sense that he wants to do the right thing. Directionless, he hooks up with two small-time hoods and becomes involved in a botched kidnapping. When he realizes that he cannot escape prosecution for his crime, he tries to imagine a way in which the woman he loves, who coaxed him into the kidnapping in the first place, will escape prosecution. The only solution he can imagine is one in which he so terrifies this woman that she is forced into killing him to save her own life. When he threatens her and then leaves his gun within her reach, she aims the gun at the back of his head. "There was one shattering explosion," Collins tells us, "and I pitched forward against the creek bank. . . . And I stayed where I was, unable to turn my face pressed into the dirt. And that was the way it should be. . . . And this—this, what had happened, was, as it had to be."[30]

What Kid Collins gives up so willingly—his life—other protagonists have taken from them. At the end of *The Grifters* (1963), small-time con man Roy Dillon and his mother, Lilly, are at odds with one another. Lilly, having recently murdered Roy's lover (who was, in turn, trying to kill Lilly), needs Roy's money in order to make a clean getaway. Roy, however, wants to keep his money because he believes that this is best for his mother—it will be the only way she will stop her life of crime. Or at least this is what he initially believes he desires. Slowly he realizes that he wants to keep his money because of deeper, less noble motives. As a child,

Roy felt sexual longing for his mother (Lilly is only fourteen years older than he). For Roy, his youth was a "*time when he had known need or desire and been denied because the denial was good for him.*"[31] Now, he realizes, if he can keep his money he can "*Keep her available*" (183), allowing him to perhaps fulfill the need that has been so long denied him. Lilly senses this, and begins to tease her son:

> "Roy . . . what if I told you I wasn't really your mother? That we weren't related?"
>
> "Huh!" He looked up startled. "Why, I—"
>
> "You'd like that, wouldn't you? Of course, you would. You don't need to tell me. Now, why would you like it Roy?"
>
> He gulped painfully, attempted a laugh of assumed nonchalance. Everything was getting out of hand. . . . The sudden awareness of his feelings, the sudden understanding of himself, all the terror and the joy and the desire held him thralled and wordless. (185)

When Lilly asks, "I want that money Roy. I've got to have it. Now, what do I have to do to get it?" (185), Roy cannot articulate his desire: "And how could he tell her? How say the unsayable?" (186). But he never has to say anything. As Roy is poised to ask for the one desire that has always been denied him—sexual possession of his mother—his mother—the very object of his desire—murders him. As Roy sits before her, taking a sip of water at her behest, Lilly, "her grip tight on the heavy purse, swung it with all her might. . . . A torrent splattered and splashed with red. . . . [Roy] rose up out of his chair, clutching at [his throat], and an ugly shard of glass oozed out between his fingers" (186). At the very moment when "desire held him thralled and wordless," Roy Dillon meets his death.

Discussing the conclusion of *The Killer Inside Me,* David Lehman notes that Thompson's novel "reaches a nihilistic orgasm."[32] Lehman's phrase is a disturbing but acutely accurate one that suggests both the consummation of desire and the nothingness and destruction at the very heart of that consummation—a suggestion that is central to Thompson's vision of desire. As with *The Killer Inside Me,* the conclusion of *The Grifters* is also marked by an explosion of violent nihilism. So too is the ending of *Savage Night* (1953), in which Charlie Bigger, like Roy Dillon, is destroyed by the very woman he most desires: "The axe flashed. My hand, my right hand, jumped and kind of leaped away from me, sliced off clean. And she swung again and all my left hand was gone but the thumb. . . . She was swinging wild. My right shoulder was hanging by a thread, and the spouting forearm dangled from it. And my scalp, my scalp and the left side of my face was dangling, and . . . and I didn't have a nose . . . or a chin . . . or. . . ."[33] The violent conclusion of *Savage Night* is surpassed only by the strangely brilliant final chapter of *A Hell of a Woman* (1954), in which, at the very end, Thompson splits his narrative in two (every other line is in italics). Thus, one of two endings are possible, both of them equally nihilistic. The protagonist, Frank Dillon, either commits suicide as he leaps out a window or is castrated by an unknown woman. We cannot know for certain which is his true fate. What we can know for certain, however, is that yet another one of Thompson's protagonists has been destroyed by his desire. In one of the two optional endings, just before he is about to be castrated, Frank characterizes his life as

> a . . . terrible tragedy and whoever was responsible for it . . . ought to be jailed. Making a guy want what he . . . couldn't get. Making him so he couldn't get much, but . . . he'd want a lot. Laying it all out for him every place he . . . turned—the swell cars and clothes and places to live . . . never letting him have anything, but always making . . . him want. Making him feel like a bastard because he . . . didn't have what he couldn't get. Making him hate . . . himself, and if a guy hates himself how can he love . . . anyone else?[34]

Frank Dillon's frantic and apocalyptic vision of life is strikingly similar to the cool and resigned vision offered by the nameless philosopher in Dostoyevsky's *Notes from Underground*, for Frank Dillon would certainly agree that desire "encompasses everything from reason down to scratching oneself." Thompson's men, however, do more than scratch themselves and, in the end, desire does more than encompass everything—it destroys everything as well. Yes, Thompson's "heroes" may begin like Sheriff Nick Corey, wanting only to be "a nothing doing nothing," but the moment they begin to pursue their desires, begin to give into the two-way pull that forces them into action and away from the zero degree, they initiate a swift process of self-annihilation in which the scratching of an itch soon becomes the tearing away of the soul. Thompson's attitude about the self-annihilation that always attends the pursuit of desire is quite clear, especially if we recall the final words of Kid Collins in *After Dark, My Sweet:* Self-destruction "was the way it should be. . . . And this—this, what had happened, was, as it had to be" (130).

The pursuit of desire that drove Frank Chambers into a world where "everything went black," is echoed in the final pages of *Savage Night,* where Charlie Bigger, lying mutilated in his basement, is left with nothing but "The darkness and myself. . . . And the little that was left of me was going, faster and faster" (147). In fact, the image of Charlie Bigger being hacked to death by the woman he most desires may be Thompson at his most Thompsonesque, and it may serve as well as a shocking reminder of the fragmented and ineffectual masculinity imaged in the *roman noir.* In the basement with Charlie, we could not be any further away from the Chandleresque vision of heroic masculinity informing the hardboiled detective novel. In the mean world in which he lives, Charlie Bigger is both tarnished and afraid. And whereas he is certainly an "unusual man," he is not a "complete" one. If anything, he is an incomplete man, first missing his right hand, then his left hand, then his scalp, his nose, his chin. Nor is there anything redemptive about his tragedy, for as O'Brien notes, "Rarely has an American writer—especially a mass market writer like Thompson—portrayed such hopeless ugliness, so unadorned a dead end."[35] Ultimately, the dead end of Thompson's fiction rests upon his dead-end vision of desire. Unlike Chandler, who envisions desire as something hierarchical and thus potentially honorable, Thompson understands desire as something unsettling and, quite literally, emasculating, leading not to heroic self-definition but to inevitable self-destruction. This dead-end vision of desire marks nearly everything Thompson ever wrote and, according to one French critic, it secures his reputation as "le plus noir, le plus amer, le plus pessimiste de tous les auteurs des romans policiers américains."[36] It is no wonder, then, that biographer Michael J. McCauley characterizes Thompson's works as "razor-sharp, pocketsized trips into the void."[37]

Seeing man as a someone who "couldn't get much, but . . .

he'd want a lot" (*Hell of a Woman,* 181), Thompson perceived the masculine condition as not only encompassed by desire but also thwarted and imprisoned by it. A Thompsonesque hero wants to be a nothing man, but he is pulled by desires that demand fulfillment, quite often against his better judgment. These desires take that hero out of his zero degree of negation and into a dangerous landscape of desperate need, a condition that will make him feel not like, "to use a rather weathered phrase, a man of honor" (Chandler, "The Simple Art of Murder," 533), but like a "bastard because he . . . didn't have what he couldn't get" (Thompson, *Hell of a Woman,* 181). For David Goodis, however, the solution to this predicament was quite simple: rewrite the landscape so that if a man "didn't have what he couldn't get" it wouldn't matter to him anyway—wouldn't make him feel like a bastard—because, ultimately, he didn't want that much to begin with. Thus, if for Thompson man was someone who "couldn't get much . . . but he'd want a lot," then for Goodis man was someone who simply couldn't get much—the "wanting," as we shall soon see, was totally erased from the equation.

IV.

David Goodis's first novel, *Retreat from Oblivion* (1938), was his first and only work of "serious" fiction. Soon, he turned to the pulps. With his second novel, however, he rescued himself, albeit momentarily, from the "oblivion" suggested by the title of his first novel and his subsequent foray into pulp fiction. This second novel, *Dark Passage* (1946), was serialized in *The Saturday Evening Post* and Warner Brothers turned it into a feature film starring Humphrey Bogart and Lauren Bacall. Immediately thereafter signed on as a Warner Brothers staff writer, Goodis had unknowingly reached the peak of his fame. After a few more hardcover publications, he was consigned to the field of paperback originals. This consignment, however, although not to Goodis's economic advantage, benefitted him as an artist. O'Brien writes:

> With the move to paperback originals, the style and content of his books changed radically. As if mirroring the failure of Goodis' higher-toned

literary ambitions, the novels turned decisively toward the lower depths. From here on he would be the chronicler of skid row, and specifically of the man fallen from his social class. . . . In this fashion David Goodis, great literary artist turned street-corner hack writer, could tell his own story and ply his trade at the same time.[38]

Goodis's first paperback hero, James Cassidy of *Cassidy's Girl* (1951), is much akin to the violent and sexually passionate protagonists of Cain and Thompson. A one-time airline pilot and war-hero, Cassidy is now a down-and-out bus driver. Years ago, he lost his airline job when, upon take-off, his co-pilot, suffering "a sudden emotional collapse, the kind that gives no warning . . . and causes a man to break up as earth breaks up when a quake hits it," "turned on Cassidy, pulled him away from the controls, grabbed the controls, and sent the plane downward when it was less than a hundred feet in the air."[39] Cassidy, the only surviving crew member in a crash that took more than seventy lives, lost his wings when it was proven that he had been drinking the night before—which he had, but that had nothing to do with the crash.

A ruined man, Cassidy drifts from job to job. A victim of another man's loss of control, what Cassidy most cherishes about his bus-driving job is that "he was at the controls. That was the thing that mattered. That was what he needed. More than anything. He knew he had lost the ability to control Cassidy, and certainly he would never be able to control Mildred [his wife], but there was one thing left in this world that he could and would control. . . . It was a wonderful bus. Because it would do what he wanted it to do" (15). But, like a Thompsonesque hero, Cassidy is engaged in a two-way pull. As much as he needs and seeks control, Cassidy will often find himself "itching for a solid session of violence" (18), itching, as it were, for a release of his passions. He is married, in turn, to a woman whom he characterizes as "a harsh and biting and downright unbearable obsession" (5). At the beginning of the novel, as we watch him take sexual possession of his wife despite her indifference, we see Cassidy, like Frank Chambers, as a man mastered by his desires: "Very deep inside of him a warning voice told him to let go of her, to leave her alone. . . . [But he] wanted this and he was going to have it and there was no other matter involved. . . . And yet, although the knowledge of her indifference was almost a physical agony, the roaring fire inside him had far greater power, and the only thing he could do was surrender himself to it" (9–10).

Pulled in two directions—one for control, the other for release—Cassidy often frequents Lundy's, a local tavern, and there we soon discover yet another one of his obsessions: alcohol. One evening, he meets Doris, an emaciated, twenty-seven-year-old woman who shares, to an even greater degree, Cassidy's passion for drink. Unlike Cassidy, however, Doris has only this one passion, and nothing else, for the "look in her eyes was the dead look far beyond caring, beyond the inclination to care" (35). There is no roaring fire inside of her. Cassidy, however, decides that he wants to shake Doris out of her degree zero, out of her "beyond caring." Looking into her expressionless eyes, Cassidy "felt the kind of pain that one feels when seeing a crippled child. And all at once he felt an enormous desire to help Doris" (41). As he makes love to her, he insists that it "has nothing to do with lust. It was desire . . . his need to caress her, to give her something of his strength" (43). Cassidy's desire, then, will be Doris' salvation.

But Shealy, Lundy's resident philosopher, warns Cassidy that such desires are misplaced and, in fact, will destroy Doris. According to Shealy, the people who frequent Lundy's, a place of "no color, no gloss, no definite shape" (20), do not want their lives complicated: "The credo I hold is based on simple arithmetic, nothing more. We can all survive and get along if we can just add one and one and get two. . . . If you don't leave her alone she won't survive. . . . Doris has only one need; and that's whisky" (48). Shealy argues that "we dragged ourselves [down to Lundy's]. Wanting it. Knowing it was just what we wanted and we'd be comfortable . . . because there's no bumps" (48). When Cassidy says that such a "comfortable" life is "rotten" and that he is "getting out" (48), Shealy sighs: "The dreams again" (50).

But Cassidy, in a flash of Chandleresque chivalry, believes that there "really was something noble to live for" (56). And while he tries to "construct a better life for himself and for Doris" (54), Mildred, his wife, and Haney, her lover, make his life a living hell. One afternoon, Haney, drunk and desperate, buys a ticket on

Cassidy's bus. Haney wants Cassidy to crawl "like a worm" (79) back to Mildred so that Mildred can have the satisfaction of throwing Cassidy out. Haney hopes that this will get Mildred's mind back on him and off of Cassidy, who deserted her for Doris. When it becomes clear that Cassidy will do no such thing, Haney strikes him over the head with his flask, knocking Cassidy unconscious and causing the bus to roll over a steep embankment. Cassidy and Haney are thrown from the bus; the other twenty-six passengers die as the bus explodes into a ball of flame.

As Cassidy lies on the side of the road, half-unconscious, Haney pours whiskey down his throat. When the police arrive, Haney, the only witness, testifies that Cassidy was drunk, and so once again Cassidy is falsely accused of killing his passengers. When the police are momentarily distracted, Cassidy escapes and spends the evening making his way back to Doris' apartment. When he arrives there, however, she is not home; she is down at Lundy's drinking again. At this moment, Cassidy is struck by the futility of his dreams: Doris' absence "expressed something completely negative, a kind of dreary pessimism, telling him that no matter what moves he made, no matter what he tried to do, he just wouldn't get anywhere" (95). But he will not give up; he cannot accept this kind of negativism. With the help of Shealy, he plans to escape to South Africa aboard a ship, with Doris by his side. He sees everyone else in his world as those "who had long ago lost the vigor and the spine and the spark. But he, Cassidy, he hadn't lost it. . . . He would never lose it. It was the marvelous substance and fire and surging and as long as it was there, as long as it revolved and throbbed, there was a chance, there was hope" (109–10).

By novel's end, however, Cassidy must jettison this "marvelous substance" of hope, this "fire and surging" of desire for something better. Cassidy's epiphany marks a profound awareness that living degree zero is the proper posture of existence—that living without desire is what others want to do and it is what he must and should want for himself:

> The moment of realization was almost tangible, like a page containing words of truth. Now he was able to understand the utter futility of his attempt to rescue Doris. There was no possibility of rescue. She didn't

want to be rescued. . . . His pity for Doris had been the reflection of pity that he felt for himself. His need for Doris had been the need to find something worthwhile and gallant within himself. (154)

"The moment ended," Goodis writes, "and for Cassidy it meant the erasing of Doris" (154). The erasing of Doris, of course, means the erasing of desire. Unlike Chandler's chivalrous Marlowe, Goodis's defeated Cassidy cannot find something "worthwhile and gallant within himself," and thus, in turn, he can find little that is worth desiring. Cassidy does not want to be here in this world of erasure, this world without desire, but Goodis is telling us that this is where he must be. When earlier in the novel Cassidy tells Shealy, "I don't know what I believe. There's part of me says I shouldn't believe in anything," Shealy responds with a sentiment that is unmistakably that of the author: "That's the sensible way. . . . Just wake up every morning and whatever happens, let it happen. Because no matter what you do, it'll happen anyway. So ride with it. Let it take you . . . down. . . . No effort. No climbing. Just slide down and enjoy the trip" (101).

For Goodis, the "sensible way" is a life of "no effort," of "no climbing." Cassidy must learn this. So too must Hart, the protagonist of *Black Friday* (1954), who begins as a man who "knew how to run [from] the emptiness."[40] Frightened by the erasure of desire that threatens to strip his life of meaning and feeling, Hart seeks constant contact with the world, even if it is a painful contact, just so as to avoid the zero degree: "He slammed his fist against the tree and pain shot through his knuckles. Not enough pain. . . . He had to hurt himself more than this, make himself realize that he couldn't continue this [emptiness]. . . . He told himself that even if he had to break his hand he had to cure himself now" (7). In the final paragraph of the novel, however, Hart can no longer outrun the emptiness that is chasing him and, like Cassidy, he embraces the erasure of desire: "He was walking very slowly, not feeling the bite of the wind, not feeling anything. And later, turning the street corners, he didn't bother to look at the street signs. He had no idea where he was going and he didn't care" (129).

Where Hart and Cassidy end up, this is where the protagonist of *Street of No Return* (1954) begins. Like Cassidy and Hart, Whitey was at an earlier time a successful man. A famous night-club singer, Whitey hooks up with Cecelia, the common-law wife of a small-time gangster. The gangster tries to convince Whitey to leave Cecelia alone, but Whitey, in classic *roman noir* fashion, tells him, "I want her. . . . I can't give her up. Just can't do without her" (76). Whitey's desire leaves the gangster no choice, and he has Whitey beaten so badly that the singer's vocal chords are forever damaged. When Cecelia fails to call him while he is in the hospital, he realizes that what he most wants, what he "can't do without," no longer wants him. After this realization, "nothing mattered" (87). He gambles away his fortune, takes up drinking, and soon he finds himself, much to his liking, "Going down. One step at a time" (89).

When the novel opens, Whitey's "slow motion suicide" (88) has long been complete. For the past seven years, he has been living on Skid Row, and every day at dawn "he'd hit the street and join the early-morning parade that moved in no special direction, the dreary assemblage of stumble bums going this way and that way and getting nowhere" (91). This nowhere is right where Whitey wants to be, for he is "a little man lost in the emptiness of a drained bottle" (2), with "nothing in his pockets and nothing in his eyes" (3). When a riot breaks out in the opening pages of the novel, "Whitey's face showed no interest at all. He wasn't even listening to the hectic noises coming from three blocks south" (6). One of Whitey's wino buddies bemoans this riot because it reminds him that "Skid Row wasn't really the hiding place it was supposed to be. . . . [Down on Skid Row, you] tried to keep away from contact with the world but somehow or other the world always made contact. The world tossed the bait and tossed it again and again, kept tossing it to get a nibble, and sooner or later the hook was taken and the line reeled in" (7).

The secret, this wino believes, is to "play it Whitey's way and not let it touch him, let nothing touch him" (9). Resist the hook of desire that the world keeps tossing at you, don't take the bait and be reeled in by wants and needs—according to the wino, this is the only way to survive. Unfortunately, Whitey, who is so good at not letting the world touch him, sees something on the other side of the street, something that forces him into contact with the world. Reeled into the "Hellhole," the place of the rioting, Whitey begins his curious odyssey. In the course of his evening in the "Hellhole," Whitey confronts the people who beat him long ago and exacts revenge upon them by foiling their plans to foment a larger, more disastrous race-riot. He even meets Cecelia again, and she is still hooked up with her gangster. He toys with the idea of trying to take her back, but he realizes that he does not want her, or anything else, bad enough.

Through it all, Whitey retains his sense of nothingness, and while the world makes contact with him, he is always aware that what he wants and seeks most is to live degree zero, to live without ambition or desire. At the beginning of Whitey's evening in the "Hellhole," an elderly black man tries to convince Whitey that he must have something to live for:

> Jones said, "You gotta care. You gotta drill it into yourself, you got to have something to live for."
>
> "Like what?" [Whitey] asked in the cracked whisper that always reminded him it was a matter of no hope, no soap, nothing at all.
>
> But the old man was still in there trying. And saying, "Like looking for an answer. No matter what the question is, there's always an answer."
>
> "Sure," he agreed, grinning again. "In this case, it's strictly zero."
>
> "It's never zero," the old man said. "Not while you're able to breathe."
>
> "I'm tired of breathing." (51)

When Whitey gets back to his corner at the end of the evening, he has not come up with anything to live for. For Whitey "the answer" is still "strictly zero." When his two wino buddies ask him where he has been and what has happened to him, "Whitey shrugged and didn't say anything" (166) because, in a way, nothing has happened to him. In his discussion of the novel, O'Brien concludes that Whitey "wanders off and comes back 175 pages later . . . only to find that all he really wants to do is go back to [his] corner" on Skid Row.[41]

The novel closes with Goodis's vision of survival, his belief that men need to live in a perpetual state of dreams deferred and desires erased in order to endure:

> The three of them walked across the street. They sat down on the pavement with their backs against the wall of the flophouse. The pavement was terribly cold and the wet wind from the river came blasting into their faces. But it didn't bother them. They sat there passing the bottle, and there was nothing that could bother them, nothing at all. (166)

Like Cassidy and Hart, Whitey ends up in a world where nothing bothers him, where nothing matters. Unlike Cassidy and Hart, however, this is the very place where Whitey begins. If *Cassidy's Girl* and *Black Friday* enact a movement from desire to the erasure of desire, then *Street of No Return* enacts no movement at all—Whitey never gets beyond the zero degree.

Shoot the Piano Player (1956), however, is a fusion of these two structures, for in it Goodis creates an existential odyssey in which his hero, Eddie Lynn, moves from wanting nothing to wanting something and back to wanting nothing once again.[42] Eddie begins as a man with "no debts or obligations" (5), "a soft-eyed, soft-mouthed nobody whose ambitions and goals aimed at exactly zero" (24). Even his smile is "something neutral. . . . It was aimed very far out there beyond all tangible targets" (24). Like Goodis's other heroes, Eddie is running from his past. Eddie was once a world-famous concert pianist, but his career fell apart when his wife, because of his neglect, took her own life. When the novel opens, Eddie is playing piano in a two-bit bar. The music he makes symbolizes the state of his soul: "The music went on, the rhythm unbroken. It was a soft, easygoing rhythm, somewhat plaintive and dreamy, a stream of pleasant sound that seemed to be saying, Nothing matters" (4). A complex set of circumstances and coincidences shake Eddie out of his easygoing rhythm of nothingness, and soon he finds himself drawn into a world of violence and, much to his disbelief, love. At the end of the novel, however, we find him right back where he started, with his "fingers caressing the keyboard" (156). And while the crowd at the bar urges him to "put some life into this joint" (156), we sense that Eddie's return to the piano marks his return to a life "aimed at exactly zero." The music will go on, the rhythm will be unbroken, and Eddie, like the author who created him, will continue to produce the "pleasant sound" that says "Nothing matters."

V.

Frank Chambers awaiting his execution, uncertain about the source and direction of his desires; Charlie Bigger crawling about in a dirt basement, what little there is left of him "going, faster and faster"; James Cassidy realizing that "no matter what moves he made, no matter what he tried to do, he just wouldn't get anywhere": These are the images of masculinity inscribed in the *roman noir,* images reflecting not the common fantasies of masculine prowess and domination but the common nightmares of impotence and ineffectuality. If, as Stephano Tani has suggested, "the mythic private detective conceived of by such writers as Dashiell Hammett and Raymond Chandler . . . [is] a creature capable of dealing efficiently with a disorderly and dangerous world,"[43] then the less-than-mythic "hero" conceived of by those other hardboiled novelists—Cain, Thompson, and Goodis—is the very nexus of danger and disorder. Instead of being defined by his ability to deal efficiently with the world—or, as we have stated the case here, being defined by his ability to deal efficiently with his contentious desires—the hero of the *roman noir* is destroyed by his very inability to do so. Lacking a Chandleresque mastery of desire, the hero of the *roman noir* has but two options. He can continue to pursue his desire until he enacts an inevitable self-annihilation, or he can embrace the zero degree and trade in self-annihilation for self-erasure. In either case, the hero is un-manned, becoming less and less like the "everything" Chandler tells us a hero must be, and more and more like, as Thompson reminds us, a "something that shouldn't ever have been." But such is the life, such is the nothingness, on the mean streets of the *roman noir.*

Notes

1. Raymond Chandler, "The Simple Art of Murder," in *The Simple Art of Murder* (Norton: New York, 1968), 533.
2. George Grella, "Murder and the Mean Streets," *Contempora* 1 (March 1970): 8.
3. John G. Cawelti, *Adventure, Mystery and Romance: Formula Stories as Art and Popular Culture* (Chicago: Univ. of Chicago Press, 1976), 151.
4. David Madden, *James M. Cain* (Boston: Twayne, 1970), 22.
5. Geoffrey O'Brien, *Hardboiled America: The Lurid Years of Paperbacks* (New York: Van Nostrand Reinhold, 1981), 68.
6. O'Brien, *Hardboiled America,* 77.

7. Cawelti, *Adventure, Mystery and Romance,* 160.
8. Dashiell Hammett, *The Novels of Dashiell Hammett* (New York: Knopf, 1965), 438.
9. Chandler, "The Simple Art of Murder," 533.
10. Chandler, "The Simple Art of Murder," 533.
11. David Goodis, *Shoot the Piano Player* (Berkeley: Black Lizard, 1987), 24.
12. Fyodor Dostoyevsky, *Notes from Underground,* trans. Andrew R. MacAndrew (New York: Signet Classic, 1961), 112.
13. O'Brien, *Hardboiled America,* 73.
14. Joyce Carol Oates, "Man under Sentence of Death: The Novels of James M. Cain," in *Tough Guy Writers of the Thirties,* ed. David Madden (Carbondale: Southern Illinois Univ. Press, 1968), 111.
15. Madden, *James M. Cain,* 66.
16. Frank Krutnick, "Desire, Transgression, and James M. Cain," *Screen* 23 (1982): 34.
17. James M. Cain, *The Postman Always Rings Twice* (New York: Vintage, 1978), 58.
18. Paul Skenazy, *James M. Cain* (New York: Ungar, 1989), 20.
19. David Goodis, *Street of No Return* (Berkeley: Black Lizard, 1987), 166.
20. O'Brien, *Hardboiled America,* 120.
21. James Wolcott, "Dead Cool," *Vanity Fair* (July 1990): 20.
22. Lawrence Block, "A Tale of Pulp and Passion: The Jim Thompson Revival," *New York Times Book Review,* 14 October 1990, 37.
23. Luc Sante, "The Gentrification of Crime," *New York Review of Books,* 28 March 1985, 18.
24. Max Allan Collins, "Jim Thompson: The Killers Inside Him," in *Murder Off the Rack: Critical Studies of Ten Paperback Masters,* ed. Jon L. Breen and Martin Harry Greenberg (Metuchen, NJ: Scarecrow Press, 1989), 38.
25. Jim Thompson, *Pop. 1280* (Berkeley: Black Lizard, 1984), 9.
26. Jim Thompson, *The Killer Inside Me* (New York: Quill, 1983), 13.
27. Jim Thompson, *The Golden Gizmo* (New York: Mysterious Press, 1989), 71.
28. Jim Thompson, *The Nothing Man* (New York: Mysterious Press, 1988), 10.
29. As Michael J. McCauley has discovered, however, Thompson's original manuscript suggested a different fate for Corey. The published novel ends with the following paragraph: "So here it is, Buck, here's my decision. I thought and I thought and then I thought some more, and I finally came to my decision. I decided I don't know no more now what to do than if I was just another lousy human bein'!" Thompson's manuscript version ends with the following lines, which Thompson scratched out with a pen: "I whirled around, drawing my

gun. We both fired at the same time." See Michael J. McCauley, *Jim Thompson: Sleep with the Devil* (New York: Mysterious Press, 1991), 243.

30. Jim Thompson, *After Dark, My Sweet* (Berkeley: Black Lizard, 1986), 130.
31. Jim Thompson, *The Grifters* (Berkeley: Black Lizard, 1985), 183.
32. David Lehman, *The Perfect Murder: A Study of Detective Fiction* (New York: Free Press, 1989), 63.
33. Jim Thompson, *Savage Night* (Berkeley: Black Lizard, 1985), 146.
34. Jim Thompson, *A Hell of a Woman* (Berkeley: Black Lizard, 1984), 181.
35. Geoffrey O'Brien, "Jim Thompson, Dimestore Dostoevsky," afterword to *Savage Night* (Berkeley: Black Lizard, 1985), 154.
36. Noel Simisolo, "Notes sur le film noir," *Cinema* 223 (July 1977): 102.
37. McCauley, *Jim Thompson*, 136.
38. Geoffrey O'Brien, "Introduction," in *Cassidy's Girl* (Berkeley: Black Lizard, 1987), ix.
39. David Goodis, *Cassidy's Girl* (Berkeley: Black Lizard, 1987), 12–13.
40. David Goodis, *Black Friday* (Berkeley: Black Lizard, 1987), 7.
41. Geoffrey O'Brien, "Introduction," in *Street of No Return* (Berkeley: Black Lizard, 1987), xii.
42. *Shoot the Piano Player* was originally published under the title *Down There.* When the novel was republished by Black Lizard Press in 1987, they opted to use a revised title, which is the English translation of the Serie Noire translation *(Tirez sur le pianiste)* of *Down There. Shoot the Piano Player* has become the accepted title of the novel because of its association with Francois Truffaut's 1960 film *Tirez sur le pianiste.*
43. Stephano Tani, *The Doomed Detective* (Carbondale: Southern Illinois Univ. Press, 1984), xi.

8

Fighting Words: The Talk of Men at War in *The Red Badge of Courage*

Alfred Habegger

Much of Stephen Crane's work, especially his perplexing novel *The Red Badge of Courage,* constitutes an intense inquiry, simultaneously sardonic and passionately involved, into what it means to negotiate the transition from youth to manhood. From the moment Crane introduces his main character, Henry Fleming, as "a youthful private," our attention is directed to his innocence, the private fears of battle that he dare not utter, and his anxiety at not measuring up to the standards of courage and performance he is afraid his fellow soldiers take for granted. Clearly introduced as someone about to be tested in combat, the youth passes through a cascading sequence of extreme experiences and states of mind, ranging from elation at repulsing the enemy's charge to panic-stricken flight and a strenuous effort to avoid seeing himself as a coward. Rather than encouraging us to share the youth's point of view, Crane's narrator sneeringly calls attention to the callowness of his daydreams and self-exculpating rationalizations, particularly when he is wandering in isolation. Once he is back with his regiment, the youth's initiatory experience culminates in "the enthusiasm of unselfishness" as he participates in a frenzied charge, which the narrator calls, almost at one and the same time, mad, savage, and sublime. At the end, though the youth is troubled by his two desertions—of his regiment and of a dying soldier who had tried to assist him—he manages to feel more comfortable about himself. In addition, his "tupenny fury"[1] at the heavens has not only been dispelled, but he feels convinced that, in the nature of things, he will be looked after:

> With this conviction came a store of assurance. He felt a quiet manhood, non-assertive but of sturdy and strong blood. He knew that he would no more quail before his guides wherever they should point. He had been to touch the great death and found that, after all, it was but the great death and was for others. He was a man.

Those readers who emphasize the irony with which the youth is regarded, and who tend to prefer the manuscript-based edition of the novel, read the "quiet manhood" passage as the height of sarcasm. For them, the youth's conviction that the great death "was for others" is a sign he has not succeeded in growing up.[2] On the other hand, those who feel the youth has completed the passage into manhood (with whatever qualifications) are uneasy about the quoted phrase, which was in fact dropped in the first (Appleton) edition.[3] "And was for others": These four words are like a rude interruption in the ennobling ceremonial language climaxing in the terse assertion, "He was a man."

The Red Badge turns out to be a test not just of Henry but of us as readers. We too are in danger, either of being lulled by the resonant organ tones of the "he was a man" paragraph or of encasing ourselves in a bristling and prophylactic irony. The problem is to reach an understanding of the changes the youth has undergone. In some ways he *has* improved. He is less anxious and defensive. He has attained the inner stability required of an effective soldier. He has learned how to take orders without quailing, and he no longer dreams of becoming a heroic leader. Given the great appeal of this foolish dream, the young man's achievement deserves respect. But it is an achievement that comes at a high cost—a loss of individuality and an illusory sense of being the darling of the universe. Fleming has learned how to follow, how to work with others, how to be a strong and sturdy member of his outfit, but these adjustments seem to entail the comforting illusion that there is a great friendliness out there. The passage says that to become a man is to become one with a group in a rather thoroughgoing sense: you don't speak up, you don't make a fool of yourself any longer, you do what you've got to do, and you've got the heavens on your side. It is all summed up in the honorific cliché, "quiet manhood," which I would imagine was a cliché in 1895.

But why is manhood *quiet? The Red Badge* is about, not grace, but silence under pressure—about the need felt by men fighting for their lives to refrain from expressing themselves and to stifle other men's more open self-expression. Crane was profoundly concerned with the competing claims of individual self-assertion and solidarity with a team. In *The Red Badge* he undertook an exploration of the costs and rewards of turning one's back on the team, and the costs and rewards of merging with it. One of the discoveries Fleming makes is that he is more afraid of being isolated from his group than of facing combat as a part of it. To be engaged in a joint battle for survival is to undergo an extreme test of the value of individual self-expression. You're going to have to learn to button up, to keep to yourself much of what you think, if you want to have the group's respect and get out alive. How much do you suppress? If learning how to become a nonassertive but effective member of a fighting team is what becoming a man is all about, then, judging from *The Red Badge,* there is good reason to feel uneasy about that hard-won quietness.

One of the reasons Crane is of interest is that the uneasiness not only pervades his writing but flagrantly calls attention to itself in his style. His bitter intensity, the conspicuously sardonic tone, and the strained diction emphatically proclaim that he is not one with Henry and the other fighting men. Yet few writers have shown such obsessive interest in the pleasures and pains of being on a fighting team (Crane himself was an expert baseball player). It is the writer's own radical instability (*his* Civil War) that drives readers to try to reach an integrated understanding of his only important novel. What I have in mind is a thematic interpretation of *The Red Badge* that neither explains away its disharmonies nor ignores the existence of different textual versions.

I.

To see what is at issue in Crane's treatment of men's reluctance or willingness to express themselves, we must pay particular attention to those scenes in which a band of men respond to an individual's loose speech. This kind of scene, which frequently reappears in Crane's work, is a powerful and defining moment for him. I would like to look at one such scene in "The Open Boat" before considering what we can learn from the characters' speech in *The Red Badge.*

Survival through solidarity is perhaps the most important lesson learned by the correspondent in "The Open Boat." Well before the conclusion of the story, this character, who is clearly a version of the author (Crane had already partly exploited the adventure in a syndicated story),[4] realizes that the experience of selfless mutual assistance is the best thing that has ever happened to him. But of course he does not express this to the three other men. Throughout the story he and they are all suitably laconic. There is one moment, however, where they all break into excited and un-self-conscious speech. At this moment the author's narrative method also changes.

As the castaways observe and comment on the tantalizing movements of a group on a beach, Crane shifts to a very intriguing sort of direct discourse. The speakers are not identified; the speeches seem much more unpremeditated than the rest of what gets uttered on the tiny dinghy; and the conversation, if this is the correct word, seems to represent a group thinking out loud rather than four individual speakers voicing their separate thoughts. Each line of dialogue (again, the term is not quite right) responds to the preceding lines, yet the attention of all four men is not on one another but on people who are obviously out of earshot. The prevailing decorum that rules self-expression on the boat has been set aside, with great relief, and the men happily enter into a cascade of eager collective commentary, a kind of prose choral ode that slowly shifts in tone from excited hope to sullen resentment. The latter feeling is directed at the man on shore whose attention-getting signal, the whirled jacket, remains maddeningly indecipherable, and of course ineffective. At the time banners and hand positions were widely used to convey messages over great distances or loud noises. This man is a loose speaker, as one of the shipwrecked men concludes: "No! He thinks we're fishing. Just giving us a merry hand. See? Ah, there, Willie."[5]

Those three last words have not drawn comment, even though their meaning seems no clearer than that of the rotated garment. Nearly everyone whom I have approached for an explanation has told me that the speaker is addressing Billie the oiler. When I proposed a query about the passage to a respected journal devoted to the elucidation of American speech, I received the same clarification from the editor:

> Since *Willie* is an alternative diminutive for *William* isn't it most reasonable to assume that "Willie" is a vocative address to Billie the oiler? Also, my memory is that Crane was pretty sloppy about details; even if he wasn't thinking of the "Willie" as a variant of "Billie," he may well have been thinking of the same character. In any case, for one of the men to call Billie "Willie" would be a perfectly natural thing, it seems to me.

This, evidently the "natural" explanation, is unsatisfactory for many reasons. In my own experience of American speech, "Billie" and "Willie" are not at all interchangeable. Within the scene, not only the speakers' names but their very identities are unguessable: so why is one of them now singled out as a *listener?* Why would the speaker of the three mysterious words suddenly abandon ordinary functional speech, and why would he do so in addressing a *working man?* Surely, we may presume that Billie already has his eye on the shore. There is no need to say "Behold!" to this man.

The mysterious exclamation must mean something well beyond the signification of the individual words. If we look at an essay written fifty years later by one of the masters of American speech, "The Secret Life of James Thurber," the general meaning of the phrase becomes apparent. This sketch, a fine put-down of Salvador Dali, exposed the vain pretensions of the artist's memoir of childhood by contrasting it with Thurber's own homely upbringing in the Midwest. Dali had known girls named Galuchka and Dullita and recollected the comforts of his mother's womb. Thurber's first memory was of accompanying his "father to a polling booth in Columbus, Ohio, where he voted for William McKinley." The only romance in Thurber's childhood came from his fascination with idioms not to be taken literally—skeleton key, leaving town under a cloud, crying one's heart out, all ears. In his conclusion, after having vindicated his "secret world of idiom" in the face of Dali's affected glamour, Thurber taunted his rival with the idiom that was now (in 1943) as antiquated and homely as Thurber's boyhood in Columbus—"Ah there, Salvador!"[6]

Evidently, at one time "Ah there" or "Ah, there, Willie" was an immediately recognizable formula expressing derision and defiance. I am not sure whether "Willie," by itself an insulting term for a homosexual man, a "Willie-boy," was part of the phrase. Neither do I know just when it was in vogue, how it got started, or even precisely what it meant. It may have served as a challenge to fight, a taunt directed at someone not considered a proper man, a victorious crowing at a rival, or something else. Perhaps it was accompanied by a gesture or movement that could not be alluded to in print. (This might explain why a distinguished expert on American speech is not familiar with the phrase.) But it was definitely an expression of rude, personal defiance. That is why the phrase forms the culminating moment of the men's excited commentary on the mystifying signal from shore. "Ah, there, Willie" epitomizes Crane's great interest in representing hoots, jeers, catcalls, threats, surly challenges, and similar utterances. But it was not just the colloquial expression of insults that caught his ear. What primarily concerned him were the social and moral aspects of jeering speech. Rude put-downs were worth recording because they articulated one of the most important means by which groups of men define, defend, and maintain themselves.

What makes Crane complicated and interesting is that he doesn't automatically say the group is always in the wrong whenever it declares a nonmember to be an outcast or a deviant. In "The Open Boat," where the group is itself in the outcast position and we as readers are made to feel that we are in the same boat, the man on shore really does look like a fool who deserves to be insulted. (But then, thinking of the gay-bashing possibly implied by "Willie," one feels uneasy.) Another story, "The Blue Hotel," is a profound investigation of the social process by which a man is defined/defines himself as a pariah. It is characteristic of Crane that this individual, a ham-handed and suspicious Swede, belongs to an ethnic group reputed not to understand the tonal intricacies (in humor, insult, tall tales) of American language. The question of responsibility, raised by two characters at the end of the story, cannot be solved precisely because the operative dynamics are sociological. And yet the story also insists that the question of responsibility is not to be evaded, as the cowboy would like. It's the reader who is left to worry about the problem.

Leaving the reader to his or her anxiety, let us now turn to Crane's most sustained exploration of the relation between a beleaguered group and the disdained outsider, *The Red Badge of Courage,* whose very title, we note, designates an insignia of attested manhood.

II.

In discussing the representation of speech in this novel,[7] I will not be concerned with talk that is metaphorical rather than literal—"the courageous words of the artillery and the spiteful sentences of the musketry." Neither will I have much to say about the many passages in which Henry Fleming's unarticulated thoughts are rendered in language and imagery he himself would not have used. "Minds, he said, were not made all with one stamp and colored green" (54). "He had been out among the dragons, he said" (72). The diction, the absence of quotation marks, and the familiarity of the narrative convention these sentences follow all announce that "said" does not mean "spoke." (Tacit though the convention may be, Crane himself called attention to it in one sentence: "But [Henry] said, *in substance,* to himself that if the earth and the moon were about to clash, many persons would doubtless plan to get upon roofs to witness the collision," 38; italics mine.) I am confining my attention to those passages that represent *spoken* language, whether that language is recorded in direct discourse or summarized by Crane in indirect discourse.

Although I will also ignore the much-discussed problem of *dialect,* using the term to refer to the presentation of regional or uncultivated speech through nonstandard orthography, it will be necessary to comment briefly on the generalized countrified traditionalism of the soldiers' talk. Some of their statements—"Well, I swan" (104), "I'm a gone coon" (21), "Be keerful, honey, you'll be a-ketchin' flies" (41)—probably had an old-timey feel for Crane's first readers. Perhaps the same was true for "kit-an'-boodle" (8, 68), "jim-hickey" (96), "chin-music" (77), "skedaddle" (14, 16), "fresh fish" (7), "fight like hell-roosters" (75), and "smart as a steel trap" (47). Most of the mild oaths and curses probably had an old-fashioned flavor by 1895—"make way, dickens [i.e., devil] take it all" (40), "by ginger [i.e., Jesus]" (62), "Great Jerusalem" (63). That Crane was able to introduce undisguised profanity into the next-to-last charge—"Where in hell yeh goin' " and "Gawd damn their souls" (89)—suggests the various euphemistic oaths were not simply an evasive concession to standards of taste. They also contributed to the general representation of how the 1890s thought the 1860s spoke.

The character with the strongest rural twang is the tattered man, whose speech—"a reg'lar jim-dandy" (46), "there's a bat'try comin' helitywhoop" (44), "first thing that feller knowed he was dead" (47)—shows none of Henry's anxiety at being taken for a greenhorn. Even so, as the last quotation shows, humor and irony are well within the tattered man's range:

> "Oh, I'm not goin' t' die yit. There too much dependin' on me fer me t' die yit. No, sir! Nary die! I can't! Ye'd oughta see th' swad a' chil'ren I've got, an' all like that."
>
> The youth glancing at his companion could see by the shadow of a smile that he was making some kind of fun. (47)

Here the bitter countrified drollery with which Crane's yokel speaks is beyond Henry's appreciation.

One could cite a few other expressions that may have struck readers in 1895 as colorful and old-fashioned—"a hull string of rifle-pits" (22), "sore feet an' damn' short rations" (23), "could tear th' stomach outa this war" (80, 106), "sech stomachs aint a-lastin' long" (7), "Gee-rod [Jesus God], how we will thump 'em" (14). Framed by the narrator's own terse, up-to-date, and highly individualized prose, these and other locutions and speeches helped give the soldiers' talk a slightly quaint, historical feel. The novel had an overwhelming historical authenticity for readers, not because it revived the history of battles and leaders and official rhetoric, but because it revived, or seemed to revive, the unofficial voices and the unexpressed experiences. The book seemed to disclose what went on *behind*—and in this sense resembles the new social history of our own time (which also uses smoke and mirrors at times). It was the *illusion* of factual excavation and reconstitution that Crane was apparently after. The glaring disparities between his language as narrator and the way his characters speak helped turn the trick.

To single out the more colorful speeches for attention, however, is to convey a misleading impression of Crane's soldiers' talk, which is flat and inexpressive and on the whole rather dull. "Billie—keep off m' feet. Yeh run—like a cow" (16). We're allus bein' chased around like rats. It makes me sick" (77). "Mebbe yeh think yeh fit th' hull battle yestirday, Flemin'." "Why, no, . . . I don't think I fit th' hull battle yestirday" (76). A general, elated that the center of his line has held, repetitiously gloats, "Yes—by Heavens—they have! . . . Yes, by Heavens, they've held 'im! They've held 'im" (34). A sort of shapeless ordinariness characterizes the language of all the speakers, ranging from the garrulous cheery-voiced man who guides Henry to his regiment to tongue-tied Henry himself.

In fact, rather than trying to make his characters sound interesting, Crane deliberately spotlights their inexpressiveness. Again and again he shows how poorly their words match their thoughts and feelings. After Henry's regiment has repulsed the first charge, he preens himself on having lived up to his ideals; all he says, however, is "Gee, aint it hot, hay?" (30). When he seems "about to deliver a philippic" (one of the narrator's many references to classical oratory), he can only say, "Hell—" (45–46). His intense effort to deliver a "rallying speech" only produces "Why—why—what—what's th' matter?" (57).[8]

It is striking how often what we hear the characters saying doesn't match in interest what we are told about their speeches. When a young girl prevents a fat soldier from stealing her horse, we hear the men saying "Gin' him thunder" and "Hit him with a stick," but the "crows and cat-calls" (12–13) that assail him when he runs off are not reported. When "a black procession of curious oaths" comes from Jim Conklin's lips, we hear nothing but another man's not very interesting questions: "Well, why don't they support us? Why don't they send supports? Do they think—" (27). In Chapter 1, it is reported that Jim Conklin and Wilson "had a rapid altercation, in which they fastened upon each other various strange epithets"; the only speeches that get reported, however, are on the order of "Oh, you think you know—" and "Huh" (9). Similarly, there is often a disparity between the claimed and the apparent tone in which speeches are delivered. When we are informed that Henry "yells in a savage voice," the spoken words hardly live up to this advance billing: "Well, yeh needn't git mad about it" (15). The cumulative impression is that, although there may be interesting language somewhere, practically everything *we* overhear is marked by an all-pervading dullness.

This flagrant inarticulateness, so pervasive and obvious in the novel, of course contributes to its realism of speech, but, more important, it contributes to an ambitious inquiry into the social and moral constraints on self-expression. From the second paragraph on, Crane makes it clear that unrestrained speech carries real risks. In fact, it is an incautious speech that gets the story moving: A soldier identified at first only as tall returns to camp "swelled with a tale" to the effect that the army is about to move. He is immediately contradicted by a sulking soldier who is tagged with the epithet "loud." Before long the two characters are given names, Jim Conklin and Wilson, and as the narrative develops, each one's changing habits of speech reflect what he has learned in battle. For now, though, they are only two different kinds of loose speakers, an expansive tall-talker and a hectoring loud-mouth.

At this early stage Conklin is another version of the jacket-whirling man on shore in "The Open Boat," whose signalling turns out to be without significance. Jim carries a garment that he waves "banner-like," and he adopts "the important air of a herald." When he speaks, it is "pompously" and "with a mighty emphasis" (1, 9). He seems to be the sort who is never at a loss for answers, as when he produces "a heavy explanation" (19) of troop movements: "I s'pose we must go reconnoiterin' 'round th' kentry jest t' keep 'em from gittin' too clost, or t'develope'm, or something" (20). The sentence makes it clear that this great windbag doesn't know the meaning of *reconnoiter* or the technical military sense of *develop*.

Later, after Conklin has sustained a mortal wound in the abdomen, he no longer talks like a blowhard. When he says to Henry, "I thought mebbe yeh got keeled over. There's been thunder t' pay t'day. I was worryin' about it a good deal" (42–43), his words ring pathetically true. His newfound gift for honest speech seems connected, paradoxically, to his effort to conceal his mortal wound. There is a grim humor, in fact, in the revelation that his abdomen has the appearance of being "chewed by wolves" (45). Crane, always aware of parallels with ancient Greece, wants us to recall the Spartan boy who was chewed to death by a fox hidden under his cloak. Conklin now knows how to govern his tongue, having learned Laconic speech the hard way. Wilson also develops for the better as a result of his combat experience. Although he begins by ordering Conklin to shut up, he soon learns to express himself more gently. What changes him is the knowledge that others, Henry in particular, have witnessed his fear and cowardice. Wilson's secret is out, and with it his loud defensiveness. His comrades are still liable to be "stung" by "language," but Wilson can no longer be "pricked" by the "little words" that "other men aimed at him" like bullets (68). This invulnerability is what chiefly distinguishes him from Henry, who remains fearful that his shameful acts will come to light. Henry's "tender flesh" is repeatedly "stung" (93) by taunts, and when he and Wilson hear themselves dismissed as "mule-driver" and "mud-digger" by an officer, it is Henry alone who sustains a wound: "arrows of scorn . . . had buried themselves in his heart" (100). Ironically, Wilson has acquired his armored immunity by rashly disclosing his fear of combat. Henry, by contrast, feels compelled by the accidents of war and his own moral weakness to conceal his desertion of the regiment and of the tattered soldier.

Thus, as far as the capacity to speak moral and emotional truth is concerned, Henry develops in an opposite way from Conklin and Wilson. At first the loud talk of these two men masks their real fears. Then they learn to express themselves: "I was worryin' about it a good deal." Henry, on the other hand, remains alternately tongue-tied and dishonest. At the beginning he does not dare give voice to his "outcry" (19) that the stupid generals are marching the men into ambush. Near the end, recalling his shameful treatment of the tattered man, he can only utter "a cry of sharp irritation and agony" followed by a covering "outburst of crimson oaths" (107). In the few instances when his tongue seems unloosed his speech is notably hollow, as when he finally expresses the thoughts that have been on his mind from the beginning and delivers "a long and intricate denunciation of the commander" (75). Such talk is foolish as well as dangerous, and he lapses back into his uneasy state of silence after being "pierced" by the "words" of a "sarcastic" voice (76). What we follow in *The Red Badge* is an account of incomplete development, an explanation, partly moral and partly circumstantial, of how a youth loses the capacity to express himself in speech. He grows up to be the kind of man who is chronically unable to speak his mind.

To say that Henry's development is incomplete is not, however, to say that he remains unchanged, as he does succeed in losing the callow daydreams, fantasies, and aspirations that are a product of his untested egotism. In some of the longer passages that were dropped from the manuscript, Henry's lofty philosophizing allows him to feel great disdain for those who do not see how nature tricks men into the risky pursuit of glory. Wandering alone away from his outfit, unable to endure the prospect of being turned into a "slang-phrase" at whom others "crowed and cackled," he sees himself alone on "the bitter pinnacle of his wisdom." He feels called to become the "prophet of a world-reconstruction." "Far down in the untouched depths of his being, among the hidden currents of his soul, he saw born a voice." This voice, grandiloquent and self-honoring, never finds an occasion to express itself in speech, for once Fleming is safely back with his regiment he begins to distance himself from his "foolish compositions." (The manuscript presents Henry as a bad writer—and thus an alternative version of the author—much more so than does the Appleton edition.) In the end he feels contempt for these "earlier gospels" and is glad to know he does not have to be a prophet: "he would no more stand upon places high and false, and denounce the distant planets." As one who has not only survived but who has shown himself capable of heroic deeds in battle, he feels "a large sympathy for the machinery of the universe." The universe is on his side after all, and it is this comforting conviction that introduces the quiet manhood paragraph.[9] He is somehow at one with the powers that be: this is the illusion on which his manhood is founded. He has grown up to the extent that he has renounced the megalomania of lonely and unhappy adolescence. But he is very far from the correspondent's wisdom at the end of "The Open Boat."

Because Wilson develops in such a different way from Henry, it is a serious mistake to take Henry's maturation as universal and inevitable. Some readers have made *The Red Badge* out to be a systemic account of war or struggle or language. In fact, it is close to being a traditional narrative of an individual's moral and social *bildung*.[10] One of its traditional elements is its use of significant contrasts that establish a context for judging the central character. The chapter in which Henry returns Wilson's packet of letters makes the key differences clear. This packet, like Wilson's original "melancholy oration" (one of the novel's countless references to forms of studied speech), constitutes a "small weapon" in Henry's hands. To use this weapon would be "to knock his friend on the head" (70–71). Henry imagines he is acting with magnanimous forbearance by saying nothing about the letters, but in actual fact he is humiliating his friend by extorting an embarrassing speech from him. In effect he has wounded Wilson on the head, so that "dark, prickling blood had flushed into his cheeks and brow." Wilson now has his own red badge, except that his shame is public in a way that Henry's will never be. Simultaneously, Henry quietly enjoys a daydream about "the stories of war" (73) he will tell his mother and the schoolgirl back home. The contrast is richly significant: while Wilson makes himself engage in a painful act of communication, Henry indulges a solitary fantasy about the self-flattering speeches he will make elsewhere. The scene brilliantly exposes the evasions of "quiet manhood."

It is surprising how many soldiers are wounded in the head in Crane's novel, and how often their head injuries are linked to the capacity for speech. When the babbling man is grazed on the head by a bullet, he responds by saying, "Oh" (28). Another man has his jaw supports shot away, "disclosing in the wide cavern of his mouth, a pulsing mass of blood and teeth. And, with it all, he made attempts to cry out. In his endeavor there was a dreadful earnestness as if he conceived that one great shriek would make him well" (100). The tattered man apparently gets his mortal wound after a friend, Tom Jamison, blurts out that his head is bleeding. Another man in the tattered man's regiment dies after being shot "plum in the head":

> Everybody yelled out t' 'im: 'Hurt, John? Are yeh hurt much?' 'No,' ses he. He looked kinder surprised an' he went on tellin' 'em how he felt. He sed he didn't feel nothin'. But, by dad, th' first thing that feller knowed he was dead. . . . So, yeh wanta watch out. Yeh might have *some queer kind 'a hurt yerself.* (47; italics mine)

Finally there is the cheery-voiced man's comrade, Jack, who answers a stranger's question at the wrong time:

> "Say, where's th' road t' th' river?" An' Jack, he never paid no attention an' th' feller kept on a-peckin' at his elbow an' sayin': "Say, where's th' road t' th' river?" Jack was a-lookin' ahead all th' time tryin' t' see th' Johnnies comin' through th' woods an' he never paid no attention t' this big fat feller fer a long time but at last he turned 'round an' he ses: "Ah, go t' hell an' find th' road t' th' river." An' jest then a shot slapped him bang on th' side th' head. (61)

In all these accounts there is an association between a terrible head wound and the articulation of thought through speech. Whether to speak up and what to say are extremely delicate questions in combat. How you resolve them may well determine whether you emerge dead or alive.

Henry himself is struck and injured on the crown of his head while confusedly attempting to declare himself, though whether he is trying "to make a rallying speech, to sing a battle-hymn," or simply to ask a question is not clear: " 'Why—Why—' stammered the youth struggling with his balking tongue." What counts is that he gets his wound while struggling unsuccessfully to express his thoughts, and, strangely, from then on his red badge marks a permanent incapacity to speak the truth about his experience in war. The tattered man has it right: Henry has sustained "some queer kind 'a hurt" in his ability to communicate through speech. *The Red Badge* is the circumstantial account of an odd injury to the central character's capacity to utter moral truth about himself.

Because we cannot know exactly what goes on in the minds of the other soldiers, it is difficult to say whether they share Henry's systematic untruth. (The question is similar to the one that bothers Henry in Chapter 1.) But there are certain features of the narrative that invite us to see him as representative of a large class of men, though not of all men. He is identified as "the youth," first of all, and the deceptive silence that characterizes him at the end seems to be the new order of the day. Significantly, the final instances of direct discourse in the novel are all rude put-downs intended to reduce others to silence:

> "Oh, shet yer mouth."
> "You make me sick."
> "G'home, yeh fool." (107–8)

The Appleton edition kept only the first of these, the command to shut one's mouth. This and the two following commands, and also the immediately preceding speeches, all by unnamed members of the regiment, are placed within the frame of Henry's agonized reflections on his abandonment of the tattered man. Evidently, the other men also feel it is best not to engage in public postmortems. Indirectly, they are telling Henry to keep his shame to himself. Confession would be sickening. The way to be a man among men is to refrain from telling what you have done or how you feel about it.

Wilson is the significant exception. The concluding exchanges between him and Henry imply that Wilson has become an outsider by virtue of his newly developed ability to talk. Like Crane's own father (whose profession was defined by formalized talk, that is, the sermon), Wilson is now "a dog-hanged parson" (77). One particular exchange establishes the final positions of the two young men relative to speech. "Well, Henry, I guess this is good-bye-John," says Wilson, and Henry answers, "Oh, shet up, yeh damn' fool" (91). Wilson's speech is not notably mawkish or embarrassing. Indeed, his use of a humorous colloquialism serves to keep his sentiment at a safe enough distance. Even so, Henry orders him to cease speaking, in this way expressing his solidarity with the final sentiment of the other men: whatever it is you have to say, keep it to yourself.

One of the most horrifying moments in the novel occurs when Jimmie Rogers, mortally wounded, is noticed by his fellows:

> When their eyes first encountered him there was a sudden halt as if they feared to go near. He was thrashing about in the grass, twisting his shuddering body into many strange postures. He was screaming loudly. This instant's hesitation seemed to fill him with a tremendous, fantastic contempt and he damned them in shrieked sentences. (81–82)

A very minor character, Jimmie is forgotten as the battle continues. In the final chapter, however, in a passage excised from the Appleton edition, Wilson remembers him:

> [H]e suddenly gestured and said: "Good Lord!"
>
> "What?" asked the youth.
>
> "Good Lord!" repeated his friend. "Yeh know Jimmie Rogers? Well, he—gosh, when he was hurt I started t' git some water fer'im an', thunder, I aint seen'im from that time 'til this. I clean forgot what I—say, has anybody seen Jimmie Rogers?"
>
> "Seen'im? No! He's dead," they told him.
>
> His friend swore. (106)

Before being deleted, this passage served to interrupt a sequence in which Henry reflects on his performance and seeks to overcome his sense of private shame. Just before the passage Henry struggles "to marshall" (106) his acts and make them "march" (106) in front of him. There follows the transition to Wilson's act of recollection: "His friend, too, seemed engaged with some retrospection" (106). Then, immediately after the Jimmie Rogers passage, our attention is called to the contrast between Wilson's act of memory and the triumphal procession that Henry is privately staging for his own benefit: "But the youth, regarding his procession of memory, felt gleeful and unregretting, for, in it, his public deeds were paraded in great and shining prominence," (106) figuratively marching "in wide purple and gold" (106) and culminating in a glorious "coronation" (106). There is an obvious contrast between Wilson's public act of recollection and the private march of triumph Henry indulges in.

Curiously, the difference between Wilson's and Henry's ways of recalling scenes of battle matches the difference between the manuscript and the Appleton edition. In suppressing the imagery of the triumphant procession along with Wilson's recollection of Jimmie Rogers (and in combination with other deletions), the latter version largely prevents us from getting a purchase on Henry's self-deceptions. Indeed, Crane even added a final sentence that closely parallels the self-flattering coronation: "Over the river a golden ray of sun came through the hosts of leaden rain clouds." In replacing the private and ironic coronation with an external and quasi divine endorsement of Henry's new faith and confidence, Crane in effect rewrote the ending *as Henry might have written it.* The private self-solacing deception in the manuscript becomes objective reality in the version of the novel that all readers regarded as authoritative until 1982, when Binder's edition first became available.

It is not necessary to explain such major alterations in the text and meaning of the novel by blaming them on Crane's editor or publisher.[11] The fact that the altered sense of the last chapter is so closely entangled with the questions at issue in the book suggests that Crane himself may well have been responsible. Belonging to a band of men was no less vital for him than was the need to go off on one's own, whether in a social or philosophical sense. *The Red Badge* emerged from a battle waged within himself, and the battle was still being fought as he moved from the manuscript to the version finally brought out by Appleton.

The instability in Crane is epitomized by a curious opposition between the way *The Red Badge* (both editions in this case) and "The Open Boat" treat the sort of scene in which a man becomes the butt of others' derisive laughter. In Henry's eyes, the worst social injury a man can sustain is to be turned into a "slang-phrase" by another man uttering "a humorous remark in a low tone" (54) to a group of men. After alternating between an incommunicable anxiety about his proven treachery and a sense of satisfaction at his public image, Henry joins the group whose identifying speech-act is the silencing jeer directed at the outsider. Wilson, however, seems to be well on his way to becoming the butt of someone's "Ah, there, Willie." We have very different feelings for the man who painfully acquires a decent kind of honesty in *The Red Badge* and for the loose signaler of "The Open Boat."

Yet, as the similarity in their names suggest, it would not be completely absurd to see them as the same man. But if they are the same man, then Crane himself must have been two very different men.

Notes

1. The quotation comes from the end of Chapter 10 of Henry Binder's edition (New York: Norton, 1982). Based on the manuscript, this edition gives considerably more attention to the pessimistic philosophy Henry Fleming indulges in while isolated from his regiment. The passages, later excised, in which he mentally labors on his new "gospels" originally constituted the conclusions of Chapters 10 and 15 (Chapter 14 in the Appleton edition), a long section in the middle of Chapter 16 (Chapter 15), and all of Chapter 12. These segments are repetitious and overwritten and are narrated with heavy sarcasm, and it is understandable that they would have been dropped. Unfortunately, they are necessary in order to make sense of certain key passages in the concluding chapter, as Hershel Parker was the first to notice. For that reason alone, my text is the one first assembled by Binder. The virtue of this text is that it gives us an idea of what the author originally had in mind in composing the novel. But there will never be an adequate final text.

   Space and time forbid any consideration of the third version of the novel, the abridgement published by a newspaper syndicate, which emphasized action over reflection and concluded with the successful capture of the rebel colors.
2. See Henry Binder, "*The Red Badge of Courage* Nobody Knows," in Stephen Crane, *The Red Badge of Courage,* ed. Henry Binder (New York: Avon, 1987), 150.
3. See Donald Pizer, " '*The Red Badge of Courage* Nobody Knows': A Brief Rejoinder," *Studies in the Novel* 11 (Spring 1979): 77–81, and "*The Red Badge of Courage:* Text, Theme, and Form," *South Atlantic Quarterly* 84 (Summer 1985): 302–13.
4. "Stephen Crane's Own Story," in *Prose and Poetry* (New York: Library of America, 1984), 875–84.
5. Stephen Crane, *Prose and Poetry* (New York: Library of America, 1984), 897.
6. James Thurber, "The Secret Life of James Thurber," *New Yorker* 19 (27 February 1943): 15–17.
7. Of those who have considered the representation of speech in the novel, W. M. Frohock, "*The Red Badge* and the Limits of Parody,"

Southern Review 6 (1970): 137–48, comments on Crane's use of free indirect discourse and Fleming's "bucolic" speech. Robert L. Hough, "Crane's Henry Fleming: Speech and Vision," *Forum* (Houston) 3 (1962): 41–42, shows that the inconsistencies in Crane's reproduction of Fleming's colloquial speech testify to Crane's lack of interest in the accurate recording of actual talk. I wish to thank Donald Pizer for calling these articles to my attention and for providing the impetus to pay closer attention to Crane.

8. See Amy Kaplan's treatment of the inadequacy of storytelling in "The Spectacle of War in Crane's Revision of History," *New Essays on the Red Badge of Courage*, ed. Lee Clark Mitchell (Cambridge: Cambridge University Press, 1986), 91–94.
9. Hershel Parker first pointed out that the deletion of the two paragraphs preceding the sentence, "With this conviction came a store of assurance," removes the referent of "this conviction."
10. For a recent example, see Christine Brooke-Rose's deconstructive reading, which maintains that "*The hero/the monster, running to/running from, separation/membership,* and *spectator/spectacle* . . . are intertwined with each other and caught up in the opposition that subsumes them-that of *courage/cowardice*" ("Ill Logics of Irony," in *New Essays on The Red Badge of Courage,* ed. Lee Clark Mitchell [Cambridge: Cambridge University Press, 1986], 129). This essay relies on Paul de Man's claim that "a narrative endlessly tells the story of its own denominational aberration" (141). Brooke-Rose's dependence on a thinker known to have concealed his Nazi collaborationism in order to construct her argument that Fleming's cowardice and savagery are exemplary for all men ravages her claim that the distinction between cowardice and courage may be safely collapsed.
11. In any case this argument has not held up to critical scrutiny. See James Colvert, "Crane, Hitchcock, and the Binder Edition of *The Red Badge of Courage,*" in *Critical Essays on Stephen Crane's Red Badge of Courage* (Boston: G. K. Hall, 1990), 238–63.

9

The Ambiguous Outlaw: John Rechy and Complicitous Homotextuality

Rafael Pérez-Torres

The Sexual Outlaw: A Documentary represents John Rechy's most overtly political novel. Although this is not a terribly interesting fact in and of itself, the text (first published in 1977) does represent for gay liberation an early and aggressive assertion of the lessons learned from the women's movement: the personal is political. Asserting this view, the book simultaneously complicates it by revealing the potentially contradictory politics of personal liberation.

The novel concerns itself with the actions of a socially marginal but sexually liberated figure as he moves through the decaying urban landscape of our postindustrial age. The protagonist—a semicomposite, semiautobiographical character named Jim—engages in a weekend "sex hunt" in and around the environs of a pre-AIDS Los Angeles sometime around the mid-1970s. Jim stands as a pastless and sexually tireless everyman who forms the moral and ethical center of the novel. He represents the image of male sexuality common to almost all of Rechy's other novels: the hustling homosexual whose actions not only address his own sexual desire, but represent a challenge to the rigid oppression of heterosexual society. Restlessly wandering the peripheries of society, the male hustler becomes for Rechy a sexual shock troop meant to disrupt and sabotage the heterosexual world. The male hustler forms a disruptive and liberating force against the repressive and rigid social order, against its narrowly defined heterosexual identity, against the social complacency and passivity that this identity engenders. His promiscuity challenges the unexamined pieties and platitudes of the repressive heterosocial world.[1]

The Sexual Outlaw thus offers a topology of homosexual masculinity, one that ostensibly maps practices of liberation and self-empowerment for a new, postrepressive age. The narrative posits an image of the homosexual hustler as a matrix of social disruption, agent and agitator for a "minority" cause, model of sexual animal *cum* revolutionary hero.

Rechy's representation of male identity as sexual outlaw emerges out of the contradictions rife within heterosocial order. The actions of the hustler—ostensibly liberating sexual practices comprised of public, anonymous sex antithetical to monogamy—position the outlaw in a tentative and limited relationship to the rest of society. The anonymity with which he performs his acts of sexual rebellion, the deserted urban terrain he claims as his own geography, serve to reinscribe the marginalization of the sexual outlaw. This marginalization is manifested most clearly by the silent codes which the hustler uses to communicate. Indeed, were it not for Rechy's text, the world it describes would remain a demimonde beyond the horizon of heterosocial vision.

More significantly, the novel reveals how the hustler can never fully reject society's repressions, contradictions, and hypocrisies. Beyond the reassertion of the homosexual as marginal, the sexual outlaw in Rechy's work embodies many of the contradictions and failures that characterize heterosociety. Conflicting modes of sociosexual organization—liberated revolutionary, entrapped sexual invert—come within the text to comprise the protagonist's identity. The homosexual hustler is constituted by the very repressive and delimiting social practices against which his own acts of erotic liberation battle. Homosexual and heterosexual practices meet in the outlaw to form an irresolvable tension. The tension becomes particularly tangible at those points where the narrative shows the hustler's sexual choreography to mirror the straight world's preoccupation with dominance and submission. Jim is compelled to power, selling his alluring body. Proving his worth by demanding money for sex, he places himself within both erotic and capital economies based in heterosocial order.

In textualizing the sexual outlaw, *The Sexual Outlaw* comes to embody numerous tensions that disrupt the semantic and semiotic order of the text. The novel valorizes a field of sexual play that seeks to trigger a form of revolt and liberation. The physical elements of this sexual play—symbolically charged clothing, actions, signals, looks—form the "silent" language of an erotic discourse that, textualized in Rechy's novel, seeks to overthrow the repressive discourses of identity imposed by heterosocial order. The "voicing" of a "silent" discourse marks one level of tension at work in *The Sexual Outlaw.* A second tension emerges at the discursive level where the homoerotic within Rechy's text, by inverting notions of heterosocial identity, unwittingly submits to them as well. Rechy's narrative seeks to construct a resistant discourse of homosexual liberation, to create, if you will, a heroic homotextuality. This homotextuality reveals the contradictions inherent both in the heterosocial world against which it speaks and in the homorevolutionary activity it champions. However, a fruitful analysis of this text cannot simply lay bare the novel's ideological enslavement to heterosocial order. While its homotextuality reinscribes elements of heterosocial order, the novel simultaneously disrupts narrative order by placing irresolvable contradictions in play. By evoking the binary structure that bolsters heterosocial order, *The Sexual Outlaw* not only inverts that binary structure but—by revealing its contradictions, contributes to its destruction.

I. The Split Narrative

The breakdown of binaries begins with the bifurcated structure of the novel. *The Sexual Outlaw* oscillates between neatly separated passages of realistic description and essayistic meditations. The descriptive passages offer in (porno)graphic detail an account of the novel's "outlaw" world. Their position as social outsider allows homosexual hustlers a critical perspective on the repressive and conformist practices of heterosocial order. Homosexuality, as defined by this order, is stigmatized, persecuted, labelled a "deviate practice." Against these negative constructions of homosexuality, the descriptive narrative represents the revolutionary function of the sexual outlaw.

The subtitle of the book, a documentary, underscores the function of the narrative as critical exposé. The work explores the sexual activities of a marginal group whose actions question and undermine heterosocial practices, practices that repressively define sexual identity in the service of social organization.[2] Sexual outlaws disrupt and destroy the operations of the heterosocial world by questioning the monological bases of its order: monogamy, reproduction, duality, stability, closure. The incessant repetition of almost identical sexual encounters detailed by these descriptive passages suggests the potentially endless lack of closure inherent in the hustler's movement from one sexual partner to another.

These (porno)graphic passages alternate with meditative "essays" that form the other half of the novel's bifurcated structure. These essays range through time and place and incorporate many different narrative forms and diverse public discourses. Part interview, part public speech, part movie montage, part meditation on gay culture, part reminiscence, these sections are mediated through and unified by an authorial voice. This voice draws together the various heterosocial voices that comment on and react to homosexuality: newspaper clippings about police harassment of gays, reports by religious and psychiatric organizations on homosexuality as evidence of moral or psychic transgression, real and imaginary audience reaction to the narrator's speeches about the gay world. These sections articulate a number of social attitudes toward homosexuality. The social discourses, then, serve as a multivocalic commentary on the outlaw's liberating practice of endless desire described in the erotic section. Rechy notes in the introduction that he, indeed, wrote the descriptive passages first, later inserting the essays at points he had marked in the manuscript. The descriptive sections serve as the erotic "center" that the "marginal" meditative passages and their evocation of social discourses critique and amplify.

One process of inversion emerges as the novel reverses sociocultural reality. Homotextuality—the discourse of homosexual liberation—is inscribed as the center of the narrative structure. The historical "center"—heterosocial order evoked by the meditative sections—becomes the novelistic "margin" whereas the homosexual Other forms the narrative core of *The Sexual Outlaw.* Thus two asymmetrical regions come to define the novel: a unitary, closed, "silent" homosexual discourse sliced through by a multiplicitous, open, "voiced" social discourse.

M. M. Bakhtin's (1981) formalist model of novelistic discourse is illustrative here. He argues that a "unitary language" (monoglossia) is a system of linguistic norms that struggles to overcome the multiplicity of meaning (heteroglossia) linguistic utterances evoke. This monoglossic system is "conceived as ideologically saturated, language as a world view, even as a concrete opinion, insuring a *maximum* of mutual understanding in all spheres of ideological life" (271). The erotic passages in Rechy's narrative are written both as a documentary description of a particular sexual world and as an "ideologically saturated" world view that informs the novel's polemic. The meditative passages, by contrast, incorporate voices questioning both the revolutionary potential of the sexual outlaw as well as the society seeking to persecute him.[3]

The unitary erotic relies on the multiplicitous heterosocial in order to find a "public" voice. Without the meditative and reflective social narrative, the erotic discourse of the male hustler would remain enclosed within a descriptive but isolated narrative. One unfamiliar with the critical and rebellious intent of the sexual outlaw—indeed, one would suspect, the majority of Rechy's reading audience—would remain wholly "outside" the narrative able to perceive only repetitive and (porno)graphic descriptions of homosexual intercourse. The rebellious note would remain unheard by those uninitiated in the hustlers' "silent" language—the elaborate choreography of clothes and signals and movements carefully detailed in the descriptive passages. The presence of the social narrative within the novel as commentary on and explanation of the erotic narrative positions both the homorevolutionary and the heterosocial arenas in a mutually reliant discursive relationship.

The narrative structure thus evokes the compromised position of the sexual outlaw as standing both within and without various social orders. The narrator, by contrast, wants to position the hustler fully outside the systems of heterosocial control. His is a tenuous, doubly marginalized position: "Existing on the fringes of the gay world, male hustlers have always been dual outsiders, outlaws from the main society, and outcasts within the main gay world of hostile non-payers and non-sellers. Desired abundantly, and envied, they are nonetheless the least cared about."[4] This position of double marginality affords the narrative of *The Sexual Outlaw* a unique and powerful critical position. In order for this position of power to be made manifest, however, the silent and hidden erotic discourse must be made public through the multivocalic narrative. Hence, whereas a strict structural separation exists between the public voices of the essays and the erotic discourse of the descriptive passages, each simultaneously reflects upon and filters the contents of the other through its own lens. The revolutionary and the repressive within *The Sexual Outlaw* become not merely inversions, negative evocations of the other. They are fully reliant and dynamic players in the homotextuality of the novel, the articulation of a male homosexual revolutionary identity.

The sense of slippage exemplified by a homorevolutionary identity attempting to stand fully outside a heterosocial order comes to the fore as the narrative emphasizes its use of realist techniques. The erotic passages evoke a literary realism, an attempt to represent a specific reality as it is lived. Rechy notes in his 1984 preface to the book that he conceived of his work as a "prose documentary." The attempt at *cinema verité* is evident in the stark ("black-and-white" Rechy calls it) imagery used to describe the sex-hunt undertaken by Jim. Rechy explains that in these sections he "wanted to create characters, including the protagonist, who might be defined 'fully'—by *inference*—only through their sexual journeys" (16). These sections of the novel describe a movement through a sexual "underworld" marked by its repetitious cycle of desire, pursuit, contact, fulfillment, and renewed desire.

The episodic quality of these descriptions stands for narrative development. "Although there is a protagonist whom the book follows intimately, minute by recorded minute for a full weekend, there is no strict plot," remarks Rechy (16). A rigidly structured sequence of erotic description replaces a sense of narrative development based upon the dynamic growth and change of the protagonist. With the exception of a few flashbacks (passages unambiguously marked "FLASHBACK" in the text), the sex scenes in the novel form a strictly chronological sequence. The passage of time marked rigorously throughout these portions of the narrative inform the reader if a particular action occurs at 6:22 P.M. or 3:07 A.M. Time becomes the principal mode of organization and lends a controlling structure to the otherwise repetitive present-tense descriptions of sodomy, fellatio, and mutual masturbation. As one scene follows another, the narrative enforces a strict temporal order. It does not, however, truly evoke a realist narrative.

The sexual descriptions, realistic as they may seem, do not move simply toward documentary expression. They form a discourse marked by unresolved desires, allowing the reader to trace strata of contradictions and conflicts. Rechy's narrative as an account in the late 1970s of a post-sexual revolution, post-gay liberation, postmodern, post-1960s social world helps locate the complexities involved in social change and political revolution. One formal constellation of this complexity—and the point at which the realist aesthetic of the novel slips into a hyperrealism—develops at the level of character psychology.

As Rechy explains in his introduction, the characters that people Jim's rebellious sexual journey are fully defined by that journey. The bourgeois individual disappears, and the male hustler stands as a figure fully traversed by social discourses—the historical, social, and moral strictures used by heterosocial order to define the individual and against which the hustler stands. While he revels in the sexual urgency of his actions, the identity of the hustler is based on the delimiting social and historical orders he resists. His is a libidinal utopia found at the margins but also, dialectically, composed of the central discursive trajectories of society's order. He stands at a point where not just the sense of the inside and the outside of individual identity blur, but where the limits of political and sexual constituencies disappear. The hustler within an ostensibly realist narrative becomes a figure fully comprised of language. The novel thus does not sustain the illusion of a realistic discourse. Fully defined by his sexual journey, the hustler represents not a rounded individual but a hyperreal figure where the contradictions of the social world come to the fore.

The gay cruising world becomes a mirror of heterosexual norms. Jim hustles for money by playing the ultra—masculine street-tough: "He's wearing Levi's and cowboy boots, no shirt. Sunglasses" (38). Making sexual connections for money, "he will most often pretend to be 'straight'—uncomfortably rationalizing the subterfuge by reminding himself that those attracted to him will usually—though certainly not always—want him to be that, like the others of his breed"(39). As top man, Jim assumes the role of the quintessential heterosexual male, appropriating the image and exaggerating it as if in a funhouse mirror. Often bodybuilders (like the narrator, the author, and the fictional Jim) and male hustlers assume both the physique and the costume—Levi's, boots, sleeveless shirts—of macho masculinity. The hustler appropriates and reflects back to masculine society a version of its own (ideal) sexual self-image.

The ultra-feminine transvestites and transsexuals represent the binary opposite to the ultra-masculine male-hustlers: "At Highland and Hollywood, the queens, awesome, defiant Amazons, are assuming their stations. The white queens are bleached and pale, the black ones shiny and purple. Extravagant in short skirts, bouffant hairdos, luminous unreal mouths and eyes. The transsexuals are haughty in their new credentials" (39). Both the queens and the hustlers assume exaggerated versions of the sexual roles circumscribed by heterosocial order. The contradictions of the gay street world are magnifications of the contradictions running through this order. A problem with the straight world, the narrative argues, is that it denies a dialectic between the masculine and feminine principles of human identity. This denial forms one basis for the split in the outlaw world Rechy's novel serves to describe.

The meditative sections of the novel criticize writers who ceaselessly flaunt their masculinity, calling them "screaming heterosexuals" and "male impersonators." The narrative seeks to redress and subvert the sense of *machismo* and homophobia found in the works of Ernest Hemingway, the "hairy godfather of heterosexual writers," and the sexual anxiety and violence invoked by the

"Tarzan-howling" Norman Mailer (195). The narrator suggests that the writers who have created the most fulfilling work—Shakespeare, Joyce, Lawrence, Proust, Genet, Burroughs—are those artists who most fully accept and integrate the "female grace" and the "male strength" of their psyches. Which is to say that the narrator values those writers who seem to challenge most successfully the binary construction of "feminine" and "masculine."

One would be terribly hard pressed, however, to find some "female grace" evident in either the graphic descriptions of the erotic narrative or the outraged authorial voice of the social narrative. Instead, the novel celebrates the power the hustler exerts over his small domain: "There is a terrific, terrible excitement in getting paid by another man for sex. A great psychological release, a feeling that this is where real sexual power lies—not only to be desired by one's own sex but to be paid for being desired, and if one chooses that strict role, not to reciprocate in those encounters, a feeling of emotional detachment as freedom—these are some of the lures . . ." (153). The narrative valorizes an image of traditional heterosexual masculinity and attitudes toward sex that involve control, detachment, freedom.

This power, ironically, often leads Jim into a position of impotence. Though excited, he will not reciprocate a sexual act unless his partner is extremely handsome. Neither will he ever initiate a sexual act: "Two beautiful male bodies lie side by side naked. . . . Used to being pursued, each waits for the other to advance first. . . . Looking away from each other, both dress hurriedly, each cut deeply by regret they did not connect" (65); "Jim wants the man to blow him first, and the man wants Jim to do it first. They separate quickly" (265). Jim's quest for power traps him in impotence, just as his domination over sexual partners leads him to a reliance upon another partner in order to affirm his power. He must be pursued as an object of desire. Repeatedly, the narrative makes evident the conflicted position of the sexual outlaw who, attempting to escape the repression and boundaries of the heterosocial world, runs again and again straight into its contradictions.

Although the narrative attempts to position the male hustler as a doubly marginal figure, it reveals him to stand both within and without heterosocial systems. His inversion of heterosexual roles is at once subversive and critical as well as imitative and conformist. The revolutionary intent of both the novel and its protagonist becomes defused as the hustler is shown to assume a reactive and thus dependent position to the center.

The interplay between silence and voice underscores this sense of dependence. The language of the hustling world—"spoken" through posture, costume, and look—represents a form of "silent" language. After his early encounters by the pier, on the beach, in the restroom, Jim realizes he has "spoken not a word to anyone today. Not one" (34). Most of the communication described in the narrative occurs through the use of gesture ("from behind blue-tinted sunglasses, he surveys those gathered here, intercepts looks—but he moves along the sand toward the ocean," 23), through sexual position ("swiftly turning his body around, torso bending forward, back to Jim, the naked youngman parts his own buttocks," 26), or through clothing ("men lie singly in that parabola of sand—the more committed in brief bikinis, or almost naked—genitals sheltered only by bunched trunks," 23). The silence, along with its suggestion of near religious commitment and sacrifice—a vow of silence—stands in contradistinction to the form the novel assumes as a publicly "voiced" disclosure of the "silent" homorevolutionary world.

The silence essential to Rechy's homosexual discourse stands in contrast to and is only made manifest by the public voices of the socially discursive sections. Which is to say, the (silent) homosexual discourse only exists in Rechy's narrative when made present by the (voiced) public language of various other discourses—a novelistic discourse, a documentary discourse, a journalistic discourse, a media discourse. The form the novel takes betrays its vision of homosexuality as a singular and impenetrable margin. The bifurcated narrative articulates a homosexual/political practice dependent upon the very social strictures against and apart from which the novel's sense of a (true) homorevolutionary identity seeks to exist.

II. Marginal Masculine Identity

The Sexual Outlaw does not just represent a story of failed rebellion. Rather, the text betrays an incessant doubling whereby the discourses of liberation and repression are ever revealing the duplicity of the other. In his studied macho posturing, in his overt strategizing for domination and power, Jim plays out a heightened image of male heterosocial dominance. Simultaneously, the narrative finds in the male hustling arena a passive-aggressive role traditionally ascribed to women within male-dominated society. Working-out incessantly in order to be desirable, passively attracting the attention of others, Jim stands as the physical manifestation of idealized manliness. He behaves, however, by a code associated with a most prim and passive form of female behavior. He must always be the object of the chase. He must never initiate contact with another man. He must always allow the other to call his attention first: "Jim sees an obvious bodybuilder. The attraction and the competition are instantly stirred. Jim is prepared to ignore the other. But the other pauses. Jim looks back. With a nod, the other invites Jim into his cubicle" (265). Jim positions himself as the center of attention, an object of worship, the focus of desire.

Pushed by the pressures of heterosocial order to remain marginal, the hustlers lay claim to abandoned public spaces as their geosexual terrain. The discourses of the heterosocial mark this rebellious claim to geographical space as much as it marks the construction of the homorevolutionary self. The sexual outlaw plays within a field bounded by the unmerciful laws behind a form of social darwinism. The struggle to survive in the heterosocial arena is carried over into the homoerotic realm of supposed liberation. Those who are old or ugly do not survive in the game of the sex hunt: "In the shadows an unattractive man is jerking off; everyone walks by, ignoring him" (75); "an unattractive loose-fleshed old man lies there naked, his hand on his spent groin. Abandoned and desperate and alone—one of the many lingering, ubiquitous, wasted, judging ghosts in the gay world. Jim avoids him" (114); "beyond the cave of the tunnel he passes a forlorn old man, waiting, alone, ignored, wasted; waiting for anybody" (203).

These lonely images stand at the fringe of the outlaw arena, denied the right to play the hunt due to their advanced age and degenerating physical appearance. The irony of Rechy's use of the term "gay world" becomes uncomfortably apparent.

The narrative thus explores the problems engendered by a practice of complicitous rebellion, one simultaneously revolutionary and restrictive. The narrative voice speaks of a sexual revolution embodied by the spirit and actions of the sexual outlaws:

> What kind of revolution is it that ends when one *looks* old, at least for most? What kind of revolution is it in which some of the revolutionaries must look beautiful? What kind of revolution is it in which the revolutionaries slaughter each other, in the sexual arenas and in the ritual of S & M?
>
> We're fighting on two fronts—one on the streets, the other inside. (285–86)

The "outside" street fight of the sexual guerrillas, amid the broken buildings of the urban wasteland and the open terrain of beach and park, stands at the point where the repressive propriety of heterosocial order proves impotent. The hustling choreography continues despite repeated repressive measures taken by the police and other state authorities. The "inside" fight, the moral imperative to overcome personal prejudice and self-hatred, occurs within a discussion of homosexual identity. The narrative suggests that an idealized vision of youth and beauty informs and infuses notions of identity and desirability. Other outlaws reject individuals unfortunate enough to be old or unappealing, and this in turn can lead to a terrible self-hatred:

> Jim faces a drunkenly swaying youngman. Not particularly attractive, the type he would not reciprocate with. Depression crowds the youngman's thin face. Jim doesn't recognize him even vaguely. . . . "You make yourself available," the drunken voice goes on tearing at the silence of the paused choreography. The shadows do not move, the spell locked. "You walk around showing off your body. You didn't even touch me, just wanted me to lick *your* body. Well, I have a body too!" (283)

The confrontation violates the hustler choreography, disturbs the "stirless dark silence," and assaults the "rigid silence" of the hunt. The moment allows the text to examine the cost of the hustler's identity: "In an unwelcome moment the ugly carnage of the sexhunt gapes at Jim—his part in it" (284). The sex hunt exacts a demanding toll, and the narrative suggests that the erotic discourse of liberation to which the sexual outlaw lays claim carries with it a repressive charge as well. The contradictions of his simultaneously revolutionary and repressive intent inextricably bind the identity of the sex hunter and the resistant intent of the novel. *The Sexual Outlaw* functions as a complicitous critique. It examines the repressive function of heterosocial order and signals the inextricable connection between that order and the homorevolutionary outlaw. In addition, it scrutinizes those repressive practices that to some degree are independent of heterosocial order. The emancipatory outlaw function described by the narrative—the homotextuality—reveals the homosexual hustler occupying a complex marginal space, one simultaneously reliant upon and resistant to central discourses of sexual identity, one implicated in a dual movement of liberation and self-repression.

Rechy's novel thus raises the specter of a complicated and compromised resistant identity. The narrative's bifurcated structure and construction of interpenetrating heterosexual and homosexual social practices mark the contradictions the text finds inscribed in the protagonist's identity. Moreover, the text suggests that repressive practices in the gay world are at moments more than manifestations of a contradictory heterosocial order. The novel thus allows one to move away from the scrutiny of textual form and individual identity toward the exploration of a complex and resistant group identity marked by a sense of conflict and capitulation, resistance and repression.

The sections of social commentary throughout the text—the "public" half of the split narrative—indicate that North American gays in the late 1970s have come to assume a "minority" consciousness. Group identity, predicated upon notions of solidarity as a stand against the oppressive attitude of the majority society, can bolster self-esteem and self-identity while simultaneously silencing critical voices. As the narrator notes: "For a gay person to criticize any aspect of the gay world is to expose himself to howls of wrath and betrayal" (246). Yet a process of critique, of a "deterritorialization" of social order, characterizes Rechy's vision of an outlaw world. The narrative thus offers insight into what one critical construction of a marginal masculine identity may look like.

Gilles Deleuze and Félix Guattari discuss deterritorialization and reterritorialization as connected processes of group consciousness. To "territorialize" is to stratify, organize, signify, attribute—to fix identity. Against this, "deterritorializations" signify those points that traverse a fixed identity. This can only be met with a move toward reterritorialization, the configuration of a new order. The critical work of these French critics suggests an endless interrelation between liberating and oppressive movements. Even if identity is questioned and social stratification dissolved, "there is still a danger that you will re-encounter organizations that restratify everything, formations that restore power to a signifier, attributions that reconstitute a subject."[5] *The Sexual Outlaw* thus serves to document how the deterritorializing activity of public homosexuality ruptures society's territorializations of sexual identity, of criminality, of sin. Even within this experience of rupture, however, movements toward new stratifications emerge: the opposition of homosexuality to racial and ethnic identity, the primary valuation of beauty and youth, the retreat into the closet from which a safe and pragmatic homosexuality can be practiced.

The revolutionary impulse of the sexual outlaw leads toward a "reterritorialization" of identity: stratified, ossified, segmented. Rechy's work explores the tension between the revolutionary impulse of its male subject and the internal and external forces that seek to contain any sense of rupture. The erotic sections are episodic and repetitious, presented as "lines of flight" away from the strictures of correctness articulated by the social discourse of the novel. Simultaneously, an irreducible tension emerges between the sense of flight and liberation suggested by the erotic discourse and the isolation and stratification its form implies: only sexuality informs these erotic sections and every other object—food and clothes and all physical movement—becomes subordinated to its drive.

The erotic discourse deterritorializes the well-defined moral and legal segments invoked in the social discourses of the novel.

This discourse also reterritorializes the significance of eroticism—sexual outlawry is and must *always* be disruptive. The narrative offers no image of the "perverse" in the sense Barthes (1985) speaks of perversion as "the search for a pleasure that is not made profitable by a social end, a benefit to the species. . . . It's on the order of bliss that exerts itself for nothing. The theme of expenditure" (232). Jim's eroticism is all-consuming, charging his clothes, food, and gesture with an eroticism itself equivalent with social rupture—a revolutionary and liberating benefit "to the species." Rechy's text thus foregrounds the theme of (capital) exchange rather than (perverse) expenditure.

The erotic discourse, in consuming and so assigning significance, silences all that is not of use to the aleatory movement of sexual outlawry. Thus Jim's ethnic background becomes subordinated to his homosexual identity:

> Jim—he calls himself that sometimes, sometimes Jerry, sometimes John—removes the bikini, lies boldly naked on the sand. Because of a mixture of Anglo and Latin bloods, his skin quickly converts the sun's rays into a tan; the tan turns his eyes bluer; long-lashed eyes which almost compromise the rugged good looks of his face, framed by dark hair. The sun licks the sweat from his body. (23)

The erotic narrative subordinates any sense of ethnic or racial identity to the erotic, the physical, the homosexual. Rechy, a Chicano, writes a narrative that makes hidden any connection to a nonsexual self. Indeed, the long lashes of his eyes "almost compromise" the protagonist's good looks. As constructed by the narrative, the racial self even threatens the sexual self.[6] In addition, the protagonist's own name—sometimes Jim, sometimes Jerry, sometimes John—has no significatory power against the segmented and wholly consuming identity of homosexual hunter.

Yet, for all this, the narrative evokes various strata of homosexual identity. Homosexual groups in the narrative function as sects with their own secret rites and rituals. In this vein, homosexuality is still tied to "the values and systems of interaction of the dominant sexuality. Its dependence upon heterosexual norms can be seen in its policy of secrecy, of concealment—due partly to the repression and partly to the sense of shame which still prevails in the 'respectable' circles."[7] The landscape Jim traverses in his journey is dotted with the glitter bars, the leather bars, the costume bars representing enclosed domains of concealed rituals of contact. Jim himself usually remains at the periphery of these bars, moving through the alleyways or parking lots outside. He attempts to be truly marginal, an outlaw/existentialist/romantic hero walking on the fringe of the already socially marginal. When Jim does enter these bars, he feels himself surrounded by churning bodies and bare torsos, a charade of ramrod poses that cause him to leave for the ostensibly liberating streets, beach fronts, and hiking trails—the open and more dangerous world of an indifferent rural/urban landscape.[8]

The social narrative examines a group who contest the grip of heterosocial power on their lives. They represent a militant homosexuality that demands its right to exist as a valid sexual, social, and moral entity. As a result, a sense of group identification begins to emerge through the text. The narrator speaks about the Hollywood Gay Parade: "There was plenty of dignity, and, embarrassing to admit—man—I felt the itchy sentiment that signals real pride. Here you are, and here they are, and here we are. I remember Ma Joad's proud speech of the Okies' eventual triumph in 'defeat.' We keep coming, she said, because we're the people" (179). This passage reveals the easy sentimentality and reliance upon cliché "hip" diction that often plague Rechy's writing. This passage compounds these problems by referring to the sentimental movie version of Steinbeck's already sentimental "proletarian" novel *The Grapes of Wrath*. Nevertheless, the passage reveals a strain of resistance manifesting itself as minority group identity. The homosexual forms a margin of opposition challenging the authority of heterosexual power. A movement away from gays having to explain themselves to the heterosexual world propels such resistance and becomes, according to Guattari, "a matter of heterosexuality's having to explain itself; the problem is displaced, the phallocratic power in general comes into question."[9] A resistant homosexual identity inverts a traditional relationship to heterosocial power. It ceases to explain its own existence and instead questions and critiques the centrality of the other's position.

Rechy's narrative, however, does not fully achieve the critical (and some might say facile) point of inversion Guattari's analysis champions. *The Sexual Outlaw* explores a homosexuality that is both reliant upon and resistant to the values and systems of the dominant society. It engages with a notion of the marginal quite distinct from the sense of pure otherness posited by Guattari. The narrative suggests that a reliance upon heterosocial norms leads to a false and destructive sense of identity while also indicating that a powerful belief in the fully resistant and militant quality of homosexual revolt can lead to a code that reterritorializes identity:

> Increasingly easy on campuses and within other enclosed groups to announce openly that one is gay. The shock is gone. . . . It is equally easy to say "gayisbeautiful—gayisproud." Almost one word, meaning obscured. But are homosexuals discovering their particular *and varied* beauty? From that of the transvestite to that of the bodybuilder? The young to the old? The effeminate to the masculine? The athletic to the intellectual? Gay must be allowed variations. It is gay fascism to decree that one *must* perform this sex act, and *must* allow that one, in order to be gay; it is gay fascism to deny *genuine* bisexuality, or to suspect all heterosexuals. (243)

The narrative calls for (but does not necessarily privilege) a genuine multiplicity of identity and sexuality. It thus explores the complicated and compromised position of a resistant homosexual minority, yet it leaves intact the sense of irresolvable contradiction it finds there. Ultimately, Rechy's text is useful less as a meditation on what homosexual "being" means than as an anticipation of how homosexual "becoming" can move beyond the binaries of heterosocial order.

III. Becoming Queer

Heterosocial order defines masculinity through a manifestation of physical and social strength. Physical prowess and politico-economic power are the marks of heterosexual machismo. In his outward appearance, the homosexual can represent an exaggerated image of male heterosocial power. Bulging muscles, cowboy boots, leather jackets, worn blue jeans as cultural icons evoke images of masculine heterosexual power. The male hustler assumes the physical role traditionally assigned to that faction most empowered by society and that most insists upon separating itself from homosexual behavior: the macho heterosexual male. One manifestation of becoming queer involves the ironic appropriation of those signs belonging to the powerful, turning those signs "queer" and resisting their circulation within heterosocial systems of exchange.[10] This appropriation does not imply the simple inversion of signifying systems, however. As Rechy's text all too clearly reveals, inversion only recreates a mirror image of asymmetrical power relations.

The Sexual Outlaw signals the inevitable repression when becoming queer is fixed (reterritorialized) as a form of homosexual being. The narrative problematizes the process of discursive appropriation as the protagonist assumes modes of being that fix trajectories of empowerment and disempowerment. In order to attain a degree of agency and control, Jim feels he must affirm his subjectivity by always being a passive object of desire as an assertion of his masculine allure. He moves through a point where, incorporating contradictory heterosocial sexual roles, those passive modes of behavior socially sanctioned for women cross with the dominant modes of behavior appropriate for men. Jim's identity incorporates the binaries of socially sanctified sexual identity, reveals their contradictions, but does not move beyond them. Homosexual being in the narrative is fixed, stuck, unable to reach out beyond the series of irreducible conflicts Jim employs to define himself. Bound by a code circumscribed by heterosocial norms, the homosexual in *The Sexual Outlaw* becomes a critical locus at which the contradictory trajectories of his dominant society converge. The novel thus posits a rebellious hero but offers us something less. In so doing, it presents an image of a compromised critique that the narrative seeks all to easily to resolve.

The narrative expresses an impossible desire for resolution and transcendence that only serves to re-entrench the contradictory position of the hustling outlaw. As the narrator explains, the "warring attempts to fuse heterosexual expectations with homosexual needs and realities create the contradictions in the gay world" (242). The homosexual world, Rechy's text implies, would be free of contradictions if freed of restraints. Or as the authorial voice articulates:

Release the heterosexual pressures on our world—convert the rage—and you release a creative energy to enrich two worlds. Pressurize the homosexual world further, and it may yet set your straight world on fire.

And when the sexual revolution is won—*if it is ever won*—what of the fighters of that war? Doesn't a won revolution end the life of the revolutionary? What of the sexual outlaw?

One will mourn his passing. (301)

The narrative points toward an apocalyptic completion of the outlaw function—toward the resolution of contradictions—as it looks forward to a social order liberated from the restraints imposed upon sexual behavior and, emblematically, upon all creative human endeavors. Such a resolution of mutual destruction posits a transcendent image of the revolutionary that the entire narrative has to this point found impossible.

Moreover, Rechy's narrative evokes a portrait of the male hustler premised on culturally inscribed discourses of rebellion, resistance, and revolution. This resistance can be viewed from a historical perspective as part of a larger movement of civil disobedience integrally related to the conditions of American civil rights activism in the 1950s and 1960s. From a cultural perspective, the resistance also evokes a romantic tradition traceable in American letters from Cooper and Emerson to (yes) Hemingway and Mailer. The artist stands as the creator of order within a disordered world, an agent of resistance to oppression and persecution. So too does the sexual outlaw.

As the narrative projects this image of the hustler, it becomes clear that the social order forming the "outside" also informs the psychosexual "inside." The novel thus describes sadomasochistic practices in the gay community as a dark imitation of heterosocial repression. In his journey through a maze of bathhouse orgies, paid sexual contact, and random encounters, Jim feels the appeal of sadomasochism as a play for power and dominance. He surrenders "to the part of him he hates," the master of "reeling scenes, spat words, rushing sensations, clashing emotions" (251). Similarly, the narrative surrenders to the strutting power of the ultramacho hustler and the garish femininity of the amazonian drag queens. Both are interiorized versions of sexual roles found in the straight world, roles against and also out of which the homosexual defines himself. The narrative thus proves ambiguous when indicating which sociosexual identities allow for a critical appropriation and which create a repressive interiorization. Rechy's novel fails to articulate adequately where critical inversion ends and slavish imitation begins.

As a repeated thematic and structural motif, the tensions and contradictions between opposites—repression and freedom, hegemony and alterity, masculinity and femininity, passivity and activity—create a picture of a fully traversed, schizophrenic world.[11] The heterosocial arena scrutinized in *The Sexual Outlaw* attempts to create a black-and-white vision in which the actions it views as wholly good seek to repress those it perceives as wholly evil. Rechy's novel reveals this to be wholly inadequate and instead disrupts the neat acts of heterosocial definition and circumscription. In so doing, however, the narrative indicates that a movement beyond binary opposition is desirable while at the same time failing to effect such a movement. The narrative seeks an answer to problems of identity through what is essentially a strategy of appropriation and inversion. In appropriating discourses of oppression, the novel oscillates between exposing and hiding, attacking and bolstering, destroying and reconstructing repressive discursive acts. Finally, the desire for a world of absolutes—the sexual outlaw as absolute other, heterosocial order as absolute evil—mirrors the repressive practices against which this desire ostensibly speaks.

Though failing to articulate a truly revolutionary function for the sexual outlaw, the novel does not represent failure. Although it calls for synthesis and transcendence, the novel cannot accomplish either. Instead, it replicates, doubles, refutes, and challenges those signs of repression and discord that map the delimiting and silencing geography through and against which the male sexual outlaw acts. Clearly the novel reveals an ideological enslavement to the binaries of heterosocial sexual identification. In its exposure of this enslavement, in its attempt to reveal that which it has in 1977 not yet the vocabulary to articulate, *The Sexual Outlaw* not only reinscribes the binary of heterosocial order. It accepts it and rejects it and reveals an impossible topology from which future constructions of sexual identity may move.

Notes

1. Eve Sedgwick (1985) employs the term *homosocial* to name the social order of heterosexual society that is a form of displaced homosexual desire. Throughout this chapter the term *heterosocial* is meant to signify the repressive sexual/social order that employs heterosexuality in order to maintain social order. I use this to distinguish from the ostensibly revolutionary and liberating "homosocial" order Rechy's sexual outlaws are meant to prefigure. This division between "heterosocial" and "homosocial" is in keeping with the basic binary constructions upon which Rechy's text rests.
2. Gayatri Spivak (1991) writes about the role of "margins" as privileged sites of questioning, those places that "haunt what we start and get done, as curious guardians" (158).
3. For a complete discussion of Bakhtin's (1981) position, see the chapter "Discourse in the Novel."
4. See Rechy (1984, 57). While the book was originally published in 1977, all further page references cited in the text refer to the 1984 edition.
5. Deleuze and Guattari discuss territorialization and reterritorialization throughout their work. This quote is from *A Thousand Plateaus* (1987, 9).
6. Though Rechy is one of the most prolific of Chicano novelists, his name is not often associated with Chicano literature. There seems to be a double silencing occurring where the Chicano community of letters by and large has refused to talk about Rechy, and Rechy, until recently, has not emphasized his Chicano identity.
7. Félix Guattari (1984) outlines some of the characteristics of "minority" group identification. See p. 233 passim.
8. The rural scenes in the novel are all enclosed by the urban world of Los Angeles. Griffith Park and the beach at Santa Monica, ostensibly oases of isolated "nature," stand surrounded by city. The "central" urban space and the "marginal" rural space form interpenetrating worlds where danger—from police or gay-bashers—is everpresent. Even the geographic within the novel underscores the dissolution of center and margin.
9. Guattari (1984) goes on to note: "In theory there is at this point a possibility of feminist and homosexual action merging" (233). Both groups question the construction of gender and sexuality in the service of social power.
10. The word *queer* here signals the radical revision of homosexual identity undertaken by such political activists as Queer Nation and the recent considerations of Queer Theory. The reappropriation of the

once pejorative term *queer* represents a discursive assertion of self-identification not available to Rechy in 1977.

11. The term *schizophrenic world* is meant to evoke a number of critical discussions surrounding postmodernity as a schizophrenic condition in which, as Fredric Jameson (1984) notes, "syntactical time breaks down, leaving behind a succession of empty signifiers, absolute moments of a perpetual present" (200). Rechy's narrative evokes a compromised world in which repressive and liberating forces problematically interpenetrate each other.

Works Cited

Bakhtin, M. M. *The Dialogic Imagination: Four Essays.* Trans. Caryl Emerson and Michael Holquist; Michael Holquist, ed. Austin: University of Texas Press, 1981.

Barthes, Roland. *The Grain of the Voice: Interviews 1962–1980.* Trans. Linda Coverdale. New York: Hill and Wang, 1985.

Deleuze, Gilles, and Félix Guattari. *A Thousand Plateaus: Capitalism and Schizophrenia.* Trans. Brian Massumi. Minneapolis: University of Minnesota Press, 1987.

Guattari, Félix. *Molecular Revolution: Psychiatry and Politics.* Trans. Rosemary Sheed. London: Penguin Books, 1984.

Jameson, Fredric. "Periodizing the 60s." In *The 60s without Apology,* ed. Sohnya Sayres, Anders Stephanson, Stanley Aronowitz, Fredric Jameson. Minneapolis: University of Minnesota Press, 1984.

Rechy, John. *The Sexual Outlaw: A Documentary.* 2nd ed. New York: Grove Press, 1984.

Sedgwick, Eve Kosofsky. *Between Men: English Literature and Male Homosocial Desire.* New York: Columbia University Press, 1985.

Spivak, Gayatri. "Theory in the Margin." In *Consequences of Theory,* ed. Jonathan Arac and Barbara Johnson, 154–80. Baltimore: Johns Hopkins Press, 1991.

10

The Lack of Gender in Frank O'Hara's Love Poems to Vincent Warren

Jim Elledge

Between August 1959 and July 1961, Frank O'Hara wrote a number of love poems chronicling his relationship with the Canadian dancer Vincent Warren, from its nervous but exuberant birth to its quietly despairing demise.[1] Despite the fact that the poems are about, on one level, one man's love for another man, readers unaware of O'Hara's homosexuality and of his relationship with Warren will not readily perceive the poems' gay concept or themes. O'Hara never identified the gender of the speaker in any of the poems in the sequence or, except in one instance—"Those Who Are Dreaming, A Play about St. Paul"—the gender of the individual to whom the poems are addressed.[2] Instead, O'Hara's speaker, an "I," offers a "you" observations about love and its high *and* low points.

Because in his poetry O'Hara typically presented his experiences as they had occurred without tampering, the reader of the Warren sequence cannot help but question why O'Hara disguised, obscured, ignored, or lied about the genders of the poems' lovers. Privately, O'Hara appears to have been relaxed about his homosexuality, because both his heterosexual and homosexual friends and acquaintances knew about it. In some cases, his sexual exploits have been recorded in the memoirs of those who knew him and published, for example, in the section of the journal

Panjandrum devoted to O'Hara and in the festschrift *Homage to Frank O'Hara.*[3] Publicly, not only in his poetry but also in his prose, he was not so open. We can ascertain at least four reasons why.

Readers must remind themselves that the atmosphere surrounding a vast majority of gays in pre-Stonewall America was one of rampant homophobia.[4] The era in which O'Hara wrote and published did not recognize homosexuality as an alternative lifestyle but deemed it either, from one extreme point of view, a crime against God, nature, and state or, from the other extreme, as quaint aberration. Martin Duberman, for example, has recalled this phenomenon in his "Gay in the Fifties," one of a number of gay memoirs currently available in print.[5] Few male or female homosexuals of those days, much less a publishing poet and a public figure who was gay and whose career had begun to thrive, willingly became victim to a heterosexual, patriarchal society eager for sacrifices. O'Hara recognized the threat. He wrote "Homosexuality," his only poem to reveal openly his view of gay life, in 1954, six years before his and Warren's relationship began, but the poem did not appear in print until May 1970, in *Poetry,* four years after his death (531). That O'Hara did not publish "Homosexuality" during his life shows his caution, because to acknowledge openly in print during the 1950s and 1960s a homosexual life-style was, for gays and lesbians, to walk to the volcano's rim and leap.

O'Hara's oeuvre, now available to the O'Hara devotee in three collections,[6] reveals that he seems to have been disinterested in using homosexuality per se as a topic for his poetry and disinterested in making his career a vehicle for political statement. O'Hara could have written any number of overtly gay poems, had he had the interest, need, or desire, and left them unpublished had he been wary only of reactions to them by a homophobic readership. He didn't. Of the hundreds of poems published posthumously in O'Hara's *Collected Poems,* only "Homosexuality" openly addresses gay life in the 1950s. O'Hara also must have realized that for him to focus overtly in any of his poems on homosexuality as subject or to acknowledge openly in his poetry his homosexual life-style or even a single sexual liaison with another man certainly would have been construed as a political statement, whether or not he meant or wanted it to be. Allen Ginsberg, O'Hara's friend, serves as an example of a poet who wrote openly homosexual poems viewed by society as political statement. Indeed, Andrew Ross has claimed that O'Hara's "blithe disregard for politics" in general was "well-known, a disregard, for example, that caused a stir when, in 1966, a minor quarrel broke out among certain literati over his refusal to sign a petition condemning U.S. involvement in Vietnam."[7] Even a quick reading of O'Hara's life's work indicates that, despite the many major, sometimes near-catastrophic sociopolitical events that occurred at the same time in which he wrote some of his best, most often anthologized work, O'Hara's poems don't reveal a political consciousness per se.

For example, "Poem [Khrushchev is coming on the right day!]," written during the cold war, opens with a reference to the leader of the Soviet Union, but ignores the importance of the Premier's visit to the United States. The poem mentions the Soviet chief only in passing and focuses, instead, in true O'Hara fashion, on the narrator's, not Khrushchev's, experiences of that particular day, on what many readers might consider unimportant minutiae of one New Yorker's everyday life: the weather, a statement remembered from a conversation of the night before, reading François Villon's poetry, and so forth. Similarly in "Personal Poem" (335–36), O'Hara frames a report of a racially motivated attack on jazz trumpeter Miles Davis with chitchat—a passage of gossip and self-absorption preceding the lines concerning Davis; one displaying black humor following them. The framing by seemingly inane lines serves to intensify the horror of the Davis incident. The framing also suggests that O'Hara viewed all experiences as equal, equally important, or equally unimportant.

We would be hard put to deny that the fear of reprisal by a homophobic society, a disinterest in homosexuality as theme or content in poetry, and a disregard for politics in general may have played a role in O'Hara's practice of omitting gender in the Warren poems. To deny them their influence on O'Hara would be foolish. However, speculation concerning the lack of gender based simply on one or any combination of the three reasons seems just as foolish and even unfair to O'Hara, who died on July 24, 1966—

three years before the birth of Gay Liberation and before activists chanted "Proud to Be Gay" and other slogans in large metropolises across the United States, especially New York and San Francisco. Both events made it "OK," at least in theory and at least among very small enclaves of artsy types and intellectuals, to be gay. Yet if we investigate the poems themselves, we learn a great deal, not only about the Warren sequence but also about O'Hara's view of gender and love in poetry.

A number of the Warren love poems "tend to be less factual, more emotional, direct, Romantic"[8] than the " 'I do this I do that' poems" (341), which readers most often associate with O'Hara. Indeed, O'Hara himself labeled them "delicate and caressing poems" in "Avenue A" (356). Although a number of the Warren poems are, for the most part, far more accessible than one often considers O'Hara's poetry to be, the sequence does contain, in typical O'Hara fashion, several poems with obscure allusions, skewed syntax, and personal references that threaten their accessibility. Readers must contend, here and there, with allusions that only O'Hara could have interpreted, such as "the clouds are imitating Diana Adams" (339), or, as in "Ballad," with unpunctuated, run-on lines and sentences that create confusing syntax. Because he often employs in his poems the names of his friends, the poems also sometimes bog down in obscurity. In "Poem [Now the violets are all gone, the rhinoceroses, the cymbals]," for example, O'Hara mentions several individuals—Janice, Kenneth, Ned—but doesn't offer their significance to the poem, if it exists.

O'Hara's practice of omitting gender identification in most of the Warren poems balances such obstacles to reader accessibility, allowing them to be understood, appreciated, and enjoyed by any reader, not by male homosexuals exclusively. For example, O'Hara's narrator addresses a "you" with quiet desire in "Now That I Am in Madrid and Can Think" and with exuberant abandon in "Steps." By ignoring the gender of "you," O'Hara frees the reader to identify "you" as anyone of any sex, any age, any race, and not simply as "Vincent Warren." He thus creates a universal "you." Simultaneously, by ignoring the gender of "I," O'Hara also creates a universal speaker, one not necessarily "Frank O'Hara" or any specific individual at all, but perhaps even the reader.

Although O'Hara obscured the identities of his lovers, a universal couple, he deftly painted their personalities, especially his speaker's. For example, O'Hara's "I," so much in love that self-restraint is impossible, virtually gushes, "oh god it's wonderful" to "love . . . so much" (371).

Because O'Hara omits gender identification from most of the Warren poems, he focuses readers' attention on matters that transcend gender, a factor that restricts the poet, the reader, and the poem. Specifically, O'Hara investigates the nature of love, its intricacies, ironies, and paradoxes—not male-male love, not male-female love, not female-female love, but individual-individual love: "I"-"you" and "you"-"I" love.

At the beginning of the sequence, the narrator of "Joe's Jacket" (329–30) contemplates the beginnings of a new love relationship. The poem concludes on Monday morning as the speaker, now at home, prepares to leave for work, borrowing "Joe's seersucker jacket," a symbol: "It is all enormity and life it has protected me and kept me here on / many occasions . . . / a precaution I loathe." Joe's jacket protects because of the friendship, that is, the platonic love, the "I" and Joe share, but the speaker both wants and does not want protection. The pun on "kept me" reveals the dilemma the "I" faces. On one hand, the jacket keeps the narrator safe by preserving and protecting; on the other, it restricts, keeping the narrator from life's successes as well as its failures. By extension, the speaker feels just as ambivalent over the new, erotic love with the poem's "you." The narrator accepts the fact that, after all, love comprises an integral part of the first day of the new week and that love has its very desirable and its less than desirable sides. The narrator, secure in the thought that, because of love, one can "face almost everything that will come up," allows the jacket simply to be "just what it is" and the future, with its potential for a lasting love, "just what happens."

In the poems that follow, O'Hara now describes the love that earlier had belonged to a "questionable moment" (330) with more emotional security and in a more favorable light. In "You Are Gorgeous and I'm Coming," for example, the narrator portrays love, and its accompanying passion, as a speeding Paris Métro train. In "Personal Poem," the speaker realizes love makes all of us happy because at least one person may be thinking of us, and love reminds the narrator in "Variations on Pasternak's 'Mein Liebchen, Was Willst Du Noch Mehr?' " (339) that, because it exists, beauty is possible. The narrator's recognition of love does even more. It offsets life's mundane moments and even the fact of our ultimate mortality. It offers the narrator warmth in "Les Luths," and in "Poem 'A la recherche d'Gertrude Stein,' " O'Hara recognizes that love strengthens life. Love makes existence as perfect as possible in an imperfect world, as the speaker in "Poem [Light clarity avocado salad in the morning]" realizes, and it affords one the possibility of understanding the darker side of life and human nature, as the narrator admits in "Poem [So many echoes in my head]." In "Now That I Am in Madrid and Can Think," love ironically lends human beings a near-divine stance in the world, and in "Cornkind," O'Hara shows it invests life and itself with meaning.

However, bliss does not characterize love in all of the Warren poems. A number of them reveal love's negative side, about which the narrator had worried in the beginning of the sequence. In "Sudden Show" (354–55), for example, the speaker, melancholy and afraid that love may be transitory, decides that "love is like the path in snow we are making / though no one else can follow, leading us only / to the ocean's sure embrace of summer." Doubt again intrudes into an otherwise happy moment in "Song" (361): "in a world where you are possible / my love / nothing can go wrong for us, tell me." The poem's last phrase, "tell me," concisely expresses the speaker's urgent need to be assured that all is well with the couple's love, while the phrase suggests the speaker's doubts. In "Those Who Are Dreaming, A Play about St. Paul" (373–75), the narrator admits to not having "known / a loveless night for so long, each night has been filled / with love" then quickly adds, afraid of jinxing the relationship, "And it might mean bad luck, to imagine / such a thing." O'Hara's speaker decides in "An Airplane Whistle (After Heine)" that too much of a good thing may be destructive to it. The concluding section of "Trying to Figure Out What You Feel" makes it apparent that the lovers are getting on one another's nerves and that the speaker has become resentful. Ultimately, O'Hara's narrator realizes love's transitory nature. Left alone in "[The light comes on by itself]" (388) to fill up time with life's mundane details, the narrator repeats five times, in urgent refrain, *I am waiting for you to love me*" after each stanza. Almost in summary, then, O'Hara asserts in "St. Paul and All That" (406–7) that love leaves one "full of anxious pleasures and pleasurable anxiety."

Although in a majority of the Warren poems O'Hara never identifies the gender of "you," he nevertheless mentions Vincent Warren by name in nearly a third of them. Yet, at the same time that he alludes to Warren, O'Hara hides the role Warren plays in the poems—and in O'Hara's line. For example, O'Hara uses Warren's first name in the opening line of "Joe's Jacket," but we are unable to ascertain from the poem anything more about "Vincent" and the poem's speaker than they, and "Jap," are traveling together. Later in the same poem, O'Hara again mentions "Vincent," but simply as a companion. The poem's "you"—the beloved of its "I"—is never linked to Warren. Instead, O'Hara employs "Vincent" simply as a part of the landscape the speaker inhabits.

In fact, even when O'Hara overtly links a poem's "you" to Warren (as happens in "The Anthology of Lonely Days," "Vincent and I Inaugurate a Movie Theater," "Vincent," "Vincent, [2]," "At Kamin's Dance Bookshop," and "St. Paul and All That"), O'Hara never discloses the romantic relationship the "I" and "you" share. We can ascertain their relationship *only* if we apply to the poems the biographical tidbits O'Hara's friends and critics have published about him.

However, O'Hara occasionally covertly refers to Warren in the poems, and for the most part, these link Warren romantically with the speaker. For example, the first letter of each line of "You Are Gorgeous and I Am Coming," an acrostic, spells *Vincent Warren,* identifying the poem's "you." Nevertheless, very few readers would think to read the poem, or any of O'Hara's work, as an acrostic. Similarly, in "Poem [That's not a cross look it's a sign of life]" (353–54), the speaker, thinking about "our elephantine history," a combination of personal and public events, repeats the name *Warren* three times, twice in "Warren G. Harding" and one in "Horace S. Warren," coyly playing with the identity of "you." Yet once again, only readers aware of O'Hara's homosexuality and his love for Vincent Warren before they approach the poem will pinpoint such obscure references and understand them.

In the Warren love poems, O'Hara presents the concept of gender as secondary to that of love. O'Hara could have used *she* to refer to the speaker's beloved, but to do so would be to lie about his relationship—and about his life. O'Hara could have used *he,* but by doing so, he would have associated love only with male-male relationships, which would have been to deny love's accessibility to, and existence in, the lives of those different than he—lesbians and heterosexuals. Indeed, to do so would be tantamount to the practice of our patriarchal, homophobic society that would have readers believe, "not by declaration but by implication,"[9] that love exists only in the realm of heterosexuality, the only territory in which it is legitimate.

Readers eager to destroy the restrictions society has placed upon the literary canon and to uphold those works historically excluded from it—a noble, laudable venture—often allow their zeal to blind them to the very work they champion and, in essence, to restrict that work exactly as those they challenge have done in the past. Readers informed about O'Hara's homosexuality may too quickly assume the lovers of the Warren poems must be male, whereas those unaware of his being gay may see no expression of homosexuality at all. By asserting their agendas upon O'Hara's work, rather than reading his poetry on its own terms, both camps reveal not only their prejudices but also their ignorance of human sexuality and human sexual practices and of the complexity of O'Hara's work. The last stanza of "Cornkind" (387), with its sexually charged concluding line, illustrates the point.

On the one hand, the stanza, "you are of me, that's what / and that's the meaning of fertility / hard and moist and moaning," will indeed suggest to some readers who are aware of O'Hara's sexual orientation that the poem is a statement of male-male love and sex. To them, the first line of the stanza will infer that the "you" and the "I" are the same sex, and those readers will continue to analyze what follows in the stanza within the perimeters that their knowledge of his homosexuality constructs around it. Indeed to them, the word *hard,* when used within the context of sexual relations, will imply a gay interpretation because, in our culture, the word is so often associated with an erect penis. On the other hand, those who read the stanza only within the perimeters of male-female sexual intercourse will see no gay possibility in "you are of me" at all. Instead, the phrase will suggest to them that the lovers share some spiritual or intellectual attribute that unites them in a manner that transcends the physical, a concept as old as, perhaps older than, the Bible. To those readers, *hard* will also suggest a male, but *moist* will connote a female, specifically vaginal fluid during intercourse. To support their interpretation, they may argue that *fertility* cannot be applied to male-male sex, because reproduction is a possibility only in male-female intercourse.

To read the stanza exclusively from the point of view of homosexuality or of heterosexuality is to deny a third possible interpretation, that the stanza actually addresses love and sexual intercourse between human beings of any sexual orientation—gay, straight, or lesbian. We can see this possibility most readily in the concluding line. Of course, *hard* may refer to an erect penis, but it may also refer to a clitoris and/or to nipples during sexual excitement. (*Hard* may also connote the type of sex in which the couple engages, some version of bondage and discipline or of sadomasochism. Such an interpretation could be supported by the last word of the stanza, *moaning,* which suggest pleasure and/or pain.) Of course, *moist* may infer vaginal fluids, but it may also refer to lubricants gays use during anal intercourse and/or to perspiration of either gender during sexual excitement. Because we can read "hard and moist" in an all-encompassing manner, *fertility* can also be interpreted not only as the heterosexual ability to reproduce oneself physically, but also, and simply, the ability of anyone to create, or give life to, anything whether physical or not: love, a poem, a child, and so forth. Similarly, "you are of me" may be interpreted as a gender reference, but we must also admit that it may refer to male-male, male-female, and female-female union of a nonphysical sort. For any reader to limit the interpretation of this stanza, or any poem in the Warren sequence, to the point of view of any one sexual orientation is to deny the stanza its obvious complexity and to be as exclusive as those who held patriarchy and heterosexuality as guiding principles when compiling the literary canon.

O'Hara's sequence of poems to Vincent Warren emphasizes the availability of love to any and all, at turns as exhilarating and depressing to one individual as to any, regardless of the sexual preferences of those who love. In short, O'Hara accepted and wrote about the experience of love as an integral part of the *human*—not the male or the female, not the heterosexual or the homosexual—condition. In his love poems to Warren, O'Hara suggests love influences life so vastly that its particulars, specifically gender, pale in comparison.

One cannot deny that fear of the repercussions from homophobia, disinterest in homosexuality as a topic of poetry, and disregard for politics may have played in varying degrees a role in O'Hara's practice of omitting gender identification. Although the omission of gender in love poetry by anyone would give meaning to the poems (as does its assertion), we cannot simply assume that O'Hara's practice of ignoring words that indicate gender only reveals a fearful, disinterested, and negligent poet. Instead, to understand most fully not only the poems but O'Hara's stance vis-à-vis the sequence and his environment, we must realize that the poet is very conscious of, and conscientious about, the effect simply common words such as *he* or *she* or *him* or *her* may have on readers. O'Hara realized that, in love poetry, omitting words that refer to gender liberates. By denying gender, O'Hara obliterated the limitations his society placed on individuals—those written about, those writing, and those reading—as well as the restrictions society placed on poems and on texts in general. Indeed, he liberated his art, and himself, by removing the obstacle to their appreciation by a homophobic society and, as important, by focussing attention on the poems' theme—love—rather than on his life. Simultaneously, by not narrowing the poems to a readership comprised solely of gays or their supporters, O'Hara gave his poems a broader possible readership. O'Hara did not want to run the risk of denying love in any of its possibilities and, consequently, chose to keep his work free of the restraints sexist language would impose upon it. While not *political* in the way that

Andrew Ross uses the word, O'Hara nevertheless made a very clear and powerful political statement by disregarding gender in his love poems for Vincent Warren. In essence, O'Hara consciously preserved, perhaps even sanctified, the universality of love by writing his love poems to Vincent Warren without regard to gender-identifying words. In fact, we may view him as having championed against the use of sexist language long before it became a cause of general concern in our society.

Notes

1. In Marjorie Perloff, *Frank O'Hara: Poet Among Painters* (New York: George Braziller, 1977), 156–63; and in Alan Feldman, *Frank O'Hara* (Boston: Twayne, 1979) 126–33 and 163, n. 7.

   Although Perloff and Feldman agree that at least some of the poems O'Hara wrote between August 1959 and July 1961 should be considered the Warren sequence, they disagree over which. They concur that the following poems belong to the sequence: "You Are Gorgeous and I'm Coming," "Saint," "To You," "Poem [Now the violets are all gone]," "Poem V(F)W," "Poem 'A la recherche d' Gertrude Stein,' " "Variations on the 'Tree of Heaven,' " "Poem [Light clarity avocado salad in the morning]," "Hôtel Transylvanie," "Poem [So many echoes in my head]," "Present," "Poem [That's not a cross look it's a sign of life]," "Sudden Snow," "Avenue A," "Now That I Am in Madrid and Can Think," "Having a Coke with You," "Song [I am stuck in traffic in a taxicab]," "An Airplane Whistle (After Heine)," "Trying to Figure Out How You Feel," "Poem [Some days I feel that I exude a fine dust]," "Cohasset," "Song [Did you see me walking by the Buick repairs?]," "Ballad," "Flag Day," "Those Who Are Dreaming, A Play about St. Paul," "Variations on Saturday," "What Appears to Be Yours," "You at the Pump," "Cornkind," "To Canada," "Vincent," "Vincent, [2]," "Poem [Twin spheres full of fur and noise]," and "St. Paul and All That."

   Perloff also includes in the sequence a number of poems Feldman ignores: "September 14, 1959 (Moon)," "Poem [Now it is the 27th]," "Poem [Wouldn't it be funny]," "Poem [O sole mio, hot diggety, nix 'I wather think I can']," "How to Get There," "Liebeslied," and "Poem [It was snowing and now}." Feldman lists several titles that Perloff excludes: "Joe's Jacket," "Personal Poem," "Variations on Pasternak's 'Mein Liebchen, Was Willst Du Noch Mehr?,' " "Les Luths," "Leafing Through Florida," "Steps," "A Warm Day for December," "[The light comes on by itself]' " "The Anthology of Lonely Days," "Vincent and I

Inaugurate a Movie Theater," "At Kamin's Dance Bookshop," and "A Chardin in Need of Cleaning."

Other poems from O'Hara's *Collected Poems* should be added to their list(s) because of the dates of the poems' composition, their concern with love, and their covert reference to Warren: "Poem [The fluorescent tubing burns like a bobby-soxer's ankles]," " 'L'Amour avait passé par là,' " "Poem [I don't know as I get what D. H. Lawrence is driving at]," "Naphtha," "Getting Up Ahead of Someone," "In Favor of One's Time," "Dances Before the Wall," "Ode to Tanaquil Leclercq," "American," "On a Birthday of Kenneth's," "Pistachio Tree at Chateau Noir," "On Rachmaninoff's Birthday #158," and "Causerie de A. F."

O'Hara's *Poems Retrieved* (See note 6), published after Perloff's and Feldman's studied, offers other poems also belonging to the Warren sequence: "Dear Vincent," "Congratulations in the Snow of Christmas Eve 1961," "Poem [You do not always seem able to decide]," "Young Girl in Pursuit of Lorca," "Poem during Poulenc's *Gloria,*" "Shooting the Shit Again," "[I will always remember]," and "Poem [lost, lost]."

2. Frank O'Hara, "Those Who are Dreaming, A Play about St. Paul," in *Collected Poems,* ed. Donald Allen (New York: Alfred A. Knopf, 1979), 373–75. All poems mentioned and quoted appear in O'Hara's *Collected Poems.* The pagination for each quoted poem is documented parenthetically within the text.
3. *Panjandrum: A Journal of Contemporary Poetry,* nos. 2–3 (1973); n. p., and *Homage to Frank O'Hara,* ed. Bill Berkson and Joe LeSueur (Berkeley, CA: Creative Arts, 1980).
4. Stonewall, a gay bar, was the site of a riot by gays in 1969, an event historically used to mark the birth of Gay Liberation.
5. In *Men's Lives,* ed. Michael S. Kimmel and Michael A. Messner (New York: Macmillan, 1989), 321–44.
6. *Early Writing,* ed. Donald Allen (Bolinas, CA: Grey Fox, 1977), and *Poems Retrieved,* ed. Donald Allen (Bolinas, CA: Grey Fox, 1977), supplement O'Hara's *Collected Poems.*
7. Andrew Ross, "The Death of Lady Day," in *Frank O'Hara: To Be True to a City,* ed. Jim Elledge (Ann Arbor: University of Michigan Press, 1990), 383.
8. Perloff, *Frank O'Hara,* 117.
9. Robert K. Martin, "Introduction," in *The Homosexual Tradition in American Poetry* (Austin: University of Texas Press, 1979), xv.

IV

Crossing Cultures, Crossing Sexualities

11

Engendering the Imperial Subject: The (De)construction of (Western) Masculinity in David Henry Hwang's *M. Butterfly* and Graham Greene's *The Quiet American*

Suzanne Kehde

By the time of his death this month at the age of eighty-six, Greene had become a kind of Grand Old Man of the left, and *The Quiet American* stood as his anti-imperialist masterpiece.

—Richard West, "Graham Greene and *The Quiet American*"

Richard West's summary judgment[1] described a text so different from the one I remembered that it sent me back to reread Greene's novel set in Vietnam at the moment when, unnoticed by the American public, the U. S. military was about to replace the French forces being driven out by the Vietminh. Written by a member of the governing classes,[2] who during the Second World War had engaged in espionage in Africa for the British government, the novel is narrated by a character who never scrutinizes his own subject position. Here Greene's imperial attitudes, embedded in a web of colonial and gender discourses, are considerably more problematic than West's formulation suggests.

A more powerful critique of imperialism is David Henry Hwang's *M. Butterfly*, which lays bare the processes of Western male engenderment supporting the structures of imperial power.

As a Chinese-American and heir to a double culture that straddles Western-Oriental alterity, Hwang is admirably situated to undertake such a critique. The play offers a useful paradigm of imperialism by exposing and elaborating the premises on which it is based.

In the *New York Times* report of a French diplomat accused of spying, who had lived for twenty years with a Chinese lover without noticing she was a man, Hwang saw an emblem of the imbrication of gender and colonial discourses. In *M. Butterfly* he lays bare the connection between Western ideas of masculinity and the rationale for imperialism by situating his critique in a rewriting of Puccini's opera. Hwang initiates his deconstruction by a gender reversal, casting his female lead with a male actor from the Beijing opera. This man, Song Liling, acts as other for René Gallimard, who projects on his lover a fantasy of femininity reflecting his own self-image—an image of the man he thinks appropriate for his class, race, and nationality. Song Liling identifies the roles in Gallimard's "favorite fantasy" as "the submissive Oriental woman and the cruel white man."[3] Gallimard, says Hwang in the Afterword, "fantasizes that he is Pinkerton and his lover is Butterfly. By the end of the piece, he realizes that he had been Butterfly, in that the Frenchman has been duped by love; the Chinese spy, who exploited that love, is therefore the real Pinkerton" (95–96). The role identified as feminine and "Oriental" in Puccini can be played by a white Frenchman; the "dominant man" can be played by a Chinese. Further, although the structure of the play does not emphasize this reversal of gender expectations to the same degree, women can also play the dominant role, sexually, as does Isabelle, Gallimard's first lay; intellectually, as does Renée, the Danish schoolgirl who interrogates Gallimard on the rationalization for male power systems; and politically, as does Comrade Chin, Song Liling's spymaster. By describing the play as his "deconstructivist *Madame Butterfly*" (95), Hwang explicitly aligns it with theoretical preoccupations, thus, in Judith Mayne's words, "submitting theory to the test of narrative."[4]

Gallimard's fascination with the scenario of Madame Butterfly centers on the masculine power manifested by Pinkerton. Conflating Chinese and Japanese under the sign of Western alterity, he observes that "Oriental girls want to be treated bad" and congratulates himself that when he leaves Beijing, "she'll know what it's like to be loved by a real man" (6), who, the play proceeds to make clear, must be white.

For Gallimard, masculinity has always been primarily associated with sexual dominance. As a boy of twelve he had become excited by his uncle's girlie magazines—not so much by lust, as he now recognizes, but by the power he imagined himself to exert over the exposed women. When he meets Song Liling, desire and power become inextricably imbricated. The position that allows him "to abuse [her] cruelly" (36) soon comes to seem "natural," to be built into the structure of the universe. He says, "God who creates Eve to serve Adam, who blesses Solomon with his harem but ties Jezebel to a burning bed—that God is a man" (38). Thus he essentializes the engenderment that has been constructed by the contingencies of power.

But the abusive relationship he thinks to enjoy with Song Liling depends on other factors besides the expectations of Western male-female sexual relationships. Gallimard would never dare treat his wife or his girlfriend in such abusive ways—perhaps because he knows he could never make them suffer as he imagines Song Liling suffers. It is her Oriental nature, he believes, to submit to his domination. Edward Said, noting that the Orient is one of the West's most persistent images of the other, has demonstrated the historical growth of the discourse of Orientalism, which he sees as "a Western style for dominating, restructuring, and having authority over the Orient."[5] Further, he maintains that "European culture gained in strength and identity by setting itself off against the Orient as a sort of surrogate and even underground self" (20). The long tradition of Orientalism that the French and British in particular have enjoyed allows Gallimard, unchallenged, to make pronouncements like "Orientals will always submit to a greater force" (46). This dominance is not accorded to him as an individual but as a function of group entitlement. He specifically denies his personal qualifications: "We, who are not handsome, nor brave, nor powerful, yet somehow believe, like Pinkerton, that we deserve a Butterfly" (10). His sense of entitlement to a submissive Oriental Butterfly comes from his membership in the governing class of a Western imperial power.

The metaphor of man as the West, woman as the Orient that hovers in the margins of the text is not constant, vehicle and tenor being subject to reversal and recirculation. During the course of the play, the relationship between man and woman enacted between Gallimard and Song Liling comes to represent the relations between the decolonized and the imperial nations. Colonization thus entails feminization of the colonized, enforced by the masculine imperialist. This mechanism is underscored by Gallimard's feminization of Song Liling. Western imperialism has "feminized" the Third World the better to exploit it. Song Liling voices this analysis: "The West thinks of itself as masculine—big guns, big industry, big money—so the East is feminine—weak, delicate, poor" (83). The Western will to power over Asian nations parallels Gallimard's masculine bullying of the submissive Oriental "woman." Vietnam in 1961, when the French had retreated and the United States had not yet openly committed troops to Indo-China, serves as the model for Asian colonial ventures in general. Gallimard expects the United States to take over Vietnam without opposition after the French leave because, he says, "Orientals simply want to be associated with whoever shows the most strength and power" (45). As Charlotte Bunch, among others, has pointed out, what starts out as colonization of women ends up as colonization of the world.[6]

The relationship between Gallimard and Song Liling thus exhibits the stereotypical signs of both male/female and imperialist/colonized relationships. As Homi Bhabha suggests, stereotyping, a fixed form of difference, exists for the production of the colonized as a fixed reality that is at once other and yet entirely knowable.[7] Thus Gallimard's stereotyping comes from his intense need to establish difference between himself and Song Liling. Conscious that he is modeling his lover on Madame Butterfly, he nonetheless seems oblivious that he is inventing a character for Song. As Bhabha says, the closer the resemblance between the colonizer and colonized, the more closely the colonizer subjects the colonized to surveillance in order to discover difference (164). By fixing his gaze on Song—by keeping him under surveillance—Gallimard can avoid scrutinizing his own subject position.

Gallimard's understanding of his relations with Song is determined by his notions of the colonial situation in a classic case of the triumph of hope over experience. As Bhabha theorizes,

> the construction of the colonial subject in discourse, and the exercise of colonial power through discourse demands an articulation of forms of difference—racial and sexual. Such an articulation becomes crucial if it is held that the body is always simultaneously inscribed in both the economy of pleasure and desire and the economy of discourse, domination and power. (150)

However, in *M. Butterfly* the "racial and sexual" are conflated; the economy of "pleasure and desire" is imbricated with the economy of "discourse, domination, and power."

The operant tool of this imbrication is the penis/phallus—the conflation of which, although resisted by some Lacanian theorists, is demonstrable in Lacan's work and, in any case, is manifest in Hwang's play. Gallimard has to read Song as woman, who signifies phallic lack. By concealing his penis Song can carry Gallimard's discourse. Throughout the play, various characters draw attention to the penis in both valorized and unvalorized states, from the anonymous Frenchman's suggestion of "misidentified equipment," to Gallimard's "How's it hangin'?" A young Danish woman meditates on "this little . . . flap of flesh." She continues:

> No one knows . . . who has the bigger . . . weenie. So, if I'm a guy with a small one, I'm going to build a really big building or take over a really big piece of land or write a really long book so the other men won't know, right? But see, it never really works, that's the problem. I mean, you conquer the country, or whatever, but you're still wearing clothes, so there's no way to prove absolutely whose is bigger or smaller. And that's what we call civilized society. The whole world run by men with pricks the size of pins. (55)

Gallimard refuses to listen to a "schoolgirl who would question the role of the penis in modern society" (58). One might perhaps conclude that his downfall stems from precisely his failure to theorize the penis—ironically, to give the function of the phallus in the symbolic register too little attention.

The trajectory of Gallimard's narrative shows the construction of (Western) male subjectivity on the establishment of sameness as well as difference. Gallimard's relationship to other men is based on what Eve Kosofsky Sedgwick calls homosociality, the order of "male homosocial desire," of the "potentially erotic" (1) which marks "the structure of men's relations with other men" (2). She pointedly refuses to essentialize, however, historicizing the particular formulation of homosociality by concentrating chiefly on "the emerging pattern [in English culture of the eighteenth and nineteenth centuries] of male friendship, mentorship, rivalry [which] was in an intimate and shifting relationship to class [and no element of which] can be understood outside of its relation to women and the gender system as a whole."[8] Although her study *Between Men* mainly confines its examples to the British novel of the mid-eighteenth to mid-nineteenth centuries, her perceptions are generally applicable to the power structures Hwang posits as the factors engendering Gallimard, who appears to have been raised in a middle-class professional French family and trained to the civil service in much the same way as his historical counterpart in Britain. Gallimard's retrospective interrogation of his sexuality is marked by a strong homosocial component. During a replay of a scene from his student years, a friend invites him to a swim party with this description: "There's no moon out, their boobs are flapping, right? You close your eyes, reach out—it's grab bag, get it? Doesn't matter whose ass is between whose legs, whose teeth are sinking into who" (8). The language of pressure to engage in aggressive, anonymous group sex suggests that the most important feature is the participation of other men.

Marc, the boyhood friend at whose father's condo this group sex took place, appears as a voice "everywhere now" (32), reinforcing throughout Gallimard's imprisonment the unacknowledged premises that have constructed Gallimard's relations to other men and to women, premises that in short have engendered him. These, the premises of homosociality, are constructed on (major) sameness as well as on (minor) difference, on the acquisition and maintenance of power on "our" side as an extension of self. The exchange of women, Sedgwick points out, is one of the major ways in which relations between men are secured (179). Just such an exchange has taken place: The image of Marc demands a return on his gift of Isabelle, whom he persuaded to initiate Gallimard into sex. Gallimard, however, pinned in the dirt under her, thought only, "So this is it?" The power relations implicit in his inferior position as much as the physical discomfort of having his buttocks pounded into the ground seem to have severely restricted his enjoyment.

The acquisition of Song Liling, the ostensibly lovesick lotus blossom he delights in humiliating and neglecting, advances Gallimard in the French colonial service. The ambassador to China, impressed by Gallimard's sexual swaggering, transfers the vice-consul and promotes Gallimard. Retrospectively Gallimard understands how the ambassador's reaction reveals the operations of the homosocial order: "Toulon . . . approves! I was learning the benefits of being a man. We form our own clubs, sit behind thick doors, smoke—and celebrate the fact that we're still boys" (46). As suggested by Lacan's dictum that the phallus is veiled, echoed here by the schoolgirl's meditation on the "weenie," any given homosocial order is felt to be in flux; the hierarchy of sameness, unlike the hierarchy of difference, can never be presumed permanently fixed.

The discourses of gender and colonialism whose operations Hwang sought to expose are omnipresent in Greene's *The Quiet American* with no critique of gender stereotypes and little of imperialist assumptions, certainly without any acknowledgment that there might be some connection between them. Like Gallimard, Fowler reads his Vietnamese lover as doubly other in her gender and nationality but, unlike him, for Fowler that fixed difference is not the focus of his most earnest scrutiny. The major strand in Fowler's engenderment—the one that occupies him most consistently, driving him at last to complicity in murder—is the homosocial, which in the colonial setting is maintained by both gender and colonial discourses. The construction of Fowler's subjectivity depends primarily on his surveillance of signs of sameness in Pyle; he needs to scrutinize all suggestion of similarity in order to focus on difference. The overt emphasis on the homosocial order throughout Greene's public school and Oxford education must have made its primacy seem natural, much in the way, satirized by Hwang, that Gallimard comes to see man's domination of woman as mandated by the universe itself.

Sedgwick's study of homosociality notes René Girard's work on "the relation of rivalry between the two active members of an erotic triangle. . . . The bond that links the two rivals is as intense and potent as the bond that links either of the rivals to the beloved." Girard's analysis focuses on the "male-centered novelistic tradition of high European culture" (Sedgwick, *Between Men,* 21), a tradition to which *The Quiet American* clearly belongs. The rivalry that forms between Fowler and Pyle runs conspicuously along the opposed axes of sameness and difference. Seen alongside the constant surveillance this rivalry demands, the construction of Phuong as doubly other is static—always-already present, it is sited in a latent nostalgia. In Bhabha's terms, Phuong is a stereotype of the exotic. Fowler mounts a satiric critique against Pyle that sweeps from his conduct as a U.S. economic adviser to his understanding of Phuong's character, intellect, and values—matters on which Fowler feels eminently qualified to pontificate. He sneers at Pyle's reasons for the ostensibly humanitarian American presence in French Indo-China, pressing for a scrutiny of the concept of democracy, which, assuming that government depends on the consent of the governed, has been a reasonably stable component of modern concepts of liberty. He mocks the simplistic evocation of the ideal by noting the express wish of Phuong, his mistress and eventually Pyle's fiancée, to see the Statue of Liberty. He attempts to call into question the idea of liberty promulgated by Pyle. Holed up in a watchtower waiting for the Viet Cong to attack, he calls across to the two Vietnamese guards, "*La liberté—qu'est ce que c'est la liberté?*", eliciting a remonstrance from Pyle: "You stand for the importance of the individual as much as I do."[9] Fowler, however, objects to Pyle not only as an individual but also as a representative of the United States, whose citizens he resents as a class: "I was tired of the whole pack of them with their private stores of Coca-Cola and their portable hospitals and their too wide cars and their not quite latest guns" (31). In short, he falls back on the unexamined assumptions of privilege due nationals of a European imperial power.

In the "natural" way one understands the hidden hierarchies

of one's own culture, Fowler knows how to negotiate the power structures of the multicultural homosocial order of Saigon. Lying in his bed smoking opium, he refuses to arise to greet the (Vietnamese) police officer who summons him to the Sureté. He is "fond of" and dependent upon Dominguez, his (male) Indian assistant who, like a well-trained American secretary (female) mediates the local culture for him. He recognizes the legal power of Vigot at the Sureté, who investigates Pyle's death but treats Fowler reciprocally as a comrade, just as Fowler treats Trouin, the pilot who takes him on a bombing raid, or the French officers he gambles with on trips up-country.

Such an amicable relationship between the two major Orientalist powers is a comparatively recent historical development. Said describes their intense late nineteenth-century competition for imperial acquisition, pointing out that the Sykes-Picot agreement of 1916 to carve up Arabia between them—which, ultimately determining national boundaries in the Middle East, led to the present unrest—was a deliberate attempt to control this rivalry. *The Quiet American* suggests that it disappeared with the collapse of both empires and, perhaps equally important, the appearance of the United States on the imperial scene. This appearance, constituting an assault on powerful members of an existing homosocial order, minimizes the focus on difference and fosters perceptions of sameness between the French and British.

Fowler mounts a verbal attack on American involvement in Vietnam in an attempt to maintain his own position in the homosocial order. Privately and publicly Fowler denies involvement, defining himself as a reporter rather than a correspondent: "I wrote what I saw. I took no action—even an opinion is a kind of action" (28). Denying that he himself has any "mental concepts" (94), he lays claim to an impossible objectivity, the hypothetical "view from nowhere." Under Pyle's questioning, he admits his sympathy toward old-style imperial colonialism: "I'd rather be an exploiter who fights for what he exploits, and dies with it" (96). In the narrative economy, he figures the British attitude toward the European colonial presence, the disengagement that Captain Trouin attributes to the whole nation: "We are fighting all of your wars, but you leave us the guilt" (151). There is historical support for Trouin's position: the British encouraged the reconquest of Vietnam in 1945, providing arms to the French soldiers interned by the Japanese during World War II. In spite of his pretence of disengagement, Fowler claims membership in the club of "the old colonial peoples" (157).

The impulse to typify, which Bhabha perceives as a ubiquitous tool in the colonial's kit, plays a large role in Fowler's management of his world. Early in the novel, Phuong's function as a symbol of Vietnam is specified; she is *"[le] pays qui te ressemble"* (14). Successful with the labels *woman* and *Oriental,* he tries to use the same technique with *American* although, as his constant scrutiny suggests, he feels less secure in his attempt to constitute a white man as a "fixed difference." He positions Pyle as "the quiet American" of the title, the man full of ironies but without ambiguities, who belongs to "a psychological world of great simplicity, where you talked of Democracy and Honor without the *u* as it's spelt on old tombstones, and you mean what your father meant by the same words" (90). Falling back on a trait associated with America from the time of Columbus, Fowler repeatedly comments on Pyle's innocence. His implication that there is an American character historically consistent and impervious to contingency essentializes Pyle.

This savage stereotyping comes from Fowler's intense need to repress his knowledge of sameness and establish difference between himself and Pyle. Invested as he is in the position of (ex)colonial disengagé, he must at all cost avoid noticing the resemblances between their situations. By fixing his gaze on Pyle—by keeping him under surveillance in his role of reporter—he can avoid self-scrutiny. However, Fowler is quite aware of the similarity in their colonial empowerment: the Vietnamese "don't want our white skins around telling them what they want" (94). In a racist conflation of the peasants and their animals, he tells Pyle that "in five hundred years . . . small boys will be sitting on the buffaloes. I like the buffaloes, they don't like our smell, the smell of Europeans. And remember—from a buffalo's point of view you are European too" (95). In order to prove Pyle wrong, Fowler insists on both their common imperial status and the continuity of Western imperialism.

In spite of Fowler's frenzied attempts to establish and maintain difference, the similarities between Fowler and Pyle are brought into focus by their common attraction to Phuong. Until Pyle declares his interest in her, Fowler regards him as "a prize pupil" (24). In a classic demonstration of the structure of the homosocial, Fowler's posture toward Pyle is paternal, with the familiarity an older man from an older culture feels free to use toward a younger one. He interrogates Pyle and berates him about the simplistic nature of his mental operations, his dependence on romantic abstractions (though Fowler's cynicism itself is merely an inversion of romanticism). When the dialogue goes in unexpected directions, Fowler blames these turns on Pyle. He complains that "my conversations with Pyle seemed to take grotesque directions. . . . Was it because of his sincerity that they so ran off the customary rails? His conversation never took the corners" (104); that is, it never follows the direction laid down by the paternal speaker, the acknowledged superior in the homosocial order. Their relationship is well established by the time Pyle becomes a rival for Phuong—a development as much a product of that relationship as a response to her. Their contest for Phuong echoes the contest between European and American imperialism: it is a question of who has the biggest resources at his disposal (Hwang's Danish schoolgirl could provide a Lacanian insight here). Pyle can offer her "security and respect" (78). Because he possesses "the infinite riches of respectability," he can marry her, whereas Fowler, whose wife refuses to divorce him, offers only a temporary home. Fowler becomes so obsessed with Pyle that he reflects, "It was as if I had been betrayed, but one is not betrayed by an enemy" (140). This perception gestures toward the structure of his relationship with Pyle but does not acknowledge it. Only with Pyle's death—in which Fowler tells himself he must connive because Pyle's endorsement of terrorist activities endangers the civilian population—and the consequent disappearance of Pyle's threat to Fowler's domestic peace can Fowler acknowledge his affection for Pyle. Pyle's death forces Fowler to ponder the similarities from which he has averted his gaze: "Was I so different from Pyle? . . . Must I too have my foot thrust in the mess of life before I saw the pain?" (186).

The Oedipal nature of the homosocial relationship[10] with its antifilial outcome is underlined by Fowler's observation that "the sight of Oedipus emerging with his bleeding eyeballs from the palace at Thebes would surely give a better training for life today" (182)—better than the American movie articulating Pyle's fantasy, in which the hero rescues a girl, kills his enemy, and leads a charmed life. In Fowler's reinscription of the Oedipus myth, the father triumphs in the ritual *agon.*

Quite capable of understanding that he is "inventing a character" (133) for Phuong (as he has for Pyle without acknowledgment), Fowler is nonetheless oblivious to his part in her expropriation. Abjuring "mental concepts" and thus construing his environment in material terms, he thinks of Phuong much as the drunken Granger does, as "a piece of tail" (36). He muses "she was the hiss of steam, the clink of the cup, she was a certain hour of the night and the promise of rest" (12), but his characteristic thought of her is of "the soft hairless skin" when he goes off to sleep with his hand between her legs—in which position, not so incidentally, he formulates his last idea about Pyle, which is inextricably imbricated with his idea of himself: "Am I the only one who really cared for Pyle?" (22). His irritated response to Pyle's concern for Phuong's best interest shows his perception of Phuong: " 'If it's only her interests you care about, for God's sake leave Phuong alone. Like any other woman she'd rather have . . .' the crash of a mortar saved Boston ears from the Anglo-Saxon word" (59). In short, in Fowler's psychological economy, Phuong is only a cunt to be had for the asking without any obligation on his part to arouse or fulfill desire.

Fowler does not scrutinize any aspect of male engenderment beyond the parameters of homosocial rivalry; he does interrogate the sign *man,* but only as regards American usage. He pretends not to understand what Granger means by "a man's man" (66) or by the compliment "Anyway you're a man" (36) to an acquaintance who accompanies Granger on a quest for girls. Fowler, himself no stranger to brothels, once again averts his gaze from self-scrutiny in order to persist in his perpetual monitoring of difference in similarity.

Articulating no regrets for the British empire itself, Fowler needs only the homosocial colonial situation. Gallimard, stripped of all support for his engenderment, forced to recognize that he is object in Song Liling's narrative as well as subject of his own, has at last no site from which to position his subjectivity. Fowler, however, can continue to exist as long as he is supported by the colonial situation, a white man still comfortably engendered in a homosocial order empowering white men bent on careers of privilege and exploitation.

But the ideology of privilege is veiled from its beneficiaries. Fowler must remain oblivious to the deep structures of gender differentiation upon which imperialism, as Hwang so eloquently shows, ultimately rests. Thus the features of imperial rule rooted in the female imaginary, which are critiqued in *M. Butterfly*, appear as "nature" in *The Quiet American*. Although Greene does suggest that the rivalry of imperial nations, specifically that of Britain and the United States, can be read through the lens of the family romance, there is no hint that he recognizes the way in which imperialism subsumes the colonized into already existent structures of gender relations. Although the defining characteristics of the imperial subject fingered by Hwang are evident in Greene, the destructiveness of the model seems merely contingent, an accident. In no way does Greene address the gender assumptions underlying the justification of imperial power. Indeed, Fowler's cynicism barely covers the traces of Greene's nostalgia for the power configurations of nation and gender prevalent before the Second World War. Benedict Anderson speaks to this situation: "It is always the ruling classes . . . that long mourn the empires, and their grief always has a stagey quality to it."[11] This observation nicely conveys the tone of *The Quiet American*, which throbs with an urgent desire to seize the day when the sun is already sinking fast.

Notes

1. Richard West, "Graham Greene and *The Quiet American*," *New York Review of Books* 24 (May 1991): 49.
2. Greene, born into an upper-middle-class professional family, was a

member of the governing classes. His father was headmaster of Berkhampsted School, where Greene himself was educated before he went up to Oxford. At both, but particularly at school, the attitudes and values appropriate to a citizen of the empire would have been inculcated: "The public schools . . . were geared to the empire's needs. Many of the ideals they aimed at, the qualities they worked to instill in their wards—notions of service, feelings of superiority, habits of authority—were derived from, and consequently dependent upon, the existence of an empire: of colonial subjects to serve, feel superior to, and exert authority over"; from Brian Porter, *The Lion's Share: A Short History of British Imperialism, 1850–1970* (London: Longman, 1975), 103.

3. David Henry Hwang, *M. Butterfly* (New York: Plume, 1989), 17. Subsequent references will be in parentheses in the text.
4. Judith Mayne, "Walking the *Tightrope* of Feminism and Male Desire," in *Men in Feminism,* ed. Alice Jardine and Paul Smith (New York: Methuen, 1987), 70.
5. Edward W. Said, *Orientalism* (New York: Vintage, 1979), 20.
6. Cited in Arthur Brittan, *Masculinity and Power* (Oxford: Blackwell, 1989), 83.
7. Homi K. Bhabha, "The Other Question: Difference, Discrimination and the Discourse of Colonialism," in *Literature, Politics and Theory* (New York: Methuen, 1986), 164.
8. Eve Kosofsky Sedgwick, *Between Men: English Literature and Male Homosocial Desire* (New York: Columbia Univ. Press, 1985) 1–2.
9. Graham Greene, *The Quiet American* (1955; reprint, New York: Penguin 1962), 97.
10. Sedgwick, *Between Men,* 22.
11. Benedict Anderson, *Imagined Communities* (London: Verso, 1983; reprint, 1991), 111.

12

J. R. Ackerley and the Ideal Friend

David Bergman

Perhaps only the lesbian transvestites is a more assiduous student of male heterosexual behavior than the homosexual man, but homosexual men—because they are males and can socialize with straight males in all-male contexts—have a privileged place from which to examine the subject. Homosexual men and lesbian transvestites are keen observers of straight masculinity for a variety of reasons, but no doubt key among them is the desire "to pass" in order to be accepted as a heterosexual male. But passing as a straight man is more than trying to take on the protective coloring that helps homosexuals and lesbian transvestites survive in an intensely homophobic society; for both groups the role has a particular allure of power and freedom, not to mention eroticism. And it is also a source of deep resentment and conflict. Straight masculinity—and let it be clear from the outset that for me the phrase is not redundant—straight masculinity is never a neutral subject of inquiry.

But homosexual men are not merely students of heterosexual masculinity; in some sense they are its creators. A number of scholars (David W. Halperin and Eve Kosofsky Sedgwick among them) have argued that both in English and German the term *homosexuality* predates the invention of the word *heterosexuality*. Indeed, heterosexual seems to have been invented to give semantic symmetry to the taxonomic label of homosexual. Who first used these terms and what was meant by them remain in doubt and perhaps never will be resolved, but whether the terms were first created by Karl Heinrich Ulrichs, Karl Maria Kertbeny, or John Addington Symonds, the fact remains that the words were coined by homosexual men.[1] Moreover, many of the most powerful images of heterosexual masculinity have been homosexual men—from Ivor Novello to Rock Hudson and James Dean; thus gay or homosexual men have been among the most enduring models of heterosexual masculinity.

Whether it is useful to think of homosexuality as giving rise to heterosexuality, or as in Sedgwick's case as poles on a spectrum of homosociality, it is important to note that their differences do not keep them far apart. They are separated not by cultural mountains and oceans, but at most by picket fences and railroad tracks. They are nodes in a highly complex interactive communications systems. They are nextdoor neighbors, with abutting property lines.

Strict constructionists of sexuality, of course, will argue that drawing a line *is* the problem, and that such categories as heterosexual and homosexual are merely imposed on the great polymorphous perversity of the population, a mere invention that has regimented itself. I do not mean to take issue with such an analysis of how sexuality should be conceptualized. Perhaps the concepts that the anthropologist Gilbert Herdt has developed can make clear the mapping of cultural boundaries I have in mind. Herdt argues for the existence of a *gay* culture, as opposed to a *homosexual* culture, in which there is a "distinctive system of rules, norms, attitudes, and, yes, beliefs from which the culture of gay men is made, a culture that sustains the social relations of same-sex desire."[2] Herdt's gay cultural space is epitomized by the gay ghetto, but is not limited to it. And just as the gay ghetto exists within the straight city, sharing many of its properties, such as fuzzy, ever-shifting borders, so to the cultural space of gay writing exists within but is ambiguously sectioned off from the straight literary practice. In homosexual culture, even more than in gay culture, boundaries were tightly sealed because of the need to keep sexuality a secret, albeit at times, an open secret.

Homosexual and gay writers have spent a great deal of energy surveying this boundary, although in the last twenty years the figure of the straight man has had a diminishing presence in gay literature, at least as an erotic object. In an as-yet-unpublished essay "Straight Women, Gay Men," Edmund White notes:

> When I was a kid back in the fifties . . . gay men hated each other so much they longed to seduce heterosexual men, "real men." . . . After the 1960s all that began to change. . . . No longer was their fondest hope (a hope by definition always frustrated) to sleep with straight men. Now those gay men who prized rough-and-ready masculinity began to embody it. In droves gay men went to the gym, sprouted mustaches, took up such professions as truck driving, heavy construction and farming. . . . Masculinity seemed more like a costume than an eternal and natural privilege.[3]

For Edmund White, the homosexual fascination with straight masculinity was structured by three interrelated myths about sexuality and gender. The first was that masculinity and sexuality were inseparable categories that were "eternal and natural." Second, that these "eternal and natural" properties gave the individual superiority, "privilege," glamour. Finally, because of his innate and abiding inferiority, the homosexual will always lack these qualities and have access to them vicariously only by loving the heterosexual male. Gay liberation, by unpacking the notion of the "eternal and natural privilege" of heterosexuality and espousing the value of same sex desire, has converted "masculinity" into a costume that can be worn by all without any particular distinction. In the debate over allowing acknowledged homosexuals into the armed forces, one of the most curious arguments surrounds the shower room where homophobes fear the lustful homosexual gaze will corrupt the sanctity of the heterosexual male body. A different fear seems to be behind this argument: the straight man's narcissistic loss of the adoring but covert gaze of homosexual men. For if the straight soldier loses his privileged licensed gaze—and what guy hasn't "clocked out his buddies"?—he will no longer be able to bask in the furtive, adoring one.

Gay writers, freed to look at gay men approvingly, have gazed less and less at their straight cohorts. Consequently the heterosexual male plays a stronger role in pre-Stonewall homosexual writing than in post-Stonewall gay writing, and perhaps no one has more assiduously charted the force fields between the homosexual and the heterosexual than J. R. Ackerley, whose entire oeuvre seems concerned with it. I turn to his work and to examine it in historical relief as a point from which contemporary gay writers have moved.

J. R. Ackerley is a difficult person to place in literary history—a little too young for Bloomsbury and a little too old for the Auden gang, he nevertheless was a close friend of E. M. Forster and a generous supporter of the young Auden. From 1935 to 1959 he was the literary editor of *The Listener.* Anthony Howard has called him "the greatest Literary Editor of his time—perhaps of all time," and *The Times* in its obituary called him an "incomparable" editor. A playwright and novelist, his strongest work as a writer was his nonfiction: a memoir of India, *Hindoo Holiday* (1932); a study of canine affection, *My Dog Tulip* (1956, rev. 1966); and an exploration of his relationship to his father, *My Father and Myself,* (1968) finished the last year of his life and published posthumously. Although Charles Monteith has called him "one of the best writers of prose of this century," his limited output and his employment of rather oddly mixed genres have kept his work from being fully appreciated.[4]

Yet as varied as these books appear to be, all of Ackerley's work deals with the same obsessive theme: losing the Ideal Friend. The Ideal Friend, like all ideals, is by definition never found, although his sighting is always rumored: in Ackerley's emotional calculus, the Ideal Friend is a sum that is approached and then fades into an approximate distance. In his masterpiece *My Father and Myself* he presents his definition of the Ideal Friend:

> I think I can put him together in a partly negative way by listing some of his main disqualifications. He should not be effeminate, indeed perfectly normal; I did not exclude education but did not want it, I could supply all that myself. . . . He should admit me but no one else; he should be physically attractive to me and younger than myself—the younger the better, as close to innocence; finally he should be on the small side, lusty, circumcised, physically healthy and clean.[5]

It is useful from the outset to see the contradictions that run through this definition. Ackerley was himself aware that his desire to find the Ideal Friend may seem a rather dubious enterprise on moral and practical grounds: "It may be thought that I had set myself a task so difficult of accomplishment as almost to put success purposely beyond my reach; it may be thought too that the reason why this search was taking me out of my own class into the working class . . . was guilt" (126). But one contradiction may escape immediate notice: English working-class males are rarely circumcised. Ackerley set himself an almost impossible task when he set out to find a man both from the working classes and circumcised. Again, Ackerley appears to favor men of a robust constitution, nevertheless he prefers those who are smaller. The Ideal Friend must be smart but not too smart, strong but not too strong, heterosexual but not too heterosexual.

The definition is quite obviously filled with internalized homophobia, of which Ackerley was also well aware. The ostensibly heterosexual Ideal Friend—what I will simply call the I.F. (the great *IF* of Ackerley's romantic desire)—maintains the elevated position of normality, while the homosexual is lowered to the abnormal, the sick, the perverse. Of the young sailor who came closest to fulfilling the requirements of I.F., Ackerley wrote:

> I did not want him to think me 'queer' and himself a part of homosexuality, a term I disliked since it included prostitutes, pansies, pouffs and queens. Though he met some of my homosexual friends, I was always on edge in case they talked in front of him the loose homosexual chatter we talked among ourselves. My sailor was a sacred cow and must be protected against all contaminations. (127)

Ackerley condescends to his I.F., whom he prefers to be poorer, smaller, as well as less educated, but despite this condescension—perhaps because of it—he wishes to protect both himself from the humiliation of being thought "queer" and the Ideal Friend from the contagion of being around homosexuals. Ackerley regards homosexuality as a contagion that might spread and that demands eternal vigilance to control. A word at the wrong time or the wrong place is all that is needed to corrupt the Ideal Friend who must remain innocent. In deference to the vulnerability of the Ideal Friend, whose innocence can never be immunized against the queer, Ackerley must adopt the manner of the heterosexual no matter how alien to himself or frustrating to the formation of genuine friendship.

But we can exaggerate the degree of condescension. The metaphor of the I.F. as a "sacred cow" sounds like a put-down, but it's not. Animals have a particularly elevated status in Ackerley's work; no one is treated with more respect than his beloved dog Queenie, who is the heroine of his novel *We Think the World of You* and *My Dog Tulip*. Queenie's special role is anticipated in Ackerley's travel book *Hindoo Holiday,* which recounts his short stay in India, where he encountered the sacredness of beasts with Sharma, the maharaja's "lover boy." "I gazed in wonder and admiration," Ackerley records,

> at the huge white marble form and calm majestic face. How peaceful were the long drooping ears! How beautiful the line of the heavy dewlap and gentle jowls. . . . The large dark glowing eyes set far apart were finely marked with black. . . . The great white face [bore] a grave wisdom and benignity of expression. . . . No wonder, I thought, these beasts are generated and the females thought to be the seat of Generation. I glanced at Sharma. . . . 'Ah, my fine young bullocks!' I thought.[6]

To be a sacred cow is to be something quite extraordinary! Powerful, peace, and privileged, the sacred cow represents a divine androgyny whose sensitivity and nurturance is never compromised by weakness or nerves.

Nor should Ackerley's desire for "innocence" be viewed as condescending because he saw himself, despite his rather large number of sex partners, as essentially innocent. For Ackerley the sure sign of innocence is a belief in romantic love between equals. In *My Father and Myself,* Ackerley recalls a Persian whom he knew from his Cambridge days when Ackerley mooned over him from afar. Ten years later they meet again. The Persian, who is gay, invites Ackerley back to his flat where, according to Ackerley, "my apparently artless ideas of love had no place in his highly sophisticated repertoire . . . and the attentions and even acrobatics he required to stimulate his jaded sex were not merely disagreeable to me but actually uncomfortable. . . . He said scathingly at last, 'The trouble with you is you're innocent' " (120). The I.F. must be innocent so that he can be Ackerley's equal. Sex that does not derive from love is tainted by the power relations of age and class. Jadedness—the sin of lower-class heterosexuals—is almost as repellent to Ackerley as the sophistication of upper-class homosexuals, because it makes him feel inferior. What Ackerley really wants is to create a space outside of either homo- or heterosexuality where he and the I.F. can live in childlike innocence, freed from the labelling that elevates one at the expense of the other.

We can, I think, regard this hypothesized space as an escape to some prelapsarian world, and frequently it is such a space. But it also can be, as Thomas Yingling has argued "a privileged site outside cultural convention from which it is possible to critique the patriarchal structures of bourgeois desire," a place that is "marginalized and potentially revolutionary."[7] Ackerley describes his place on the sexual map as beyond labels; nevertheless, he "stood among the men, not among the women. Girls I despised; vain, silly creatures. . . . Their place was the harem, from which they should never have been released; true love, equal and understanding love, occurred only between men. I saw myself therefore in the tradition of the Classic Greeks surrounded and supported by all the famous homosexuals of history" (118).

I do not want to excuse Ackerley's misogyny or his gynophobia undisguised in this and other passages. But I do not want his misogyny to obscure the revolutionary potential of the equality he wishes to achieve with other men—the "equal and understanding love" that he feels occurs "only between men." Such mutuality of affection *is* a radical departure for an Englishman of his generation. Significantly, Ackerley locates that equality within "the Greek view of life," an ideology he inherited from Goldsworthy Lowes Dickinson, the teacher of E. M. Forster and his closest friend and mentor, and from Edward Carpenter, himself an apostle of Whitmanian adherence.

The impulse among British homosexuals to seek sexual partners from a different class is one of the more problematic elements in the structure of their desires. It is all too simple to see this tendency as exploitation of the poor. No doubt exploitation was involved. As Jeffrey Weeks points out, Roger Casement was in the habit of recording not only the size of his pick-ups' penises, but their price.[8] Yet for Edward Carpenter, "The blending of Social Strata in masculine love seems . . . one of its pronounced, and social hopeful features,"[9] and Carpenter's life-long relationship to George Merrill appears to have been unmarred by economic exploitation. Ackerley's relationship with working-class men was neither as exploitive as Casement's nor as idealistic as Carpenter's. W. H. Auden, I believe, shrewdly sees both the appeal and the necessity of Ackerley's arrangement:

All sexual desire presupposes that the loved one is in some way "other" than the lover: the eternal and, probably, insolvable problem for the homosexual is finding a substitute for the natural differences, anatomical and psychic, between a man and a woman. . . . A homosexual who is like Mr. Ackerley, an intellectual and reasonably well-off is very apt to become romantically enchanted by the working class, whose lives, experiences, and interests are so different from their own, and to whom, because they are poorer, the money and comforts he is able to provide can be a cause for affectionate gratitude.[10]

For Auden, Ackerley's involvement with the working class is explained by mutual give and take. Ackerley could share with his working-class lovers the pleasure of exchanging different sorts of experience, and for the material benefits Ackerley could provide they could return the pleasure of having truly helped. Auden is impatient with anyone who might question the morality of such an arrangement. "A great deal of nonsense has been spoken and written about the sinfulness of giving and receiving money for sexual favors," and Auden wants none of it.[11]

But Weeks suggests another strain to the cross-class tendencies of English homosexuals. He finds these liaisons "suggestive of the guilt-ridden fear of relationships within their own class."[12] Ackerley's anxiety about what his friends might say or do in the presence of the I.F. suggests his discomfort with his own class status. Ackerley's hold on upper-middle-class status was extremely loose. His parents were from the lower classes, and through hard work and good luck, Roger Ackerley made a fortune in the fruit importing business by finding successful ways of promoting bananas. (One of his more amusing stunts was running a contest awarding £1000 to the first person to discover a "perfectly straight banana.")[13] When Roger died, he left his family in straightened conditions, and J. R. Ackerley struggled all his life to earn enough to maintain his mother, aunt, and neurotic sister.

As Ackerley views it, the "equal and understanding love" of the I.F. is threatened on three flanks: on the right by silly, manipulative girls; on his left by competitive capitalism and materialism, which breaks down the compassion necessary for real equality and emotional mutuality, and from his rear by heartless pouffs and queens. Only homosexuals, like himself, who honored " 'the manly respectability' of our relationship" are capable of achieving equality, mutuality, and understanding (127). Indeed, one might trace Ackerley's misogyny to the competition between heterosexual women and homosexual men over the pool of I.F.s. As he wrote in *My Father and Myself:* "The girlfriend was a situation all too liable to be found in the lives of normal boys, and . . . they had to be admitted; I never suffered much from jealousy and the Ideal Friend could have a girl or wife if he wished, so long as she did not interfere with me. No wife ever failed to interfere with me" (137). For Ackerley, female homophobia results from female possessiveness. Under the conditions of late capitalism, women "traffick in men," as exchange quantities that establish their value.

No doubt, here both Ackerley and I risk strenuous opposition. Michael Pollak has argued that "of all the different types of masculine sexual behavior, homosexuality is undoubtedly the one whose functioning is most strongly suggestive of the market."[14] Traditionally both in Europe and Asia, homosexual behavior has had no other institutional structure but the house of prostitution. But just as homosexuals have entered into the sexual market, they have also complained most vehemently against it. What I think needs to be explored is not merely the way men treat others as objects, but how they objectify themselves.

It is odd, to say the least, that feminist theory—which has developed a subtle, elaborate, and accurate analysis of how men objectify women—has failed to see in its equally subtle, elaborate, and accurate analysis of heterosexual male ego structure the very same objectification. If, as Nancy Chodorow has argued, masculinity is defined through greater ego independence and firmness of ego boundaries that block both emotional expression and empathetic understanding, then masculinity is by far the more objectlike gender role.[15] If men don't complain about such objectification, it is because objectification rather than chaffing against a man's sense of his masculinity, confirms and extols it. This desire for objectification becomes the greatest obstacle in becoming the Ideal Friend.

I want to look at two instances in Ackerley's work where the drive *for* objectification becomes the obstacle to ideal friendship. The first occurs in his play *Prisoners of War,* his first published work. The action takes place during the Great War in a hotel in the Alps where the Germans have interned captured British officers. In many ways this magic mountain ought to be the marginal site where ideal friendship should be able to blossom, but it's not. The play follows two pairs of homoerotic relations between Tetford and Rickman, and between Conrad and Grayle. Tetford and Conrad are older, socially higher, and homosexual; Rickman and Grayle are younger, of a lower class, and assertively heterosexual. Tetford's relations with Rickman work out by the end of the play because their relationship has been squarely placed within the objectifying context of a business partnership. In Act III, they decide to go to Canada—Rickman's country—to work together. Tetford's suggestion is carefully monitored to erase any strong emotions: "I thought we might start something [in Canada] on our own. We'd pull along all right together, I guess—and you need me to keep hold on you." Rickman agrees, but with one caveat, "Well, you ain't what one's call extra tough; and you need to be tough out there." Tetford replies "scornfully," "I bet I'm as tough as you—at the moment." They shake on their "partnership" and according to stage directions "*Something passes between them.*"[16] The preconditions of toughness and business—both objectifying conditions—are necessary before any contact can be made.

Conrad's relationship to Grayle—his "holy grail," so to speak—is less successful. Suffering from depression, Conrad asks Grayle while stroking "the curly head affectionately," if he'll "stick by" him. Grayle, who suffers this affection because—again according to the stage directions—he had "been educated at a good public school," breaks away as soon as others appear. Grayle cannot deal with Conrad's increasing demands to empathize with his subjective experience. When Conrad suffers a psychotic break, Grayle is unwilling to be left alone in the room with him, and it is Tetford who upbraids Conrad for his lack of sympathy, "Can't you be decent to him even now?" Grayle's need for objectification—his fear of subjectivity—is exemplified by his affair with Madame Louis, the Jewish widow, who in the antisemitism of the day is quite transparently a fortune hunter. Grayle can manage his relationship with Mme Louis because it is a mercantile exchange that requires no intersubjectivity. In some of the more famous lines of the play, Mme Louis asks Conrad whether it is true that he "does not like much the fair sex." "The fair sex?" Conrad asks her in reply, "Which sex is that?" (119) As a Jew, she is neither "fair" in coloring nor in her business deals. She exemplifies the commodification of sex that Ackerley associates with heterosexuality.

The second incident takes place in India—again a locale that Ackerley hopes might take him outside of capitalist relations. But colonialization and patriarchy once more have warped the concept of masculinity despite the rhetoric extolling friendship. Ackerley is told that during *Holi,* a festival in honor of Krishna, "all men are equal and may be treated so in the name of Friendship" (201), but the reality falls far short. Narayan and Sharma are best friends, who, although married, sleep together, but without sex. Once Sharma, who is the maharaja's paramour, kissed Narayan who pretended to sleep. Sharma tells Narayan that if Narayan dies, he could not continue living. Ackerley sees in this relationship the asymmetry that ruins all his own friendships. Narayan's feelings for Sharma are not as honest and simple as Sharma's feelings. Ackerley comments that Narayan's affection "is based chiefly on possession; he is proud of the influence he has over this wild handsome creature, Sharma's unquestioning, unswerving devotion and respect. . . . Narayan is not unkind to him, but he is . . . contemptuous of the childish mind, and treats him usually as if he were a slave or a hopelessly backward student"(244). Heterosexual males, then, fall into two categories: They either objectify others and themselves, contemptuously treating the innocence that is necessary for true love and intersubjective understanding; or they are vulnerably innocent, subject to exploitation or corruption. Only under the protection of a noneffeminate homosexual can the heterosexual be protected, and his egalitarian feelings cultivated.

And yet, even Ackerley cannot protect himself or his potential Ideal Friends from the corruption and competition of heterosexuality and capitalism. He finds himself using a ploy "akin to my father's technique of bribery in advance for special . . . service" (*My Father,* 136). But finally the I.F. is a highly conflicted figure, always already lost, because he is the screen for Ackerley's incestuous desires for his father. *My Father and Myself* is not merely an account of Ackerley's search for the real man beneath the successful Edwardian exterior, but also a love letter to revive and consummate his desires for his father. If the only copulative Ackerley can engage in is the one in the title, it is a sign that he has sublimated his incestuous wishes and belated his desires. For although Ackerley doesn't spell it out, it is his father who is best described by his formula for the Ideal Friend; his father was generous, clean, seemingly innocent, less educated, and bisexual. Ackerley's discovery that his father headed an entirely different family in the same neighborhood and had probably worked as a homosexual prostitute allows him to fantasize the imaginary home he might have had with his own father, the illicit and egalitarian love he never found.

Although Ackerley traveled in Japan, India, Italy, and England, he found no place where friendship can flourish between equals; nor could he find the male free from the forces of objectification and competition. All men would sooner or later betray the love he would give them, as he himself betrayed his own feelings in the silence and the distance he put between everyone. Ironically, although no human could occupy the space of the Ideal Friend, his beloved Queenie, the German shepherd to whom he dedicated *My Father and Myself* and about whom he wrote so lovingly in *My Dog Tulip,* came as close as he was ever to find.

Notes

1. For a lengthy treatment of this issue see David M. Halperin, *One Hundred Years of Homosexuality* (New York: Routledge, 1990), 155, n. 1; 158, n. 17; Eve Kosofsky Sedgwick, *Epistemology of the Closet* (Berkeley: University of California Press, 1990), 2.
2. Gilbert Herdt, "Introduction," in *Gay Culture in America: Essays from the Field,* ed. Gilbert Herdt (Boston: Beacon, 1992), 5.
3. "Straight Women, Gay Men," unpublished manuscript in my personal possession.

4. All these critical comments may be found in Peter Parker, *Ackerley: The Life of J. R. Ackerley* (New York: Farrar Straus, 1989), 1–2.
5. J. R. Ackerley, *My Father and Myself* (New York: Harcourt Brace Jovanovich, 1968), 125. Subsequent references will be in parentheses in the text.
6. J. R. Ackerley, *Hindoo Holiday: An Indian Journal* (New York: Poseidon Press, 1960), 253. Subsequent references to this work will be in parentheses in the text.
7. Yingling, Thomas E., *Hart Crane and the Homosexual Text: New Thresholds, New Anatomies* (Chicago: University of Chicago Press, 1990), 30.
8. Weeks, Jeffrey. *Coming Out: Homosexual Politics in Britain, from the Nineteenth Century to the Present.* (London: Quartet, 1977), 40.
9. Quoted in Weeks, *Coming Out,* 41.
10. W. H. Auden, "Papa Was a Wise Old Sly-Boots," in *Forwards and Afterwards* (New York: Vintage, 1974), 451.
11. Auden, *Papa,* 451.
12. Weeks, *Coming Out,* 41.
13. Parker, *Ackerley,* 43.
14. Michael Pollak, "Male Homosexuality; or Happiness in the Ghetto," in *Western Sexuality: Practices and Precept in Past and Present Times,* ed. Phillippe Arias and Andre Bejin (Oxford: Oxford University Press, 1985), 44.
15. Nancy Chodorow, *The Reproduction of Mothering: Psychoanalysis and the Sociology of Gender* (Berkeley: University of California Press, 1976), 167–69.
16. J. R. Ackerley, *The Prisoners of War,* in *Gay Plays,* ed. Michael Wilcox, vol. 3 (London: Methuen, 1925), 128–29. Subsequent references will be in parentheses in the text.

13

E. M. Forster at the End

Richard Dellamora

In the 1890s in England there occurred both a renaissance of cultural production by male homosexuals and a major onslaught against them that took as its focus Oscar Wilde, the cynosure of upper-class masculine difference. The successful prosecution of Wilde on charges of "gross indecency" in 1895 brought this renewal to an end with a crash that has continued to be heard across several generations of middle-class men, sexually and emotionally attracted to other men. The effect on the generation born around 1880 was particularly severe as instances the case of E. M. Forster, who was 16 years of age at the time of Wilde's debacle. Young men like John Gray, Aubrey Beardsley, and Alfred Douglas, who were in their late teens or early to mid-twenties between 1890 and 1894, experienced moral and practical support when they questioned hegemonic values. Forster also found friendship and encouragement among homosexuals such as Oscar Browning, G. Lowes Dickinson, and others; and he became romantically entangled with H. O. Meredith while an undergraduate at King's College, Cambridge. But Meredith was at least nominally straight, and sexual fulfillment eluded Forster for many years. Not until he fell in love with a young man named Mohammed el Adl while in Alexandria during World War I did he become sexually experienced.

In the meantime, Forster enjoyed friendships with homosexual men and supportive women while also undergoing a series of intense, sexually frustrated relationships with heterosexual or bisexual men. Whereas no definitive answer is available as to why Forster's homosexuality was for so long blocked at the site of the genitals, the end of relatively open homosexual self-expression posed major difficulties in his personal life and in the career that unfolded for him during the first decade of the new century—as an ironic observer of the tragicomedy of English upper-middle-class life and manners.

"Albergo Empedocle" (1903), Forster's first published short story, was suitable for publication in one of the homosexual magazines that had appeared at Oxford and London early in the decade. After 1895 these were gone or else under changed editorial policies. Wilde had made writing for a double audience the height of chic, but the glamour disappeared after male homosexuality had been negated in the most public fashion. Male heterosexual writers too lost the opportunity critically to assess gender norms.[1] The relatively public opportunities for socializing and collaborative work that male homosexuals had briefly enjoyed ceased to exist. As a young homosexual writer with a keen eye for the details of bourgeois domestic life, Forster found himself without a suitable social or publishing context. That he overcame these limits in a string of successful novels, climaxing in the publication of *Howards End* in 1910, was a triumph that could not be sustained indefinitely. Forster expresses the situation as early as a diary entry of June 16, 1911. Shortly after the success of *Howards End* and at a time when he was in his early thirties, he writes: "Weariness of the only subject that I both can and may treat—the love of men for women & vice versa."[2]

Even when Forster in his fiction resolutely focuses on male-female relations, they have as a limiting term the dangers posed by excessive investments between men. The threat of what Victorian sexologists defined as sexual inversion actively shapes the representation of conventional sexuality in Forster's writing, and this fact is already true in "Albergo Empedocle." In referring to this novel situation, which pertains not only to Forster's difficulties but to his social milieu, I use the term the *heterosexual contract*, by which I mean the prescribed investment of young men in relations with women whose main significance is their relation to social (re)production.[3] This contract, which defines both male-female relations and the male relations that frame them, marks a significant change from the male homosocial construction of sexuality prevalent in the mid-Victorian period. The contract demands a "forgetting" of desire between men that Forster figures at the literal level through the use of amnesia. As for young women, in their roles as fiancées or wives, they must sacrifice the slightest suggestion of a female difference that might exist outside the limits of the phallogocentric order.[4]

The new context has implications for the structure of Forster's fiction, in particular for the function of irony with respect to the reader as an excluded third term who is, nonetheless, implicated in the text by the way in which desire is structured between a narrator and narratee.[5] In a recent study, Ross Chambers has argued that oppositional writing depends primarily upon irony, a trope that can be put into operation only in the presence of a reader, who provides a necessary third term in addition to the first two. Chambers distinguishes two such operations: an irony of negation, which negates values of the dominant culture to whose members the text is in the first instance addressed; and an irony of appropriation, whereby the text suggests different desires to a reader or group of readers in opposition, wittingly or unwittingly, to the values of the dominant group.[6] Remaining for the most part within the limits of reader-response theory, Chambers does not exploit the possibility that structural irony affords for calling into existence as yet indeterminate social groupings. "Albergo Empedocle," while addressed to conventional readers of *Temple Bar,* the journal in which it first appeared, appeals to a second set of readers who share Forster's need both to express and to dissemble a special interest in male intimacy.

This latter group are in an oppositional relation to the heterosexual contract along with its affiliations of class, rank, and nationality—even if, like Harold, the protagonist of the story, they aren't quite aware of the fact. In "Albergo Empedocle," male-male desire places one at the margin of the heterosexual contract but not altogether outside it.[7] This positioning at the margin is necessary if the processes of group formation are to occur but also opens possibilities of self-deception and of failure in personal relations that neither Harold nor Tommy, the framing narrator of the story, escapes.

The significance of the setting of Forster's story amid Greek ruins on Sicily brings to mind the end during the 1890s of the discussion, dating from the late Enlightenment, of the significance of intimacy between males in the institution of pederasty as it had existed in different forms at ancient Athens and Sparta. While Forster as a boy was recoiling from the philistine atmosphere of Tonbridge School, Victorian philology entered a final phase as Walter Pater and Wilde, between 1890 and 1892, continued ironically to undercut the uses to which Greek models were conventionally put in elite education. Even when Greek studies were used to serve the political, social, and economic purposes of male elites, philology performed a useful function in foregrounding the connection between male intimacy and cultural and social production. As part of conventional education, such ties were subjected to critique by writers like Pater and Wilde; on the other hand, the debates compelled homosexual polemicists to theorize connections between masculine desire and positive outcomes in cultural and social relations. In slightly different terms, male homosexual discourses were necessarily preoccupied with the utilities of male intimacy. The forced abandonment of this project for young people of Forster's generation was to have negative consequences for the process of transforming Great Britain into a fully democratic state.[8]

In "Albergo Empedocle" Forster responds to both of these endings by drawing on tropes of metempsychosis and amnesia. On a visit with his bride-to-be and her parents to Sicily, Harold dreams that he has lived before as a Greek at Girgenti, the site of the former city of Acragas, a major commercial and cultural center during the Age of Pericles. The experience seems to suggest that whereas it may no longer be possible to *think Greek,* it is possible to *become Greek.* This rapture, however, can be achieved only at the cost of disconnection from normal existence; in other words, only at a moment when it has become impossible to envisage a hermeneutics of Greek love does the protagonist overleap the work of intellection by assuming for himself a metaphoric identification with the Other. This projection is precipitated by the refusal of

Mildred, Harold's fiancée, and her family to comprehend the possibility of being different. Harold is pushed into a breakdown and has to be repatriated by force to that other island, Great Britain, the counter to Sicily in the story. There he becomes the permanent ward of a mental hospital: "Long before Harold reached the asylum his speech had become absolutely unintelligible: indeed by the time he arrived at it, he hardly ever uttered a sound of any kind" (62).

Under the pressure of rejection by others, metempsychosis becomes an identification that captures the subject within a virtually complete solipsism. The recovery of a prior existence is incompatible with modern life because "we" (that is, we late Victorians) are amnesiacs. "We" have forgotten what it means to think Greek—even though as few years ago as the early 1890s writers were showing us how to do so.[9] Accordingly, although philology retains the grammar and syntax of ancient Greek, in Forster's rhetoric it has lost—as have modern subjects generally—the capacity of enunciation. Only Tommy, whose avowals of "love" for Harold equivocally frame the story, shares his friend's belief: "I firmly believe that he has been a Greek—nay, that he is a Greek, drawn by recollection back into his previous life. He cannot understand our speech because we have lost his pronunciation" (62). Tommy, however, does not speak Harold's language either or, rather, he can speak it only with the language of the body, the most equivocal of utterances, in the kiss that he receives from Harold at the end of the story. The role that Tommy plays needs to be regarded warily because his witness leaves Harold fixed in place as the subject of an existence almost totally estranged from "ours" and onto which, in view of Harold's muteness, Tommy is free to project what he will. Yet his fidelity to a love that cannot be voiced in return is the one space that Forster finds for expressing desire between men.

The extremity of Harold's situation suggests yet one more ending, this time generic, implied in Forster's short story; that is, the end of realist narrative, particularly in the novel, as a story in which two male rivals struggle for possession of a woman.[10] When Forster uses male-homosocial triangulation, he uses it differently so as to show that, at least in his fiction, the mediation of desire between men in a female object has ceased to constitute the terms of normal sexuality. Writing from a tacit homosexual subject-position, Forster frames relations between men and women with an eye to desire between men. This framing poses the possibility of another narrative trajectory to some readers while presenting male-female relations not so much as normal but as representative of the institution of heterosexuality. In this context, Forster describes the implications for female subjectivity of the position of women as "wife" or "woman" within this order. This representation, particularly in Mildred, contributes to the critique of marriage but operates as well so as to limit Forster's awareness of the ways in which female subjectivities can exist in resistance to the formation of gender. Forster demonstrates the cost to women of their positioning within heterosexuality but at the expense of failing to respond to their capacity to differ from their prescribed roles.

In "Albergo Empedocle," the triangle of Harold, Mildred, and Tommy focuses on Harold. Despite the fact that Tommy and Harold's mutual if asymmetrical desires for each other set the interpretive horizons of the story, after Harold's experience Mildred reveals another, more forceful triangle at work: that of herself, her future husband, and her father, Sir Edwin. Mildred takes the following view of Harold's experience: "Worn out," Harold "had fallen asleep, and, . . . had indulged in a fit of imagination on awaking. She had fallen in with it, and they had encouraged each other to fresh deeds of folly. All was clear. And how was she to hide it from her father?" (55) As the family expedition indicates, Harold is marrying not just Mildred but also her family. In return, the contract guarantees Mildred a fixed place in the scheme of things.

As Eve Kosofsky Sedgwick has shown in her discussion of Charles Dickens's *Our Mutual Friend* (1864–65), woman's work in the triangle, as it functions in mid-Victorian fiction, is to save the male from his own indecisive and unrecognized desires. Harold conforms to this script when he insists that Mildred validate his dream by kissing him with passion, something previously absent in their relations. His demand for her knowing acceptance belongs yet more properly to a moment late in male homosocial existence when, as Sedgwick shows, this time by way of her reading of James's "The Beast in the Jungle," woman as "friend" serves the function of cherishing the secret of John Marcher, a man so deeply closeted that he forgets that he has told her his "secret."[11]

Like a number of late Victorian wives who married men attracted to other men,[12] Mildred's ambivalent relation to her status as woman makes her initially prepared to undertake this exacting role but only on condition that she too can become Greek—that is, that within her role as wife she can occupy the place of an imaginary Other to Harold and thereby become more nearly his equal. When she decides that supporting Harold will, to the contrary, require self-sacrifice on her part while reinforcing her subordination as woman and her exclusion from "Greek" culture, she turns on him with remarkable vehemence. As for Harold, he is innocent of what his secret might be or why it needs to be a secret at all. His incomprehension signals that the male-homosocial role of woman as the friend or wife who keeps a man's secret does not in this story provide an effective bound to errant desires. Harold's Greek experience has begun to move him outside the terms of the contract. What he needs are interlocutors who can share his memories.

I. A Roman Ending

"Albergo Empedocle" begins with a letter that seems to set in place the sort of male homosocial triangulation that is a familiar aspect of realist narrative in Victorian fiction. As described by Harold, however, the situation sounds not quite right:

> We've just come from Pompeii. On the whole it's decidedly no go and very tiring. What with the smells and the beggars and the mosquitoes we're rather off Naples altogether, and we've changed our plans and are going to Sicily. The guidebooks say you can run through it in no time; only four places you have to go to, and very little in them. That suits us to a T. Pompeii and the awful Museum here have fairly killed us—except of course Mildred, and perhaps Sir Edwin.
>
> Now why don't you come too? I know you're keen on Sicily, and we all would like it. You would be able to spread yourself no end with your archaeology. For once in my life I should have to listen while you jaw.

You'd enjoy discussing temples, gods, etc., with Mildred. She's taught me a lot, but of course it's no fun for her, talking to us. Send a wire; I'll stand the cost. Start at once and we'll wait for you. The Peaslakes say the same, especially Mildred.

My not sleeping at night, and my headaches are all right now, thanks very much. As for the blues, I haven't had any since I've been engaged, and don't intend to. So don't worry any more.

Yours,
Harold (36)

In fairly evident transcoding, Harold's dissatisfaction with traveling expresses an underlying awareness that the engagement mentioned at the end of the letter is a mistake. The prenuptial tour is, in reality, a series of detours that "go" nowhere and whose predetermined stops on the way have "very little" in them, except, that is, for threatening Harold with annihilation. "Pompeii" and its "awful museum" are associated in his mind with marriage, the family, philistine culture, and the burdens of imperium: in other words, with the responsibilities upon which he is about to enter. For his part, Harold would rather be on another trip, one that would "suit" him "to a T"—that is, to a *T/Tommy*.

In this light, it is not surprising to find Harold resisting his fiancée in her role of *cicerone*. As Tommy writes, submaliciously, a bit later: "Mildred . . . was the fount of information. It was she who generally held the Baedeker and explained it. She had been expecting her continental scramble for several years, and had read a fair amount of books for it, which a good memory often enabled her to reproduce" (37). The key word here is memory, figured in the Baedeker, which connotes repetition. Memory in this sense only appears to "scramble" because it knows where it's headed, having learned its object by rote before meeting it. In contrast to this work of memory is recollection or metempsychosis or the belief, held by Empedocles who once lived at Acragas, in "the transmigration of souls" (41). This latter condition, implicitly recalling efforts within nineteenth-century philology to recover Greek consciousness, enables one to be constituted as wholly other.

Early on in the story, Mildred defends Harold's capacity for imagination against her father, who doubts that Harold has any. As well, it is Mildred who sets matters in motion by telling Harold en route to Girgenti that "today you must imagine you are a Greek" (42). Yet Mildred's capacity for sympathy is put cruelly to the test when Harold experiences his prior existence at Acragas. His continuing psychic stability depends on her sharing this belief with him; with no sense of exaggeration, he says to her: "I might have died if you hadn't believed me" (50). And Mildred does try. "Oh, Harold," she says, "I too may remember. . . . Oh, Harold! I am remembering! . . . . In the wonderful youth of Greece did I speak to you and know you and love you. We walked through the marble streets, we led solemn sacrifices, I armed you for the battle, I welcomed you from the victory. The centuries have parted us, but not for ever. Harold, I too have lived at Acragas!" (53) Without a guidebook to con, however, Mildred fails. She can become Greek only by translating Greece and Greek love into the parodic form of suburban bliss. One imagines her waving Harold from the door as he carries his briefcase into the urban fray. Her difference, which accommodates no difference, is fake, as she says later: "pure imagination, the result of sentimental excitement" (54). Harold's sleep, however, has converted him into a truth-sayer. In response to her claim to have lived at Acragas, he quietly responds: " 'No, Mildred darling, you have not' " (53).

The reader shortly learns that, contrary to his report to Tommy, headaches and insomnia do continue to trouble Harold. Mildred shows no awareness of these symptoms of bodily and spiritual disease. To her as to her father, Harold might just as well be a piece of classical statuary. His external deportment conforms to the observation of an educator like Benjamin Jowett that:

> You may look at a Greek statue and be struck with the flexure of the limbs, the majestic folds of the drapery, the simplicity, the strength. And yet scarcely any topics arise in the mind of the uncritical [viewer]. . . . The highest art is colorless like water, it has been said; it is a surface without prominences or irregularities over which the eye wanders impressed by the beauty of the whole with nothing to detain it at a particular point. . . . It is a smooth surface over which the hand may pass without interruption, but the curious work lies beneath the surface: the effect only is seen from without. The finer the workmanship the more completely is the art concealed.[13]

This remark is, if not colored, then shadowed by the preterition that draws attention to while denying the fact that Greek "limbs" may draw "the eye" (and "the hand") to a "particular point," a point that redirects attention from a surface without openings to "the curious work" accessible only from the inside. Precisely Harold's presentation of "a surface without prominences or irregularities" makes him a suitable candidate as son-in-law, almost too suitable.

In Sicily, however, Harold betrays a disturbing propensity to imagine that he is "someone else," a "dodge" (39) he confesses that he occasionally resorts to when he has trouble falling asleep, or when he has "the blues" (40). When Sir Edwin discovers this capacity, he is shocked: "It is never safe to play tricks with the brain," he admonishes. "I must say I'm astonished: you of all people!" (40) It's even worse after Harold's dream when Sir Edwin demands that unless the young man acknowledges that he has been deluded, the marriage will not take place. What is troubling ("queer" in Sir Edwin's usage) is Harold's ability to change when he encounters something or someone different.

As the mention of Sir Edwin in Harold's letter indicates, Harold's contract is only incidentally with Mildred even as it is only incidental that she has something to say about the Greek temples at Girgenti: she can repeat what she has read. Similarly, in the role of wife and mother, she will repeat the genealogy of the Peaslakes. The corporate character of the engagement is implicitly extended in the brief reference at opening to another ending, the destruction of Herculaneum and Pompeii as a result of an eruption of Vesuvius in 79 A.D. "Pompeii" signifies English as an analogue of Roman culture both in the static density of existence as recovered from the ashes in archaeological digs and in the characteristic twinning of Roman with British imperium in nineteenth-century English thought.[14] The sense of closure impressed on Harold during his visit to "the awful Museum" helps set the stage for the crisis at Girgenti.

On the train from Palermo, Harold's view of Sicily comments ironically on England's economic and political position at the end of the century: "They had hardly crossed the watershed of the island. It was the country of the mines, barren and immense, absolutely destitute of grass or trees, producing nothing but cakes of sallow sulphur, which were stacked on the platform of every wayside station. Human beings were scanty, and they were stunted and dry, mere withered vestiges of men. And far below at the bottom of the yellow waste was the moving living sea, which embraced Sicily when she was green and delicate and young, and embraces her now, when she is brown and withered and dying" (42). This vision suggests both the actual as opposed to the putative effects of Empire because Sicily's denudation is a result of centuries of foreign invasion and domination. Tommy/Forster's outburst contrasts, however, to the commentary of the tenth edition of *The Encyclopaedia Britannica* (1902), which blandly remarks on the systematic transfer of capital from Sicily to the north after the unification of Italy:

> Like all southern Italy, Sicily in 1860 was poor, notwithstanding the possession of notable reserves of monetary capital. On the completion of Italian unity part of this pecuniary capital was absorbed by the sudden increase of taxation, and a much greater part was employed by private individuals in the purchase of lands formerly belonging to the suppressed religious corporations. . . . Both the revenues acquired by taxation and the proceeds of the land sales were almost entirely spent by the State in northern Italy, where the new Government, for administrative and military reasons, had been obliged to establish its principal organizations, and consequently its great centers of economic consumption. (vol. 9, 618)

The Peaslakes identify with Sicily's conquerors. After the small upset that occurs when Sir Edwin learns about Harold's "dodge," Mildred restores quiet by returning to the guidebook: she "passed on to the terrible sack of Acragas by the Romans. Whereat their faces relaxed, and they regained their accustomed spirits" (41).[15]

Tommy's "keen" interest in Sicilian archaeology, however, associates him with the world, both pastoral and civic, of *Greek* Sicily, which appears to offer in Acragas a far different model of colonization from Italian, Roman, or English. Harold's letter betokens the wish to recover this existence in company with Tommy (even if the wish can only be uttered in negation and displaced onto Mildred). In the absence of Tommy, the possibility of recovery is open to Harold only in something like the form of his experience at Girgenti, where he falls asleep in the afternoon sun between the legs of a toppled colossal statue of Atlas and wakes convinced that, in an earlier life, he has lived as a citizen of Acragas.

> [There] were two fallen columns, lying close together, and the space that separated them had been silted up and was covered with flowers. On it, as on a bed, lay Harold, fast asleep, his cheek pressed against the hot stone of one of the columns, and his breath swaying a little blue iris that had rooted in one of its cracks. . . .
>
> Sleep has little in common with death, to which men have compared it. Harold's limbs lay in utter relaxation, but he was tingling with life, glorying in the bounty of the earth and the warmth of the sun, and the little blue flower bent and fluttered like a tree in a gale. The light beat upon his eyelids and the grass leaves tickled his hair, but he slept on, and the lines faded out of his face as he grasped the greatest gift that the animal life can offer. (47–48)

Mildred frames the scene as a tourist should: "He looked so picturesque, and she herself, sitting on the stone watching him, must look picturesque too. She knew that there was no one to look at her, but from her mind the idea of a spectator was never absent for a moment. It was the price she had paid for becoming cultivated" (47).

By 1903, high culture, including Greek culture, had been thoroughly commodified for the consumption and adornment of members of Mildred's class. Exotic locales provided the props for situating members of this group in preformulated ways. Mildred responds to such a scene as a masculist observer would. Her gaze is from the position of one who is already an object within such a scene. This framing excludes the possibility that instead of responding in a "cultivated" way Mildred might be changed by contact with "animal life" or by a pastoral existence that combines both spontaneous and cultivated responses. Hence the metonymic function of the travel book, whose mapping determines before one leaves home what knowledge will or will not be ascertained while abroad.[16]

For a middle- or upper-class male homosexual, Greek culture could be commodified in another way in the form of sexual tourism—whether the object of desire remained fantasmatic as it did for Forster on his Italian and Greek tours of 1902 and 1903 or whether it was acquired in more practicable ways. When Baron von Gloeden, for instance, photographs young Sicilian peasants in the ungarb of ancient youth, the discrepancy between sign and signifier indicates the inability of representation to suture the difference between material and imaginary reality. Nonetheless, these images, with the blessing of local Sicilians, drew homosexuals to the villa at Taormina from which von Gloeden sold his postcards.[17] Forster pitches the attraction in another register. In "Albergo Empedocle," Greek culture provides the opportunity of imagining a "better love," as presumably it does for Tommy, whose interest in Sicily is described as that of an archaeologist, not of a tourist. Yet even when resolutely scientific or high-minded, trips like Forster's 1902 visit to Girgenti exist within a structure of erotic fantasy that is marked by class and ethnic snobbery. Forster/Harold/Tommy's aspiration to a better love is distinguishable but not dissociable from the other meanings of fin-de-siècle tourism. For these men, absorption in Greek culture, though oppositional in Chambers's use of the word, signifies economic and national distinction.

Against these significations, Forster buttresses the oppositional meaning of Harold's experience through intertextual reference to polemical texts of the homosexual renaissance of a few years before. Mildred's gaze at Harold recalls that of the Prior at the sleeping figure of Apollo/Apollyon in Pater's "Apollo in Picardy," an imaginary portrait of 1893.[18] In the story, Pater uses the setting of a monastic community in order to analyze the psychological effects of homophobia on a male homosocial subject. The blue iris recalls the hyacinths that blossom after the murder, probably at the hands of the Prior, of his young companion, Hyacinth. Harold's habit of looking out the window of the asylum recalls the Prior's similar practice after he is judged to be insane and placed under house arrest. "Gazing . . . daily for many hours, he would mistake mere blue distance, when that was visible, for blue flowers, for hyacinths, and wept at the sight."[19] In Forster's less ironic text, we simply don't know what Harold sees. The references to Pater, however, provide textual means of overcoming the limiting terms of the "spectator" envisaged by Mildred.

II. Sweet Nothings

At the end of "Albergo Empedocle," the narrator observes:

> Most certainly he is not unhappy. His own thoughts are sweet to him, and he looks out of the window hour after hour and sees things in the sky and sea that we have forgotten. But of his fellow men he seems utterly unconscious. He never speaks to us, nor hears us when we speak. He does not know that we exist.
>
> So at least I thought till my last visit. I am the only one who still goes to see him; the others have given it up. Last time, when I entered the room, he got up and kissed me on the cheek. I think he knows that I understand him and love him: at all events it comforts me to think so. (63)

Just as the story begins with a missive from Harold to Tommy, it ends with another, with Harold's chaste kiss. In a story in which the reader has learned something of the semiotics of kissing, this kiss is a bodily sign of Greek love in contrast both to the proffered kiss of conscious desire that Mildred rejects at Girgenti and to the "decorous peck" (50) that had earlier sealed her engagement. In a world that has become amnesiac by resolutely turning away from *thinking Greek*—and Tommy includes himself among the "we" who have forgotten—Tommy can at best be only nearly sure what the language of the body means when, in the final words of the story, he says: "I think he knows that I understand and love him: at all events it comforts me to think so" (63). Tommy needs comfort because, though his absence from Sicily was necessary, it meant that he was not at hand at Harold's moment of truth. Accordingly, Tommy has missed, perhaps for good, his own chance to reenter Greek subjectivity.

In adhering to the Christian counsel to visit the sick, Tommy does on the other hand give witness to his love for Harold. Indeed, in Tommy's telling, his love frames the story even though at the start that love appears to have been baffled and remains so throughout. Harold, Tommy confides, is "the man I love most in the world" (37). Yet the role of witness and the confidence with which Tommy uses the verb are odd in view of the ignorances that usually attend love within the story. In addition, by proffering this knowledge to the reader as though it were fairly straightforward, Tommy posits a line of shared cognition between Harold, himself, and the reader despite the fact that the story is structured in such a way as to leave such a possibility in suspension. At no time do Harold and Tommy clearly understand love in the same way. Instead, the assumption of intelligibility on Tommy's part depends on a reading-effect. In the experience of readers of the story, there may exist relations that will complete Tommy and Harold's untold, unconsummated "love." Tommy makes a utopian appeal to a reader who has recovered the ability to *think Greek,* who understands touch, and who has enough imagination to project a world in which it would make sense to say as Harold does: "I was better, I saw better, heard better, thought better. . . . I loved very differently. . . . Yes, I loved better too" (51, 52). By this appeal, Tommy calls into being a reader of the future who may be described as the subject of a gay erotics. Moving beyond the frame of the heterosexual contract, the text implies the potential existence of cultural and social spaces in which men will be able to voice and to enact their mutual sexual and emotional bonds.

At this point, the ends that accompany Forster's hesitant beginnings as a writer help explain discrepancy between hope and contingencies. Forster, who was born on New Years Day 1879, was sixteen years old during the Wilde trials of 1895. As "a little cissy" aware of the distances—including distances of desire—between himself and others his age, Forster was both appalled and instructed by the punishment meted out to Wilde, the only homosexual of his class who seemed able simultaneously to appeal to newly emergent groups, including male homosexual and lesbian ones; sharply to satirize the powers that be; yet to continue to enjoy entry and success in the worlds both of middlebrow and highbrow culture.[20] Two years later, when Forster left Tonbridge School to enter King's College, he found a place at which the conditions for a life of Greek harmony still seemed to exist:

> Body and spirit, reason and emotion, work and play, architecture and scenery, laughter and seriousness, life and art—these pairs which are elsewhere contrasted were there fused into one. People and books reinforced one another, intelligence joined hands with affection, speculation became a passion, and discussion was made profound by love.[21]

Forster achieved this sense of wholeness especially as a result of being selected for membership in the Apostles, the Cambridge undergraduate society of which Alfred Tennyson and Arthur Henry Hallam had been early members and that achieved new distinction at the turn of the century through the membership of men like Bertrand Russell, Alfred North Whitehead, Lytton Strachey, Leonard Woolf, and John Maynard Keynes.[22] Moreover, the line into this group was affective: Forster was sponsored for membership by H. O. ("Hom") Meredith, a handsome, bright, athletic, sexually confused young man, with whom Forster fell in love.[23] Although arguments in defense of male homosexuality were put forward at the weekly meetings, members kept quiet about their sexual involvements; and Forster and Meredith's intimacies were confined to "kisses and embraces."[24]

In a biography of Forster that is marked by homophobia, Francis King comments that "Meredith, a basically heterosexual man, probably took the physical lead, either out of kindness or out of curiosity, but Forster was the one who was in love."[25] Yet there is evidence that Meredith signed the heterosexual contract with difficulty. Shortly after he and Forster became friends, Meredith became engaged to Caroline Graveson, then "had a nervous breakdown."[26] In 1906, Meredith wrote to Keynes from Manchester: "I think I am dead really now. . . . Or perhaps I should say I realize now what was plain to others two years ago. I come to life temporarily when I meet Forster." Furbank remarks: "Forster, as was his habit in friendship, made vigorous efforts to rouse Meredith out of his apathy. They would go for long walks, endlessly discussing Meredith's problems, or sometimes walking in total silence while he brooded."[27] In this relationship, Forster appears to have played the role of "Tommy."

Homosexual members of the Apostles or, later, Bloomsbury lived in a country in which their exchanges could subject them to ignominy, blackmail, and legal prosecution. Under the relatively new terms of the Labouchère amendment, the prohibition of "gross indecency" brought a far wider range of acts between men, including kissing, within the net of the Law. Indeed, even those Saturday night deliberations about the nobility of male love were potentially liable to prosecution. Within these circumstances, Forster, referring to himself as a homosexual, uses the term "*minority*." Returning from a trip to Greece in 1904, he describes himself as though he were part of a barren Mediterranean landscape:

> I'd better eat my soul for I certainly shan't have it. I'm going to be a minority if not a solitary, and I'd best make copy out of my position. There is nothing contemptible or cynical in this. I too have sweet waters though I shall never drink them. So I can understand the drought of others, though they will not understand my abstinence.[28]

For Forster being a minority at that time meant living privately and celibately. Faced with this sort of isolation, it is not surprising that the insulation of groups like the Apostles increased or that homosexual involvements came to appear to outsiders to be a part of a "cult."[29]

Forster's decision not to reprint "Albergo Empedocle" during his lifetime is in keeping with the extreme sense of apartness expressed in the preceding quotation. Yet it is a part of the continuing interest of this story that it calls into existence the members of a minority *group*. This structure depends in turn upon contingencies: on the existence of a homosexual radical culture before 1895, on its subsequent suppression, and on the continuing effects of the work of gender in Victorian Greek studies. Even when it was no longer possible to contest the meaning of masculinity within philological inquiry, the efforts of writers like Pater, Wilde, and others continued to lend fortitude to men like Forster.

Forster is often thought of as a man with a double career: the first climaxed with the publication of *A Passage to India* in 1924, after which he ceased to publish new fiction. The second career is a posthumous one as the writer of gay short stories and the novel *Maurice,* which were published after his death in 1970. The two parts of Forster's career, however, and the frustration of his work as a novelist after 1924 are conditioned by the institution of heterosexuality, which both impels the novels that deal with conventional sexuality and ensures that, in various ways as in "Albergo Empedocle," they work out a complex relationship to a specifically homosexual desire. In this sense, there are not two careers but one marked by continual compromise and resistance.

III. Another Difference

And, finally, Mildred, archetype of what Noel Annan refers to as "the self-satisfied, uneducated, conventional Edwardian girl, whom Forster knew so well, corseted by the conventions of her class and determined, come what may, to impose her will."[30] Her representation in "Albergo Empedocle" demonstrates the production of "woman"—in marriage or a picturesque setting—as a heterosexual institution. Viewed in this light, the sympathetic woman of the James short story is a logical impossibility. In a story that refers in many ways to the love that dare not speak its name, Mildred vindictively insists on naming Harold a "charlatan and cad" (56). She does so, moreover, in defense of herself as a woman, convinced that in turning back her wish to participate in his other life, Harold means to subordinate her:

> How patiently he had heard her rapturous speech, in order that he might prove her silly to the core! How diabolically worded was his retort—"No, Mildred darling, you have not lived at Acragas." It implied: "I will be kind to you and treat you well when you are my wife, but recollect that you are silly, emotional, hypocritical; that your pretensions to superiority are gone for ever; that I have proved you inferior to me, even as all women are inferior to all men. Dear Mildred, you are a fool!" (55–56)

Mildred's reaction shows that, in her scrutiny of Baedeker, she has been in search of cultural capital for herself, something she needs to offset the assured superiority of her better educated male coevals. This capital prominently includes the Greek studies that put a premium on male relations—so that the translation of Harold into Greek experience must either be recoded by Mildred or else be felt by her to be utterly demeaning.

Mildred responds in terms of her position as a future wife: what is implicitly in contest is her rivalry over Harold with Tommy, which she translates into archaeological terms. Mildred perceives her failure to be one of "archaeology" (55), the field of Tommy's expertise. The knowledge possessed by male subjects of elite education excludes her. She won't bear it. She lashes out. In a barely concealed metaphor, she kills Harold. Or, at least, Tommy thinks so: "I . . . believe that if things had happened otherwise he might be living that greater life among us, instead of among friends of two thousand years ago, whose names we never heard. That is why I shall never forgive Mildred Peaslake as long as I live" (63).

As enforcer of the contract and an outmoded novelistic realism, Mildred merits Tommy's anger. Yet the word *cad* suggests some of the ambiguities in gender and sexual relations in these years. Forster himself would use the term at Alexandria a number of years later at a moment when anxieties of class, gender, and race combined to prompt him to lose confidence in his first lover, Mohammed el Adl. In a letter of April 4, 1918, to Florence Barger, the wife of a former Cambridge classmate and a lifelong friend and confidante, Forster writes: "I thought he had meant to insult me, and left in a fury. He was puzzled and distressed, but very dignified. All through it is *I* who have endangered the thing. . . . I have found it so hard to believe he was neither a traitor or [*sic*] cad."[31] Poised on the fine line that separated friend from traitor, lover from cad, Forster was in a position to understand the volatile insecurity that a young upper-class woman might feel shortly before her marriage.

The writer of "Albergo Empedocle" was younger, less experienced, and less reflective than the Forster of 1918. He represents Mildred through the medium of Tommy's animosity, an effect reinforced by the way in which other characters likewise see her. Mildred's father, for instance, is confident that, despite occasional flights of fancy, "she could be trusted to behave in a thoroughly conventional manner" (45). This comment in indirect discourse, written by Tommy/Forster, is as reliable but only as reliable as is the narrator. Tommy assures the reader: "I am well acquainted with all who went then, and have had circumstantial information of all that happened, I think that my account of the affair will be as intelligible as anyone's" (36). Well, yes. . . .

The containment of Mildred's subjectivity within her function as "woman" prompts questions about the capacities of the narrator to envisage feminine difference. As for Forster, in contrast to his ability to register masculine differences, he gives no clue that Mildred might have a capacity to be different from the roles that she has been called upon to play. Yet the nonnegotiability of Mildred in the role of a May Bartram or a Florence Barger does indicate the high price that women who invested in such a compromise had to be willing to pay. Her refusal to pay this price is a noteworthy revolt and could be admirable though unfortunately, in Forster's ironic presentation, she revolts not in the direction of dis-identification with "woman" but in the direction of an accentuated identification with her place in the heterosexual contract. The expression of feminine differences would have to wait for writers such as Radclyffe Hall, who, in "Miss Ogilvy Finds Herself" (1926), writes her own story of a subject of same-sex desire who is rapt into another world. But in Hall's story, the protagonist is *Miss* Ogilvy.

Notes

1. The scandal attending publication of *Jude the Obscure* later in 1895 indicates the negative impact for male heterosexual writers of the Wilde scandal. See Richard Dellamora, *Masculine Desire: The Sexual Politics of Victorian Aestheticism* (Chapel Hill, NC: University of North Carolina Press, 1990), 212–17.
2. Quoted in Oliver Stallybrass, "Introduction," in E. M. Forster, *The Life to Come and Other Stories* (Harmondsworth: Penguin, 1975), 16. Citations from "Albergo Empedocle" refer to this edition and appear in parentheses in text. Unless otherwise cited, biographical information is from Claude Summers, *E. M. Forster* (New York: Frederick Ungar, 1983), chap. 1.
3. I adapt the phrase from Teresa de Lauretis, "The Female Body and Heterosexual Presumption," *Semiotica* 67, no. 3/4 (1987): esp. pp. 260, 277 n. 1; and from Monique Wittig, *The Straight Mind and Other Essays,* trans. Louise Turcotte (Boston: Beacon Press, 1992), 24–25. See also Teresa De Lauretis, "Eccentric Subjects: Feminist Theory and Historical Consciousness," *Feminist Studies* 16 (Spring 1990): 128–29. I supplement her work by suggesting that the contract is implemented with special aggressivity in the years immediately following Wilde's imprisonment.
4. My suggested dates for the installation of this shift in the construction of conventional sexuality parallel the development, in Continental psychoanalysis, of Freud's model of female sexual difference, a model that Mary Jacobus argues instates "the phallus" as "an arbitrary and divisive mark around which sexuality is constructed" (*Reading Woman: Essays in Feminist Criticism* [New York: Columbia University Press, 1986], 122). For a discussion of the problematic of

"woman" in male modernity, see Alice Jardine, *Gynesis: Configurations of Woman and Modernity* (Ithaca, NY: Cornell University Press, 1985), chap. 4.

5. See Ross Chambers, *Room for Maneuver: Reading (the) Oppositional (in) Narrative* (Chicago: University of Chicago Press, 1991), 24, 32.
6. Chambers, *Room for Maneuver,* 237–41.
7. Chambers, *Room for Maneuver,* 217.
8. I follow Alan Sinfield's argument in *Literature, Politics, and Culture in Postwar Britain* (Berkeley: University of California Press, 1989), esp. chap. 5.
9. I mean showing us how in the sense described by David Halperin in a discussion of heroic male friendship in the *Iliad* and other early texts. Halperin argues that interpretations of "homosexuality" in these works tell us more about the understanding of sexuality in the culture of the interpreter than in the cultures in which the works themselves were first performed or written (*One Hundred Years of Homosexuality and Other Essays on Greek Love* [New York: Routledge, 1990], 87).
10. See Eve Kosofsky Sedgwick, *Between Men: English Literature and Male Homosocial Desire* (New York: Columbia University Press, 1985), especially chapter 9. Subsequent page references to this book are included in the text.
11. Eve Kosofsky Sedgwick, *Epistemology of the Closet* (Berkeley: University of California Press, 1990), 210.
12. For the wives of Oscar Wilde and Edmund Gosse, see, respectively, Anne Clark Amor, *Mrs. Oscar Wilde: A Woman of Some Importance* (London: Sidgwick and Jackson, 1983) and Ann Thwaite, *Edmund Gosse: A Literary Landscape: 1849–1928* (Chicago: University of Chicago Press, 1984). See also Francis King, *E. M. Forster* (London: Thames and Hudson, 1988), 22–23.
13. Quoted in Lesley Higgins, "Essaying 'W. H. Pater Esq.': New Perspectives on the Tutor/Student Relationship between Pater and Hopkins," in *Pater in the 1990s,* ed. Laurel Brake and Ian Small (Greensboro, NC: ELT Press, 1991), 90.
14. Linda Dowling, "Roman Decadence and Victorian Historiography," *VS* 28 (Summer 1985): 579–607. Similarly, in "Ansell," another early story, the narrator's upper-class father is distressed when his son loses interest in the history of Rome after he makes friends with a garden boy: "My father did not like my entire separation from rational companions and pursuits. I had suddenly stopped reading and no longer cared to discuss with him the fortunes of the Punic War or the course of Aeneas from Troy" (Forster, *The Life to Come,* 28).
15. Acragas is the Greek name of Girgenti, known to the Romans as Agrigentum and, since 1927, as Agrigento, a change of name conso-

nant with the fascist program of invoking an earlier empire. Forster visited the town in April 1902.

16. See John Frow, "Tourism and the Semiotics of Nostalgia," *October* 57 (Summer 1991): 123–51.
17. Tom Waugh, "Photography, Passion and Power," *The Body Politic* (March 1984): 30. Additional information provided by Tom Waugh in a phone conversation on August 11, 1992.
18. For a discussion of "Apollo in Picardy," see Dellamora, *Masculine Desire,* chap. 9. For the connections between Pater and Forster, see Robert Martin, "The Paterian Mode in Forster's Fiction: *The Longest Journey* to *Pharos and Pharillon,*" in *E. M. Forster: Centenary Revaluations,* ed. Judith Scherer Herz and Robert K. Martin (Toronto: University of Toronto Press, 1982), 99–112.
19. Walter Pater, *Miscellaneous Studies* (London: 1910. Reprint. New York: Johnson Reprint Co., 1967), 170.
20. Quoted in King, *E. M. Forster,* 17. One of the features of the last fifteen years of the century, as discussed in George Gissing's *New Grub Street* (1891) and in such recent studies as Jonathan Freedman's *Professions of Taste: Henry James, British Aestheticism, and Commodity Culture* (Stanford, CA: Stanford University Press, 1990), is the emergence of what is now referred to as "middlebrow" taste. Middlebrow taste, which might be described as the revenge of Philistinism on Matthew Arnold, was—and is—averse to *thinking Greek.*
21. Quoted in King, *E. M. Forster,* 19.
22. For a discussion of the sexual politics of the Apostles in the 1830s, see Dellamora, *Masculine Desire,* chap. 1.
23. P. N. Furbank, *E. M. Forster: A Life* (London: Secker and Warburg, 1977), vol. 1, 78.
24. Furbank, *Forster,* vol. 1, 98.
25. King, *E. M. Forster,* 34.
26. Furbank, *Forster,* vol. 1, 140.
27. Furbank, *Forster,* vol. 1, 141.
28. Furbank, *Forster,* vol. 1, 111.
29. See Noel Gilroy Annan, *Our Age: English Intellectuals Between the World Wars—A Group Portrait* (New York: Random House, 1990), chaps. 7, 8.
30. Annan, *Our Age,* 111.
31. Quoted in Philis Gardner, "The Evolution of E. M. Forster's *Maurice,*" in *E. M. Forster: Centenary Revaluations,* ed. Judith Scherer Herz and Robert K. Martin (Toronto: University of Toronto Press, 1982), 218. The letter is not included in E. M. Forster, *Selected Letters: Volume 1, 1879–1920,* ed. Mary Lago and P. N. Furbank (Cambridge: Harvard University Press, 1983).

14

Richard Rodriguez's Poetics of Manhood

Martin A. Danahay

"I became a man by becoming a public man."
—Richard Rodriguez
Hunger of Memory: The Education of Richard Rodriguez

In his ethnographic study of a Cretan village, *The Poetics of Manhood,* Michael Herzfeld has emphasized the way in which masculinity is enacted in the process of narrating a story. Herzfeld analyzes the ways in which Cretan men construct their masculinity in telling stories; when relating their tales of sheep stealing Cretan men are dramatizing their masculine status. Herzfeld describes the self-dramatization of Cretan men as a "poetics," a "performance of selfhood" that "depends upon an ability to identify the self with larger codes of identity."[1] Herzfeld's ethnography is concerned with "the poetics of being a true Glendiot man" (46), and analyzes the various ways in which Glendiot males perform their masculinity in public, particularly in sheep-stealing narratives in which the speaker's performance demonstrates that one is "good *at being* a man" (46, 209). Herzfeld provides a particularly fruitful theoretical model for the analysis of narratives in terms of their staging of masculinity as a public performance.[2] Taking my cue from his book, in the following pages I will analyze Richard Rodriguez's *Hunger of Memory: The Education of Richard Rodriguez* as a "poetics of manhood" that dramatizes his status as a man, especially as a "public" man engaged in writing an autobiography.[3]

Richard Rodriguez's *Hunger of Memory: The Education of Richard Rodriguez* has been analyzed, even by myself, as primarily a text about ethnicity and the problems of growing up as the child of Hispanic immigrants in Anglo America.[4] However, I wish to give a different reading of the book here, and suggest that it be viewed as a meditation on being *masculine* in America. In other words, the book dramatizes the condition of being masculine and plays out a dialectic between ways of being masculine and being feminine in contemporary America. *Hunger of Memory* therefore represents a fascinating complementary text to contemporary autobiographies written by women, such as Maxine Hong Kingston's *The Woman Warrior* and Maya Angelou's *I Know Why the Caged Bird Sings.*

Rodriguez claims, like Maxine Hong Kingston in *The Woman Warrior,* to be breaking an injunction to silence in writing his autobiography. Rodriguez claims that he is "writing about the very things my mother asked me not to reveal" (175) in publishing *Hunger of Memory,* just as Kingston in *Woman Warrior* represents herself as breaking her mother's injunction "Don't tell."[5] However, where Kingston's *Woman Warrior* focuses almost entirely upon her mother as a symbol of her relationship to the Chinese community, Rodriguez's text enacts a complex set of identifications with both his mother and father. In particular, Rodriguez identifies his father with silence, and opposes him to his mother's acquisition of English and success as a secretary to the governor of California.

As the title of his book indicates, Rodriguez's story is about the effects of American socialization on him as a male from a Hispanic background. The word that sums up the effect of this education as Rodriguez sees it is "separation." Summarizing his educational career, Rodriguez says: "What I am about to say has taken me more than twenty years to admit: *A primary reason for my success in the classroom was that I couldn't forget that schooling was changing me and separating me from the life I enjoyed before becoming a student*" (45).

Rodriguez equates his successful career as a student with his increasing alienation from his family, and apparently accepts this as the inevitable cost of his "success."[6] Rather than record with ambivalence his separation from his family and his community, Rodriguez celebrates his learning of English as a sign of his gaining autonomy and a public identity. Rodriguez's text is not written in opposition to the cultural hegemony of education as a process that deracinates its subjects. For Rodriguez, his education was fundamentally a benign exercise of turning him into a citizen of the United States. Education gave him a voice. This education was also explicitly a matter of class, as he uses "American" and "middle-class" as synonyms. He calls his narrative "an American story" (5) and a "middle class pastoral." (6) When Rodriguez says that "I had grown culturally separated from my parents," (72) he is describing what he sees as a natural and all-American process of turning the lower-class immigrant kid into a middle-class American citizen.

Rodriguez's attitude to his socialization can be accounted for in terms of gender. *Hunger of Memory,* like such narratives as *The Autobiography of Malcolm X* by Alex Haley, is a masculine success story. Malcolm X's story records the way in which he escaped the ghetto, his drug habit, and jail and is told as a conversion narrative in which he finds Allah and is saved. Rodriguez's is an educational success story in which he receives a Ph.D. as the ultimate reward. Rodriguez therefore interprets his increasing estrangement from his family as an ambiguous development; on the one hand he is losing contact with his parents, especially his father, but on the other he is enjoying increased success in his academic work.

Hunger of Memory is thus a form of bildungsroman; it describes the career of a middle-class male from his successes as a "scholarship boy" to his studies as a graduate student at Berkeley. Rodriguez is clearly ambivalent about this success, but it is this success story that gives his narrative coherence. The narrative dramatizes how Rodriguez becomes a "public man," and dramatizes his masculine status in the process. Although Rodriguez questions racial categories, his narrative rests on a fundamental dichotomy in terms of gender that reinscribes the gendered division of labor in American society.

Rodriguez's public work, writing, involves a denial of the feminine, private part of his life embodied in his Mexican family. Much of Rodriguez's book concerns the disappointments he experienced in his chosen work, and his consequent romanticization of family life. Andrew Tolson explains this aspect of masculinity as an inevitable result of the gendered division of labor: "In capitalist societies, with their highly developed divisions of labour, and the widening split between 'work' and 'home,' masculine expectations can only be maintained at the price of psychological unity. At work, a man's gender identity is no longer complete—it is slowly split apart."[7]

Rodriguez registers this split in American masculine gender identity in his insistence on the separation of male and female aspects of his narrative. *Hunger of Memory* is a eulogy for those aspects of his identity that he feels he must reject, such as intimacy and the domestic life of the Spanish-speaking family, but also romanticizes. This process has been described by Jonathan Rutherford in *Men's Silences* in the following terms:

> Masculinity is defined in dividing off the elements it must disavow and projecting them into the subordinate term of femininity, filling it with the antithesis of its own identity. The female body in its very alienness is both idealised and loathed by men. . . . To maintain the fiction of its own identity, the masculine must maintain the binary distinction. Splitting and projection illustrate how psychic processes are mobilised in defence of frontiers.[8]

In order to create a unified self in the face of the split between masculine and feminine, Rodriguez valorizes the masculine "public man" over the private and feminine. Equating speaking Spanish with the domestic and feminine, he comes to the conclusion that to be a man he must separate himself from his family. This is the source of Rodriguez's ambivalence toward his socialization; he sees his separation from his family as natural, but he also projects values such as intimacy into the feminine domestic sphere that he rejects. Rodriguez therefore views separation from his family in positive terms as an assertion of autonomy, and subscribes to an interpretation of his life history as one of increasing distance from his family and from Hispanic culture. *Hunger of Memory* would not be a very interesting or complicated book, however, if Rodriguez's attitude was monovocal and unified in its appreciation of the effects of his socialization upon him. In the latter stages of the book he describes visiting home after being away at college, and feeling like an intruder in the house: "Living with my parents for the summer, I remained an academic—a kind of anthropologist in the family kitchen, searching for evidence of our 'cultural ties' as we ate dinner together" (160).

Hunger of Memory becomes a eulogy for a lost intimacy embodied in his Spanish-speaking childhood, an Eden lost for Rodriguez in becoming an "academic." The most striking aspect of this quotation is the way that "academic" and "anthropologist" are used as the antithesis of "family." Rodriguez sees his professional, public persona as inimical to the intimacy he equates with family. Rodriguez feels that "I had shattered the intimate bond that had once held the family close" (30) by learning English, and the "hunger" in *Hunger of Memory* is for this lost intimacy. However, "intimacy" in the book is seen as inimical to a number of other of Rodriguez's "public" identities, especially his masculinity and his profession.

Rodriguez's subject position as "male academic" turns him into an "anthropologist" in his own family kitchen. Like many men, Rodriguez both celebrates and marginalizes intimacy, making it into a value that is fundamentally at odds with the public performance of masculinity. He simultaneously praises intimacy and makes it into a "lost" ideal that he once possessed but reluctantly has had to forego in order to become a public man. His sentiments here corroborate Tolson's description in *The Limits of Masculinity* of the radical separation of work and home, and the psychic cost for men. Rodriguez experiences masculine and feminine and work and home as diametric opposites that are mutually exclusive. Constructing a masculine identity involves denying the incompatible aspects of his personality.

Rodriguez's success story is complicated, however, by the way in which he identifies with Anglo culture in gendered terms, and his view of his chosen profession as a "feminine" form of work. A set of counteridentifications works against the simple equation of public as masculine and private as feminine. He identifies his own success in school with his mother's accomplishments in learning

English and finding herself a job. He sees the negative effects of his education in terms of his father's inability to get ahead in his new environment and his difficulty with the English language. The book ends with a sudden realization of his father's silence during a family gathering. His father asks him a question and Rodriguez realizes that is "the only thing he has said to me all evening" (95); the story of his own success, therefore, is implicitly contrasted with his father's increasing silence. His book ends with an image of his father's silence that, like the silence of other marginalized figures, "remains to oppress them" (185). His father through his silence is associated with figures like *los pobres,* poor Mexican immigrants who are unable to adopt the "public" voice of spoken English and thus become victims of exploitation and oppression.

Describing his parents' reaction to their children's increased use of English at home, Rodriguez says that his mother spoke more, his father less:

> My mother and father, for their part, responded differently as their children spoke to them less. She grew restless, seemed troubled and anxious at the scarcity of words exchanged in the house. It was she who would question me about my day when I came home from school. . . . By contrast my father seemed reconciled to the new quiet. Though his English improved somewhat, he retired into silence. (24)

As a result, it was his mother who "became the public voice of the family" and would talk to Anglo officials and strangers (24). In the public/private dichotomy that underlies Rodriguez's story, it is his mother, not his father, who is identified with the "public" world of spoken English. Rodriguez comes to associate the two languages, through his parents, with different ways of being masculine and feminine. Reacting against the description of his father as "shy," Rodriguez points out that when speaking Spanish his father's behavior changed:

> But my father was not shy, I realized, when I'd watch him speaking Spanish with relatives. Using Spanish he was quickly effusive. Especially when talking with other men, his voice would spark, flicker, flare alive with sounds. In Spanish, he expressed ideas and feelings he rarely revealed in English. With firm Spanish sounds, he conveyed confidence and authority English would never allow him. (25)

The "firm" and masculine sounds of his father's Spanish voice contrast with his increasing silence in English. For Rodriguez silence becomes synonymous with victimization and exclusion from the public, Anglo world, so that his father is a figure who symbolizes the silence that Rodriguez himself both valorizes and rejects. His father as a symbol of masculinity becomes a symbol of Rodriguez's ambivalence about his education and his profession.

Rodriguez's ambivalent attitude to his father is made into the overt theme of *Days of Obligation,* the subtitle of which is *An Argument with My Mexican Father.* This subtitle is misleading. Rodriguez's father does indeed appear in this autobiographical essay, but the subtitle makes little sense if one understands it to mean that the text is a literal argument with an individual identifiable as his father. The "father" in the title is not an individual but a symbol, standing for Rodriguez's Mexican family and his ambivalent attitude to its Mexican past. The book opens with Rodriguez travelling through Mexico with a foreign T.V. camera crew searching for the archetypal Mexican village that will stand for his parents' origins. The text moves on from this opening to dramatize Rodriguez's own opposed tendencies, one to search for and venerate his family's Mexican past and the other to embrace the forgetfulness and rejection of the past by Puritan American culture. His journey in search of the sites of ruined Catholic missions in Protestant California is another version of this meditation on the relationship between his past and present, as is his movement back and forth over several weeks between Tijuana and San Diego. His father comes to represent the past for Rodriguez, his mother someone who has succeeded in entering Anglo America.

Days of Obligation, like *Hunger of Memory,* is organized around gendered dichotomies. This is startling because the text has many astute and sometimes hilarious observations about the condition of being a mestizo, which in Mexican Spanish means "mixed, confused."[9] The book explores the many contradictions in Rodriguez's identity as an American mestizo returning to Mexico, and the many contradictions and dichotomies within his relationship to American and Mexican culture. The book is grounded, however, in starkly drawn gendered opposites, as is *Hunger of Memory.* Whereas Rodriguez explores with great sensitivity the blurred boundaries between racial categories, he uses "masculine" and "feminine" as unproblematic polar opposites. In *Days of Obligation* Mexico is female, whereas America as Uncle Sam is male: "you betray Uncle Sam by favoring private over public life" (in other words, by favoring feminine over masculine), whereas "Mama Mexico" is private and intimate and feminine (62–63). In religion, Protestantism is male, Catholicism is voluptuous and female (181). Rodriguez reads the movement of young Mexican males from Mexico to the United States as a version of his own autobiography in which they leave behind "Mama Mexico" and become a man: "*You are a boy from a Mexican village. You have come into the country on your knees with your head down. You are a man*" (78).

The gender dichotomies in *Days of Obligation* are much more strongly delineated than in *Hunger of Memory,* largely because Rodriguez's mother is largely absent from this "argument" between father and son. In *Hunger of Memory* Rodriguez's mother is a focal point for his anxieties about the gendered associations of teaching and literary criticism. Teaching in America is viewed as a "feminine" occupation, especially at the primary and high school levels where the majority of teachers are women. As a man who has, at least initially, chosen a career in education, Rodriguez wrestles with the gender-based assumptions about teaching as work. This identification of his occupation in gender-based terms is heightened by his having chosen *literature* as his area of expertise within academic specializations, because this subject is traditionally associated with "feelings" and "emotions," all of which for Rodriguez connote femininity. Rodriguez worries at one point that "education was making me effeminate" (127), a worry that leads him to consider his education within the context of *machismo:* "I knew that I had violated the ideal of the *macho* by becoming such a dedicated student of language and literature. *Machismo* was a word never exactly defined by the persons who used it. (It was best described by the 'proper' behavior of men.)" (128).

This is a succinct statement of one of the cultural dichotomies underlying Rodriguez's autobiography; in order to be a successful Anglo professional he has to become a student of language, thereby "violating" the tenets of *machismo.* A "real" man "never verbally revealed his emotions" (128–29), although "it was permitted a woman to be gossipy and chatty" (128). In obeying his teachers' injunctions to speak in class, Rodriguez implicitly aligns himself with a "chatty" feminine way of behaving, and distances himself from his father's more reserved, or in Spanish *formal,* way of behaving. As Rodriguez's remarks make clear, at stake here is a gender-based way of *behaving,* that is, of performing one's masculinity in public. The more "successful" Rodriguez is in school or in work, the less "masculine" he is in the terms of *machismo.* He finds himself caught between two culturally defined ways of behaving that are in conflict with one another. If he were to follow his father's behavior he would be *macho,* and identify himself with reserve, silence, and the repression of emotion. He finds himself, however, drawn to a Protestant, Anglo model of behavior that aligns him with the feminine. This gendered dichotomy leads him to identify more and more closely with his mother:

> I often was proud of my way with words. Though, on other occasions, for example, when I would hear my mother busily speaking to women, it would occur to me that my attachment to words made me like her. Her son. Not *formal* like my father. At such times I even suspected that my nostalgia for sounds—the noisy, intimate Spanish sounds of my past—was nothing more than effeminate yearning. (129)

At this point the nexus of gendered identifications at work in *Hunger of Memory* becomes clear; intimacy, literature, and speaking English become associated with the "feminine" aspects of Rodriguez's personality, whereas silence, sexuality, and power become associated with his father and the "masculine" aspects of his personality. In order to resist his effeminization, Rodriguez must reject his "effeminate yearning" for the intimate sounds of Spanish. The Spanish sounds of his past become the locus of an intense nostalgia for a set of associations embodied in his mother. Rodriguez's father is a problematic symbol of masculinity in *Hunger of Memory* because of his increasing silence. Rodriguez values a *formal* way of behaving, but associates it with silence and victimization in Anglo America. This simultaneous appreciation and rejection of silence as a marker of masculinity is made most obvious in Rodriguez's attitude to *los braceros,* the working-class manual laborers who come to symbolize "real" men's work in the text, as opposed to the "effeminate" labor of the intellectual. Rodriguez calls *los braceros* "powerful, powerless men" (114); they are "powerful" because their muscles represent for Rodriguez a muscular, *macho,* silent form of masculinity; and "powerless" because their very silence marks them for him as oppressed victims of Anglo cultural dominance. These men become for Rodriguez objects of simultaneous fear and desire:

I continued to see the *braceros,* those men I resembled in one way and, in another way, didn't resemble at all. On the watery horizon of a Valley, I'd see them. And though I feared looking like them, it was with silent envy that I regarded them still. I envied them their physical lives, their freedom to violate the taboo of the sun. Closer to home I would notice the shirtless construction workers, the roofers, the sweating men tarring the street in front of the house. I was unwilling to admit the attraction of their lives. I tried to deny it by looking away. But what was denied became strongly desired. (126)

The *braceros* come to represent for Rodriguez those aspects of his masculinity that he would deny in himself, namely his body and the darkness of his skin. They also become symbols of a repressed sexual desire; the "attraction" of these men is partly erotic. Rodriguez to an extent internalizes the racist categories of Anglo culture that associate "white" with good and "dark" with the evil and dangerous. This is also, however, a typical reaction by an intellectual, especially a male academic, to images of working-class, muscular labor. Rodriguez idealizes working-class manual labor because American intellectual labor devalues the physical in favor of the mental, seeing the two as in some way opposed. Rodriguez began to associate with a self-consciously intellectual group of students who would refer to fellow students playing baseball or football as "animals" (126). As Rodriguez explains, "the sensations that first had excited in me a sense of my maleness, I denied" (126). The *braceros* come to symbolize the denied and repressed masculinity embodied in *machismo,* and thus function as both objects of fear (because they represent the repressed body) and desire (because they represent a sexuality he denies in himself).

Rodriguez turns to literature and intellectual pursuits as compensation, a deliberate turn to the "feminine," that excludes the repressed masculine body and masculine desire. Rodriguez turns to literature to recapture in a vicarious and mediated form the "intimacy" he associates with his mother and early family life. While literature cannot be "intimate," it approximates what he is looking for in terms of the "personal." Literature comes to represent the lost community of Spanish culture, albeit in attenuated form. Listening to a nun reading aloud in his school, Rodriguez glimpses the possibilities of written communication as a form of "fellowship": "I sat there and sensed for the very first time some possibility of fellowship between a reader and a writer, a communication never *intimate* like that I heard spoken words convey, but one nonetheless *personal*" (60).

Reading for the young Rodriguez from this moment comes to represent a compensation for the estrangement from his family. It restores a lost intimacy in the imaginary relationship between a writer and a reader. The urgent autobiographical confessions of his books in this context become imaginary compensations for the domestic intimacy he has lost in becoming a "public" man. He says that lyric poetry especially came to function as a reminder of the kind of intimacy he felt he had lost when he grew apart from his family: "As public artifact, the poem can never duplicate intimate sound. But by imitating such sound, the poem helps me recall the intimate times of my life. I read in my room—alone—and grow conscious of being alone, sounding my voice, in search of another" (38).

The poem serves as a "memory device," reminding Rodriguez of lost intimacy, but as he makes clear, it can never replace intimacy. In some ways it makes him even more acutely aware of his isolation, and thus precipitates an even more desperate search for more intimacy. Rodriguez writes that "I vacuumed books for epigrams, scraps of information, ideas, themes—anything to fill the hollow within me and make me feel educated." (64) As the metaphors of "vacuum" and "hollow" make clear here, Rodriguez imagines that he has lost something essential that reading English literature can only partially compensate for.

Like his ambivalent attitude toward his body, Rodriguez's ambivalent attitude toward education is inflected by gender contrasts. Rodriguez strongly identifies with a description of "the scholarship boy" as a figure who "does not straddle, cannot reconcile, the two great opposing cultures of his life" (66). This is in some ways an accurate description of the way his mind works, in that he continually poses dichotomies, like public/private or masculine/feminine, and then finds himself unable to reconcile them. The larger pattern of *Hunger of Memory* is the creation of such dichotomies, then the despairing rejection of one side of the dichotomy in favor of the other. However, the term boy in "scholarship boy" also underlines the extent to which Rodriguez experiences American education as a diminishment of his masculinity. Education is for boys, not men. As in his idealization of the *braceros,* Rodriguez represents education, his chosen field of work, as inimical to masculinity.

Although reading books holds out the promise of an attenuated intimacy, it also connotes for Rodriguez isolation and withdrawal. When describing the experience of reading poetry in the quotation Rodriguez emphasizes that he reads poetry *alone* in his room. As Rodriguez progresses in his career he comes to feel increasingly isolated, so that he begins to wonder, "Was my dissertation much more than an act of social withdrawal?" (70). Through his studies Rodriguez gains a sense of vicarious community of scholars "united by a common respect for the written word and for scholarship," but this was a "union" in which "we remained distant for one another." (70) Rodriguez's academic research and writing thus come, like his reading when younger, to both assuage a need for intimacy, and to further exacerbate his feelings of isolation and estrangement from any community.

Rodriguez continually compares his current position as a male academic in disparaging terms with other forms of social identity. Calling himself "a citizen of the secular city" (107), Rodriguez reads his autobiography as part of a wider social movement away from the "communal Catholicism" of his youth. Once again, Rodriguez reads this aspect of his life in terms of both his loss of intimacy with his family and the development of his masculine identity. When it occurs to him to ask himself if God is dead, he answers the question with an affirmation of his faith: "I would cry into the void. . . . If I should lose my faith in God, I would have no place to go where I could feel myself a man. The Catholic Church of my youth mediated with special grace between the public and private realms of my life, such was the extent of its faith in itself" (108–9).

Rodriguez dramatizes here his self-conflict between his past as Catholic boy, and his adult persona, which he labels "individualist Protestant." He claims that "I have become like a Protestant Christian" and become a member of a sect whose experience of community is as "a community of those who share with each other only the experience of standing alone before God" (110). Rodriguez's religious experience here comes to sound exactly like his experience of becoming a professional academic; he loses his sense of belonging to a community and finds it replaced by an individualistic gathering of people with only a weak sense of connection to one another.

We should not accept this master narrative at face value, however. As the previous quotation shows, Rodriguez's sense of religion, like his professional identity, is bound up with his image of himself as masculine; only in church, he says, can "I feel myself a man." However, he is only aware of this aspect of himself because he has already withdrawn from his community, and separated from his family. This awareness is predicated upon an act of withdrawal from the start. This apparently paradoxical combination of "social withdrawal" and desire for community is expressed with particular force in his attitude toward silence in the closing pages of *Hunger of Memory*. As the story nears closure, Rodriguez describes the process of writing the book itself. The "poetics of manhood" that lie behind the tale become apparent when in a parenthetical aside Rodriguez says: "(In writing this autobiography, I am actually describing the man I have become—the man in the present.)" (176).

At this moment Rodriguez names *Hunger of Memory* as about the process of "becoming a man," and of staging that masculinity in the narrative. In writing about this process Rodriguez confronts some of his central self-contradictions, especially in his radically opposite valuations of silence and writing. In order to complete the manuscript, Rodriguez shuts himself in his apartment "to closet myself in the silence I both need and fear" (176). Like the figures of the *braceros,* silence is a source of both desire and danger. The desire finds its source in the *macho* image of men as essentially silent about matters of emotion; the fear comes from Rodriguez not wanting to be identified with *los pobres,* poor Mexican immigrants who, unlike him, have not found a public voice.

Rodriguez claims that in writing *Hunger of Memory* he has overcome the dichotomies that underlie the book, especially that between public and private:

> The loneliness I have felt many mornings, however, has not made me forget that I am engaged in a highly public activity. I sit here in silence writing this small volume of words and it seems to me the most public thing I ever have done. My mother's letter has served to remind me; I am making my personal life public. (176)

Such a description implies that he has in some way transcended the dichotomies that inform the text. This is not the case, as his final image of his almost silent father makes clear. Rodriguez has opted in publishing *Hunger of Memory* to become a "public man." He has chosen, as his mother recognizes, to establish an identity that in his terms separates him from the "private" life of his family. Publishing *Hunger of Memory* is a declaration of independence on his part.

Perhaps the most courageous aspect of *Hunger of Memory* is Rodriguez's unflinching insistence on the cost that lies behind the statement that "I became a man by becoming a public man." Given the gendered dichotomies within which he works, becoming a "public man" means renouncing the "private," feminine-identified aspects of his identity, including his profession as an effeminate form of work. Rodriguez summarizes the damaging effects of conventional American masculinity; to be masculine men must be "public," they must be professional, they must be "silent" on emotional matters. The American ideal is close to the definition of *macho* Rodriguez gives in *Days of Obligation* when he says "there is sobriety in the male, and silence, too—a severe limit on emotional range. The male isn't weak. The male wins a Purple Heart or he turns wife beater. The male doesn't cry" (57). While the easy transition from not being "weak" to wife beating is disturbing, this collection of phrases summarizes many of the stereotypes of American masculinity.[10]

As the intense nostalgia for intimacy and community in *Hunger of Memory* shows, this idea entails repressing and denying one's family and any real sense of community. Such a definition of masculinity leads to intense feelings of isolation that such vicarious communities as literature and scholarship can only partially assuage. *Hunger of Memory,* therefore, makes dramatic statements about being masculine in contemporary America. Rodriguez's attitude toward masculinity is given particular ethnic inflections by his attitudes to the ideal of *machismo,* but overall the book has far more to say about being an American middle-class man than any other subject. The autobiography is a "middle-class pastoral" (6) that tells the story of how he became "the man that I have become" (176). *Hunger of Memory* captures extremely well the dichotomies underlying masculine self-fashioning in America.

Rodriguez's texts are problematic when one tries to account for their positions on race and gender. His attitude toward race is so radical that it subverts conventional popular political categories; *Hunger of Memory* can be cited both as a justification for and a refutation of bilingual education, and thus serves both left- and right-wing arguments. Overall, especially in *Days of Obligation,* Rodriguez deconstructs with breathtaking insight the racial categories operating in American English. He is particularly insightful and ironic on the uses of the term *Indian.* His position on gender roles, however, is more troubling. I am left wondering after reading his books whether it makes any sense whatsoever to characterize Protestantism as "male," literature as "feminine," or Mexico as "female." The essentializing and stereotyping in such moves makes the gender-based categories upon which he is relying seem like blunt instruments that do violence to their subject. However, Rodriguez in the final analysis is a courageous writer. He tackles in personal terms the issues that are dealt with more obliquely by academic writers. Peter Middleton's recent theoretical analysis of masculine conventions is an interesting example of the way in which the issues addressed through autobiography by Rodriguez are transmuted into academic discourse by professional critics. Middleton begins his book by describing the ways in which he first tried to write about masculinity: "My first attempts were poems. My first discursive writing about masculinity was intended to be a prose fiction about the violence of writing.... Whenever I tried to write, the ball-point would dig deeper and deeper into the paper, incising the words and then tearing through" (1).

Middleton's description of writing is striking in its emphasis upon violence. His analysis in *The Inward Gaze* of myths such as Superman documents the cost to its subjects of contemporary versions of masculinity. He does so, however, within the measured vocabulary of academic theory; the violence of the poems and fiction with which he started writing is muted by the conventions of academic discourse in his literary analysis.[11] Rodriguez deals with a similar subject, but more overtly. The self-inflicted violence implicit in becoming a "public man" is registered overtly in *Hunger of Memory*. Rodriguez gains his masculinity by rejecting aspects of himself associated with the "feminine": Mexico, intimacy, and Catholicism. Turning vice into virtue, he suggests such rejection is part of growing up an American male and a necessary prerequisite to entry into public life. As the increasing rate of publication on questions of masculinity attests, men are beginning to question whether such self-inflicted violence is necessary, and whether or not the cost is too high.

The emotional investment in Rodriguez's books rescues them from the stereotyping of gender roles on which they depend. Responding as a male academic myself, I value Rodriguez's books most for their relentless questioning of masculine myths of success. Rodriguez is involved in an unflinching cataloguing of the costs for himself of becoming a successful, "public" man. The elegiac tones of his autobiographies bespeak his sense of loss in his transformation. Rodriguez articulates the cost of being masculine in America.

Notes

1. Michael Herzfeld, *The Poetics of Manhood: Contest and Identity in a Cretan Mountain Village* (Princeton: Princeton University Press, 1985), 10. Hereafter cited parenthetically in text.
2. Jeff Hearn has argued that masculinity in the late nineteenth and

twentieth centuries is connected to a widening of the sphere of the "public man" and linked to organizations such as the state. See Jeff Hearn, *Men in the Public Eye: The Construction and Deconstruction of Public Men and Public Patriarchies* (New York: Routledge, 1992).

3. Richard Rodriguez, *Hunger of Memory: The Education of Richard Rodriguez* (New York: Bantam Books, 1983), 7. Hereafter cited parenthetically in text.
4. See Martin A. Danahay, "Breaking the Silence: Symbolic Violence and the Teaching of Contemporary 'Ethnic' Autobiography," *College Literature* 18, no. 3 (October 1991): 64-79; George Yuridice, "Marginality and the Ethics of Survival," in *Universal Abandon?: The Politics of Postmodernism* (Minneapolis: University of Minnesota Press, 1988); Michael M. J. Fischer, "Ethnicity and the Postmodern Arts of Memory," in *Writing Culture: The Poetics and Politics of Culture* (Berkeley: University of California Press, 1986); Werner Sollors, *Beyond Ethnicity: Consent and Descent in American Culture* (New York: Oxford University Press, 1986).
5. Rodriguez's attitude to silence shares some features with the role of silence in *Woman Warrior* and *I Know Why the Caged Bird Sings*; however, it also differs in the way Rodriguez links silence to his father, and speech to his mother. For analyses of silence in *Woman Warrior,* see King-Kok Cheung, "Don't Tell: Imposed Silence in *The Color Purple* and *The Woman Warrior,*" *PMLA* 103, no. 2 (March 1988): 162–74; Elaine H. Kim, "Defining Asian American Realities through Literature," in *Cultural Critique* 6 (Spring 1987); Sally L. Kitch, "Gender and Language: Dialect, Silence and the Disruption of Discourse," *Women's Studies* 14, no. 1 (1987); and Sidonie Smith, *A Poetics of Women's Autobiography* (Bloomington: Indiana University Press, 1987).
6. In this Rodriguez parallels the account of masculine socialization in such studies as Nancy Chodorow's *The Reproduction of Mothering: Psychoanalysis and the Sociology of Gender* (Berkeley: University of California Press, 1978) and Arthur Brittan's *Masculinity and Power* (New York: Basil Blackwell, 1989). On pages 190–92, Brittan critiques the essentialist aspects of Chodorow's account, and argues that such gendered characteristics are socially constructed.
7. Andrew Tolson, *The Limits of Masculinity* (New York: Harper and Row, 1979), 48.
8. Jonathan Rutherford, *Men's Silences: Predicaments in Masculinity* (New York: Routledge, 1992), 78.
9. Richard Rodriguez, *Days of Obligation: An Argument with My Mexican Father* (New York: Viking Penguin, 1992), 2. Hereafter cited parenthetically in text.
10. Rodriguez's characterization of masculinity echoes analyses of male

attitudes toward emotion and intimacy by literary critics. For instance, Peter Middleton in *The Inward Gaze: Masculinity and Subjectivity in Modern Culture* (New York: Routledge, 1992) points out that "men in most Western cultures are not supposed to show any emotion in public other than anger . . . because anger is masculine power at its most impressive" (212). Hereafter cited parenthetically in text.

11. I am acutely aware that the same is true of my own analysis; although this article is motivated by strong personal interests, they do not appear overtly in the text. I am performing a "public" role here that relies upon the kind of separation of work and "private" life that Tolson describes in *The Limits of Masculinity*.

Contributors

David Bergman is the author of *Gaiety Transfigured: Gay Self-Representation in American Literature* (University of Wisconsin Press, 1991) and the winner of the George Elliston Poetry Prize for *Cracking the Code* (Ohio State University Press, 1985). He edited John Ashberry's *Reported Sightings: Art Chronicles 1957–87* (Knopf, 1989).

Miriam Cooke is Professor of Arabic at Duke University. In 1993 she edited, with Angela Woolacott, *Gendering War Talk* (Princeton University Press). Her anthology of Arab women's feminist writings in translation, *Opening the Gates: One Hundred Years of Arab Feminist Writing,* was published by Indiana University Press in the United States and by Virago in the United Kingdom. It has been translated into Dutch and German. Professor Cooke is the author of *The Anatomy of an Egyptian Intellectual: Yahya Haqqi* (Three Continents, 1984) and *War's Other Voices: Women Writers on the Lebanese Civil War* (Cambridge University Press, 1988). She has translated Haqqi's novel, *Good Morning! and Other Stories* (Three Continents, 1987).

Martin A. Danahay is a British, white, masculine middle-class subject and an Assistant Professor of English at Emory University, where he teaches courses on Victorian literature and the theory and practice of autobiography. He has published articles on ethnic autobiography, Victorian autobiography, and Victorian painting. His book, *A Community of One: Masculine Autobiography and Autonomy in Nineteenth-Century British Literature,* was published by the State University of New York Press in 1993.

Richard Dellamora, who recently completed a year as a Visiting Fellow in the department of English at Princeton University, lives in Toronto and teaches in the Departments of English and Cultural Studies at Trent University in Peterborough, Ontario. He is the author of *Masculine Desire: The Sexual Politics of Victorian Aestheticism,* (University of North Carolina Press, 1990) and *Apocalyptic Overtures: Sexual Politics and the Sense of an Ending* (forthcoming from Rutgers University Press 1994).

Leonard Duroche, whose major teaching and research areas are the literary representations of masculinity and the social construction of gender narratives, is an Associate Professor of German at the University of Minnesota. He is a former editorial board member of *Men's Studies Review,* is currently an associate editor of *The Journal of Men's Studies,* and is also editing an encyclopedia of men's studies. His publications include a book, *Aspects of Criticism* (Mouton, 1967), and articles on German, comparative literature, and male gender studies in various American and German scholarly journals. He is also a contributor to *Men, Masculinity and Social Theory,* edited by Jeff Hearn and David Morgan (Unwin and Hyman, 1990).

Jim Elledge has edited a collection of essays and reviews on Frank O'Hara, *Frank O'Hara: To Be True to a City* (University of Michigan Press, 1990). He wrote the article on O'Hara for the *Reader's Encyclopedia of American Literature* and published an essay on him, " 'Never Argue with the Movies': Love and the Cinema in Frank O'Hara's Poetry," in *Poet & Critic.* His critical essays have appeared in *Contemporary Poets* (4th and 5th eds.), *American Poetry, Tar River Poetry, Studies in Short Fiction,* among others. His books include *Weldon Kees: A Critical Introduction; Standing "Between the Dead and the Living": The Elegiac Technique of Wilfred Owen's War Poems; Various Envies: Poems; Nothing Nice: Poems;* and *Sweet Nothings: An Anthology of Rock and Roll in American Poetry.* He is an Associate Professor of English at Illinois State University and is the editor of *The Illinois Review.*

Alfred Habegger is a Professor of English at the University of Kansas. He is the author of *Gender, Fantasy and Realism in Ameri-*

can Literature (Columbia University Press, 1982) and *Henry James and the "Woman Business"* (Cambridge University Press, 1989). He has published in *PMLA, Novel, American Literature, New England Quarterly, Women's Studies,* and many other journals; his story, "A Little Spoon," appeared in *The New Yorker.* His current project, *The Father: A Life of Henry James, Sr.,* will be published by Farrar, Straus & Giroux.

Suzanne Kehde's article, "Voices from the Margin" appeared in *Feminism and Dialogics,* edited by Dale Bower and Susan Jaret McKinstry (SUNY Press, 1991); "Spivak, Bakhtin, Vygotsky and the Bag Lady" was published in *Perigraph* (Fall 1988); "Walter Van Tilburg Clark and the Withdrawal of Landscape" is forthcoming in *Western Landscape—Real and Imagined: Essays on Space and Place,* edited by Leonard Engel (University of New Mexico Press). Her play, *Everything You Always Wanted,* was produced at Wichita State University Theatre in November 1989. Kehde is a lecturer at California Polytechnic State University, San Luis Obispo.

David Leverenz is the author of *Manhood and the American Renaissance* (Cornell University Press, 1989), *The Language of Puritan Feeling* (Rutgers University Press, 1980), and various articles on American literature. He has also co-edited *Mindful Pleasures: Essays on Thomas Pynchon* (Little, Brown, 1976). From 1969 to 1985 he taught at Rutgers, where he chaired the Department of English at Livingston College for five years. He is now a Professor of English at the University of Florida.

Christopher Metress is an Assistant Professor of English at Samford University in Birmingham, Alabama. His work has appeared in *Essays in Literature, Studies in the Novel,* and *Studies in Short Fiction.* He is currently editing a collection of critical essays on Dashiell Hammet for Greenwood Press.

Peter F. Murphy is the Assistant Dean and an Assistant Professor of Cultural Studies at SUNY Empire State College. He has been a Fulbright Teaching Fellow at the Universidade Federal do Rio

Grande do Sul, in Porto Alegre, Brazil. His essay on John Hawkes, "The Woman Writer and Male Authority in *Virginie: Her Two Lives*" will be published in *Men Writing the Feminine: Literature, Theory, and the Question of Genders,* edited by Thaïs Morgan (SUNY Press, 1994). "Cultural Studies as Praxis" appeared in the June 1992 issue of *College Literature.*

Rafael Pérez-Torres is an Assistant Professor of English at the University of Pennsylvania. He teaches contemporary American literature for the Department of English and has published articles on the novels of Rudolpho Anaya, Luís Rafael Sánchez, and Toni Morrison. His most recent projects include *Against Myths, Against Margins—Movement in Chicano Poetry,* a book-length study of the course of Chicano poetic expression, and two forthcoming critical articles: "Nomads and Migrants—Negotiating a Multicultural Postmodernism" in *Cultural Critique* and "Feathering the Serpent: Chicano Mythic 'Memory,'" in *The Uses of Memory in Multi-Ethnic Literatures,* edited by Joseph Skerrett and Amritjit Singh. Pérez-Torres is also the academic coordinator for the Institute for Recruitment of Teachers, a program that encourages gifted college students of color to become teachers at the secondary and university level.

David Radavich is a poet, playwright, and literary critic. In addition to a play, *Nevertheless . . .* (Aran, 1988) and a collection of poems, *Slain Species* (Court Poetry, 1980), he has published a wide variety of poetry in the United States and abroad. His plays have been performed by the Charleston Alley Theatre, Mid-America Playwrights Theatre, and the Missouri Association of Playwrights, among others. He has also published academic articles on drama, poetry, and the contemporary writing scene. From 1979 to 1981 he taught as a Fulbright Junior Lecturer at the Universität Stuttgart, West Germany; currently he is Professor of English at Eastern Illinois University.

Peter Schwenger teaches English at St. Vincent University in Halifax, Nova Scotia. He is the author of *Phallic Critiques: Masculinity* *and Twentieth-Century Literature* and *Letter Bomb: Nuclear Holocaust and the Exploding Word.* The chapter included in this book was originally delivered as the keynote address for a conference on *Gender and the Curriculum* sponsored jointly by St. John's University and the College of St. Benedict in Minnesota.

Index

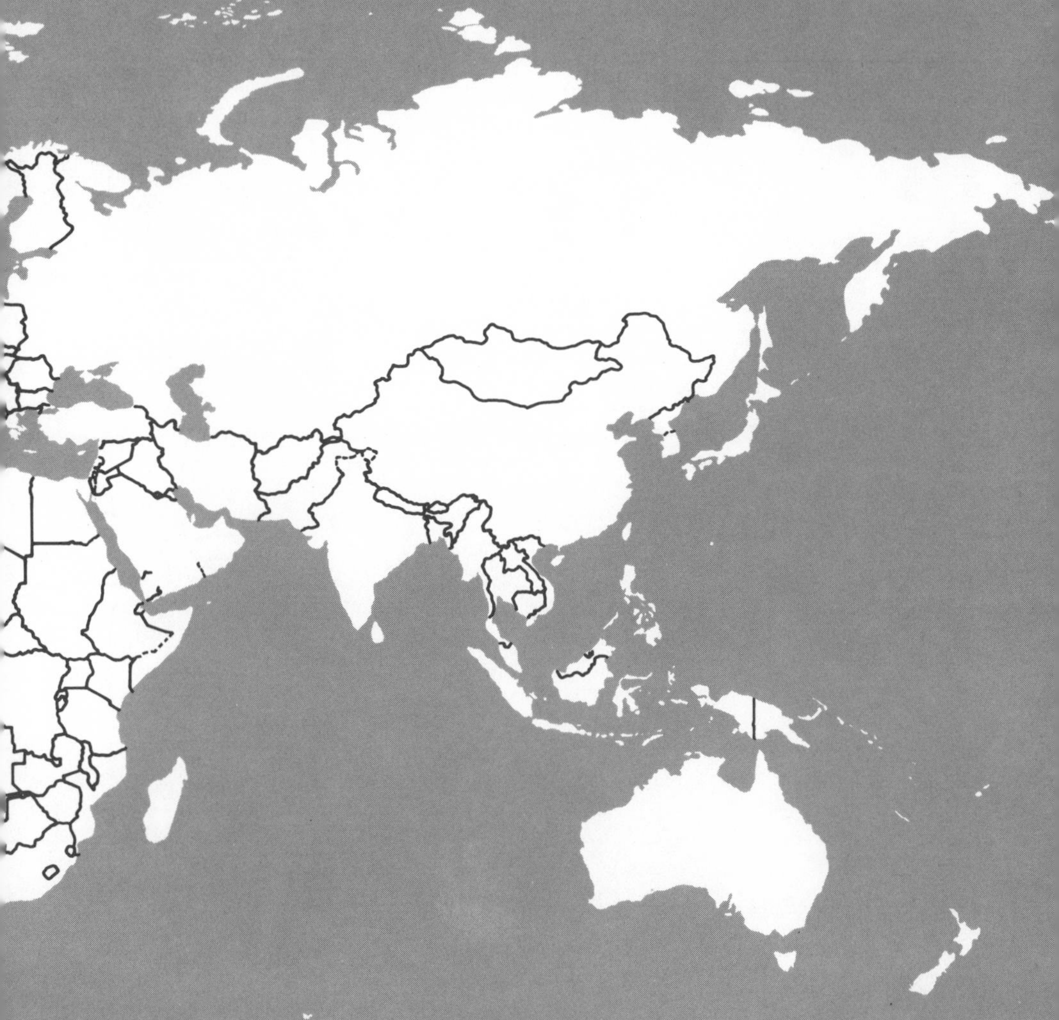

Iran
a country study

Federal Research Division
Library of Congress
Edited by Helen Chapin Metz
Research Completed
December 1987

On the cover: A fifth century B.C. drinking vessel in the shape of a winged lion, from Hamadan

Fourth Edition, 1989; First Printing, 1989.

Library of Congress Cataloging-in-Publication Data

Iran: a Country Study.

Area handbook series, DA Pam.; 550-68
Supt. of Docs. No.: D 101.22:550-68/987
Research completed October 1987.
Bibliography: p. 309.
Includes index.
1. Iran. I. Metz, Helen Chapin, 1928- . II. Library of Congress. Federal Research Division. III. Series. IV. Series: DA Pam.; 550-68.
DS254.5.I742 1989 955 88-600484

Headquarters, Department of the Army
DA Pam 550-68

For sale by the Superintendent of Documents, U.S. Government Printing Office
Washington, D.C. 20402

Foreword

This volume is one in a continuing series of books now being prepared by the Federal Research Division of the Library of Congress under the Country Studies—Area Handbook Program. The last page of this book lists the other published studies.

Most books in the series deal with a particular foreign country, describing and analyzing its political, economic, social, and national security systems and institutions, and examining the interrelationships of those systems and the ways they are shaped by cultural factors. Each study is written by a multidisciplinary team of social scientists. The authors seek to provide a basic understanding of the observed society, striving for a dynamic rather than a static portrayal. Particular attention is devoted to the people who make up the society, their origins, dominant beliefs and values, their common interests and the issues on which they are divided, the nature and extent of their involvement with national institutions, and their attitudes toward each other and toward their social system and political order.

The books represent the analysis of the authors and should not be construed as an expression of an official United States government position, policy, or decision. The authors have sought to adhere to accepted standards of scholarly objectivity. Corrections, additions, and suggestions for changes from readers will be welcomed for use in future editions.

Louis R. Mortimer
Acting Chief
Federal Research Division
Library of Congress
Washington, D.C. 20540

Acknowledgments

The authors wish to acknowledge the contributions of the writers of the 1978 edition of *Iran: A Country Study,* edited by Richard F. Nyrop. Their work provided general background for the present volume.

The authors are grateful to individuals in various government agencies and private institutions who gave of their time, research materials, and expertise to the production of this book. The authors also wish to thank members of the Federal Research Division staff who contributed directly to the preparation of the manuscript. These people included Thomas Collelo, the substantive reviewer of all the graphic and textual material; Richard F. Nyrop, who reviewed all drafts and served as liaison with the sponsoring agency; Marilyn L. Majeska, who edited chapters; and Martha E. Hopkins, who edited chapters and managed editing and book production.

Also involved in preparing the text were editorial assistants Barbara Edgerton, Nerissa Dixon, Monica Shimmin, and Izella Watson; Vincent Ercolano and Ruth Nieland, who edited chapters; Carolyn Hinton, who performed the prepublication editorial review; and Shirley Kessell of Communicators Connection, who compiled the index.

Graphics were prepared by David P. Cabitto, assisted by Sandra K. Cotugno and Kimberly A. Lord. Harriett R. Blood prepared the physical features map. Carolina Forrester reviewed map drafts, and Greenhorne and O'Mara prepared the final maps. Special thanks are owed to Theresa E. Kamp, who designed the cover artwork and the illustrations on the title page of each chapter. Diann Johnson, of the Library of Congress Composing Unit, prepared the camera-ready copy under the supervision of Peggy Pixley.

The authors would like to thank several individuals who provided research and operational support. Afaf S. McGowan obtained photographs, Rhonda E. Boris assisted in editorial research, and Gwendolyn B. Batts performed word-processing.

Finally, the authors acknowledge the generosity of the many individuals and public and private agencies who allowed their photographs to be used in this study.

Contents

List of Figures

Preface

Like its predecessor, this study is an attempt to treat in a concise and objective manner the dominant social, political, economic, and military aspects of contemporary Iranian society. Sources of information included scholarly journals and monographs, official reports of governments and international organizations, foreign and domestic newspapers, and numerous periodicals. Relatively up-to-date statistical data in the economic and social fields were unfortunately unavailable, even from the United Nations and the World Bank. Although the Introduction mentions events as late as June 1989, the cut-off date for research for this volume was December 31, 1987. It should be noted that Houman Sadri wrote the section on the Iran-Iraq War in chapter 5, and that Joseph A. Kechichian wrote the remainder of that chapter. Chapter bibliographies appear at the end of the book; brief comments on some of the more valuable sources suggested as possible further reading appear at the end of each chapter. Measurements are given in the metric system; a conversion table is provided to assist those readers who are unfamiliar with metric measurements (see table 1, Appendix).

The transliteration of Persian words and phrases posed a particular problem, and Dr. Eric Hooglund was most helpful in resolving these difficulties. For words that are of direct Arabic origin—such as Muhammad (the Prophet), Muslim, and Quran—the authors followed a modified version of the system for Arabic adopted by the United States Board on Geographic Names and the Permanent Committee on Geographic Names for British Official Use, known as the BGN/PCGN system. (The modification is a significant one, entailing the deletion of all diacritical marks and hyphens.) The BGN/PCGN system was also used to transliterate Persian words, again without the diacritics. In some instances, however, place-names were so well known by another spelling that to have used the BGN/PCGN system might have caused confusion. For example, the reader will find Basra for the city rather than Al Basrah.

An effort has been made to limit the use of foreign words and phrases. Those deemed essential to an understanding of the society have been briefly defined at the place where they first appear in a chapter or are explained in the Glossary.

Country Profile

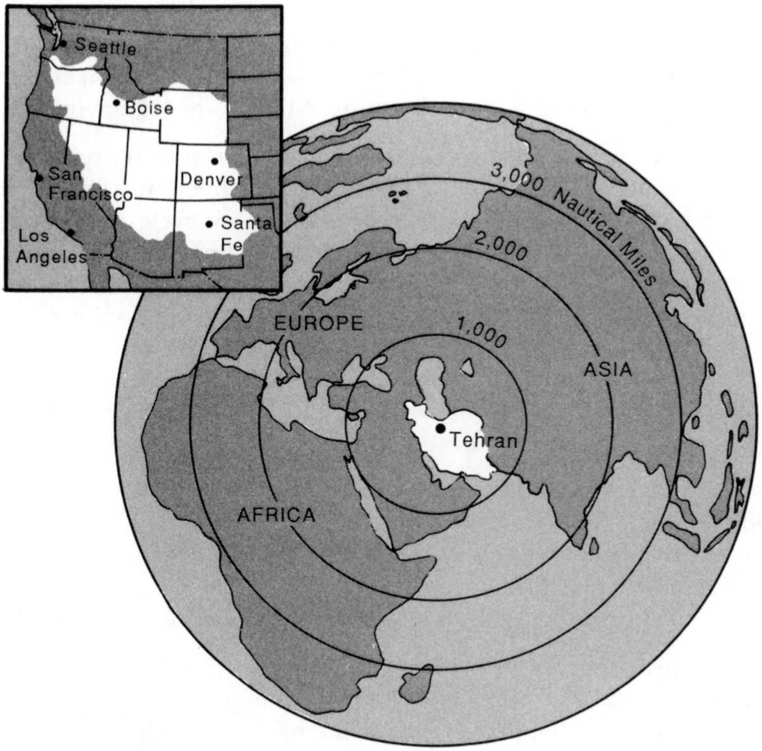

Country

Formal Name: Islamic Republic of Iran.

Short Form: Iran.

Term for Citizens: Iranian.

Capital: Tehran.

Geography

Size: Land area of about 1,648,000 square kilometers; sovereignty claimed over territorial waters up to 12 nautical miles.

Topography: Large Central Plateau surrounded on three sides by rugged mountain ranges. Highest peak Mount Damavand, approximately 5,600 meters; Caspian Sea about 27 meters below sea level.

Society

Population: Preliminary results of October 1986 census listed total population as 48,181,463, including approximately 2.6 million refugees from Afghanistan and Iraq. Population grew at rate of 3.6 percent per annum between 1976 and 1986. Government figures showed 50 percent of population under fifteen years of age in 1986.

Education: School system consists of five years of primary (begun at seven years of age), three years of middle school, and four years of high school education. High school has three cycles: academic, science and mathematics, and vocational technical. Government announced 11.5 million students in above school system in academic year 1986–87; percentage of school age population in school not published. Postrevolution decrease in university enrollments, particularly percentage of women students, which declined from 40 percent in prerevolutionary period to 10 percent in 1984. Number of students abroad also declined.

Health: Iranian Medical Association reported 12,300 doctors in 1986; 38,000 additional doctors needed to provide population with minimally adequate health care. Most medical personnel located in large cities. High infant mortality rate. Gastrointestinal, parasitic, and respiratory diseases other chief causes of mortality.

Languages: Persian official language and native tongue of over half the population. Spoken as a second language by majority of the remainder. Other Indo-European languages, such as Kirmanji (the collective term in Iran for the dialects spoken by Kurds), as well as Turkic languages and Arabic also important.

Religion: Shia Islam official religion with at least 90 percent adherence. Also approximately 8 percent Sunni Muslims and smaller numbers of Bahais, Armenian and Assyrian Christians, Jews, and Zoroastrians.

Economy

Gross Domestic Product: About US$168 billion in 1985, US$165 billion in 1986, and US$176 billion (estimated) in 1987 (figure given at official rate; unofficial rate as much as 10 times higher for United States dollar value of rial). Percentage of GDP growth 1.5 percent (real) in 1985 and 10 percent (estimated) in 1986. Inflation rate estimated at 20 percent in 1985, 30 percent in 1986, and 35 percent in 1987. Figures must be regarded with caution as official sources seriously underestimate rate of inflation and currency depreciation.

Gross National Product: 1986 estimate US$82.4 billion.

Industry: Oil major industry. In 1986 oil production averaged 1.9 million barrels per day; in January 1987 crude oil production averaged 2.2 million barrels per day, of which exports averaged between 1.5 million and 1.7 million barrels per day. Reported reserves of 48.5 billion barrels in 1986 ranked Iran fourth behind Saudi Arabia, Soviet Union, and Kuwait. Damage to Iranian oil installations during 1986–87 reduced oil production and exports substantially. Natural gas reserves claimed by government to be 13.8 trillion cubic meters in 1987. Oil and gas produced estimated 8 percent of GDP in FY 1986–87. Non-oil industry mainly agricultural products, carpets, textiles, and war-related manufacturing such as munitions. Industry employed approximately 31 percent of work force in 1987. Manufacturing and mining produced estimated 23 percent of GDP in FY 1986–87. Services produced estimated 48 percent of GDP in FY 1986–87.

Agriculture: Accounted for estimated 21 percent of GDP in FY 1986–87 and employed approximately 38 percent of work force. Despite regime efforts to promote self-sufficiency, Iran more dependent on agricultural imports in 1987 than in 1970s. Lack of progress resulted from unresolved land reform issues, government policies that did not provide incentives for farmers to invest, and migration to cities.

Imports: In 1983–84 about US$18.1 billion. Principal imports: road vehicles and machines (35 percent), manufactures and iron and steel (29 percent), and food and live animals (13 percent).

Exports: In 1985 about US$13.4 billion, of which all but about US$270 million from oil and gas. Oil exports in FY 1986–87 estimated between US$10.5 billion and US$11.5 billion; about US$900 million non-oil exports.

Major Trade Areas: In 1985 about 16 percent of imports from Federal Republic of Germany (West Germany), 13 percent from Japan, 7 percent from Britain, and 6 percent each from Italy and Turkey. In 1985 about 16 percent of exports to Japan and 9 percent each to Italy and Turkey.

Transportation and Communications

Roads: In 1984 a total of 136,381 kilometers of roads, of which 41 percent paved; of paved roads 16,551 kilometers of main roads and 34,838 kilometers of secondary roads.

Railroads: About 4,700 kilometers of railroads in 1987, including newly electrified track in north between Tabriz and Jolfa for Soviet imports; also rail connection with Turkey.

Pipelines: About 5,900 kilometers for crude oil; 3,900 kilometers for refined products; 3,300 kilometers for natural gas in 1987; some possibly inoperable as result of war damage.

Airports: In 1987 three international airports: Tehran, Abadan, and Esfahan. Other airports being expanded and construction for new ones planned.

Communications: In 1986 about 1.5 million telephones; 3,000 out of 70,000 rural communities had telephones in 1987 compared with 300 in 1979. Further telephone expansion planned. Additional microwave links opened between Tehran, Ankara, and Karachi in early 1980s.

Government and Politics

Government: Islamic Republic under Constitution of 1979, with Ayatollah Sayyid Ruhollah Musavi Khomeini as *faqih* (see Glossary) for life and ultimate decision maker. Executive branch included elected president, responsible for selecting prime minister and cabinet, which must be approved by parliament, or Majlis (see Glossary), elected legislative assembly. Judiciary independent of both executive and Majlis. Council of Guardians, consisting of six religious scholars appointed by *faqih* and six Muslim lawyers approved by Majlis, ensured conformity of legislation with Islamic law.

Politics: Islamic Republican Party, created in 1979, dissolved in 1987 because its factions made it unmanageable. Iran Freedom Movement, a nonreligious political party, existed in 1987 but had been intimidated into silence. Opposition political parties existed in exile abroad: monarchists, democrats, Kurds, Islamic groups, and Marxists. Regime stressed mass political participation through religious institutions, such as mosques, rather than political parties. Factories, schools, and offices had Islamic associations similar to mosque voluntary associations. Fervent religious zeal and support for the Revolution promoted by the Pasdaran (Pasdaran-e Enghelab-e Islami, or Islamic Revolutionary Guard Corps, or Revolutionary Guards).

Administrative Divisions: Country divided into twenty-four provinces (*ostans*), each under a governor general (*ostandar*); provinces subdivided into counties (*shahrestans*), each under a governor (*farmandar*). Most administrative officials appointive and answerable to central Ministry of Interior. In addition, each county had clerical *imam jomeh* chosen from among county senior clergy. *Imam jomeh* served as representative of *faqih.*

Foreign Affairs: Policy of Islamic revolutionary government based on export of Islamic revolution and liberation of Islamic and Third World countries generally. Other major policy was independence from both West and East, especially United States, the ''Great Satan,'' and Soviet Union, the ''Lesser Satan.'' War with Iraq, which began in 1980, had been very costly in men and matériel. War ended with Iran's acceptance of a cease-fire in July 1988.

National Security

Armed Forces: In 1986 army, 305,000; navy, 14,500; air force, 35,000. Two-thirds of army conscripted; majority of navy and air force volunteers. Pasdaran (Revolutionary Guards)—approximately 350,000.

Combat Units and Major Equipment: (Note: because of wartime losses, equipment estimates were highly tentative.) Army had three mechanized divisions, each with three brigades—each of which in turn had three armored and six mechanized battalions, seven infantry divisions, one airborne brigade, one Special Forces division composed of four brigades, one Air Support Command, some independent armored brigades including infantry and ''coastal force,'' twelve surface-to-air missile (SAM) battalions with improved Hawk missiles, reserve Qods battalion of ex-servicemen, about 1,000 tanks, and about 320 combat helicopters. Navy had fifteen combat vessels and thirty naval aircraft in 1986; by late 1987 only some small patrol craft and a few Hovercraft believed operable; three marine battalions; naval air had about thirty aircraft, mainly helicopters. Air force consisted of eight fighter and fighter-bomber squadrons, one reconnaissance squadron, two joint tanker-transport squadrons, five light transport squadrons, and five SAM squadrons; about ninety operational aircraft in 1986. Pasdaran had possibly eight divisions loosely organized in eleven regional commands and numerous independent brigades.

Paramilitary: Basij ''Popular Mobilization Army'' volunteers—strength varied; in 1986 said to be 3 million.

Military Budget: (figures varied and unreliable) In 1985–86 military budget estimated at US$14.1 billion; total war-related expenses by 1987 estimated at US$100 billion.

Police and Internal Security Agencies: In 1986 Gendarmerie about 70,000, including border guard; National Police, approximately 200,000; SAVAMA secret police, number unknown.

Figure 1. Administrative Divisions

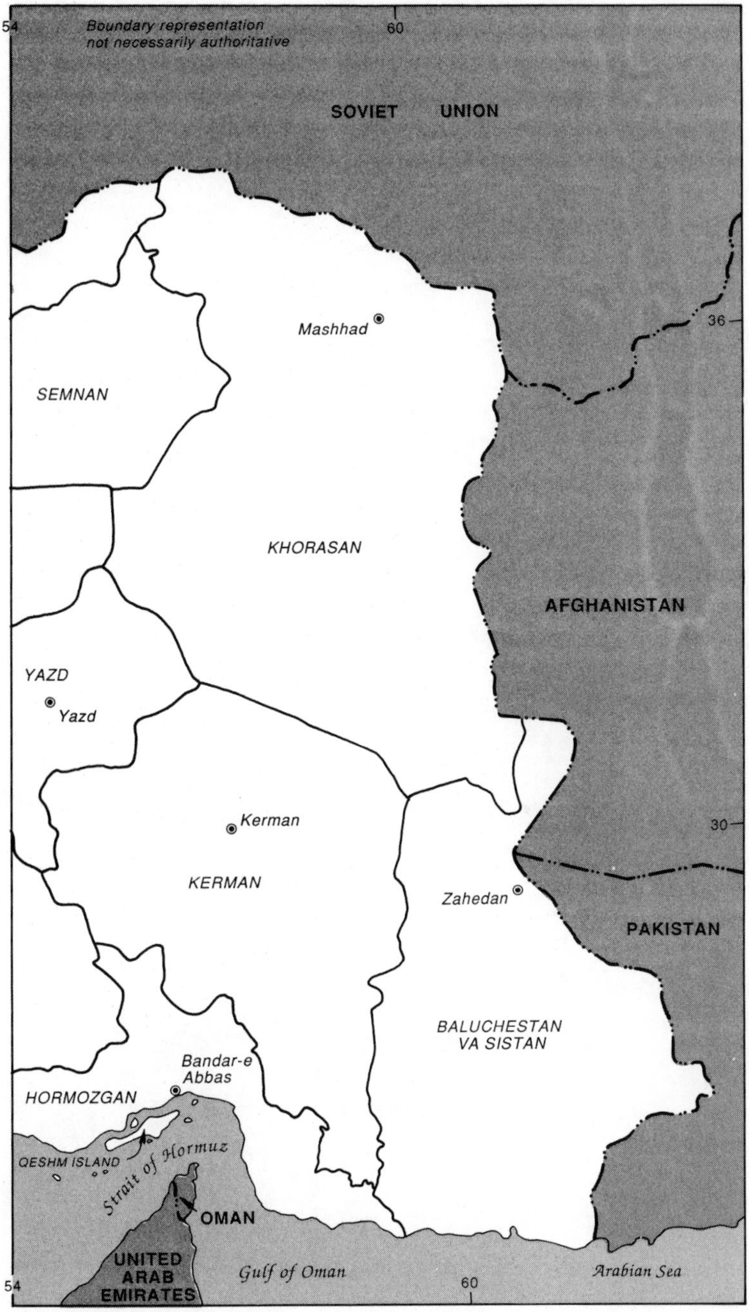
54
Boundary representation
not necessarily authoritative
60
SOVIET UNION
36
Mashhad
SEMNAN
KHORASAN
AFGHANISTAN
YAZD
Yazd
30
Kerman
KERMAN
Zahedan
PAKISTAN
BALUCHESTAN
VA SISTAN
Bandar-e
Abbas
HORMOZGAN
QESHM ISLAND
Strait of Hormuz
OMAN
UNITED
ARAB
EMIRATES
Gulf of Oman
Arabian Sea
54
60

Introduction

DURING IRAN'S LONG HISTORY, the country has evolved its own great Persian civilization, in addition to forming a part of a number of world empires. Iran has created sophisticated institutions, many of which still influenced its Islamic regime in the 1980s. Despite the turmoil surrounding the establishment of its revolutionary government, Iran's development has shown continuity. Major trends affecting Iran throughout much of its history have been a tradition of monarchical government, represented in the twentieth century by Mohammad Reza Shah Pahlavi; the important political role of the Shia (see Glossary) Islamic clergy, seen most recently in Ayatollah Sayyid Ruhollah Musavi Khomeini; and, since the late nineteenth century, pressure for Westernization or modernization.

Iran has been distinguished for having regimes that not only conquered neighboring areas but also devised ingenious institutions. The Achaemenids (550–330 B.C.)—who ruled the first Iranian world empire, which stretched from the Aegean coast of Asia Minor to Afghanistan, as well as south to Egypt—created the magnificent structures at Persepolis, the remains of which still exist. The Achaemenids also inaugurated a vast network of roads, a legal code, a coinage system, and a comprehensive administrative system that allowed some local autonomy, and they engaged in wide-ranging commerce. Iran has also influenced its conquerors. Following its conquest of Iran, the Muslim Umayyad Empire (A.D. 661–750) adopted many Iranian institutions, such as Iran's administrative system and coinage. Moreover, Tamerlane (1381–1405), the famous Mongol ruler, made use of Iranian administrators in governing his far-flung territories.

Despite their primarily tribal origin, for most of the country's history the people of Iran have known only monarchical government, often of an absolutist type. For example, the Sassanids who ruled Iran for four centuries, beginning in A.D. 224, revived the Achaemenid term *shahanshah* (king of kings) for their ruler and considered him the "shadow of God on earth." This concept was again revived in the late eighteenth century by the Qajar monarchy, which remained in power until Reza Khan, a military commander, had himself crowned as Reza Shah Pahlavi in 1925. Many considered Reza Shah's son, Mohammad Reza Shah, to be an absolutist ruler in his later days, especially because of his use of the internal security force SAVAK (Sazman-e Ettelaat va Amniyat-e Keshvar) to repress domestic opposition.

After the Muslim conquest, Iran was strongly influenced by Islam and, specifically, the political role exercised by the Shia clergy. Such influence was established under the indigenous dynastic reign of the Safavids (1501–1722). The Safavids belonged to a Sufi religious order and made Shia Islam the official religion of Iran, undertaking a major conversion campaign of Iranian Muslims. The precedent was revived in 1979 in a much more thoroughgoing theocratic fashion by Ayatollah Khomeini.

In contrast to this traditional element in Iranian history has been the pressure toward Westernization that began in the late nineteenth century. Such pressures initially came from Britain, which sought to increase its commercial relations with Iran by promoting modernization of Iran's infrastructure and liberalization of its trade. British prodding had little effect, however, until Iranian domestic reaction to the growing corruption of the Qajar monarchy led to a constitutional revolution in 1905–1906. This revolution resulted in an elected parliament, or Majlis (see Glossary), a cabinet approved by the Majlis, and a constitution guaranteeing certain personal freedoms of citizens. Within less than twenty years, the program of Reza Shah stressed measures designed to reduce the powers of both tribal and religious leaders and to bring about economic development and legal and educational reforms along Western lines. Mohammad Reza Shah, like his father, promoted such Westernization and largely ignored the traditional role in Iranian society of conservative Shia religious leaders (see Shia Islam in Iran, ch. 2).

Mohammad Reza Shah also strengthened the military by considerably expanding its role in internal security matters to counteract the domestic opposition that arose after Mohammad Mossadeq's prime ministership (see Mossadeq and Oil Nationalization, ch. 1). In addition, the shah stressed defense against external enemies because he felt threatened by the Soviet Union, which had occupied Iranian territory during and after World War II. To counter such a threat, the shah sought United States military assistance in the form of advisory personnel and sophisticated weaponry. He also harshly repressed the communist Tudeh Party and other dissident groups such as the Islamic extremist Mojahedin (Mojahedin-e Khalq, or People's Struggle) and Fadayan (Cherikha-ye Fadayan-e Khalq, or People's Guerrillas) organizations.

Meanwhile, the shah promoted Iran's economic development by implementing a series of seven- and five-year economic development plans, of which the first was launched in 1949. The programs emphasized the creation of the necessary infrastructure and the establishment of capital-intensive industry, initially making use of Iran's enormous oil revenues but seeking ultimately to diversify the country's economy by expanding heavy industry. In the 1960s, the shah also paid attention to land reform, but the redistribution of land to peasants was slow, and in many instances the amount of land allocated to individual farmers was inadequate for economically viable agricultural production. Moreover, Iran experienced high inflation as a result of the shah's huge foreign arms purchases and his unduly rapid attempts at industrial development and modernization. Members of the bazaar, or small merchant class, benefited unevenly from the modernization and gained less proportionately than the shah's Westernizing elite (see Urban Society, ch. 2). This lack of benefit from reforms was also true of the inhabitants of most small villages, who remained without electricity, running water, or paved roads (see Oil Revenues and Acceleration of Modernization, 1960–79, ch. 3).

Many factors contributed to the fall of the shah (see The Coming of the Revolution, ch. 1). Observers most often cited such factors as concern over growing Western influences and secularization, the ignoring of the religious leaders, the repression of potential dissidents and of the Tudeh Party, and the failure of the bazaar class to achieve significant benefits from the shah's economic development programs. Following a brief secular provisional government after the shah was overthrown in 1979, clerical forces loyal to Ayatollah Khomeini took control and launched a far-reaching Islamic revolution.

In Khomeini's revolutionary regime, the Ayatollah himself acted as policy guide and ultimate decision maker in his role as the pious jurist, or *faqih* (see Glossary), in accordance with the doctrine of *velayat-e faqih* (see Glossary), under which religious scholars guided the community of believers. Iran, officially renamed the Islamic Republic of Iran, became a theocratic state with the rulers representing God in governing a Muslim people, something not attempted previously even by the twelve Shia Imams (see Glossary).

The Constitution of 1979 designates Khomeini as the *faqih* for life. The Assembly of Experts in 1985 designated Hojjatoleslam Hosain Ali Montazeri as the deputy to Khomeini and thus in line as successor. In 1988 it was not clear, however, whether the country would accept the choice of the experts when Khomeini died.

Other than appointing Khomeini *faqih* for life, the revolutionary Constitution provides for political institutions to implement the legislative aspects of the government. An elected legislative assembly, the Majlis, charged with approving legislation devised by the executive, was dominated by Muslim religious leaders. The Constitution also created the Council of Guardians to ensure that laws passed by the Majlis conformed with Islam. In practice, the Council of Guardians has been conservative about economic legislation, blocking Majlis measures on land reform, for example. To overcome this blocking of legislation, in January 1988 Ayatollah Khomeini created a special council to adjudicate conflicts among the Council of Guardians, the Majlis, and the executive. He said the state could set aside provisions of the Quran temporarily if it were for the good of the Islamic community as a whole.

Other than through legislative instititutions, political expression occurred in principle through political parties. However, the dominant political faction, the largely clergy-led Islamic Republican Party established in early 1979, was dissolved in 1987 because it had become unmanageable. Subsequently, only one legally recognized political party, the Iran Freedom Movement (Nehzat-e Azadi-yi Iran), which had been established by former Prime Minister Mehdi Bazargan, operated in Iran. Estimates of the number of persons opposed to the government or in prison varied. Officially, the latter number was given as 9,000, but the antigovernment Mojahedin maintained that 140,000 was a more realistic figure. In 1988 opposition parties existed in exile, primarily in Western Europe, and included ethnic Kurdish movements and the Mojahedin Islamic extremists, as well as Marxists and monarchists (see Opposition Political Parties in Exile, ch. 4). The Mojahedin also had created the Iranian National Army of Liberation, which operated out of northern Iraq against the Khomeini regime.

After the Ayatollah's government came to power, it initially executed or imprisoned many members of the shah's regime, including officers of the various armed services. But, following the outbreak of the war with Iraq in 1980, substantial numbers of military men were released from prison to provide essential leadership on the battlefield or in the air war (see Iranian Resistance and Mobilization, ch. 5). As early as June 1979, a counterforce to the regular military was created in the form of the Pasdaran (Pasdaran-e Enghelab-e Islami, or Islamic Revolutionary Guard Corps, or Revolutionary Guards), an organization charged with safeguarding the Revolution. The Pasdaran became a significant military force in its own right and was overseen by a cabinet-level minister (see Special and Irregular Armed Forces, ch. 5).

By 1988 the eight-year-old war with Iraq had evolved through various stages of strategy and tactics (see The Iran-Iraq War, ch. 5). Because Iran's population was approximately three times that of

Iraq, Iran's military manpower pool was vastly superior. Capitalizing on this advantage, in the early stages of the war Iran engaged extensively in "human-wave" assaults against Iraqi positions, frequently using youths in their early teens. This war strategy proved extremely costly to Iran in terms of human casualties; it was estimated that between 180,000 and 250,000 Iranians had been killed by 1987, and estimated losses of matériel were also large. The hostilities included a tanker war in the Persian Gulf and the mining of the Gulf by Iran, events that led to the involvement of the United States and other Western nations, which sought to protect their shipping and safeguard their strategic, economic, and political interests in the area. Furthermore, a "war of cities" was inaugurated in 1985, with each side bombarding the other's urban centers with missiles. Iran expended considerable effort in developing a domestic arms industry capable of manufacturing or modifying weapons and war matériel obtained from outside sources. Iran's principal arms supplier was China, from which it acquired Silkworm HY-2 surface-to-surface missiles, among other weapons systems. Iran received no missiles from the Soviet Union, which attempted to maintain amicable relations with both sides in the Iran-Iraq War. In addition, in the ground war, which initially had favored Iraq but then turned strongly in Iran's favor, in April 1988 Iraq succeeded in regaining the Faw Peninsula. Iraq thus recovered a significant part of the territory it had lost earlier to Iran.

The war has severely strained Iran's economy by depleting its foreign exchange reserves and causing a balance of payments deficit. It has also redirected manpower that would otherwise have increased the ranks of the unemployed (see The War's Impact on the Economy, ch. 3). By 1987 Iran's overall war costs were calculated at approximately US$350 billion. Moreover, wartime damage to urban centers in western Iran, such as Abadan, Ahvaz, Dezful, and Khorramshahr, caused refugees to flood into Tehran and other cities, further aggravating the housing shortage. The destruction of petroleum producing, processing, and shipping installations on the Persian Gulf had reduced Iran's oil production and its export capability, thereby cutting revenues. Sales of other domestic commodities, such as carpets, agricultural products, and caviar, were unable to compensate for the lost oil revenue, which was further reduced by a world oil glut. Thus, in 1988 the revolutionary regime faced a straitened economic future in which basic structural problems—such as the degree of state involvement in the economy and the successful implementation of agricultural reform—remained to be addressed.

Iran's economic situation has influenced its foreign policy to some extent. Although ideological considerations based on revolutionary principles dominated in the early days of the Revolution, Iran's policies became more pragmatic as the war with Iraq continued. For example, because of its need for weapons and other military matériel, the Khomeini regime was willing to purchase arms from Western nations and even from Israel. Initially, the revolutionary government had made a radical foreign policy change from the pro-Western stance of the shah. The United States, because of its support of the shah, was branded as the "Great Satan" and the Soviet Union as the "Lesser Satan." Both capitalism and socialism were condemned as materialistic systems that sought to dominate the Third World. In practice, however, the United States was the major target, as evidenced most clearly in the seizure of the United States embassy in Tehran and the taking of American diplomats as hostages in November 1979.

Because of the Khomeini regime's desire to export revolution, regional monarchies with Western associations, such as Saudi Arabia, the Gulf states, and Jordan, were regarded with some hostility, particularly after these countries came to the support of Iraq in the Iran-Iraq War (see Relations with Regional Powers, ch. 4). Iran's militant foreign policy in the region was reflected in the August 1, 1987, demonstrations during the Mecca pilgrimage. As a result, over 400 pilgrims were killed (the majority of them Iranian). As a protest against Iranian actions in the Gulf, in late April 1988 Saudi Arabia severed diplomatic relations with Iran. Another instance of Iran's militant policy was its funding and sponsorship of Islamic extremist organizations in Lebanon, particularly Islamic Amal and Hizballah, which contributed to the ongoing civil war in Lebanon.

In 1988 the country with which Iran had the most cordial relationship was Syria. Iran also maintained active economic relations with the Soviet Union, especially with respect to direct trade, joint fisheries, and the transshipment of goods via the Soviet Union to Western Europe.

Iran's future course in the late 1980s hinged upon a number of factors. These included the smoothness with which it would be able to make the transition to Ayatollah Khomeini's successor; the duration, cost, and settlement terms of the war with Iraq; the direction of Iran's foreign policy, in relation both to the superpowers and to the remainder of the world, particularly the countries of the region; and the skill of Iranian technocrats in taking the necessary steps to address the country's economic difficulties.

June 20, 1988

* * *

After the manuscript was completed in June 1988, two significant events occurred in July 1988 that contributed to Iran's decision on July 18 to accept the United Nations (UN) proposal of 1987 for a cease-fire to the Iran-Iraq War. On July 3, 1988, the United States Navy shot down in error a civilian Iranian airliner that it believed was planning to attack a United States Navy ship in the Persian Gulf. In a step indicative of moderation, Iran took the downing of Iran Air Flight 655 to the UN, a body to which it had paid little heed since 1981 because Iran felt the UN was supporting the Iraqi position in the Iran-Iraq hostilities. Just prior to the UN debate, President Ronald Reagan announced that the United States, without accepting blame for the accident, was prepared to make an *ex gratia* payment to the victims' relatives.

In the more immediate conduct of the war, on July 13 Iraqi forces advanced on the south central front, capturing Dehloran, thirty kilometers inside Iran. They took about 5,000 prisoners as well as substantial amounts of Iranian military equipment during their three-day occupation of the area. Foreign experts surmised that Iraq sought to strengthen its bargaining position in the event peace negotiations were forthcoming.

On July 18 Iran announced its acceptance of UN Resolution 598 of July 1987, which called for a cease-fire. Khomeini, taking responsibility for accepting this "poisonous chalice," while at the same time recognizing the great sacrifices of the nation, stated that, in view of recent "unspecified events" (presumably Iraq's "war of cities" and its use of chemical warfare, together with the intervention of the "Great Satan") and the advice of Iranian political and military experts, he believed the cease-fire to be in the interest of the Revolution. As of mid-May 1989, although the cease-fire was holding, no significant progress had been made in UN-sponsored Iranian-Iraqi peace negotiations, and Iraq was insisting on sovereignty over the entire Shatt al Arab as a condition for the settlement.

Khomeini had often stated that he would not agree to an end of the war without the overthrow of Iraqi President Saddam Husayn's regime. His reversal of position raised questions concerning the future of the Revolution. There was evidence in the spring of 1989 that factionalism was increasing among revolutionary leaders. The most dramatic example of this was Ayatollah Montazeri's being obliged in late March to resign as successor to Khomeini. Montazeri apparently fell from grace because he had become unduly critical in public of the regime's policies. He had repeatedly criticized the continued execution of numerous individuals on the ground that they were hostile to the Revolution and had questioned whether Iran had actually won the war with Iraq.

The realignments taking place among the top hierarchy were not clear as of mid-May 1989. For example, in early March Khomeini had concurred with the appointment of Hojjatoleslam Abdullah Nouri, a friend of Majlis Speaker Ali Akbar Hashemi-Rafsanjani, as his personal representative to the Pasdaran. This move was thought to be part of Rafsanjani's strategy to diminish the influence of the Pasdaran and to integrate them more closely with the army, because the regime considered the army a more loyal force than the Pasdaran in the postwar period. Even before the war ended, in early 1988, the government had begun following a pragmatic policy, seeking to regain friends for Iran in the world community through such means as reestablishing diplomatic relations with France, Canada, and Britain. Relations with Britain were again severed, however, in late February 1989, as a result of Khomeini's imposition of the death sentence on February 14 on British writer Salman Rushdie for his authorship of *The Satanic Verses*.

Since the end of the war in July 1988 a major issue among the different factions in the government has been the degree of foreign involvement to be permitted in Iran's reconstruction. Despite some dissent in this regard, the government has sought to obtain loans and credits for Iran from various West European sources and from Japan because oil income is not projected to be adequate to meet rebuilding needs, let alone allow for development projects. Preoccupation with reconstruction and the lack of funds had obliged the revolutionary regime to postpone, if not abandon, any measures to export the Revolution. Instead, Iran was seeking a reconciliation with some of the Persian Gulf states and with the Soviet Union. Furthermore, it appeared that in its budgetary allocations for the new Iranian year beginning March 21 and for the proposed new five-year development plan, the regime was increasing its spending on agriculture and water projects and stressing education, health, and social measures, all of which were designed to show Islamic concern for the downtrodden.

A second issue among the various factions concerned the extent to which governmental centralization was appropriate. One faction maintained that more centralized policy direction was needed for the successful implementation of reconstruction programs, and that to achieve this end the presidency needed to be strengthened. Rafsanjani supported this position and was one of more than 100 signatories of a proposal made to Khomeini that one of the ways of strengthening the executive would be to eliminate the office of prime minister. In this connection, a letter was published in the Iranian press on April 16, 1989, and signed by 166 Majlis delegates, asking Khomeini to establish a committee to amend the Constitution in three areas: the *faqih,* the presidency, and the judiciary. Khomeini responded in late April by appointing twenty members to a Commission for the Revision of the Constitution, with the Majlis appointing five additional members. Khomeini set out guidelines for the commission to use in looking at eight areas of the Constitution, including the three requested. Other aspects to be examined included the role of the Discernment Council, appointed to reconcile differences among the Council of Guardians, the Majlis, and the government. By mid-May the commission had met several times.

The press has reported that the deliberations included debate on draft proposals for amending the articles of the Constitution pertaining to qualifications for the post of *faqih* so that lower-ranking clergy could serve on a collective council of *faqihs*. This would permit Rafsanjani and Khamenehi, for example, to serve. Other debate centered around proposed changes in the presidency that would entail the elimination of the post of prime minister or allow the president to appoint the prime minister without Majlis approval, thus making the prime minister responsible to the president. As early as January 1989, Rafsanjani had hinted that he might run for president to succeed Khamenehi when the latter's term ended in August 1989. Although as of mid-May Rafsanjani had not publicly committed himself to running, he had gained the endorsement for this post from revolutionary leaders of all factions. It appeared, therefore, that the revolutionary regime was on the way to some major changes in the executive structure and in its leadership.

May 18, 1989 — Helen Chapin Metz

* * *

As this volume was in press, Ayatollah Khomeini died on June 3, 1989, of a heart attack, following intestinal surgery two weeks earlier. After lengthy deliberations, on June 4 President Khamenehi was named Khomeini's successors as *faqih* by a two-thirds majority of the Assembly of Experts. The future of Iran's government in the light of possible collective leadership and the proposed reforms to the constitution affecting the executive, judicial, and administrative structures remained unclear.

June 5, 1989 Helen Chapin Metz

Chapter 1. Historical Setting

Members of the Achaemenid royal bodyguard, from a bas-relief at Persepolis

THE ISLAMIC REVOLUTION in 1979 brought a sudden end to the rule of the Pahlavi dynasty, which for fifty years had been identified with the attempt to modernize and Westernize Iran. The Revolution replaced the monarchy with an Islamic republic and a secular state with a quasi-theocracy. It brought new elites to power, altered the pattern of Iran's foreign relations, and led to the transfer of substantial wealth from private ownership to state control. There were continuities across the watershed of the Revolution, however; bureaucratic structure and behavior, attitudes toward authority and individual rights, and the arbitrary use of power remained much the same. In 1987, nearly a decade after the Revolution, it was still too early to determine whether the continuities—always striking over the long sweep of Iran's history—or the changes would prove the more permanent.

The Revolution ended a pattern of monarchical rule that, until 1979, had been an almost uninterrupted feature of Iranian government for nearly 500 years. The tradition of monarchy itself is even older. In the sixth century B.C., Iran's first empire, the Achaemenid Empire, was already established. It had an absolute monarch, centralized rule, a highly developed system of administration, aspirations of world rule, and a culture that was uniquely Iranian even as it borrowed, absorbed, and transformed elements from other cultures and civilizations. Although Alexander the Great brought the Achaemenid Empire to an end in 330 B.C., under the Sassanids (A.D. 224–642) Iran once again became the center of an empire and a great civilization.

The impact of the Islamic conquest in the seventh century was profound. It introduced a new religion and a new social and legal system. The Iranian heartland became part of a world empire whose center was not in Iran. Nevertheless, historians have found striking continuities in Iranian social structure, administration, and culture. Iranians contributed significantly to all aspects of Islamic civilization; in many ways they helped shape the new order. By the ninth century, there was a revival of the Persian (Farsi) language and of a literature that was uniquely Iranian but was enriched by Arabic and Islamic influences.

The breakup of the Islamic empire led, in Iran as in other parts of the Islamic world, to the establishment of local dynasties. Iran, like the rest of the Middle East, was affected by the rise to power of the Seljuk Turks and then by the destruction wrought first by the Mongols and then by Timur, also called Tamerlane (Timur the Lame).

With the rise of the Safavids (1501–1732), Iran was reconstituted as a territorial state within borders not very different from those prevailing today. Shia (see Glossary) Islam became the state religion, and monarchy once again became a central institution. Persian became unquestionably the language of administration and high culture. Although historians no longer assert that under the Safavids Iran emerged as a nation-state in the modern sense of the term, nevertheless by the seventeenth century the sense of Iranian identity and Iran as a state within roughly demarcated borders was more pronounced.

The Qajars (1795–1925) attempted to revive the Safavid Empire and in many ways patterned their administration after that of the Safavids. But the Qajars lacked the claims to religious legitimacy available to the Safavids; they failed to establish strong central control; and they faced an external threat from technically, militarily, and economically superior European powers, primarily Russia and Britain. Foreign interference in Iran, Qajar misrule, and new ideas on government led in 1905 to protests and eventually to the Constitutional Revolution (1905–07), which, at least on paper, limited royal absolutism, created in Iran a constitutional monarchy, and recognized the people as a source of legitimacy.

The rise of Reza Shah Pahlavi, who as Reza Khan seized power in 1921 and established a new dynasty in 1925, reflected the failure of the constitutional experiment. His early actions also reflected the aspirations of educated Iranians to create a state that was strong, centralized, free of foreign interference, economically developed, and sharing those characteristics thought to distinguish the more advanced states of Europe from the countries of the East.

This work of modernization and industrialization, expansion of education, and economic development was continued by the second Pahlavi monarch, Mohammad Reza Shah Pahlavi. He made impressive progress in expanding employment and economic and educational opportunities, in building up strong central government and a strong military, in limiting foreign influence, and in giving Iran an influential role in regional affairs.

Such explosions of unrest as occurred during the 1951–53 oil nationalization crisis and the 1963 riots during the Muslim month of Moharram, indicated that there were major unresolved tensions in Iranian society, however. These stemmed from inequities in wealth distribution; the concentration of power in the hands of the crown and bureaucratic, military, and entrepreneurial elites; the demands for political participation by a growing middle class and members of upwardly mobile lower classes; a belief that Westernization posed a threat to Iran's national and Islamic identity; and a growing polarization between the religious classes and the state.

These tensions and problems gave rise to the Islamic Revolution. In the late 1980s, they continued to challenge Iran's new rulers.

Ancient Iran

Pre-Achaemenid Iran

Iran's history as a nation of people speaking an Indo-European language did not begin until the middle of the second millennium B.C. Before then, Iran was occupied by peoples with a variety of cultures. There are numerous artifacts attesting to settled agriculture, permanent sun-dried-brick dwellings, and pottery-making from the sixth millennium B.C. The most advanced area technologically was ancient Susiana, present-day Khuzestan Province (see fig. 1). By the fourth millennium, the inhabitants of Susiana, the Elamites, were using semipictographic writing, probably learned from the highly advanced civilization of Sumer in Mesopotamia (ancient name for much of the area now known as Iraq), to the west.

Sumerian influence in art, literature, and religion also became particularly strong when the Elamites were occupied by, or at least came under the domination of, two Mesopotamian cultures, those of Akkad and Ur, during the middle of the third millennium. By 2000 B.C. the Elamites had become sufficiently unified to destroy the city of Ur. Elamite civilization developed rapidly from that point, and, by the fourteenth century B.C., its art was at its most impressive.

Immigration of the Medes and the Persians

Small groups of nomadic, horse-riding peoples speaking Indo-European languages began moving into the Iranian cultural area from Central Asia near the end of the second millennium B.C. Population pressures, overgrazing in their home area, and hostile neighbors may have prompted these migrations. Some of the groups settled in eastern Iran, but others, those who were to leave significant historical records, pushed farther west toward the Zagros Mountains.

Three major groups are identifiable—the Scythians, the Medes (the Amadai or Mada), and the Persians (also known as the Parsua or Parsa). The Scythians established themselves in the northern Zagros Mountains and clung to a seminomadic existence in which raiding was the chief form of economic enterprise. The Medes settled over a huge area, reaching as far as modern Tabriz in the north and Esfahan in the south. They had their capital at Ecbatana (present-day Hamadan) and annually paid tribute to the Assyrians. The Persians were established in three areas: to the south of Lake Urmia (the traditional name, also cited as Lake Orumiyeh, to which it has reverted after being called Lake Rezaiyeh under the Pahlavis), on the northern border of the kingdom of the Elamites; and in the environs of modern Shiraz, which would be their eventual settling place and to which they would give the name *Parsa* (what is roughly present-day Fars Province).

During the seventh century B.C., the Persians were led by Hakamanish (Achaemenes, in Greek), ancestor of the Achaemenid dynasty. A descendant, Cyrus II (also known as Cyrus the Great or Cyrus the Elder), led the combined forces of the Medes and the Persians to establish the most extensive empire known in the ancient world.

The Achaemenid Empire, 550–330 B.C.

By 546 B.C., Cyrus had defeated Croesus, the Lydian king of fabled wealth, and had secured control of the Aegean coast of Asia Minor, Armenia, and the Greek colonies along the Levant (see fig. 2). Moving east, he took Parthia (land of the Arsacids, not to be confused with Parsa, which was to the southwest), Chorasmis, and Bactria. He besieged and captured Babylon in 539 and released the Jews who had been held captive there, thus earning his immortalization in the Book of Isaiah. When he died in 529, Cyrus's kingdom extended as far east as the Hindu Kush in present-day Afghanistan.

His successors were less successful. Cyrus's unstable son, Cambyses II, conquered Egypt but later committed suicide during a revolt led by a priest, Gaumata, who usurped the throne until overthrown in 522 by a member of a lateral branch of the Achaemenid family, Darius I (also known as Darayarahush or Darius the Great). Darius attacked the Greek mainland, which had supported rebellious Greek colonies under his aegis, but as a result of his defeat at the Battle of Marathon in 490 was forced to retract the limits of the empire to Asia Minor.

The Achaemenids thereafter consolidated areas firmly under their control. It was Cyrus and Darius who, by sound and farsighted administrative planning, brilliant military maneuvering, and a humanistic worldview, established the greatness of the Achaemenids and in less than thirty years raised them from an obscure tribe to a world power.

The quality of the Achaemenids as rulers began to disintegrate, however, after the death of Darius in 486. His son and successor,

Xerxes, was chiefly occupied with suppressing revolts in Egypt and Babylonia. He also attempted to conquer the Greek Peloponnesus, but encouraged by a victory at Thermopylae, he overextended his forces and suffered overwhelming defeats at Salamis and Plataea. By the time his successor, Artaxerxes I, died in 424, the imperial court was beset by factionalism among the lateral family branches, a condition that persisted until the death in 330 of the last of the Achaemenids, Darius III, at the hands of his own subjects.

The Achaemenids were enlightened despots who allowed a certain amount of regional autonomy in the form of the satrapy system. A satrapy was an administrative unit, usually organized on a geographical basis. A satrap (governor) administered the region, a general supervised military recruitment and ensured order, and a state secretary kept official records. The general and the state secretary reported directly to the central government. The twenty satrapies were linked by a 2,500-kilometer highway, the most impressive stretch being the royal road from Susa to Sardis, built by command of Darius. Relays of mounted couriers could reach the most remote areas in fifteen days. Despite the relative local independence afforded by the satrapy system however, royal inspectors, the "eyes and ears of the king," toured the empire and reported on local conditions, and the king maintained a personal bodyguard of 10,000 men, called the Immortals.

The language in greatest use in the empire was Aramaic. Old Persian was the "official language" of the empire but was used only for inscriptions and royal proclamations.

Darius revolutionized the economy by placing it on a silver and gold coinage system. Trade was extensive, and under the Achaemenids there was an efficient infrastructure that facilitated the exchange of commodities among the far reaches of the empire. As a result of this commercial activity, Persian words for typical items of trade became prevalent throughout the Middle East and eventually entered the English language; examples are *bazaar, shawl, sash, turquoise, tiara, orange, lemon, melon, peach, spinach,* and *asparagus.* Trade was one of the empire's main sources of revenue, along with agriculture and tribute. Other accomplishments of Darius's reign included codification of the *data,* a universal legal system upon which much of later Iranian law would be based, and construction of a new capital at Persepolis, where vassal states would offer their yearly tribute at the festival celebrating the spring equinox.

In its art and architecture, Persepolis reflected Darius's perception of himself as the leader of conglomerates of people to whom he had given a new and single identity. The Achaemenid art and architecture found there is at once distinctive and also highly

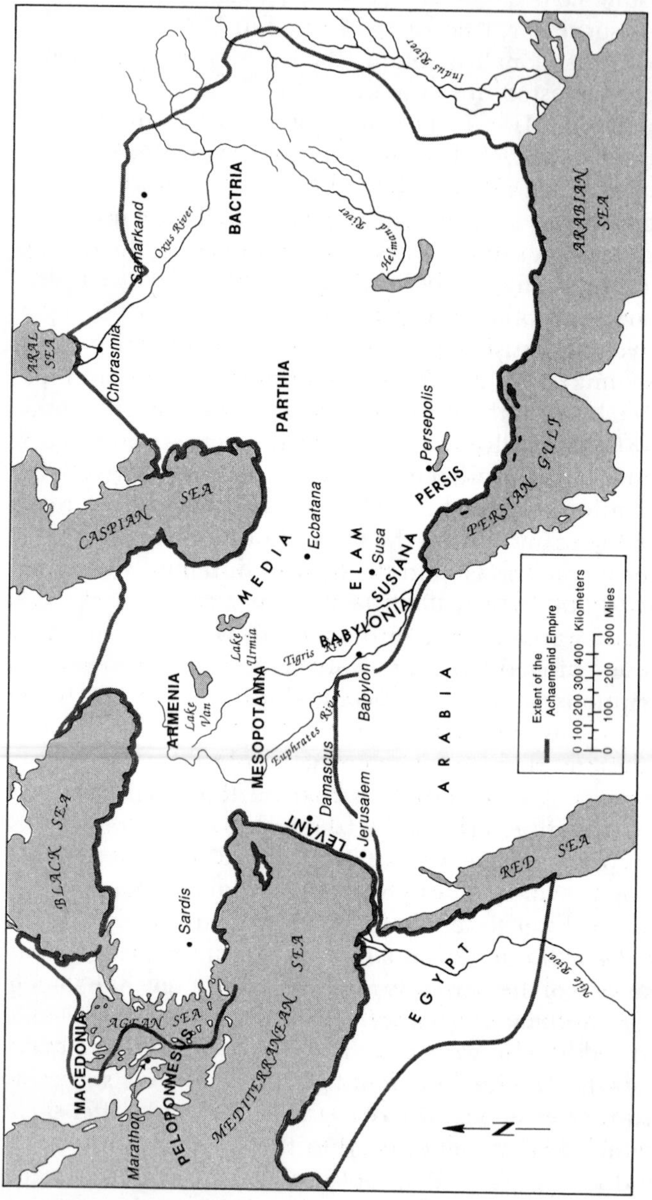

Source: Based on information from *Hammond World Atlas*, Maplewood, New Jersey, 1971; and Herbert Vreeland, *Iran*, New Haven, 1957.

Figure 2. Persian Empire, ca. 500 B.C.

eclectic. The Achaemenids took the art forms and the cultural and religious traditions of many of the ancient Middle Eastern peoples and combined them into a single form. This Achaemenid artistic style is evident in the iconography of Persepolis, which celebrates the king and the office of the monarch.

Alexander the Great, the Seleucids, and the Parthians

Envisioning a new world empire based on a fusion of Greek and Iranian culture and ideals, Alexander the Great of Macedon accelerated the disintegration of the Achaemenid Empire. He was first accepted as leader by the fractious Greeks in 336 B.C. and by 334 had advanced to Asia Minor, an Iranian satrapy. In quick succession he took Egypt, Babylonia, and then, over the course of two years, the heart of the Achaemenid Empire—Susa, Ecbatana, and Persepolis—the last of which he burned. Alexander married Roxana (Roshanak), the daughter of the most powerful of the Bactrian chiefs (Oxyartes, who revolted in present-day Tadzhikistan), and in 324 commanded his officers and 10,000 of his soldiers to marry Iranian women. The mass wedding, held at Susa, was a model of Alexander's desire to consummate the union of the Greek and Iranian peoples. These plans ended in 323 B.C., however, when Alexander was struck with fever and died in Babylon, leaving no heir. His empire was divided among four of his generals. Seleucus, one of these generals, who became ruler of Babylon in 312, gradually reconquered most of Iran. Under Seleucus's son, Antiochus I, many Greeks entered Iran, and Hellenistic motifs in art, architecture, and urban planning became prevalent.

Although the Seleucids faced challenges from the Ptolemies of Egypt and from the growing power of Rome, the main threat came from the province of Fars (Partha to the Greeks). Arsaces (of the seminomadic Parni tribe), whose name was used by all subsequent Parthian kings, revolted against the Seleucid governor in 247 B.C. and established a dynasty, the Arsacids, or Parthians. During the second century, the Parthians were able to extend their rule to Bactria, Babylonia, Susiana, and Media, and, under Mithradates II (123–87 B.C.), Parthian conquests stretched from India to Armenia. After the victories of Mithradates II, the Parthians began to claim descent from both the Greeks and the Achaemenids. They spoke a language similar to that of the Achaemenids, used the Pahlavi script, and established an administrative system based on Achaemenid precedents.

Meanwhile, Ardeshir, son of the priest Papak, who claimed descent from the legendary hero Sasan, had become the Parthian governor in the Achaemenid home province of Persis (Fars). In

A.D. 224 he overthrew the last Parthian king and established the Sassanid dynasty, which was to last 400 years.

The Sassanids, A.D. 224–642

The Sassanids established an empire roughly within the frontiers achieved by the Achaemenids, with the capital at Ctesiphon (see fig. 3). The Sassanids consciously sought to resuscitate Iranian traditions and to obliterate Greek cultural influence. Their rule was characterized by considerable centralization, ambitious urban planning, agricultural development, and technological improvements. Sassanid rulers adopted the title of *shahanshah* (king of kings), as sovereigns over numerous petty rulers, known as *shahrdars*. Historians believe that society was divided into four classes: the priests, warriors, secretaries, and commoners. The royal princes, petty rulers, great landlords, and priests together constituted a privileged stratum, and the social system appears to have been fairly rigid. Sassanid rule and the system of social stratification were reinforced by Zoroastrianism, which became the state religion. The Zoroastrian priesthood became immensely powerful. The head of the priestly class, the *mobadan mobad,* along with the military commander, the *eran spahbod,* and the head of the bureaucracy, were among the great men of the state.

Rome had replaced Greece as Iran's principal Western enemy, and hostilities between the two empires were frequent. Shahpur I (241–72), son and successor of Ardeshir, waged successful campaigns against the Romans and in 260 even took the emperor Valerian prisoner.

Chosroes I (531–79), also known as Anushirvan the Just, is the most celebrated of the Sassanid rulers. He reformed the tax system and reorganized the army and the bureaucracy, tying the army more closely to the central government than to local lords. His reign witnessed the rise of the *dihqans* (literally, village lords), the petty landholding nobility who were the backbone of later Sassanid provincial administration and the tax collection system. Chosroes was a great builder, embellishing his capital, founding new towns, and constructing new buildings. Under his auspices, too, many books were brought from India and translated into Pahlavi. Some of these later found their way into the literature of the Islamic world. The reign of Chosroes II (591–628) was characterized by the wasteful splendor and lavishness of the court.

Toward the end of his reign Chosroes II's power declined. In renewed fighting with the Byzantines, he enjoyed initial successes, captured Damascus, and seized the Holy Cross in Jerusalem. But counterattacks by the Byzantine emperor Heraclius brought enemy forces deep into Sassanid territory.

Years of warfare exhausted both the Byzantines and the Iranians. The later Sassanids were further weakened by economic decline, heavy taxation, religious unrest, rigid social stratification, the increasing power of the provincial landholders, and a rapid turnover of rulers. These factors facilitated the Arab invasion in the seventh century.

Islamic Conquest

The beduin Arabs who toppled the Sassanid Empire were propelled not only by a desire for conquest but also by a new religion, Islam. The Prophet Muhammad, a member of the Hashimite clan of the powerful tribe of Quraysh, proclaimed his prophetic mission in Arabia in 612 and eventually won over the city of his birth, Mecca, to the new faith (see Religious Life, ch. 2). Within one year of Muhammad's death in 632, Arabia itself was secure enough to allow his secular successor, Abu Bakr, the first caliph, to begin the campaign against the Byzantine and Sassanid empires.

Abu Bakr defeated the Byzantine army at Damascus in 635 and then began his conquest of Iran. In 637 the Arab forces occupied the Sassanid capital of Ctesiphon (which they renamed Madain), and in 641–42 they defeated the Sassanid army at Nahavand. After that, Iran lay open to the invaders. The Islamic conquest was aided by the material and social bankruptcy of the Sassanids; the native populations had little to lose by cooperating with the conquering power. Moreover, the Muslims offered relative religious tolerance and fair treatment to populations that accepted Islamic rule without resistance. It was not until around 650, however, that resistance in Iran was quelled. Conversion to Islam, which offered certain advantages, was fairly rapid among the urban population but slower among the peasantry and the *dihqans*. The majority of Iranians did not become Muslim until the ninth century.

Although the conquerors, especially the Umayyads (the Muslim rulers who succeeded Muhammad from 661–750), tended to stress the primacy of Arabs among Muslims, the Iranians were gradually integrated into the new community. The Muslim conquerors adopted the Sassanid coinage system and many Sassanid administrative practices, including the office of vizier, or minister, and the *divan,* a bureau or register for controlling state revenue and expenditure that became a characteristic of administration throughout Muslim lands. Later caliphs adopted Iranian court ceremonial practices and the trappings of Sassanid monarchy. Men of Iranian origin served as administrators after the conquest, and

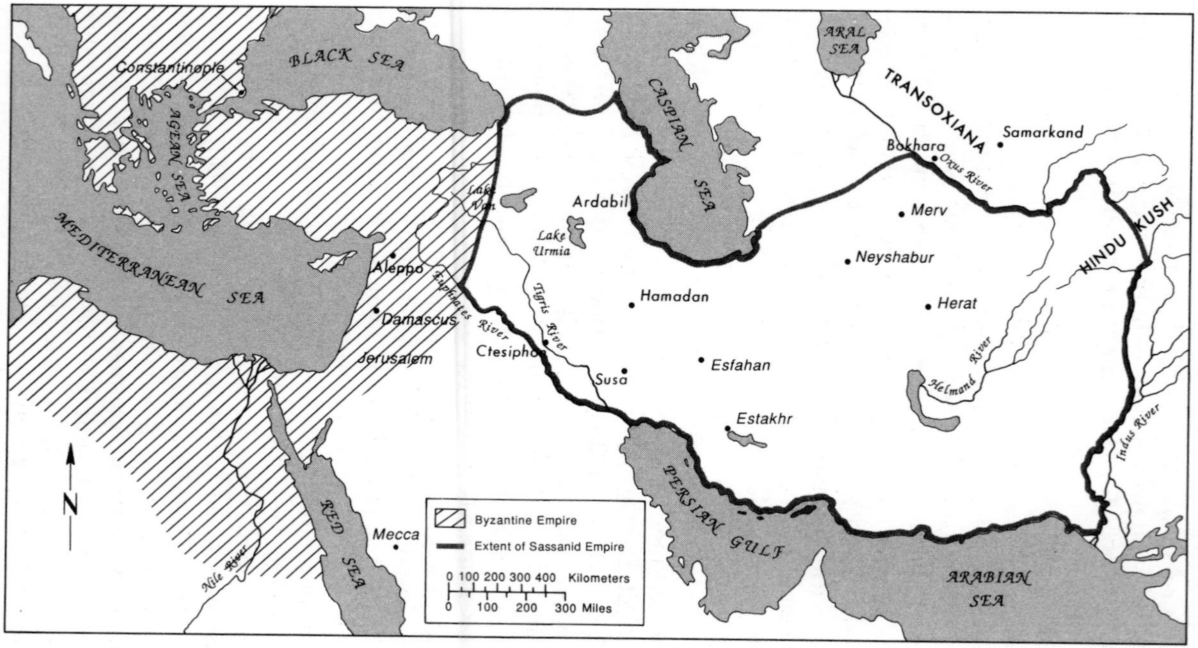

Source: Based on information from *Historical Atlas of the Muslim Peoples,* Amsterdam, 1957; and Jere L. Bacharach, *A Middle East Studies Handbook,* Seattle, 1984.

Figure 3. Sassanid Empire, Sixth Century A.D.

Iranians contributed significantly to all branches of Islamic learning, including philology, literature, history, geography, jurisprudence, philosophy, medicine, and the sciences.

The Arabs were in control, however. The new state religion, Islam, imposed its own system of beliefs, laws, and social mores. In regions that submitted peacefully to Muslim rule, landowners kept their land. But crown land, land abandoned by fleeing owners, and land taken by conquest passed into the hands of the new state. This included the rich lands of the Sawad, a rich, alluvial plain in central and southern Iraq. Arabic became the official language of the court in 696, although Persian continued to be widely used as the spoken language. The *shuubiyya* literary controversy of the ninth through the eleventh centuries, in which Arabs and Iranians each lauded their own and denigrated the other's cultural traits, suggests the survival of a certain sense of distinct Iranian identity. In the ninth century, the emergence of more purely Iranian ruling dynasties witnessed the revival of the Persian language, enriched by Arabic loanwords and using the Arabic script, and of Persian literature.

Another legacy of the Arab conquest was Shia Islam, which, although it has come to be identified closely with Iran, was not initially an Iranian religious movement. It originated with the Arab Muslims. In the great schism of Islam, one group among the community of believers maintained that leadership of the community following the death of Muhammad rightfully belonged to Muhammad's son-in-law, Ali, and to his descendants. This group came to be known as the Shiat Ali, the partisans of Ali, or the Shias. Another group, supporters of Muawiya (a rival contender for the caliphate following the murder of Uthman), challenged Ali's election to the caliphate in 656. After Ali was assassinated while praying in a mosque at Kufa in 661, Muawiya was declared caliph by the majority of the Islamic community. He became the first caliph of the Umayyad dynasty, which had its capital at Damascus.

Ali's youngest son, Husayn, refused to pay the homage commanded by Muawiya's son and successor Yazid I and fled to Mecca, where he was asked to lead the Shias—mostly those living in present-day Iraq—in a revolt. At Karbala, in Iraq, Husayn's band of 200 men and women followers, unwilling to surrender, were finally cut down by about 4,000 Umayyad troops. The Umayyad leader received Husayn's head, and Husayn's death in 680 on the tenth of Moharram continues to be observed as a day of mourning for all Shias (see Religious Life, ch. 2).

The largest concentration of Shias in the first century of Islam was in southern Iraq. It was not until the sixteenth century, under the Safavids, that a majority of Iranians became Shias. Shia Islam became then, as it is now, the state religion.

The Abbasids, who overthrew the Umayyads in 750, while sympathetic to the Iranian Shias, were clearly an Arab dynasty. They revolted in the name of descendants of Muhammad's uncle, Abbas, and the House of Hashim. Hashim was an ancestor of both the Shia and the Abbas, or Sunni (see Glossary), line, and the Abbasid movement enjoyed the support of both Sunni and Shia Muslims. The Abbasid army consisted primarily of Khorasanians and was led by an Iranian general, Abu Muslim. It contained both Iranian and Arab elements, and the Abbasids enjoyed both Iranian and Arab support.

Nevertheless, the Abbasids, although sympathetic to the Shias, whose support they wished to retain, did not encourage the more extremist Shia aspirations. The Abbasids established their capital at Baghdad. Al Mamun, who seized power from his brother, Amin, and proclaimed himself caliph in 811, had an Iranian mother and thus had a base of support in Khorasan. The Abbasids continued the centralizing policies of their predecessors. Under their rule, the Islamic world experienced a cultural efflorescence and the expansion of trade and economic prosperity. These were developments in which Iran shared.

Iran's next ruling dynasties descended from nomadic, Turkic-speaking warriors who had been moving out of Central Asia into Transoxiana for more than a millennium. The Abbasid caliphs began enlisting these people as slave warriors as early as the ninth century. Shortly thereafter the real power of the Abbasid caliphs began to wane; eventually they became religious figureheads while the warrior slaves ruled. As the power of the Abbasid caliphs diminished, a series of independent and indigenous dynasties rose in various parts of Iran, some with considerable influence and power. Among the most important of these overlapping dynasties were the Tahirids in Khorasan (820–72); the Saffarids in Sistan (867–903); and the Samanids (875–1005), originally at Bukhara (also cited as Bokhara). The Samanids eventually ruled an area from central Iran to India. In 962 a Turkish slave governor of the Samanids, Alptigin, conquered Ghazna (in present-day Afghanistan) and established a dynasty, the Ghaznavids, that lasted to 1186.

Several Samanid cities had been lost to another Turkish group, the Seljuks, a clan of the Oghuz (or Ghuzz) Turks, who lived north of the Oxus River (present-day Amu Darya). Their leader, Tughril Beg, turned his warriors against the Ghaznavids in Khorasan. He moved south and then west, conquering but not wasting the cities in his path. In 1055 the caliph in Baghdad gave Tughril Beg robes, gifts, and the title King of the East. Under Tughril Beg's successor, Malik Shah (1072–92), Iran enjoyed a cultural and scientific renaissance, largely attributed to his brilliant Iranian vizier, Nizam al Mulk. These leaders established the observatory where Umar (Omar) Khayyam did much of his experimentation for a new calendar, and they built religious schools in all the major towns. They brought Abu Hamid Ghazali, one of the greatest Islamic theologians, and other eminent scholars to the Seljuk capital at Baghdad and encouraged and supported their work.

A serious internal threat to the Seljuks, however, came from the Ismailis, a secret sect with headquarters at Alumut between Rasht and Tehran. They controlled the immediate area for more than 150 years and sporadically sent out adherents to strengthen their rule by murdering important officials. The word *assassins,* which was applied to these murderers, developed from a European corruption of the name applied to them in Syria, *hashishiyya,* because folklore had it that they smoked hashish before their missions.

Invasions of the Mongols and Tamerlane

After the death of Malik Shah in 1092, Iran once again reverted to petty dynasties. During this time, Genghis (Chinghis) Khan brought together a number of Mongol tribes and led them on a devastating sweep through China. Then, in 1219, he turned his 700,000 forces west and quickly devastated Bukhara, Samarkand, Balkh, Merv, and Neyshabur. Before his death in 1227, he had reached western Azarbaijan, pillaging and burning cities along the way.

The Mongol invasion was disastrous to the Iranians. Destruction of *qanat* irrigation systems destroyed the pattern of relatively continuous settlement, producing numerous isolated oasis cities in a land where they had previously been rare (see Water, ch. 3). A large number of people, particularly males, were killed; between 1220 and 1258, the population of Iran dropped drastically.

Mongol rulers who followed Genghis Khan did little to improve Iran's situation. Genghis's grandson, Hulagu Khan, turned to foreign conquest, seizing Baghdad in 1258 and killing the last Abbasid caliph. He was stopped by the Mamluk forces of Egypt at Ain Jalut in Palestine. Afterward he returned to Iran and spent the rest of his life in Azarbaijan.

A later Mongol ruler, Ghazan Khan (1295–1304), and his famous Iranian vizier, Rashid ad Din, brought Iran a partial and brief economic revival. The Mongols lowered taxes for artisans, encouraged agriculture, rebuilt and extended irrigation works, and improved the safety of the trade routes. As a result, commerce increased dramatically. Items from India, China, and Iran passed easily across the Asian steppes, and these contacts culturally enriched Iran. For example, Iranians developed a new style of painting based on a unique fusion of solid, two-dimensional Mesopotamian painting with the feathery, light brush strokes and other motifs characteristic of China. After Ghazan's nephew, Abu Said, died in 1335, however, Iran again lapsed into petty dynasties—the Salghurid, Muzaffarid, Inju, and Jalayirid—under Mongol commanders, old Seljuk retainers, and regional chiefs.

Tamerlane, variously described as of Mongol or Turkic origin, was the next ruler to achieve emperor status. He conquered Transoxiana proper and by 1381 established himself as sovereign. He did not have the huge forces of earlier Mongol leaders, so his conquests were slower and less savage than those of Genghis Khan or Hulagu Khan. Nevertheless, Shiraz and Esfahan were virtually leveled. Tamerlane's regime was characterized by its inclusion of Iranians in administrative roles and its promotion of architecture and poetry. His empire disintegrated rapidly after his death in 1405, however, and Mongol tribes, Uzbeks, and Bayundur Turkomans ruled roughly the area of present-day Iran until the rise of the Safavid dynasty, the first native Iranian dynasty in almost 1,000 years.

The Safavids, 1501–1722

The Safavids, who came to power in 1501, were leaders of a militant Sufi order. They traced their ancestry to Shaykh Safi ad Din (died circa 1334), the founder of their order, who claimed descent from Shia Islam's Seventh Imam, Musa al Kazim. From their home base in Ardabil, they recruited followers among the Turkoman tribesmen of Anatolia and forged them into an effective fighting force and an instrument for territorial expansion. Sometime in the mid-fifteenth century, the Safavids adopted Shia Islam, and their movement became highly millenarian in character. In 1501, under their leader Ismail, the Safavids seized power in Tabriz, which became their capital. Ismail was proclaimed shah of Iran. The rise of the Safavids marks the reemergence in Iran of a powerful central authority within geographical boundaries attained by former Iranian empires. The Safavids declared Shia Islam the state religion and used proselytizing and force to convert the large majority of Muslims in Iran to the Shia sect. Under the early Safavids, Iran was a theocracy in which state and religion were closely intertwined. Ismail's followers venerated him not only as the *murshid-kamil,* the perfect guide, but also as an emanation of the Godhead. He combined in his person both temporal and spiritual authority. In the

Part of the Porch of Xerxes at Persepolis
Courtesy LaVerle Berry

new state, he was represented in both these functions by the *vakil,* an official who acted as a kind of alter ego. The *sadr* headed the powerful religious organization; the vizier, the bureaucracy; and the *amir alumara,* the fighting forces. These fighting forces, the *qizilbash,* came primarily from the seven Turkic-speaking tribes that supported the Safavid bid for power.

The Safavids faced the problem of integrating their Turkic-speaking followers with the native Iranians, their fighting traditions with the Iranian bureaucracy, and their messianic ideology with the exigencies of administering a territorial state. The institutions of the early Safavid state and subsequent efforts at state reorganization reflect attempts, not always successful, to strike a balance among these various elements. The Safavids also faced external challenges from the Uzbeks and the Ottomans. The Uzbeks were an unstable element along Iran's northeastern frontier who raided into Khorasan, particularly when the central government was weak, and blocked the Safavid advance northward into Transoxiana. The Ottomans, who were Sunnis, were rivals for the religious allegiance of Muslims in eastern Anatolia and Iraq and pressed territorial claims in both these areas and in the Caucasus.

The Safavid Empire suffered a serious setback in 1524, when the Ottoman sultan Selim I defeated the Safavid forces at Chaldiran and occupied the Safavid capital, Tabriz. Although he was forced to withdraw because of the harsh winter and Iran's scorched earth policy, and although Safavid rulers continued to assert claims to spiritual leadership, the defeat shattered belief in the shah as a semidivine figure and weakened the hold of the shah over the *qizilbash* chiefs. In 1533 the Ottoman sultan Süleyman occupied Baghdad and then extended Ottoman rule to southern Iraq. Except for a brief period (1624–38) when Safavid rule was restored, Iraq remained firmly in Ottoman hands. The Ottomans also continued to challenge the Safavids for control of Azarbaijan and the Caucasus until the Treaty of Qasr-e Shirin in 1639 established frontiers both in Iraq and in the Caucasus that remain virtually unchanged in the late twentieth century.

The Safavid state reached its apogee during the reign of Shah Abbas (1587–1629). The shah gained breathing space to confront and defeat the Uzbeks by signing a largely disadvantageous treaty with the Ottomans. He then fought successful campaigns against the Ottomans, reestablishing Iranian control over Iraq, Georgia, and parts of the Caucasus. He counterbalanced the power of the *qizilbash* by creating a body of troops composed of Georgian and Armenian slaves who were loyal to the person of the shah. He extended state and crown lands and the provinces directly administered by the state, at the expense of the *qizilbash* chiefs. He relocated tribes to weaken their power, strengthened the bureaucracy, and further centralized the administration.

Shah Abbas made a show of personal piety and supported religious institutions by building mosques and religious seminaries and by making generous endowments for religious purposes. His reign, however, witnessed the gradual separation of religious institutions from the state and an increasing movement toward a more independent religious hierarchy.

In addition to his political reorganization and his support of religious institutions, Shah Abbas also promoted commerce and the arts. The Portuguese had previously occupied Bahrain and the island of Hormoz off the Persian Gulf coast in their bid to dominate Indian Ocean and Persian Gulf trade, but in 1602 Shah Abbas expelled them from Bahrain, and in 1623 he used the British (who sought a share of Iran's lucrative silk trade) to expel the Portuguese from Hormoz. He significantly enhanced government revenues by establishing a state monopoly over the silk trade and encouraged internal and external trade by safeguarding the roads and welcoming British, Dutch, and other traders to Iran. With the encouragement of the shah, Iranian craftsmen excelled in producing fine silks, brocades, and other cloths, carpets, porcelain, and metalware. When Shah Abbas built a new capital at Esfahan, he adorned it with fine mosques, palaces, schools, bridges, and a bazaar. He patronized the arts, and the calligraphy, miniatures, painting, and agriculture of his period are particularly noteworthy.

Although there was a recovery with the reign of Shah Abbas II (1642–66), in general the Safavid Empire declined after the death of Shah Abbas. The decline resulted from weak rulers, interference by the women of the harem in politics, the reemergence of *qizilbash* rivalries, maladministration of state lands, excessive taxation, the decline of trade, and the weakening of Safavid military organization. (Both the *qizilbash* tribal military organization and the standing army composed of slave soldiers were deteriorating.) The last two rulers, Shah Sulayman (1669–94) and Shah Sultan Hosain (1694–1722), were voluptuaries. Once again the eastern frontiers began to be breached, and in 1722 a small body of Afghan tribesmen won a series of easy victories before entering and taking the capital itself, ending Safavid rule.

Afghan supremacy was brief. Tahmasp Quli, a chief of the Afshar tribe, soon expelled the Afghans in the name of a surviving member of the Safavid family. Then, in 1736, he assumed power in his own name as Nader Shah. He went on to drive the Ottomans from Georgia and Armenia and the Russians from the Iranian coast on the Caspian Sea and restored Iranian sovereignty over Afghanistan. He also took his army on several campaigns into India and in 1739 sacked Delhi, bringing back fabulous treasures. Although Nader Shah achieved political unity, his military campaigns and extortionate taxation proved a terrible drain on a country already ravaged and depopulated by war and disorder, and in 1747 he was murdered by chiefs of his own Afshar tribe.

A period of anarchy and a struggle for supremacy among Afshar, Qajar, Afghan, and Zand tribal chieftains followed Nader Shah's death. Finally Karim Khan Zand (1750–79) was able to defeat his rivals and to unify the country, except for Khorasan, under a loose form of central control. He refused to assume the title of shah, however, and ruled as *vakil al ruaya,* or deputy of the subjects. He is remembered for his mild and beneficent rule.

The Qajars, 1795–1925

At Karim Khan's death, another struggle for power among the Zands, Qajars, and other tribal groups once again plunged the country into disorder and disrupted economic life. This time Aga Mohammad Qajar defeated the last Zand ruler outside Kerman in 1794 and made himself master of the country, beginning the Qajar dynasty that was to last until 1925. Under Fath Ali (1797–1834), Mohammad Shah (1834–48), and Naser ad Din Shah (1848–96) a degree of order, stability, and unity returned to the country. The Qajars revived the concept of the shah as the shadow of God on earth and exercised absolute powers over the servants of the state. They appointed royal princes to provincial governorships and, in the course of the nineteenth century, increased their power in relation to that of the tribal chiefs, who provided contingents for the shah's army. Under the Qajars, the merchants and the ulama, or religious leaders, remained important members of the community. A large bureaucracy assisted the chief officers of the state, and, in the second half of the nineteenth century, new ministries and offices were created. The Qajars were unsuccessful, however, in their attempt to replace the army based on tribal levies with a European-style standing army having regular training, organization, and uniforms.

Early in the nineteenth century, the Qajars began to face pressure from two great world powers, Russia and Britain. Britain's interest in Iran arose out of the need to protect trade routes to India, while Russia's came from a desire to expand into Iranian territory from the north. In two disastrous wars with Russia, which ended with the Treaty of Gulistan (1812) and the Treaty of Turkmanchay (1828), Iran lost all its territories in the Caucasus north of the Aras

The tomb of Ibn Sina (known as Avicenna by the West), a famous mathematician who died in A.D. 1037
Courtesy LaVerle Berry

River. Then, in the second half of the century, Russia forced the Qajars to give up all claims to territories in Central Asia. Meanwhile, Britain twice landed troops in Iran to prevent the Qajars from reasserting a claim to Herat, lost after the fall of the Safavids. Under the Treaty of Paris in 1857, Iran surrendered to Britain all claims to Herat and territories in present-day Afghanistan.

The two great powers also came to dominate Iran's trade and interfered in Iran's internal affairs. They enjoyed overwhelming military and technological superiority and could take advantage of Iran's internal problems. Iranian central authority was weak; revenues were generally inadequate to maintain the court, bureaucracy, and army; the ruling class was divided and corrupt; and the people suffered exploitation by their rulers and governors.

When Naser ad Din acceded to the throne in 1848, his prime minister, Mirza Taqi Khan Amir Kabir, attempted to strengthen the administration by reforming the tax system, asserting central control over the bureaucracy and the provincial governors, encouraging trade and industry, and reducing the influence of the Islamic clergy (see Glossary) and foreign powers. He established a new school, the Dar ol Fonun, to educate members of the elite in the new sciences and in foreign languages. The power he concentrated in his hands, however, aroused jealousy within the bureaucracy and fear in the king. He was dismissed and put to death in 1851, a fate shared by earlier powerful prime ministers.

In 1858 officials like Malkam Khan began to suggest in essays that the weakness of the government and its inability to prevent foreign interference lay in failure to learn the arts of government, industry, science, and administration from the advanced states of Europe. In 1871, with the encouragement of his new prime minister, Mirza Hosain Khan Moshir od Dowleh, the shah established a European-style cabinet with administrative responsibilities and a consultative council of senior princes and officials. He granted a concession for railroad construction and other economic projects to a Briton, Baron Julius de Reuter, and visited Russia and Britain himself. Opposition from bureaucratic factions hostile to the prime minister and from clerical leaders who feared foreign influence, however, forced the shah to dismiss his prime minister and to cancel the concession. Nevertheless, internal demand for reform was slowly growing. Moreover, Britain, to which the shah turned for protection against Russian encroachment, continued to urge the shah to undertake reforms and open the country to foreign trade and enterprise as a means of strengthening the country. In 1888 the shah, heeding this advice, opened the Karun River in Khuzestan to foreign shipping and gave Reuter permission to open the country's first bank. In 1890 he gave another British company a monopoly over the country's tobacco trade. The tobacco concession was obtained through bribes to leading officials and aroused considerable opposition among the clerical classes, the merchants, and the people. When a leading cleric, Mirza Hasan Shirazi, issued a *fatva* (religious ruling) forbidding the use of tobacco, the ban was universally observed, and the shah was once again forced to cancel the concession at considerable cost to an already depleted treasury.

The last years of Naser ad Din Shah's reign were characterized by growing royal and bureaucratic corruption, oppression of the rural population, and indifference on the shah's part. The tax machinery broke down, and disorder became endemic in the provinces. New ideas and a demand for reform were also becoming more widespread. In 1896, reputedly encouraged by Jamal ad Din al Afghani (called Asadabadi because he came from Asadabad), the well-known Islamic preacher and political activist, a young Iranian assassinated the shah.

The Constitutional Revolution

The shah's son and successor, Muzaffar ad Din (1896–1907), was a weak and ineffectual ruler. Royal extravagance and the absence of incoming revenues exacerbated financial problems. The shah quickly spent two large loans from Russia, partly on trips to Europe. Public anger fed on the shah's propensity for granting concessions to Europeans in return for generous payments to him and his officials. People began to demand a curb on royal authority and the establishment of the rule of law as their concern over foreign, and especially Russian, influence grew.

The shah's failure to respond to protests by the religious establishment, the merchants, and other classes led the merchants and clerical leaders in January 1906 to protest by taking sanctuary in mosques in Tehran and outside the capital. When the shah reneged on a promise to permit the establishment of a "house of justice," or consultative assembly, 10,000 people, led by the merchants, took sanctuary in June in the compound of the British legation in Tehran. In August the shah was forced to issue a decree promising a constitution. In October an elected assembly convened and drew up a constitution that provided for strict limitations on royal power, an elected parliament, or Majlis (see Glossary), with wide powers to represent the people, and a government with a cabinet subject to confirmation by the Majlis. The shah signed the constitution on December 30, 1906. He died five days later. The Supplementary Fundamental Laws approved in 1907 provided, within limits, for freedom of press, speech, and association, and for security of life and property. According to scholar Ann K.S. Lambton, the Constitutional Revolution marked the end of the medieval period in Iran. The hopes for constitutional rule were not realized, however.

Muzaffar ad Din's successor, Mohammad Ali Shah, was determined to crush the constitution. After several disputes with the members of the Majlis, in June 1908 he used his Russian-officered Persian Cossack Brigade to bomb the Majlis building, arrest many of the deputies, and close down the assembly. Resistance to the shah, however, coalesced in Tabriz, Esfahan, Rasht, and elsewhere. In July 1909, constitutional forces marched from Rasht and Esfahan to Tehran, deposed the shah, and reestablished the constitution. The ex-shah went into exile in Russia.

Although the constitutional forces had triumphed, they faced serious difficulties. The upheavals of the Constitutional Revolution and civil war had undermined stability and trade. In addition, the ex-shah, with Russian support, attempted to regain his throne, landing troops in July 1910. Finally, the hope that the Constitutional Revolution would inaugurate a new era of independence from the great powers ended when, under the Anglo-Russian Agreement of 1907, Britain and Russia agreed to divide Iran into spheres of influence. The Russians were to enjoy exclusive right to pursue their interests in the northern sphere, the British in the south and east; both powers would be free to compete for economic and political advantage in a neutral sphere in the center. Matters came to a head when Morgan Shuster, a United States administrator hired as treasurer general by the Persian government to reform its finances, sought to collect taxes from powerful officials who were Russian protégés and to send members of the treasury gendarmerie, a tax department police force, into the Russian zone. When in December 1911 the Majlis unanimously refused a Russian ultimatum demanding Shuster's dismissal, Russian troops, already in the country, moved to occupy the capital. To prevent this, on December 20 Bakhtiari chiefs and their troops surrounded the Majlis building, forced acceptance of the Russian ultimatum, and shut down the assembly, once again suspending the constitution. There followed a period of government by Bakhtiari chiefs and other powerful notables.

World War I

Iran hoped to avoid entanglement in World War I by declaring its neutrality, but ended up as a battleground for Russian, Turkish, and British troops. When German agents tried to arouse the southern tribes against the British, Britain created an armed force, the South Persia Rifles, to protect its interests. Then a group of Iranian notables led by Nezam os Saltaneh Mafi, hoping to escape Anglo-Russian dominance and sympathetic to the German war effort, left Tehran, first for Qom and then for Kermanshah (renamed Bakhtaran after the fall of Mohammad Reza Shah in 1979), where they established a provisional government. The provisional government lasted for the duration of the war but failed to capture much support.

At the end of the war, because of Russia's preoccupation with its own revolution, Britain was the dominant influence in Tehran. The foreign secretary, Lord Curzon, proposed an agreement under which Britain would provide Iran with a loan and with advisers to the army and virtually every government department. The Iranian prime minister, Vosuq od Dowleh, and two members of his cabinet who had received a large financial inducement from the British, supported the agreement. The Anglo-Persian Agreement of 1919 was widely viewed as establishing a British protectorate over Iran. It aroused considerable opposition, and the Majlis refused to approve it. The agreement was already dead when, in February 1921, Persian Cossack Brigade officer Reza Khan, in collaboration with prominent journalist Sayyid Zia ad Din

Tabatabai, marched into Tehran and seized power, inaugurating a new phase in Iran's modern history.

The Era of Reza Shah, 1921-41

Tabatabai became prime minister and Reza Khan became commander of the armed forces in the new government. Reza Khan, however, quickly emerged as the dominant figure. Within three months, Tabatabai was forced out of the government and into exile. Reza Khan became minister of war. In 1923 Ahmad Shah agreed to appoint Reza Khan prime minister and to leave for Europe. The shah was never to return. Reza Khan seriously considered establishing a republic, as Atatürk had done in Turkey, but abandoned the idea as a result of clerical opposition. In October 1925, a Majlis dominated by Reza Khan's men deposed the Qajar dynasty; in December the Majlis conferred the crown on Reza Khan and his heirs. The military officer who had become master of Iran was crowned as Reza Shah Pahlavi in April 1926.

Even before he became shah, Reza Khan had taken steps to create a strong central government and to extend government control over the country. Now, as Reza Shah, with the assistance of a group of army officers and younger bureaucrats, many trained in Europe, he launched a broad program of change designed to bring Iran into the modern world (see Historical Background, ch. 5). To strengthen the central authority, he built up Iran's heterogeneous military forces into a disciplined army of 40,000, and in 1926 he persuaded the Majlis to approve a law for universal military conscription. Reza Shah used the army not only to bolster his own power but also to pacify the country and to bring the tribes under control. In 1924 he broke the power of Shaykh Khazal, who was a British protégé and practically autonomous in Khuzestan. In addition, Reza Shah forcibly settled many of the tribes.

To extend government control and promote Westernization, the shah overhauled the administrative machinery and vastly expanded the bureaucracy. He created an extensive system of secular primary and secondary schools and, in 1935, established the country's first European-style university in Tehran. These schools and institutions of higher education became training grounds for the new bureaucracy and, along with economic expansion, helped create a new middle class. The shah also expanded the road network, successfully completed the trans-Iranian railroad, and established a string of state-owned factories to produce such basic consumer goods as textiles, matches, canned goods, sugar, and cigarettes.

Many of the Shah's measures were consciously designed to break the power of the religious hierarchy. His educational reforms ended the clerics' near monopoly on education. To limit further the power of the clerics, he undertook a codification of the laws that created a body of secular law, applied and interpreted by a secular judiciary outside the control of the religious establishment. He excluded the clerics from judgeships, created a system of secular courts, and transferred the important and lucrative task of notarizing documents from the clerics to state-licensed notaries. The state even encroached on the administration of *vaqfs* (religious endowments) and on the licensing of graduates of religious seminaries.

Among the codes comprising the new secular law were the civil code, the work of Justice Minister Ali Akbar Davar, enacted between 1927 and 1932; the General Accounting Act (1934–35), a milestone in financial administration; a new tax law; and a civil service code.

Determined to unify what he saw as Iran's heterogeneous peoples, end foreign influence, and emancipate women, Reza Shah imposed European dress on the population. He opened the schools to women and brought them into the work force. In 1936 he forcibly abolished the wearing of the veil.

Reza Shah initially enjoyed wide support for restoring order, unifying the country, and reinforcing national independence, and for his economic and educational reforms. In accomplishing all this, however, he took away effective power from the Majlis, muzzled the press, and arrested opponents of the government. His police chiefs were notorious for their harshness. Several religious leaders were jailed or sent into exile. In 1936, in one of the worst confrontations between the government and religious authorities, troops violated the sanctity of the shrine of Imam Reza in Mashhad, where worshipers had gathered to protest Reza Shah's reforms. Dozens of worshipers were killed and many injured. In addition, the shah arranged for powerful tribal chiefs to be put to death; bureaucrats who became too powerful suffered a similar fate. Reza Shah jailed and then quietly executed Abdul Hosain Teimurtash, his minister of court and close confidant; Davar committed suicide.

As time went on, the shah grew increasingly avaricious and amassed great tracts of land. Moreover, his tax policies weighed heavily on the peasants and the lower classes, the great landowners' control over land and the peasantry increased, and the condition of the peasants worsened during his reign. As a result, by the mid-1930s there was considerable dissatisfaction in the country.

Meanwhile, Reza Shah initiated changes in foreign affairs as well. In 1928 he abolished the capitulations under which Europeans in Iran had, since the nineteenth century, enjoyed the privilege of being subject to their own consular courts rather than to the Iranian judiciary. Suspicious of both Britain and the Soviet Union, the shah circumscribed contacts with foreign embassies. Relations with the Soviet Union had already deteriorated because of that country's commercial policies, which in the 1920s and 1930s adversely affected Iran. In 1932 the shah offended Britain by canceling the agreement under which the Anglo-Persian Oil Company produced and exported Iran's oil. Although a new and improved agreement was eventually signed, it did not satisfy Iran's demands and left bad feeling on both sides. To counterbalance British and Soviet influence, Reza Shah encouraged German commercial enterprise in Iran. On the eve of World War II, Germany was Iran's largest trading partner.

World War II and the Azarbaijan Crisis

At the outbreak of World War II, Iran declared its neutrality, but the country was soon invaded by both Britain and the Soviet Union. Britain had been annoyed when Iran refused Allied demands that it expel all German nationals from the country. When Hitler invaded the Soviet Union in 1941, the Allies urgently needed to transport war matériel across Iran to the Soviet Union, an operation that would have violated Iranian neutrality. As a result, Britain and the Soviet Union simultaneously invaded Iran on August 26, 1941, the Soviets from the northwest and the British across the Iraqi frontier from the west and at the head of the Persian Gulf in the south. Resistance quickly collapsed. Reza Shah knew the Allies would not permit him to remain in power, so he abdicated on September 16 in favor of his son, who ascended the throne as Mohammad Reza Shah Pahlavi. Reza Shah and several members of his family were taken by the British first to Mauritius and then to Johannesburg, South Africa, where Reza Shah died in July 1944.

The occupation of Iran proved of vital importance to the Allied cause and brought Iran closer to the Western powers. Britain, the Soviet Union, and the United States together managed to move over 5 million tons of munitions and other war matériel across Iran to the Soviet Union. In addition, in January 1942 Iran signed a tripartite treaty of alliance with Britain and the Soviet Union under which Iran agreed to extend nonmilitary assistance to the war effort. The two Allied powers, in turn, agreed to respect Iran's independence and territorial integrity and to withdraw their troops from Iran within six months of the end of hostilities. In September 1943, Iran declared war on Germany, thus qualifying for membership in the United Nations (UN). In November at the Tehran Conference, President Franklin D. Roosevelt, Prime Minister Winston Churchill, and Prime Minister Josef Stalin reaffirmed a commitment to

Iran's independence and territorial integrity and a willingness to extend economic assistance to Iran.

The effects of the war, however, were very disruptive for Iran. Food and other essential items were scarce. Severe inflation imposed great hardship on the lower and middle classes, while fortunes were made by individuals dealing in scarce items. The presence of foreign troops accelerated social change and also fed xenophobic and nationalist sentiments. An influx of rural migrants into the cities added to political unrest. The Majlis, dominated by the propertied interests, did little to ameliorate these conditions. With the political controls of the Reza Shah period removed, meanwhile, party and press activity revived. The communist Tudeh Party was especially active in organizing industrial workers. Like many other political parties of the left and center, it called for economic and social reform.

Eventually, collusion between the Tudeh and the Soviet Union brought further disintegration to Iran. In September 1944, while American companies were negotiating for oil concessions in Iran, the Soviets requested an oil concession in the five northern provinces. In December, however, the Majlis passed a law forbidding the government to discuss oil concessions before the end of the war. This led to fierce Soviet propaganda attacks on the government and agitation by the Tudeh in favor of a Soviet oil concession. In December 1945, the Azarbaijan Democratic Party, which had close links with the Tudeh and was led by Jafar Pishevari, announced the establishment of an autonomous republic. In a similar move, activists in neighboring Kordestan established the Kurdish Republic of Mahabad. Both autonomous republics enjoyed the support of the Soviets, and Soviet troops remained in Khorasan, Gorgan, Mazandaran, and Gilan. Other Soviet troops prevented government forces from entering Azarbaijan and Kordestan. Soviet pressure on Iran continued as British and American troops evacuated in keeping with their treaty undertakings. Soviet troops remained in the country. Prime Minister Ahmad Qavam had to persuade Stalin to withdraw his troops by agreeing to submit a Soviet oil concession to the Majlis and to negotiate a peaceful settlement to the Azarbaijan crisis with the Pishevari government. In April the government signed an oil agreement with the Soviet Union; in May, partly as a result of United States, British, and UN pressure, Soviet troops withdrew from Iranian territory. Qavam took three Tudeh members into his cabinet. Qavam was able to reclaim his concessions to the Soviet Union, however. A tribal revolt in the south, partly to protest communist influence, provided an opportunity to dismiss the Tudeh cabinet officers. In December, ostensibly in preparation for new Majlis elections, he sent the Iranian army into Azarbaijan. Without Soviet backing, the Pishevari government collapsed, and Pishevari himself fled to the Soviet Union. A similar fate befell the Kurdish Republic of Mahabad. In the new Majlis, a strong bloc of deputies, organized in the National Front and led by Mohammad Mossadeq, helped defeat the Soviet oil concession agreement by 102 votes to 2. The Majlis also passed a bill forbidding any further foreign oil concessions and requiring the government to exploit oil resources directly.

Soviet influence diminished further in 1947, when Iran and the United States signed an agreement providing for military aid and for a United States military advisory mission to help train the Iranian army. In February 1949, the Tudeh was blamed for an abortive attempt on the shah's life, and its leaders fled abroad or were arrested. The party was banned.

Mossadeq and Oil Nationalization

From 1949 on, sentiment for nationalization of Iran's oil industry grew. In 1949 the Majlis approved the First Development Plan (1948–55), which called for comprehensive agricultural and industrial development of the country (see The Beginnings of Modernization: The Post-1925 Period, ch. 3). The Plan Organization was established to administer the program, which was to be financed in large part from oil revenues. Politically conscious Iranians were aware, however, that the British government derived more revenue from taxing the concessionaire, the Anglo-Iranian Oil Company (AIOC—formerly the Anglo-Persian Oil Company), than the Iranian government derived from royalties. The oil issue figured prominently in elections for the Majlis in 1949, and nationalists in the new Majlis were determined to renegotiate the AIOC agreement. In November 1950, the Majlis committee concerned with oil matters, headed by Mossadeq, rejected a draft agreement in which the AIOC had offered the government slightly improved terms. These terms did not include the fifty-fifty profit-sharing provision that was part of other new Persian Gulf oil concessions.

Subsequent negotiations with the AIOC were unsuccessful, partly because General Ali Razmara, who became prime minister in June 1950, failed to persuade the oil company of the strength of nationalist feeling in the country and in the Majlis. When the AIOC finally offered fifty-fifty profit-sharing in February 1951, sentiment for nationalization of the oil industry had become widespread. Razmara advised against nationalization on technical grounds and was assassinated in March 1951 by Khalil Tahmasebi, a member of the militant Fadayan-e Islam. On March 15, the Majlis voted to nationalize the oil industry. In April the shah yielded to Majlis pressure and demonstrations in the streets by naming Mossadeq prime minister.

Oil production came to a virtual standstill as British technicians left the country, and Britain imposed a worldwide embargo on the purchase of Iranian oil. In September 1951, Britain froze Iran's sterling assets and banned export of goods to Iran. It challenged the legality of the oil nationalization and took its case against Iran to the International Court of Justice at The Hague. The court found in Iran's favor, but the dispute between Iran and the AIOC remained unsettled. Under United States pressure, the AIOC improved its offer to Iran. The excitement generated by the nationalization issue, anti-British feeling, agitation by radical elements, and the conviction among Mossadeq's advisers that Iran's maximum demands would, in the end, be met, however, led the government to reject all offers. The economy began to suffer from the loss of foreign exchange and oil revenues.

Whereas Mossadeq's popularity was growing, political disorder also increased, leading to United States intervention. Mossadeq had come to office on the strength of support from the National Front and other parties in the Majlis and as a result of his great popularity. His popularity, growing power, and intransigence on the oil issue were creating friction between the prime minister and the shah. In the summer of 1952, the shah refused the prime minister's demand for the power to appoint the minister of war (and, by implication, to control the armed forces). Mossadeq resigned, three days of pro-Mossadeq rioting followed, and the shah was forced to reappoint Mossadeq to head the government.

As domestic conditions deteriorated, however, Mossadeq's populist style grew more autocratic. In August 1952, the Majlis acceded to his demand for full powers in all affairs of government for a six-month period. These special powers were subsequently extended for a further six-month term. He also obtained approval for a law to reduce, from six years to two years, the term of the Senate (established in 1950 as the upper house of the legislature), and thus brought about the dissolution of that body. Mossadeq's support in the lower house, the Majlis, was dwindling, however, so on August 3, 1953, the prime minister organized a plebiscite for the dissolution of the Majlis, claimed a massive vote in favor of the proposal, and dissolved the legislative body.

The administration of President Harry S Truman initially had been sympathetic to Iran's nationalist aspirations. Under the administration of President Dwight D. Eisenhower, however, the

United States came to accept the view of the British government that no reasonable compromise with Mossadeq was possible and that, by working with the Tudeh, Mossadeq was making probable a communist-inspired takeover. Mossadeq's intransigence and inclination to accept Tudeh support, the Cold War atmosphere, and the fear of Soviet influence in Iran also shaped United States thinking. In June 1953, the Eisenhower administration approved a British proposal for a joint Anglo-American operation, code-named Operation Ajax, to overthrow Mossadeq. Kermit Roosevelt of the United States Central Intelligence Agency (CIA) traveled secretly to Iran to coordinate plans with the shah and the Iranian military, which was led by General Fazlollah Zahedi.

In accord with the plan, on August 13 the shah appointed Zahedi prime minister to replace Mossadeq. Mossadeq refused to step down and arrested the shah's emissary. This triggered the second stage of Operation Ajax, which called for a military coup. The plan initially seemed to have failed, the shah fled the country, and Zahedi went into hiding. After four days of rioting, however, the tide turned. On August 19, pro-shah army units and street crowds defeated Mossadeq's forces. The shah returned to the country. Mossadeq was sentenced to three years' imprisonment for trying to overthrow the monarchy, but he was subsequently allowed to remain under house arrest in his village outside Tehran until his death in 1967. His minister of foreign affairs, Hosain Fatemi, was sentenced to death and executed. Hundreds of National Front leaders, Tudeh Party officers, and political activists were arrested; several Tudeh army officers were also sentenced to death.

The Post-Mossadeq Era and the Shah's White Revolution

To help the Zahedi government through a difficult period, the United States arranged for immediate economic assistance of US$45 million. The Iranian government restored diplomatic relations with Britain in December 1953, and a new oil agreement was concluded in the following year (see Concession Agreements, ch. 3). The shah, fearing both Soviet influence and internal opposition, sought to bolster his regime by edging closer to Britain and the United States. In October 1955, Iran joined the Baghdad Pact, which brought together the "northern tier" countries of Iraq, Turkey, and Pakistan in an alliance that included Britain, with the United States serving as a supporter of the pact but not a full member. (The pact was renamed the Central Treaty Organization—CENTO—after Iraq's withdrawal in 1958.) In March 1959, Iran signed a bilateral defense agreement with the United States (see Foreign Influences in Weapons, Training, and Support Systems, ch. 5). In the Cold War atmosphere, relations with the Soviet Union were correct but not cordial. The shah visited the Soviet Union in 1956, but Soviet propaganda attacks and Iran's alliance with the West continued. Internally, a period of political repression followed the overthrow of Mossadeq, as the shah concentrated power in his own hands. He banned or suppressed the Tudeh, the National Front, and other parties; muzzled the press; and strengthened the secret police, SAVAK (Sazman-e Ettelaat va Amniyat-e Keshvar—see Law Enforcement Agencies, ch. 5). Elections to the Majlis in 1954 and 1956 were closely controlled. The shah appointed Hosain Ala to replace Zahedi as prime minister in April 1955 and thereafter named a succession of prime ministers who were willing to do his bidding.

Attempts at economic development and political reform were inadequate. Rising oil revenues allowed the government to launch the Second Development Plan (1955–62) in 1956 (see The Beginnings of Modernization: The Post-1925 Period, ch. 3). A number of large-scale industrial and agricultural projects were initiated, but economic recovery from the disruptions of the oil nationalization period was slow. The infusion of oil money led to rapid inflation and spreading discontent, and strict controls provided no outlets for political unrest. When martial law, which had been instituted in August 1953 after the coup, ended in 1957, the shah ordered two of his senior officials to form a majority party and a loyal opposition as the basis for a two-party system. These became known as the Melliyun and the Mardom parties. These officially sanctioned parties did not satisfy demands for wider political representation, however. During Majlis elections in 1960, contested primarily by the Melliyun and the Mardom parties, charges of widespread fraud could not be suppressed, and the shah was forced to cancel the elections. Jafar Sharif-Emami, a staunch loyalist, became prime minister. After renewed and more strictly controlled elections, the Majlis convened in February 1961. But as economic conditions worsened and political unrest grew, the Sharif-Emami government fell in May 1961.

Yielding both to domestic demands for change and to pressure for reform from President John F. Kennedy's administration, the shah named Ali Amini, a wealthy landlord and senior civil servant, as prime minister. Amini was known as an advocate of reform. He received a mandate from the shah to dissolve parliament and rule for six months by cabinet decree. Amini loosened controls on the press, permitted the National Front and other political parties to resume activity, and ordered the arrest of a number of former senior officials on charges of corruption. Under Amini, the cabinet approved the Third Development Plan (1962–68) and undertook a program to reorganize the civil service. In January 1962, in the single most important measure of the fourteen-month Amini government, the cabinet approved a law for land distribution.

The Amini government, however, was beset by numerous problems. Belt-tightening measures ordered by the prime minister were necessary, but in the short term they intensified recession and unemployment. This recession caused discontent in the bazaar and business communities. In addition, the prime minister acted in an independent manner, and the shah and senior military and civilian officials close to the court resented this challenge to royal authority. Moreover, although enjoying limited freedom of activity for the first time in many years, the National Front and other opposition groups pressed the prime minister for elections and withheld their cooperation. Amini was unable to meet a large budget deficit; the shah refused to cut the military budget, and the United States, which had previously supported Amini, refused further aid. As a result, Amini resigned in July 1962.

He was replaced by Asadollah Alam, one of Mohammad Reza Shah's close confidants. Building on the credit earned in the countryside and in urban areas by the land distribution program, the shah in January 1963 submitted six measures to a national referendum. In addition to land reform, these measures included profit-sharing for industrial workers in private sector enterprises, nationalization of forests and pastureland, sale of government factories to finance land reform, amendment of the electoral law to give more representation on supervisory councils to workers and farmers, and establishment of a Literacy Corps to allow young men to satisfy their military service requirement by working as village literacy teachers. The shah described the package as his White Revolution (see Glossary), and when the referendum votes were counted, the government announced a 99-percent majority in favor of the program. In addition to these other reforms, the shah announced in February that he was extending the right to vote to women.

These measures earned the government considerable support among certain sectors of the population, but they did not deal immediately with sources of unrest. Economic conditions were still difficult for the poorer classes. Many clerical leaders opposed land reform and the extension of suffrage to women. These leaders were also concerned about the extension of government and royal authority that the reforms implied. In June 1963, Ayatollah Sayyid Ruhollah Musavi Khomeini, a religious leader in Qom, was arrested after a fiery speech in which he directly attacked the shah.

The arrest sparked three days of the most violent riots the country had witnessed since the overthrow of Mossadeq a decade earlier. The shah severely suppressed these riots, and, for the moment, the government appeared to have triumphed over its opponents.

State and Society, 1964–74

Elections to the twenty-first Majlis in September 1963 led to the formation of a new political party, the Iran Novin (New Iran) Party, committed to a program of economic and administrative reform and renewal. The Alam government had opened talks with the National Front leaders earlier in the year, but no accommodation had been reached, and the talks had broken down over such issues as freedom of activity for the front. As a result, the front was not represented in the elections, which were limited to the officially sanctioned parties, and the only candidates on the slate were those presented by the Union of National Forces, an organization of senior civil servants and officials and of workers' and farmers' representatives, put together with government support.

After the elections, the largest bloc in the new Majlis, with forty seats, was a group called the Progressive Center. The center, an exclusive club of senior civil servants, had been established by Hasan Ali Mansur in 1961 to study and make policy recommendations on major economic and social issues. In June 1963, the shah had designated the center as his personal research bureau. When the new Majlis convened in October, 100 more deputies joined the center, giving Mansur a majority. In December, Mansur converted the Progressive Center into a political party, the Iran Novin. In March 1964, Alam resigned and the shah appointed Mansur prime minister, at the head of an Iran Novin-led government.

The events leading to the establishment of the Iran Novin and the appointment of Mansur as prime minister represented a renewed attempt by the shah and his advisers to create a political organization that would be loyal to the crown, attract the support of the educated classes and the technocratic elite, and strengthen the administration and the economy. The Iran Novin drew its membership almost exclusively from a younger generation of senior civil servants, Western-educated technocrats, and business leaders. Initially, membership was limited to 500 hand-picked persons, and it was allowed to grow very slowly. In time it came to include leading members of the provincial elite and its bureaucratic, professional, and business classes. Even in the late 1960s and early 1970s, when trade unions and professional organizations affiliated themselves with the party, full membership was reserved for a limited group.

In carrying out economic and administrative reforms, Mansur created four new ministries and transferred the authority for drawing up the budget from the Ministry of Finance to the newly created Budget Bureau. The bureau was attached to the Plan Organization and was responsible directly to the prime minister. In subsequent years it introduced greater rationality in planning and budgeting. Mansur appointed younger technocrats to senior civil service posts, a policy continued by his successor. He also created the Health Corps, modeled after the Literacy Corps, to provide primary health care to rural areas.

In the Majlis the government enjoyed a comfortable majority, and the nominal opposition, the Mardom Party, generally voted with the government party. An exception, however, was the general response to the Status of Forces bill, a measure that granted diplomatic immunity to United States military personnel serving in Iran, and to their staffs and families. In effect, the bill would allow these Americans to be tried by United States rather than Iranian courts for crimes committed on Iranian soil. For Iranians the bill recalled the humiliating capitulatory concessions extracted from Iran by the imperial powers in the nineteenth century. Feeling against the bill was sufficiently strong that sixty-five deputies absented themselves from the legislature, and sixty-one opposed the bill when it was put to a vote in October 1964.

The measure also aroused strong feeling outside the Majlis. Khomeini, who had been released from house arrest in April 1964, denounced the measure in a public sermon before a huge congregation in Qom. Tapes of the sermon and a leaflet based on it were widely circulated and attracted considerable attention. Khomeini was arrested again in November, within days of the sermon, and sent into exile in Turkey. In October 1965, he was permitted to take up residence in the city of An Najaf, Iraq—the site of numerous Shia shrines—where he was to remain for the next thirteen years.

Although economic conditions were soon to improve dramatically, the country had not yet fully recovered from the recession of the 1959–63 period, which had imposed hardships on the poorer classes. Mansur attempted to make up a budget deficit of an estimated US$300 million (at then prevalent rates of exchange) by imposing heavy new taxes on gasoline and kerosene and on exit permits for Iranians leaving the country. Because kerosene was the primary heating fuel for the working classes, the new taxes proved highly unpopular. Taxicab drivers in Tehran went on strike, and Mansur was forced to rescind the fuel taxes in January, six weeks after they had been imposed. An infusion of US$200 million in new revenues (US$185 million from a cash bonus for five offshore oil concessions granted to United States and West European firms and US$15 million from a supplementary oil agreement concluded with the Consortium, a group of foreign oil companies) helped the government through its immediate financial difficulties.

With this assistance, Mohammad Reza Shah was able to maintain political stability despite the assassination of his prime minister and an attempt on his own life. On January 21, 1965, Mansur was assassinated by members of a radical Islamic group. Evidence made available after the Islamic Revolution revealed that the group had affiliations with clerics close to Khomeini. A military tribunal sentenced six of those charged to death and the others to long prison terms. In April there was also an attempt on the shah's life, organized by a group of Iranian graduates of British universities. To replace Mansur as prime minister, the shah appointed Amir Abbas Hoveyda, a former diplomat and an executive of the National Iranian Oil Company (NIOC—see Oil and Gas Industry, ch. 3). Hoveyda had helped Mansur found the Progressive Center and the Iran Novin and had served as his minister of finance.

Hoveyda's appointment marked the beginning of nearly a decade of impressive economic growth and relative political stability at home. During this period, the shah also used Iran's enhanced economic and military strength to secure for the country a more influential role in the Persian Gulf region, and he improved relations with Iran's immediate neighbors and the Soviet Union and its allies. Hoveyda remained in office for the next twelve years, the longest term of any of Iran's modern prime ministers. During this decade, the Iran Novin dominated the government and the Majlis. It won large majorities in both the 1967 and the 1971 elections. These elections were carefully controlled by the authorities. Only the Mardom Party and, later, the Pan-Iranist Party, an extreme nationalist group, were allowed to participate in them. Neither party was able to secure more than a handful of Majlis seats, and neither engaged in serious criticism of government programs.

In 1969 and again in 1972, the shah appeared ready to permit the Mardom Party, under new leadership, to function as a genuine opposition, i.e., to criticize the government openly and to contest elections more energetically, but these developments did not occur. The Iran Novin's domination of the administrative machinery was further made evident during municipal council elections held in 136 towns throughout the country in 1968. The Iran Novin won control of a large majority of the councils and every seat in 115 of them. Only 10 percent of eligible voters cast ballots in Tehran, however, a demonstration of public indifference that was not confined to the capital.

Under Hoveyda the government improved its administrative machinery and launched what was dubbed "the education revolution." It adopted a new civil service code and a new tax law and appointed better qualified personnel to key posts. Hoveyda also created several additional ministries in 1967, including the Ministry of Science and Higher Education, which was intended to help meet expanded and more specialized manpower needs. In mid-1968 the government began a program that, although it did not resolve problems of overcrowding and uneven quality, increased the number of institutions of higher education substantially, brought students from provincial and lower middle-class backgrounds into the new community colleges, and created a number of institutions of high academic standing, such as Tehran's Arya Mehr Technical University (see Education, ch. 2).

The shah had remarried in 1959, and the new queen, Farah Diba Pahlavi, had given birth to a male heir, Reza, in 1960. In 1967, because the crown prince was still very young, steps were taken to regularize the procedure for the succession. Under the constitution, if the shah were to die before the crown prince had come of age, the Majlis would meet to appoint a regent. There might be a delay in the appointment of a regent, especially if the Majlis was not in session. A constituent assembly, convened in September 1967, amended the constitution, providing for the queen automatically to act as regent unless the shah in his lifetime designated another individual. In October 1967, believing his achievements finally justified such a step, the shah celebrated his long-postponed coronation. Like his father, he placed the crown on his own head. To mark the occasion, the Majlis conferred on the shah the title of Arya-Mehr, or "Light of the Aryans."

This glorification of the monarchy and the monarch, however, was not universally popular with the Iranians. In 1971 celebrations were held to mark what was presented as 2,500 years of uninterrupted monarchy (there were actually gaps in the chronological record) and the twenty-fifth centennial of the founding of the Iranian empire by Cyrus the Great. The ceremonies were designed primarily to celebrate the institution of monarchy and to affirm the position of the shah as the country's absolute and unchallenged ruler. The lavish ceremonies (which many compared to a Hollywood-style extravaganza), the virtual exclusion of Iranians from the celebrations in which the honored guests were foreign heads of state, and the excessive adulation of the person of the shah in official propaganda generated much adverse domestic comment. A declaration by Khomeini condemning the celebrations and the regime received wide circulation. In 1975, when the Majlis, at government instigation, voted to alter the Iranian calendar so that year one of the calendar coincided with the first year of the reign of Cyrus rather than with the beginning of the Islamic era, many Iranians viewed the move as an unnecessary insult to religious sensibilities.

Iran, meantime, experienced a period of unprecedented and sustained economic growth. The land distribution program launched in 1962, along with steadily expanding job opportunities, improved living standards, and moderate inflation between 1964 and 1973, help explain the relative lack of serious political unrest during this period.

In foreign policy, the shah used the relaxation in East-West tensions to improve relations with the Soviet Union. In an exchange of notes in 1962, he gave Moscow assurances he would not allow Iran to become a base for aggression against the Soviet Union or permit foreign missile bases to be established on Iranian soil. In 1965 Iran and the Soviet Union signed a series of agreements under which the Soviets provided credits and technical assistance to build Iran's first steel mill in exchange for shipments of Iranian natural gas. This led to the construction of the almost 2,000-kilometer-long trans-Iranian gas pipeline from the southern fields to the Iranian-Soviet frontier. The shah also bought small quantities of arms from the Soviet Union and expanded trade with East European states. Although Soviet officials did not welcome the increasingly close military and security cooperation between Iran and the United States, especially after 1971, Moscow did not allow this to disrupt its own rapprochement with Tehran.

In 1964 the shah joined the heads of state of Turkey and Pakistan to create an organization, Regional Cooperation for Development (RCD), for economic, social, and cultural cooperation among the three countries "outside the framework of the Central Treaty Organization." The establishment of RCD was seen as a sign of the diminishing importance of CENTO and, like the rapprochement with the Soviet Union, of the shah's increasing independence in foreign policy. The three RCD member states undertook a number of joint economic and cultural projects, but never on a large scale.

The shah also began to play a larger role in Persian Gulf affairs. He supported the royalists in the Yemen Civil War (1962–70) and, beginning in 1971, assisted the sultan of Oman in putting down a rebellion in Dhofar (see Historical Background, ch. 5). He also reached an understanding with Britain on the fate of Bahrain and

Shah Mohammad Reza Pahlavi distributes land deeds to a peasant woman under a land reform program
Courtesy United States Information Agency

three smaller islands in the Gulf that Britain had controlled since the nineteenth century but that Iran continued to claim. Britain's decision to withdraw from the Gulf by 1971 and to help organize the Trucial States into a federation of independent states (eventually known as the United Arab Emirates—UAE) necessitated resolution of that situation. In 1970 the shah agreed to give up Iran's long-standing claim to Bahrain and to abide by the desire of the majority of its inhabitants that Bahrain become an independent state. The shah, however, continued to press his claim to three islands, Abu Musa (controlled by the shaykh of Sharjah) and the Greater and Lesser Tunbs (controlled by the shaykh of Ras al Khaymah). He secured control of Abu Musa by agreeing to pay the shaykh of Sharjah an annual subsidy, and he seized the two Tunbs by military force, immediately following Britain's withdrawal.

This incident offended Iraq, however, which broke diplomatic relations with Iran as a result. Relations with Iraq remained strained until 1975, when Iran and Iraq signed the Algiers Agreement, under which Iraq conceded Iran's long-standing demand for equal navigation rights in the Shatt al Arab, and the shah agreed to end support for the Kurdish rebellion in northern Iraq.

With the other Persian Gulf states, Tehran maintained generally good relations. Iran signed agreements with Saudi Arabia and other Gulf states delimiting frontiers along the continental shelf in the Persian Gulf, began cooperation and information-sharing on security matters with Saudi Arabia, and encouraged closer cooperation among the newly independent Gulf shaykhdoms through the Gulf Cooperation Council.

To enhance Iran's role in the Gulf, the shah also used oil revenues to expand and equip the Iranian army, air force, and navy. His desire that, in the aftermath of the British withdrawal, Iran would play the primary role in guaranteeing Gulf security coincided with President Richard M. Nixon's hopes for the region. The Nixon Doctrine, enunciated in 1969, sought to encourage United States allies to shoulder greater responsibility for regional security. Then, during his 1972 visit to Iran, Nixon took the unprecedented step of allowing the shah to purchase any conventional weapon in the United States arsenal in the quantities the shah believed necessary for Iran's defense (see Foreign Influences in Weapons, Training, and Support Systems, ch. 5). United States-Iranian military cooperation deepened when the shah allowed the United States to establish two listening posts in Iran to monitor Soviet ballistic missile launches and other military activity.

Renewed Opposition

In the years that followed the riots of June 1963, there was little overt political opposition. The political parties that had been prominent in the 1950–63 period were weakened by arrests, exile, and internal splits. Political repression continued, and it proved more difficult to articulate a coherent policy of opposition in a period of economic prosperity, foreign policy successes, and such reform measures as land distribution. Nonetheless, opposition parties gradually reorganized, new groups committed to more violent forms of struggle were formed, and more radical Islamic ideologies were developed to revive and fuel the opposition movements.

Both the Tudeh and the National Front underwent numerous splits and reorganizations. The Tudeh leadership remained abroad, and the party did not play a prominent role in Iran until after the Islamic Revolution. Of the National Front parties that managed to survive the post-1963 clampdown, the most prominent was the Nehzat-e Azadi-yi Iran, or the Iran Freedom Movement (IFM), led by Mehdi Bazargan. Bazargan worked to establish links between his movement and the moderate clerical opposition. Like others who looked to Islam as a vehicle for political mobilization, Bazargan was active in preaching the political pertinence of Islam to a younger generation of Iranians. Among the best known thinkers associated with the IFM was Ali Shariati, who argued for an Islam committed to political struggle, social justice, and the cause of the deprived classes.

Khomeini, in exile in Iraq, continued to issue antigovernment statements, to attack the shah personally, and to organize supporters. In a series of lectures delivered to his students in An Najaf in 1969 and 1970 and later published in book form under the title of *Velayat-e Faqih* (The Vice Regency of the Islamic Jurist), he argued that monarchy was a form of government abhorrent to Islam, that true Muslims must strive for the establishment of an Islamic state, and that the leadership of the state belonged by right to the *faqih*, or Islamic jurist. A network of clerics worked for Khomeini in Iran, returning from periods of imprisonment and exile to continue their activities. Increasing internal difficulties in the early 1970s gradually won Khomeini a growing number of followers.

In the meantime, some younger Iranians, disillusioned with what they perceived to be the ineffectiveness of legal opposition to the regime and attracted by the example of guerrilla movements in Cuba, Vietnam, and China, formed a number of underground groups committed to armed struggle. Most of these groups were uncovered and broken up by the security authorities, but two survived: the Fadayan (Cherikha-ye Fadayan-e Khalq, or People's Guerrillas), and the Mojahedin (Mojahedin-e Khalq, or People's Struggle). The Fadayan were Marxist in orientation, whereas the Mojahedin sought to find in Islam the inspiration for an ideology of political struggle and economic radicalism (see Antiregime Opposition Groups, ch. 5). Nevertheless, both movements used similar tactics in attempting to overthrow the regime: attacks on police stations; bombing of United States, British, and Israeli commercial or diplomatic offices; and assassination of Iranian security officers and United States military personnel stationed in Iran. In February 1971, the Fadayan launched the first major guerrilla action against the state with an armed attack on an Imperial Iranian Gendarmerie (the internal security and border guard) post at Siahkal in the Caspian forests of northern Iran. Several similar actions followed. A total of 341 members of these guerrilla movements died between 1971 and 1979 in armed confrontations with security forces, by execution or suicide, or while in the hands of their jailers. Many more served long terms in prison.

The Coming of the Revolution

By late 1976 and early 1977, it was evident that the Iranian economy was in trouble. The shah's attempt to use Iran's vastly expanded oil revenues after 1973 for an unrealistically ambitious industrial and construction program and a massive military buildup greatly strained Iran's human and institutional resources and caused severe economic and social dislocation. Widespread official corruption, rapid inflation, and a growing gap in incomes between the wealthier and the poorer strata of society fed public dissatisfaction.

In response, the government attempted to provide the working and middle classes with some immediate and tangible benefits of the country's new oil wealth. The government nationalized private secondary schools, declared that secondary education would be free for all Iranians, and started a free meal program in schools. It took over private community colleges and extended financial support to university students. It lowered income taxes, inaugurated an ambitious health insurance plan, and speeded up implementation of a program introduced in 1972, under which industrialists were required to sell 49 percent of the shares of their companies to their employees.

The programs were badly implemented, however, and did not adequately compensate for the deteriorating economic position of the urban working class and those, who, like civil servants, were on fixed salaries. To deal with the disruptive effects of excessive spending, the government adopted policies that appeared threatening to the propertied classes and to bazaar, business, and industrial elements who had benefited from economic expansion and might have been expected to support the regime. For example, in an effort to bring down rents, municipalities were empowered to take over empty houses and apartments and to rent and administer them in place of the owners. In an effort to bring down prices in 1975 and 1976, the government declared a war on profiteers, arrested and fined thousands of shopkeepers and petty merchants, and sent two prominent industrialists into exile.

Moreover, by 1978 there were 60,000 foreigners in Iran—45,000 of them Americans—engaged in business or in military training and advisory missions. Combined with a superficial Westernization evident in dress, life styles, music, films, and television programs, this foreign presence tended to intensify the perception that the shah's modernization program was threatening the society's Islamic and Iranian cultural values and identity. Increasing political repression and the establishment of a one-party state in 1975 further alienated the educated classes.

The shah was aware of the rising resentment and dissatisfaction in the country and the increasing international concern about the suppression of basic freedoms in Iran. Organizations such as the International Council of Jurists and Amnesty International were drawing attention to mistreatment of political prisoners and violation of the rights of the accused in Iranian courts. More important, President Jimmy Carter, who took office in January 1977, was making an issue of human rights violations in countries with which the United States was associated. The shah, who had been pressed into a program of land reform and political liberalization by the Kennedy administration, was sensitive to possible new pressures from Washington.

Beginning in early 1977, the shah took a number of steps to meet both domestic and foreign criticism of Iran's human rights record. He released political prisoners and announced new regulations to protect the legal rights of civilians brought before military courts. In July the shah replaced Hoveyda, his prime minister of twelve years, with Jamshid Amuzegar, who had served for over a decade in various cabinet posts. Unfortunately for the shah, however, Amuzegar also became unpopular, as he attempted to slow the overheated economy with measures that, although generally thought necessary, triggered a downturn in employment and private sector profits that would later compound the government's problems.

Leaders of the moderate opposition, professional groups, and the intelligentsia took advantage of the shah's accommodations and the more helpful attitude of the Carter administration to organize and speak out. Many did so in the form of open letters addressed to prominent officials in which the writers demanded adherence to the constitution and restoration of basic freedoms. Lawyers, judges, university professors, and writers formed professional associations to press these demands. The National Front, the IFM, and other political groups resumed activity.

The protest movement took a new turn in January 1978, when a government-inspired article in *Etalaat,* one of the country's leading newspapers, cast doubt on Khomeini's piety and suggested that he was a British agent. The article caused a scandal in the religious community. Senior clerics, including Ayatollah Kazem Shariatmadari, denounced the article. Seminary students took to the streets in Qom and clashed with police, and several demonstrators were killed. The Esfahan bazaar closed in protest. On February 18, mosque services and demonstrations were held in several cities to honor those killed in the Qom demonstrations. In Tabriz these demonstrations turned violent, and it was two days before order could be restored. By the summer, riots and antigovernment demonstrations had swept dozens of towns and cities. Shootings inevitably occurred, and deaths of protesters fueled public feeling against the regime.

The cycle of protests that began in Qom and Tabriz differed in nature, composition, and intent from the protests of the preceding year. The 1977 protests were primarily the work of middle-class intellectuals, lawyers, and secular politicians. They took the form of letters, resolutions, and declarations and were aimed at the restoration of constitutional rule. The protests that rocked Iranian cities in the first half of 1978, by contrast, were led by religious elements and were centered on mosques and religious events. They drew on traditional groups in the bazaar and among the urban working class for support. The protesters used a form of calculated violence to achieve their ends, attacking and destroying carefully selected targets that represented objectionable features of the regime: nightclubs and cinemas as symbols of moral corruption and the influence of Western culture; banks as symbols of economic exploitation; Rastakhiz (the party created by the shah in 1975 to run a one-party state) offices and police stations as symbols of political repression. The protests, moreover, aimed at more fundamental change: in slogans and leaflets, the protesters attacked the shah and demanded his removal, and they depicted Khomeini as their leader and an Islamic state as their ideal. From his exile in Iraq, Khomeini continued to issue statements calling for further demonstrations, rejected any form of compromise with the regime, and called for the overthrow of the shah.

The government's position deteriorated further in August 1978, when more than 400 people died in a fire at the Rex Cinema in Abadan. Although evidence available after the Revolution suggested that the fire was deliberately started by religiously inclined students, the opposition carefully cultivated a widespread conviction that the fire was the work of SAVAK agents. Following the Rex Cinema fire, the shah removed Amuzegar and named Jafar Sharif-Emami prime minister. Sharif-Emami, a former minister and prime minister and a trusted royalist, had for many years served as president of the Senate. The new prime minister adopted a policy of conciliation. He eased press controls and permitted more open debate in the Majlis. He released a number of imprisoned clerics, revoked the imperial calendar, closed gambling casinos, and obtained from the shah the dismissal from court and public office of members of the Bahai religion, a sect to which the clerics strongly objected (see Non-Muslim Minorities, ch. 2). These measures, however, did not quell public protests. On September 4, more than 100,000 took part in the public prayers to mark the end of Ramazan, the Muslim fasting month. The ceremony became an occasion for antigovernment demonstrations that continued for the next two days, growing larger and more radical in composition and in the slogans of the participants. The government declared martial law in Tehran and eleven other cities on the night of September 7–8, 1978. The next day, troops fired into a a crowd of demonstrators at Tehran's Jaleh Square. A large number of protesters, certainly many more than the official figure of eighty-seven, were killed. The Jaleh Square shooting came to be known as "Black Friday." It considerably radicalized the opposition movement and made compromise with the regime, even by the moderates, less likely.

In October the Iraqi authorities, unable to persuade Khomeini to refrain from further political activity, expelled him from the country. Khomeini went to France and established his headquarters at Neauphle-le-Château, outside Paris. Khomeini's arrival in France provided new impetus to the revolutionary movement. It gave Khomeini and his movement exposure in the world press and media. It made possible easy telephone communication with lieutenants in Tehran and other Iranian cities, thus permitting better coordination of the opposition movement. It allowed Iranian political and religious leaders, who were cut off from Khomeini while he was in Iraq, to visit him for direct consultations. One of these visitors was National Front leader Karim Sanjabi. After a meeting with Khomeini early in November 1978, Sanjabi issued a three-point statement that for the first time committed the National Front to the Khomeini demand for the deposition of the shah and the establishment of a government that would be "democratic and Islamic."

Scattered strikes had occurred in a few private sector and government industries between June and August 1978. Beginning in September, workers in the public sector began to go on strike on a large scale. When the demands of strikers for improved salary and working benefits were quickly met by the Sharif-Emami government, oil workers and civil servants made demands for changes in the political system. The unavailability of fuel oil and freight transport and shortages of raw materials resulting from a customs strike led to the shutting down of most private sector industries in November.

On November 5, 1978, after violent demonstrations in Tehran, the shah replaced Sharif-Emami with General Gholam-Reza Azhari, commander of the Imperial Guard. The shah, addressing the nation for the first time in many months, declared he had heard the people's "revolutionary message," promised to correct past mistakes, and urged a period of quiet and order so that the government could undertake the necessary reforms. Presumably to placate public opinion, the shah allowed the arrest of 132 former leaders and government officials, including former Prime Minister Hoveyda, a former chief of SAVAK, and several former cabinet ministers. He also ordered the release of more than 1,000 political prisoners, including a Khomeini associate, Ayatollah Hosain Ali Montazeri.

The appointment of a government dominated by the military brought about some short-lived abatement in the strike fever, and oil production improved. Khomeini dismissed the shah's promises as worthless, however, and called for continued protests. The Azhari government did not, as expected, use coercion to bring striking government workers back to work. The strikes resumed, virtually shutting down the government, and clashes between demonstrators and troops became a daily occurrence. On December 9 and 10, 1978, in the largest antigovernment demonstrations in a year, several hundred thousand persons participated in marches in Tehran and the provinces to mark Moharram, the month in which Shia mourning occurs.

In December 1978, the shah finally began exploratory talks with members of the moderate opposition. Discussions with Karim Sanjabi proved unfruitful: the National Front leader was bound by his agreement with Khomeini. At the end of December another National Front leader, Shapour Bakhtiar, agreed to form a government on condition the shah leave the country. Bakhtiar secured a vote of confidence from the two houses of the Majlis on January 3, 1979, and presented his cabinet to the shah three days later. The shah, announcing he was going abroad for a short holiday, left the country on January 16, 1979. As his aircraft took off, celebrations broke out across the country.

The Bakhtiar Government

Once installed as prime minister, Bakhtiar took several measures designed to appeal to elements in the opposition movement. He lifted restrictions on the press; the newspapers, on strike since November, resumed publication. He set free remaining political prisoners and promised the dissolution of SAVAK, the lifting of martial law, and free elections. He announced Iran's withdrawal from CENTO, canceled US$7 billion worth of arms orders from the United States, and announced Iran would no longer sell oil to South Africa or Israel.

Although Bakhtiar won the qualified support of moderate clerics like Shariatmadari, his measures did not win him the support of Khomeini and the main opposition elements, who were now committed to the overthrow of the monarchy and the establishment of a new political order. The National Front, with which Bakhtiar had been associated for nearly thirty years, expelled him from the movement. Khomeini declared Bakhtiar's government illegal. Bazargan, in Khomeini's name, persuaded the oil workers to pump enough oil to ease domestic hardship, however, and some normalcy returned to the bazaar in the wake of Bakhtiar's appointment. But strikes in both the public and the private sector and large-scale demonstrations against the government continued. When, on January 29, 1979, Khomeini called for a street "referendum" on the monarchy and the Bakhtiar government, there was a massive turnout.

Bakhtiar sought unsuccessfully to persuade Khomeini to postpone his return to Iran until conditions in the country were normalized. Khomeini refused to receive a member of the regency council Bakhtiar sent as an emissary to Paris and after some hesitation rejected Bakhtiar's offer to come to Paris personally for consultations. Bakhtiar's attempt to prevent Khomeini's imminent return by closing the Mehrabad Airport at Tehran on January 26, 1979, proved to be only a stopgap measure.

Khomeini arrived in Tehran from Paris on February 1, 1979, received a rapturous welcome from millions of Iranians, and announced he would "smash in the mouth of the Bakhtiar government." He labeled the government illegal and called for the strikes and demonstrations to continue. A girls' secondary school at which Khomeini established his headquarters in Tehran became the center of opposition activity. A multitude of decisions, and the coordination of the opposition movement, were handled here by what came to be known as the *komiteh-ye Imam,* or the Imam's committee. On February 5, Khomeini named Mehdi Bazargan as prime minister of a provisional government. Although Bazargan did not immediately announce a cabinet, the move reinforced the conditions of dual authority that increasingly came to characterize the closing days of the Pahlavi monarchy. In many large urban centers local *komitehs* (revolutionary committees) had assumed responsibility for municipal functions, including neighborhood security and the distribution of such basic necessities as fuel oil. Government ministries and such services as the customs and the posts remained largely paralyzed. Bakhtiar's cabinet ministers proved unable to assert their authority or, in many instances, even to enter their offices. The loyalty of the armed forces was being seriously eroded by months of confrontation with the people on the streets. There were instances of troops who refused to fire on the crowds, and desertions were rising. In late January, air force technicians at the Khatami Air Base in Esfahan became involved in a confrontation with their officers.

In his statements, Khomeini had attempted to win the army rank and file over to the side of the opposition. Following Khomeini's arrival in Tehran, clandestine contacts took place between Khomeini's representatives and a number of military commanders. These contacts were encouraged by United States ambassador William Sullivan, who had no confidence in the Bakhtiar government, thought the triumph of the Khomeini forces inevitable, and believed future stability in Iran could be assured only if an accommodation could be reached between the armed forces and the Khomeini camp. Contacts between the military chiefs and the Khomeini camp were also being encouraged by United States general Robert E. Huyser, who had arrived in Tehran on January 4, 1979, as President Carter's special emissary. Huyser's assignment was to keep the Iranian army intact, to encourage the military to maintain support for the Bakhtiar government, and to prepare the army for a takeover, should that become necessary. Huyser began a round of almost daily meetings with the service chiefs of the army, navy, and air force, plus heads of the National Police and the Gendarmerie who were sometimes joined by the chief of SAVAK. He dissuaded those so inclined from attempting a coup immediately upon Khomeini's return to Iran, but he failed to get the commanders to take any other concerted action. He left Iran on February 3, before the final confrontation between the army and the revolutionary forces.

On February 8, uniformed airmen appeared at Khomeini's home and publicly pledged their allegiance to him. On February 9, air force technicians at the Doshan Tappeh Air Base outside Tehran mutinied. Units of the Imperial Guard failed to put down the insurrection. The next day, the arsenal was opened, and weapons were distributed to crowds outside the air base. The government announced a curfew beginning in the afternoon, but the curfew was universally ignored. Over the next twenty-four hours, revolutionaries seized police barracks, prisons, and buildings. On February 11, twenty-two senior military commanders met and announced that the armed forces would observe neutrality in the confrontation between the government and the people. The army's withdrawal from the streets was tantamount to a withdrawal of support for the Bakhtiar government and acted as a trigger for a general uprising. By late afternoon on February 12, Bakhtiar was in hiding, and key points throughout the capital were in rebel hands. The Pahlavi monarchy had collapsed.

The Revolution

Bazargan and the Provisional Government

Mehdi Bazargan became the first prime minister of the revolutionary regime in February 1979. Bazargan, however, headed a government that controlled neither the country nor even its own bureaucratic apparatus. Central authority had broken down. Hundreds of semi-independent revolutionary committees, not answerable to central authority, were performing a variety of functions in major cities and towns across the country. Factory workers, civil servants, white-collar employees, and students were often in control, demanding a say in running their organizations and choosing their chiefs. Governors, military commanders, and other officials appointed by the prime minister were frequently rejected by the lower ranks or local inhabitants. A range of political groups, from the far left to the far right, from secular to ultra-Islamic, were vying for political power, pushing rival agendas, and demanding immediate action from the prime minister. Clerics led by Ayatollah Mohammad Beheshti established the Islamic Republican Party (IRP). The party emerged as the organ of the clerics around Khomeini and the major political organization in the country. Not to be outdone, followers of more moderate senior cleric Shariatmadari established the Islamic People's Republican Party (IPRP) in 1979, which had a base in Azarbaijan, Shariatmadari's home province.

Moreover, multiple centers of authority emerged within the government. As the supreme leader, Khomeini did not consider himself bound by the government. He made policy pronouncements, named personal representatives to key government organizations, established new institutions, and announced decisions without consulting his prime minister. The prime minister found he had to share power with the Revolutionary Council, which Khomeini had established in January 1979 and which initially was composed of clerics close to Khomeini, secular political leaders identified with Bazargan, and two representatives of the armed forces. With the establishment of the provisional government, Bazargan and his colleagues left the council to form the cabinet. They were replaced by Khomeini aides from the Paris period, such as Abolhassan Bani Sadr and Sadeq Qotbzadeh, and by protégés of Khomeini's clerical associates. The cabinet was to serve as the executive authority. But the Revolutionary Council was to wield supreme decision-making and legislative authority.

Differences quickly emerged between the cabinet and the council over appointments, the role of the revolutionary courts and other revolutionary organizations, foreign policy, and the general direction of the Revolution. Bazargan and his cabinet colleagues were eager for a return to normalcy and rapid reassertion of central authority. Clerics of the Revolutionary Council, more responsive to the Islamic and popular temper of the mass of their followers, generally favored more radical economic and social measures. They also proved more willing and able to mobilize and to use the street crowd and the revolutionary organizations to achieve their ends.

In July 1979, Bazargan obtained Khomeini's approval for an arrangement he hoped would permit closer cooperation between the Revolutionary Council and the cabinet. Four clerical members of the council joined the government, one as minister of interior and three others as undersecretaries of interior, education, and defense, while Bazargan and three cabinet colleagues joined the council. (All eight continued in their original positions as well.) Nevertheless, tensions persisted.

Even while attempting to put in place the institutions of the new order, the revolutionaries turned their attention to bringing to trial and punishing members of the former regime whom they considered responsible for carrying out political repression, plundering the country's wealth, implementing damaging economic policies, and allowing foreign exploitation of Iran. A revolutionary court set to work almost immediately in the school building in Tehran where Khomeini had set up his headquarters. Revolutionary courts were established in provincial centers shortly thereafter. The Tehran court passed death sentences on four of the shah's generals on February 16, 1979; all four were executed by firing squad on the roof of the building housing Khomeini's headquarters. More executions, of military and police officers, SAVAK agents, cabinet ministers, Majlis deputies, and officials of the shah's regime, followed on an almost daily basis.

The activities of the revolutionary courts became a focus of intense controversy. On the one hand, left-wing political groups and populist clerics pressed hard for "revolutionary justice" for miscreants of the former regime. On the other hand, lawyers' and human rights' groups protested the arbitrary nature of the revolutionary courts, the vagueness of charges, and the absence of defense lawyers. Bazargan, too, was critical of the courts' activities. At the prime minister's insistence, the revolutionary courts suspended their activities on March 14, 1979. On April 5, new regulations governing the courts were promulgated. The courts were to be established at the discretion of the Revolutionary Council and with Khomeini's permission. They were authorized to try a variety of broadly defined crimes, such as "sowing corruption on earth," "crimes against the people," and "crimes against the Revolution." The courts resumed their work on April 6. On the following day, despite international pleas for clemency, Hoveyda, the shah's prime minister for twelve years, was put to death. Attempts by Bazargan to have the revolutionary courts placed under the judiciary and to secure protection for potential victims through amnesties issued by Khomeini also failed. Beginning in August 1979, the courts tried and passed death sentences on members of ethnic minorities involved in antigovernment movements. Some 550 persons had been executed by the time Bazargan resigned in November 1979.

Bazargan had also attempted, but failed, to bring the revolutionary committees under his control. The committees, whose members were armed, performed a variety of duties. They policed neighborhoods in urban areas, guarded prisons and government buildings, made arrests, and served as the execution squads of the revolutionary tribunals. The committees often served the interests of powerful individual clerics, revolutionary personalities, and political groups, however. They made unauthorized arrests, intervened in labor-management disputes, and seized property. Despite these abuses, members of the Revolutionary Council wanted to bring the committees under their own control, rather than eliminate them. With this in mind, in February 1979 they appointed Ayatollah Mohammad Reza Mahdavi-Kani head of the Tehran revolutionary committee and charged him with supervising the committees countrywide. Mahdavi-Kani dissolved many committees, consolidated others, and sent thousands of committeemen home. But the committees, like the revolutionary courts, endured, serving as one of the coercive arms of the revolutionary government.

In May 1979 Khomeini authorized the establishment of the Pasdaran (Pasdaran-e Enghelab-e Islami, Islamic Revolutionary Guard Corps or Revolutionary Guards—see Special and Irregular Armed Forces, ch. 5). The Pasdaran was conceived by the men around Khomeini as a military force loyal to the Revolution and the clerical leaders, as a counterbalance for the regular army, and as a force to use against the guerrilla organizations of the left, which were also arming. Disturbances among the ethnic minorities accelerated the expansion of the Pasdaran.

Two other important organizations were established in this formative period. In March Khomeini established the Foundation for the Disinherited (Bonyad-e Mostazafin—see Treatment of Veterans and Widows, ch. 5). The organization was to take charge of the assets of the Pahlavi Foundation and to use the proceeds to assist low-income groups. The new foundation in time came to be one of the largest conglomerates in the country, controlling hundreds of expropriated and nationalized factories, trading firms, farms, and apartment and office buildings, as well as two large newspaper chains. The Crusade for Reconstruction (Jihad-e Sazandegi or Jihad), established in June, recruited young people for construction of clinics, local roads, schools, and similar facilities in villages and rural areas. The organization also grew rapidly, assuming functions in rural areas that had previously been handled by the Planning and Budget Organization (which replaced the Plan Organization in 1973) and the Ministry of Agriculture.

Trouble broke out among the Turkomans, the Kurds, and the Arabic-speaking population of Khuzestan in March 1979 (see Peoples and Languages, ch. 2). The disputes in the Turkoman region of Gorgan were over land rather than claims for Turkoman cultural identity or autonomy. Representatives of left-wing movements, active in the region, were encouraging agricultural workers to seize land from the large landlords. These disturbances were put down, but not without violence. Meanwhile, in Khuzestan, the center of Iran's oil industry, members of the Arabic-speaking population organized and demanded a larger share of oil revenues for the region, more jobs for local inhabitants, the use of Arabic as a semi-official language, and a larger degree of local autonomy. Because Arab states, including Iraq, had in the past laid claim to Khuzestan as part of the "Arab homeland," the government was bound to regard an indigenous movement among the Arabic-speaking population with suspicion. The government also suspected that scattered instances of sabotage in the oil fields were occurring with Iraqi connivance. In May 1979, government forces responded to these disturbances by firing on Arab demonstrators in Khorramshahr. Several demonstrators were killed; others were shot on orders of the local revolutionary court. The government subsequently quietly transferred the religious leader of the Khuzestan Arabs, Ayatollah Mohammad Taher Shubayr al Khaqani, to Qom, where he was kept under house arrest. These measures ended further protests.

The Kurdish uprising proved more deep-rooted, serious, and durable. The Kurdish leaders were disappointed that the Revolution had not brought them the local autonomy they had long desired. Scattered fighting began in March 1979 between government and Kurdish forces and continued after a brief cease-fire; attempts at negotiation proved abortive. One faction, led by Ahmad Muftizadeh, the Friday prayer leader in Sanandaj, was ready to accept the limited concessions offered by the government, but the Kurdish Democratic Party, led by Abdol-Rahman Qasemlu, and a more radical group led by Shaykh Ezz ad Din Husaini issued demands that the authorities in Tehran did not feel they could accept. These included the enlargement of the Kordestan region to include all Kurdish-speaking areas in Iran, a specified share of the national revenue for expenditure in the province, and complete autonomy in provincial administration. Kurdish was to be recognized as an official language for local use and for correspondence with the central government. Kurds were to fill all local government posts and to be in charge of local security forces. The central government would remain responsible for national defense, foreign affairs, and central banking functions. Similar autonomy would be granted other ethnic minorities in the country. With the rejection of these demands, serious fighting broke out in August 1979. Khomeini, invoking his powers as commander in chief, used the army against other Iranians for the first time since the Revolution. No settlement was reached with the Kurds during Bazargan's prime ministership.

Because the Bazargan government lacked the necessary security forces to control the streets, such control passed gradually into the hands of clerics in the Revolutionary Council and the IRP, who ran the revolutionary courts and had influence with the Pasdaran, the revolutionary committees, and the club-wielding *hezbollahis* (see Glossary), or "partisans of the party of God." The clerics deployed these forces to curb rival political organizations. In June the Revolutionary Council promulgated a new press law and began a crackdown against the proliferating political press. On August 8, 1979, the revolutionary prosecutor banned the leading left-wing newspaper, *Ayandegan.* Five days later *hezbollahis* broke up a Tehran rally called by the National Democratic Front, a newly organized left-of-center political movement, to protest the *Ayandegan* closing. The Revolutionary Council then proscribed the front itself and issued a warrant for the arrest of its leader. *Hezbollahis* also attacked the headquarters of the Fadayan organization and forced the Mojahedin to evacuate their headquarters. On August 20, forty-one opposition papers were proscribed. On September 8, the two largest newspaper chains in the country, Kayhan and Etalaat, were expropriated and transferred to the Foundation for the Disinherited.

In June and July 1979, the Revolutionary Council also passed a number of major economic measures, whose effect was to transfer considerable private sector assets to the state. It nationalized banks, insurance companies, major industries, and certain categories of urban land; expropriated the wealth of leading business and industrial families; and appointed state managers to many private industries and companies.

The New Constitution

Khomeini had charged the provisional government with the task of drawing up a draft constitution. A step in this direction was taken on March 30 and 31, 1979, when a national referendum was held to determine the kind of political system to be established. Khomeini rejected demands by various political groups and by Shariatmadari that voters be given a wide choice. The only form of government to appear on the ballot was an Islamic republic, and voting was not by secret ballot. The government reported an overwhelming majority of over 98 percent in favor of an Islamic republic. Khomeini proclaimed the establishment of the Islamic Republic of Iran on April 1, 1979.

The Khomeini regime unveiled a draft constitution on June 18. Aside from substituting a strong president, on the Gaullist model, for the monarchy, the constitution did not differ markedly from the 1906 constitution and did not give the clerics an important role in the new state structure (see Constitutional Framework, ch. 4). Khomeini was prepared to submit this draft, virtually unmodified, to a national referendum or, barring that, to an appointed council of forty representatives who could advise on, but not revise, the document. Ironically, as it turned out, it was the parties of the left who most vehemently rejected this procedure and demanded that the constitution be submitted for full-scale review by a constituent assembly. Shariatmadari supported these demands.

A newly created seventy-three-member Assembly of Experts convened on August 18, 1979, to consider the draft constitution. Clerics, and members and supporters of the IRP dominated the assembly, which revamped the constitution to establish the basis for a state dominated by the Shia clergy. The Assembly of Experts completed its work on November 15, and the Constitution was approved in a national referendum on December 2 and 3, 1979, once again, according to government figures, by over 98 percent of the vote.

In October 1979, when it had become clear that the draft constitution would institutionalize clerical domination of the state, Bazargan and a number of his cabinet colleagues had attempted to persuade Khomeini to dissolve the Assembly of Experts, but Khomeini refused. Now opposition parties attempted to articulate their objections to the Constitution through protests led by the IPRP. Following the approval of the Constitution, Shariatmadari's followers in Tabriz organized demonstrations and seized control of the radio station. A potentially serious challenge to the dominant clerical hierarchy fizzled out, however, when Shariatmadari wavered in his support for the protesters, and the pro-Khomeini forces organized massive counterdemonstrations in the city in 1979. In fear of condemnation by Khomeini and of IRP reprisals, the IPRP in December 1979 announced the dissolution of the party.

Few foreign initiatives were possible in the early months of the Revolution. The Bazargan government attempted to maintain correct relations with the Persian Gulf states, despite harsh denunciations of the Gulf rulers by senior clerics and revolutionary leaders. Anti-American feeling was widespread and was fanned by Khomeini himself, populist preachers, and the left-wing parties. Bazargan, however, continued to seek military spare parts from Washington and asked for intelligence information on Soviet and Iraqi activities in Iran. On November 1, 1979, Bazargan met with President Carter's national security adviser, Zbigniew K. Brzezinski, in Algiers, where the two men were attending Independence Day celebrations. Meanwhile, the shah, who was seriously ill, was admitted to the United States for medical treatment. Iranians feared that the shah would use this visit to the United States to secure United States support for an attempt to overthrow the Islamic Republic. On November 1, 1979, hundreds of thousands marched in Tehran to demand the shah's extradition, while the press denounced Bazargan for meeting with a key United States official. On November 4, young men who later designated themselves "students of the Imam's line" (imam—see Glossary), occupied the United States embassy compound and took United States diplomats hostage. Bazargan resigned two days later; no prime minister was named to replace him.

The Revolutionary Council took over the prime minister's functions, pending presidential and Majlis elections. The elections for the new president were held in January 1980; Bazargan, fearing further personal attacks, did not run. The three leading candidates were Jalal od Din Farsi, representing the IRP, the dominant clerical party; Abolhasan Bani Sadr, an independent associated with Khomeini who had written widely on the relationship of Islam to politics and economics; and Admiral Ahmad Madani, a naval officer who had served as governor of Khuzestan Province and commander of the navy after the Revolution. Farsi, however, was disqualified because of his Afghan origin, leaving Bani Sadr and Madani as the primary challengers. Bani Sadr was elected by 75 percent of the vote.

The Bani Sadr Presidency

Bani Sadr's program as president was to reestablish central authority, gradually to phase out the Pasdaran and the revolutionary courts and committees and to absorb them into other government organizations, to reduce the influence of the clerical hierarchy, and to launch a program for economic reform and development. Against the wishes of the IRP, Khomeini allowed Bani Sadr to be sworn in as president in January 1980, before the convening of the Majlis. Khomeini further bolstered Bani Sadr's position by appointing him chairman of the Revolutionary Council and delegating to the president his own powers as commander in chief of the armed forces. On the eve of the Iranian New Year, on March 20, Khomeini issued a message to the nation designating the coming year as "the year of order and security" and outlining a program reflecting Bani Sadr's own priorities.

Nevertheless, the problem of multiple centers of power and of revolutionary organizations not subject to central control persisted to plague Bani Sadr. Like Bazargan, Bani Sadr found he was competing for primacy with the clerics and activists of the IRP. The struggle between the president and the IRP dominated the political life of the country during Bani Sadr's presidency. Bani Sadr failed to secure the dissolution of the Pasdaran and the revolutionary courts and committees. He also failed to establish control over the judiciary or the radio and television networks. Khomeini himself appointed IRP members Ayatollah Mohammad Beheshti as chief justice and Ayatollah Abdol-Karim Musavi-Ardabili as prosecutor general (also seen as attorney general). Bani Sadr's appointees to head the state broadcasting services and the Pasdaran were forced to resign within weeks of their appointments.

Parliamentary elections were held in two stages in March and May 1980, amid charges of fraud. The official results gave the IRP and its supporters 130 of 241 seats decided (elections were not completed in all 270 constituencies). Candidates associated with Bani Sadr and with Bazargan's IFM each won a handful of seats; other left-of-center secular parties fared no better. Candidates of the radical left-wing parties, including the Mojahedin, the Fadayan, and the Tudeh, won no seats at all. IRP dominance of the Majlis was reinforced when the credentials of a number of deputies representing the National Front and the Kurdish-speaking areas, or standing as independents, were rejected. The consequences of this distribution of voting power soon became evident. The Majlis began its deliberations in June 1980. Hojjatoleslam Ali Akbar Hashemi-Rafsanjani, a cleric and founding member of the IRP, was elected Majlis speaker. After a two-month deadlock between the president and the Majlis over the selection of the prime minister, Bani Sadr was forced to accept the IRP candidate, Mohammad Ali Rajai. Rajai, a former street peddler and schoolteacher, was a Beheshti protégé. The designation of cabinet ministers was delayed because Bani Sadr refused to confirm cabinet lists submitted by Rajai. In September 1980, Bani Sadr finally confirmed fourteen of a list of twenty-one ministers proposed by the prime minister. Some key cabinet posts, including the ministries of foreign affairs, labor, commerce, and finance, were filled only gradually over the next six

Demonstrators outside the United States Embassy
in Tehran in late 1979
Copyright Lehtikuva/PHOTRI

months. The differences between president and prime minister over cabinet appointments remained unresolved until May 1981, when the Majlis passed a law allowing the prime minister to appoint caretakers to ministries still lacking a minister.

The president's inability to control the revolutionary courts and the persistence of revolutionary temper were demonstrated in May 1980, when executions, which had become rare in the previous few months, began again on a large scale. Some 900 executions were carried out, most of them between May and September 1980, before Bani Sadr left office in June 1981. In September the chief justice finally restricted the authority of the courts to impose death sentences. Meanwhile a remark by Khomeini in June 1980 that "royalists" were still to be found in government offices led to a resumption of widespread purges. Within days of Khomeini's remarks some 130 unofficial purge committees were operating in government offices. Before the wave of purges could be stopped, some 4,000 civil servants and between 2,000 and 4,000 military officers lost their jobs. Around 8,000 military officers had been dismissed or retired in previous purges.

The Kurdish problem also proved intractable. The rebellion continued, and the Kurdish leadership refused to compromise on its demands for local autonomy. Fighting broke out again in April

1980, followed by another cease-fire on April 29. Kurdish leaders and the government negotiated both in Mahabad and in Tehran, but, although Bani Sadr announced he was prepared to accept the Kurdish demands with "modifications," the discussions broke down and fighting resumed. The United States hostage crisis was another problem that weighed heavily on Bani Sadr. The "students of the Imam's line" and their IRP supporters holding the hostages were using the hostage issue and documents found in the embassy to radicalize the public temper, to challenge the authority of the president, and to undermine the reputations of moderate politicians and public figures. The crisis was exacerbating relations with the United States and West European countries. President Carter had ordered several billion dollars of Iranian assets held by American banks in the United States and abroad to be frozen. Bani Sadr's various attempts to resolve the crisis proved abortive. He arranged for the UN secretary general to appoint a commission to investigate Iranian grievances against the United States, with the understanding that the hostages would be turned over to the Revolutionary Council as a preliminary step to their final release. The plan broke down when, on February 23, 1980, the eve of the commission's arrival in Tehran, Khomeini declared that only the Majlis, whose election was still several months away, could decide the fate of the hostages.

The shah had meantime made his home in Panama. Bani Sadr and Foreign Minister Qotbzadeh attempted to arrange for the shah to be arrested by the Panamanian authorities and extradited to Iran. But the shah abruptly left Panama for Egypt on March 23, 1980, before any summons could be served.

In April the United States attempted to rescue the hostages by secretly landing aircraft and troops near Tabas, along the Dasht-e Kavir desert in eastern Iran. Two helicopters on the mission failed, however, and when the mission commander decided to abort the mission, a helicopter and a C-130 transport aircraft collided, killing eight United States servicemen.

The failed rescue attempt had negative consequences for the Iranian military. Radical factions in the IRP and left-wing groups charged that Iranian officers opposed to the Revolution had secretly assisted the United States aircraft to escape radar detection. They renewed their demand for a purge of the military command. Bani Sadr was able to prevent such a purge, but he was forced to reshuffle the top military command. In June 1980, the chief judge of the Army Military Revolutionary Tribunal announced the discovery of an antigovernment plot centered on the military base in Piranshahr in Kordestan. Twenty-seven junior and warrant officers were arrested. In July the authorities announced they had uncovered a plot centered on the Shahrokhi Air Base in Hamadan. Six hundred officers and men were implicated. Ten of the alleged plotters were killed when members of the Pasdaran broke into their headquarters. Approximately 300 officers, including two generals, were arrested, and warrants were issued for 300 others. The government charged the accused with plotting to overthrow the state and seize power in the name of exiled leader Bakhtiar. Khomeini ignored Bani Sadr's plea for clemency and said those involved must be executed. As many as 140 officers were shot on orders of the military tribunal; wider purges of the armed forces followed.

In September 1980, perhaps believing the hostage crisis could serve no further diplomatic or political end, the Rajai government indicated to Washington through a diplomat of the Federal Republic of Germany (West Germany) that it was ready to negotiate in earnest for the release of the hostages. Talks opened on September 14 in West Germany and continued for the next four months, with the Algerians acting as intermediaries. The hostages were released on January 20, 1981, concurrently with President Ronald Reagan's taking the oath of office. The United States in return released US$11 to US$12 billion in Iranian funds that had been frozen by presidential order. Iran, however, agreed to repay US$5.1 billion in syndicated and nonsyndicated loans owed to United States and foreign banks and to place another US$1 billion in an escrow account, pending the settlement of claims filed against Iran by United States firms and citizens. These claims, and Iranian claims against United States firms, were adjudicated by a special tribunal of the International Court of Justice at The Hague, established under the terms of the Algiers Agreement. As of 1987, the court was still reviewing outstanding cases, of which there were several thousand.

The hostage settlement served as a further bone of contention between the Rajai government, which negotiated the terms, and Bani Sadr. The president and the governor of the Central Bank (Central Bank of the Islamic Republic of Iran—established originally in 1960 as Bank Markazi Iran), a presidential appointee, charged the Iranian negotiators with accepting terms highly disadvantageous to Iran.

One incentive to the settling of the hostage crisis had been that in September 1980 Iran became engaged in full-scale hostilities with Iraq. The conflict stemmed from Iraqi anxieties over possible spillover effects of the Iranian Revolution. Iranian propagandists were spreading the message of the Islamic Revolution throughout the Gulf, and the Iraqis feared this propaganda would infect the Shia Muslims who constituted a majority of Iraq's population.

The friction between Iran and Iraq led to border incidents, beginning in April 1980. The Iraqi government saw in the disturbed situation in Iran the opportunity to undo the 1975 Algiers Agreement concluded with the shah (not to be confused with the 1980 United States-Iran negotiations). There is also evidence the Iraqis hoped to bring about the overthrow of the Khomeini regime and to establish a more moderate government in Iran. On September 17, President Saddam Husayn of Iraq abrogated the Algiers Agreement. Five days later Iraqi troops and aircraft began a massive invasion of Iran (see The Iran-Iraq War, ch. 5).

The war did nothing to moderate the friction between Bani Sadr and the Rajai government with its clerical and IRP backers. Bani Sadr championed the cause of the army; his IRP rivals championed the cause of the Pasdaran, for which they demanded heavy equipment and favorable treatment. Bani Sadr accused the Rajai government of hampering the war effort; the prime minister and his backers accused the president of planning to use the army to seize power. The prime minister also fought the president over the control of foreign and domestic economic policy. In late October 1980, in a private letter to Khomeini, Bani Sadr asked Khomeini to dismiss the Rajai government and to give him, as president, wide powers to run the country during the war emergency. He subsequently also urged Khomeini to dissolve the Majlis, the Supreme Judicial Council, and the Council of Guardians so that a new beginning could be made in structuring the government. In November Bani Sadr charged that torture was taking place in Iranian prisons and that individuals were executed "as easily as one takes a drink of water." A commission Khomeini appointed to investigate the torture charges, however, claimed it found no evidence of mistreatment of prisoners.

There were others critical of the activities of the IRP, the revolutionary courts and committees, and the club-wielding *hezbollahis* who broke up meetings of opposition groups. In November and December, a series of rallies critical of the government was organized by Bani Sadr supporters in Mashhad, Esfahan, Tehran, and Gilan. In December, merchants of the Tehran bazaar who were associated with the National Front called for the resignation of the Rajai government. In February 1981, Bazargan denounced the government at a mass rally. A group of 133 writers, journalists, and academics issued a letter protesting the suppression of basic freedoms. Senior clerics questioned the legitimacy of the revolutionary courts, widespread property confiscations, and the power exercised by Khomeini as *faqih*. Even Khomeini's son, Ahmad Khomeini, initially spoke on the president's behalf. The IRP retaliated by using its *hezbollahi* gangs to break up Bani Sadr rallies in various cities and to harass opposition organizations. In November it arrested Qotbzadeh, the former foreign minister, for an attack on the IRP. Two weeks later, the offices of Bazargan's paper, *Mizan,* were smashed.

Khomeini initially sought to mediate the differences between Bani Sadr and the IRP to prevent action that would irreparably weaken the president, the army, or the other institutions of the state. He ordered the cancellation of a demonstration called for December 19, 1980, to demand the dismissal of Bani Sadr as commander in chief. In January 1981, he urged nonexperts to leave the conduct of the war to the military. The next month he warned clerics in the revolutionary organizations not to interfere in areas outside their competence. On March 16, after meeting with and failing to persuade Bani Sadr, Rajai, and clerical leaders to resolve their differences, he issued a ten-point declaration confirming the president in his post as commander in chief and banning further speeches, newspaper articles, and remarks contributing to factionalism. He established a three-man committee to resolve differences between Bani Sadr and his critics and to ensure that both parties adhered to Khomeini's guidelines. This arrangement soon broke down. Bani Sadr, lacking other means, once again took his case to the public in speeches and newspaper articles. The adherents of the IRP used the revolutionary organizations, the courts, and the *hezbollahi* gangs to undermine the president.

The three-man committee appointed by Khomeini returned a finding against the president. In May, the Majlis passed measures to permit the prime minister to appoint caretakers to ministries still lacking a minister, to deprive the president of his veto power, and to allow the prime minister rather than the president to appoint the governor of the Central Bank. Within days the Central Bank governor was replaced by a Rajai appointee.

By the end of May, Bani Sadr appeared also to be losing Khomeini's support. On May 27, Khomeini denounced Bani Sadr, without mentioning him by name, for placing himself above the law and ignoring the dictates of the Majlis. On June 7, *Mizan* and Bani Sadr's newspaper, *Enqelab-e Eslami,* were banned. Three days later, Khomeini removed Bani Sadr from his post as the acting commander in chief of the military. Meanwhile, gangs roamed the streets calling for Bani Sadr's ouster and death and clashed with Bani Sadr supporters. On June 10, participants in a Mojahedin rally at Revolution Square in Tehran clashed with *hezbollahis.* On June 12, a motion for the impeachment of the president was presented by 120 deputies. On June 13 or 14, Bani Sadr, fearing for his life, went into hiding. The speaker of the Majlis, after initially blocking the motion, allowed it to go forward on June 17. The next day, the Mojahedin issued a call for "revolutionary resistance in all its forms." The government treated this as a call for rebellion and moved to confront the opposition on the streets. Twenty-three protesters were executed on June 20 and 21, as the Majlis debated the motion for impeachment. In the debate, several speakers denounced Bani Sadr; only five spoke in his favor. On June 21, with 30 deputies absenting themselves from the house or abstaining, the Majlis decided for impeachment on a vote of 177 to 1. The revolutionary movement had brought together a coalition of clerics, middle-class liberals, and secular radicals against the shah. The impeachment of Bani Sadr represented the triumph of the clerical party over the other members of this coalition.

Terror and Repression

Following the fall of Bani Sadr, opposition elements attempted to reorganize and to overthrow the government by force. The government responded with a policy of repression and terror. The government also took steps to impose its version of an Islamic legal system and an Islamic code of social and moral behavior.

Bani Sadr remained in hiding for several weeks. Believing he was illegally impeached, he maintained his claim to the presidency, formed an alliance with Mojahedin leader Masoud Rajavi, and in July 1981 escaped with Rajavi from Iran to France. In Paris, Bani Sadr and Rajavi announced the establishment of the National Council of Resistance (NCR) and committed themselves to work for the overthrow of the Khomeini regime. They announced a program that emphasized a form of democracy based on elected popular councils; protection for the rights of the ethnic minorities; special attention to the interests of shopkeepers, small landowners, and civil servants; limited land reform; and protection for private property in keeping with the national interest. The Kurdish Democratic Party, the National Democratic Front, and a number of other small groups and individuals subsequently announced their adherence to the NCR.

Meanwhile, violent opposition to the regime in Iran continued. On June 28, 1981, a powerful bomb exploded at the headquarters of the IRP while a meeting of party leaders was in progress. Seventy-three persons were killed, including the chief justice and party secretary general Mohammad Beheshti, four cabinet ministers, twenty-seven Majlis deputies, and several other government officials. Elections for a new president were held on July 24, and Rajai, the prime minister, was elected to the post. On August 5, 1981, the Majlis approved Rajai's choice of Ayatollah Mohammad Javad-Bahonar as prime minister.

Rajai and Bahonar, along with the chief of the Tehran police, lost their lives when a bomb went off during a meeting at the office of the prime minister on August 30. The Majlis named another cleric, Mahdavi-Kani, as interim prime minister. In a new round of elections on October 2, Hojjatoleslam Ali Khamenehi was elected president. Division within the leadership became apparent, however, when the Majlis rejected Khamenehi's nominee, Ali Akbar Velayati, as prime minister. On October 28, the Majlis elected Mir-Hosain Musavi, a protégé of the late Mohammad Beheshti, as prime minister.

Although no group claimed responsibility for the bombings that had killed Iran's political leadership, the government blamed the Mojahedin for both. The Mojahedin did, however, claim responsibility for a spate of other assassinations that followed the overthrow of Bani Sadr. Among those killed in the space of a few months were the Friday prayer leaders in Tabriz, Kerman, Shiraz, Yazd, and Bakhtaran; a provincial governor; the warden of Evin Prison, the chief ideologue of the IRP; and several revolutionary court judges, Majlis deputies, minor government officials, and members of revolutionary organizations.

In September 1981, expecting to spark a general uprising, the Mojahedin sent their young followers into the streets to demonstrate against the government and to confront the authorities with their own armed contingents. On September 27, the Mojahedin used machine guns and rocket-propelled grenade launchers against units of the Pasdaran. Smaller left-wing opposition groups, including the Fadayan, attempted similar guerrilla activities. In July 1981, members of the Union of Communists tried to seize control of the Caspian town of Amol. At least seventy guerrillas and Pasdaran members were killed before the uprising was put down. The government responded to the armed challenge of the guerrilla groups by expanded use of the Pasdaran in counterintelligence activities and by widespread arrests, jailings, and executions. The executions were facilitated by a September 1981 Supreme Judicial Council circular to the revolutionary courts permitting death sentences for "active members" of guerrilla groups. Fifty executions a day became routine; there were days when more than 100 persons were executed. Amnesty International documented 2,946 executions in the 12 months following Bani Sadr's impeachment, a conservative figure because the authorities did not report all executions. The pace of executions slackened considerably at the end of 1982, partly as a result of a deliberate government decision but primarily because, by then, the back of the armed resistance movement had largely been broken. The radical opposition had, however, eliminated several key clerical leaders, exposed vulnerabilities in the state's security apparatus, and posed the threat, never realized, of sparking a wider opposition movement.

By moving quickly to hold new elections and to fill vacant posts, the government managed to maintain continuity in authority, however, and by repression and terror it was able to crush the guerrilla movements. By the end of 1983, key leaders of the Fadayan, Paykar (a Marxist-oriented splinter group of the Mojahedin), the Union of Communists, and the Mojahedin in Iran had been killed, thousands of the rank and file had been executed or were in prison, and the organizational structure of these movements was gravely weakened. Only the Mojahedin managed to survive, and even it had to transfer its main base of operations to Kordestan, and later to Kurdistan in Iraq, and its headquarters to Paris (see Antiregime Opposition Groups, ch. 5).

During this period, the government was also able to consolidate its position in Kordestan. Fighting had resumed between government forces and Kurdish rebels after the failure of talks under Bani Sadr in late 1980. The Kurds held parts of the countryside and were able to enter the major cities at will after dark. With its takeover of Bukan in November 1981, however, the government reasserted control over the major urban centers. Further campaigns in 1983 reduced rebel control over the countryside, and the Kurdish Democratic Party had to move its headquarters to Iraq, from which it made forays into Iran. The Kurdish movement was further weakened when differences between the Kurdish Democratic Party and the more radical Komala (Komala-ye Shureshgari-ye Zahmat Keshan-e Kordestan-e Iran, or Committee of the Revolutionary Toilers of Iranian Kordestan), a Kurdish Marxist guerrilla organization, resulted in open fighting in 1985.

The government also moved against other active and potential opponents. In April 1982, the authorities arrested former Khomeini aide and foreign minister Qotbzadeh and charged him with plotting with military officers and clerics to kill Khomeini and to overthrow the state. Approximately 170 others, including 70 military men, were also arrested. The government implicated the respected religious leader Shariatmadari, whose son-in-law had allegedly served as the intermediary between Qotbzadeh and Shariatmadari. At his trial, Qotbzadeh denied any design on Khomeini's life and claimed he had wanted only to change the government, not to overthrow the Islamic Republic. Shariatmadari, in a television interview, said he had been told of the plot but did not actively support it. Qotbzadeh and the military men were executed, and Shariatmadari's son-in-law was jailed. In an unprecedented move, members of the Association of the Seminary Teachers of Qom voted to strip Shariatmadari of his title of *marja-e taqlid* (a jurist who is also an object of emulation). Shariatmadari's Center for Islamic Study and Publications was closed, and Shariatmadari was placed under virtual house arrest.

In June 1982, the authorities captured Qashqai leader Khosrow Qashqai, who had returned to Iran after the Revolution and had led his tribesmen in a local uprising. He was tried and publicly hanged in October.

All these moves to crush opposition to the Republic gave freer rein to the Pasdaran and revolutionary committees. Members of these organizations entered homes, made arrests, conducted searches, and confiscated goods at will. The government organized "Mobile Units of God's Vengeance" to patrol the streets and to impose Islamic dress and Islamic codes of behavior. Instructions issued by Khomeini in December 1981 and in August 1982 admonishing the revolutionary organizations to exercise proper care in entering homes and making arrests were ignored. "Manpower renewal" and "placement" committees in government ministries and offices resumed widescale purges in 1982, examining officeholders and job applicants on their beliefs and political inclinations. Applicants to universities and military academies were subjected to similar examinations.

By the end of 1982, the country experienced a reaction against the numerous executions and a widespread feeling of insecurity because of the arbitrary actions of the revolutionary organizations and the purge committees. The government saw that insecurity was also undermining economic confidence and exacerbating economic difficulties. Accordingly, in December 1982 Khomeini issued an eight-point decree prohibiting the revolutionary organizations from entering homes, making arrests, conducting searches, and confiscating property without legal authorization. He also banned unauthorized tapping of telephones, interference with citizens in the privacy of their homes, and unauthorized dismissals from the civil service. He urged the courts to conduct themselves so that the people felt their life, property, and honor were secure.

The government appointed a follow-up committee to ensure adherence to Khomeini's decree, to look into the activities of the revolutionary organizations, and to hear public complaints against government officials. Some 300,000 complaints were filed within a few weeks. The follow-up committee was soon dissolved, but the decree nevertheless led to a marked decrease in executions, tempered the worst abuses of the Pasdaran and revolutionary committees, and brought a measure of security to individuals not engaged in opposition activity.

The December decree, however, implied no increased tolerance for the political opposition. The Tudeh had secured itself a measure of freedom during the first three years of the Revolution by declaring loyalty to Khomeini and supporting the clerics against liberal and left-wing opposition groups. But the government showed less tolerance for the party after the impeachment of Bani Sadr and the repression of left-wing guerrilla organizations. The party's position further deteriorated in 1982, as relations between Iran and the Soviet Union grew more strained over such issues as the war with Iraq and the Soviet presence in Afghanistan. The government began closing down Tudeh publications as early as June 1981, and in 1982 officials and senior clerics publicly branded the members of the Tudeh as agents of a foreign power.

In February 1983, the government arrested Tudeh leader Nureddin Kianuri, other members of the party Central Committee, and more than 1,000 party members. The party was proscribed, and Kianuri confessed on television to spying for the Soviet Union and to "espionage, deceit, and treason." Possibly because of Soviet intervention, none of the leading members of the party was brought to trial or executed, although the leaders remained in prison. Many rank and file members, however, were put to death.

By 1983 Bazargan's IFM was the only political group outside the factions of the ruling hierarchy that was permitted any freedom of activity. Even this group was barely tolerated. For example, the party headquarters was attacked in 1983, and two party members were assaulted on the floor of the Majlis.

In 1984 Khomeini denounced the Hojjatiyyeh, a fundamentalist religious group that rejected the role assigned to the *faqih* under the Constitution. The organization, taking this attack as a warning, dissolved itself.

Consolidation of the Revolution

As the government eliminated the political opposition and successfully prosecuted the war with Iraq, it also took further steps to consolidate and to institutionalize the achievements of the Revolution. The government took several measures to regularize the status of revolutionary organizations. It reorganized the Pasdaran and the Crusade for Reconstruction as ministries (the former in November 1982 and the latter in November 1983), a move designed to bring these bodies under the aegis of the cabinet, and placed the revolutionary committees under the supervision of the minister of interior. The government also nominally incorporated the revolutionary courts into the regular court system and in 1984 reorganized the security organization led by Mohammadi Rayshahri, concurrently the head of the Army Military Revolutionary Tribunal, as the Ministry of Information and Security. These measures met with only limited success in reducing the considerable autonomy, including budgetary independence, enjoyed by the revolutionary organizations.

An Assembly of Experts (not to be confused with the constituent assembly that went by the same name) was elected in December 1982 and convened in the following year to determine the successor to Khomeini. Khomeini's own choice was known to be Montazeri. The assembly, an eighty-three-member body that is required to convene once a year, apparently could reach no agreement on a successor during either its 1983 or its 1984 session, however. In 1985 the Assembly of Experts agreed, reportedly on a split vote, to name Montazeri as Khomeini's ''deputy'' (*qaem maqam*), rather than ''successor'' (*ja-neshin*), thus placing Montazeri in line for the succession without actually naming him as the heir apparent (see The Faqih, ch. 4).

Elections to the second Majlis were held in the spring of 1984. The IFM, doubting the elections would be free, did not participate, so the seats were contested only by candidates of the IRP and other groups and individuals in the ruling hierarchy. The campaign revealed numerous divisions within the ruling group, however, and the second Majlis, which included several deputies who had served in the revolutionary organizations, was more radical than the first. The second Majlis convened in May 1984 and, with some prodding from Khomeini, gave Mir-Hosain Musavi a renewed vote of confidence as prime minister. In 1985 it elected Khamenehi, who was virtually unchallenged, to another four-year term as president.

Bazargan, as leader of the IFM, continued to protest the suppression of basic freedoms. He addressed a letter on these issues to Khomeini in August 1984 and issued a public declaration in February 1985. He also spoke out against the war with Iraq and urged a negotiated settlement. In April 1985 Bazargan and forty members of the IFM and the National Front urged the UN secretary general to negotiate a peaceful end to the conflict. In retaliation, in February 1985, the *hezbollahis* smashed the offices of the party, and the party newspaper was once again shut down. Bazargan was denounced from pulpits and was not allowed to run for president in the 1985 elections.

There were, however, increasing signs of factionalism within the ruling group itself over questions of social justice in relation to economic policy, the succession, and, in more muted fashion, foreign policy and the war with Iraq. The debate on economic policy arose partly from disagreement over the more equitable distribution of wealth and partly from differences between those who advocated state control of the economy and those who supported private sector control. Divisions also arose between the Majlis and the Council of Guardians, a group composed of senior Islamic jurists and other experts in Islamic law and empowered by the Constitution to veto, or demand the revision of, any legislation it considers in violation of Islam or the Constitution. In this dispute, the Council of Guardians emerged as the collective champion of private property rights.

In May 1982, the Council of Guardians had vetoed a law that would have nationalized foreign trade. In the fall of 1982, the council forced the Majlis to pass a revised law regarding the state takeover of urban land and to give landowners more protection. In January of the following year, the council vetoed the Law for the Expropriation of the Property of Fugitives, a measure that would have allowed the state to seize the property of any Iranian living abroad who did not return to the country within two months.

In December 1982, the Council of Guardians also vetoed the Majlis' new and more conservative land reform law. This law had been intended to help resolve the issue of land distribution, left unresolved when the land reform law was suspended in November 1980. The suspension had also left unsettled the status of 750,000 to 850,000 hectares of privately owned land that, as a result of the 1979–80 land seizures and redistributions, was being cultivated by persons other than the owners, but without transfer of title.

The debate between proponents of state and of private sector control over the economy was renewed in the winter of 1983–84, when the government came under attack and leaflets critical of the Council of Guardians were distributed. Undeterred, the council blocked attempts in 1984 and 1985 to revive measures for nationalization of foreign trade and for land distribution, and it vetoed a measure for state control over the domestic distribution of goods. As economic conditions deteriorated in 1985, there was an attempt in the Majlis to unseat the prime minister. Khomeini, however, intervened to maintain the incumbent government in office (see The Consolidation of Theocracy, ch. 4).

These differences over major policy issues persisted even as the Revolution was institutionalized and the regime consolidated its hold over the country. The differences remained muted, primarily because of Khomeini's intervention, but the debate threatened to grow more intense and more divisive in the post-Khomeini period. Moreover, while in 1985 Montazeri appeared slated to succeed Khomeini as Iran's leader, there was general agreement that he would be a far less dominant figure as head of the Islamic Republic than Khomeini has been.

* * *

The projected eight-volume *The Cambridge History of Iran* provides learned and factual essays by specialists on history, literature, the sciences, and the arts for various periods of Iranian history from the earliest times. Six volumes, covering history through the Safavid era, had been published by 1987.

For the history of ancient Iran and the period from the Achaemenids up to the Islamic conquest, R. Ghirshman's *Iran: From the Earliest Times to the Islamic Conquest* and A.T. Olmstead's *History of the Persian Empire* are somewhat dated but continue to be standard works. More recent books on the period are Richard Frye's *The Heritage of Persia* and its companion volume *The Golden Age of Persia.*

For the early Islamic period, there are few books devoted specifically to Iran, and readers must consult standard works on early Islamic history. A good study to consult is Marshall G.S. Hodgson's three-volume work, *The Venture of Islam.* Much useful information, for the early as well as the later Islamic period, can be culled from E.G. Browne's four-volume *A Literary History of Persia.* Ann K.S. Lambton's *Landlord and Peasant in Persia* is excellent for both administrative history and land administration until the 1950s.

For studies of single Islamic dynasties in Iran, the following are interesting and competent: E.C. Bosworth's *The Ghaznavids,* Vasilii Bartold's *Turkestan to the Mongol Invasion,* Bertold Spuler's *Die Mongolen in Iran,* and Roy P. Mottahedeh's study of the Buyids, *Loyalty and Leadership in an Early Islamic Society.*

On the Safavid and post-Safavid periods, in addition to the excellent pieces by H.R. Roemer and others in *The Cambridge History of Iran,* volume 6, there is also Laurence Lockhart's *The Fall of the Safavid Dynasty and the Afghan Occupation of Persia* and his *Nadir Shah* and Roger Savory's *Iran under the Safavids.* Said Amir Arjomand's *The Shadow of God and the Hidden Imam* focuses on the relationship of the religious establishment to the state under the Safavids. The Zand period is covered in straightforward fashion by John R. Perry in *Karim Khan Zand.*

For the modern period, *Roots of Revolution* by Nikki R. Keddie provides an interpretative survey from the rise of the Qajars in 1795 to the fall of the Pahlavis in 1979; *Iran Between Two Revolutions* by Ervand Abrahamian is a detailed political history of Iran from the period of the Constitutional Revolution of 1905–1907 to the Islamic

Revolution of 1979. Ruhollah K. Ramazani's *The Foreign Policy of Iran, 1500–1941* is factual and comprehensive on foreign policy issues for the period from 1800 to the abdication of Reza Shah. On nineteenth-century economic history, Charles Issawi's *The Economic History of Iran, 1800–1914,* a collection of documents with extensive commentary, is still unsurpassed.

For the period of Reza Shah, *A History of Modern Iran* by Joseph M. Upton is concise and incisive. *Modern Iran* by L.P. Elwell-Sutton, although written in the 1940s, is still a useful study; and Amin Banani's *The Modernization of Iran, 1921–1941,* covering the same period and along the same lines, looks less at political developments under Reza Shah than at the changes introduced in such areas as industry, education, legal structure, and women's emancipation. Donald Wilber's *Riza Shah Pahlavi, 1878–1944* is basically a factual but not strongly interpretative biography of the founder of the Pahlavi dynasty. J. Bharier's *Economic Development in Iran, 1900–1970,* as the name suggests, provides an economic history of the late Qajar and much of the Pahlavi period.

For the period of Mohammad Reza Shah, in addition to books by Abrahamian and Keddie (cited above), *Iran: The Politics of Groups, Classes, and Modernization* by James A. Bill and *The Political Elite of Iran* by Marvin Zonis are both studies of elite politics and elite structure. Fred Halliday's *Iran: Dictatorship and Development* is a critical account of the nature of the state and the shah's rule, and Robert Graham's *Iran: The Illusion of Power* casts an equally critical eye on the last years of the shah's reign. More sympathetic assessments can be found in George Lenczowski's *Iran under the Pahlavis.* Relations between the state and the religious establishment for the whole of the Pahlavi period are covered in Shahrough Akhavi's *Religion and Politics in Contemporary Iran.* Iran's foreign policy is surveyed in Ramazani's *Iran's Foreign Policy, 1941–1973.*

The United States-Iranian relationship in the period 1941–80 is the focus of Barry Rubin's *Paved with Good Intentions.* The United States-Iranian relationship in the period following the Islamic Revolution is covered in Gary Sick's *All Fall Down.* The foreign policy of the Islamic Republic is covered in Ramazani's *Revolutionary Iran. Reign of the Ayatollahs* by Shaul Bakhash is a political history of the Islamic Revolution up to 1986. *The State and Revolution in Iran, 1962–1982* by Hossein Bashiriyeh is an interpretative essay on the Revolution and its background. Roy P. Mottahedeh's *The Mantle of the Prophet* is at once a biography of a modern-day Iranian cleric, a study of religious education in Iran, and an intriguing interpretation of Iran's cultural history. (For further information and complete citations, see Bibliography.)

Chapter 2. The Society and Its Environment

Two men who came to pay tribute to Darius, ca. 500 B.C., from a bas-relief at Persepolis

IRAN HAS BEEN EXPERIENCING significant social changes since the 1979 Islamic Revolution that overthrew the monarchy. Ayatollah Sayyid Ruhollah Musavi Khomeini, the spiritual leader of the Revolution, and his supporters, who were organized in the Islamic Republican Party (IRP), were determined to desecularize Iranian society. They envisaged the destruction of the royal regime as a prelude to the creation of an Islamic society whose laws and values were derived from the Quran and religious texts sacred to Shia (see Glossary) Islam. The flight into foreign exile of the royal family and most of the prerevolutionary political elite, and the imprisonment or cooptation of those who chose to remain, effectively enabled the Shia Islamic clergy (see Glossary) to take over governmental institutions and to use the power and authority of the central government to implement programs designed to accomplish this goal.

The creation of the Islamic Republic of Iran in 1979 resulted in the destruction of the power and influence of the predominantly secular and Western-oriented political elite that had ruled Iran since the early part of the twentieth century. The new political elite that emerged was composed of Shia clergymen and lay technocrats of middle-class origins. The major consequence of their programs has been cultural, that is, the desecularization of public life in Iran. By 1987 this new political elite had not adopted policies that would have caused any major restructuring of the country's economy. While there has been controversy regarding the appropriate role of the government in regulating the national economy, the overall philosophy of this new political elite has been that private property is respected and protected under Islam.

The establishment of an "ideal" religious society has been impeded by foreign war. Iran became involved in a protracted war with its neighbor, Iraq, in September 1980, when the latter country invaded Iran's oil-rich southwestern province of Khuzestan. This conflict has meant a total war for Iran. By 1987 at least 200,000 Iranians had been killed and another 350,000 to 500,000 wounded. At any one time, 600,000 men were under arms. Property destruction, including the complete leveling of one major city, several towns, and scores of villages, as well as extensive damage to industrial infrastructure and residential neighborhoods of other urban areas, was estimated at billions of dollars. The war also created the need to provide for as many as 1.5 million persons who had become refugees; to ration a wide variety of foodstuffs; to retool most major industries for the production of war-related goods; and to expend a substantial proportion of government resources, including revenues from the sale of petroleum, on the war effort.

Although the war with Iraq has imposed extraordinary burdens on the economy and society, the government of the Republic has continued its efforts to recast society according to religiously prescribed behavioral codes. These policies have resulted in a significant enhancement of the role that the mosque plays in society. The Shia clergy have become the major political actors not only at the national level but also at the local level, where the chief cleric in each town has assumed the functions of a de facto district governor (see Local Government, ch. 4). Thus, local mosques, in addition to fulfilling their traditional roles as places for prayer, have become primary sources of social services that formerly were obtained from various government ministries. Mosques also have become one of the principal institutions for enforcing the observance of public morals.

All the major cultural and social groups in Iran have been affected by the changes resulting from the establishment of the Republic. The secularized, Western-educated, upper and middle classes of the prerevolutionary period have been frequent targets of criticism by the clergy and lay political leaders, who have accused them of "immoral life-styles." These secular groups have tended to resent the laws that regulate individual behavior. In particular, they dislike *hejab* (see Glossary), the dress codes that require women to be covered in public except for their faces and hands, and the prohibition of all alcoholic beverages. Members of these classes, who predominated in the upper levels of the civil service and in the professions, have also been compelled to undergo "re-education classes" in Islam to retain their positions.

In contrast, the religious middle class, generally identified as the bazaar class, has tended to support the laws the secularized groups disliked because these laws reflect the ideal life-style that the bazaar traditionally has tried to follow. Similarly, the lower classes in both urban and rural areas have not necessarily tended to perceive laws regulating behavior as intrusions because the religious sanctions have for the most part merely reinforced the values of their generally conservative life-styles.

Geography

Iran is one of the world's most mountainous countries. Its mountains have helped to shape both the political and the economic history of the country for several centuries. The mountains enclose several broad basins, or plateaus, on which major agricultural and urban settlements are located. Until the twentieth century, when major highways and railroads were constructed through the mountains to connect the population centers, these basins tended to be relatively isolated from one another. Typically, one major town dominated each basin, and there were complex economic relationships between the town and the hundreds of villages that surrounded it. In the higher elevations of the mountains rimming the basins, tribally organized groups practiced transhumance, moving with their herds of sheep and goats between traditionally established summer and winter pastures. There are no major river systems in the country, and historically transportation was by means of caravans that followed routes traversing gaps and passes in the mountains. The mountains also impeded easy access to the Persian Gulf and the Caspian Sea.

With an area of 1,648,000 square kilometers, Iran ranks sixteenth in size among the countries of the world. Iran is about one-fifth the size of the continental United States, or slightly larger than the combined area of the contiguous states of California, Arizona, Nevada, Oregon, Washington, and Idaho.

Located in southwestern Asia, Iran shares its entire northern border with the Soviet Union. This border extends for more then 2,000 kilometers, including nearly 650 kilometers of water along the southern shore of the Caspian Sea. Iran's western borders are with Turkey in the north and Iraq in the south, terminating at the Shatt al Arab (which Iranians call the Arvand Rud). The Persian Gulf and Gulf of Oman littorals form the entire 1,770-kilometer southern border. To the east lie Afghanistan on the north and Pakistan on the south. Iran's diagonal distance from Azarbaijan in the northwest to Baluchestan va Sistan in the southeast is approximately 2,333 kilometers.

Topography

Iran consists of rugged, mountainous rims surrounding high interior basins. The main mountain chain is the Zagros Mountains, a series of parallel ridges interspersed with plains that bisect the country from northwest to southeast. Many peaks in the Zagros exceed 3,000 meters above sea level, and in the south-central region of the country there are at least five peaks that are over 4,000 meters. As the Zagros continue into southeastern Iran, the average elevation of the peaks declines dramatically to under 1,500 meters. Rimming the Caspian Sea littoral is another chain of mountains, the narrow but high Alborz Mountains. Volcanic Mount Damavand (5,600 meters), located in the center of the Alborz, is not only the country's highest peak but also the highest mountain on the Eurasian landmass west of the Hindu Kush (see fig. 4).

The center of Iran consists of several closed basins that collectively are referred to as the Central Plateau. The average elevation of this plateau is about 900 meters, but several of the mountains that tower over the plateau exceed 3,000 meters. The eastern part of the plateau is covered by two salt deserts, the Dasht-e Kavir and the Dasht-e Lut. Except for some scattered oases, these deserts are uninhabited.

Iran has only two expanses of lowlands: the Khuzestan plain in the southwest and the Caspian Sea coastal plain in the north. The former is a roughly triangular-shaped extension of the Mesopotamia plain and averages about 160 kilometers in width. It extends for about 120 kilometers inland, barely rising a few meters above sea level, then meets abruptly with the first foothills of the Zagros. Much of the Khuzestan plain is covered with marshes. The Caspian plain is both longer and narrower. It extends for some 640 kilometers along the Caspian shore, but its widest point is less than 50 kilometers, while at some places less than 2 kilometers separate the shore from the Alborz foothills. The Persian Gulf coast south of Khuzestan and the Gulf of Oman coast have no real plains because the Zagros in these areas come right down to the shore.

There are no major rivers in the country. Of the small rivers and streams, the only one that is navigable is the Karun, which shallow-draft boats can negotiate from Khorramshahr to Ahvaz, a distance of about 180 kilometers. Several other permanent rivers and streams also drain into the Persian Gulf, while a number of small rivers that originate in the northwestern Zagros or Alborz drain into the Caspian Sea. On the Central Plateau, numerous rivers, most of which have dry beds for the greater part of the year, form from snow melting in the mountains during the spring and flow through permanent channels, draining eventually into salt lakes that also tend to dry up during the summer months. There is a permanent salt lake, Lake Urmia (the traditional name, also cited as Lake Urmiyeh, to which it has reverted after being called Lake Rezaiyeh under Mohammad Reza Shah), in the northwest, whose brine content is too high to support fish or most other forms of aquatic life. There are also several connected salt lakes along the Iran-Afghanistan border in the province of Baluchestan va Sistan.

Climate

Iran has a variable climate. In the northwest, winters are cold with heavy snowfall and subfreezing temperatures during December and January. Spring and fall are relatively mild, while summers are dry and hot. In the south, winters are mild and the summers are very hot, having average daily temperatures in July exceeding 38° C. On the Khuzestan plain, summer heat is accompanied by high humidity.

In general, Iran has an arid climate in which most of the relatively scant annual precipitation falls from October through April. In most of the country, yearly precipitation averages 25 centimeters or less. The major exceptions are the higher mountain valleys of the Zagros and the Caspian coastal plain, where precipitation averages at least 50 centimeters annually. In the western part of the Caspian, rainfall exceeds 100 centimeters annually and is distributed relatively evenly throughout the year. This contrasts with some basins of the Central Plateau that receive ten centimeters or less of precipitation annually.

Population

In November 1986, the government reported that the preliminary count in the fourth national census, which had been conducted during October, showed a total population of 48,181,463. According to the government, this total included about 2.6 million refugees who had come from Afghanistan and Iraq since 1980. The population of Iranian nationals, approximately 45.6 million, represented an increase of about 12 million over the 33.7 million enumerated in the 1976 census. This indicated that the Iranian population had grown at an annual rate of 3.6 percent between 1976 and 1986. A population increase in excess of 3.3 percent per year puts Iran's population growth rate among the higher rates in the world.

The preliminary report on the 1986 census showed that Iran's population had been growing at a faster rate since 1976 than during earlier periods. Throughout the first half of the twentieth century, estimates and scattered population surveys indicated that the average population growth rate was less than 2 percent annually. After World War II, however, the population growth rate began to rise. Between the first national census in 1956, when Iran's population numbered 19 million, and the second national census in 1966, when the population count was 25.3 million, the annual growth rate averaged 2.9 percent. The results of the 1976 national census, however, indicated a slight decrease in the average annual growth rate to 2.7 percent.

The sharp increase in the population growth rate from 2.7 percent to nearly 3.6 percent per year between 1976 and 1986 appeared to be related to the Revolution in 1979. Prior to the Revolution, the government had promoted a family planning program; however, following the Revolution, the new government ceased all official

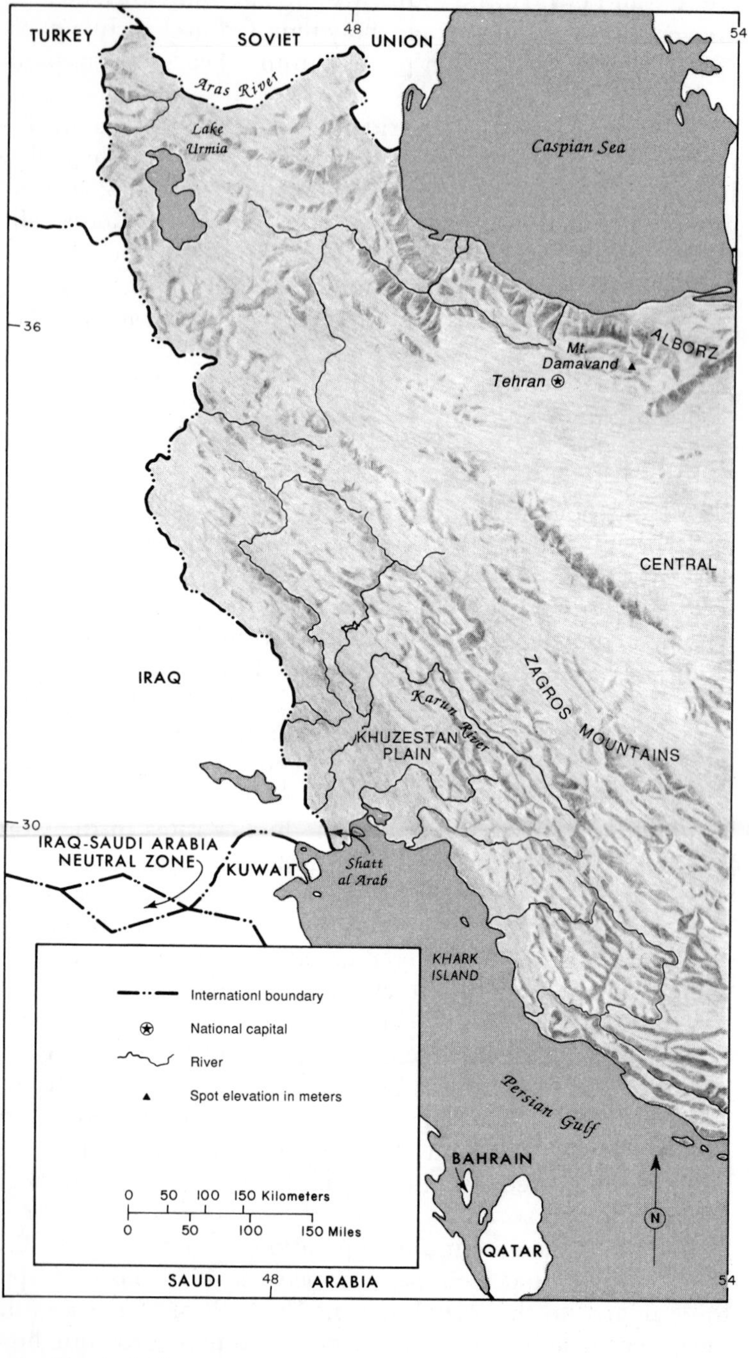

Figure 4. Physical Features

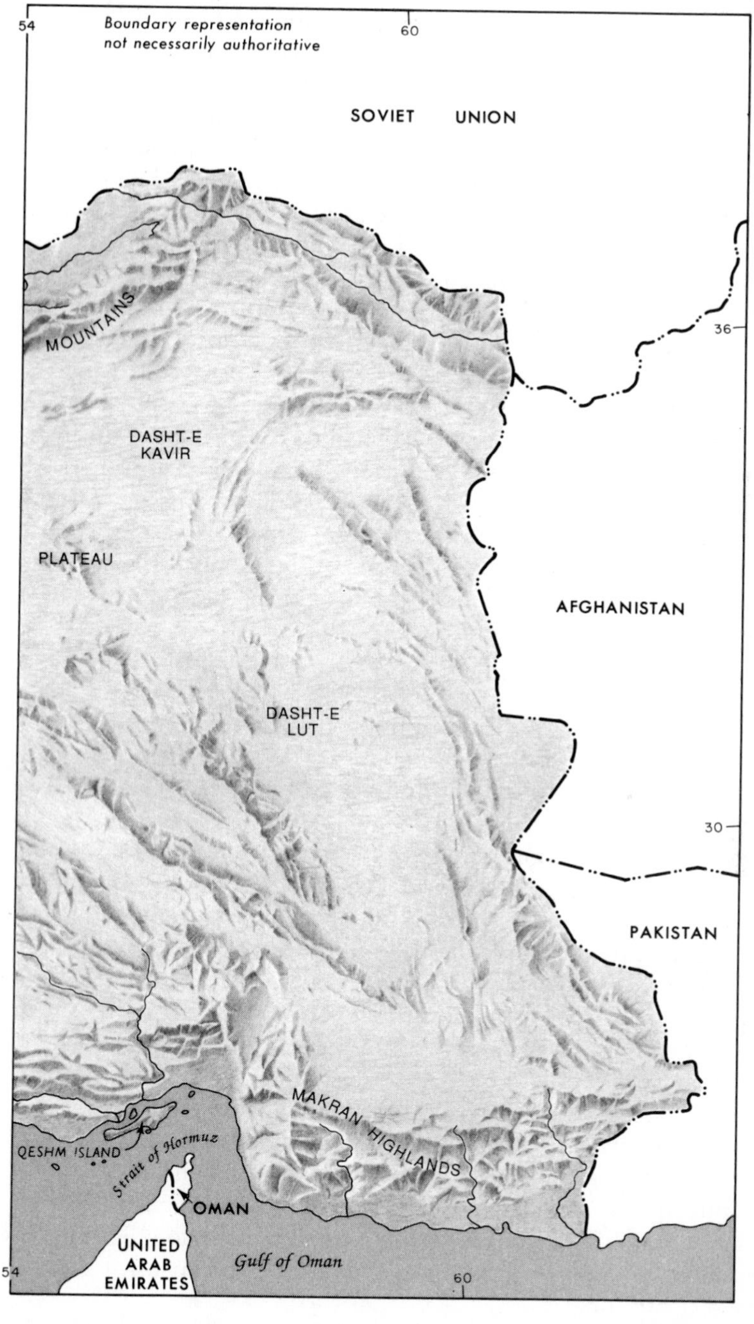
54
Boundary representation
not necessarily authoritative
60
SOVIET UNION
36
MOUNTAINS
DASHT-E
KAVIR
PLATEAU
AFGHANISTAN
DASHT-E
LUT
30
PAKISTAN
MAKRAN HIGHLANDS
QESHM ISLAND
Strait of Hormuz
OMAN
UNITED
ARAB
EMIRATES
Gulf of Oman
54
60

involvement in family planning. Although there has been no religious prohibition on birth control, government pronouncements and literature have tended to extol the virtues of large families.

In mid-1987, data on vital statistics from the 1986 preliminary census were incomplete, but some demographic changes were already evident. The 1976 census data had indicated that 51.4 percent of the population was male and 48.6 was female. The median age of the population was 16.5 years, and less than 3.5 percent of the population was over 65. The relatively large population increase between 1976 and 1986 had the effect of increasing the already extreme youthfulness of the population. In 1986 the government announced that 50 percent of the population was under 15 years of age, and about 45 percent was in the 15- to 59-year age group, while only 5 percent was over the age of 60.

According to the preliminary results of the 1986 census, the average population density for the country was twenty-nine persons per square kilometer. In some regions, especially along the Caspian coast and in East Azarbaijan, the average density was significantly higher, while in the more arid regions of the Central Plateau and Baluchestan va Sistan, average population density was ten or fewer persons per square kilometer.

Major Cities

Tehran, the capital, is the country's largest city and the second most populous city in the Middle East after Cairo. Tehran is a comparatively young city, the origins of which date back about 700 years. The old part of the city is a few kilometers to the northwest of ancient Rey, an important city that was destroyed by the Mongol invasions of the thirteenth century. Tehran was founded by refugees from Rey, but remained an insignificant small town until the end of the eighteenth century, when the founder of the Qajar dynasty chose it to be his capital (see The Qajars, 1795–1925, ch. 1). Tehran has been the capital of the country ever since.

The centralization of the government and the expansion of the bureaucracy under the Pahlavis, the last royal dynasty, were major factors in Tehran's rapid growth after 1925. The city's population doubled between 1926 and 1940 and tripled between 1940 and 1956, when it reached more than 1.5 million. Tehran's population continued to grow rapidly, exceeding 2.7 million by 1966. Its population in the 1986 census was slightly over 6 million. This figure represented a 35 percent increase over the 1976 census of slightly under 4.5 million.

In 1986 Iran had one other city, Mashhad, with a population over 1 million. Mashhad's population of more than 1.4 million represented an increase of 110 percent since 1976. Much of its growth was attributed to the large number of Afghan refugees, approximately 450,000, who were living in the city. The historical origins of Mashhad are similar to those of Tehran inasmuch as the city essentially developed after the centuries-old city of Tus, near modern Mashhad, was destroyed by the Mongols. Mashhad has served as the principal commercial center of Khorasan since the nineteenth century, although its major growth has occurred only since the mid-1950s. It also has become an important manufacturing center and has numerous carpet, textile, and food-processing factories.

Iran's other major cities include Esfahan, Tabriz, and Shiraz, all of which had populations of 800,000 or more in 1986. Like Mashhad, these cities have experienced relatively rapid growth since the mid-1950s. All three of these cities are important manufacturing centers, especially Esfahan, where many of Iran's heavy industries are concentrated. Smaller cities (populations of 100,000 to 500,000) such as Ahvaz, Bakhtaran (before the Revolution Kermanshah), Hamadan, Karaj, Kerman, Qazvin, Qom, Rasht, and Urumiyeh (or Urmia, formerly known as Rezaiyeh) also have grown considerably since 1956 (see table 2, Appendix). A total of 30 cities, more than double the number in the 1966 census, had populations exceeding 100,000 in 1986.

Emigration

Since the Revolution, there has been a small but steady emigration of educated Iranians. Estimates of the number vary from 750,000 to 1.5 million. Most such emigrants have preferred to settle in Western Europe or the United States, although there are also sizable communities of Iranians in Turkey. Newspapers in Istanbul claimed during 1986 that as many as 600,000 Iranians were living in Turkey, although the Turkish Ministry of Interior has reported that there are only about 30,000 Iranians in the country. The United States census for 1980 found 122,000 Iranians living in the United States. By 1987 it was estimated this number exceeded 200,000, with the largest concentration found in southern California.

Iranian emigrants tended to be highly educated, many holding degrees from American and West European universities. A sizable proportion were members of the prerevolutionary political elite. They had been wealthy before the Revolution, and many succeeded in transferring much of their wealth out of Iran during and after the Revolution.

Other Iranians who have emigrated include members of religious minorities, especially Bahais and Jews; intellectuals who had opposed the old regime, which they accused of suppressing free thought and who have the same attitude toward the Islamic Republic; members of ethnic minorities; political opponents of the government in Tehran; and some young men who deserted from the military or sought to avoid conscription. There were virtually no economic emigrants from Iran, although a few thousand Iranians have continued to work in Kuwait, Qatar, and other Persian Gulf states, as before the Revolution.

Refugees

The preliminary 1986 national census figures included approximately 2.6 million persons listed as refugees of foreign nationality. The largest number, consisting of slightly more than 2.3 million, were Afghans. The refugees from Afghanistan were concentrated in several refugee camps in eastern Iran, but approximately one-third of them were living in such cities as Mashhad, Shiraz, and Tehran at the time of the census. In addition, there were nearly 300,000 refugees from Iraq, with which Iran had been at war since 1980.

The influx of foreign refugees was the direct result of war on Iran's borders. Since early 1980, the Afghan refugees had been fleeing the fighting in their country between various Afghan resistance groups and government forces assisted by more than 100,000 Soviet troops. The Iraqi refugees were expelled by their own government, which claimed that they were really Iranian descendants of persons who had immigrated to Iraq from Iran many years ago. In addition to refugees of foreign origins, Tehran has had to cope with several hundred thousand Iranian civilian refugees from the war zones.

The Iraqi advance into Khuzestan in the fall of 1980 resulted in extensive damage to the residential areas of two of Iran's major cities, Abadan and Khorramshahr, as well as the destruction of numerous small towns and villages (see The Original Iraq Offensive, ch. 5). The intensive shelling of the large cities of Ahvaz and Dezful also destroyed residential neighborhoods. Consequently, tens of thousands of civilians fled southwestern Iran in 1980 and 1981, and the government set up refugee reception areas in Shiraz, Tehran, and other cities removed from the battle zone. During the Iraqi occupation of Khuzestan, the government had to shelter up to 1.5 million refugees. Efforts to resettle at least some of the refugees were undertaken in 1983 after Iran had recaptured much of Khuzestan from Iraq; however, continued fighting in the area and Iraqi air strikes on cities and towns in western Iran resulted in a steady stream of displaced civilians in need of food and shelter.

During the period 1980 to 1981, the government of Iraq expelled into Iran about 200,000 persons whom it claimed were Iranians. Most were Iraqi citizens, sometimes whole families, who were or had been residents of Iraq's Shia shrine cities and also were descendants of Iranian clergy and pilgrims who had settled in the religious centers as far back as the eighteenth century. In most cases, the refugees had never been to Iran and could speak no Persian (Farsi). Furthermore, they were required to leave the greater part of their possessions in Iraq. Thus, the Iranian government had to provide them with basic food and shelter.

Developing policies to deal with the Afghan refugees became a major burden for the government as early as 1984 because the number of Afghan refugees had continued to increase almost daily since the first group crossed the border in 1980. Iran, however, received virtually no international assistance for the Afghan refugees. It set up several camps in eastern Iran where the refugees were processed and provided with basic shelter and rations. These camps were located in or near towns in Khorasan and were provided with certain municipal services such as free access to public schools for registered refugee children. Although no data have been published on the gender and age composition of the refugees, press reports indicate that most were probably women, children, and men too old to fight, as in the Afghan refugee camps in Pakistan. Most of the young men probably remained with the Afghan resistance forces for the greater part of the year.

Although the Afghans were required to live in the special refugee camps, by 1986 an estimated one-third of them had left the camps and were living in residential areas of large cities such as Mashhad, Shiraz, and Tehran. The Afghans apparently came to the cities in order to earn money to support families who remained in the camps. They engaged in street vending and worked on construction sites or in factories. The Iranian press periodically reported on the roundup of such Afghans and their forcible return to the camps. The Afghans needed special work permits, but it was not clear whether these were difficult or easy to obtain or whether private employers required them as a condition of employment.

Peoples and Languages

Iran has a heterogeneous population speaking a variety of Indo-Iranian, Semitic, and Turkic languages. The largest language group consists of the speakers of Indo-Iranian languages, who in 1986 comprised about 70 percent of the population. The speakers of Indo-Iranian languages are not, however, a homogeneous group. They include speakers of Persian, the official language of the country, and its various dialects; speakers of Kirmanji, the term for related dialects spoken by the Kurds who live in the cities, towns, and villages of western Iran and adjacent areas of Iraq and Turkey; speakers of Luri, the language of the Bakhtiaris and Lurs who live in the Zagros; and Baluchi, the language of the seminomadic people who live in southeastern Iran and adjacent areas of Afghanistan and Pakistan. Approximately 28 percent of the population speaks various dialects of Turkish. Speakers of Semitic languages include Arabs and Assyrians (see fig. 5).

The Persian Language

The official language of Iran is Persian (the Persian term for which is Farsi). It is the language of government and public instruction and is the mother tongue of half of the population. Persian is spoken as a second language by a large proportion of the rest. Many different dialects of Persian are spoken in various parts of the Central Plateau, and people from each city can usually be identified by their speech. Some dialects, such as Gilaki and Mazandari, are distinct enough to be virtually unintelligible to a Persian speaker from Tehran or Shiraz.

Persian is an ancient language that has developed through three historical stages. Old Persian dates back to at least 514 B.C. and was used until about A.D. 250. It was written in cuneiform and used exclusively for royal proclamations and announcements. Middle Persian, also known as Pahlavi, was in use from about A.D. 250 to 900. It was the official language of the Sassanid Empire and of the Zoroastrian priesthood. It was written in an ideographic script called Huzvaresh.

Modern Persian is a continually evolving language that began to develop about A.D. 900. Following the Arab conquest of the Sassanid Empire in the seventh century and the gradual conversion of the population to Islam, Arabic became the official, literary, and written language, but Persian remained the language of court records. Persian, however, borrowed heavily from Arabic to enrich its own vocabulary and eventually adopted the Arabic script. In subsequent centuries, many Turkic words also were incorporated into Persian.

As part of the Indo-European family of languages, Persian is distantly related to Latin, Greek, the Slavic and Teutonic languages, and English. This relationship can be seen in such cognates as *beradar* (brother), *pedar* (father), and *mader* (mother). It is a relatively easy language for English-speaking people to learn compared with any other major language of the Middle East. Verbs tend to be regular, nouns lack gender and case distinction, prepositions are much used, noun plural formation tends to be regular, and word order is important. The difficulty of the language lies in the subtlety and variety of word meanings according to context. Persian is written right to left in the Arabic script with several modifications. It has four more consonants than Arabic—*pe, che, zhe,* and *gaf*—making a total of thirty-two letters. Most of the letters have four forms in writing, depending on whether they occur at the beginning, in the middle, or at the end of a word or whether they stand separately. The letters stand for the consonants and the three long vowels; special marks written above or below the line are used to denote short vowels. These signs are used only in dictionaries and textbooks, so that a reader must have a substantial vocabulary to understand a newspaper, an average book, or handwriting.

Persian is the most important of a group of several related languages that linguists classify as Indo-Iranian. Persian speakers regard their language as extremely beautiful, and they take great pleasure in listening to the verses of medieval poets such as Ferdowsi, Hafez, and Sadi. The language is a living link with the past and has been important in binding the nation together.

There is no accepted standard transliteration of Persian into Latin letters, and Iranians write their names for Western use in a variety of ways, often following French spelling. Among scholars and librarians a profound dispute exists between those who think Persian should be transliterated in conformity with the rules for Arabic and those who insist that Persian should have its own rules because it does not use all of the same sounds as Arabic.

Among educated Persians, there have been sporadic efforts as far back as the tenth century to diminish the use of Arabic loanwords in their language. Both Pahlavi shahs supported such efforts in the twentieth century. During the reign of Reza Shah Pahlavi (1925–41), serious consideration was given to the possibility of Romanizing the writing of Persian as had been done with Turkish, but these plans were abandoned. Since the Revolution, a contrary tendency to increase the use of Arabic words in both spoken and written Persian has emerged among government leaders.

The Persian-speaking People

The Persians constitute the largest ethnic component in Iran. They predominate in the major urban areas of central and eastern Iran—in the cities of Tehran, Esfahan, Mashhad, Shiraz, Arak, Kashan, Kerman, Qom, and Yazd—and in the villages of the Central Plateau. An estimated 50 to 60 percent of the population speaks Persian as a first language.

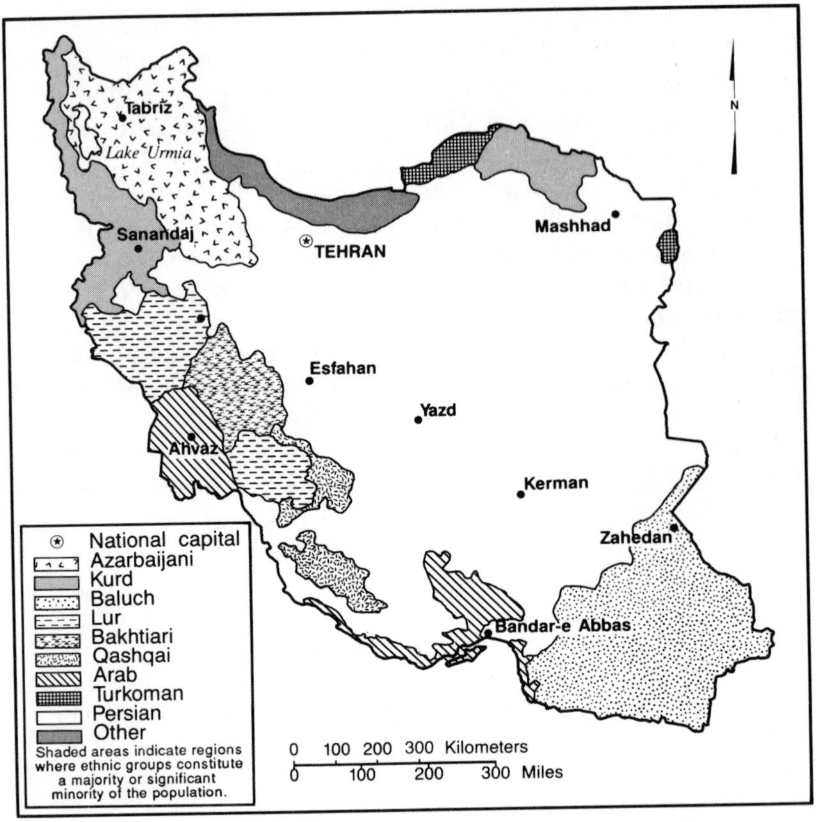

Figure 5. Major Ethnic Groups

In music, poetry, and art the Persians consider themselves—and are generally considered by other groups—as the leaders of the country. This feeling is strengthened by a consciousness of a heroic past and a rich literary heritage. Both before the Revolution and since, Persians have filled the majority of government positions.

The vast majority of Persians are Shia Muslims (see Shia Islam in Iran, this ch.). The Shia religion serves as a source of unity among Persians and other Iranian Shias. Since at least the beginning of the nineteenth century, Persians have dominated the higher ranks of the Shia clergy and have provided important clerical revolutionary leaders such as ayatollahs Khomeini and Hosain Ali Montazeri. Fewer than 500,000 Persians are followers of other faiths. These include Bahais, Jews, or members of the pre-Islamic Zoroastrian faith.

Indo-Iranian-speaking Groups

Lurs and Bakhtiaris

In the central and southern Zagros live the Bakhtiaris and the Lurs, two groups that speak Luri, a language closely related to Persian. Linguists have identified two Luri dialects: Lur Buzurg, which is spoken by the Bakhtiari, Kuhgiluyeh, and Mamasani tribes; and Lur Kuchik, which is spoken by the Lurs of Lorestan. Like the Persians, the Bakhtiaris and Lurs are Shia Muslims. Historically, each of the two groups was organized into several tribes. The tribal leaders or *khans*, especially those of the Bakhtiari tribes, were involved in national politics and were considered part of the prerevolutionary elite (see table 3, Appendix).

The Bakhtiaris have been considered both a political and a tribal entity separate from other Lurs for at least two centuries. They are concentrated in an area extending southward from Lorestan Province to Khuzestan Province and westward from Esfahan to within eighty kilometers of the present-day Iraqi border. A pastoral nomadic tribe called Bakhtiari can be traced back in Iranian history to as early as the fourteenth century, but the important Bakhtiari tribal confederation dates only from the nineteenth century. At the height of Bakhtiari influence, roughly from 1870 to 1930, the term *Bakhtiari* came to be associated not just with the nomadic tribes that provided the military prowess of the confederation but also with the villagers and even town dwellers who were under Bakhtiari jurisdiction. Thus, some Arabic-, Persian-, and Turkic-speaking peasants were considered part of the Bakhtiari. Beginning in the 1920s, the Pahlavi shahs gradually succeeded in establishing the authority of the central government in the Bakhtiari area. Several campaigns also were undertaken to settle forcibly the nomadic pastoral component of the Bakhtiari. The combined political and economic pressures resulted in a significant decline in the power of the Bakhtiari confederation. Detribalized Bakhtiaris, especially those who settled in urban areas and received an education in state schools, tended to be assimilated into Persian culture. By the time of the Revolution in 1979 the term *Bakhtiari* tended to be restricted to an estimated 250,000 tribespeople, most of whom still practiced pastoral nomadism.

Historically, the Bakhtiaris have been divided into two main tribal groups. The Chahar Lang are located in the northwest of the Bakhtiari country and until the middle of the nineteenth century retained the leadership of all the Bakhtiari tribes. The Haft Lang, the southwestern group, have been more closely associated with modern Iranian politics than the Chahar Lang and in some instances have exercised significant influence.

The Lurs (closely related to the Bakhtiaris) live in the Zagros to the northwest, west, and southeast of the Bakhtiaris. There were about 500,000 Lurs in Iran in the mid-1980s. The Lurs are divided into two main groups, the Posht-e Kuhi and the Pish-e Kuhi. These two groups are subdivided into more than sixty tribes, the most important of which include the Boir Ahmadi, the Kuhgiluyeh, and the Mamasani. Historically, the Lurs have included an urban segment based in the town of Khorramabad, the provincial capital of Lorestan. Prior to 1900, however, the majority of Lurs were pastoral nomads. Traditionally, they were considered among the fiercest of Iranian tribes and had acquired an unsavory reputation on account of their habit of preying on both Lur and non-Lur villages. During the 1920s and 1930s, the government of Reza Shah undertook several coercive campaigns to settle the nomadic Lurs. Following the abdication of Reza Shah in 1941, many of the recently settled tribes reverted to nomadism. Mohammad Reza Shah Pahlavi's government attempted with some success through various economic development programs to encourage the remaining nomadic Lurs to settle. By 1986 a majority of all Lurs were settled in villages and small towns in the traditional Lur areas or had migrated to cities.

Baluchis

The Baluchis—who constitute the majority of the population in Baluchestan va Sistan—numbered approximately 600,000 in Iran in the mid-1980s. They are part of a larger group that forms the majority of the population of Baluchistan Province in Pakistan and of some areas in southern Afghanistan. In Iran the Baluchis are concentrated in the Makran highlands, an area that stretches eastward along the Gulf of Oman coast to the Pakistan border and includes some of the most desolate country in the world. The Baluchis speak an Indo-Iranian language that is distantly related to Persian and more closely related to Pashtu, one of the major languages of Afghanistan and Pakistan. Historically, Baluchi has been only an oral language, although educated Baluchis in Pakistan have developed a written script that employs the Arabic alphabet. Unlike the majority of Persians, the majority of Baluchis are Sunni (see Glossary) rather than Shia Muslims. This religious difference has been a source of tension in the past, especially in the ethnically mixed provincial capital of Zahedan. Religious tensions have been exacerbated since the establishment of the Republic.

About half of the Baluchis are seminomadic or nomadic; the remainder are settled farmers or townsmen. Tribal organization remains intact among nomadic and seminomadic Baluchis; tribal patterns of authority and obligation have also been retained by the majority of settled Baluchis. The Baluchis have been one of the most difficult tribal groups for the central government to control, in large part because of poor communications between Tehran and Baluchestan va Sistan. With the exception of the city of Zahedan, neither the monarchy nor the Republic invested any significant funds in local development projects. As a result, the Baluchis are one of the poorest and least educated peoples in Iran. Most of the principal Baluchi tribes in Iran border Pakistan or Afghanistan. They include the Yarahmadzai, the Nauri, the Gomshadzai, the Saravan, the Lashari, and the Barazani. Along the coast of the Gulf of Oman live the important tribes of Sadozai and Taherza.

Kurds

The Kurds speak a variety of closely related dialects, which in Iran are collectively called Kirmanji. The dialects are divided into northern and southern groups, and it is not uncommon for the Kurds living in adjoining mountain valleys to speak different dialects. There is a small body of Kurdish literature written in a modified Arabic script. Kurdish is more closely related to Persian than is Baluchi and also contains numerous Persian loanwords. In large Kurdish cities, the educated population speaks both Persian and Kurdish.

There are approximately 4 million Kurds in Iran. They are the third most important ethnic group in the country after the Persians and Azarbaijanis and account for about 9 percent of the total population (see Turkic-speaking Groups, this ch.). They are concentrated in the Zagros Mountain area along the western frontiers with Turkey and Iraq and adjacent to the Kurdish populations of both those countries. Kurds also live in the Soviet Union and Syria. The Kurdish area of Iran includes most of West Azarbaijan, all of Kordestan, much of Bakhtaran (formerly known as Kermanshahan) and Ilam, and parts of Lorestan. Historically, the Kurds of Iran have been both urban and rural, with as much as half the rural population practicing pastoral nomadism in different periods of history. By the mid-1970s, fewer than 15 percent of all Kurds were nomadic. In addition, during the 1970s there was substantial migration of rural Kurds to such historic Kurdish cities as Bakhtaran (known as Kermanshah until 1979), Sanandaj, and Mahabad, as well as to larger towns such as Baneh, Bijar, Ilam, Islamabad (known as Shahabad until 1979), Saqqez, Sar-e Pol-e Zahab, and Sonqor. Educated Kurds also migrated to non-Kurdish cities such as Karaj, Tabriz, and Tehran.

There are also scatterings of Kurds in the provinces of Fars, Kerman, and Baluchestan va Sistan, and there is a large group of approximately 350,000 living in a small area of northern Khorasan. These are all descendants of Kurds whom the government forcibly removed from western Iran during the seventeenth century.

Most of the rural Kurds retain a tribal form of social organization, although the position of the chief is less significant among the majority of Kurds who live in villages than it is among the unsettled pastoralists. An estimated forty Kurdish tribes and confederations of tribes were still recognized in the mid-1980s. Many of these were organized in the traditional manner, which obligated several subordinate clans to pay dues in cash or produce and provide allegiance to a chief clan. The land reform program of the 1960s did not disrupt this essentially feudal system among most tribally organized Kurds.

The majority of both rural and urban Kurds in West Azarbaijan and Kordestan practice Sunni Islam. There is more diversity of religious practice in southern Kurdish areas, especially in the Bakhtaran area, where many villagers and townspeople follow Shia beliefs. Schismatic Islamic groups, such as the Ahl-e Haqq and the Yazdis, both of which are considered heretical by orthodox Shias, traditionally have had numerous adherents among the Kurds of the Bakhtaran region. A tiny minority of Kurds are adherents of Judaism.

The Kurds have manifested an independent spirit throughout modern Iranian history, rebelling against central government efforts to restrict their autonomy during the Safavid, Qajar, and Pahlavi periods. The most recent Kurdish uprising took place in 1979 following the Revolution. Mahabad, which has been a center of Kurdish resistance against Persian authority since the time of the Safavid monarch Shah Abbas (1587–1629), was again at the forefront of the Kurdish autonomy struggle. Intense fighting between government forces and Kurdish guerrillas occurred from 1979 to 1982, but since 1983 the government has asserted its control over most of the Kurdish area.

Other Groups

Scattered throughout central, southern, and eastern Iran are small groups speaking many different Indo-Iranian languages. In the southern part of the Central Plateau are such small nomadic and seminomadic tribes. Other tribes, related to groups in neighboring Afghanistan and the Soviet Union, are found in Khorasan. Also in Khorasan are an estimated 25,000 Tajiks, a settled farming people related to the Tajiks of Afghanistan and the Soviet

Union. Distinguishable, but comparatively smaller, Indo-Iranian-speaking minorities are the following tribally organized settled groups: the Hazareh, Barbai, Teimuri, Jamshidi, and Afghani in Khorasan; the Qadikolahi and Palavi in Mazandaran; and the Sasani and Agajani in the Talesh region of Gilan.

Turkic-speaking Groups

The second major element of the population is composed of various Turkic-speaking groups. The Turkic languages belong to the Ural-Altaic family, which includes many languages of Soviet Central Asia and western China, as well as Turkish, Hungarian, and Finnish. The various Turkic languages spoken in Iran tend to be mutually intelligible. Of these, only Azarbaijani is written to any extent. In Iran it is written in the Arabic script, in contrast to the Azarbaijani in Turkey, which is written in the Roman script, and that of the Soviet Union, which is written in the Cyrillic script. Unlike Indo-European languages, Turkic languages are characterized by short base words to which are added numerous prefixes and suffixes, each addition changing the meaning of the base. They are also distinguished by their vowel harmony, which means that the kind of vowel used in the base word and the additives must agree. Thus, lengthy words might be filled with "o's" and "u's" or with "a's" and "e's," but not with mixtures of the two.

Turkic speakers make up as much as 25 percent of Iran's total population. They are concentrated in northwestern Iran, where they form the overwhelming majority of the population of East Azarbaijan and a majority of West Azarbaijan. They also constitute a significant minority in the provinces of Fars, Gilan, Hamadan, Khorasan, Mazandaran, and Tehran. Except for the Azarbaijanis, most of the Turkic groups are tribally organized. Some of the Turkic tribes continue to follow a nomadic or seminomadic life. Educated Turkic speakers in the large cities speak and understand Persian.

Azarbaijanis

By far the largest Turkic-speaking group are the Azarbaijanis, who account for over 85 percent of all Turkic speakers in Iran. Most of the Azarbaijanis are concentrated in the northwestern corner of the country, where they form the majority population in an area between the Caspian Sea and Lake Urmia and from the Soviet border south to the latitude of Tehran. Their language, Azarbaijani (also called Azeri or Turkish), is structurally similar to the Turkish spoken in Turkey but with a strikingly different accent. About half of all Azarbaijanis are urban. Major Azarbaijani cities include Tabriz, Urmia, Ardabil, Zanjan, Khoy, and Maragheh. In addition, an estimated one-third of the population of Tehran is Azarbaijani and there are sizable Azarbaijani minorities in other major cities, such as Hamadan, Karaj, and Qazvin. The life styles of urban Azarbaijanis do not differ from those of Persians, and there is considerable intermarriage among the upper classes in cities of mixed populations. Similarly, customs among Azarbaijani villagers do not appear to differ markedly from those of Persian villagers. The majority of Azarbaijanis, like the majority of Persians, are Shia Muslims. A tiny minority of Azarbaijanis are Bahais (see Non-Muslim Minorities, this ch.).

Qashqais

The Qashqais are the second largest Turkic group in Iran. The Qashqais are a confederation of several Turkic-speaking tribes in Fars Province numbering about 250,000 people. They are pastoral nomads who move with their herds of sheep and goats between summer pastures in the higher elevations of the Zagros south of Shiraz and winter pastures at low elevations north of Shiraz. Their migration routes are considered to be among the longest and most difficult of all of Iran's pastoral tribes. The majority of Qashqais are Shias.

The Qashqai confederation emerged in the eighteenth century when Shiraz was the capital of the Zand dynasty. During the nineteenth century, the Qashqai confederation became one of the best organized and most powerful tribal confederations in Iran, including among its clients hundreds of villages and some non-Turkic-speaking tribes. Under the Qashqais' most notable leader, Khan Solat ad Doleh, their strength was great enough to defeat the British-led South Persia Rifles in 1918. Reza Shah's campaigns against them in the early 1930s were successful because the narrow pass on the route from their summer to winter pastures was blocked, and the tribe was starved into submission. Solat and his son were imprisoned in Tehran, where Solat was subsequently murdered. Many Qashqais were then settled on land in their summer pastures, which averages 2,500 meters above sea level.

The Qashqais, like the Bakhtiaris and other forcibly settled tribes, returned to nomadic life upon Reza Shah's exile in 1941. Army and government officials were driven out of the area, but the Qashqais, reduced in numbers and disorganized after their settlement, were unable to regain their previous strength and independence. In the post-World War II period, the Qashqai khans supported the National Front of Prime Minister Mohammad Mossadeq. Following the 1953 royalist coup d'état against Mossadeq,

A nomadic Qashqai family moving to new grazing ground
Courtesy United Nations (S. Jackson)

the Qashqai khans were exiled, and army officers were appointed to supervise tribal affairs. The Qashqais revolted again in the period 1962 to 1964, when the government attempted to take away their pastures under the land reform program. A full-fledged military campaign was launched against them, and the area was eventually pacified. Since the mid-1960s, many Qashqais have settled in villages and towns. According to some estimates, as many as 100,000 Qashqais may have been settled by 1986. This change from pastoral nomadism to settled agriculture and urban occupations proved to be an important factor hindering the Qashqai tribes from organizing effectively against the central government after the Revolution in 1979 when exiled tribal leaders returned to Iran hoping to rebuild the confederation.

By the 1980s, the terms *Qashqai* and *Turk* tended to be used interchangeably in Fars, especially by non-Turkic speakers. Many Turkic groups, however, such as the urban Abivardis of Shiraz and their related village kin in nearby rural areas and the Baharlu, the Inalu, and other tribes, were never part of the Qashqai confederation. The Baharlu and Inalu tribes actually were part of the Khamseh confederacy created to counterbalance the Qashqais. Nevertheless, both Qashqai and non-Qashqai Turks in Fars recognize a common ethnic identity in relation to non-Turks. All of these Turks speak mutually intelligible dialects that are closely related to Azarbaijani. The total Turkic-speaking population of Fars was estimated to be about 500,000 in 1986.

Other Groups

Many other Turkic-speaking groups are scattered throughout Iran, but mainly along the northern tier of provinces. In the northeastern part of East Azarbaijan live some fifty tribes collectively called the Ilsavan (formerly known as Shahsavan). The Ilsavan, who may number as many as 100,000, are pastoral and take their flocks to summer pastures on the high slopes of Mount Sabalan and to winter pastures in the Dasht-e Moghan, adjacent to the Aras River, which forms the frontier between Iran and the Soviet Union. The Ilsavan first appeared in Iranian history as staunch supporters of the Safavid dynasty, which originated during the fifteenth century in Ardabil, a town located in a valley on the south side of Mount Sabalan.

The Qajars, from whom came the royal family that Reza Shah dethroned, form a Turkic-speaking enclave among the Mazandarani. Some are settled agriculturists while others are pastoral nomads. In the northeastern part of Mazandaran, in a region known as the Turkoman Sahra, live several tribes of Turkomans, some of which are sections of larger tribes living across the border in the Soviet Union. In 1986 the number of Turkomans in Iran was estimated to be about 250,000. Several small, nomadic, Turkic-speaking groups, including Qarapakhs and Uzbeks, live in Khorasan. Small numbers of Qarapakhs also live in northwestern Iran along the southern shore of Lake Urmia.

The Afshars are one of the most scattered of the Turkic-speaking groups. A seminomadic people who speak a dialect akin to Azarbaijani, they are found along the shore of Lake Urmia, around Zanjan, along the borders of Kordestan, south of Kerman, and in Khorasan. These separated groups are estimated to total 100,000, but they do not share any consciousness of a common identity nor do they have any political unity. Nevertheless, they all refer to themselves as Afshars and differentiate themselves from other groups, both Turk and non-Turk, that surround them.

Semitic Language Groups

Arabic and Assyrian are the two Semitic languages spoken in Iran. The Arabic dialects are spoken in Khuzestan and along the Persian Gulf coast. They are modern variants of the older Arabic that formed the base of the classical literary language and all the colloquial languages of the Arabic-speaking world. As a Semitic language, Arabic is related to Hebrew, Syriac, and Ethiopic. Like these other Semitic languages, Arabic is based on three-consonant roots, whose meanings vary according to the combinations of vowels that are used to separate the consonants. Written Arabic often is difficult to learn because of the tendency not to indicate short vowels by diacritical marks. There is no linguistic family relationship between Arabic and Persian, although Persian vocabulary has been heavily influenced by Arabic. The Arabic loanwords incorporated into Persian have been modified to fit the Persian sound patterns. Arabic also continues to be the language of prayer of all Muslims in Iran. Children in school learn to read the Quran in Arabic. Persian- and Turkic-speaking Iranians who have commercial interests in the Persian Gulf area often learn Arabic for business purposes.

In 1986 there were an estimated 530,000 Arabs in Iran. A majority lived in Khuzestan, where they constituted a significant ethnic minority. Most of the other Arabs lived along the Persian Gulf coastal plains, but there also were small scattered tribal groups living in central and eastern Iran. About 40 percent of the Arabs were urban, concentrated in such cities as Abadan, Ahvaz, and Khorramshahr. The majority of urban Arab adult males were unskilled workers, especially in the oil industry. Arabs also worked in commerce and services, and there was a small number of Arab professionals. Some urban Arabs and most rural Arabs are tribally organized. The rural Arabs of Khuzestan tend to be farmers and fishermen. Many of the Arabs who live along the Persian Gulf coastal plains are pastoral nomads who keep herds of cattle, sheep, and camels.

Both the urban and the rural Arabs of Khuzestan are intermingled with the Persians, Turks, and Lurs who also live in the province. The Khuzestan Arabs are Shias. While this physical and spiritual closeness has facilitated intermarriage between the Arabs and other Iranians, the Arabs have tended to regard themselves as separate from non-Arabs and have usually been so regarded by other Iranians. Among the Khuzestan Arabs there has been a sense of ethnic solidarity for many years. The government of neighboring Iraq, both before and after the 1979 Revolution in Iran, has claimed that the Khuzestan Arabs are discriminated against and has asserted at various times that it has assisted those desiring "liberation" from Tehran. When Iraq invaded Iran in 1980 and occupied much of Khuzestan for nearly two years, however, an anticipated uprising of the Arab population did not occur, and most of the local Arabs fled the area along with the non-Arab population.

Apart from Khuzestan there is little sense of ethnic unity among the scattered Arab settlements. The Arabs in the area stretching from Bushehr to Bandar-e Abbas tend to be Sunnis. This has helped to strengthen their differentiation from most non-Arab Iranians and even from the Arabs of Khuzestan.

The other Semitic people of Iran are the Assyrians, a Christian group that speaks modern dialects of Assyrian, an Aramaic language that evolved from old Syriac. Language and religion provide a strong cohesive force and give the Assyrians a sense of identity with their coreligionists in Iraq, in other parts of the Middle East, and also in the United States. Most Assyrians adhere to the Assyrian Church of the East (sometimes referred to as the Chaldean Church or Nestorian Church). Many theologians regard this church as the oldest in Christendom. In the nineteenth century, Protestant and Roman Catholic missionaries proselytized among the Assyrians and converted many of them.

There were about 32,000 Assyrians in Iran at the time of the 1976 census. Many of them emigrated after the Revolution in 1979, but at least 20,000 were estimated still to be living in Iran in 1987. The traditional home of the Assyrians in Iran is along the western shore of Lake Urmia. During World War I virtually the entire Assyrian population fled the area, which had become a battleground for opposing Russian and Turkish armies. Thousands of Assyrians perished on the overland flight through the Zagros to the safety of British-controlled Iraq. Eventually, many of the Iranian Assyrians settled among the Assyrian population of Iraq or emigrated to the United States. During the reign of Reza Shah, Assyrians were invited back to Iran to repopulate their villages. A few thousand did return, but, since the 1940s, most young Assyrians have migrated to Tehran and other urban centers.

Armenians

Armenians, a non-Muslim minority that traditionally has lived in northwestern Iran adjacent to the historic Armenian homeland located in what today are eastern Turkey and Soviet Armenia, speak an Indo-European language that is distantly related to Persian. There were an estimated 300,000 Armenians in the country at the time of the Revolution in 1979. There has been considerable emigration of Armenians from Iran since, although in 1986 the Armenian population was still estimated to be 250,000. In the past there were many Armenian villages, especially in the Esfahan area, where several thousand Armenian families had been forcibly resettled in the early seventeenth century during the reign of the Safavid ruler, Shah Abbas. By the 1970s, the Armenians were predominantly urban. Approximately half lived in Tehran, and there were sizable communities in Esfahan, Tabriz, and other cities. The Armenians tend to be relatively well educated and maintain their own schools and Armenian-language newspapers.

Most Armenians are Gregorian Christians, although there are some Roman Catholic and Protestant Armenians as a result of European and American missionary work in Iran during the nineteenth and early twentieth centuries. The Armenian Orthodox Church is divided between those who give their allegiance to the patriarch based at Echmiadzin, near Yerevan in the Armenian Soviet Socialist Republic, and those who support his rival, the patriarch of Cicile at Antilyas, near Beirut in Lebanon. Since 1949 a majority of Armenian Gregorians have followed the patriarch of Cicile. Clergy from Soviet Armenia were at one time active among the Iranian Armenians and had some success in exploiting their sense of community with their coreligionists in the Soviet Union. Several thousand Armenians emigrated from Iran to Soviet Armenia during World War II, and, except for occasional interruptions by one government or another, such emigration has continued. There has also been steady emigration of Iranian Armenians from Iran to the United States.

Structure of Society

Iranians have a very strong sense of class structure. In the past they referred to their society as being divided into tiers, or *tabagheh,* which were identified by numbers: the first tier corresponded to the upper classes; the second, to the middle classes; and the third, to the lower classes. Under the influence of revolutionary ideology, society is now perceived as being divided into the wealthy, a term generally prefixed with negative adjectives; the middle classes; and the *mostazafin,* a term that literally means disinherited. In reality, Iranian society has always been more complex than a three-tier division implies because each of the three broad classes is subdivided into several social groups. These divisions have existed in both urban and rural areas.

Urban Society

Historically, towns in Iran have been administrative, commercial, and manufacturing centers. The traditional political elite consisted of families whose wealth was derived from land and/or trade and from which were recruited the official representatives of the central government. In larger cities, these families could trace their power and influence back several generations. Influential families were also found among the Shia clergy in the largest cities. The middle stratum included merchants and owners of artisan workshops.

The lowest class of urban society included the artisans, laborers, and providers of personal services, such as barbers, bath attendants, shoemakers, tailors, and servants. Most of these, especially the artisans, who were organized into trade associations or guilds, worked in the covered bazaars of the towns.

The urban bazaar historically has been the heart of the Iranian town. In virtually all towns the bazaar is a covered street, or series of streets and alleyways, lined with small shops grouped by service or product. One part of the bazaar contains the shops of cloth and apparel dealers; another section those of carpet makers and merchants; and still another, the workshops of artisans making goods of copper, brass, or other metals, leather, cotton, and wool. In small towns the bazaar might be the equivalent of a narrow, block-long street; in the largest cities, such as Tehran, Esfahan, Mashhad, Tabriz, and Shiraz, the bazaar is a warren of streets that contains warehouses, restaurants, baths, mosques, schools, and gardens in addition to hundreds and hundreds of shops.

The modernization policies of the Pahlavi shahs both preserved and transformed all of these aspects of urban society. This process also led to the rapid growth of the urban population. The extension of central government authority throughout the country fostered the expansion of administrative apparatuses in all major provincial centers. By the 1970s, such cities were sites not just of the principal political and security offices but also of the local branches of diverse government offices such as education, justice, taxation, and telecommunications.

The establishment of modern factories displaced the numerous artisan workshops. Parts of old bazaars were destroyed to create wide streets. Merchants were encouraged to locate retail shops along these new streets rather than in the bazaars. Many of the stores that opened to meet the increased demand for commerce and services from the rapidly expanding urban population were in the new streets. The political elite in the last years of the Pahlavi dynasty spoke of the bazaars as symbols of backwardness and advanced plans to replace some of them with modern shopping malls.

The Urban Political Elite

Prior to the Revolution of 1979, the political elite of the towns consisted of the shah and his family and court in Tehran and the representatives of the monarchy in the provincial towns. These representatives included provincial governors and city mayors, all of whom were appointed by Tehran; high-level government officials; high-ranking military officers; the wealthiest industrialists and financiers; the most prominent merchants; and the best known professionals in law, medicine, and education. The highest ranks of the Shia clergy—the clerics who had obtained the status of ayatollah—were no longer considered part of the national elite by the mid-1970s, although this social group had been very important in the elite from the seventeenth to the mid-twentieth century.

The Revolution of 1979 swept aside this old elite. Although the old political elite was not physically removed, albeit many of its members voluntarily or involuntarily went into exile, it was stripped of its political power. The new elite consisted first and foremost of the higher ranks of the Shia clergy. The most important administrative, military, and security positions were filled by lay politicians who supported the rule of the clergy. The majority of the lay political elite had their origins in the prerevolutionary middle class, especially the bazaar families (see Political Dynamics, ch. 4).

The Bazaar

Opposing the political elite through much of the twentieth century has been the bazaar, an important political, economic, and social force in Iran since at least the time of the Qajar dynasty. The Pahlavi shahs viewed the bazaar as an impediment to the modern society that they wished to create and sought to enact policies that would erode the bazaar's importance. They were aware that the alliance of the mercantile and artisan forces of the bazaar with the Shia clergy posed a serious threat to royal government, as occurred in 1890 and again during the Constitutional Revolution of 1905–07. The emergence of such an alliance in the period from 1923 to 1924 is believed by many scholars to have convinced Reza Shah not to establish a republic, as Atatürk had done in Turkey, but to establish a new dynasty based upon his family.

Reza Shah recognized the potential power of the bazaar, and he was apparently determined to control it. As his secularization programs had adversely affected the clergy, many of his economic reforms hurt the bazaar. His son also sought to control the influence of the bazaar. As a consequence, the bazaar remained a locus of opposition to both Pahlavi shahs. During 1978 the bazaar spearheaded the strikes that paralyzed some sectors of the economy and provided support for the political actions of the Shia clergy. In essence, the feared alliance of the bazaar and clergy had once again come to play a pivotal role in effecting political change in Iran.

The Republic has been much more solicitous of the bazaar than was the Pahlavi dynasty. Several of the early economic programs implemented by the governments of the Republic have benefited the interests of the bazaar; nevertheless, the complexities of managing an economy under the impact of a total war have also forced the central government to adopt economic policies that the bazaar has opposed. Generally, the government leaders have favored varying degrees of state regulation over such economic issues as the pricing of basic commodities and foreign trade, while entrepreneurs, bazaar merchants, and some prominent clergy have opposed such restrictions. These economic issues have been among the main reasons for the emergence of two contentious factions among the political elite (see The Consolidation of Theocracy, ch. 4).

Social Class in Contemporary Iran

Prior to the Revolution of 1979, political connections were considered a key measure of one's social status. In other words, the amount of access that one was perceived to have to the highest levels of decision making was the major determinant of prestige. Wealth was important, but acquiring and maintaining wealth tended to be closely intertwined with access to political power. Consequently, members of the political elite were generally involved in numerous complex interrelationships. For example, some members of the Senate (the upper house of the parliament, or Majlis—see Glossary), a legislative body that included many members of the political elite appointed by the shah, were also on the boards of several industrial and commercial enterprises and were owners of extensive agricultural lands. Since being part of an elite family was an important prerequisite for entry into the political elite, marital relationships tended to bind together important elite families.

The other classes attempted to emulate the political elite in seeking connections to those with political power, whether on the provincial, town, or village level. By the 1970s, however, the nonelite of all classes perceived education as important for improving social status. Education was seen as providing entry into high-status jobs that in turn would open up opportunities for making connections with those who had political power. Despite a great expansion in educational opportunities, the demand far outstripped the ability or willingness of the elite to provide education; this in turn became a source of resentment. By the late 1970s, the nonelite groups, especially the middle classes, rather than admiring the elite and desiring to emulate them, tended to resent the elite for blocking opportunities to compete on an equal basis.

As a result of the lack of field research in Iran after the Revolution, it was difficult in the late 1980s to determine whether the traditional bases for ascribing class status had changed. It is probable that access to political power continued to be important for ascribing status even though the composition of the political elite had changed. It also appears that education continued to be an important basis for determining status.

The Upper Classes

The postrevolutionary upper classes consisted of some of the same elements as the old elite, such as large landowners, industrialists, financiers, and large-scale merchants. They remained part of the upper class by virtue of having stayed in Iran and having retained a considerable part of their wealth. For the most part, however, such persons no longer had any political influence, and in the future the absence of such influence could impede the acquisition of new wealth. The element of the upper classes with greatest political influence was a new group, the senior clergy. Wealth was apparently no longer an attribute of authority, as the example of Khomeini demonstrated. Religious expertise and piety became the major criteria for belonging to the new political elite. Thus, key government administrators held their positions because of their perceived commitment to Shia Islam. They were part of the new political elite, although not members of the old social elite.

The Middle Classes

After the Revolution of 1979, the composition of the middle class was no different from what it had been under the monarchy. There were several identifiable social groups, including entrepreneurs, bazaar merchants, professionals, managers of private and nationalized concerns, the higher grades of the civil service, teachers, medium-scale landowners, military officers, and the junior ranks of the Shia clergy. Some middle-class groups apparently had more access to political power than they had had before the Revolution because the new political elite had been recruited primarily from the middle class.

Prior to the Revolution, the middle class was divided between those possessed of a Western education, who had a secular outlook, and those suspicious of Western education, who valued a role for religion in both public and private life. In general, the more secularly oriented tended to be found among those employed in the bureaucracy, the professions, and the universities, while the more religiously oriented were concentrated among bazaar merchants and the clergy. Among entrepreneurs and especially primary and secondary school teachers, the secular and religious points of view may have had roughly equal numbers of proponents. Since the Revolution, these two outlooks have been in contention. The religious outlook has dominated politics and society, but it appears that the secular middle class has resented laws and regulations that were perceived as interfering with personal liberties.

The middle class was divided by other issues as well. Before the Revolution, an extremely high value had been placed upon obtaining a foreign education. The new political elite, however, regarded a foreign education with suspicion; accordingly, many members of the middle class who were educated abroad have been required to undergo special Islamic indoctrination courses to retain their jobs. In some cases, refusal to conform to religiously prescribed dress and behavior codes has resulted in the loss of government jobs. As a result of these tensions, thousands of Western-educated Iranians have emigrated since 1979.

The Working Class

The working class has been in the process of formation since the early twentieth century. The industrialization programs of the Pahlavi shahs provided the impetus for the expansion of this class. By the 1970s, a distinct working-class identity, *kargar,* had been established, although those who applied this term to themselves did not actually constitute a unified group. The working class was divided into various groups of workers: those in the oil industry, manufacturing, construction, and transportation; and mechanics and artisans in bazaar workshops. The most important component, factory workers, numbered about 2.5 million on the eve of the Revolution, double the number in 1965, and they accounted for 25 percent of Iran's total employed labor force (see Labor Force, ch. 3).

The workers within any one occupation, rather than sharing a common identity, were divided according to perceived skills. For example, skilled construction workers, such as carpenters, electricians, and plumbers, earned significantly higher wages than the more numerous unskilled workers and tended to look down upon them. Similar status differences were common among workers in the oil industry, textile manufacturing, and metal goods production. The heaviest concentration of unskilled workers was in construction, which on the eve of the Revolution employed 9 percent of the entire labor force. In addition to relatively low wages, unskilled construction workers had no job security.

The unions played only a passive role from the viewpoint of workers. Under both the monarchy and the Republic, union activity was strictly controlled by the government. Both the shah and the government of the Islamic Republic considered strikes to be unpatriotic and generally suppressed both strikes and independent efforts to organize workers. Although strikes played an important role in undermining the authority of the government during the final

An elderly, blind cleric
Courtesy United Nations
(John Isaac)

months of the monarchy, once the Republic had been established the new government embraced the view of its royalist predecessor regarding independent labor activities. Thus the government has considered strikes to be un-Islamic and has forcibly suppressed them. A long history of factionalism among different working-class occupational groups and between skilled and unskilled workers within an industry traditionally has contributed to the relative success of governments in controlling the working class.

The Lower Class

Members of the urban lower class can be distinguished by their high illiteracy rate, performance of manual labor, and generally marginal existence. The lower class is divided into two groups: those with regular employment and those without. Those who have regular work include domestic servants, bath attendants, porters, street cleaners, peddlers, street vendors, gardeners, office cleaners, laundry workers, and bakery workers. Thousands work only occasionally or seasonally at these or other jobs. Among the marginally employed there is much reliance on begging. In the past, some members of this group also resorted to prostitution, gambling, smuggling, and drug selling. Since the Revolution, there have been severe penalties for persons convicted of moral offenses, although newspaper reports of the uncovering of various crime rings would indicate that the new codes have not been successful in eliminating such activities.

At the time of the Revolution, it was estimated that as much as one-third of the population of Tehran and one-quarter of the population of other large cities consisted of persons living on the margins of urban society. Life was typified by squalid slums, poverty, malnutrition, lack of health and educational facilities, and crime. In 1987 there was no evidence of measures undertaken by the new government to alleviate conditions in the urban slums.

Urban Migration

A main characteristic of the working class has been its peasant origins. The rapid growth of the working class in the 1960s and 1970s was the result of migration from villages to cities. There also has been some migration from small towns to larger cities and from economically depressed areas, such as Baluchestan and Kordestan, to more economically vital regions. The result of these population transfers has been an inability of urban services to keep pace with the population growth and the consequent spread of slum areas. In 1987 south Tehran was still Iran's most extensive urban slum, but other large cities also had notable slum sections. It was in these areas that marginally employed and unskilled workers were concentrated. Immediately after the Revolution, the government announced its intention of making living and working conditions in rural areas more attractive as a means of stemming rural-to-urban migration. Although the slowdown in the economy since the Revolution may have contributed to a generally reduced rate of urban growth, there was no evidence that migration from the villages had ceased. The preliminary results from the 1986 census indicated that such cities as Mashhad and Shiraz have grown at even faster rates than before the Revolution.

Rural Society

At the time of the Revolution there were about 68,000 villages in Iran. They varied from mere hamlets of a few families up to sizable settlements with populations of 5,000. Social organization in these villages was less stratified than in urban areas, but a hierarchy of political and social relationships and patterns of interaction could be identified. At the top of the village social structure was the largest landowner or owners. In the middle stratum were peasants owning medium to small farms. In the larger villages the middle stratum also included local merchants and artisans. The lowest level, which predominated in most villages, consisted of landless villagers.

Immediately before the Revolution in 1979, Iran's agriculturally productive land totaled about 16.6 million hectares. Approximately one-half of this land was owned by some 200,000 absentee landlords who resided in urban areas. Such owners were represented in the villages by agents who themselves were generally large landowners. The property of the large-scale owners tended to be among the most fertile in the country and generally was used for the production of such cash crops as cotton, sugar beets, fruit, and high-demand vegetables. Agricultural workers were recruited from among the landless villagers and were given either a share of the crop or a cash wage. In some cases, landlords contracted with small peasant owners to farm their fields in return for a share of the crop. Such agreements netted for the landlords from 20 to 70 percent of the harvest, depending upon the crop and the particular inputs provided by the respective parties.

In 1979 about 7 million hectares were divided among approximately 2 million peasant families, whose holdings ranged from less than 1 hectare up to 50. They had acquired ownership as a result of a land reform program implemented between 1962 and 1971. In a typical village a few families owned sufficient land—ten or more hectares—to engage in farming for profit. About 75 percent of the peasant owners, however, had less than 7 hectares, an amount generally insufficient for anything but subsistence agriculture.

Approximately 50 percent of all villagers owned no land. Within individual villages the landless population varied from as little as 10 percent of the total to more than 75 percent. The landless villagers were composed of three distinct social groups: village merchants, village artisans and service workers, and agricultural laborers. Village merchants were found primarily in the larger villages. Their interests tended to coincide with those of the peasant owners, and it was not uncommon for the better-off merchants to acquire agricultural landholdings. Village artisans included blacksmiths, carpenters, cobblers, and coppersmiths. The increasing availability of urban-manufactured goods throughout the 1960s and 1970s had caused a sharp decline in the numbers of village artisans, although carpenters were still important in the larger villages.

The largest group of landless villagers consisted of agricultural laborers who subsisted by contracting with landlords and larger peasant owners to work in their fields on a daily or seasonal basis. In return for their labor they received a wage, based upon the nature of the work performed, or, in some cases, a share of the crop. This group also provided many of the migrants from rural areas in the 1970s. In some areas the migration rate was so great that landlords were compelled to import foreign workers, primarily unskilled

Afghans, to work their lands. The Afghan and other foreign workers were rounded up immediately after the Revolution and expelled from Iran.

Traditionally, in each village the *kadkhuda* (see Glossary)—not to be confused with the head of the smallest tribal unit, a clan—was responsible for administering its affairs and for representing the village in relations with governmental authorities and other outsiders. Before land reform, landlords appointed the *kadkhudas* from among the peasants. Sometimes *kadkhudas* also served as the landlord's agent in the village, although the tendency was for these two positions to be filled by separate persons. After land reform, the office of *kadkhuda* became, at least in theory, elective. However, since the *kadkhuda* was the primary channel through which the government transacted its affairs with the villages, any villager desiring to be a *kadkhuda* had to demonstrate that he had sufficient political access to government officials in the nearest town to protect the interests of the village. In effect, this meant that *kadkhudas* were actually selected by government officials. In general, "elected" *kadkhudas* tended to be among the richest peasant landowners. The land reform and various rural development programs undertaken prior to the Revolution did not produce positive results for the majority of villagers. Economic conditions for most village families stagnated or deteriorated precisely at the time that manufacturing and construction were experiencing an economic boom in urban areas. Consequently, there was a significant increase in rural-to-urban migration. Between the 1966 and the 1976 censuses, a period when the population of the country as a whole was growing at the rate of 2.7 percent per year, most villages actually lost population, and the overall growth rate for the rural population was barely 0.5 percent annually. This migration was primarily of young villagers attracted to cities by the prospect of seasonal or permanent work opportunities. By the late 1970s, this migration had seriously depleted the labor force of many villages. This was an important factor in the relative decline in production of such basic food crops as cereals because many farming families were forced to sow their agricultural land with less labor-intensive crops.

The problems of rural stagnation and agricultural decline had already surfaced in public debate by the eve of the Revolution. During the immediate turmoil surrounding the fall of the monarchy, peasants in many villages took advantage of the unsettled conditions to complete the land redistribution begun under the shah, i.e., they expropriated the property of landlords whom they accused of being un-Islamic. In still other villages, former landlords who had lost property as a result of land reform tried to regain it by flaunting their commitment to Islam and their antagonism to the deposed shah.

Thus, from the beginning the republican government was compelled to tackle the land problem. This proved to be a difficult issue because of the differences among the political elite with respect to the role of private property under Islam. Some officials wanted to legitimize the peasant expropriations as a means of resolving the problem of inequitable land distribution resulting from the shah's land reform program. Such officials generally believed in the principle that the peasant who actually tilled the soil should also be the owner. In contrast, other officials opposed legitimizing land expropriations on the ground that private property is both sanctioned and protected by Islamic law. By 1987 no consensus had been reached, and the question of land redistribution remained unresolved.

The government, however, has demonstrated considerable interest in rural development. A new organization for rebuilding villages, the Crusade for Reconstruction (Jihad-e Sazandegi or Jihad), was created in 1979. It consisted of high-school-educated youth, largely from urban areas, who were charged with such village improvement tasks as providing electrification and piped water, building feeder roads, constructing mosques and bath houses, and repairing irrigation networks.

Nomadic Society

There has never been a census of pastoral nomads in Iran. In 1986 census officials estimated that nomads totaled 1.8 million. The number of tribally organized people, both nomadic and sedentary, may be twice that figure, or nearly 4 million. The nomadic population practices transhumance, migrating in the spring and in the fall. Each tribe claims the use of fixed territories for its summer and winter pastures and the right to use a specified migration route between these areas. Frequently summer and winter camps are widely separated, in some cases by as much as 300 kilometers. Consequently, the semiannual migrations, with families, flocks, and household equipment, may take up to two months to complete. The nomadic tribes are concentrated in the Zagros, but small groups are also found in northeastern and southeastern Iran.

The movements of the tribes appear to be an adaptation to the ecology of the Zagros. In the summer, when the low valleys are parched from insufficient rainfall, the tribes are in the higher elevations. When the snows begin to fall and cover the pastures of the higher valleys, the tribes migrate to low-lying pastures that remain green throughout the winter because of the seasonal rainfall.

Traditionally, the nomadic tribes have kept large herds of sheep and goats, which have provided the main source of red meat for Iran. During migrations the tribes trade their live animals, wool, hair, hides, dairy products, and various knotted and woven textiles with villagers and townspeople in return for manufactured and agricultural goods that the nomads are unable to produce. This economic interdependence between the nomadic and settled populations of Iran has been an important characteristic of society for several centuries.

During the Qajar period (1795–1925), when the central government was especially weak, the nomadic tribes formed tribal confederations and acquired a great deal of power and influence. In many areas these tribal confederations were virtually autonomous and negotiated with the local and national governments for extensive land rights. The largest tribal confederations, such as those of the Bakhtiari and the Qashqai, were headed by a paramount leader, or *ilkhan*. Individual tribes within a confederation were headed by a *khan, beg, shaykh,* or *sardar*. Subtribes, generally composed of several clans, were headed by *kalantars*. The head of the smallest tribal unit, the clan, was called a *kadkhuda*.

Reza Shah moved against the tribes with the new national army that he began creating while minister of war and prime minister (1921–25). After he became shah, his tribal policy had two objectives: to break the authority and power of the great tribal confederation leaders, whom he perceived as a threat to his goal of centralizing power, and to gain the allegiance of urban political leaders who had historically resented the power of the tribes. In addition to military maneuvers against the tribes, Reza Shah used such economic and administrative techniques as confiscation of tribal properties and the holding of chiefs' sons as hostages. Eventually, many nomads were subdued and placed under army control. Some were given government-built houses and forced to follow a sedentary life. As a result, the herds kept by the nomads were unable to obtain adequate pasturage, and there was a drastic decline in livestock. When Reza Shah abdicated in 1941, many nomadic tribes returned to their former life-styles.

Mohammad Reza Shah continued the policy of weakening the political power of the nomadic tribes, but efforts to coerce them to settle were abandoned. Several tribal leaders were exiled, and the military was given greater authority to regulate tribal migrations. Tribal pastures were nationalized during the 1960s as a means of permitting the government to control access to grazing. In addition, various educational, health, and vocational training programs were implemented to encourage the tribes to settle voluntarily.

Following the Revolution, several former tribal leaders attempted to revitalize their tribes as major political and economic forces. Many factors impeded this development, including the hostile attitude of the central government, the decline in nomadic populations as a result of the settlement of large numbers of tribespeople in the 1960s and 1970s, and the consequent change in attitudes, especially of youth raised in villages and towns.

By the mid-1980s, it seemed that the nomadic tribes were no longer a political force in Iranian society. For one thing, the central government had demonstrated its ability to control the migration routes. Moreover, the leadership of the tribes, while formally vested in the old families, effectively was dispersed among a new generation of nonelite tribespeople who tended to see themselves as ethnic minorities and did not share the views of the old elite.

The Family

For most Iranians the reciprocal obligations and privileges that define relations between kinsfolk—from the parent-child bond to more distant ones—have been more important than those associated with any other kind of social alignment. Economic, political, and other forms of institutional activity have been significantly colored by family ties. This has been true not only for the nuclear family of parents and offspring but also for the aggregate kinsfolk, near and distant, who together represent the extended family at its outermost boundary.

Historically, an influential family was one that had its members strategically distributed throughout the most vital sectors of society, each prepared to support the others in order to ensure family prestige and family status. Since the Revolution, this has meant that each of the elite families of Tehran and the major provincial centers included a cadre of clergy, bureaucrats, and Pasdaran (Pasdaran-e Enghelab-e Islami, or Islamic Revolutionary Guard Corps, or Revolutionary Guards—see Special and Irregular Armed Forces, ch. 5). Business operations have continued to be family affairs; often large government loans for business ventures have been obtained simply because the owners were recognized as members of families with good Islamic and revolutionary credentials. Political activities also followed family lines. Several brothers or first cousins might join the Islamic Republican Party. Another group of siblings might become members of a clandestine opposition group such as the Mojahedin (Mojahedin-e Khalq, or People's Struggle) (see Opposition Political Parties in Exile, ch. 4). Similarly, one member of a family might join the clergy, another the Pasdaran or the armed forces. Successful members were expected to assist less successful ones to get their start. Iranians have viewed this inherent nepotism as a positive value, not as a form of corruption. A person without family ties has little status in the society at large. The severing of ties is acceptable only if a family member has done something repugnant to Islam. Even then, the family is encouraged to make the person aware of his deviance and encourage repentance.

Religious law supports the sanctity of the family in diverse ways, defining the conditions for marriage, divorce, inheritance, and guardianship. Additional laws have been passed by the Majlis that reinforce and refine religious law and are designed to protect the integrity of the family (see The Judiciary, ch. 4).

The head of the household—the father and the husband—expects obedience and respect from others in the family. In return, he is obligated to support them and to satisfy their spiritual, social, and material needs. In practice, he is more a strict disciplinarian. He also may be a focus of love and affection, and family members may feel a strong sense of duty toward him. Considerable conflict and irresolution have resulted in many families, especially in urban areas, because young Iranians, imbued with revolutionary religious views or secular values, have not been able to reconcile these new ideas with the traditional values of their fathers.

Marriage regulations are defined by Shia religious law, although non-Shias are permitted to follow their own religious practices. Before the Revolution, the legal marriage age was eighteen for females and twenty-one for males, although in practice most couples, especially among lower-class urban and rural families, actually were younger than the law permitted when they married. Consequently, the average marriage age for both sexes was 18.9 years. Since the Revolution, the minimum legal age for marriage for both males and females has been lowered to fifteen and thirteen years, respectively, although even younger boys and girls may be married with the permission of their fathers. The average age of marriage is believed to have fallen as a result of official encouragement of earlier marriages.

The selection of a marriage partner is normally determined by customary preference, economic circumstances, and geographic considerations. Among the Christians, Jews, and Zoroastrians, the choice may be restricted by religious practice. There is a distinct preference for marriage within extended kin networks, and a high incidence of marriages among first and second cousins exists. A traditionally preferred marriage is between the children of two brothers, although this kind of consanguineous marriage was declining among the old regime elite and secular middle class by the eve of the Revolution.

Marriage arrangements in villages and among the lower and traditional middle classes of urban areas tend to follow traditional patterns. When a young man is judged ready for marriage, his parents will visit the parents of a girl whom they believe to be a suitable match. In many cases, the man will have already expressed an interest in the girl and have asked his parents to begin these formalities. If the girl's parents show similar interest in the union, the conversation quickly turns to money. There must be an agreement on the amount of the bride-price that will be given to the bride's family at the time of marriage. In principle this payment is supposed to compensate the girl's family for her loss, but in practice it is used primarily to finance the cost of the wedding. The exact sum varies according to the wealth, social position, and degree of kinship of the two families.

Once the two families have agreed to the marriage, the prospective bride and groom are considered engaged. The courtship period now commences and may extend for a year or more, although generally the engagement lasts less than twelve months. The actual wedding involves a marriage ceremony and a public celebration. The ceremony is the signing of a marriage contract in the presence of a mullah (see Glossary). One significant feature of the marriage contract is the *mahriyeh,* a stipulated sum that the groom gives to his new bride. The *mahriyeh* usually is not paid at the time of the marriage, especially in marriages between cousins. The contract notes that it is to be paid, however, in the event of divorce or, in case of the husband's death, to be deducted from his estate before the inheritance is divided according to religious law. If the *mahriyeh* is waived, as sometimes happens in urban areas, this too must be stipulated in the marriage contract.

Marriage customs among the secularized middle and upper classes tend to follow practices in the United States and Europe. The prenuptial bride-price may be paid in installments or even eliminated altogether, especially if a substantial *mahriyeh* is guaranteed. It is typical for the marriage partners to have chosen one another. The bride and groom usually sit together at the reception, to which both male and female guests are invited.

Polygyny in Iran is regulated by Islamic custom, which permits a man to have as many as four wives simultaneously, provided that he treats them equally. During the reign of Mohammad Reza Shah, the government attempted to discourage polygyny through legal restrictions, such as requiring the permission of the first wife before the state would register a second marriage. The practice of kin marriages also tended to work against polygynous marriages, since families would exert pressure on men not to take a second wife.

No reliable figures existed on the number of polygynous marriages in the 1960s and 1970s, but they were believed to be on the decline and largely confined to the older generation. After the Revolution, the republican government abolished the secular codes relating to marriage and decreed polygyny acceptable as long as such marriages were in accordance with Shia religious law.

Shia Islam, unlike Sunni Islam, also recognizes a special form of temporary marriage called *muta.* In a *muta* marriage, the man and woman sign a contract agreeing to live together as husband and wife for a specified time, which can be as brief as several hours or as long as ninety-nine years. The man agrees to pay a certain amount of money for the duration of the contract. Provision is also made for the support of any offspring. There is no limit on the number of *muta* marriages that a man may contract. Traditionally, *muta* marriages have been common in Shia pilgrimage centers such as Mashhad and An Najaf in Iraq. Under the monarchy, the government refused to grant any legal recognition to *muta* marriages in an effort to discourage the practice. Since the Revolution, however, *muta* marriages have again become acceptable.

Under both Islamic law and traditional practice, divorce in Iran historically has been easier for a man to obtain than for a woman. Men could exercise the right of repudiation of wives according to the guidelines of Islamic law. Women were permitted to leave their husbands on narrowly defined grounds, such as insanity or impotence. Beginning in the mid-1960s, the royal government attempted to broaden the grounds upon which women could seek divorce through the Family Protection Law. This legislation was frequently criticized by the clergy and was one of the first laws abrogated after the Revolution. In 1985, however, legislation was passed permitting women to initiate divorce proceedings in certain limited circumstances.

Statistics on divorce since the Revolution were unavailable in early 1987. The government claimed that the divorce rate in Iran was much lower than in industrialized countries. Furthermore, members of the clergy have preached that divorce is "reprehensible" under Islam even though it is tolerated.

The Sexes

Traditional Attitudes Toward Segregation of the Sexes

With the notable exception of the Westernized and secularized upper and middle classes, Iranian society before the Revolution practiced public segregation of the sexes. Women generally practiced use of the *chador* (or veil) when in public or when males not related to them were in the house. In the traditional view, an ideal society was one in which women were confined to the home, where they performed the various domestic tasks associated with managing a household and rearing children. Men worked in the public sphere, that is, in the fields, factories, bazaars, and offices. Deviations from this ideal, especially in the case of women, tended to reflect adversely upon the reputation of the family. The strength of these traditional attitudes was reflected in the public education system, which maintained separate schools for boys and girls from the elementary through the secondary levels.

The traditional attitudes on the segregation of women clashed sharply with the views and customs of the secularized upper and middle classes, especially those in Tehran. Mixed gatherings, both public and private, were the norm. During the Pahlavi era the government was the main promoter of change in traditional attitudes toward sexual segregation. It sought to discourage veiling of women at official functions and encouraged mixed participation in a variety of public gatherings. The result was to bring the government into social conflict with the Shia clergy, who sought to defend traditional values.

Impact of Western Ideas on the Role of Women

Among the ideas imported into Iran from the West was the notion that women should participate in the public sphere. The Pahlavi government encouraged women to get as much education as possible and to participate in the labor force at all levels. After 1936, when Reza Shah banned the *chador,* veiling came to be perceived among the minority of elite and secular middle-class women as a symbol of oppression. Before the Revolution, Iranian society was already polarized between the traditionally minded majority and a minority of involved women who were dedicated to improving the status of women. As early as 1932, Iranian women held a meeting of the Oriental Feminine Congress in Tehran at which they called for the right of women to vote, compulsory education for both boys and girls, equal salaries for men and women, and an end to polygyny. In 1963 women were given the right to vote and to hold public office.

Female Participation in the Work Force

Prior to the Revolution, three patterns of work existed among women. Among the upper classes, women either worked as professionals or undertook voluntary projects of various kinds. Whereas secular middle-class women aspired to emulate such women, traditional middle-class women worked outside the home only from dire necessity. Lower class women frequently worked outside the home, especially in major cities, because their incomes were needed to support their households.

Women were active participants in the Revolution that toppled the shah. Most activists were professional women of the secular middle classes, from among whom political antagonists to the regime had long been recruited. Like their male counterparts, such women had nationalist aspirations and felt that the shah's regime was a puppet of the United States. Some women also participated in the guerrilla groups, especially the Mojahedin and the Fadayan (see Anti-Regime Opposition Groups, ch. 5). More significant, however, were the large numbers of lower class women in the cities who participated in street demonstrations during the latter half of 1978 and early 1979. They responded to the call of Khomeini that it was necessary for all Muslims to demonstrate their opposition to tyranny.

Following the Revolution, the status of women changed. The main social group to inherit political power—the traditional middle class—valued most highly the traditional role of women in a segregated society. Accordingly, laws were enacted to restrict the role of women in public life; these laws affected primarily women of the secularized middle and upper classes. *Hejab,* or properly modest attire for women, became a major issue. Although it was not mandated that women who had never worn a *chador* would have to wear this garment, it was required that whenever women appeared in public they had to have their hair and skin covered, except for the face and hands. The law has been controversial among secularized women, although for the majority of women, who had worn the *chador* even before the Revolution, the law probably has had only negligible impact.

Religious Life

The overwhelming majority of Iranians—at least 90 percent of the total population—are Muslims who adhere to Shia Islam. In contrast, the majority of Muslims throughout the world follow Sunni Islam. Of the several Shia sects, the Twelve Imam (see Glossary) or Twelver (*ithna-ashari*), is dominant in Iran; most Shias in Bahrain, Iraq, and Lebanon also follow this sect. All the Shia sects originated among early Muslim dissenters in the first three centuries following the death of the Prophet Muhammad in A.D. 632 (see Islamic Conquest, ch. 1).

The principal belief of Twelvers, but not of other Shias, is that the spiritual and temporal leadership of the Muslim community passed from Muhammad to Ali and then sequentially to eleven of

Esfahan women attend a literacy class concerned with home economics
Courtesy United Nations

Ali's direct male descendants, a tenet rejected by Sunnis. Over the centuries various other theological differences have developed between Twelver Shias and Sunnis.

Shia Islam in Iran

Distinctive Beliefs

Although Shias have lived in Iran since the earliest days of Islam, and there was one Shia dynasty in part of Iran during the tenth and eleventh centuries, it is believed that most Iranians were Sunnis until the seventeenth century. The Safavid dynasty made Shia Islam the official state religion in the sixteenth century and aggressively proselytized on its behalf. It is also believed that by the mid-seventeenth century most people in what is now Iran had become Shias, an affiliation that has continued.

All Shia Muslims believe there are seven pillars of faith, which detail the acts necessary to demonstrate and reinforce faith. The first five of these pillars are shared with Sunni Muslims. They are *shahada,* or the confession of faith; *namaz,* or ritualized prayer; *zakat,* or almsgiving; *sawm,* fasting and contemplation during daylight hours during the lunar month of Ramazan; and hajj, or pilgrimage to the holy cities of Mecca and Medina once in a lifetime if financially feasible. The other two pillars, which are not shared with

Sunnis, are jihad—or crusade to protect Islamic lands, beliefs, and institutions, and the requirement to do good works and to avoid all evil thoughts, words, and deeds.

Twelver Shia Muslims also believe in five basic principles of faith: there is one God, who is a unitary divine being in contrast to the trinitarian being of Christians; the Prophet Muhammad is the last of a line of prophets beginning with Abraham and including Moses and Jesus, and he was chosen by God to present His message to mankind; there is a resurrection of the body and soul on the last or judgment day; divine justice will reward or punish believers based on actions undertaken through their own free will; and Twelve Imams were successors to Muhammad. The first three of these beliefs are also shared by non-Twelver Shias and Sunni Muslims.

The distinctive dogma and institution of Shia Islam is the Imamate, which includes the idea that the successor of Muhammad be more than merely a political leader. The Imam must also be a spiritual leader, which means that he must have the ability to interpret the inner mysteries of the Quran and the *shariat* (see Glossary). The Twelver Shias further believe that the Twelve Imams who succeeded the Prophet were sinless and free from error and had been chosen by God through Muhammad.

The Imamate began with Ali, who is also accepted by Sunni Muslims as the fourth of the "rightly guided caliphs" to succeed the Prophet. Shias revere Ali as the First Imam, and his descendants, beginning with his sons Hasan and Husayn (also seen as Hosein), continue the line of the Imams until the Twelfth, who is believed to have ascended into a supernatural state to return to earth on judgment day. Shias point to the close lifetime association of Muhammad with Ali. When Ali was six years old, he was invited by the Prophet to live with him, and Shias believe Ali was the first person to make the declaration of faith in Islam. Ali also slept in Muhammad's bed on the night of the *hijra,* or migration from Mecca to Medina, when it was feared that the house would be attacked by unbelievers and the Prophet stabbed to death. He fought in all the battles Muhammad did except one, and the Prophet chose him to be the husband of his favorite daughter, Fatima.

In Sunni Islam an imam is the leader of congregational prayer. Among the Shias of Iran the term *imam* traditionally has been used only for Ali and his eleven descendants. None of the Twelve Imams, with the exception of Ali, ever ruled an Islamic government. During their lifetimes, their followers hoped that they would assume the rulership of the Islamic community, a rule that was believed to have been wrongfully usurped. Because the Sunni caliphs were cognizant of this hope, the Imams generally were persecuted during the

Umayyad and Abbasid dynasties. Therefore, the Imams tried to be as unobtrusive as possible and to live as far as was reasonable from the successive capitals of the Islamic empire.

During the ninth century Caliph Al Mamun, son of Caliph Harun ar Rashid, was favorably disposed toward the descendants of Ali and their followers. He invited the Eighth Imam, Reza (A.D. 765–816), to come from Medina to his court at Marv (Mary in the present-day Soviet Union). While Reza was residing at Marv, Mamun designated him as his successor in an apparent effort to avoid conflict among Muslims. Reza's sister Fatima journeyed from Medina to be with her brother but took ill and died at Qom. A shrine developed around her tomb, and over the centuries Qom has become a major Shia pilgrimage and theology center.

Mamun took Reza on his military campaign to retake Baghdad from political rivals. On this trip Reza died unexpectedly in Khorasan. Reza was the only Imam to reside or die in what is now Iran. A major shrine, and eventually the city of Mashhad, grew up around his tomb, which has become the most important pilgrimage center in Iran. Several important theological schools are located in Mashhad, associated with the shrine of the Eighth Imam.

Reza's sudden death was a shock to his followers, many of whom believed that Mamun, out of jealousy for Reza's increasing popularity, had him poisoned. Mamun's suspected treachery against Reza and his family tended to reinforce a feeling already prevalent among his followers that the Sunni rulers were untrustworthy.

The Twelfth Imam is believed to have been only five years old when the Imamate descended upon him in A.D. 874 at the death of his father. The Twelfth Imam is usually known by his titles of Imam-e Asr (the Imam of the Age) and Sahib az Zaman (the Lord of Time). Because his followers feared he might be assassinated, the Twelfth Imam was hidden from public view and was seen only by a few of his closest deputies. Sunnis claim that he never existed or that he died while still a child. Shias believe that the Twelfth Imam remained on earth, but hidden from the public, for about seventy years, a period they refer to as the lesser occultation (*gheybat-e sughra*). Shias also believe that the Twelfth Imam has never died, but disappeared from earth in about A.D. 939. Since that time the greater occultation (*gheybat-e kubra*) of the Twelfth Imam has been in force and will last until God commands the Twelfth Imam to manifest himself on earth again as the Mahdi, or Messiah. Shias believe that during the greater occultation of the Twelfth Imam he is spiritually present—some believe that he is materially present as well—and he is besought to reappear in various invocations and prayers. His name is mentioned in wedding invitations, and his birthday is one of the most jubilant of all Shia religious observances.

The Shia doctrine of the Imamate was not fully elaborated until the tenth century. Other dogmas were developed still later. A characteristic of Shia Islam is the continual exposition and reinterpretation of doctrine. The most recent example is Khomeini's expounding of the doctrine of *velayat-e faqih* (see Glossary), or the political guardianship of the community of believers by scholars trained in religious law. This has not been a traditional idea in Shia Islam and is, in fact, an innovation. The basic idea is that the clergy, by virtue of their superior knowledge of the laws of God, are the best qualified to rule the society of believers who are preparing themselves on earth to live eternally in heaven. The concept of *velayat-e faqih* thus provides the doctrinal basis for theocratic government, an experiment that Twelver Imam Shias had not attempted prior to the Iranian Revolution in 1979.

Religious Obligations

In addition to the seven principal tenets of faith, there are also traditional religious practices that are intimately associated with Shia Islam. These include the observance of the month of martyrdom, Moharram, and pilgrimages to the shrines of the Twelve Imams and their various descendants. The Moharram observances commemorate the death of the Third Imam, Husayn, who was the son of Ali and Fatima and the grandson of Muhammad. He was killed near Karbala in modern Iraq in A.D. 680 during a battle with troops supporting the Umayyad caliph. Husayn's death is commemorated by Shias with passion plays and is an intensely religious time.

Pilgrimage to the shrines of imams is a specific Shia custom. The most important shrines in Iran are those for the Eighth Imam in Mashhad and for his sister Fatima in Qom. There are also important secondary shrines for other relatives of the Eighth Imam in Rey, adjacent to south Tehran, and in Shiraz. In virtually all towns and in many villages there are numerous lesser shrines, known as *imamzadehs,* which commemorate descendants of the imams who are reputed to have led saintly lives. Shia pilgrims visit these sites because they believe that the imams and their relatives have power to intercede with God on behalf of petitioners. The shrines in Iraq at Karbala and An Najaf are also revered by Shias.

Religious Institutions and Organizations

Historically, the single most important religious institution in Iran has been the mosque. In towns, congregational prayers, as well as prayers and rites associated with religious observances and important phases in the lives of Muslims, took place in mosques. Iranian Shias before the Revolution did not generally attach great significance to institutionalization, however, and there was little emphasis on mosque attendance, even for the Friday congregational prayers. Mosques were primarily an urban phenomenon, and in most of the thousands of small villages there were no mosques. Mosques in the larger cities began to assume more important social roles during the 1970s; during the Revolution they played a prominent role in organizing people for the large demonstrations that took place in 1978 and 1979. Since that time their role has continued to expand, so that in 1987 mosques played important political and social roles as well as religious ones.

Another religious institution of major significance was a special building known as a *hoseiniyeh. Hoseiniyehs* existed in urban areas and traditionally served as sites for recitals commemorating the martyrdom of Husayn, especially during the month of Moharram. In the 1970s, some *hoseiniyehs,* such as the Hoseiniyeh Irshad in Tehran, became politicized as prominent clerical and lay preachers used the symbol of the deaths as martyrs of Husayn and the other Imams as thinly veiled criticism of Mohammad Reza Shah's regime, thus helping to lay the groundwork for the Revolution in 1979.

Institutions providing religious education include *madrasehs* and *maktabs. Madrasehs,* or seminaries, historically have been important for advanced training in Shia theology and jurisprudence. *Madrasehs* are generally associated with noted Shia scholars who have attained the rank of ayatollah. There are also some older *madrasehs,* established initially through endowments, at which several scholars may teach. Students, known as *talabehs,* live on the grounds of the *madrasehs* and are provided stipends for the duration of their studies, usually a minimum of seven years, during which they prepare for the examinations that qualify a seminary student to be a low-level preacher, or mullah. At the time of the Revolution, there were slightly more than 11,000 *talabehs* in Iran; approximately 60 percent of these were studying at the *madrasehs* in the city of Qom, another 25 percent were enrolled in the important *madrasehs* of Mashhad and Esfahan, and the rest were at *madrasehs* in Tabriz, Yazd, Shiraz, Tehran, Zanjan, and other cities.

Maktabs, primary schools run by the clergy, were the only educational institutions prior to the end of the nineteenth century when the first secular schools were established. *Maktabs* declined in numbers and importance as the government developed a national public school system beginning in the 1930s. Nevertheless, *maktabs*

A prayer meeting at the University of Tehran
Courtesy United Nations (John Isaac)

continued to exist as private religious schools right up to the Revolution. Since 1979 the public education system has been desecularized and the *maktabs* and their essentially religious curricula merged with government schools (see Education, this ch.).

Another major religious institution in Iran is the shrine. There are more than 1,100 shrines that vary from crumbling sites associated with local saints to the imposing shrines of Imam Reza and his sister Fatima in Mashhad and Qom, respectively. These more famous shrines are huge complexes that include the mausoleums of the venerated Eighth Imam and his sister, tombs of former shahs, mosques, *madrasehs,* and libraries. Imam Reza's shrine is the largest and is considered to be the holiest. In addition to the usual shrine accoutrements, Imam Reza's shrine contains hospitals, dispensaries, a museum, and several mosques located in a series of courtyards surrounding his tomb. Most of the present shrine dates from the early fourteenth century, except for the dome, which was rebuilt after being damaged in an earthquake in 1673. The shrine's endowments and gifts are the largest of all religious institutions in the country. Traditionally, free meals for as many as 1,000 people per day are provided at the shrine. Although there are no special times for visiting this or other shrines, it is customary for pilgrimage traffic to be heaviest during Shia holy periods. It has been estimated that more than 3 million pilgrims visit the shrine annually.

Visitors to Imam Reza's shrine represent all socioeconomic levels. Whereas piety is a motivation for many, others come to seek the spiritual grace or general good fortune that a visit to the shrine is believed to ensure. Commonly a pilgrimage is undertaken to petition Imam Reza to act as an intermediary between the pilgrim and God. Since the nineteenth century, it has been customary among the bazaar class and members of the lower classes to recognize those who have made a pilgrimage to Mashhad by prefixing their names with the title *mashti.*

The next most important shrine is that of Imam Reza's sister, Fatima, known as Hazarat-e Masumeh (the Pure Saint). The present shrine dates from the early sixteenth century, although some later additions, including the gilded tiles, were affixed in the early nineteenth century. Other important shrines are those of Shah Abdol Azim, a relative of Imam Reza, who is entombed at Rey, near Tehran, and Shah Cheragh, a brother of Imam Reza, who is buried in Shiraz. A leading shrine honoring a person not belonging to the family of Imams is that of the Sufi master Sayyid Nimatollah Vali near Kerman. Shias make pilgrimages to these shrines and the hundreds of local *imamzadehs* to petition the saints to grant them special favors or to help them through a period of troubles.

Because Shias believe that the holy Imams can intercede for the dead as well as for the living, cemeteries traditionally have been located adjacent to the most important shrines in both Iran and Iraq. Corpses were transported overland for burial in Karbala in southern Iraq until the practice was prohibited in the 1930s. Corpses are still shipped to Mashhad and Qom for burial in the shrine cemeteries of these cities.

The constant movement of pilgrims from all over Iran to Mashhad and Qom has helped bind together a linguistically heterogeneous population. Pilgrims serve as major sources of information about conditions in different parts of the country and thus help to mitigate the parochialism of the regions.

A traditional source of financial support for all religious institutions has been the *vaqf,* a religious endowment by which land and other income-producing property is given in perpetuity for the maintenance of a shrine, mosque, *madraseh,* or charitable institution such as a hospital, library, or orphanage. A *mutavalli* administers a *vaqf* in accordance with the stipulations in the donor's bequest. In many *vaqfs* the position of *mutavalli* is hereditary. Under the Pahlavis, the government attempted to exercise control over the administration of *vaqfs,* especially those of the larger shrines. This was a source of conflict with the clergy, who perceived the government's efforts as lessening their influence and authority in traditional religious matters.

The government's interference with the administration of *vaqfs* led to a sharp decline in the number of *vaqf* bequests. Instead, wealthy and pious Shias chose to give financial contributions directly to the leading ayatollahs in the form of *zakat,* or obligatory alms. The clergy in turn used the funds to administer their *madrasehs* and to institute various educational and charitable programs, which indirectly provided them with more influence in society. The access of the clergy to a steady and independent source of funding was an important factor in their ability to resist state controls and ultimately helped them direct the opposition to the shah.

Religious Hierarchy

From the time that Twelver Shia Islam emerged as a distinct religious denomination in the early ninth century, its clergy, or ulama, have played a prominent role in the development of its scholarly and legal tradition; however, the development of a distinct hierarchy among the Shia clergy dates back only to the early nineteenth century. Since that time the highest religious authority has been vested in the *mujtahids,* scholars who by virtue of their erudition in the science of religion (the Quran, the traditions of

Muhammad and the imams, jurisprudence, and theology) and their attested ability to decide points of religious conduct, act as leaders of their community in matters concerning the particulars of religious duties. Lay Shias and lesser members of the clergy who lack such proficiency are expected to follow *mujtahids* in all matters pertaining to religion, but each believer is free to follow any *mujtahid* he chooses. Since the mid-nineteenth century it has been common for several *mujtahids* concurrently to attain prominence and to attract large followings. During the twentieth century, such *mujtahids* have been accorded the title of *ayatollah.* Occasionally an ayatollah achieves almost universal authority among Shias and is given the title of *ayatollah ol ozma,* or grand ayatollah. Such authority was attained by as many as seven *mujtahids* simultaneously, including Ayatollah Khomeini, in the late 1970s.

To become a *mujtahid,* it is necessary to complete a rigorous and lengthy course of religious studies in one of the prestigious *madrasehs* of Qom or Mashhad in Iran or An Najaf in Iraq and to receive an authorization from a qualified *mujtahid.* Of equal importance is either the explicit or the tacit recognition of a cleric as a *mujtahid* by laymen and scholars in the Shia community. There is no set time for studying a particular subject, but serious preparation to become a *mujtahid* normally requires fifteen years to master the religious subjects deemed essential. It is uncommon for any student to attain the status of *mujtahid* before the age of thirty; more commonly students are between forty and fifty years old when they achieve this distinction.

Most seminary students do not complete the full curriculum of studies to become *mujtahids.* Those who leave the *madrasehs* after completing the primary level can serve as prayer leaders, village mullahs, local shrine administrators, and other religious functionaries. Those who leave after completing the second level become preachers in town and city mosques. Students in the third level of study are those preparing to become *mujtahids.* The advanced students at this level are generally accorded the title of *hojjatoleslam* when they have completed all their studies.

The Shia clergy in Iran wear a white turban and an *aba,* a loose, sleeveless brown cloak, open in front. A *sayyid,* who is a clergyman descended from Muhammad, wears a black turban and a black *aba.*

Unorthodox Shia Religious Movements

Shah Ismail, the founder of the Safavid dynasty, who established Twelver Shia Islam as the official religion of Iran at the beginning of the sixteenth century, was revered by his followers as a Sufi master. Sufism, or Islamic mysticism, has a long tradition in Iran. It developed there and in other areas of the Islamic empire during the ninth century among Muslims who believed that worldly pleasures distracted from true concern with the salvation of the soul. Sufis generally renounced materialism, which they believed supported and perpetuated political tyranny. Their name is derived from the Arabic word for wool, *suf,* and was applied to the early Sufis because of their habit of wearing rough wool next to their skin as a symbol of their asceticism. Over time a great variety of Sufi brotherhoods was formed, including several that were militaristic, such as the Safavid order, of which Ismail was the leader.

Although Sufis were associated with the early spread of Shia ideas in the country, once the Shia clergy had consolidated their authority over religion by the early seventeenth century, they tended to regard Sufis as deviant. At various periods during the past three centuries some Shia clergy have encouraged persecution of Sufis, but Sufi orders have continued to exist in Iran. During the Pahlavi period, some Sufi brotherhoods were revitalized. Some members of the secularized middle class were especially attracted to them, but the orders appear to have had little following among the lower classes. The largest Sufi order was the Nimatollahi, which had *khanehgahs,* or teaching centers, in several cities and even established new centers in foreign countries. Other important orders were the Dhahabi and Kharksar brotherhoods. Sufi brotherhoods such as the Naqshbandi and the Qadiri also existed among Sunni Muslims in Kordestan. There is no evidence of persecution of Sufis under the Republic, but the brotherhoods are regarded suspiciously and generally have kept a low profile.

Iran also contains Shia sects that many of the Twelver Shia clergy regard as heretical. One of these is the Ismaili, a sect that has several thousand adherents living primarily in northeastern Iran. The Ismailis, of whom there were once several different sects, trace their origins to the son of Ismail who predeceased his father, the Sixth Imam. The Ismailis were very numerous and active in Iran from the eleventh to the thirteenth century; they are known in history as the "Assassins" because of their practice of killing political opponents. The Mongols destroyed their center at Alamut in the Alborz Mountains in 1256. Subsequently, their living imams went into hiding from non-Ismailis. In the nineteenth century, their leader emerged in public as the Agha Khan and fled to British-controlled India, where he supervised the revitalization of the sect. The majority of the several million Ismailis in the 1980s live outside Iran.

Another Shia sect is the Ahl-e Haqq. Its adherents are concentrated in Lorestan, but small communities also are found in

Kordestan and Mazandaran. The origins of the Ahl-e Haqq are believed to lie in one of the medieval politicized Sufi orders. The group has been persecuted sporadically by orthodox Shias. After the Revolution, some of the sect's leaders were imprisoned on the ground of religious deviance.

Sunni Muslims

Sunni Muslims constitute approximately 8 percent of the Iranian population. A majority of Kurds, virtually all Baluchis and Turkomans, and a minority of Arabs are Sunnis, as are small communities of Persians in southern Iran and Khorasan. The main difference between Sunnis and Shias is that the former do not accept the doctrine of the Imamate. Generally speaking, Iranian Shias are inclined to recognize Sunnis as fellow Muslims, but as those whose religion is incomplete. Shia clergy tend to view missionary work among Sunnis to convert them to true Islam as a worthwhile religious endeavor. Since the Sunnis generally live in the border regions of the country, there has been no occasion for Shia-Sunni conflict in most of Iran. In those towns with mixed populations in West Azarbaijan, the Persian Gulf region, and Baluchestan va Sistan, tensions between Shias and Sunnis existed both before and after the Revolution. Religious tensions have been highest during major Shia observances, especially Moharram.

Non-Muslim Minorities

Bahais

The largest non-Muslim minority in Iran is the Bahais. There were an estimated 350,000 Bahais in Iran in 1986 (see table 4, Appendix). The Bahais are scattered in small communities throughout Iran with a heavy concentration in Tehran. Most Bahais are urban, but there are some Bahai villages, especially in Fars and Mazandaran. The majority of Bahais are Persians, but there is a significant minority of Azarbaijani Bahais, and there are even a few among the Kurds.

Bahaism is a religion that originated in Iran during the 1840s as a reformist movement within Shia Islam. Initially it attracted a wide following among Shia clergy and others dissatisfied with society. The political and religious authorities joined to suppress the movement, and since that time the hostility of the Shia clergy to Bahaism has remained intense. In the latter half of the nineteenth century, the Bahai leader fled to Ottoman Palestine—roughly present-day Israel—where he and his successors continued to elaborate Bahai doctrines by incorporating beliefs from other world religions. By the early twentieth century, Bahaism had evolved into a new religion that stressed the brotherhood of all peoples, equality of the sexes, and pacifism.

The Shia clergy, as well as many Iranians, have continued to regard Bahais as heretics from Islam. Consequently, Bahais have encountered much prejudice and have sometimes been the objects of persecution. The situation of the Bahais improved under the Pahlavi shahs when the government actively sought to secularize public life. Bahais were permitted to hold government posts (despite a constitutional prohibition) and allowed to open their own schools, and many were successful in business and the professions. Their position was drastically altered after 1979. The Islamic Republic did not recognize the Bahais as a religious minority, and the sect has been officially persecuted. More than 700 of their religious leaders were arrested, and several of them were executed for apostasy; their schools were closed; their communal property was confiscated; they were prohibited from holding any government employment; and they were not issued identity cards. In addition, security forces failed to protect Bahais and their property from attacks by mobs.

Christians

Iran's indigenous Christians include an estimated 250,000 Armenians, some 32,000 Assyrians, and a small number of Roman Catholic, Anglican, and Protestant Iranians converted by missionaries in the nineteenth and twentieth centuries. The Armenians are predominantly urban and are concentrated in Tehran and Esfahan; smaller communities exist in Tabriz, Arak, and other cities. A majority of the Assyrians are also urban, although there are still several Assyrian villages in the Lake Urmia region. Armenians and Assyrians were recognized as official religious minorities under the 1906 constitution. Although Armenians and Assyrians have encountered individual prejudice, they have not been subjected to persecution. During the twentieth century, Christians in general have participated in the economic and social life of Tehran. The Armenians, especially, achieved a relatively high standard of living and maintained a large number of parochial primary and secondary schools.

The new, republican Constitution of 1979 also recognized the Armenians and Assyrians as official religious minorities (see Constitutional Framework, ch. 4). They are entitled to elect their own representatives to the Majlis and are permitted to follow their own religious laws in matters of marriage, divorce, and inheritance. Other Christians have not received any special recognition, and there have been a number of incidents of persecution of Iranian

Anglicans. All Christians are required to observe the new laws relating to attire, prohibition of alcohol, and segregation by sex at public gatherings. Christians have resented these laws because they have infringed on their traditional religious practices. In addition, the administration of the Armenian schools has been a source of tension between Christians and the government. The Ministry of Education has insisted that the principals of such schools be Muslims, that all religion courses be taught in Persian, that any Armenian literature classes have government approval, and that all female students observe *hejab* inside the schools.

Jews

In 1986 there were an estimated 50,000 Jews in Iran, a decline from about 85,000 in 1978. The Iranian Jewish community is one of the oldest in the world, being descended from Jews who remained in the region following the Babylonian captivity, when the Achaemenid rulers of the first Iranian empire permitted Jews to return to Jerusalem. Over the centuries the Jews of Iran became physically, culturally, and linguistically indistinguishable from the non-Jewish population. The overwhelming majority of Jews speak Persian as their mother language, and a tiny minority, Kurdish. The Jews are predominantly urban and by the 1970s were concentrated in Tehran, with smaller communities in other cities, such as Shiraz, Esfahan, Hamadan, and Kashan.

Until the twentieth century the Jews were confined to their own quarters in the towns. In general the Jews were an impoverished minority, occupationally restricted to small-scale trading, money-lending, and working with precious metals. Since the 1920s, Jews have had greater opportunities for economic and social mobility. They have received assistance from a number of international Jewish organizations, including the American Joint Distribution Committee, which introduced electricity, piped water, and modern sanitation into Jewish neighborhoods. The Jews have gradually gained increased importance in the bazaars of Tehran and other cities, and after World War II some educated Jews entered the professions, particularly pharmacy, medicine, and dentistry.

The Constitution of 1979 recognized Jews as an official religious minority and accorded them the right to elect a representative to the Majlis. Like the Christians, the Jews have not been persecuted. Unlike the Christians, the Jews have been viewed with suspicion by the government, probably because of the government's intense hostility toward Israel. Iranian Jews generally have many relatives in Israel—some 45,000 Iranian Jews emigrated from Iran to Israel between 1948 and 1977—with whom they are in regular contact.

Since 1979 the government has cited mail and telephone communications as evidence of "spying" in the arrest, detention, and even execution of a few prominent Jews. Although these individual cases have not affected the status of the community as a whole, they have contributed to a pervasive feeling of insecurity among Jews regarding their future in Iran and have helped to precipitate large-scale emigration. Most Jews who have left since the Revolution have settled in the United States.

Zoroastrians

In 1986 there were an estimated 32,000 Zoroastrians in Iran. They speak Persian and are concentrated in Tehran, Kerman, and Yazd. Zoroastrianism initially developed in Iran during the seventh century B.C. Later, it became the official religion of the Sassanid Empire, which ruled over Iran for approximately four centuries before being destroyed by the Arabs in the seventh century A.D. After Iran's incorporation into the Islamic empire, the majority of its population was gradually converted from Zoroastrianism to Islam, a process that was probably completed by the tenth century.

During the Qajar era there was considerable prejudice against Zoroastrians. In the mid-nineteenth century, several thousand Zoroastrians emigrated from Iran to British-ruled India to improve their economic and social status. Many eventually acquired wealth in India and subsequently expended part of their fortunes on upgrading conditions in the Zoroastrian communities of Iran. The emphasis placed on Iran's pre-Islamic heritage by the Pahlavis also helped Zoroastrians to achieve a more respected position in society. Many of them migrated from Kerman and Yazd to Tehran, where they accumulated significant wealth as merchants and in real estate. By the 1970s, younger Zoroastrians were entering the professions.

Like the Christians and Jews, the Zoroastrians are recognized as an official religious minority under the Constitution of 1979. They are permitted to elect one representative to the Majlis and, like the other legally accepted minorities, may seek employment in the government. They generally enjoy the same civil liberties as Muslims. Although Zoroastrians probably have encountered individual instances of prejudice, they have not been persecuted because of their religious beliefs.

Education

Prior to the mid-nineteenth century, it was traditional in Iran for education to be associated with religious institutions. The clergy, both Shia and non-Shia, assumed responsibility for instructing youth in basic literacy and the fundamentals of religion. Knowledge of reading and writing was not considered necessary for all the population, and thus education generally was restricted to the sons of the economic and political elite. Typically, this involved a few years of study in a local school, or *maktab*. Those who desired to acquire more advanced knowledge could continue in a religious college, or *madraseh,* where all fields of religious science were taught. A perceived need to provide instruction in subjects that were not part of the traditional religious curriculum, such as accounting, European languages, military science, and technology, led to the establishment of the first government school in 1851. For many years this remained the only institution of higher learning in the country.

By the early twentieth century there were several schools teaching foreign languages and sciences, including a few for girls. These schools were run by foreign missionaries, private Iranians, and the government. Their function was to educate the children of the elite. During the Constitutional Revolution (1905–1907), a number of reform-minded individuals proposed the establishment of a nationwide, public, primary school system. Progress in opening new schools was steady but slow, and by the end of the Qajar dynasty (1925) there were approximately 3,300 government schools with a total enrollment of about 110,000 students.

During the Pahlavi era (1925–79), the government implemented a number of policies aimed at modernizing the country and expanded the education system. The Ministry of Education was given responsibility for regulating all public and private schools and drafted a uniform curriculum for primary and for secondary education. The entire public system was secular and for many years remained based upon the French model. Its objective was to train Iranians for modern occupations in administration, management, science, and teaching. This education system was the single most important factor in the creation of the secularized middle class.

The goal of creating a nationwide education system was never achieved during the Pahlavi era. In 1940 only 10 percent of all elementary-age children were enrolled in school, and less than 1 percent of youths between the ages of 12 and 20 were in secondary school. These statistics did not increase significantly until the early 1960s, when the government initiated programs to improve and expand the public school system. By 1978 approximately 75 percent of all elementary-age children were enrolled in primary schools, while somewhat less than 50 percent of all teenagers were attending secondary schools.

Modern college and university education also was developed under the Pahlavis; by the 1920s, the country had several institutes of higher education. In 1934 the institutes associated with government ministries were combined to form the University of Tehran, which was coeducational from its inception. Following World War II, universities were founded in other major cities, such as Tabriz, Esfahan, Mashhad, Shiraz, and Ahvaz. During the 1970s, these universities were expanded, and colleges and vocational institutes were set up in several cities.

One of the first measures adopted by the government after the Revolution in 1979 was the desecularization of the public school system. This was a three-pronged program that involved purging courses and textbooks believed to slander Islam and substituting courses on religion; purging teachers to ensure that only those who understood the true meaning of Islam (i.e., were not secular) remained in the schools; and regulating the behavior and dress of students.

Although the government reintroduced the study of religion into the public school curriculum from primary grades through college, it did not act to alter the basic organization of the education system. Thus, as late as the school year 1986–1987, schools had not changed significantly from the pattern prior to the Revolution. Students studied in primary schools for five years, beginning the first grade at about age seven. Then they spent three years, designated the guidance cycle, in a middle school. In this cycle, the future training of students was determined by their aptitude as demonstrated on examinations. Students were then directed into one of three kinds of four-year high schools: the academic cycle, preparing for college; the science and mathematics cycle, preparing for university programs in engineering and medicine; and the vocational technical cycle.

The Ministry of Education announced that nearly 11.5 million students were registered for elementary and secondary schools during the academic year 1986–1987. Statistics on the percentage of young people aged seven through nineteen enrolled in school have not been available since the Revolution. It is generally estimated that the percentages have remained similar to those before the Revolution: school attendance of about 78 percent of elementary-age children and less than 50 percent of secondary-age youth.

Since the Revolution, higher education has experienced significantly more drastic changes than elementary and secondary education. The university campuses became centers of conflict between students who supported a thorough desecularization of administrations, faculties, and curricula and students who wanted to retain a secular system. There were violent clashes at several universities in the 1979–1980 school year; as a result the government closed all 200 institutes of higher learning in April 1980. The universities then were purged of professors and students considered insufficiently Islamic and were not completely reopened until the fall of 1983. When the colleges resumed classes, they enrolled only a fraction of the 1979 to 1980 student body. At the University of Tehran, Iran's largest, student enrollment was reduced from 17,000 to 4,500; similarly large declines were registered at other institutions. The decline in the number of female students was even more dramatic: whereas on the eve of the revolution women had constituted about 40 percent of the total number of students in higher education, after 1983 they formed only 10 percent.

An educational problem in Iran since the early twentieth century has been the general perception among the upper and middle classes that foreign education is superior to Iranian. Thus, there have been large numbers of Iranians studying abroad. As long as the foreign-educated students returned to Iran, they were able to apply their skills for the overall benefit of the country; however, under both the monarchy and the Republic, thousands of Iranians have elected not to return to their homeland, creating a veritable "brain drain." Since the Revolution, the government has tried to discourage Iranians from going abroad to study, although it has not prevented the practice.

Health and Welfare

Medical Personnel and Facilities

According to the Iranian Medical Association (IMA), in 1986 there were 12,300 physicians and 1,700 dentists in Iran. Medical support personnel of all kinds were in short supply, with the total number of nurses estimated at around 7,000. There were about 550 hospitals throughout the country, with a total of 62,100 beds.

The regional distribution of medical personnel was uneven. The ratio of patients to physicians in 1986 averaged more than 1,000 to 1 for Tehran, Mashhad, Esfahan, and Shiraz; more than 2,000 to 1 in all other large cities (with more than 100,000 in population); and more than 4,500 to 1 elsewhere. An estimated 70 percent of all specialists practiced in Tehran.

Even before the Revolution there was a high rate of emigration of physicians, most of whom settled in the United States. In March 1976 when there were 12,196 physicians practicing in Iran, there were an estimated 10,000 other Iranian physicians practicing abroad. During the revolution there was a major exodus of physicians; the IMA has estimated that about 7,000—40 percent of the

A worker sprays to rid area of mosquitoes during a malaria-eradication campaign
Courtesy World Health Organization

total—have left the country since the Revolution, contributing to a severe shortage.

The Islamic Republic has sought to increase the number of all medical personnel and to expand medical facilities. Health clinics and dispensaries have been constructed in lower income neighborhoods of the large cities, in small towns, and in villages. The medical schools at Tehran and Shiraz universities have developed programs for training paramedical personnel, and more students have been admitted to medical schools. Nevertheless, the facilities for training physicians remained inadequate, and fewer than 750 doctors were graduated from medical schools between 1980 and 1986. The IMA has said that Iran needs a total of at least 50,000 physicians to provide the whole population with minimally adequate health care.

Health Hazards and Preventive Medicine

During the 1970s, apart from a high infant mortality rate, the chief causes of death were gastrointestinal, respiratory, and parasitic diseases. The incidence of cancer, diabetes, and heart disease was increasing. Several contagious diseases, such as grippe and influenza, conjunctivitis, scarlet fever, whooping cough, pulmonary tuberculosis, and typhoid fever were common. There is no evidence that the incidence of these diseases or the major causes of mortality have declined during the 1980s.

Drug addiction was a serious problem before the Revolution and reportedly has worsened since 1979. The Ministry of Health estimated in 1986 that there may have been as many as 1 million addicts in the country. Opium is the most commonly used drug. Since the end of the nineteenth century, opium has been smoked as a recreational drug at social gatherings. The Shia clergy have tried to discourage this practice by declaring the use of opium religiously prohibited. There is also some heroin use in the country.

In the 1970s and 1980s, the Ministry of Health carried out vaccination campaigns in both urban and rural areas. Periodic campaigns have included immunizations against measles, tuberculosis, diphtheria, tetanus, whooping cough, and poliomyelitis for infants and children, and general vaccinations against smallpox and cholera. These campaigns have prevented the outbreak of major epidemics.

Water Supply and Sanitation

In the mid-1980s, polluted water supplies remained one of the main reasons for the high incidence of parasitic and gastrointestinal diseases. Tehran and other large cities had chlorinated water systems, but contaminated water has continued to be a major problem in the smaller towns and villages. The disposal of waste also remained unsatisfactory. Tehran in 1986 still did not have a sewage system serving the entire city. Most of the other cities had only partial sewage systems, and in small towns and villages there were none at all.

Welfare

Religious and social traditions profoundly influence attitudes toward welfare. There is a general belief that fate determines living conditions, but most Iranians feel an obligation to help the needy in accordance with religious tenets. This idea has been reinforced since the Revolution by the persistent exhortations of the clergy to help the poorest people in society, the *mostazafin*. The giving of alms (*zakat*) is one of the mandatory obligations of the Islamic faith. As a consequence, donors of real property and monetary bequests are anxious that their names be attached to their gifts. Charitable donations may be distributed at any time, but Friday, the day of congregational prayers, is regarded as a particularly appropriate day, and even those of modest means regularly distribute food to the poor.

There is a long history in Iran of wealthy individuals' bequeathing part of their estates in the form of perpetual endowments, *vaqfs*, for a specified charitable purpose (see Religious Institutions and

Organizations, this ch.). The last dynasty established the Pahlavi Foundation, which funded programs ranging from low-cost housing projects to the preservation of national relics. After the Revolution, the government took over administration of the Pahlavi Foundation and renamed it the Foundation for the Disinherited (Bonyad-e Mostazafin). Some of its former programs, such as granting scholarships and operating cooperatives, have been continued, but others were redesigned or dropped entirely in favor of new projects that are in accord with religious ideology.

Government-funded social insurance programs have not been as important as the private *vaqfs*. The first workers in the country to benefit from a public retirement program were government employees. Legislation during the 1960s and 1970s provided for the extension of social security benefits to broader categories of employees, but by the time of the Revolution less than 10 percent of the total work force was actually covered by social security. The government of the Islamic Republic has said that extending coverage to all employed persons is one of its priorities, but as of 1986 no information was available about what measures may have been adopted to extend coverage.

The first public housing projects were built in the 1960s in the southern part of Tehran. These were developments of small, single-family homes that were sold to the occupants at subsidized cost over several years. Public housing projects expanded to other cities during the 1970s. After the Revolution, the Republic continued to budget funds for the construction of low-cost public housing, although prior to 1985 its efforts in this area focused primarily on the provision of interest-free, long-term loans to encourage private construction on public land.

Since 1985 the government has built low-cost public housing, particularly in Tehran and in large cities that suffered considerable damage during the war, such as Ahvaz and Dezful. Priority for such housing has been given to widows of men killed during the war.

This housing is an example of the kind of social program that the revolutionary regime felt ideologically committed to provide as a way of assisting the less fortunate, the *mostazafin*. Other examples of concern for the poorer elements of society were the construction of elementary schools, bathhouses, and health clinics in villages and low-income urban areas and the emphasis on religious charitable giving to the disadvantaged. This concern for the deprived members of society was a traditional element of Islam that had been neglected to a considerable degree under the shah but which was being emphasized by the revolutionary government.

* * *

The most complete analysis of Iranian society prior to the Revolution is *Iran Between Two Revolutions* by Ervand Abrahamian. *Roots of Revolution* by Nikki R. Keddie is an excellent study of the cultural tensions between the secularized middle and upper classes and the religiously oriented bazaar class, and it examines the relationship of this social conflict to the Revolution. The background of Shia clerical opposition to secular state policies is thoroughly examined in Shahrough Akhavi's *Religion and Politics in Contemporary Iran.* The most detailed study of social class divisions is *Iran: Dictatorship and Development* by Fred Halliday. A detailed analysis of several important policies implemented during the early years of the Republic is *The Reign of the Ayatollahs* by Shaul Bakhash. A fascinating fictionalized account of how the secularized classes have reacted to the Islamic Republic is *Sorraya in a Coma* by Ismail Fassih. (For further information and complete citations, see Bibliography.)

Chapter 3. The Economy

A ninth century ceramic plate from Neyshabur

REGARDLESS OF THE CHANGES in politics and ideology brought about by each successive regime in Iran, the one constant has been lack of fundamental economic change for the majority of Iran's people. Since the Islamic Revolution in 1979, Iran has repudiated the Western-style modernization initiated by Reza Shah Pahlavi and continued by his son, Mohammad Reza Shah Pahlavi. The postrevolutionary government of Ayatollah Sayyid Ruhollah Musavi Khomeini condemned the Pahlavi policy of allowing all countries to invest in, and trade freely with, Iran as unsatisfactory on political and cultural grounds and initiated a program of "self-reliance." Moreover, the modern production techniques introduced by the Pahlavis had eventually proved inappropriate for Iran because they required large capital investments. Having rejected Western models as inimical to the needs of Iran and being obliged to manage a wartime economy, the post-revolutionary government cut imports of luxury goods, began rationing subsistence items, nationalized industries, and expanded direct taxation. By late 1987, the result was a shortage of many goods that had once been imported, an insufficiently productive agricultural system, high unemployment, and a greater dependence than ever on revenues from oil and gas exports.

In the early 1920s, only a few large or modern industrial plants were in operation in Iran. The population was overwhelmingly rural, and transportation remained primitive. Except for the petroleum industry, still in its formative stage, production was geared to small, local markets. Increasing quantities of oil were produced for the international market, but with little impact on the domestic economy.

After establishing the Pahlavi dynasty in 1925, Reza Shah began to modernize Iran by developing a strong central government and entering Western markets. The results were mixed. The government improved communications, built an education system modeled on the Western example, and began construction of the Trans-Persian Railway. Centralization led, however, to authoritarianism, a state monopoly on foreign trade, and stagnant agricultural productivity. Many Iranians continued to reside in small, isolated settlements, and an estimated one-quarter of the population consisted of fiercely independent nomadic tribesmen. Modernization threatened the nomads' way of life and generally brought little benefit to Iran's undereducated, underemployed population because it focused on the development of capital-intensive industries rather than of labor-intensive enterprises.

When Mohammad Reza assumed power in 1941, he attempted to continue his father's modernization efforts (see The Post-Mossadeq Era and the Shah's White Revolution, ch. 1). By 1978 Iran had experienced great changes, but progress had been uneven for various elements of the population and different parts of the country over the preceding half-century. The Revolution of 1979 substituted "self-reliance" for Westernization as the focus of development. The importing of luxury goods, such as color televisions and stereos, was stopped, and the funding for development and construction in particular was cut significantly. Reductions in construction spending affected the entire economy and sent the gross national product (GNP—see Glossary) on a downward spiral. The budget cuts made in the name of "self-reliance," after the Revolution in 1979 and the onset of the war with Iraq in 1980, did additional damage to the economy.

During the 1970s, oil and gas exports remained Iran's main source of foreign exchange. This dependence increased in the years immediately following the Revolution, as the price of oil peaked at US$40 per barrel. Although non-oil exports began to drop sharply because of the 1980 international recession, earnings from oil exports remained high until the mid-1980s, when the price of oil began to decline. Oil revenues began to fall in 1984 and by 1985 averaged only US$1 billion per month, the approximate equivalent of the cost of continuing the war with Iraq. By 1986 monthly oil revenues averaged US$6.5 million per month. After 1984 the decline in oil revenues and the cost of the war created budget deficits. Consequently, the government reduced nonmilitary spending, which did further damage to the national economy. Domestic food production became insufficient, which forced Iran to import 65 percent of the food that it needed and to ration essential items such as meat, rice, and dairy products. Black marketing, long lines for consumer goods, and high unemployment exacerbated the effects of nonmilitary budget cuts. To ameliorate the situation, the government tried to reduce its dependence on declining oil revenues by investing in other key industries, such as copper and steel production. As of late 1987, however, economic problems remained severe and essential commodities scarce.

The Revolution of 1979 held forth to the Iranian populace the promise of "national integrity" through "self-reliance." Although intended to change Iran's economic and political course, the Revolution had produced no structural changes in the economy by late

1987. The growing need to sell oil on the international market demonstrated Iran's continuing inability to isolate its economy.

By late 1987, Iran was actually more dependent on oil than ever before. As in Reza Shah's time, attempts at modernization had been initiated by an autocratic government that stressed Iran's "unique" identity. In the late 1980s, that identity increasingly has been defined by Islam, rather than by any particular economic policy. Although much economic activity has occurred within Iran since 1979, the lack of fundamental change has been the constant. Oil earnings have fluctuated, banks have been nationalized, industries have developed—yet the power structure has merely shifted from the shah's circle to the clerical class.

Role of the Government

The central economic role of government in post-World War II Iran has been the manipulation and allocation of oil revenues. Since the beginning of the production of petroleum in commercial quantities in the 1920s, government oil policies have reflected the varying priorities of the different regimes and have exacerbated economic and cultural cleavages within the society.

During the reign of Reza Shah (1925–41), oil revenues were modest, and most of the proceeds from oil went to Britain through the Anglo-Iranian Oil Company (AIOC). For its revenues, the regime relied upon indirect taxes (customs duties and excise taxes) on items such as tea and sugar. In contrast, after 1951, the government of Mohammad Reza Shah (1941–79) relied on oil income to finance the policies of centralization by which it was able to control most aspects of Iranian society until nearly the end of the shah's rule.

Reza Shah's regime financed its development programs through modest oil royalties, customs revenues, personal income taxes, and state monopolies. During his reign, oil production royalties, although still low, quadrupled in terms of the rial (for value of the rial—see Glossary); this money was spent on defense and industrial development. Between 1926 and 1941, higher tariffs boosted annual customs revenues from approximately US$5.6 million to US$16.3 million. Institution of a small income tax replaced the local levies and enabled the government to extend its influence into the provinces; by 1941 the income tax provided annual revenues of US$10.8 million. Finally, the government relied upon state monopolies on consumer goods such as sugar, tobacco, tea, and fuel, which contributed approximately US$46.5 million annually by the early 1940s.

The Beginnings of Modernization: The Post-1925 Period

Reza Shah introduced the concept of centralized economic planning to Iran at the expense of older societal values and traditions (see The Era of Reza Shah, 1921–41, ch. 1). Reza Shah consolidated power by developing support in three areas: the army, the government bureaucracy, and the court circle. Once his power was consolidated, he pursued economic, social, and cultural reforms. Reza Shah believed that the secret of modernization lay in replacing many religious and social norms of traditional society with the values of a twentieth-century nation-state. Reza Shah's policies favored the urban over the rural, the wealthy over other classes, and industry in general over agriculture. Developing this "new order" gradually cost Reza Shah most of his base of support. Nevertheless, government centralization enabled him to achieve full control over the economy.

Economic development began with the expansion of the transportation system. The first project was the expansion of the Trans-Persian Railway. In the first five years of his reign, Reza Shah developed a network of railroads that connected ports to inland cities, thereby encouraging trade between rural and urban centers. By 1941 railroads crossed Iran from north to south and from east to west (see Transportation and Telecommunications, this ch.).

The existence of a modern transportation system by the 1930s encouraged industrial growth, which was further promoted by government financial incentives. Construction of modern manufacturing plants was a high priority, as was the development of whole industries rather than small, individual factories. Financial incentives included government-sanctioned monopolies, low-interest loans to prospective factory owners, and financial backing for plants and equipment by the Ministry of Industry. The number of industrial plants (excluding those processing petroleum) increased 1,700 percent during Reza Shah's reign.

In 1925 only about twenty modern plants existed, of which five were relatively large, employing about fifty workers each. By 1941 the number of modern plants had risen to 346, of which 146 were large installations. These large plants included thirty-seven textile mills, eight sugar refineries, eleven match factories, eight chemical companies, two glassworks, one tobacco-processing plant, and five tea-processing plants.

Between 1926 and 1941, the oil industry labor force increased from 20,000 to 31,000. By 1941 the oil industry employed 16,000 workers at the Abadan refinery and another 4,800 at drilling sites in Khuzestan. These wage earners, in conjunction with those

A copper artisan plies his trade on a street in Esfahan
Courtesy United Nations

employed in emerging modern industrial enterprises, formed a working class of about 170,000 and represented about 4 percent of the total labor force in 1941.

Rapid industrial growth created a modern, urban working class that nonetheless coexisted with people who had more traditional occupations, values, and ways of life. This new industrial work force developed in the five major centers, where 75 percent of the modern factories were located: the towns of Tehran, Tabriz, and Esfahan, and the provinces of Gilan and Mazandaran. Tehran's population alone increased from more than 196,000 in 1922 to about 700,000 by 1941. Modernization accelerated the pace of life through changes in culture, education, and traditional social norms, including those governing the role of women.

The cost of developing the military establishment, centralized ministries, large-scale industrial plants, and institutions of higher education increased the budget nearly 1,800 percent during Reza Shah's reign. The Iranian national budget grew from approximately US$15 million in 1925 to US$166.5 million in 1941 (based on the 1936 exchange rate). Because industrial development was predicated on oil revenues, the government's lack of control over the oil industry created periodic tensions with foreign oil companies. The emphasis on industrial development also demonstrated the need for development planning.

The concept of development planning by the government dates back to 1947, when it was initiated by Mohammad Reza Shah's government as a series of seven-year cycles. The Plan Organization consisted of leading government officials, who provided guidelines from which a development strategy was formed. Planning had a direct impact on the public sector because of its effect on allocations of capital expenditures. In Iran's mixed economy, however, the planners had no direct power over private sector investments and development; instead, they had to rely on indirect measures, such as fiscal and financial incentives.

The First Development Plan (1948–55) failed, except for strengthening the role of the Plan Organization, which, after 1973 was called the Planning and Budget Organization and in January 1985 was transformed by the parliament, or Majlis (see Glossary), into a ministry. The basic development strategy was the pragmatic approach of accelerating growth by incorporating the latest technology into large-scale, capital-intensive industry. Expansion of the infrastructure, however, preceded the development of industry. The planners often built ahead of demand, creating physical and economic incentives for the private sector. Diversification of industry was also a goal, although the planners recognized that the excessive dependence on oil revenues would have to continue at first to provide the capital to diversify. Diversification was intended to facilitate import substitution, and development of large-scale industry meant that many plants producing for export could achieve economies of scale.

The Second Development Plan (1955–62) focused on public sector expenditures, with an investment program to be funded by foreign loans and 80 percent of oil revenues. The government spent so much money, however, that the regime faced severe inflation and depleted foreign currency reserves by fiscal year (FY—see Glossary) 1959. Although Iran was experiencing economic problems, the plan provided for the construction of several reservoir dams, the most important of which were located on the Dez, Safid, and Karaj rivers. Simultaneously, private sector investment in light industry remained strong until the economic crisis that began in 1959.

During the middle and late 1950s, economic instability exacerbated chronic social problems, such as overcentralization of government, concentration of land in the hands of relatively few wealthy landlords, enormous bureaucracy, and regressive tax laws. As early as 1949, the shah voiced his intention to consider needed changes, especially in land reform. It was not until the 1960s, however, that he actually instituted agrarian reform. The intervening decade was a period of consolidation following the regime of Reza Shah; it also featured a period of government control by Mohammad Mossadeq (see Mossadeq and Oil Nationalization, ch. 1).

Oil Revenues and the Acceleration of Modernization, 1960–79

During the reign of Mohammad Reza Shah, significant increases in oil revenues, coincident with the centralization of the economy, compounded societal stress and imbalance. The modernization that continued throughout the shah's rule affected the economic infrastructure but not the monarchical political structure. The gap between the two was accentuated by the Western industrial policies promulgated by the shah.

In the 1960s, economic planning focused on four main goals. The first was rapid development of large industries by capital-intensive methods and the use of the latest technology; the second was employment of foreign advisers and technicians to guide the modern industrial complex. The third was encouragement of large industrial profits, and the fourth was control of wages by reallocating savings from labor costs to capital investment. It was assumed that wealthy industrialists would reinvest their capital in the economy, thereby stimulating economic development. But such investment did not occur, and the gap in income between industrial owners and the commercial class, or bazaar (traditional middle class merchants), was never closed, which contributed to the revolutionary pressures that eventually brought down the regime. The bazaar did not benefit from the 1974–78 oil boom; as a consequence, bazaar members helped lead and finance the Revolution.

The series of national reforms and development programs that Mohammad Reza Shah had embarked on in the 1950s came to be known in 1963 as the "White Revolution" (see The Post-Mossadeq Era and the Shah's White Revolution, ch. 1). The White Revolution was simultaneously the shah's attempt at economic modernization and his attempt at political stabilization. He intended to accelerate nation-building and to enhance his regime's image as the promoter and guardian of the public welfare.

Land reform was a major element of the shah's economic development program. Land reform affected both the economic structure and the social mores of the agrarian component of society. The Third Development Plan (1962–68) and the Fourth Development Plan (1968–73) together infused US$1.2 billion into agriculture through land reclamation, subsidized irrigation projects, and land redistribution programs. These programs undermined traditional rural authority figures, encouraged commercial farming, and transformed the rural class structure. By the 1970s, the rural class was divided into three components: absentee farmers, independent farmers, and rural wage earners (see Land Use, this ch.).

The third plan was transitional to a new time frame of five years for development plans. Oil revenues supported the US$1.9 billion national budget, which fostered an economic boom in the public and private sectors. The government concentrated its activities on heavy industries, dam building, and public utilities, as well as on expansion of oil and gas production. Private industry benefited from bank credits given as part of the third plan.

The fourth plan accelerated economic growth and integrated sectoral and regional concerns into a national development program. During the fourth plan, the annual rate of growth in gross domestic product (GDP—see Glossary) averaged 11.8 percent, which exceeded the growth target. The strongest growth occurred in industry, petroleum, transportation, and communications. Several large projects under construction during the fourth plan included a steel mill, an aluminum smelter, a petrochemical complex, a tractor plant, and a gas pipeline leading to the Soviet border. Farming and crop production were given low priority during this period of industrialization, which widened the large gap between the industrial and agricultural sectors.

The third and fourth development plans affected the urban population in particular because of the emphasis on the increased production of consumer goods and the expansion of industries such as gas and oil. Between 1963 and 1977, many industrial facilities were constructed, primarily in urban areas.

The Fifth Development Plan (1973–78) set investment at US$36.5 billion; this figure almost doubled to US$70 billion as a result of large increases in oil revenues during the period. Almost two-thirds of the capital allocated under the fifth plan was concentrated in housing, manufacturing and mining, oil and gas projects, and transportation and communications. Some additional oil revenues were spent on ad hoc defense and construction projects rather than on the fifth plan's priority areas.

In the period between the quadrupling of oil prices in 1973 and mid-1977, Mohammad Reza Shah pushed both industrialization and the establishment of a modern, mechanized military much too rapidly. As a result, inflation increased, corruption became commonplace, and rural-to-urban migration intensified. In addition, because of a lack of technically trained Iranian personnel, the shah increasingly brought foreign consultants into Iran. This further exacerbated an already severe housing shortage in Tehran.

In mid-1977, the shah appointed Jamshid Amuzegar as prime minister, and the latter immediately launched a deflationary program. This sudden slowdown in the economy led to widespread unemployment, especially among unskilled and semiskilled workers, which further increased the gap between rich and poor. The economic slowdown was a major factor in radicalizing large segments of the population and turning them against the shah.

Some argue that rapid modernization created the disequilibrium that brought about the shah's fall. Others, however, stress the importance of the way in which the rapid modernization was implemented. After the economy's initial development, inequalities in income distribution were not addressed. Those at the lower end of the economic spectrum—for example, small merchants and businessmen, urban migrants, and artisans—felt disadvantaged in relation to workers in large businesses, industries, and enterprises with foreign associations. Western-educated Iranians rapidly became a well-paid elite, as did factory workers. Bazaar merchants, students, and the ulama, however, did not benefit so directly from modernization.

The increased availability of health and educational resources in towns and cities that resulted from Mohammad Reza Shah's programs contributed to an explosion of the urban population. In the 1950s, urban areas accounted for 31 percent of the population; by the late 1970s, that number had increased to about 50 percent. The urban population became stratified into an upper class, a propertied middle class, a salaried (managerial) class that included the bazaar, and a wage-earning working class.

The Post-1979 Period

The disparity between the economic promises of the shah's regime and the results as perceived by the majority of Iran's citizens contributed to a revolutionary climate in the late 1970s. When the revolutionary regime came to power in 1979 (on the heels of the economic downturn of the late 1970s), it claimed that modernization and Westernization had nothing to offer Iran, as the recession had made evident. Islam, not economic planning, was cited as the basis for correcting the perceived ills of Iranian society stemming from the alleged excesses of the shah. The regime came to power criticizing Mohammad Reza Shah's failed agricultural policies and promising self-sufficiency and economic independence. The government adopted an emphasis on agriculture as the foundation of its program. To consolidate power quickly among the rural poor, the Khomeini regime capitalized on popular resentment of the shah for having largely ignored the agricultural sector.

All six of the development plans designed under the shah aimed at economic development; the Sixth Development Plan, intended for 1978–83, was never implemented because the Revolution occurred in early 1979. The First Development Plan of the Islamic Republic (1983–88) proclaimed that its goals were to establish Iran's economic independence through self-sufficiency in foodstuffs and to reduce the country's dependence on oil exports.

The first "republican" plan focused on five points: expanding education, representing the interests of the *mostazafin* (the disinherited), achieving economic independence, diversifying the economy to lessen the dependence on oil and gas exports, and developing agriculture. The development plan did not include a factor for defense expenditures. Criticism of this plan resulted in its revision in 1984, although the changes were not approved by the Majlis until January 1986. The revision included an increase in the investment in agriculture (from 15.5 to 16.7 percent of the national budget) and a smaller investment in non-oil industry (the share fell to 52 percent). Projected oil revenues in this version of the plan were based on the lower oil price prevailing in 1985.

The budget for the first republican plan was US$166 billion, but the allocation of funds was delayed because of political and economic pressures. The political pressures came from newly empowered groups and individuals interested in using the social disruption caused by the Revolution to create their own financial empires, free of state control. The war with Iraq also affected funding for the first republican plan.

Oil revenue shortfalls caused the first republican plan to be revised again in early 1987. The shortfalls, in combination with the expenses associated with the Iran-Iraq War, resulted in nearly half the budget being allocated to military goods. Imports of consumer products were cut in half, and projects under the development plan were given low priority (see fig. 6). Austerity measures and increased unemployment resulted.

Gauging the relationship between government economic policy and actual operation of the economy subsequent to the Revolution of 1979 is difficult because official economic policy has been obscured by religious and ideological themes. Iran's financial system began adhering to Islamic principles after the Revolution, a process that accelerated in the 1980s. Although the Planning and Budget Organization prepared budgets, in coordination with several other ministries, the Majlis, the majority of whose members were Muslim religious leaders, was responsible for ratification (see The Majlis, ch. 4).

The budget presented a financial outline within which outlays were planned for military purposes, education, and other government activities. There was an increasing discrepancy between budget estimates for the war and actual costs. Whereas the government claimed in 1982 that 13 percent of the total budget was spent on defense, independent analysts claimed that the figure rose from 11.5 percent of the budget in 1979 to 46.9 percent in 1982. However unreliable the Iranian claims about defense spending, one thing was increasingly clear: the Iranian government dedicated virtually all foreign exchange resources, including both advance drawings on revenues and uncollectible receivables (which were counted as assets), to prosecution of the war.

Inflation was a serious issue in the mid-1980s. The increase in prices, which was beyond the control of the monetary authorities and the Central Bank—founded originally in 1960 as Bank Markazi Iran and renamed Central Bank (Bank Markazi) of the Islamic Republic of Iran in December 1983—began in the 1970s with the rapid rise in oil revenues and equally rapid increases in government expenditures. The latter had a multiplier effect on the money supply and added to the demand for goods and services, thereby inducing price rises. The monetary authorities attempted to minimize the multiplier effect by increasing the cost of borrowing and tightening credit. Imports increased as a result of lower duties, relaxed quotas, and an increase in government purchases of foreign goods. Bottlenecks at the ports and elsewhere in the transportation system limited the capacity of imports to satisfy demand, however.

Efforts to reduce inflation date to 1973, when a serious price control program was initiated. The government took additional measures to curb inflation in May 1980 by linking the rial to the Special Drawing Rights (SDRs—see Glossary) of the International Monetary Fund (IMF—see Glossary) instead of the United States dollar and by encouraging investment in the private sector and growth in non-oil industries. In addition, subsidies on basic goods were increased to keep their prices down. Nevertheless, a 30-percent inflation rate persisted, a black market rate on the United States dollar flourished, and foreign exchange controls continued.

Inflation was continually understated by the government. The government asserted that the inflation rate had fallen from 32.5 percent in FY 1980 to 17 percent in FY 1983 and to 5.5 percent in FY 1985; independent analysts, however, claimed that a more accurate inflation rate for 1985 was 50 percent. As essential goods grew scarcer in the wartime economy, import controls fed inflation. Prices of basic foodstuffs and consumer goods increased faster than the Central Bank admitted. The increasing cost of rental property in urban areas and continued subsidies for consumers on basic foods reflected a serious inflationary problem in the mid-1980s.

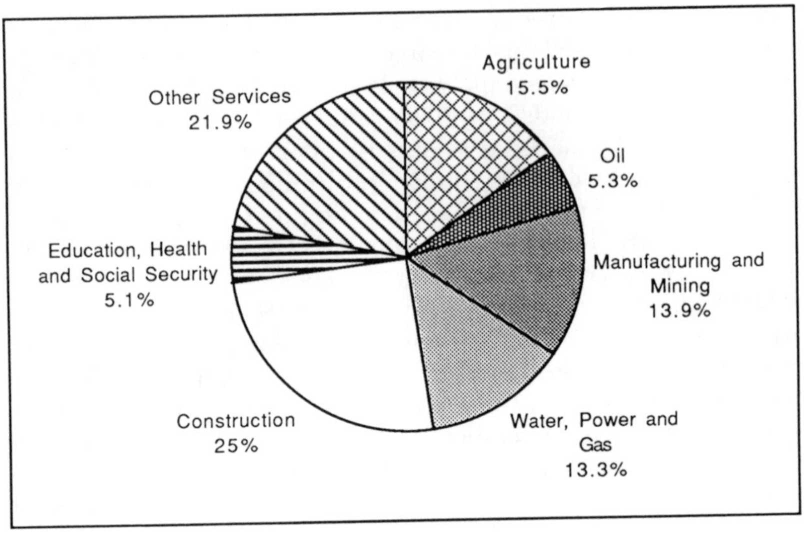

Source: Based on information from Iranian government publications and Economist Intelligence Unit, *Iran Country Profile, 1986–87,* London, 1987.

Figure 6. First Development Plan of Islamic Republic of Iran, 1983–88

To the surprise of many, the Majlis increased the FY 1986 budget in March 1986, even though oil revenues were projected downward. The increase went mainly to finance military spending and the steel and nuclear industries. The rising costs of the war, coupled with falling oil prices in 1986, led to the use of non-oil exports to generate revenue because oil income was no longer a guaranteed source of foreign currency (see Non-Oil Exports, this ch.). To finance short-term debts, Iran drained its small reserve of foreign currency by allowing advance drawing on revenues.

The FY 1987 budget also reflected the priority of the war effort. The government again promised to curb inflation, to continue to subsidize basic foodstuffs, and to make available to the import sector a revolving fund of US$7 billion, presumably for consumer use.

Monetary and Fiscal Policy

The Iranian fiscal year begins on March 21 and runs through March 20 of the following calendar year. The budget, presented to the Majlis by the Planning and Budget Organization, consists of three sections: ordinary, plan, and defense allocations. Because of conflict between the Revolution's stated opposition to the massive defense expenditures of the shah and the high cost of the war with Iraq that began less than one year after the Revolution, as of late 1987 there had been no fiscal year in which defense expenditures were not severely understated for domestic political reasons. As a result, attempting to set forth actual figures on the money supply, especially as a function of fiscal policy, was almost pointless.

Banking

Western-style banks and insurance came late to Iran, but protected and stimulated by the government and fed by expanding economic activity, banking became one of the fastest growing sectors of the economy in the 1960s. The insurance industry had barely started in 1960 and had a negligible role in the accumulation of funds to finance development, largely because insurance was not used by most of the population.

Before the modern era in Iranian banking, which dates to the opening of a branch of a British bank in 1888, credit was available only at high rates from noninstitutional lenders such as relatives, friends, wealthy landowners, and bazaar moneylenders. In 1988 these noninstitutional sources of credit were still available, particularly in the more isolated rural communities. Institutional banking spread rapidly in the late 1960s; by 1988 almost all small towns were served by at least one bank. None of these operations were private because banks were nationalized in 1979.

In 1960 Bank Markazi Iran was established as the central bank. Later legislation further defined its powers and responsibilities. The bank issued notes and acted as banker for the government, keeping accounts, marketing government securities, maintaining foreign exchange reserves, and overseeing international transactions. It also set standards for the supervised financial institutions, established credit and monetary policies, and took measures to enforce credit and monetary policies. The banking laws limited foreign participation to 40 percent in any banks operated in Iran (except the Soviet bank, which had been founded much earlier). Subsequently, the Central Bank limited foreign ownership in new banks to 35 percent.

By 1977 the banking system consisted of the Central Bank, twenty-four commercial banks, twelve specialized banks, and three savings and loan associations (these numbers decreased after the Revolution). The commercial banks had more than 7,400 branches, including a few in other countries. The specialized banks focused mostly on a particular kind of lending (e.g., industrial or agricultural loans), although three regional banks specialized in financing local development projects. In addition, in 1977 approximately seventy foreign banks (primarily from the major industrial nations) had representative offices in Iran, but they conducted no local banking business. Their purpose was to facilitate trade relations.

All domestic banks and insurance companies in Iran were nationalized in 1979. In 1980 the twenty-nine domestic banks remaining after the Revolution were consolidated into nine units. Foreign banks in Iran declined in number to thirty by 1987 and included the representative office of a small Soviet bank that financed trade. French banks were excluded from the Iranian market in 1983, leaving those of the Federal Republic of Germany (West Germany), as well as Swiss, Japanese, and British banks to finance about 30 percent of total trade.

Immediately after the Revolution, the government called for the establishment of an Islamic banking system (which became law in March 1984) that would replace interest payments with profit sharing. In Islamic terms, this meant that profit (interest) was acceptable only if a lender's money were ''not at risk.'' The introduction of Islamic banking procedures was gradual; confusion and delays disrupted the initial stages of implementation. In March 1985, the Islamic code was extended to include bank loans and advances. By late 1987, however, only certain banks were fully Islamicized, and only about 10 percent of private deposits were subject to Islamic rules.

The Central Bank controlled the issuance of letters of credit. These were deferred payment instruments that relieved the cash-flow problem Iran experienced after oil prices began to decline in 1983. The government financed many imports with these high-interest letters of credit. Originally a letter of credit was to be repaid within 180 days, but by 1987 Iranian customers wanted 720 days' credit. Up to US$4 billion in letters of credit remained outstanding in early 1987, but the government did not include these supplier credits when assessing its foreign debt.

The Central Bank established a good reputation in international banking circles in the 1980s. It had practically no long-term foreign debt in early 1987—only US$5 million—and was recognized as an international creditor. Between 1979 and 1984, the government paid cash for US$66 billion worth of imports, and it repaid immediately US$7 billion of existing debts. The Central Bank's reputation for honoring its financial obligations, however, did not change the attitudes of West European bankers, who, in a 1987 poll, expressed their unwillingness to lend money to Iran. To help relieve its cash-flow problem after 1983, the government sought repayment from several countries of money they borrowed from Iran during the reign of the Mohammad Reza Shah.

In the first quarter of 1986, Iranian deposits in international banks fell by US$570 million, reducing Iran's holdings to US$7.1 billion. This reduction coincided with the continued fall in oil revenues, and foreign exchange deposits were expected to decrease further in the late 1980s.

Taxes

In the past, Iranian officials had focused on increasing non-oil tax revenues, particularly through direct taxes on personal and business income. A major reform of the tax laws in 1967 nearly doubled direct tax revenues within two years. Additional legislation in the 1970s had the effect of increasing the importance of direct taxes, which grew to US$2.5 billion in FY 1976, up from US$156 million in FY 1967.

Like most developing countries that produced oil, Iran had relied on indirect taxes (customs duties and excise taxes) for most of its non-oil revenue. Indirect taxes accounted for 72 percent of non-oil tax revenues in FY 1962, 60 percent in FY 1972, and 45 percent in FY 1976. In FY 1986, indirect taxes fell 12 percent as a result of a 30-percent reduction in customs duties.

The rapid increase in oil production and oil revenues in the 1970s freed Iranian officials from having to develop the tax system. As a consequence, the narrow tax base focused on consumers generally and on the urban, salaried middle class specifically. In 1977 fiscal authorities attempted to reform the tax system. But the numerous exemptions, particularly those that had been granted to industries to encourage private investment, presented obstacles to the continued expansion of direct taxes.

By 1985 government workers were paying a disproportionate amount of Iran's taxes—nearly three-quarters of all taxes in FY 1984—according to the government. For example, in the last few months of 1984 about US$16 million was collected from individuals in the private sector and US$510 million (or 76 percent of tax revenues) from government employees.

Taxes were expected to contribute US$15.7 billion to the budget in FY 1987, an amount 11.2 percent less than that approved the previous year. In the FY 1987 budget, direct taxes were reduced to a level that accounted for 46 percent of tax income, while indirect taxes accounted for 53 percent. Companies accounted for most of the direct taxes (54 percent). Of the indirect taxes, 40 percent came from taxes on imports, and 60 percent from consumption and sales taxes. A decrease in imports resulted in an overall decline in tax revenue.

The decline in revenue from indirect taxes (such as customs duties) in FY 1986 caused total tax revenues to fall 1 percent below the FY 1985 level. The collection of direct taxes simultaneously increased by 9.5 percent, partly because of a new option that permitted payment of taxes into a regional development fund. Businesses paid income taxes at a higher rate than individuals, and the tax rate on government corporations was higher than that on private businesses.

The War's Impact on the Economy

Iraq's attack on Iran in September 1980 provided the new Iranian government with an external scapegoat to divert attention from its own economic mismanagement. The war created economic dislocation, decreased industrial and petroleum development, and caused further deterioration of the agricultural sector, which had already suffered from the flight of landlords in 1979 and 1980.

Oil Exports

Iraq attacked Iranian ports, the oil terminal at Khark (then the main export terminal for crude oil, also cited as Kharg) Island and, beginning in 1984, tankers shuttling between Khark and Sirri islands in the Persian Gulf. The heavy damage to refineries and pipelines, factories, and industrial sites hurt oil production but did not significantly slow the export of oil until 1986; between 1982 and 1986, Iran produced 2.3 million barrels per day (bpd—see Glossary) on average (see table 5, Appendix). The combined effects of decreased oil production and falling oil prices, however, created an economic crisis and a shortage of foreign exchange by 1986. The destruction in 1980 of the important Abadan refinery (which produced an average of 628,000 bpd), the bombing of refineries and shuttle tankers, and the continued embargo on purchases of Iranian oil by Japan, the United States, and France contributed to the crisis. By November 1987, Iranian oil exports were estimated at 1 million bpd, down from an estimated 1.9 million bpd the previous month.

The Iraqi strategy of interrupting Iran's export supply line dated back to February 1984, when Iraq attacked tankers shuttling between Khark and Sirri islands. The terminal and cargo handling jetties on Khark Island were hit, reducing the island's export capacity from 6.5 million bpd to 2.5 million bpd within 3 months. This new tactic did not halt Iranian oil exports, but it did decrease them. As a consequence of lower export earnings, the new budgets showed deficits in fiscal years 1985 and 1986.

After the bombings of Khark Island, Iran developed Sirri Island as an alternate terminal. Operations began on Sirri Island in February 1985. Iraq attacked the refinery there on August 12, 1986, temporarily disrupting Iran's oil exports, and again in the fall of 1986, this time inflicting damage from which Iran took longer to recover.

As a consequence of the early 1984 bombings, insurance rates for tankers in the Gulf increased. The increase prompted Iran to extend special incentives to tankers to compensate for the risk involved. During the Iraqi attacks, Iran's main crude oil customer, Japan, banned its tankers from the Khark-Sirri shuttle. After Iran began giving preferential treatment to certain customers, Japan resumed its shipments in July 1984.

The August 1986 attacks on Sirri Island caused oil exports to fall to about one-third of their normal volume (from 1.6 million bpd to 600,000 bpd). An effort was made to develop Larak Island as a loading point, but monsoon winds temporarily closed Abu al Bukush, Larak Island's main oil terminal, in September 1986. Iraqi attacks on Larak Island's chief remaining oil export terminal in November and December 1986 further damaged it. By November 1987, Larak Island had recovered and had become Iran's main export point because of its distance from Iraq's air bases and because of its air defense system.

The oil export terminal at Lavan Island, which for years had exported 200,000 bpd, was also severely damaged in an attack in September 1986. The success of this attack made it clear that Iraq was gradually destroying Iran's export industry. By the end of 1986, the Iraqis had bombed Khark, Sirri, and Larak islands, as well as the shuttle tankers to Sirri and Larak; thirteen tankers had been damaged in missile attacks in August 1986 alone. The war also postponed the completion (projected for 1989) of a large petrochemical plant at Bandar-e Khomeini (formerly known as Bandar Shahpur, but renamed after the Revolution), an Iranian-Japanese venture.

War Costs

Half of Iran's revenue was spent on arms imports in the mid-1980s. In order to dedicate half its budget to military expenditures, Iran was forced to reduce such essential imports as food, for which it spent about US$4 billion annually from 1983 to 1987. Rationing of essentials such as meat, rice, and dairy products after the beginning of the war resulted in long lines at shops and an active black market. Sometimes the need occurred, as in the spring of 1987, to add nonfood consumer items to the rationing list. These austerity measures gave rise to the possibility of political instability.

Because of the war, trade had to be rerouted through the Soviet Union and Turkey, which increased transportation costs. The war also caused Iran to deplete its foreign reserves and to depend on foreign suppliers for needed goods. Military equipment accounted for about 25 percent of total imports by the mid-1980s, and the budget for FY 1987 showed that funds for the war exceeded financial allocations to all other economic sectors. The total cost of the war from its beginning in 1980 until early 1987 was more than US$240 billion (based on a total of US$200 billion by the end of 1984 and a cost of US$20 billion for each year thereafter). If lost oil revenues were taken into account, the cost of the war through 1987 would be even higher.

Labor Force

Data on Iran's labor force after the Revolution were incomplete in mid-1987, but the economically active population was estimated to be about 12.5 million. Unemployment had been a serious problem since 1979. In the autumn of 1986, the government announced that 1.8 million persons—about 14.5 percent of the labor force—were registered as unemployed. This was a high percentage by comparison with the 1975 International Labour Organisation's unemployment estimate of 3.5 percent. In 1987 economists believed that underemployment was also relatively high.

Agriculture remained the principal source of employment in the late 1980s. The decline in the size of the agricultural work force had been much more gradual since the Revolution than during 1949–79. At the end of World War II, approximately 60 percent of the work force was employed in agriculture; by 1979 the percentage of workers in agriculture had fallen to just under 40 percent. In 1987 an estimated 38 percent of the work force, or nearly 4.8 million workers, was employed in agriculture.

The industrial sector in 1987 employed about 31 percent of the work force, the same percentage as on the eve of the Revolution. From the 1920s until 1978, the industrial work force grew rapidly, especially during the 1970s, when industrial employment grew at an annual rate of 14 percent. The relative stasis of industrial employment in comparison to its rapid expansion before the Revolution has been attributed by economists to the war with Iraq, especially to the destruction of important industrial infrastructure in the southwestern part of the country (see fig. 7).

According to an Iranian government report for FY 1984, the industrial work force employed in factories with 10 or more laborers totaled some 593,000. About 25 percent of this number, or 145,000 workers, was employed in the textile and leather industries. Another 141,000 workers were employed in heavy industries.

The service sector employed about 31 percent of the work force in 1987. All commercial activity and most civil service jobs were considered part of this sector. A substantial proportion of service sector employment, however, was in marginal activities such as custodial work, street vending, and personal services such as barbering, attendant work at public baths, consumer goods repairs, and the performance of porter duties in town bazaars.

At the time of the Revolution in 1979, an estimated 1.3 million Iranians (13 percent of the work force) were women. (Rural women working the fields were not counted as part of the work force.) Female employment was highest in manufacturing, which accounted for an estimated 60 percent of all working females. Women were employed extensively in the textile mills and in labor-intensive manufacturing jobs requiring few skills and offering relatively low pay, such as carpet making and other handicrafts undertaken in factories, small workshops, and homes. Many women were employed in services as well. About 20 percent of working females were employed in domestic and other personal services and accounted for nearly 17 percent of all employment in this category. Less than 20 percent of working women were government employees, and a tiny minority held professional positions.

After the Revolution, work opportunities for professional women and those working in offices were severely constricted. The government opposed having women work in jobs that would enable them to render legal opinions or supervise males. Official statistics, however, indicated that the number of women in the labor force remained relatively constant because women were needed to work in war-related plant jobs. The government survey for FY 1984 reported that females made up more than 12.6 percent of the urban labor force and 6 percent of the industrial work force. The total number of women in the labor force in 1985 was 1.6 million, of whom about 18 percent were unemployed. Of the 1.3 million women actively employed, approximately 43 percent worked in urban areas; 61 percent of urban women workers were government employees.

Two factors for which there were no reliable data in 1988 affected the labor force after 1980: the war with Iraq and the presence of Afghan refugees. On the one hand, more than 500,000 working-age males were removed from the labor force at any given time for military service. War-related casualties removed additional tens of thousands of potential workers. On the other hand, many Afghan refugees, of whom there were slightly more than 2.3 million

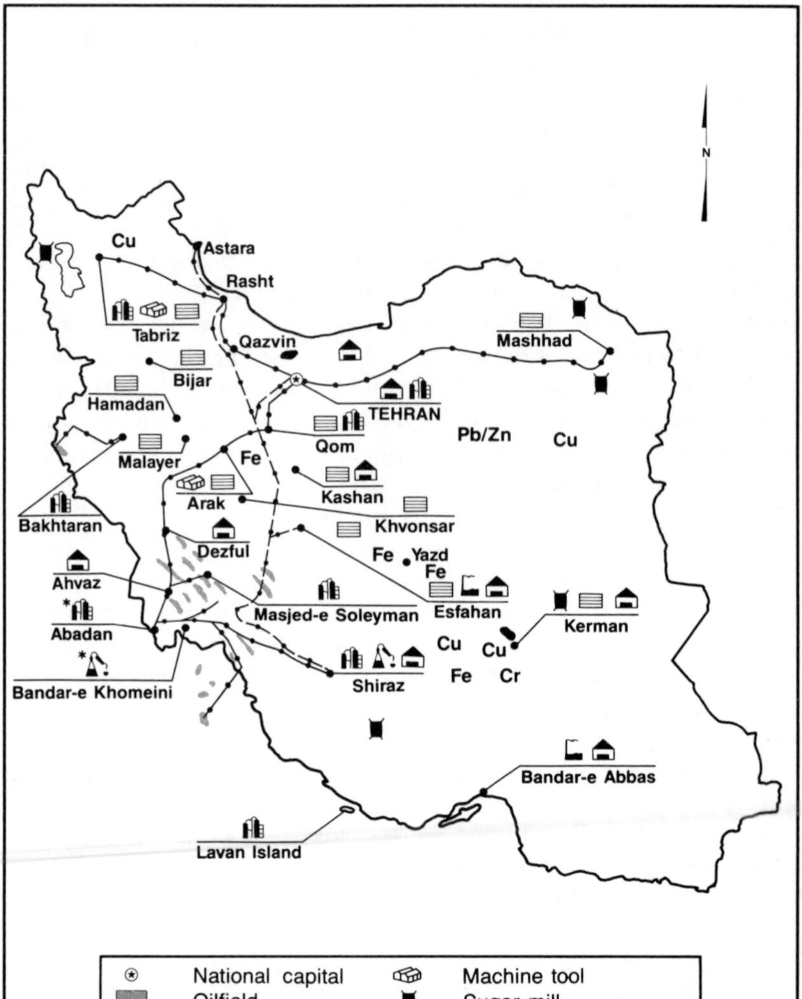

Figure 7. Industry and Mining, 1987

according to the preliminary 1986 figures, were working in Iran after 1980, most in unskilled jobs (see Refugees, ch. 2). There were no meaningful estimates of the number of workers who may have lost jobs because of the extensive war-inflicted destruction of industrial sites and commercial enterprises between 1980 and 1987.

Petroleum Industry

Following the quadrupling of oil prices in the last quarter of 1973, prices remained relatively stable from 1975 to 1978. During this period, Mohammad Reza Shah encouraged a high level of oil production and increased spending on imported goods and services and on military and economic aid to a small number of Iran's allies. Khomeini's government shifted the emphasis by decreeing a policy of oil conservation, with production reduced to a level sufficient to do no more than meet foreign exchange needs.

The efforts, initiated by the shah, to develop the petrochemical industry were thwarted by the Iran-Iraq War. The shah had begun a large petrochemical plant at Bandar Shahpur (now Bandar-e Khomeini) to produce fertilizers and sulfur; the plan was to expand production to include aromatics and olefins in a joint venture with Mitsui, a Japanese consortium. The plant, which cost US$3 billion, had almost been completed at the time of the Revolution. Iraqi planes bombed the still-unfinished plant in late 1986. Other petrochemical plants were completed soon after 1979, including the Khemco sulfur plant on Khark Island and a fertilizer plant at Marv Dasht near Shiraz.

The global recession of the early 1980s depressed the demand for oil. Iranian exports were also affected by the increased production by countries that were not members of the Organization of Petroleum Exporting Countries (OPEC—see Glossary). The resulting glut on the market caused a decline in Iranian oil revenues, which in turn lowered the value of the Iranian GNP. From September to October 1980, output fell from 1.3 million bpd to 450,000 bpd. Iran's petroleum production increased, however, to 2.4 million bpd in both 1982 and 1983, which enabled the government to end domestic rationing (see table 5, Appendix). However, production fell again in 1986 to 1.9 million bpd. OPEC prices for crude oil meanwhile fell from US$34 per barrel in 1982 to US$29 in March 1983. The government reduced oil exports in the early 1980s to promote a higher price per barrel and to foster conservation. Oil production fell as planned, although not as low as during 1980–81. By 1987 oil and gas exports produced only enough revenue to meet basic needs.

Oil revenues financed the import of weapons, food, medicine, and other critical goods and services by the mid-1980s. Whether or not the oil sector would be able to sustain losses as Iraq continued to target Iranian oil production and transportation facilities remained to be seen in late 1987. In addition to bombings of Iranian shuttle tankers, the Iranian oil industry was also troubled by fluctuating prices. Oil revenues decreased in 1985 and early 1986, remained steady in late 1986, and rose gradually in 1987. The government attempted to compensate for lost revenues in 1987 by further reductions in nonmilitary programs.

Oil and Gas Industry

Petroleum has been the main industry in Iran since the 1920s. Iran was the world's fourth largest producer of crude oil and the second largest exporter of petroleum at the peak of its oil industry in the mid-1970s. The war with Iraq cut Iran's production in the 1980s, although Iranian oil reserves remained the fourth largest in the world.

Nationalization of the oil industry in 1951 resulted in temporary political and financial chaos. Production did not resume until late 1954 (see Mossadeq and Oil Nationalization, ch. 1). As part of the nationalization process, the government formed the National Iranian Oil Company (NIOC). As owner, the government directed NIOC policy. As a result of the Consortium Agreement reached in 1954 between the government and a consortium of foreign oil companies, industry control of the oil companies was left virtually intact, but the agreement greatly increased the government's share of income from each barrel of oil produced. The combination of the larger share of income and rising oil production provided the government with increased revenues with which to finance industrial development. In addition, slow but steady progress was made in reestablishing Iran's relations with Western powers in the aftermath of nationalization. The resolution of the oil crisis in 1954 (nationalization of oil and the signing of the Consortium Agreement) led to a policy of increased economic and political cooperation between Iran and states outside the Soviet sphere of influence. In 1961 Iran joined with other major oil-exporting countries to form OPEC, whose members acted in concert to increase each country's control over its own production and to maximize its revenues.

When Iran's economy worsened after the outbreak of war with Iraq, its willingness to abide by OPEC guidelines decreased. From 1983 to 1984, OPEC priced oil at US$29 per barrel, but Iran undercut OPEC prices at US$28 per barrel through October 1984 and subsequently reduced it even further to US$26.50 per barrel. Iran continued deliberate undercutting until the pricing crisis in July 1986, when prices dropped below US$10 per barrel and the oil-exporting countries met to reach agreement on both price and production levels. The thirteen members of OPEC, and several non-OPEC countries, agreed in December 1986 to a price of US$18 per barrel, with a maximum differential of US$2.65 between light and heavy crude oil. (Light crude is the source of products such as gasoline and is more expensive, whereas heavy crude provides the components used in products such as residual fuel, oil coke, and waxes.) By January 1987, as a result of war damage and government conservation policies, crude production averaged 2.2 million bpd, about 100,000 bpd below Iran's OPEC quota.

Production and Reserves

In 1986 Iran's reported crude oil reserves of 48.5 billion barrels ranked behind only those of Saudi Arabia, the Soviet Union, and Kuwait. By February 1987, the NIOC estimated that Iran's recoverable oil reserves had nearly doubled from the 1986 level to 93 billion barrels, a figure that could not be verified by outside specialists. In the first half of 1986, Iran had produced 1.9 million bpd of oil, of which 800,000 bpd went for domestic consumption and 1.1 million bpd for export. Production dropped during 1986 as a result of the oil pricing crisis and the bombings of Khark Island and Sirri Island. By early 1987, oil exports had increased and neared the level set in OPEC's December 1986 agreement, averaging 1.5 to 1.7 million bpd.

Iran made strides in the development of the gas industry as well, with efforts dating back to the 1960s. One area of emphasis was the extraction of "associated" gas, natural gas found in solution with oil, which previously had been flared. In 1966 Iran reached agreement with the Soviet Union to deliver up to 28 million cubic meters of gas per day. In return, the Soviets committed equipment and expertise to build a steel mill, an engineering plant, and other related facilities. In 1966 the government also formed the National Iranian Gas Company, a wholly owned subsidiary of NIOC, to produce gas for both domestic consumption and export. By October 1970, the Iranian gas trunkline had been completed, capable of moving gas from the southwestern Iranian oil fields to the Soviet border at Astara on the Caspian Sea. Spur lines branched off the trunkline to major Iranian cities, supplying gas primarily for industrial use. Pipeline capacity reached 45.3 million cubic meters per day by 1975. Iran had made a heavy investment in developing the gas industry by 1977, anticipating a decline in oil production in the early 1980s.

Gas production increased from 20 billion cubic meters in 1980 to about 35 billion cubic meters in 1985. Much of this increased production, however, was flared (an inefficient but inexpensive process), peaking in 1982 at over 50 percent of gas produced (14.2 billion cubic meters flared of 24.5 billion cubic meters produced), largely as a result of Iraqi destruction of facilities for producing and reinjecting natural gas. Recovery of natural gas improved thereafter, with flaring accounting for less than 22 percent of production in 1984 and 17 percent in 1985.

The development of the Iranian gas industry was bolstered by the discovery of several natural gas fields in 1973 and 1974. Reserves in 1974 stood at 7.5 trillion cubic meters, and by 1977 known natural gas reserves amounted to 10.6 trillion cubic meters. According to Iranian sources, natural gas reserves in Iran were the second largest in the world at 13.8 trillion cubic meters in proven reserves as of 1987. This was more than the combined reserves of the entire Western world. Additional gas deposits were discovered in Baluchestan va Sistan Province in August 1986. Only Soviet reserves, estimated to be some 3.5 times larger, surpassed Iran's. Despite its enormous reserves, Iran exported no gas from 1980, when a pricing agreement with the Soviet Union was canceled and the gas trunkline to the Soviet Union was closed, to 1987. Because the Soviets refused to pay Iran's price, Iran turned its gas reserves to domestic industrial, commercial, and residential use. In August 1986, Iran announced that it would resume the export of natural gas to the Soviet Union, with the expectation of returning eventually to the previous export level of 10 billion cubic meters per year. Subsequently, the resumption of natural gas export was postponed and no deliveries had occurred as of the end of 1987.

Concession Agreements

Commercial extraction of oil began at the turn of the century, when exploration and exploitation rights were granted to foreigners. The first of these was an Englishman, W.K. D'Arcy, who in 1908 discovered commercial quantities of petroleum. D'Arcy's discovery led to the formation of the Anglo-Persian Oil Company in 1909, which, after 1935, operated as the Anglo-Iranian Oil Company (AIOC).

Disagreements over revenues arose almost immediately between the government and the newly formed oil company. The interpretative agreement reached in 1920 temporarily quieted matters. When revenues fell sharply at the beginning of the Great Depression, however, Iran canceled the concession, causing Britain to take the case to the League of Nations in 1932. Before the league came to

Petroleum is the engine that drives the Iranian economy
Courtesy United Nations (E. Adams)

a decision, a significant modification of the original concession was negotiated by Iran and the company acting on their own. Royalty payments, previously a share of company profits, were supplanted by a fixed payment per ton of oil produced. Minimum payments to the government were established, and the life of the concession was extended by 32 years (until 1993), although the concession area was reduced about 80 percent.

After continued disputes over the terms of the contract with the AIOC, the Majlis voted to nationalize the petroleum industry in 1951. In 1954 the AIOC was renamed the Consortium, reflecting the 40-percent ownership held by British Petroleum, 14 percent by Royal Dutch Shell; 7 percent each by Gulf Oil, Socony-Mobil, Esso (later Exxon), Standard Oil of California, and Texaco; 6 percent by Compagnie Française des Pétroles; and 5 percent by various interests collectively known as the Iricon Agency. The Consortium's concession was to run through 1979, with the expectation of negotiable fifteen-year options. Instead, at the request of the Iranian government, in 1973 the Consortium agreed to form a new agency to market Iranian petroleum. The Consortium members in return received a privileged buyer status for a twenty-year supply of crude petroleum.

This agreement was interrupted because of strikes in the oil fields in 1978 during the rebellion against Mohammad Reza Shah.

Petroleum exporting was not resumed until his departure on January 16, 1979. Subsequently, the NIOC canceled the 1973 marketing agreement with former Consortium members, offering them instead a special nine-month supply agreement, after which they lost special buyer status.

Refining and Transport

At the beginning of 1977, Iran had six refineries in operation, with a combined capacity of more than 800,000 bpd. In 1986 Iran had refineries operating in Esfahan, Tabriz, Bakhtaran (formerly known as Kermanshah), Shiraz, Qom, Tehran, and Lavan Island, with a combined capacity of more than 1 million bpd. All contributed to the domestic supply of petroleum products, but the Abadan refinery in the late 1970s produced primarily for export. The high cost of transportation led to regional location of refineries. Pipelines brought the crude oil from the fields to the refineries for processing and regional distribution of products.

The Abadan refinery, located on the Persian Gulf, was completed in 1912 and, until bombed and destroyed in 1980 by Iraq, remained one of the world's largest, with a capacity of 628,000 bpd. Foreign oil companies had operated it until the 1973 NIOC takeover. About 20 percent of its production had gone to the domestic market in the early 1970s, but in 1973 the NIOC geared the industry toward domestic needs and local consumption. The Abadan refinery was linked by pipeline to several fields and a seaport; the pipeline ran from Abadan north to Tehran, and then along Iran's northern border from Tabriz in the west to Mashhad in the east.

The other refineries were smaller than the one at Abadan. Two, built and operated by the NIOC, were located near Tehran to supply that market; one was completed in 1968 and the other in 1975. Both were supplied by pipelines from the southwestern oil fields. An additional pipeline also carried petroleum products from the Abadan refinery for distribution in the Tehran area.

Crude oil for the Bakhtaran refinery came from a field close to the Iraqi border; the Shiraz refinery, completed in 1973 with a capacity of 40,000 bpd, distributed its products in the southern and eastern parts of the country. A topping plant (see Glossary), constructed in the 1930s, operated at Masjed-e Soleyman in southwestern Iran. It supplied oil for the domestic market and sent distillates by pipeline to the Abadan refinery.

A refinery in Tabriz, constructed in 1975 and having a capacity of 80,000 bpd, supplied the northwestern area of the country. Petroleum consumption had increased rapidly in the northwest, and a pipeline was completed by 1976 from Tehran to Tabriz to supply crude to the refinery.

Khark Island, located 483 kilometers from the mouth of the Persian Gulf and about 25 kilometers off the coast of Iran, was the principal sea terminal until bombed by the Iraqis in 1985 and 1986; it had been the world's largest offshore crude oil terminal. Export of refined products then reverted to the terminal at Bandar-e Mashur in southwestern Iran, which had been used before the construction of the Khark Island installation.

The availability of new oil terminals allowed Iran to expand its oil production. In the 1960s, crude was sent to Abadan, then exported from Abadan and Bandar-e Mashur. The construction of the Khark Island terminal to export crude oil permitted use of Bandar-e Mashur exclusively for product exports. Some 95 percent of the crude oil came from the producing fields of Agha Jari, Karenj, Marun, Pariz, Bibi Hakimeh, and Ahvaz.

During the 1980s, the Khark Island terminal continued to be responsible for 80 percent of oil exports. Khark Island had two terminals, one on a jetty and the other on a small island off the west coast of the island. The first was a complete complex, and the second was used for quick loading of ships. The jetty was bombed by Iraq to disrupt Iran's main shipping point in early 1985 and again more heavily in September 1985. Shipments were slowed at the jetty, and the island terminal section was devastated.

Aside from Bandar-e Mashur, other export facilities were developed both inside and outside the Persian Gulf. To reduce the threat from Iraq, facilities were expanded at the port of Jask, located just outside the Persian Gulf on the Gulf of Oman, and Sirri Island became an alternative loading point. A petroleum shuttle was initiated between Khark and Sirri islands, and Khark Island continued to export most of the country's oil until additional Iraqi bombing in January 1986. Reduced exports remained possible through the use of the shuttle service to Sirri Island, with its floating terminal for storage and reloading. The August 1986 bombing of shuttle tankers to Sirri and the resulting increase in insurance rates, however, prevented even this level of exports. Because the pipelines for Khark converge at a pumping station at Ganaveh (about forty kilometers northeast of Khark on the Gulf) before going underwater, Ganaveh replaced Khark as the western terminus of the oil shuttle to Sirri Island in the mid-1980s.

Non-Oil Industry

Government incentives to bolster domestic industry were offered in the mid-1980s, but they were offset by the effects of the war.

Factories were forced to lay off workers or to shut down because of declines in imports of as much as nearly 50 percent. This decline resulted in raw material shortages. Other state and private industrial enterprises converted to production of military matériel.

In the mid-1980s, Iran halted importation of domestically producible machinery. As an incentive to domestic production, industries that produced war matériel were granted about US$400 million to replace items whose import value would have exceeded US$1.3 billion. Domestic production increases by 1986 resulted in local manufacture of 80 percent of required munitions, including an antitank missile and such items as gas masks for protection against Iraqi chemical weapons. Industrial production held steady in early 1987, following a 20 percent drop in 1985 from 1984. The Ministry of Heavy Industries anticipated US$75 million in industrial exports in FY 1986.

Among the projects scheduled for funding in FY 1987 were a pesticides plant at Qazvin and the completion of a steel plant at Mobarakeh. There were also plans to construct mineral processing plants in the northwestern city of Zanjan that would produce 40,000 tons of lead and 60,000 tons of zinc annually.

The non-oil industrial sector represented a small portion of the economy, but it provided labor-intensive domestic employment, such as the hand knotting of rugs. Foreign sales of Iran's non-oil products also generated badly needed hard currency. Iran exported US$2.3 billion worth of non-oil goods between 1982 and 1987. Of this total, agricultural products accounted for 32.2 percent, carpets 29.3 percent, textiles 10.9 percent, and caviar 4.9 percent (see Non-Oil Exports, this ch.).

In 1986 Iran started placing greater emphasis on non-oil sectors to offset falling oil prices and revenue. Non-oil revenue totaled about US$700 million in 1986, in comparison with oil revenues of less than US$1 billion. Although it had increased by US$200 million over the previous year, non-oil revenue fell short of the official goal of US$1 billion. Carpet sales accounted for most of the increase, whereas exports of such items as industrial goods and minerals decreased. The FY 1987 target for non-oil exports was doubled to US$1.4 billion, including US$50 million in locally made goods.

Carpets

After the 1979 Revolution, the customary high volume of carpet exports was sharply reduced because of the new regime's policy of conserving carpets as national treasures and its refusal to export them to "corrupt Westerners." This policy was abandoned in 1984

The manufacturing of carpets and rugs is an important element in Iran's economy
Courtesy United Nations (John Isaac)

in view of carpets' importance as a source of foreign exchange. Carpet exports more than tripled in value (from US$35 million to US$110 million) and doubled in weight (from 1,154 tons to 2,845 tons) between March and August 1986, which contributed to a fall in world carpet prices.

Construction

The economic prosperity fueled by the growing oil revenues of the mid-1970s encouraged a construction boom. The expansion of the construction industry slowed, however, and all but stopped after the Revolution. Construction continued to decline until 1984. The domestic recession, created by deliberate government reductions in oil production in 1979, caused a drop in new construction starts, fewer buyers, and a decreased demand for materials.

In FY 1983, the government decided once again to encourage private sector participation in construction. The subsequent increase in loans to private industries by commercial banks revived the construction industry by 1984, although it could not keep pace with housing needs in urban areas.

The housing shortage became severe by 1986. Exacerbated by population pressures, the shortage was an especially serious problem in Tehran. The allocation of credit for building construction accounted for 7 to 8 percent of the GNP. Half of all the 900,000 housing applicants countrywide were in Tehran, yet only half of these received housing. Tehran issued 25 percent of the country's housing permits, with fixed construction investment accounting for 2 percent of the GNP. The government deliberately discouraged further expansion in Tehran, and new building construction regulations in 1986 tied construction permits to the ownership of land through an earlier order from a religious magistrate. According to the director of the Urban Land Organization, a government body created in June 1979 to administer the transfer of nationalized land to deserving families for housing purposes, the housing sector in early 1986 needed about US$10 billion to alleviate the shortage. The banks could only provide about US$4 billion of this total.

Manufacturing and Industrial Development

The first phase of modern industrial development occurred under Reza Shah in the 1930s. When Mohammad Reza Shah succeeded his father in 1941, he began a planning process designed to hasten economic modernization. During the mid-1950s, the state encouraged and supported the building of fertilizer, sugar-refining, cement, textile, and milling plants. By the late 1950s, the government had provided a role for private business by authorizing generous credits from the Plan Organization.

Industrialization led to a rapid increase in manufacturing output. Many new industries were established between 1962 and 1972. The impressive new range of domestic manufacturing enterprises included iron and steel, machine tools, agricultural implements, tractors, communications equipment, television sets, refrigerators, car and bus assembly, and petrochemical products.

Higher oil revenues in the 1970s accelerated economic development. A number of large-scale industrial projects were undertaken during the period of the Fifth Development Plan (1973–78), with government investments concentrated in petrochemicals and basic metal industries as well as crude oil production. Domestic and international private investment was projected to furnish 64 percent of a planned total of US$11 billion for manufacturing investments between FY 1973 and FY 1977. The economy proved incapable of absorbing such feverish growth, however; some projects were postponed, and completion dates were extended for others. Nevertheless, industrial production grew at close to 20 percent per year, and a diversified industrial base was established. By FY 1975, manufacturing and mining (excluding electric power and construction) contributed about 10 percent of GDP.

Shortages of skilled labor and equipment adversely affected production from 1977 onward. Business failures and a generally declining economy led to strikes and political instability in 1978 and 1979. The flight of capital and factory owners after the 1979 Revolution led to the nationalization of industries in the summer of 1979. The decline of the industrial sector was hastened by the war with Iraq; Iraqi bombing of petrochemical and steel plants in Abadan, Ahvaz, and Bandar-e Khomeini in 1980 and 1981 caused further disruption. Recovery began in 1982, but only among smaller industries. Efforts to revive the larger industrial and petrochemical plants began in 1982 and 1983. As a result of technical advances, the Esfahan steel mill was expected to produce 700,000 tons of iron rods in FY 1987—enough to meet domestic needs. In May 1987, Iran's minister of mines and metals reported that twenty exploration projects were under way, aimed at supplying raw materials for the country's steel plants.

The war with Iraq slowed industrial production but also created a new industry, the manufacture of prosthetics. In August 1986, the head of the Iranian Rehabilitation Agency stated that more than 2 million handicapped individuals had sought the rehabilitation services offered by his agency in 1985 but that the agency was capable of serving only 40,000 newly handicapped persons annually. In response to this need, Iran reportedly planned to increase to six the number of factories producing artificial limbs and other prosthetic devices.

Mining and Quarrying

Iran's mineral wealth, in addition to oil and gas, includes chromite, lead, zinc, copper, coal, gold, tin, iron, manganese, ferrous oxide, and tungsten. Commercial extraction of significant reserves of turquoise, fireclay, and kaolin is also possible. Most mining was small scale until modernization efforts in the 1960s led to the systematic recording of known deposits, as well as the systematic search for new ones. Industrialization increased the need for steel, which in turn boosted demand for coal, iron ore, and limestone. Construction of new roads and railroads since the 1960s improved transportation among mining centers throughout the country, especially around the Kerman-Bafq area of south-central Iran.

Prior to the Revolution in 1979, the government intended to develop the copper industry to the point that it would rival oil as a source of foreign exchange. Iranian copper deposits are among the world's largest, and mining is particularly advanced southwest of Kerman near Sirjan. The Iran-Iraq War risks and declining world copper prices inhibited copper extraction, which prior to

FY 1982 had remained insignificant. The government, however, promoted private sector investment in copper in FY 1982, which may have been responsible for the improved copper output in 1983.

In the 1980s, Iran's major nonmetallic mineral exports were chromite and construction stone. Iran's total chromite reserves were estimated at 20 to 30 million tons in 1987. Exports of construction stone to the Persian Gulf countries increased 200 percent in 1986 over the previous year.

The government conducted surveys in the 1970s to ascertain the commercial potential of known mineral deposits. By 1977 about half the country had been surveyed from the air, but less than one-fifth had been explored on the ground. Studies of mineral deposits throughout the country were completed in the mid-1980s, detailing the most recent discoveries of reserves of silica, limestone, granite, and iron ore. In addition, several uranium deposits were discovered in Baluchestan va Sistan in August 1986, and in September 1986 another 750,000 tons of white kaolin deposits on the Iran-Afghanistan border near Birjand were reported.

The extent of mineral resources was indicated by the fact that approximately 2.7 million tons of minerals were extracted from 27 active mines in Yazd Province in FY 1986. Iran earned a total of US$85 million from mineral exports in that year.

Utilities

In 1963 the Iranian government created a hydroelectric management authority. Its functions were incorporated into the Ministry of Water and Power in 1967. The electric power industry had been nationalized in 1965 so that a large, integrated system might be built. In 1967 all water resources were nationalized except generators attached to industrial plants (see Water, this ch.).

The Fourth Development Plan (1968–73) ushered in a new phase of utility development designed to add 4,915 million cubic meters of storage capacity for water, which in turn would generate electricity. Projects designed under this program were completed after the Revolution; they included dam projects in Halil Rud (Jiroft), Shahrud (Taleghan), Lar, Minab, and Qeshlaq.

By 1972, about one-quarter of the population had electricity, and approximately 3,218 kilometers of transmission and distribution lines had been constructed as the start of a national system. Two smaller, separate networks were centered on Kerman in the south central area and Mashhad in the northeast.

During the 1960s and early 1970s, the rapid growth of manufacturing, increasing urbanization, and the extension of electrical service to more of the population put great pressure on planners to

Laborers weigh and process jute in a small mill
Courtesy United States Information Agency

build ahead of demand. They did not always succeed, even with extensive foreign advice. For example, industrial development was temporarily held up in the vicinity of Bandar-e Abbas because of insufficient power, and by mid-1977 brownouts and blackouts were frequently disrupting industry. Nevertheless, many experts favored building a network with large, interconnected power stations rather than the more costly and inefficient construction of separate facilities to head off each impending local shortage. The near doubling of investment goals for the fifth plan compounded the problem of keeping the power supply ahead of demand, however, for it meant a substantial increase in the number of industrial consumers.

In the 1980s, the government began to emphasize the development of steam-powered plants, as part of a plan to reduce hydroelectric power from 25 percent to 10 percent of available national energy by the end of the century. Reversing this policy in the mid-1980s, Minister of Energy Mohammad Taqi Banki stated that hydroelectric power had once again been given priority for reasons of environmental safety and higher productivity.

By the end of 1986, 17 dams were operating with a total energy generation capacity of 7,000 megawatts, a 10-percent increase over 1985. Construction on the Qom River of a US$130 million dam with a 200-million-cubic-meter capacity was scheduled to begin in December 1986. It would supply the northern city of Qom, seventy kilometers away, with drinking and irrigation water. A three-megawatt power station was planned nearby. A feasibility study for a US$1 billion hydroelectric dam on the Karun River was submitted in early 1987. This dam, which would take 6 years to build, would generate 800 megawatts of electricity and replace 2 other proposed dams.

Iran's total electric power capacity was approximately 12 million kilowatts in 1985, the most recent year for which statistics were available in 1987. It produced almost 42 billion kilowatt-hours in 1985, compared with 33 billion kilowatt-hours in 1983. In the FY 1987 budget, the Ministry of Water and Power was authorized to raise electricity rates for consumers who used more than 250 kilowatts, with a further increase for those using more than 400 kilowatts, in order to boost revenues by US$830.4 million.

The national supply of electricity dropped 40 percent in early 1986 because of Iraqi bombing of power plants. The minister of energy announced that the shortages began in January because of severe gas shortages at the power plants in Esfahan, Lowshan, Rasht, Rey, and several other locations. Again, in December 1986, the minister of energy announced impending power cuts as a result of shortfalls in generation.

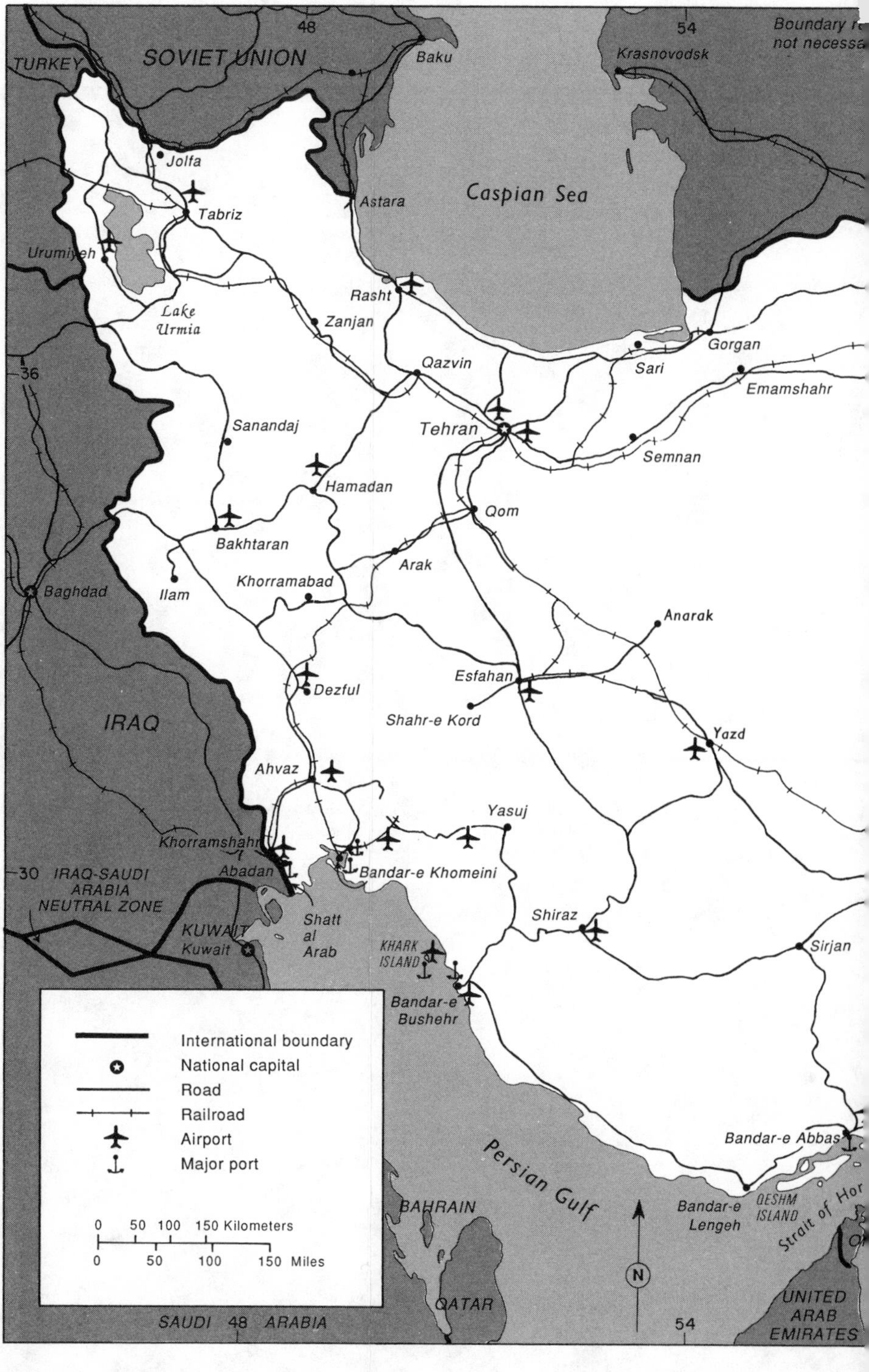

Figure 8. Transportation System, 1987

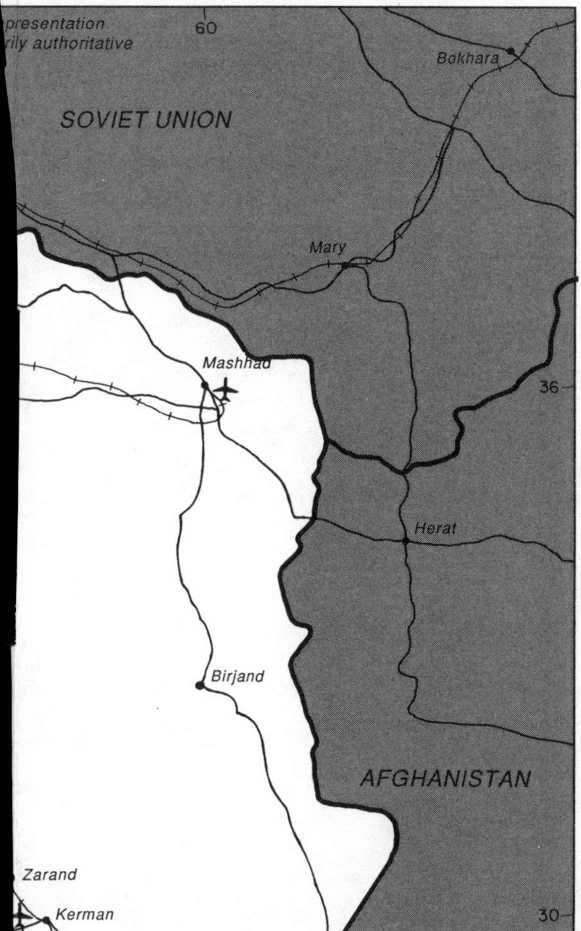

presentation
rily authoritative
60
Bokhara
SOVIET UNION
Mary
Mashhad
36
Herat
Birjand
AFGHANISTAN
Zarand
Kerman
30
Zahedan
Nok
Kundi
PAKISTAN
Jask
Bandar-e Beheshti
Gulf of Oman
60

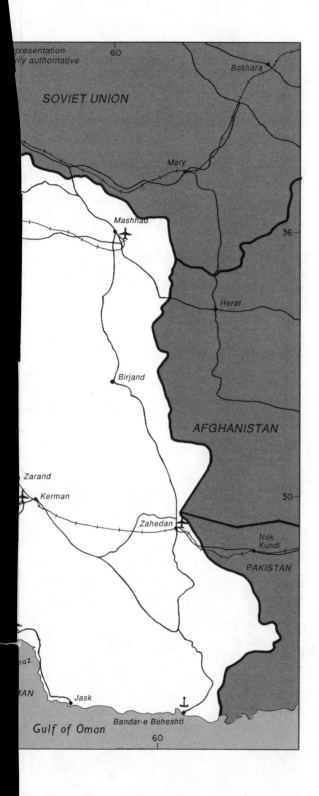

Iranian officials had earlier opted for nuclear power plants to meet part of the demand for electricity, entering into discussions with representatives from West Germany and France. The plants under consideration were pressurized water reactors using enriched uranium. They were to be built near the Persian Gulf because of the need for large quantities of water for cooling. The decision in favor of nuclear power stemmed from policy decisions to develop non-oil energy sources.

Nuclear power was not abandoned in the 1980s. The Atomic Energy Organization of Iran, set up in 1973 to produce nuclear energy for electricity needs, focused in 1987 on the exploration and use of uranium deposits and on the use of nuclear energy in industry, agriculture, and medicine. The construction of the nuclear power plant in Bushehr ceased in 1982 as a result of a fire in the plant; additional damage stemmed from three Iraqi attacks in 1985 and 1986. In 1987 an Argentine-Spanish firm was negotiating to finish construction of the nuclear power plant. Designed to have two 1,200-megawatt reactors, it was expected to take 3 years to complete.

Transportation and Telecommunications

As part of Reza Shah's development plan, modernization of the transportation and telecommunications sectors began in the 1930s and received huge infusions of capital investment from the mid-1960s onward under Mohammad Reza Shah's regime. In May 1979, Mehdi Bazargan's government created an organization called the Crusade for Reconstruction (Jihad-e Sazandegi or Jihad), which focused on rural reconstruction. In 1982 the organization claimed to have built 12,872 kilometers of roads, or nearly 1 kilometer per village.

Transportation

The rugged terrain and sheer size of Iran made the expansion of transportation facilities difficult. Emphasis was placed on linking the major population centers and economic centers by rail and road; superimposed on a map, such main arteries would form a "T," with the crossbar extending from the northwestern corner to the northeast along the southern coast of the Caspian Sea. The vertical line would run through Tehran down to the Gulf (see fig. 8).

In 1925 Iran had only 3,218 kilometers of railroad—much of it in disrepair, but in 1931 a railroad was built to link the two bodies of water on Iran's northern and southern borders, the port of Bandar-e Shah (known as Bandar-e Torkaman after the Revolution of 1979) on the Caspian Sea near Gorgan was linked by rail to the port of Bandar-e Shahpur (known as Bandar-e Khomeini after the 1979 Revolution) on the southwestern coast, passing through Tehran, and in 1941 the northern regions of Iran were connected by rail from west to east (from Tabriz to Mashhad). This was accomplished with the aid of foreign technicians and engineers. The railroad had expanded southeast from Tabriz to Kerman by 1977, and roads and air travel linked many parts of the country. Roads in good condition in 1941 totaled 22,526 kilometers; by 1984 there were 51,389 kilometers of paved roads. These roads, built primarily for military use, had the effect of stimulating development.

The leg of the "T" from Tehran to the Gulf was the most intensively used transportation corridor, accounting for half of all road traffic and two-thirds of all rail traffic by 1978. Domestic and foreign trade from the Gulf traversed this portion of road. Key ports were connected to each other and to Tehran through the "T" network. Foreign trade came through the Gulf ports of Khorramshahr, Bandar-e Shahpur, Bushehr, and Bandar-e Abbas. Khorramshahr handled trade primarily for the private sector, and Bandar-e Shahpur handled imports for the governments. Other foreign trade traversed the northwestern part of Iran. This area was connected by road and railroad with Turkey and the Soviet Union and with two minor ports on the Caspian Sea.

The transportation system became incapable of meeting trade demands during the oil boom of the mid-1970s. Neither the ports nor the transportation infrastructure leading from the ports could handle the volume of goods. As a consequence, long lines of ships formed, some waiting months to unload and adding more than US$1 billion a year to freight costs. Perishable goods spoiled, and delayed deliveries of durable goods disrupted production and construction schedules. Consequently, the government gave the expansion of port and transportation facilities high priority. By 1976 the 6 major ports of Bandar-e Abbas, Bandar-e Shahpur, Chah Bahar (known as Bandar-e Beheshti after the 1979 Revolution), Bushehr, Abadan, and Khorramshahr had a capacity of 12 million tons, with expansion projects underway. By late 1977, unloading delays were no longer a problem. As a result of war damage, the ports of Abadan and Khorramshahr were closed in 1980, leaving the other four main ports and twelve minor ports in operation.

The construction of fourteen jetties along the Gulf coast was planned in 1986; one of these, at Jask near the Strait of Hormuz, opened in February 1986. Built at a cost of approximately US$20 million, it included a covered warehouse, a passenger terminal building, and a 130-meter-long jetty for the use of small ships up to 2,000 tons. Especially after the Revolution, the government expanded roads as well as port facilities. The total length of roads in 1974 was about 50,000 kilometers, of which 14 percent was hard-surfaced. A major post-1979 increase in road construction helped boost total road length in 1984 to 136,381 kilometers, of which 41 percent was paved. Main or national roads comprised 16,551 kilometers and secondary roads 34,838 kilometers of this total.

Post-Revolution maintenance of roads and railroads suffered, as did road access to the ports. The State Railways Organization extended Iran's 4,567 kilometers of railroad track by the completion in 1987 of approximately 130 kilometers of electrified track in the north between Tabriz and Jolfa for imports from the Soviet Union. An additional 1,300 kilometers were scheduled to be added to the network by 1989, although war conditions made it unlikely that this goal would be realized. Other legs were planned between Mashhad in the northeast and the Soviet border at Sarakhs and in the north from Gorgan to Gonbad. A joint economic agreement between Iran and the Soviet Union in August 1987 reportedly called for a railroad route for the export of Soviet goods through Iran to the Gulf. A 560-kilometer extension to the World War II-era railroad linking Iran to Pakistan via Zahedan in southeastern Iran was completed in 1987 to join Zahedan to Kerman and thence to Tehran.

Iran's two principal international airports were located in Tehran (Mehrabad Airport) and Abadan. A new international airport in Esfahan began operations in 1986, and another airport forty kilometers south of Tehran was under construction in 1987. In addition, an international airport was scheduled to be built at Gorgan, east of the Caspian Sea. In developments affecting smaller, national airports, the runway at Kerman was extended in FY 1986. Plans in 1987 called for the airports at Ardabil, Iranshahr, Mashhad, Sari, and Zabol to be lengthened and widened to accommodate larger airplanes and for a new runway to be built at Zahedan.

Telecommunications

Reza Shah emphasized telecommunications as a focus of modernization in the 1930s. Telecommunications was reemphasized in the 1960s as part of Mohammad Reza Shah's White Revolution (see Glossary). Development was financed by a consortium of international firms that established satellite links for Iran's telecommunications. By the late 1970s, Iran had telegraph, television, and data communications capabilities. The National Iranian Radio and Television Organization had sufficient television transmission capability and enough relay stations to reach about 60 percent of the population. Iran had 1.7 million television sets in 1976 and 2.1 million by 1984.

The principal complaint about the telecommunications system remained the average citizen's inability to obtain a telephone. Although the number of telephone lines increased from 400,000 to 800,000 between 1972 and 1977, hundreds of thousands of customers waited as long as two years for a telephone. By 1980 the number of telephones had increased to about 1.2 million, and by 1986 to 1.5 million. About 3,000 of 70,000 rural communities had telephones in 1987, compared with 300 in 1979. To meet the demand for telephones, authorities decided to seek local production of digital equipment, and in May 1987 the British company Plessey Major Systems was negotiating a US$166.3 million contract to supply the Ministry of Posts, Telephones, and Telegraph with almost 1 million lines of telephone exchange equipment. Automatic telephone facilities were also included in project planning.

As a result of the opening of additional microwave links between Tehran, Ankara, and Karachi, international service generally improved in the early 1980s. Temporary disruption was caused, however, by an Iraqi attack on a communications installation near Hamadan on June 8, 1986.

Tourism

The disincentives resulting from the war, the anti-Western stance of the revolutionary regime, and the restrictions on visas all discouraged tourism after 1979. Visitors to the famous sites of Persepolis, Pasargard, and Esfahan dwindled; the number of tourists fell from a high of 695,500 in 1977 to 62,373 in 1982. By 1984, however, the number of tourists had increased to 157,000. This increase had a virtually negligible effect, however, on the economy.

Agriculture

After nearly achieving agricultural self-sufficiency in the 1960s, Iran reached the point in 1979 where 65 percent of its food had to be imported. Declining productivity was blamed on the use of modern fertilizers, which had inadvertently scorched the thin Iranian soil. Unresolved land reform issues, a lack of economic incentives to raise surplus crops, and low profit ratios combined to drive increasingly large segments of the farm population into urban areas.

The 1979 Revolution sought self-sufficiency in foodstuffs as part of its overall goal of decreased economic dependence on the West. Higher government subsidies for grain and other staples and expanded short-term credit and tax exemptions for farmers complying with government quotas were intended by the new regime to promote self-sufficiency. But by early 1987, Iran was actually more dependent on agricultural imports than in the 1970s.

Water

Iran's land surface covers 165 million hectares, more than half of which is uncultivable. A total of 11.5 million hectares is under cultivation at any time, of which 3.5 million hectares were irrigated in 1987, and the rest watered by rain. Only 10 percent of the country receives adequate rainfall for agriculture; most of this area is in western Iran. The water shortage is intensified by seasonal rainfalls. The rainy season occurs between October and March, leaving the land parched for the remainder of the year. Immense seasonal variations in flow characterize Iran's rivers. The Karun River and other rivers passing through Khuzestan (in the southwest at the head of the Gulf) carry water during periods of maximum flow that is ten times the amount borne in dry periods. Several of the government's dam projects are on these rivers. In numerous localities, there may be no precipitation until sudden storms, accompanied by heavy rains, dump almost the entire year's rainfall in a few days. Often causing floods and local damage, the runoffs are so rapid that they cannot be used for agricultural purposes.

Water shortages are compounded by the unequal distribution of water. Near the Caspian Sea, rainfall averages about 128 centimeters per year, but in the Central Plateau and in the lowlands to the south it seldom exceeds 10 to 12 centimeters, far below the 26 to 31 centimeters usually required for dry farming (see Climate, ch. 2).

Scarcity of water and of the means for making use of it have constrained agriculture since ancient times. To make use of the limited amounts of water, the Iranians centuries ago developed man-made underground water channels called *qanats* that were still in use in 1987. They usually are located at the foot of a mountain and are limited to land with a slope. A *qanat* taps water that has seeped into the ground and channels it via straight tunnels to the land surface. The *qanats* are designed to surface in proximity to village crops.

The chief advantage of the *qanat* is that its underground location prevents most of the evaporation to which water carried in surface channels is subject. In addition, the *qanat* is preferable to the modern power-operated deep well because it draws upon underground water located far from the villages. The chief disadvantages of the *qanat* are the costs of construction and maintenance and a lack of flexibility; the flow cannot be controlled, and water is lost when it is not being used to irrigate crops.

In the late 1980s, an estimated 60,000 *qanats* were in use, and new units were still being dug (although not in western Iran, where rainfall is adequate). To assist villagers, the government undertook a program to clean many *qanats* after the Revolution in 1979. *Qanat* water is distributed in various ways: by turn, over specified periods; by division into shares; by damming; and by the opening of outlets through which the water flows to each plot of land. So important is the *qanat* system to the agricultural economy and so complex is the procedure for allocating water rights (which are inherited), that a large number of court cases regularly deal with adjudication of conflicting claims.

Construction of large reservoir dams since World War II has made a major contribution to water management for both irrigation and industrial purposes. Dam construction has centered in the province of Khuzestan in the southwest as a result of the configuration of its rivers flowing from the Zagros Mountains. The upper courses flow in parallel stretches before cutting through the surrounding mountains in extremely narrow gorges called *tangs*. The terrain in Khuzestan provides good dam sites. The government set up the Khuzestan Water and Power Authority in 1959 to manage natural resources in that province. All economic development plans emphasized the need to improve water supplies and reservoirs so as to improve crop production. Large reservoirs were built throughout the country, beginning with the Second Development Plan. The first dams were built on the Karaj, Safid, and Dez rivers.

The first of the major dams had a significant impact on the Iranian economy. Completed in 1962, the Mohammad Reza Shah Dam on the Dez River was designed to irrigate the Khuzestan plain and to supply electricity to the province. After several years of operation, the dam had achieved only a small part of its goals, and the government decided that the lands below the dam and other dams nearing completion required special administration. As a consequence, a law was passed in 1969 nationalizing irrigable lands downstream from dams. The lands below the Mohammad Reza Shah Dam were later leased to newly established domestic and foreign companies that became known as agribusinesses.

Land Use

Desert, wasteland, and barren mountain ranges cover about half of Iran's total land area. Of the rest, in the 1980s about 11 percent was forested, about 8 percent was used for grazing or pastureland, and about 1.5 percent was made up of cities, villages, industrial centers, and related areas. The remainder included land that was cultivated either permanently or on a rotation, dry-farming basis (about 14 percent) and land that could be farmed with adequate

Siphon irrigation being used in a sugar-beet field near Qazvin
Courtesy United Nations

irrigation (about 15 to 16 percent). Some observers considered the latter category as pastureland.

In most regions, the natural cover is insufficient to build up much organic soil content, and on the steeper mountain slopes much of the original earth cover has been washed away. Although roughly half of Iran is made up of the arid Central Plateau, some of the gentler slopes and the Gulf lowlands have relatively good soils but poor drainage. In the southeast, a high wind that blows incessantly from May to September is strong enough to carry sand particles with it. Vegetation can be destroyed, and the lighter soils of the region have been stripped away.

In mountain valleys and in areas where rivers descending from the mountains have formed extensive alluvial plains, much of the soil is of medium to heavy texture and is suited to a variety of agricultural uses when brought under irrigation. Northern soils are the richest and the best watered. The regions adjacent to Lake Urmia (also cited as Lake Urumiyeh and formerly known as Lake Rezaiyeh under the Pahlavis) and the Caspian Sea make up only about 25 percent of the country's area but produce 60 percent or more of its major crops.

The land reform program of 1962 affected agricultural lands and the production of crops. Implemented in three stages, the program redistributed agricultural lands to the peasantry, thereby lessening the power of the feudal landlords. By the time the program was declared complete in 1971, more than 90 percent of the farmers who held rights to cultivation had become owners of the land they farmed. The new owners, however, became disillusioned with the government and its policies as their real economic situation worsened by the late 1970s.

On average, the minimal landholding for subsistence farming in Iran is about seven hectares. If each of the 3.5 million sharecroppers and landowners in villages (as of 1981) were given an equal share of land (from the 16.6 million hectares of cropland), each family would be entitled to only 4.7 hectares, not enough land for subsistence farming. Even if there were sufficient arable land, many of the sharecroppers could not afford to buy more than four of the seven hectares needed for subsistence farming.

The basic rural landholding infrastructure did not change after the Revolution. A minority of landowners continued to profit by exploiting the labor of sharecroppers. Prior to the land reform program, feudal and absentee landlords, including religious leaders responsible for *vaqf* land, comprised the ruling elite. Over the years, *vaqf* landholdings grew considerably, providing many Iranian clergy with a degree of economic independence from the central government. Redistribution of the land resulted in power being transferred to farmers who acquired ten or more hectares of land and to the rural bourgeoisie (see State and Society, 1964–74, ch. 1). Uncertainty about the prospect of effective land reform under Khomeini contributed to a massive loss of farm labor—5 million people—between 1982 and 1986.

Emphasis on subsistence agriculture persisted because of the lack of capital allocated after the Revolution, perhaps because the regime's technocrats were from urban areas and therefore uninformed about agriculture, or because the bazaar class, which constituted a disproportionate share of the 1979 government, did not represent the interests of agriculture. Uncertainties about future landownership, as well as the war with Iraq, caused further disruption of agriculture. Ten percent of agricultural land fell into Iraqi hands between 1980 and 1982, although the territory was subsequently regained by Iran. The war stifled agricultural development by causing a loss of revenue and by draining the already shrinking agricultural labor pool through heavy conscription.

Crop Production

By 1987, eight years after the Revolution, there had been no progress toward agricultural self-sufficiency. By the end of the first year following the 1979 Revolution, agricultural output had fallen by 3.5 percent, and it continued to decline, except for those growing seasons characterized by above-normal rainfall, such as FY 1982 and FY 1985. Sugar, wheat, cotton, and rice production increased in FY 1982, whereas wheat, barley, and rice production increased in FY 1985. Iran was the largest world supplier of pistachios, with 95,000 tons produced in 1982 to 1983 and 97,000 tons in 1986. The war did not inhibit the production of pistachios, which are grown in south-central Iran (see table 6, Appendix).

Grains

Overall grain production increased throughout the 1970s, peaking in the late 1970s and again in the early 1980s and decreasing somewhat by 1985. Wheat is Iran's main grain crop; its production increased in the early 1980s from that in the 1970s, along with that of barley.

Wheat is a staple for most of the population. Bread is the most important single item in the Iranian diet, except in certain parts of the Caspian lowlands where rice is more commonly grown. Wheat and barley are planted on dry-farmed and irrigated lands and on mountain slopes and plains. Wheat is used almost exclusively for human consumption, and barley is used mainly as animal feed.

Rice is the only crop grown exclusively under irrigation. The long-grain rice of Iran grows primarily in the wet Caspian lowlands in the northern provinces of Gilan and Mazandaran, where heavy rainfall facilitates paddy cultivation. Population growth and the rising standard of living stimulated production of the high-quality rice that could be used for export. Although the Ministry of Agriculture and Rural Development sought to develop rice as an export crop as early as 1977, by the end of that year 326,000 tons of rice had to be imported to meet domestic needs. In 1985 rice imports increased 3 percent over the previous year's 710,000 tons.

Other grain imports fell in 1985 by 43 percent compared with 1984 levels. Wheat, flour, and feed grain imports declined as output increased.

Sugar

During the early and mid-1970s, sugar output increased annually at a rate of 5 to 6 percent, but consumption rose at a rate of 10 percent or more. With an increased production of beet and cane sugar in the early 1970s, it was expected that Iran would export sugar by 1977. Instead, 300,000 tons of raw sugar were imported that year. To supplement sugar production, the government in 1976 initiated a large beekeeping and honey-processing operation at a site near Qom, which produced about 2,000 tons of honey annually.

The production of raw sugar decreased from 687,000 tons in 1976 to 412,000 tons in 1985. Sugar production dropped to a low of 380,000 tons in 1980.

Sugar cane production increased from about 1.7 million tons in FY 1981 to about 2 million tons in FY 1983. Sugar beet production, however, declined by 15.5 percent, from 4.3 million tons in FY 1982 to 3.7 million tons in FY 1983.

Livestock

The value of livestock increased annually after 1981, but the decreases in livestock in the early revolutionary period were such that by 1985 the overall value of livestock remained below the 1976 level. Severe shortages of meat and eggs, coupled with high demand and the absence of price controls, encouraged the raising of livestock and were expected to improve livestock availability.

Livestock-raising methods were generally unsophisticated. Sheep and goats were kept by nomadic tribesmen and by sedentary villagers who supported a few animals as a sideline to farming. These animals had diets of grass and shrubs that often left them diseased and malnourished; in turn, the herders obtained little profit in the way of meat, milk, hair, and hides.

Fisheries

The Caspian Sea and the Persian Gulf remained the country's two largest fishing areas. A variety of fish were found in both bodies of water; catches totaled 44,800 tons in 1981 and 34,500 tons in 1983. Fishing in the Persian Gulf has declined since the onset of war with Iraq. By 1986 national freshwater catches totaled only 25,000 to 35,000 tons per year.

Commercial fishing was controlled by two state-owned enterprises, the Northern Fishing Company operating in the Caspian Sea and the Southern Fisheries Company in the Persian Gulf and the Gulf of Oman. Sturgeon, white salmon, whitefish, carp, bream, pike, and catfish predominate in the Caspian, and sardines, sole, tuna, bream, snapper, mackerel, swordfish, and shrimp predominate in the Persian Gulf.

The Caspian sturgeon was of particular importance because it produces the roe that is processed into caviar. Known as "gray pearls," Iranian caviar is said to be the finest in the world and commands a high price. The main importers of Iranian caviar were the Soviet Union and the West European countries. Increasing pollution in the Caspian Sea, however, posed a threat to the industry.

Forestry

Some of Iran's forest resources were nationalized under Mohammad Reza Shah's development plans, beginning in 1963. Since then, the state has gradually gained control over forest use. The plentiful commercial timber in the Alborz and Zagros mountains was diminished by illegal cutting that did not show up in official statistics; approximately 6.5 million cubic meters were cut in 1986 alone. Of an estimated 18 million hectares of forest lands, only about 3.2 million hectares near the Caspian Sea can be regarded as commercially productive.

Plentiful rainfall, a mild climate, and a long growing season have combined to create a dense forest of high-quality timber in the Caspian region. There is an extensive growth of temperate-zone hardwoods, including oak, beech, maple, Siberian elm, ash, walnut, ironwood, alder, basswood, and fig. About half of the Caspian forests consists of these trees; the remainder is low-grade scrub. The Zagros Mountains in the west and areas in Khorasan and Fars provinces abound in oak, walnut, and maple trees. Shiraz is renowned for its cypresses.

To curtail indiscriminate forest destruction, the government in 1967 moved to nationalize all forests and pastures. A forest service was established; by 1970 more than 3,000 forest rangers and guards were employed, and 1.3 million saplings had been planted on 526,315 hectares of land. The value of exported forest products was six times greater in 1973 than in 1984; the decrease in exports probably resulted from increased domestic and war-related consumption.

Foreign Trade

Imports

Overall trade contracted in 1986, with import restrictions matching falling export earnings. The trade statistics did not, however, reflect the flourishing black market for foreign goods. Gasoline was available on the black market for five times the official rate; food and other goods were available at similarly inflated prices. Rising prices and salaries (among civil servants, for example) compounded the rate of inflation, which ranged between 10 and 50 percent, depending on the kind of goods purchased.

Capital and consumer goods imports decreased after the 1979 Revolution, with capital goods falling from 30 percent of total imports in 1979 to 15 percent by 1982. Importation of luxury goods was restricted to conserve foreign currency and preserve the balance of payments. Food imports increased to more than US$2 billion by FY 1983, despite the emphasis on agricultural self-sufficiency. Rice imports alone increased by 200,000 tons in 1986, despite increased rice production.

Food imports in early 1986 consumed as much as 20 percent of total foreign exchange. Iran had become one of the largest per capita purchasers of wheat in the world, buying 3.4 million tons annually. The nation spent about US$3 billion per year on food items such as wheat, rice, meat, vegetable oil, eggs, chicken, tea, and sugar. By December 1986, Iran's imports of meat and dairy products alone exceeded the value of the country's entire industrial output.

Between March and June 1986, imports declined to US$2.6 billion, a drop of 16 percent compared with the same period the previous year. Shrinking imports reflected a conscious government effort to contain the financial crisis by further restricting the entry of luxury goods into the country. Discretionary imports for private consumption were expected to be halved in FY 1987 to US$5 billion, from the FY 1986 low of US$8 to US$10 billion.

Iran resorted to barter agreements with some countries in 1986 and 1987, trading oil for goods such as tea from Sri Lanka, rice from Thailand, wheat from Argentina, and various foodstuffs from Turkey. Failure to pay its debts caused Iran to lose its contract with Peugeot-Talbot for automobile assembly kits. Although the contract was suspended officially in November 1986, no new kits had been shipped since January 1986, and Iran lost business worth US$190 million per year as production of the Peykan automobile ceased. Iran also lost its barter agreement with New Zealand after failing to pay cash debts for imported goods; thus, in 1987 Iran paid for 90,000 tons of imported lamb in cash rather than with oil, as it had for 135,000 tons of New Zealand lamb imported in 1986.

Non-Oil Exports

In 1985 the government announced its new goal of doubling non-oil exports in 1986. Although the value of non-oil exports increased 70 percent between March and June 1986, this increase shrank to 59 percent by August 1986. Because inflation had reduced the value of non-oil exports, the government abandoned its goal for non-oil exports.

Despite government encouragement, non-oil exports in 1985 accounted for only 10 percent of total exports. Industrial and mineral exports together accounted for 25 percent of the value of non-oil exports in 1985 but only 5 percent in 1986. The export of manufactured goods and cotton also declined appreciably as a result of the war. A further 25 percent of non-oil export income came from carpets and fruit. Carpet exports were the exception to the overall downturn in non-oil exports in 1985. Carpet exports more than tripled from 1985 to 1986, but as carpet output increased, prices on the international market fell.

The other key non-oil export was agricultural produce. Some agricultural exports increased in FY 1986, whereas industrial exports continued to decline. Official figures showed that agricultural exports were up in value 46 percent for the period March–August 1986, as compared with the same period during the preceding fiscal year. This figure is misleading, however, because there was a decline in the ratio of the value of agricultural exports to agricultural imports. In the mid-1980s, the agricultural sector operated at a subsistence level, growing food primarily to feed the general population and producing for export only the financially lucrative cash crops whose production varied according to seasonal fluctuations in rainfall. A halting though generally upward trend in the production and export of cash crops began just before the Revolution.

Fruit and vegetable exports increased in 1986 as a result of good weather, a big market in the Persian Gulf area for fresh produce, and incentives to grow and market cash crops, whose prices the government did not regulate. Fruit and vegetable exports accounted for 30 percent of the country's non-oil exports in the first half of FY 1987. Previously, fruit had not exceeded 5 percent of total non-oil exports.

Bumper crops of pistachios sold at the international market rate and bumper crops of fruit and vegetables were the only exceptions to a general decline in agricultural production. Production of pistachios was so competitive that the United States Department of Commerce imposed a 318-percent duty on imports of Iranian roasted pistachios in the fall of 1986, causing a decline in exports to the United States.

Through 1986, Iranian caviar exports in the 1980s fluctuated between US$20 million and US$40 million. In 1986 the exports were worth only about US$20 million. That year, Iran sought to recapture the Italian market (estimated at US$900,000 annually) from the Soviet Union. Iran had sold only US$100,000 worth of caviar (about 11 percent of the market) to Italy in 1985.

Trade Partners

Before 1979 Iran had relied on the industrial West for trade. Little changed in subsequent years except rhetoric. Although the government purportedly sought to develop trade relations with other

Islamic countries, figures showed that in 1985 approximately 64 percent of Iran's imports came from the West, 28 percent from developing countries, and 8 percent from Eastern Europe. These figures, although representing an absolute increase in trade with Third World countries, actually indicated only a small percentage increase in total trade. Economic necessity mandated that Iran trade with whatever country was willing, notwithstanding policy pronouncements regarding self-sufficiency and Third World communities of interest. Nearly all foreign trade occurred through government-controlled purchasing and distribution companies, which were charged with enforcing government trade policies and regulating the quantity and quality of imports.

Despite trade sanctions applied in 1980 by the United States, the European Economic Community, and Japan, Iranian imports from the West actually increased 13.5 percent from FY 1980 to FY 1981. West Germany remained Iran's primary supplier in 1985, followed by Japan, Britain, Italy, and Turkey (see table 7, Appendix).

As a result of United States trade restrictions following the Tehran embassy takeover in 1979, imports from the United States dropped dramatically. This lost market, coupled with the decline in oil revenues, forced the government to consider bartering Iranian oil for non-oil goods. It was estimated that total trade with new Islamic and Third World trade partners would increase from 20 percent in the mid-1980s to 35 percent in 1987 through barter.

Barter agreements became commonplace in 1984 to compensate for the fall in revenue from oil exports (see Balance of Payments, this ch.). These revenues were 15 percent less (or US$1.7 billion) than expected in FY 1984, with barter arrangements making up the difference. About one-quarter of 1984 oil exports resulted from barter or bilateral trade agreements. Barter became a point of contention between the Ministry of Oil, which opposed it, and the Ministry of Foreign Affairs, which supported barter as a key element of foreign policy. Bartering ceased in late 1985 as a result of disagreement between the ministries but resumed in 1986 because of economic necessity occasioned by depressed oil prices. Bartering with other countries, especially in Eastern Europe, mitigated the effects of the economy's structural problems but failed to solve them.

The United States resumed trade with Iran in FY 1981, with direct sales totaling US$300 million. United States exports to Iran fell to less than half that amount, however, in FY 1982. This led to Iran's renewal of the Regional Cooperation for Development pact with Pakistan and Turkey in October 1984, which by 1985 had greatly increased trade among these partners. By early 1987, trade among the three countries was worth over US$3 billion, as compared with US$100 million before the Revolution.

In 1986 the United States imported US$612 million worth of Iranian products, principally crude oil, caviar, rugs, furs, spices, and gems. Of those imports, crude oil represented US$508.8 million, pistachios and other nuts US$15 million, carpets US$5.5 million, and caviar about US$2 million. In the first five months of 1987, the United States imported US$418.5 million in Iranian goods. The increase was probably caused by fluctuations in petroleum spot prices and in the demand for oil in general.

In 1986 Iran acknowledged the role of the Soviet Union as a major future trade partner by announcing its plans to complete the electrification of the railroad between Tabriz and the Soviet city of Jolfa. Moreover, the construction of railroad lines—to be completed by 1989—linking other points in Iran with the Soviet Union and with Pakistan indicated the growing Iranian intent to deal with both countries as trade partners (see Transportation and Telecommunications, this ch.). In August 1987, Iran and the Soviet Union agreed to large-scale joint economic projects, including oil pipelines and a railroad to the Gulf. Despite the apparent intention on both sides to do business, overall Iranian-Soviet trade in FY 1986 was one-quarter that in FY 1985.

Balance of Payments

Oil revenues in the mid-1970s brought Iran a foreign exchange surplus. But when oil revenues fell sharply in 1978, an economic crisis resulted. Iran went from being a long-term lender in the 1970s to a short-term borrower in the 1980s, with the acquisition of foreign currency a perennial problem. The revolutionary government resorted to barter with several countries in the mid-1980s, but some customers soon insisted on receiving payment from Iran before shipment because of disagreements over the terms of payment. Problems arose when countries wanted to renegotiate barter contracts in 1986, to reflect the lower cost of oil, and Iran insisted on the original terms. Also, barter did not improve the foreign currency situation; to maintain a foreign exchange balance, Iran would have had to earn at least US$1 billion more than the sums received from civilian non-oil exports.

Another method used by the government to improve its balance of payments was the collection of funds owed to Iran by foreign suppliers and governments. The Iranian government estimated in 1986 that several countries, chiefly Egypt, the United States, and France, owed Iran US$5 to US$6 billion. Clearly, the continued costs of the war coupled with falling oil revenues afforded the economy little elasticity.

Iran had a US$5.4 billion balance of payments deficit during 1986, largely as a result of low oil prices and the disruption of oil shipments caused by Iraqi bombing. Oil prices fell from US$27 per barrel in November 1985 to US$12 in February 1986. Although prices rose in the fall of 1986, the average price of oil for the year was US$13 per barrel, half that in 1985. The estimated US$10 billion in export earnings in 1986 was the lowest since 1973.

As a result of its high balance of payments deficit and foreign exchange shortage, Iran reduced its imports and divested itself of foreign financial assets acquired by Mohammad Reza Shah. For example, in 1986 it sold 25.6 percent of its holdings, worth approximately US$150 million, in the West German engineering firm Deutsche Babcock. Iran's efforts to cope with its economic crisis by making barter agreements, repossessing funds, cutting imports, and divesting itself of foreign financial assets were superficial responses to deeper structural problems within the economy, such as the need for land and agricultural reforms and the redistribution of income.

The country's balance of payments looked bleak for the final years of the 1980s. The continuing war with Iraq, declining oil revenues, high unemployment, reduced consumer imports, severe inflation, a rising foreign debt, and a severe foreign currency shortage tested the economic policies of the revolutionary regime. The economy produced essential products and addressed in some measure the problems facing the national budget, a remarkable feat given the war, but failed to address basic structural issues.

* * *

Despite the disruptive influences of war on all aspects of the national life, a surprising number of good publications on the Iranian economy were readily available in the late 1980s. The Central Bank (Bank Markazi) of the Islamic Republic publishes reliable annual statistics on the state of the economy, the budget, finances, and balance of payments. A publication from Tehran called *Iran Press Digest* has a superb weekly update of economic and political events. *Iran Monitor,* a monthly publication based in Switzerland, provides an up-to-date account of international financial and trade issues. *Iran Times,* an independent weekly newspaper with sections in English and Persian, details current economic developments and statistics. Two other sources of consistently good coverage of Iran are the *Middle East Economic Digest (MEED),* published in London, and *Middle East Research and Information Project (MERIP) Reports,* published in Washington.

Eric Hooglund provides an understanding of land reform issues in *Land and Revolution in Iran, 1960–1980.* For concise reports on the economic situation in Iran, the following sources are helpful: Patrick Clawson's "Islamic Iran's Economic Policies and Prospects"; Sohrab Behdad's *Foreign Exchange Gap, Structural Constraints and the Political Economy of Exchange Rate Determination in Iran;* and Wolfgang Lautenschlager's "The Effects of an Overvalued Exchange Rate on the Iranian Economy, 1979–1984." (For further information and complete citations, see Bibliography.)

Chapter 4. Government and Politics

A bas-relief of a bearded sphinx, ca. 500 B.C., from Persepolis

THE IRANIAN ISLAMIC REVOLUTION of 1979 resulted in the replacement of the monarchy by the Islamic Republic of Iran. The inspiration for the new government came from Ayatollah Sayyid Ruhollah Musavi Khomeini, who first began formulating his concept of an Islamic government in the early 1970s, while in exile in the Shia Islam learning and pilgrimage center of An Najaf in Iraq. Khomeini's principal objective was that government should be entrusted to Islamic clergy (see Glossary) who had been appropriately trained in Islamic theology and jurisprudence. He referred to this ideal government as a *velayat-e faqih,* or the guardianship of the religious jurist. Khomeini did not, however, elaborate concrete ideas about the institutions and functions of this ideal Islamic government. The translation of his ideas into a structure of interrelated governmental institutions was undertaken by the special Assembly of Experts, which drafted the Constitution of the Islamic Republic during the summer and fall of 1979. Subsequently, this Constitution was ratified by popular vote in December 1979.

The political institutions established under the Constitution have been in the process of consolidation since 1980. These institutions have withstood serious challenges, such as the impeachment and removal from office of the first elected president and the assassination of the second one; the assassination of a prime minister, several members of the cabinet, and deputies of the parliament, or Majlis (see Glossary); an effort to overthrow the government by armed opposition; and a major foreign war. By 1987 the constitutional government's demonstrated ability to survive these numerous crises inspired confidence among the political elite.

At the top of the government structure is the *faqih* (see Glossary), the ultimate decision maker. The Constitution specifically names Khomeini as the *faqih* for life and provides a mechanism for choosing his successors. The role of the *faqih* has evolved into that of a policy guide and arbitrator among competitive views. Below the *faqih* a distinct separation of powers exists between the executive and legislative branches. The executive branch includes an elected president, who selects a prime minister and cabinet that must be approved by the elected legislative assembly, the Majlis. The judiciary is independent of both the executive and the Majlis.

Until 1987 the government was dominated by a single political party, the Islamic Republican Party (IRP). Other political parties were permitted as long as they accepted the Constitution and the basic principles of *velayat-e faqih*. In practice, however, few other political parties have been permitted to operate legally since 1981. Most of the political parties that were formed in the immediate aftermath of the Revolution have disbanded, gone underground, or continued to operate in exile.

The Constitution stipulates that the government of the Republic derives its legitimacy from both God and the people. It is a theocracy in the sense that the rulers claim that they govern the Muslim people of Iran as the representatives of the divine being and the saintly Twelve Shia Imams (see Glossary). The people have the right to choose their own leaders, however, from among those who have demonstrated both religious expertise and moral rectitude. At the national level this is accomplished through parliamentary and presidential elections scheduled at four-year intervals. All citizens who have attained sixteen years of age are eligible to vote in these elections. There are also local elections for a variety of urban and rural positions.

Constitutional Framework

The government is based upon the Constitution that was approved in a national referendum in December 1979. This republican Constitution replaced the 1906 constitution, which, with its provisions for a shah to reign as head of state, was the earliest constitution in the Middle East. Soon after the Revolution, however, on March 30 and 31, 1979, the provisional government of Mehdi Bazargan asked all Iranians sixteen years of age and older to vote in a national referendum on the question of whether they approved of abolishing the monarchy and replacing it with an Islamic republic. Subsequently, the government announced that a 98-percent majority favored abrogating the old constitution and establishing such a republic. On the basis of this popular mandate, the provisional government prepared a draft constitution drawing upon some of the articles of the abolished 1906 constitution and the French constitution written under Charles de Gaulle in 1958. Ironically, the government draft did not allot any special political role to the clergy or even mention the concept of *velayat-e faqih*.

Although the provisional government initially had advocated a popularly elected assembly to complete the Constitution, Khomeini indicted that this task should be undertaken by experts. Accordingly the electorate was called upon to vote for an Assembly of Experts from a list of names approved by the government. The draft constitution was submitted to this seventy-three member assembly, which was dominated by Shia clergy. The Assembly of Experts convened in August 1979 to write the constitution in final form for approval by popular referendum. The clerical majority was generally dissatisfied with the essentially secular draft constitution and was determined to revise it to make it more Islamic. Produced after three months of deliberation, the final document, which was approved by a two-thirds majority of the Assembly of Experts, differed completely from the original draft. For example, it contained provisions for institutionalizing the office of supreme religious jurist, or *faqih,* and for establishing a theocratic government.

The first presidential elections took place in January 1980, and elections for the first Majlis were held in March and May of 1980. The Council of Guardians, a body that reviews all legislation to ensure that laws are in conformity with Islamic principles, was appointed during the summer of 1980. Presidential elections were held again in 1981 and 1985. The second Majlis was elected in 1984.

The Faqih

The preamble to the Constitution vests supreme authority in the *faqih.* According to Article 5, the *faqih* is the just and pious jurist who is recognized by the majority of the people at any period as best qualified to lead the nation. In both the preamble and Article 107 of the Constitution, Khomeini is recognized as the first *faqih.* Articles 108 to 112 specify the qualifications and duties of the *faqih.* The duties include appointing the jurists to the Council of Guardians; the chief judges of the judicial branch; the chief of staff of the armed forces; the commander of the Pasdaran (Pasdaran-e Enghelab-e Islami, or Islamic Revolutionary Guards Corps, or Revolutionary Guards); the personal representatives of the *faqih* to the Supreme Defense Council; and the commanders of the army, air force, and navy, following their nomination by the Supreme Defense Council. The *faqih* also is authorized to approve candidates for presidential elections. In addition, he is empowered to dismiss a president who has been impeached by the Majlis or found by the Supreme Court to be negligent in his duties (see fig. 9).

Articles 5 and 107 of the Constitution also provide procedures for succession to the position of *faqih.* After Khomeini, the office of *faqih* is to pass to an equally qualified jurist. If a single religious leader with appropriate qualifications cannot be recognized consensually, religious experts elected by the people are to choose from among themselves three to five equally distinguished jurists who then will constitute a collective *faqih,* or Leadership Council.

In accordance with Article 107, an eighty-three-member Assembly of Experts was elected in December 1982 to choose a successor

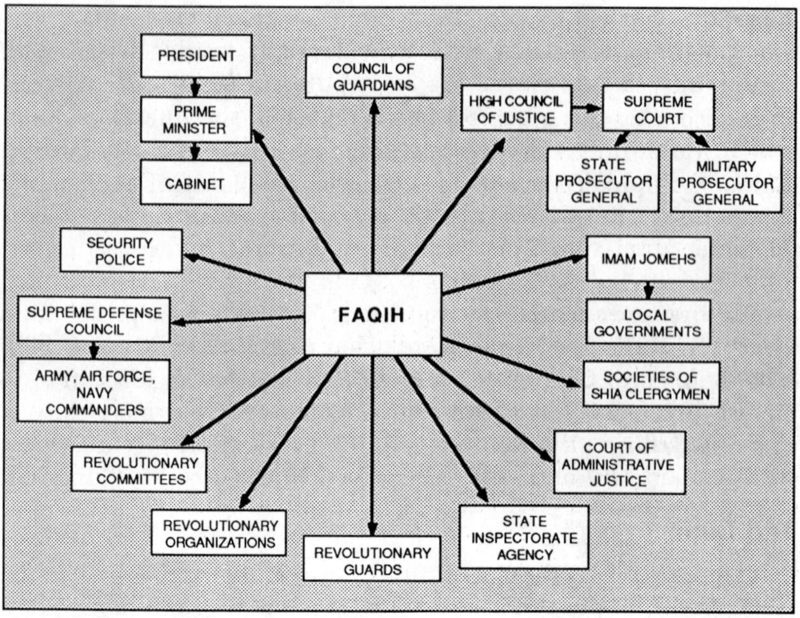

Source: Based on information from Shahrough Akhavi in N. Keddie and E. Hooglund (eds.), *The Iranian Revolution and the Islamic Republic,* Syracuse, New York, 1986.

Figure 9. Powers of the Faqih

to Khomeini. Even before the first meeting of the Assembly of Experts in the spring of 1983, some influential members of the clergy had been trying to promote Ayatollah Hosain Ali Montazeri (born 1923), a former student of Khomeini, as successor to the office of *faqih.* As early as the fall of 1981, Khomeini himself had indicated in a speech that he considered Montazeri the best qualified to be *faqih.* Hojjatoleslam Ali Akbar Hashemi-Rafsanjani, who as of late 1987 had been the speaker of the Majlis since its formation in 1980, also supported Montazeri's succession. Rafsanjani, in fact, nominated him at the first deliberations of the Assembly of Experts, as well as at subsequent conventions in 1984 and 1985. At the third meeting, Montazeri was designated "deputy" rather than "successor," but this put him in line to be Khomeini's successor. Since November 1985, the press and government radio and television broadcasts have referred to Montazeri as the *faqih*-designate.

The Presidency

The Constitution stipulates that the president is "the holder of the highest official power next to the office of *faqih.*" In effect, the president is the head of state of the Islamic Republic. Articles 113 to 132 of the Constitution pertain to the qualifications, powers, and responsibilities of the president. The president is elected for a four-year term on the basis of an absolute majority vote of the national electorate and may be reelected for one additional term. The president must be a Shia Muslim and a man "of political and religious distinction." He is empowered to choose the prime minister, approve the nominations of ministers, sign laws into force, and veto decrees issued by the Council of Ministers, or cabinet.

Elected in January 1980, Abolhasan Bani Sadr was Iran's first president under the Constitution of 1979. His tenure of office was marked by intense rivalry with the IRP-dominated Majlis. Within one year of his election, relations between the president and his opponents in the Majlis had deteriorated so severely that the Majlis initiated impeachment proceedings against Bani Sadr. In June 1981, a majority of Majlis deputies voted that Bani Sadr had been negligent in his duties and requested that Khomeini dismiss him from office as specified under the Constitution.

Iran's second president, Mohammad Ali Rajai, was elected in July 1981 but served only a brief term before being assassinated in a bombing at the prime minister's office on August 30, 1981. The third president, Hojjatoleslam Ali Khamenehi, was elected in October 1981 and reelected to a second term in 1985. During his tenure, relations between the presidency and the Majlis have been relatively cooperative. Not only was Khamenehi an important religious figure but he also was secretary general of the IRP until its dissolution in 1987.

The Prime Minister and the Council of Ministers

The prime minister is chosen by the president and must be approved by the Majlis. According to Article 135 of the Constitution, the prime minister may remain in office as long as he retains the confidence of the Majlis, but he must submit a letter of resignation to the president upon losing a confidence vote. The prime minister is responsible for choosing the ministers who will form his government, known as the Council of Ministers (also known as the cabinet). In 1987 the Council of Ministers totaled twenty-five members. Each minister had to be approved by both the president and the Majlis. The prime minister and his cabinet establish government policies and execute laws.

Following each of his elections, President Khamenehi chose Mir-Hosain Musavi as prime minister. Musavi generally had consistent support in the Majlis, although a vocal minority of deputies opposed many of his economic policies. Policies pertaining to the nationalization of large industries and foreign trade and the expropriation of large-scale agricultural landholdings for redistribution among peasants were especially controversial in the years 1982 to 1987.

The Majlis

Articles 62 through 90 of the Constitution of 1979 invest legislative power in the Islamic Consultative Assembly, the parliament, or Majlis (see Glossary). Deputies are elected by direct, secret ballot once every four years. Each deputy represents a geographic constituency, and every person sixteen years of age and older from a given constituency votes for one representative. The Majlis cannot be dissolved: according to Article 63, "elections of each session should be held before the expiration of the previous session, so that the country may never remain without an assembly." Article 64 establishes the number of representatives at 270, but it also provides for adding one more deputy, at 10-year intervals, for each constituency population increase of 150,000. Five of the 270 seats are reserved for the non-Muslim religious minorities: one each for Assyrian Christians, Jews, and Zoroastrians, and two for Armenian Christians.

The Constitution permits the Majlis to draft its own regulations pertaining to the election of a speaker and other officers, the formation of committees, and the holding of hearings. When the first Majlis convened in the summer of 1980, the deputies voted to have annual elections for the position of speaker. Rafsanjani was elected as speaker of the first Majlis; he was reelected six times through the beginning of 1987. The speaker is assisted by deputy speakers and the chairmen of various committees.

The Majlis not only has the responsibility of approving the prime minister and cabinet members but also has the right to question any individual minister or anyone from the government as a whole about policies. Articles 88 and 89 require ministers to appear before the Majlis within ten days to respond to a request for interpellation. If the deputies are dissatisfied with the information obtained during such questioning, they may request the Majlis to schedule a confidence vote on the performance of a minister or the government.

Article 69 stipulates that Majlis sessions be open to the public, that regular deliberations may be broadcast over radio and television, and that minutes of all meetings be published. Since 1980 sessions of the Majlis have been broadcast regularly. The public airing of Majlis meetings has demonstrated that the assembly has been characterized by raucous debate. Economic policies, with the notable exception of oil policy, have been the most vigorously debated issues.

The Council of Guardians

The Constitution also provides for the Council of Guardians, which is charged with examining all legislation passed by the Majlis to ensure that it conforms to Islamic law. According to Article 91, the Council of Guardians consists of twelve members; six of them must be "just and pious" clergymen who are chosen by the *faqih* or the Leadership Council. The other six must be Muslim lawyers who are first selected by the High Council of Justice, then approved by a majority vote of the Majlis. The members of the Council of Guardians serve six-year terms, with half the members being changed every three years.

The responsibilities of the Council of Guardians are delineated in Articles 94 through 99. The members must review each law voted by the Majlis and determine, no later than ten days after the assembly has submitted a bill for consideration, whether or not it conforms with Islamic principles. If ten days are insufficient to study a particular piece of legislation, the Council of Guardians may request a ten-day extension. A majority of the clerical members of the Council of Guardians must agree that any given law does not violate religious precepts. If the Council of Guardians decides that a law contradicts Islam, the bill is returned to the Majlis for revision. If the Council of Guardians decides that a law conforms with Islam, that law is ratified.

During its first two years of operation, the Council of Guardians did not challenge Majlis bills and generally played a passive role in the political process. In May 1982, however, the Council of Guardians established its independent role by vetoing a law to nationalize all foreign trade. Since that time, the Council of Guardians has refused to ratify several pieces of legislation that would restrict property rights. In particular, the Council of Guardians has opposed the efforts of the Majlis to enact comprehensive land reform statutes.

The Judiciary

Article 156 of the Constitution provides for an independent judiciary. According to Articles 157 and 158, the highest judicial office is the High Council of Justice, which consists of five members who serve five-year, renewable terms. The High Council of Justice consists of the chief justice of the Supreme Court and the attorney general (also seen as State Prosecutor General), both of whom must be Shia *mujtahids* (members of the clergy whose demonstrated erudition in religious law has earned them the privilege of interpreting laws), and three other clergy chosen by religious jurists. The responsibilities of the High Council of Justice include establishing appropriate departments within the Ministry of Justice to deal with civil and criminal offenses, preparing draft bills related to the judiciary, and supervising the appointment of judges. Article 160 also stipulates that the minister of justice is to be chosen by the prime minister from among candidates who have been recommended by the High Council of Justice. The minister of justice is responsible for all courts throughout the country.

Article 161 provides for the Supreme Court, whose composition is based upon laws drafted by the High Council of Justice. The Supreme Court is an appellate court that reviews decisions of the lower courts to ensure their conformity with the laws of the country and to ensure uniformity in judicial policy. Article 162 stipulates that the chief justice of the Supreme Court must be a *mujtahid* with expertise in judicial matters. The *faqih,* in consultation with the justices of the Supreme Court, appoints the chief justice for a term of five years.

In 1980 Ayatollah Mohammad Beheshti was appointed by Khomeini as the first chief justice. Beheshti established judicial committees that were charged with drafting new civil and criminal codes derived from Shia Islamic laws. One of the most significant new codes was the Law of Qisas, which was submitted to and passed by the Majlis in 1982, one year after Beheshti's death in a bomb explosion (see The Rise and Fall of Bani Sadr, this ch.). The Law of Qisas provided that in cases of victims of violent crime, families could demand retribution, up to and including death. Other laws established penalties for various moral offenses, such as consumption of alcohol, failure to observe *hejab* (see Glossary), adultery, prostitution, and illicit sexual relations. Punishments prescribed in these laws included public floggings, amputations, and execution by stoning for adulterers.

The entire judicial system of the country has been desecularized. The attorney general, like the chief justice, must be a *mujtahid* and is appointed to office for a five-year term by the *faqih* (Article 162). The judges of all the courts must be knowledgeable in Shia jurisprudence; they must meet other qualifications determined by rules established by the High Council of Justice. Since there were insufficient numbers of qualified senior clergy to fill the judicial positions in the country, some former civil court judges who demonstrated their expertise in Islamic law and were willing to undergo religious training were permitted to retain their posts. In practice, however, the Islamization of the judiciary forced half of the former civil court judges out of their positions. To emphasize the independence of judges from the government, Article 170 stipulates that they are "duty bound to refrain from executing governmental decisions that are contrary to Islamic laws."

Local Government

As of 1987, Iran was divided into twenty-four provinces (*ostans*). Each province was subdivided into several counties (*shahrestans*). *Shahrestans* numbered 195, each of which was centered on the largest town within its boundaries. Most *shahrestans* took their names from those towns that served as county seats. All of the *shahrestans* consisted of two or more districts, or *bakhshs*. The 498 *bakhshs* were further subdivided into rural subdistricts (*dehestans*). Each *dehestan* consisted of several villages dispersed over an average area of 1,600 square kilometers.

The prerevolutionary provincial administrative structure was still employed in 1987. Thus, each province was headed by a governor general (*ostandar*), who was appointed by the minister of interior. Each county was headed by a governor (*farmandar*), also appointed by the minister of interior. Local officials, such as the chiefs of districts (*bakhshdars*), rural subdistricts (*dehyars*), and villages (*kadkhudas*—see Glossary), were appointed by the provincial governors general and county governors; these local officials served as representatives of the central government.

Prior to the Revolution, the governor general was the most powerful person in each province. Since 1979, however, the clerical *imam jomehs,* or prayer leaders, have exercised effective political power at the provincial level. The *imam jomeh* is the designated representative of the *faqih* in each county. Until 1987 each *imam jomeh* was appointed from among the senior clergy of the county. In June 1987, Khomeini approved guidelines for the election of *imam jomehs*. The *imam jomehs* have tended to work closely with the *komitehs* (revolutionary committees) and the Pasdaran, and in most counties these organizations are subordinate to the *imam jomehs*.

Political Dynamics

The Revolution replaced the old political elite, which had consisted of the Pahlavi family, wealthy families of the former Qajar dynasty, and wealthy industrialists and financiers, with a new political elite of Shia clergy and lay politicians of middle and lower middle class origin. The roots of most members of this new elite lay in the bazaar middle class (see Urban Society, ch. 2). Thus, the values of the new elite and the attitudes they professed were the ones most esteemed by the bazaar: respect for entrepreneurial skill, distrust of capitalist methods, and religious conservatism. Since the Revolution, they have striven to create a political order that incorporates their shared vision of an ideal society based upon Islamic principles.

Although the new political elite has been relatively united as to the overall goals envisaged for the Islamic Republic, its members have been deeply divided over various political, social, and economic policies deemed appropriate for achieving long-term objectives. These divisions have been manifested in political developments and struggles in the years since 1979. This period has been characterized by four phases, each dominated by distinct political issues. The first phase coincided with the provisional government of Prime Minister Bazargan, from February to November 1979. The next phase, which lasted until June 1981, was marked by the political rise and fall of Bani Sadr. During the third phase, which ended in December 1982, the government survived a major armed insurrection. During the next phase, which began in 1983, the political elite has been involved in the process of consolidating the theocratic regime, and that process was continuing in late 1987.

The Provisional Government

The government under the monarchy had been highly centralized. Although in theory the shah was a constitutional monarch, in practice he wielded extraordinary power as head of state, chief executive, and commander in chief of the armed forces. The shah was actively involved in day-to-day decision making and played a pivotal role as the most important formulator of national goals and priorities.

During the Revolution, the authority that had been concentrated in the shah and exercised through the bureaucracy based in Tehran was severely eroded; many governmental functions were usurped by several hundred *komitehs* that sprang up in urban neighborhoods, towns, and villages throughout the country. By the time the provisional government of Bazargan had acceded to power, these *komitehs,* usually attached to local mosques, were reluctant to surrender to the central government any of the wide-ranging powers they had assumed. Their determination to retain substantial power was supported by most members of the Revolutionary Council, a body formed by Khomeini in January 1979 to supervise the transition from monarchy to republic. The Revolutionary Council remained independent of the provisional government and undertook actions, or sanctioned those actions carried out by the revolutionary committees, that were in conflict with the policies pursued by the

The shah and his family, with eldest son, Reza Cyrus Pahlavi standing in rear. (Photo taken in the mid-1970s)

Bazargan cabinet. Inevitably, the provisional government, which wanted to reestablish the authority of the central government, would come into conflict with the *komitehs* and the proliferation of revolutionary organizations.

Bazargan's lack of essential backing from the Revolutionary Council, and ultimately from Khomeini, made it virtually impossible for his government to exercise effective control over arrests, trials, the appointment of officials, military-civilian relations, and property confiscations. Consequently, the various revolutionary organizations and the *komitehs* persistently challenged the authority of the provisional government throughout its brief tenure. Bazargan's apparent powerlessness even extended to the realm of foreign policy. When a group of college students overran the United States embassy in downtown Tehran, Bazargan and his cabinet were unable to prevent American personnel from being held as hostages. Acknowledging the impotence of his administration, Bazargan resigned after only nine months in office.

The issue of central versus local control that had plagued the Bazargan government continued to be a matter of political contention in 1987. Although the extreme diffusion of power that characterized the Bazargan government no longer prevailed in 1987, in comparison with the prerevolutionary situation, political power in Iran was relatively decentralized. This arrangement represented a balance between two vocal factions within the political elite. A procentralization faction has argued that the goals of an Islamic republic can best be achieved and maintained only if the institutions of government are strong. In contrast, a decentralization faction has insisted that bureaucratization is inherently destructive of long-term objectives and that the future of the Revolution can only be ensured through extensive popular participation in numerous revolutionary organizations.

The Rise and Fall of Bani Sadr

Bani Sadr was the first popularly elected president of the Islamic Republic. He assumed office with a decisive electoral vote—75 percent—and with the blessing of Khomeini. Within seventeen months, however, he had been impeached by the Majlis, and dismissed from office. Bani Sadr was destroyed, at least in part, by the same issue that had brought down Bazargan, that is, the efforts of the government to reestablish its political authority. Ironically, prior to his election as president, Bani Sadr had advocated decentralization of political power and had even helped to undermine the Bazargan government. As president, Bani Sadr became a convert to the principle that centralization of power was necessary;

soon, he was embroiled in a bitter political dispute with his former allies. The downfall of Bani Sadr, however, also involved a more fundamental issue, namely, the distribution of power among the new political institutions of the Republic. The fate of Bani Sadr demonstrated that the legislature was independent from and at least equal to the executive, the reverse situation of the Majlis under the Pahlavi shahs.

The conflict between Bani Sadr and the Majlis, which was dominated by the IRP, began when the assembly convened in June 1980. The first issue of controversy concerned the designation of a prime minister. Although the Constitution provides for the president to select the prime minister, it also stipulates that the prime minister must have the approval of the Majlis. After a protracted political struggle, the Majlis forced Bani Sadr to accept its own nominee, Rajai, as prime minister. The president, who had aspired to serve as a strong figure similar to de Gaulle when he was president of France, was unable to reconcile his differences with the prime minister, who preferred to formulate government policies in consultation with the Majlis. As Bani Sadr continued to lose influence over political developments to the Majlis, his own credibility as an effective leader was undermined.

The Majlis also frustrated Bani Sadr's attempts to establish the authority of the presidency in both domestic and foreign affairs. For example, the leaders of the IRP in the Majlis manipulated Bani Sadr's efforts to deal with Iran's international crises, the dispute with the United States over the hostages, and the war with Iraq that began in September 1980, in order to discredit him. When Bani Sadr tried to ally himself with the interests of the disaffected, secularized middle class, the IRP mobilized thousands of supporters, who were incited to assault persons and property derisively identified as "liberal," the euphemism used for any Iranian whose values were perceived to be Western. Bani Sadr attempted to defend his actions by writing editorials in his newspaper, *Enqelab-e Islami,* that criticized IRP policies and denounced the Majlis and other IRP-dominated institutions as being unconstitutional. Eventually, the leaders of the IRP convinced Khomeini that Bani Sadr was a danger to the Revolution. Accordingly, in June 1981 the Majlis initiated impeachment proceedings against the president and found him guilty of incompetence. Bani Sadr went into hiding even before Khomeini issued the decree dismissing him from office. At the end of July, he managed to flee the country in an airplane piloted by sympathetic air force personnel.

The Reign of Terror

The dismissal of Bani Sadr on June 21, 1981, brought to a head the underlying conflicts within the political elite and between its members and other groups contesting for power. In the final three months of Bani Sadr's presidency, political violence had intensified as organized gangs of *hezbollahis* (see Glossary) attacked individuals and organizations considered to be enemies of the Revolution. One of the main opposition parties, the Mojahedin (Mojahedin-e Khalq, or People's Struggle), rose up in a nationwide armed rebellion (see Opposition Political Parties in Exile, this ch.). Although the Mojahedin's uprising was quickly contained, during the following eighteen months the country was in a virtual state of siege as the government used extraordinary measures to suppress not only the Mojahedin but also other opposition movements. The government's fears of the opposition's capabilities were exacerbated by several sensational acts of terrorism directed at regime officials. These included the bombing of the IRP headquarters on June 28, 1981, which killed at least seventy top leaders of the party, including Beheshti, the secretary general of the party and the chief justice of the Supreme Court; the bombing at the prime minister's office on August 30, which killed several more leaders including former prime minister Rajai, who had replaced Bani Sadr as president, and the cleric Mohammad Javad Bahonar, who was Rajai's prime minister; and the assassinations of several key officials in Tehran and important provincial cities.

The government responded to the Mojahedin challenge by carrying out mass arrests and executions. At the height of the confrontation, an average of 50 persons per day were executed; on several days during September 1981, the total number executed throughout the country exceeded 100. Although the government dramatized its resolve to crush the uprising by conducting many of these mass executions in public, officials showed little interest in recording the names and numbers of the condemned. Thus, no statistics exist for the total number executed. Nevertheless, by the end of 1982 an estimated 7,500 persons had been executed or killed in street battles with the Pasdaran. Approximately 90 percent of the deaths had been associated with the Mojahedin, and the rest with smaller political groups that had joined the Mojahedin in the attempt to overthrow the government by armed force.

The efforts to root out the Mojahedin were accompanied by a general assault on procedural rights. The Pasdaran and specially recruited gangs of *hezbollahis* patrolled urban neighborhoods, ostensibly looking for the safe houses in which supporters of the Mojahedin

Voters cast their ballots in presidential election in January 1980
Copyright Lehtikuva/PHOTRI

and other opposition groups were suspected of hiding. They invaded such homes and arrested occupants without warrants. Persons suspected of insufficient loyalty to the regime were harassed and often subjected to arbitrary arrest and expropriation of their property. Extensive purges were initiated within all government ministries, and thousands of employees who failed loyalty tests were dismissed. Complaints were voiced that government agents eavesdropped on telephone conversations and opened private mail to collect information to use against citizens. The courts generally failed to protect individuals against violations of due process during this period.

The reign of terror officially ended in December 1982 when Khomeini issued an eight-point decree that effectively instructed the courts to ensure that the civil and due process rights of citizens be safeguarded. The decree forbade forcible entry of homes and businesses, arrest and detention without judges' orders, property expropriation without court authorization, and all forms of government spying on private persons. Special councils were to be established to investigate all complaints about court violations of individual rights.

The Consolidation of Theocracy

By the time Khomeini issued his judicial decree, the armed opposition had been suppressed. Although isolated acts of terrorism continued to take place after December 1982, the political elite no longer perceived such incidents as threatening to the regime. Both religious and lay leaders remained generally intolerant of dissent, but a gradual decline was noted in government abuses of civil liberties in line with the provisions of the eight-point decree. As preoccupation with internal security abated, the leaders began to establish consensus on the procedures that they believed were necessary to ensure the continuity of the new political institutions. Accordingly, elections were held for the Assembly of Experts, which chose a successor to Khomeini, and regulations were promulgated for the smooth functioning of the ministerial bureaucracies. The politicians also were determined to restore relative normalcy to society, albeit within prescribed Islamic bounds. Thus, they permitted the universities, which had been closed in 1980, to reopen, and they tried to control the excesses of the *hezbollahis*.

The refocusing of political energies on consolidating the regime also brought into the open the debate among members of the political elite over government policies. Two main issues dominated this debate: the role of the revolutionary organizations that operated fairly autonomously of the central government; and government intervention in the economy. The government of Prime Minister Mir-Hosain Musavi, which was approved by the Majlis in October 1981 and won a second parliamentary mandate in October 1985, tried to restrain the revolutionary organizations and advocated broad regulatory economic control. The Majlis served as the principal arena in which these issues were debated. Opposition from the Majlis blocked some laws outright and forced the government to accept compromises that diluted the effects of other policies.

Political Parties

During the final years of the Pahlavi monarchy, only a single, government-sponsored political party, the Rastakhiz, operated legally. Nevertheless, several legally proscribed political parties continued to function clandestinely. These included parties that advocated peaceful political change and those that supported the armed overthrow of Mohammad Reza Shah Pahlavi. Among the former parties were the National Front, which actually was a coalition of democratically inclined political parties and other organizations that originally had been founded in 1949; the Nehzat-e Azadi-yi Iran, or the Iran Freedom Movement (IFM), established in 1961 by democratically inclined clergy and laymen; and the Tudeh Party, a Marxist party that had been founded in 1941. The two most important guerrilla organizations were the Islamic Mojahedin and the Marxist Fadayan (Cherikha-ye Fadayan-e Khalq, or People's

While adults pray, a boy holds up a picture of Ayatollah Khomeini
Courtesy United Nations (John Isaac)

Guerrillas), both of which had been largely suppressed after carrying out several sensational terrorist actions in the early 1970s.

The overthrow of the Pahlavi monarchy allowed a full spectrum of Islamic, leftist, and secular ideas supporting the Revolution to flourish. With the exception of the monarchist Rastakhiz, which had dissolved, the prerevolutionary parties were reactivated, including the Mojahedin and Fadayan. In addition, several new parties were organized. These included secular parties, such as the National Democratic Front and the Radical Party; religious parties, such as the IRP and the Muslim Peoples' Republican Party; and leftist parties, such as the Paykar. All these parties operated openly and competitively until August 1979, when the Revolutionary Council forced the provisional government to introduce regulations to restrict the activities of most political parties.

The Domination of the Islamic Republican Party

Created in February 1979 by clergy who had been students of Khomeini before his exile from the country in 1964, the IRP emerged as the country's dominant political force. Core members included ayatollahs Beheshti, Abdol-Karim Musavi-Ardabili, and Mohammad Reza Mahdavi-Kani and hojjatoleslams Khamenehi, Rafsanjani, and Bahonar. All had been active in mobilizing large crowds for the mass demonstrations during the Revolution. Following the overthrow of the shah, the IRP leaders continued to use their extensive contacts with religious leaders throughout the country to mobilize popular support. The IRP leaders perceived the secular, leftist, and more liberal Islamic parties as threats to their own political goals. As early as the summer of 1979, the IRP encouraged its supporters to attack political rallies and offices of these other parties.

Although Khomeini himself never became a member of the IRP, the party leaders exploited their close association with him to project a popular image of the IRP as the party following the line of the imam Khomeini. This implicit identification helped IRP candidates win a majority of seats in the elections for the Assembly of Experts that drafted the Constitution. During the 1980 elections for the first Majlis, IRP candidates and independents sympathetic with most IRP positions again won a majority of the seats. The party's effective control of the Majlis emboldened the IRP in its harassment of opponents. Throughout 1980 IRP-organized gangs of *hezbollahis* used intimidation tactics against supporters of other political parties, and consequently, most of the secular parties were cowed into silence as their leaders fled to foreign exile.

By 1981 the only political party that could seriously challenge the IRP was the Mojahedin. This Islamic organization had grown rapidly in two years from a few hundred supporters to a membership of 150,000, mostly educated young men and women in the cities, who were attracted by the Mojahedin's liberal, even radical, interpretations of traditional Shia concepts. The ideological conflict between the Mojahedin and the IRP was serious because the former rejected the IRP argument of a religious basis for the political principle of *velayat-e faqih.* In fact, in June 1980 Khomeini denounced the Mojahedin on account of the organization's insistence that laymen were as qualified as clergy to interpret religious doctrines. Although the Mojahedin closed most of its branch offices following this verbal assault, unlike the secular political parties it was not easily intimidated by IRP-organized political violence. On the contrary, Mojahedin members engaged in armed clashes with *hezbollahis.* Tensions between Mojahedin and IRP partisans intensified during the political conflict between Bani Sadr and the IRP leaders. The Mojahedin lent its support to the beleaguered president; after Bani Sadr was impeached, the organization rose in armed rebellion against the IRP-dominated government.

Several of the small leftist parties joined the Mojahedin uprising. These included the Paykar, a prerevolutionary Marxist splinter from the Mojahedin, and the Fadayan Minority. The latter had split from the main Fadayan (thereafter referred to as the Fadayan Majority) in 1980 after a majority of the party's Central Committee had voted to support the government. Both the Paykar and the Fadayan Minority shared the view of the Mojahedin that the IRP was "merely a group of fascist clerics blocking a true revolution." The Mojahedin had a much broader base of support than did either of its allies, but the combined strength of all the parties could not match the capabilities of the IRP in terms of mobilizing masses of committed supporters. Thus, the government eventually was able to break the back of the armed opposition. The Mojahedin survived largely because its leader, Masud Rajavi, escaped to France, where he reorganized the party while in exile.

Not all of the leftist parties supported the Mojahedin's call to arms. Significantly, both the Tudeh and the Fadayan Majority condemned the insurrection and proclaimed their loyalty to the constitutional process. Even though these parties were permitted to function within narrowly circumscribed limits, the IRP leaders remained deeply suspicious of them. Both parties were distrusted because of their espousal of Marxist ideas. In addition, a widespread perception prevailed that the Tudeh was subservient to the Soviet Union, an attitude derived from the Tudeh's historic practice of basing its own foreign policy stances upon the line of the Soviet Union. In the autumn of 1982, toleration for the Tudeh dissipated quickly once the party began to criticize the decision to take the Iran-Iraq War into Iraqi territory. In February 1983, the government simultaneously arrested thirty top leaders of the Tudeh and accused them of treason. The party was outlawed, its offices closed, and members rounded up. Subsequently, Tudeh leaders were presented on television, where they confessed to being spies for the Soviet Union.

After the spring of 1983, the only nonreligious political party that continued to operate with legal sanction was the IFM. Prominent members included the former prime minister, Bazargan, and the former foreign minister, Ibrahim Yazdi, both of whom were elected to the first Majlis in 1980. The IFM opposed most of the policies of the IRP. Whenever Bazargan or another IFM member dared to speak out against IRP excesses, however, gangs of *hezbollahis* ransacked party offices. Bazargan was subjected to verbal abuse and even physical assault. He was powerless to protect one of his closest associates from being tried and convicted of treason for actions performed as an aide in the provisional government. The IFM boycotted the 1984 Majlis elections and Bazargan was barred from being a candidate in the 1985 presidential elections.

In practice, the IFM has been intimidated into silence, and thus its role as a loyal opposition party has been largely symbolic.

The IRP's success in silencing or eliminating organized opposition was directed not only at political parties but also was extended to other independent organizations. Even religious associations were not exempt from being forcibly disbanded if they advocated policies that conflicted with IRP goals. Although it emerged as the dominant political party, the IRP leadership failed to institutionalize procedures for developing the IRP into a genuine mass party. IRP offices were set up throughout the country, but in practice these did not function to recruit members. Rather, the offices served as headquarters for local clergy who performed a variety of political roles distinct from purely party functions. At both the national and the local levels, the IRP's clerical leaders perceived themselves as responsible for enforcing uniform Islamic behavior and thought. Thus, they generally viewed the party as a means of achieving this goal and not as a means of articulating the political views of the masses. In actuality, therefore, the IRP remained essentially an elitist party.

The debate within the political elite on power distribution and economic policy also adversely affected the IRP. Intensified dissent over economic programs, beginning in 1986, virtually paralyzed the party. Consequently, President Khamenehi, who had become the IRP's secretary general in 1981 following the death of Beheshti and several other key party leaders, decided it would be politically expedient to disband the IRP. Khamenehi and Rafsanjani jointly signed a letter to Khomeini in June 1987, in which they notified him of the party's polarization and requested his consent to dissolve the party. The *faqih* agreed, and the political party that had played such an important role during the first eight years of the Republic ceased to exist.

Opposition Political Parties in Exile

Many of the opposition parties that were suppressed inside the country were reorganized abroad. In 1987 more than a dozen political parties were active among the Iranian exile communities in Western Europe, the United States, and Iraq. All of these parties belonged to one of four broad ideological groups: monarchists, democrats, Islamicists, and Marxists. With the notable exception of the Mojahedin and the ethnic Kurdish parties, the expatriate opposition parties eschewed the use of political violence to achieve their shared goal of overthrowing the regime in Tehran.

Monarchists

The several monarchist political parties supported the restoration of a royalist regime in Iran. With varying degrees of enthusiasm the monarchists contended that Reza Cyrus Pahlavi, the eldest son (born 1960) of the last shah, was the legitimate ruler of the country. The former crown prince proclaimed himself Shah Reza II in 1980 following his father's death. Subsequently, he announced that he wanted to reign as a constitutional monarch and have a role similar to the role of the king of Spain. The most active monarchist group has been the Paris-based National Resistance Movement of Iran under the leadership of Shapour Bakhtiar, the last royalist prime minister. The National Resistance Movement's official position was to restore the 1906 constitution as its original drafters intended, with a shah that reigns rather than rules. In 1983 Bakhtiar's group agreed to cooperate with another Paris-based party, the Iran Liberation Front, which was led by elder statesman and former royalist prime minister Ali Amini. In general, the monarchist parties have been weakened by personality conflicts among the several leaders. When Manuchehr Ganji, a former royalist cabinet officer, broke with Amini in 1986, many Iran Liberation Front followers joined him in forming a new rival party called the Banner of Kaveh, after the legendary pre-Islamic blacksmith hero who defeated an evil tyrant and restored the rule of ancient Iran to a just shah.

Democratic Parties

The democratic parties also consisted of several groups, all of which supported a republican form of government; some of them, such as the National Democratic Front and the Kurdish Democratic Party of Iran (KDP), also espoused varying forms of socialism. The National Front, under the nominal leadership of Karim Sanjabi, and the National Democratic Front of Hedayatollah Matin-Daftari were both headquartered in Paris. Neither the National Front nor the National Democratic Front has engaged in significant political activity since 1982, although the latter party joined the Mojahedin-dominated National Council of Resistance in that year and was still a member in 1987. In contrast, the KDP, which advocated political and cultural rights for the Kurdish ethnic minority within a federally organized government, has been fighting against the Islamic Republic since 1979. By the beginning of 1986, however, KDP forces had been driven out of Iranian Kordestan, although they continued to conduct sporadic hit-and-run operations against units of the army and Pasdaran from bases in Iraqi and Turkish Kurdistan.

Islamic Groups

In 1987 the principal Islamic party in opposition to the government of Iran was the Mojahedin, which had been founded in 1965 by a group of religiously inspired young Shias. All were college graduates who believed that armed struggle was the only way to overthrow the shah. In the early 1970s, the Mojahedin engaged in armed confrontations with the military and carried out acts of terrorism, including the assassination of an American military adviser. The Mojahedin was crushed for the most part by 1975, but it reemerged in early 1979 and revitalized itself. Its interpretations of Islam, however, soon brought the organization into conflict with the IRP. During the summer of 1981, the Mojahedin unsuccessfully attempted an armed uprising against the government. More than 7,500 Mojahedin followers were killed during the conflict, and within one year the organization had once again been crushed (see The Domination of the Islamic Republican Party, this ch.).

Rajavi, the leader of the Mojahedin, managed to escape from Iran with Bani Sadr in July 1981. In France he reorganized the Mojahedin and tried to broaden its appeal by inviting all nonmonarchist parties to join the National Council of Resistance, which he and Bani Sadr established to coordinate opposition activities. Although most of the political parties refrained from cooperating with the Mojahedin, it nevertheless was most successful in recruiting new members and establishing a loyal following in United States and West European cities with sizable Iranian communities. From the perspective of the other political parties, one of the Mojahedin's most controversial positions was its public endorsement of direct contacts with Iraq, beginning in 1983. This was a contentious issue even within the National Council of Resistance and eventually led to Bani Sadr's break with Rajavi in 1984.

The Mojahedin maintained clandestine contact with sympathizers in Iran, and these underground cells regularly carried out isolated terrorist acts. For this reason, Tehran was more concerned about the Mojahedin than any other opposition group based abroad. The freedom of operation that the Mojahedin enjoyed in France became one of the issues that led to increasingly strained relations between the Iranian and French governments after 1982. When Paris actively sought to improve relations in late 1985, Prime Minister Musavi set restrictions on the Mojahedin as one of the conditions for normalizing relations. In June 1986, France pressured the

Mojahedin to curtail its activities. This move prompted Rajavi to accept an invitation from President Saddam Husayn of Iraq for the Mojahedin to establish its headquarters in Baghdad. Following the move to Iraq, the Mojahedin set up military training camps near the war front and periodically claimed that its forces had crossed into Iran and successfully fought battles against the Pasdaran. In June 1987, Rajavi announced the formation of the newly reorganized and expanded National Army of Liberation, open to non-Mojahedin members, to help overthrow the government of Iran.

Marxists

Like the Mojahedin, several Marxist political parties have maintained clandestine cells inside the country. Tudeh leaders, who managed to escape the government's mass arrests and forcible dissolution of their party in early 1983, reestablished the Tudeh in exile in the German Democratic Republic (East Germany). The Fadayan Majority, which later in 1983 suffered the same fate as the Tudeh, was decimated by government persecution; its surviving members eventually joined the Tudeh. The Komala (Komala-ye Shoreshgari-ye Zahmatkeshan-e Kordestan-e Iran, or Committee of the Revolutionary Toilers of Iranian Kordestan), a predominantly, but not exclusively, Kurdish party, had rejected as early as 1979 the Tudeh and Fadayan Majority policy of cooperation with the regime and continued to fight against central government forces up to the end of 1985, when it was forced to retreat to Iraqi Kurdistan. The Fadayan Minority had joined the Mojahedin uprising in 1981 and consequently lost most of its cadres in the ensuing confrontation with the regime. It has party offices in several West European cities and on university campuses in the United States. The Paykar, which also joined the Mojahedin's unsuccessful rebellion, was largely destroyed by 1982, although secret cells were believed still to exist in 1987.

Political Orientations

The Revolution of 1979 brought about a fundamental change in Iranian attitudes toward politics. Under the monarchy the political culture had been elitist in the sense that all major governmental decisions were made by the shah and his ministers. Most of the population acquiesced in this approach to politics. The fusion of traditional Shia Islamic ideals with political values during the Revolution resulted in the emergence of a populist political culture. The principal characteristics of this political culture are pervasive feelings that the government is obligated to ensure social justice and that every citizen should participate in politics. These feelings are acknowledged by the political leadership, which constantly expresses its concern for the welfare of the *mostazafin* (disinherited) and persistently praises the people's work in a host of political and religious associations.

The transformation of the political culture owed much to the charisma of Khomeini. He was determined not simply to overthrow the monarchy but also to replace it with a new society that derived its values from Islam. Khomeini believed that the long-term success of such an ideal Islamic government was dependent on the commitment and involvement of the masses. He envisaged the clergy as responsible for providing religious guidance, based on their expertise in Islamic law, to the people as they worked to create a new society in which religion and politics were fused. Khomeini's reputation for piety, learning, and personal integrity, as well as his forceful personality, have been important factors in the mobilization of thousands of committed followers to carry out the desecularization of the country's political institutions.

Mass political involvement has been both an objective and a characteristic of postrevolutionary Iran. Political participation, however, is not through political parties but through religious institutions. The mosque has become the single most important popular political institution. Participation in weekly congregational prayers, at which a political sermon is always delivered, is considered both a religious and a civic duty. For political aspirants, attendance at the weekly prayers is mandatory. Numerous religiopolitical associations are centered on the mosques. These organizations undertake a wide variety of activities, such as distributing ration coupons, investigating the religious credentials of aspirants for local offices, conducting classes in subjects ranging from the study of Arabic to superpower imperialism, and setting up teams to monitor shop prices and personal behavior. These organizations tend to be voluntary associations whose members devote several hours per week to their activities. Although most of these voluntary associations are for men, several are specifically for women.

Religious, rather than secular, organizations thus have the most important political roles. Factories, schools, and offices also have Islamic associations that undertake functions similar to those of the mosque voluntary associations. Although many secular groups exist, the majority of such associations as industrial and professional unions, university clubs, and mercantile organizations have acquired religious overtones. These private organizations generally have religious advisers who provide guidance to members on prayer ritual, Islamic law, and Shia history. Associations that try

A street vendor sells photographs of political leaders in the early 1980s
Courtesy United Nations (John Isaac)

to avoid mixing religion with business are suspected of being anti-Islamic and risk having their articles of incorporation revoked.

The Iranians who accept the dominant role of religion refer to themselves as *hezbollahis*. They tend to be fervent both in their profession of religious belief and in their loyalty to the Islamic Republic. Self-identified *hezbollahis* join the numerous mosque-related voluntary associations, the Pasdaran, and the personal staffs of the leading ayatollahs. Given their strong commitment to the regime, it was inevitable that *hezbollahis* would resent those whom they perceived as critical of the government. By 1987, however, it was still not possible, owing to the lack of field research in Iran from the time of the Revolution, to estimate what percent of the adult population considered themselves true *hezbollahis,* what percent was generally indifferent and simply acquiesced to regime policies, or what percent strongly disapproved of the government.

The Mass Media

The Constitution provides for freedom of the press as long as published material accords with Islamic principles. The publisher of every newspaper and periodical is required by law to have a valid publishing license. Any publication perceived as being anti-Islamic is not granted a publication license. In practice, the criteria for being anti-Islamic have been broadly interpreted to encompass all materials that include an antigovernment sentiment. In 1987 all the papers and magazines in circulation supported the basic political institutions of the Islamic Republic.

The major daily newspapers for the country are printed in Tehran. The leading newspapers include *Jumhori-yi Islami, Resalat, Kayhan, Abrar,* and *Etalaat.* The *Tehran Times* and *Kayhan International* are two English-language dailies in Tehran. While all these newspapers are considered to be appropriately Islamic, they do not endorse every program of the central government. For example, *Jumhori-yi Islami,* the official organ of the IRP before its dissolution in 1987, presents the official government line of prime minister Musavi. In contrast, *Resalat* is consistently critical of government policies, especially those related to the economy. The other newspapers criticize various aspects of governmental policies but do not have a consistent position.

No prior censorship of nonfiction exists, but any published book that is considered un-Islamic can be confiscated, and both the author and the publisher are liable for attempting to offend public morals or Islam. Private publishing companies thus tend to restrict their titles to subjects that will not arouse official ire. Numerous new books in history, science, geography, and classical poetry and literature have been published since 1987, including many manuscripts that had been banned under the shah. Although fiction is subject to prior censorship, numerous novels have been published.

All radio and television broadcasting is controlled by the government. Television and radio stations exist in Tehran and the major provincial cities. Stations in Azerbaijan and Kordestan are permitted to broadcast some programs in Azeri Turkish and Kurdish. Several of the banned opposition groups broadcast into Iran from stations in Iraq or the Caucasus republics of the Soviet Union. Both the British Broadcasting Company and the Voice of America broadcast Persian-language news and feature programs to FM radio channels in Iran.

Foreign Policy

Iran's foreign policy was dramatically reversed following the Revolution. After World War II, Iranian leaders considered their country to be part of the Western alliance system. They actively cultivated relations with the United States, both as a means of protecting their country from perceived political pressures emanating from the Soviet Union and as a matter of genuine ideological conviction.

The Revolution, which was laden with anti-American rhetoric, brought new leaders to power who disapproved of Iran's relationship with the United States. The new leaders were convinced that Washington had tried to maintain the shah in power, despite the mass demonstrations calling for his downfall, and were deeply suspicious of American intentions toward their Revolution. These leaders believed that the United States was plotting to restore the shah to power and were unresponsive to persistent efforts by American diplomats to persuade them that the United States had no ill intentions toward the new regime.

The more radical revolutionaries were determined to eradicate all traces of American influence from Iran. Fearing that the provisional government was seeking an accommodation with the United States, some of these radicals precipitated the seizure of the American embassy in November 1979. Subsequently, they exploited the protracted hostage crisis between Tehran and Washington to achieve their objective of terminating normal relations with the United States. The severing of ties with the United States was regarded not only as essential for expunging American influence from the country but also was considered a prerequisite for implementing their revolutionary foreign policy ideology. This new ideology consisted of two concepts: export of revolution and independence from both the East and the West. By the time the hostage crisis was finally resolved in January 1981, these ideas were embraced by the entire political elite.

Concept of Export of Revolution

The concept of exporting the Islamic Revolution derives from a particular worldview that perceives Islamic revolution as the means whereby Muslims and non-Muslims can liberate themselves from the oppression of tyrants who serve the interests of international imperialism. Both the United States and the Soviet Union are perceived as the two principal imperialist powers that exploit Third World countries. A renewed commitment to Islam, as the experience of Iran in overthrowing the shah demonstrated, permits oppressed nations to defeat imperialism. According to this perspective, by following Iran's example any country can free itself from imperialist domination.

Although the political elite agrees upon the desirability of exporting revolution, no unanimity exists on the means of achieving this goal. At one end of the spectrum is the view that propaganda efforts to teach Muslims about the Iranian example is the way to export revolution. Material assistance of any form is not necessary because oppressed people demonstrate their readiness for Islamic revolution by rising against dictatorial governments. Those who subscribe to this line of reasoning argue that Iranians received no external assistance in their Revolution but were successful as a result of their commitment to Islam. Furthermore, they cite Khomeini's often stated dictum that Iran has no intention of interfering in the internal affairs of other countries. This view is compatible with the maintenance of normal diplomatic relations between Iran and other countries.

At the opposite end of the spectrum is the view of Iran as the vanguard of a world revolutionary movement to liberate Muslim countries specifically, and other Third World countries generally, from imperialist subjugation. This activist perspective contends that the effective export of revolution must not be limited to propaganda efforts but must also include both financial and military assistance. Advocates of this view also cite Khomeini to justify their position and frequently quote his statements on the inevitability of the spread of Islamic revolution throughout the world.

Although various viewpoints fall between these two perspectives, since 1979 the two extreme views have been in contention in the formulation of foreign policy. In general, those who advocate exporting revolution solely through education and example have dominated the Ministry of Foreign Affairs, while those who favor active assistance to nonstate revolutionary groups have not served in important government positions relating to foreign policy. Nevertheless, because the supporters of an activist approach include some prominent political leaders, they have been able to exercise influence over certain areas of foreign relations. This has been especially true with respect to policy toward Lebanon and, to a lesser degree, policy in the Persian Gulf (see Relations with Regional Powers, this ch.).

The earliest organization promoting the active export of revolution was Satja, established in the spring of 1979 by Mohammad Montazeri and his close associate, Mehdi Hashemi. Satja's contacts with numerous nonstate groups throughout the Arab Middle East soon brought the organization into direct conflict with both the IRP leadership and the provisional government. Ayatollah Hosain Ali Montazeri, the father of Mohammad Montazeri, rebuked his son publicly, saying his son had been suffering illusions since being tortured by the former shah's secret police. Satja was forced to disband, but Mohammad Montazeri and Hashemi then joined the Pasdaran, where they eventually set up within that organization the Liberation Movements Office. Mohammad Montazeri was subsequently killed in the June 1981 bombing of the IRP headquarters that claimed the lives of over seventy prominent politicians. Following that development, Hashemi emerged as the principal leader of those advocating both moral and material support for revolutionaries around the world.

Under Hashemi's direction, the Liberation Movements Office operated autonomously of the Ministry of Foreign Affairs and maintained contact with opposition movements in several countries. Inevitably, its goal of promoting revolution abroad conflicted with the government's objective of normalizing relations with at least some of the governments that the Liberation Movements Office was helping to overthrow. Control over the direction of foreign policy was eventually resolved in favor of the Ministry of Foreign Affairs. In 1984 the Liberation Movements Office was removed from the jurisdiction of the Pasdaran, and its functions were transferred to the Ministry of Foreign Affairs and Ministry of Information and Security. Dissatisfied with these arrangements, Hashemi resigned from his posts and went to Qom. There he obtained a position within the large bureaucracy of Ayatollah Montazeri, who supervised six seminaries, several charitable organizations, a publishing house, and numerous political offices. Having lost none of his zeal for exporting revolution, Hashemi succeeded in setting up the Office for Global Revolution, which, although nominally part of Montazeri's staff, actually operated independently. By 1986 Hashemi's activities had once again brought him into conflict with the Ministry of Foreign Affairs. In October he and several of his associates were arrested, and the Office for Global Revolution was closed. During the summer of 1987, Hashemi and some of his colleagues were tried for "deviating from Islam"; Hashemi was found guilty and subsequently executed.

Concept of Neither East nor West

During the Revolution, Khomeini and his associates condemned both the United States and the Soviet Union as equally malevolent forces in international politics. They believed the United States, because of its close relationship with the regime of the shah, was the superpower that posed the most immediate danger to their revolution. Thus, they referred to the United States as the "Great Satan," a term that continued to be used in 1987. In contrast, they regarded the Soviet Union, because it had not been as closely involved with the shah, as the "Lesser Satan." The United States represented the West, or capitalism, while the Soviet Union represented the East, or socialism. The revolutionaries embraced Khomeini's view that these materialist ideologies were ploys to help maintain imperialist domination of the Third World, and thus they were inherently inimical to Islam. Consequently, a major foreign policy goal from the time of the Revolution has been to preclude all forms of political, economic, and cultural dependence on either Western capitalism or Eastern socialism and to rely solely upon Islam.

The most dramatic symbol of the revolutionary determination to assert independence of both the East and the West was the hostage crisis between Iran and the United States. Although the seizure of the American embassy in Tehran in November 1979 initially had been undertaken by nongovernmental groups to demonstrate their anger at the admission of the shah into the United States, this incident rapidly developed into a major international crisis when Khomeini and the Revolutionary Council gave their ex post facto sanction to it. The crisis lasted for 444 days, during which time those political leaders who were most hostile to Western influences used it to help achieve their aim of severing diplomatic and other ties between Tehran and Washington.

After 1980 Iran adopted positions opposed to those of the United States on a wide variety of international issues. Although officials in both countries eventually approved of some secret contacts, most notably those involving clandestine arms shipments to Iran from Israel and the United States during 1985 and 1986, the bitterness that the hostage crisis left on both sides made it difficult for either country to consider normalizing relations as late as the end of 1987.

The West European allies of the United States were also viewed with suspicion. France, in particular, was singled out as a "mini-Satan" that collaborated with the United States in the oppression of Muslims. Although initially Iran's political elite were favorably disposed toward France because Paris had provided refuge to Khomeini when he was expelled from Iraq in 1978, relations between the two countries steadily deteriorated after 1980. Two issues were the source of the Iranian hostility: France's support of Iraq, especially its provision of weapons, and the fact that since 1981 France has been the headquarters for most of the expatriate opposition groups. France and Iran also had opposing perspectives on several international issues, most notably developments in Lebanon. In the spring of 1986, the French government initiated a policy of trying to reduce tensions with the Islamic Republic. As part of this effort, France pressured the Mojahedin to close its Paris headquarters and agreed to repay the Iranian government part of a US$1 billion loan that had been extended to a French nuclear energy consortium during the reign of the shah. France was unwilling, however, to accede to Iran's demand that it cease arms sales to Iraq. Consequently, relations between Paris and Tehran vacillated between correctness and tension.

This was dramatically illustrated in July 1987, when the two countries became involved in a major diplomatic confrontation. The Iranian embassy in Paris provided haven to an Iranian national who had been summoned to appear in court in connection with a series of terrorist bombings in the French capital. Although France broke diplomatic relations with Iran over this issue and a series of related incidents, both countries seemed determined to salvage their rapprochement policy. In December France agreed to expel more Iranian Mojahedin activists and to repay Iran a second installment on its outstanding loan, in return for Iranian mediation efforts in obtaining the release of French citizens being held as hostages in Lebanon. Diplomatic relations were restored as of the end of 1987.

Iran's postrevolutionary relations with the Soviet Union and its allies have been significantly less dramatic. Tehran has expressed its opposition to numerous Soviet international policies. For example, Iran severely criticized the Soviet Union for dispatching its troops into Afghanistan at the end of 1979 and took the lead several months later in denouncing Moscow at a conference of foreign ministers of Islamic countries. Soviet support for the Marxist-Leninist regime in Kabul continued to be a source of friction between the two countries in 1987. Soviet support of Iraq, especially the provision of weapons, has been another area of contention between Moscow and Tehran. Iran also has accused the Soviet Union of assisting Iranian opposition groups, especially the Tudeh. Nevertheless, Iran and the Soviet Union have maintained diplomatic relations, and the two countries have striven to keep their relations correct, if not always cordial.

Although Iran remained distrustful of the Soviet Union's international policies, it generally avoided injecting its anti-imperialist ideology into economic relations. Thus, trade with the Soviet Union became relatively important after 1979. This included not only direct trade between Iran and the Soviet Union but also transit trade from Iran through the Soviet Union to markets in Europe. Tensions over economic matters continued, however, particularly over the issue of natural gas shipments to the Caucasus republics via the pipeline that had been constructed before the Revolution. When in 1980 Moscow resisted Tehran's attempt to raise the price charged for this natural gas, the pipeline was closed. In the summer of 1986, the two countries worked out a new agreement but as of December 1987 natural gas shipments had not been resumed.

The Iran-Iraq War

One of the earliest focuses of Iran's interest in exporting revolution was the Persian Gulf area. The revolutionary leaders viewed the Arab countries of the Gulf, along with Iraq, as having tyrannical regimes subservient to one or the other of the superpowers. Throughout the first half of 1980, Radio Iran's increasingly strident verbal attacks on the ruling Baath (Arab Socialist Resurrection) Party of Iraq irritated that government, which feared the impact of Iranian rhetoric upon its own Shias, who constituted a majority of the population. Thus, one of the reasons that prompted Iraqi President Saddam Husayn to launch the invasion of Iran in the early autumn of 1980 was to silence propaganda about Islamic revolution. Baghdad believed that the postrevolutionary turmoil in Iran would permit a relatively quick victory and lead to a new regime in Tehran more willing to accommodate the interests of Iran's Arab neighbors. This hope proved to be a false one for Iraq.

From the point of view of foreign relations, Iran's war with Iraq had evolved through four phases by 1987. During the first phase, from the fall of 1980 until the summer of 1982, Iran was on the defensive, both on the battlefield and internationally. The country was preoccupied with the hostage crisis at the outbreak of the war, and most diplomats perceived its new government as generally ineffective. During the second phase, from 1982 to the end of 1984, the success of Iran's offensives alarmed the Arab states, which were concerned about containing the spread of Iran's Revolution. The third phase, 1985 to 1987, was characterized by Iranian efforts to win diplomatic support for its war aims. The fourth phase began in the spring of 1987 with the involvement of the United States in the Persian Gulf.

The Iraqi invasion and advance into Khuzestan during phase one surprised Iran. The Iraqis captured several villages and small towns in the provinces of Khuzestan and Ilam and, after brutal hand-to-hand combat, captured the strategic port city of Khorramshahr (see The Iran-Iraq War, ch. 5). The nearby city of Abadan, with its huge oil-refining complex, was besieged; Iraqi forces moved their offensive lines close to the large cities of Ahvaz and Dezful. Although the Iranians stemmed the Iraqi advance by the end of 1980, they failed to launch any successful counteroffensives. Consequently, Iraq occupied approximately one-third of Khuzestan Province, from which an estimated 1.5 million civilians had fled. Property damage to factories, homes, and infrastructure in the war zone was estimated in the billions of dollars.

Although the war had settled into a stalemate by the end of 1980, during the following eighteen months Iranian forces made gradual advances and eventually forced most of the Iraqi army to withdraw across the border. During this period, Iran's objectives were to end the war by having both sides withdraw to the common border as it had existed prior to the invasion. Baghdad wanted Tehran's consent to the revision of a 1975 treaty that had defined their common riparian border as the middle channel of the Shatt al Arab (which Iranians call the Arvand Rud). Baghdad's proclaimed reason for invading Iran, in fact, had been to rectify the border; Iraq claimed that the international border should be along the low water of the Iranian shore, as it had been prior to 1975. In international forums, Iran generally failed to win many supporters to its position.

The second phase of the war began in July 1982, when Iran made the fateful decision, following two months of military victories, to invade Iraqi territory. The change in Iran's strategic position also brought about a modification in stated war aims. Khomeini and other leaders began to say that a simple withdrawal of all forces to the pre-September 1980 borders was no longer sufficient. They now demanded, as a precondition for negotiations, that the aggressor be punished. Iran's leaders defined the new terms explicitly: the removal from office of Iraqi president Saddam Husayn and the payment of reparations to Iran for war damages in Khuzestan. The Iranian victories and intransigence on terms for peace coincided with the Israeli invasion of Lebanon; consequently, Iran decided to dispatch a contingent of its own Pasdaran to Lebanon to aid the Shia community there. These developments revived fears of Iranian-induced political instability, especially among the Arab rulers in the Persian Gulf. In 1983 Iraq acquired French-made Exocet missiles, which were used to launch attacks on Iranian oil facilities in the Persian Gulf. Iran retaliated by attacking tankers loaded with Arab oil, claiming that the profits of such oil helped to finance loans and grants to Iraq. Iraq responded by attacking ships loaded with Iranian oil, thus launching what became known as the tanker war.

By the beginning of 1985, the third phase of the war had begun. During this phase, Iran consciously sought to break out of its diplomatic isolation by making overtures to various countries in an effort to win international support for its war objectives. Iran's diplomatic efforts concentrated particularly on the countries of the Arab world. The Iranian initiatives led to significantly improved relations with such countries as Oman and Saudi Arabia.

Iraq responded to Iran's diplomatic initiatives by intensifying its attacks on Iran-related shipping in the Persian Gulf. Iranian retaliation increasingly focused on Kuwaiti shipping. By early 1987, Iran's actions prompted Kuwait to request protection for its shipping from both the Soviet Union and the United States. By the summer of 1987, most European and Arab governments were blaming Iran for the tensions in the Gulf, and Iran again found itself diplomatically isolated.

Relations with Regional Powers

The Persian Gulf States

Although the shah had been unpopular among the rulers of the six states on the Arab side of the Persian Gulf, the Revolution in Iran, nevertheless, was a shock to them. Iran under the shah had been the main guarantor of political stability in the region. Under the Republic, Iran was promising to be the primary promoter of revolution. All six countries—Bahrain, Kuwait, Oman, Qatar, Saudi Arabia, and the United Arab Emirates (UAE)—were ruled by hereditary monarchs who naturally feared the new rhetoric from Tehran. Indeed, during the first year following the Revolution, throughout the Gulf region numerous acts of political sabotage and violence occurred, claiming inspiration from the Iranian example. The most sensational of these was the assault by Muslim dissidents on the Grand Mosque in the holy city of Mecca, Saudi Arabia. Other clashes occurred between groups of local Shias and security forces in Saudi Arabia, Kuwait, and Bahrain.

The outbreak of war between Iran and Iraq further alarmed the Persian Gulf Arab states. In 1981 they joined together in a collective

Foreign Minister Ali Akbar Velayati addressing
the United Nations General Assembly in 1982
Courtesy United Nations

defense alliance known as the Gulf Cooperation Council (GCC). Although the GCC announced its neutrality with respect to the Iran-Iraq War, Iran perceived its formation as part of the Iraqi war effort and generally was hostile toward it. The GCC for its part suspected Iran of supporting antigovernment groups throughout the Persian Gulf. These concerns were heightened in December 1981, when authorities in Bahrain announced the discovery of a clandestine group that had plans to carry out sabotage and terrorist acts as part of an effort to overthrow the government; several of the plotters had links to Iranian clerics. In December 1983, a series of bombings occurred in Kuwait, including incidents at the American and French embassies; the Arab nationals who were captured and charged with these acts of terrorism were members of an Iraqi Shia movement, Ad Dawah, that was headquartered in Tehran. In May 1985, a suicide driver unsuccessfully tried to kill the ruler of Kuwait.

Despite GCC suspicions of Iranian involvement in subversive activities, until 1987 more cooperation than confrontation was found between Iran and the GCC members. In general, Iran avoided dealing with the GCC as an entity, preferring to ignore its existence and to treat each country separately. Iran's relations with the six component states varied from friendliness to hostility. For example, Iran and the UAE maintained relatively cordial relations. The political ties between the two countries were reinforced by economic ties. An Iranian mercantile community in the UAE was concentrated in Dubayy, a city that emerged—following the destruction of Khorramshahr—as an important transit center where international goods destined for Iran were offloaded into smaller boats capable of entering small Iranian fishing towns that served as ports of entry despite their lack of docking facilities. In Bahrain, where the ruling family was Sunni Muslim and a majority of the population was Shia, lingering suspicions of Iranian intentions did not inhibit the government from improving diplomatic relations with Tehran. Because there were no outstanding issues between Iran and Qatar, relations between them were generally correct.

Iran's relations with the other three GCC members—Kuwait, Oman, and Saudi Arabia—have been more complex and, throughout the early and mid-1980s, have been characterized by alternating periods of tension and mutual accommodation. For example, immediately after the Revolution, Iranian propaganda singled out the sultan of Oman as an example of the kind of "un-Islamic tyrant" who should be overthrown. This hostility sprang from the revolutionaries' perception of the Omani ruler as having been a close friend of the shah. Iran's view had developed in the 1970s when the shah sent military assistance, including an Iranian military contingent, to help the sultan crush a long-term rebellion. More significant, however, the Iranian leaders regarded the sultan as subservient to the United States. They denounced his policies of supporting the Camp David Accords, providing facilities for American air crews who attempted the unsuccessful rescue of the hostages in April 1980, signing an agreement for American military use of the air base on Masirah Island, and discussing with the United States construction of an airfield on the Musandam Peninsula overlooking the Strait of Hormuz. Oman generally refrained from responding to Iranian charges and consequently avoided an escalation of the verbal barrages. Despite the many areas of friction, tensions between Iran and Oman gradually abated after 1981. The movement toward more correct diplomatic relations culminated in 1987 with a state visit of the Omani foreign minister to Iran.

Iran's relations with Saudi Arabia and Kuwait were strained because both of these countries provided major financial support to Iraq after the Iran-Iraq War began. In addition, Iran accused them of providing logistical assistance for Iraqi bombing raids on Iranian oil installations. For their part, Saudi Arabia and Kuwait believed that Iran supported subversive activities among their Shia minorities. They also resented Iranian attacks on their shipping.

Saudi Arabia annually confronted embarrassing incidents during the pilgrimage season when Iranians tried to stage political demonstrations. Nevertheless, both Saudi Arabia and Kuwait made efforts to seek a rapprochement with Iran in 1985 and 1986. The Saudi efforts were more successful and resulted in an exchange of visits of the Saudi and Iranian foreign ministers in 1985. The Saudis and Iranians also began to cooperate in some areas of mutual interest, such as international oil policy. In contrast, relations between Kuwait and Iran did not improve significantly. In the fall of 1986, Iran began to single out Kuwait's ships for retaliatory attacks, and this led to a worsening of diplomatic relations.

Political tensions between Tehran and Kuwait increased significantly after the United States agreed to reflag Kuwaiti oil tankers. Iran accused Kuwait and its neighbors, especially Saudi Arabia, of being mere puppets of the "Great Satan." During the pilgrimage to Mecca in the summer of 1987, Iran encouraged the pilgrims—150,000 of whom had come from Iran—to demonstrate against the United States and the corrupt rulers of the Gulf. More than 400 pilgrims, including at least 300 Iranians, were killed in a stampede in Mecca when Saudi security forces attempted to break up a demonstration.

Turkey, Pakistan, and Afghanistan

Relations with Turkey and Pakistan since the Revolution generally have been amicable and without any major issues. Before the Revolution, Iran had joined both countries in a defensive alliance (that included Britain with the United States as an observer), the Central Treaty Organization, and in an economic agreement, the Regional Cooperation for Development. Iran withdrew from both agreements after the Revolution. Nevertheless, Iran's economic ties with Pakistan and Turkey have expanded significantly. Both countries have become important trade partners of Iran. Turkey also has become the major transit route for goods traveling by truck and rail between Europe and Iran. The increased volume of trade with Turkey and Pakistan has been facilitated both by their location and by the ideology of "neither East nor West," which advocates reducing imports from the industrialized nations in favor of importing more from Muslim and Third World countries.

Although Iran maintained diplomatic relations with Afghanistan in 1987, Iran was critical of both the Marxist-Leninist government in Kabul and the presence of Soviet troops in the country. Although distrustful of the ideologies of most groups, Iran's leaders generally supported the cause of the Afghan resistance. Iran provided financial and limited military assistance to those Afghan resistance forces whose leaders had pledged loyalty to the Iranian vision of Islamic revolution. Iran also hosted about 2.3 million refugees who had fled Afghanistan.

Israel and the Non-Gulf Arab States

Prior to the Revolution, Iran and Israel had been de facto allies in the Middle East. One of the very first acts of the provisional government was to denounce that relationship and to turn over the former Israeli mission in Tehran to the Palestine Liberation Organization. All trade with Israel was banned, especially the sale of oil. Iranian leaders contended that Israel's existence was illegitimate, because it came about as a result of the destruction of Palestine. Therefore, Iran advocated eradicating Israel and reconstituting Palestine. Those Arabs who advocated compromise with Israel, such as Anwar as Sadat of Egypt, were excoriated as traitors. In general, Iran's relations with the Arab states have been based on perceptions of each state's relations with Israel. Thus, Iran has been hostile toward those states it regarded as willing to accept Israel's existence—Egypt, Jordan, Morocco, and Tunisia—and friendly toward those it regarded as sharing Iranian views—Algeria, Libya, and Syria. Despite its uncompromising position, however, Iran is known to have purchased weapons clandestinely from Israel as recently as 1985.

Syria has been revolutionary Iran's principal ally in the Middle East. This relationship involved both political and economic ties. The de facto alliance between the two countries emerged at the beginning of 1982. At that time, Iran supported the government of Hafiz al Assad against the Muslim Brotherhood, which had risen in rebellion against the secularizing policies of the ruling Baath Party. Iran's backing of the Syrian government was significant because the Muslim Brotherhood was the first Islamic political group to claim the Iranian Revolution as the primary inspiration for its rebellion. Soon after the Muslim Brotherhood had been crushed, Damascus shut down the pipeline through which Iraqi oil crossed Syria to reach Mediterranean ports. This action against another Arab state, which also was ruled by a Baath party, was an important gesture in support of the Iranian war effort. The action was also a hostile blow against Iraq because Iraqi Persian Gulf ports had been blockaded since the beginning of the war, and the only other exit route for its oil exports was through a smaller pipeline traversing Turkey. Iran had agreed to provide Syria 20,000 barrels of oil per day free of charge as compensation for the transit fees Syria would lose by closing the pipeline. Iran also agreed to sell Syria additional oil it required, at a heavily discounted price.

In 1987 this agreement was again renewed. Syria also provided Iran arms from its own stock of Soviet- and East European-made weapons.

Iran's Role in Lebanon

The Shia clergy in Iran have long had an interest in the Shia population of Lebanon. Clergy for the Lebanese Shia communities were trained in Iran before the Revolution, and intermarriage between clerical families in both countries had been occurring for several generations. Lebanon's most prominent Shia cleric, Imam Musa as Sadr, who mysteriously disappeared in 1978 while on a trip to Libya, was born in Iran into a clerical family with relatives in Lebanon, a fact that facilitated his acceptance in the latter country. Musa as Sadr was a political activist, like so many clerics of his generation trained in Qom and An Najaf, and he succeeded in politicizing the Lebanese Shias. Thus, it was natural that the Shia community of Lebanon should become one of the earliest to which Iranian advocates of exporting revolution turned their attention. Their analysis of the political situation in Lebanon in 1979 and 1980 convinced them that the country was ripe for achieving an Islamic revolution and that conditions were also favorable for eradicating Israel and recreating Palestine.

The main constraint on Iran's political involvement in Lebanon was Amal, the political organization established by Musa as Sadr. After Sadr's disappearance, Amal had fallen under the influence of secularized Shias who preferred the political integration of the Shia community within a pluralistic state and regarded the Iranian vision of Islamic revolution as inappropriate for Lebanon. The Israeli invasion of southern Lebanon in 1982, however, provided Iran an opportunity to circumvent Amal's domination of the Shias. Syria permitted a contingent of several hundred Pasdaran members to enter Lebanon, ostensibly to help fight against Israel. The Pasdaran established posts in the eastern Biqa Valley and from there proselytized on behalf of Islamic revolution among poor and uprooted Shia young people. The ideas of Islamic revolution appealed to many of the Shias who were recruited by new political groups such as Islamic Amal and the Hizballah, both of which opposed the comparative moderation of Amal. The support of the Pasdaran provided these groups with a direct link to Tehran, and this permitted Iran to become one of the foreign powers exerting influence in Lebanon. In 1987 an estimated 500 members of the Pasdaran were in Lebanon.

Iran and International Organizations

Iran is a charter member of the United Nations (UN). Although it belongs to all UN specialized agencies, the Republic has not participated as actively as the monarchy in the world organization. Iran criticized the UN for nonsupport during the Iran-United States crisis over the hostages. Iran also criticized the UN for failing to condemn Iraq as an "aggressor" following the Iraqi invasion of Iran in 1980.

As a major oil producer and exporter, Iran is a founding member of the Organization of Petroleum Exporting Countries (OPEC—see Glossary). Both under the monarchy and under the Republic the government has advocated that OPEC maintain high prices for the oil that members sell on the international market. Iran supported lower production quotas for members as a means of keeping international oil prices high. Between 1979 and 1985, Iran generally was regarded as uncooperative at the semi-annual OPEC ministerial conferences. Since 1985, however, Iran has worked with Saudi Arabia, the largest oil producer within OPEC, to draft production and pricing compromises acceptable to the whole OPEC membership.

* * *

The most detailed examination of the government of Iran during the first four years following the Revolution is Shaul Bakhash's *The Reign of the Ayatollahs.* Considerable detail about various policies pursued by the government can be found in Dilip Hiro's *Iran under the Ayatollahs.* A collection of essays that analyze the role of the clergy in politics, the postrevolutionary economy, the aspects of the "new" Islamic ideology, the opposition, and Iran's relations with the superpowers is found in *The Iranian Revolution and the Islamic Republic,* edited by Nikki Keddie and Eric Hooglund. *Revolutionary Iran* by Ruhollah Ramazani examines Iran's foreign policy in the Middle East since 1979. (For further information and complete citations, see Bibliography.)

Chapter 5. National Security

A sword and scabbard from a bas-relief at Persepolis, ca. 500 B.C.

DURING THE 1970s, imperial Iran developed one of the most impressive military forces in the Middle East, and it used those forces to assume a security role in the Persian Gulf after the British military withdrawal in 1971. The defense of the strategic Strait of Hormuz preoccupied the shah, as it did the other conservative monarchs in the area. Freedom of navigation in the Gulf was important for international shipping, and the shah was perceived, at least in certain quarters, as the undeclared "policeman of the West in the Gulf." When independent observers concluded that Iran's military buildup exceeded its defensive needs, the shah declared that his responsibilities extended beyond Iran and included the protection of the Gulf. Increasingly, the military played a pivotal role in promoting this policy and, in doing so, gained a privileged position in society. Under the Nixon Doctrine of 1969, according to which aiding local armed forces was considered preferable to direct United States military intervention, Washington played an important part in upgrading the Iranian military forces. The United States supplied Iran with sophisticated hardware and sent thousands of military advisers and technicians to help Iran absorb the technology.

By 1979 the United States military presence in Iran had drawn the wrath of Iranians. Ayatollah Sayyid Ruhollah Musavi Khomeini specifically identified the shah's pro-American policies as detrimental to Iranian interests and called on his supporters to oppose the United States presence. He cited special legal privileges granted United States personnel in Iran as an example of the shah's excessive identification of Iran's interests with those of Washington.

Following the Islamic Revolution of 1979, the armed forces underwent fundamental changes. The revolutionary government purged high-ranking officials as well as many mid-ranking officers identified with the Pahlavi regime and created a loyal military force, the Pasdaran (Pasdaran-e Enghelab-e Islami, or Islamic Revolutionary Guard Corps, or Revolutionary Guards), whose purpose was to defend the Revolution. When the Iran-Iraq War began, however, the revolutionary government had to acknowledge its need for the professional services of many of the purged officers to lead the armed forces in defending the country against Iraq. The army was unexpectedly successful in the war, even though, as of 1987, the regular armed forces continued to be regarded with considerable suspicion. Within the Iranian military there was competition between the regular and irregular armed forces. The Islamic clergy (see Glossary) continued to rely more heavily on the loyal Pasdaran to defend the regime. Moreover, most of the casualties were members of the Pasdaran and Basij volunteers who composed the irregular armed forces. In the late 1980s, in addition to defending the Revolution, Iran continued to follow certain national security policies that had remained constant during the previous four decades.

Armed Forces

Historical Background

The importance of the armed forces in Iran flows from Iran's long history of successive military empires. For over 2,500 years, starting with the conquests of the Achaemenid rulers of the sixth century B.C., Iran developed a strong military tradition. Drawing on a vast manpower pool in western Asia, the Achaemenid rulers raised an army of 360,000, from which they could send expeditions to Europe and Africa.

Iranian early military history boasts the epic performances of such great leaders as Cyrus the Great and Darius I. The last great Iranian military ruler was Nader Shah, whose army defeated the Mughals of India in 1739. Since then, however, nearly all efforts to conquer more territory or check encroaching empires have failed. During much of the nineteenth and early twentieth centuries, Iran was divided and occupied by British and Russian military forces. When their interests coincided in 1907, London and St. Petersburg entered into the Anglo-Russian Agreement, which formally divided Iran into two spheres of influence. During World War I, the weak and ineffective Qajar Dynasty, allegedly hindered by the effects of the Constitutional Revolution of 1905–1907, could not prevent increasing British and Russian military interventions, despite Iran's declaration of neutrality (see World War I, ch. 1).

In 1918 the Qajar armed forces consisted of four separate foreign-commanded military units. Several provincial and tribal forces could also be called on during an emergency, but their reliability was highly questionable. More often than not, provincial and tribal forces opposed the government's centralization efforts, particularly because Tehran was perceived to be under the dictate of foreign powers. Having foreign officers in commanding positions over Iranian troops added to these tribal and religious concerns. Loyal, disciplined, and well trained, the most effective government unit was the 8,000-man Persian Cossacks Brigade. Created in 1879 and commanded by Russian officers until the 1917 Bolshevik Revolution, after which its command passed into Iranian hands, the brigade represented the core of the new Iranian armed forces.

Swedish officers commanded the 8,400-man Gendarmerie (later the Imperial Gendarmerie and after 1979 the Islamic Iranian Gendarmerie), organized in 1911 as the first internal security force. The 6,000-man South Persia Rifles unit was financed by Britain and commanded by British officers from its inception in 1916. Its primary task was to combat tribal forces allegedly stirred up by German agents during World War I. The Qajar palace guard, the Nizam, commanded by a Swedish officer, was a force originally consisting of 2,000 men, although it deteriorated rapidly in numbers because of rivalries. Thus, during World War I the 24,400 troops in these four separate military units made up one of the weakest forces in Iranian history.

Upon signing the Treaty of Brest-Litovsk with Germany and Turkey on December 15, 1917, Russia put in motion its eventual withdrawal from Iran, preparing the way for an indigenous Iranian military. A hitherto little-known colonel, Reza Khan (later known as Reza Shah Pahlavi, founder of the Pahlavi dynasty), assumed leadership of the Persian Cossacks Brigade in November 1918, after the expulsion of its Russian commanders. In February 1921, Reza Khan and Sayyid Zia ad Din Tabatabai, a powerful civilian conspirator, entered Tehran at the head of 1,500 to 2,500 Persian Cossacks and overthrew the Qajar regime. Within a week, Tabatabai formed a new government and made Reza Khan the army chief. Recognizing the importance of a strong and unified army for the modern state, Reza Khan rapidly dissolved all "independent" military units and prepared to create a single national army for the first time in Iranian history.

Riding on a strong nationalist wave, Reza Khan was determined to create an indigenous officer corps for the new army, though an exception was made for a few Swedish officers serving in the Gendarmerie. Within a matter of months, officers drawn from the Persian Cossacks represented the majority. Nevertheless, Reza Khan recognized the need for Western military expertise and sent Iranian officers to European military academies, particularly St. Cyr in France, to acquire modern technical know-how. In doing so, he hoped the Iranian army would increase its professionalism without jeopardizing the country's still fragile social, political, and religious balance.

By 1925 the army had grown to a force of 40,000 troops, and Reza Khan, under the provisions of martial law, had gradually assumed control of the central government. His most significant political accomplishment came in 1925 when the parliament, or Majlis (see Glossary), enacted a universal military conscription law. In December 1925, Reza Khan became the commander in chief of the army; with the assistance of the Majlis, he assumed the title of His Imperial Majesty Reza Shah Pahlavi (see The Era of Reza Shah, 1921–41, ch. 1).

Reza Khan created the Iranian army, and the army made him shah. Under the shah, the powerful army was used not only against rebellious tribes but also against anti-Pahlavi demonstrations. Ostensibly created to defend the country from foreign aggression, the army became the enforcer of Reza Shah's internal security policies. The need for such a military arm of the central government was quite evident to Reza Shah, who allocated anywhere from 30 to 50 percent of total yearly national expenditures to the army. Not only did he purchase modern weapons in large quantities, but, in 1924 and 1927, respectively, he created an air force and a navy as branches of the army, an arrangement unchanged until 1955. With the introduction of these new services, the army established two military academies to meet the ever-rising demand for officers. The majority of the officers continued to be trained in Europe, however, and upon their return served either in the army or in key government posts in Tehran and the provinces. By 1941 the army had gained a privileged role in society. Loyal officers and troops were well paid and received numerous perquisites, making them Iran's third wealthiest class, after the shah's entourage and the powerful merchant and landowning families. Disloyalty to the shah, evidenced by several coup attempts, was punished harshly.

By 1941 the army stood at 125,000 troops—five times its original size—and was considered well trained and well equipped. Yet, when the army faced its first challenge, the shah was sorely disappointed; the Iranian army failed to repulse invading British and Soviet forces. London and Moscow had insisted that the shah expel Iran's large German population and allow shipments of war supplies to cross the country en route to the Soviet Union. Both of these conditions proved unacceptable to Reza Shah; he was sympathetic to Germany, and Iran had declared its neutrality in World War II. Iran's location was so strategically important to the Allied war effort, however, that London and Moscow chose to overlook Tehran's claim of neutrality. Against the Allied forces, the Iranian army was decimated in three short days, the fledgling air force and navy were totally destroyed, and conscripts deserted by the thousands. His institutional power base ruined, Reza Shah abdicated in favor of his young son, Mohammad Reza Shah Pahlavi.

In the absence of a broad political power base and with a shattered army, Mohammad Reza Shah faced an almost impossible task of rebuilding. There was no popular sympathy for the army in view of the widespread and largely accurate perception that it was a brutal tool used to uphold a dictatorial regime. The young shah, distancing Tehran from the European military, in 1942 invited the United States to send a military mission to advise in the reorganization effort. With American advice, emphasis was placed on quality rather than quantity; the small but more confident army was capable enough to participate in the 1946 campaign in Azarbaijan to put down a Soviet-inspired separatist rebellion (see World War II and the Azarbaijan Crisis, ch. 1).

Unlike its 1925 counterpart, the 1946 Majlis was suspicious of the shah's plans for a strong army. Many members of the parliament feared that the army would once again be used as a source of political power. To curtail the shah's potential domination of the country, they limited his military budgets.

Although determined to build an effective military establishment, the shah was forced to accept the ever-rising managerial control of the Majlis. Prime Minister Mohammad Mossadeq, backed by strong Majlis support, demanded and received the portfolio of minister of war in 1952. For the better part of a year, Mossadeq introduced changes in the high command, dismissing officers loyal to the shah and replacing them with pro-Mossadeq nationalists. With the assistance of British and United States intelligence, however, officers dismissed by Mossadeq staged the August 1953 coup d'état, which overthrew the prime minister and returned the shah to power (see Mossadeq and Oil Nationalization, ch. 1).

In a classic housecleaning, several hundred pro-Mossadeq officers were arrested, allegedly for membership in the communist Tudeh Party. Approximately two dozen were executed, largely to set an example and to demonstrate to the public that the shah was firmly in command. Within two years, the shah had consolidated his rule over the armed forces, as well as over the much-weakened Majlis. Separate commands were established for the army, air force, and navy; and all three branches of the military embarked on massive modernization programs, which flourished throughout the 1960s and 1970s.

Nonetheless, the shah's military was probably crippled as early as 1955. Mohammad Reza Shah, mistrustful of his subordinates as well as his close advisers, instituted an unparalleled system of control over all his officers. Not only did the monarch make all decisions pertaining to purchasing, promotions, and routine military affairs, but he also permitted little interaction among junior and senior officers. Even less was tolerated among senior officers. No meetings grouping all his top officers in the same room were ever held. Rather, the shah favored individual "audiences" with each service chief; he then delegated assignments and duties according to his overall plans. This approach proved effective for the shah, at least until his downfall in 1979. For the Iranian armed forces, it proved devastating.

As internal security agencies assumed the critical role of maintaining public order, the Imperial Iranian Armed Forces (IIAF) were charged with defending the country against foreign aggression. First among threats was the Soviet Union, which shares a 2,000-kilometer border with Iran. The shah feared that Moscow would try to gain access to warm-water port facilities, a Russian goal since Peter the Great, and seek to destabilize what the Soviets surely perceived to be a pro-Western, if not pro-American, regime. The majority of Iranian troops, therefore, were stationed in the north for the better part of the early 1960s. The resulting high level of tension between two mismatched neighboring forces was not a satisfactory arrangement for the politically and militarily astute monarch. Taking a pragmatic approach, the shah pursued economic cooperation to improve relations with the Soviet Union and thereby reduced military tensions along the border. Having softened Iran's Cold War rhetoric in relation to Moscow, the shah focused his attention on the Persian Gulf. When in 1971 Britain terminated its treaties of protection with the several small Arab shaykhdoms or amirates of the Arabian Peninsula, the shah's primary security concerns shifted to the border with Iraq.

When petroleum exports from the Gulf expanded rapidly in the 1970s and British withdrawal from the conservative shaykhdoms created a security vacuum, the Iranian military expanded its plans to include the defense of sea-lanes, especially the Strait of Hormuz, although navigation through the strait generally takes place entirely in Oman's territorial waters. Iran has always considered the forty-one-kilometer-wide strait vital to its oil exports and, since 1968, has made every effort to exert as much influence as possible there. The shah referred to the strait as Iran's "jugular vein," and the revolutionary regime has been similarly concerned with its security (see fig. 10).

In March 1975, Iran reached a geographic-political agreement with Iraq. This pact, called the Algiers Agreement, accomplished two important military objectives. First, because the existence of the agreement allowed Iran to terminate aid to the Kurdish rebels in Iraq, Iran could deploy more of its forces in areas other than the Iraqi border. Second, Baghdad's acceptance of Iran's boundary claim to a thalweg (the middle of the main navigable channel) in the Shatt al Arab settled a security issue, freeing the Iranian navy to shift its major facilities from Khorramshahr on the Iraqi border to Bandar-e Abbas near the strait and to upgrade its naval forces in the southern part of the Gulf.

Despite frequent public expressions of reserve, the weaker conservative Arab monarchies of the Persian Gulf supported the shah's military mission of guaranteeing freedom of navigation in and through the Gulf. They strongly objected, however, to Iran's military occupation in November 1971 of the islands of Abu Musa, belonging to Sharjah, and the Greater and Lesser Tunbs, belonging to Ras al Khaymah. These two members of the United Arab Emirates could offer no resistance to Tehran's swift military action, however. The Iranian navy used its Hovercraft to transport occupying troops, and it eventually installed military facilities on two of the islands. Despite its earlier agreement to respect Sharjah's claim to Abu Musa, Tehran justified the occupation of Abu Musa and the Tunbs on strategic grounds. Located near the strait between the deepest navigation lanes, the islands offered ideal bases from which to watch over shipping in the Gulf.

This action was only the precursor of other regional operations by which a strong Iranian military would deter foreign, especially Soviet or Soviet-inspired, incursions into the Gulf. Twice, during the 1970s, the shah provided military assistance—to Oman and Pakistan—to overcome internal rebellions. By doing so, he established Iran as the dominant regional military power.

The most significant combat operation involving Iranian (along with British and Jordanian) troops took place in Oman's Dhofar Province. Iran aided Sultan Qabus in fighting the Popular Front for the Liberation of Oman, which was supported by the People's Democratic Republic of Yemen (South Yemen) and the Soviet Union. Starting with an initial force of 300 in late 1972, the Iranian contingent grew in strength to 3,000 before its withdrawal in January 1977. The shah was proud that his forces had participated in the defeat of the guerrilla rebellion, even though the performance of Iranian troops in Oman was mixed. The air force received the most favorable reports from the battle zone. Reconnaissance flights provided valuable information, and helicopters proved effective in the rugged Dhofar region. Ground forces fared less well, suffering significant casualties, with 210 Iranian soldiers killed in 1976 alone. The high casualty rate was attributed to the overall lack of combat experience. Nearly 15,000 Iranian soldiers were rotated through Oman during the five-year period.

In 1976 Iranian counterinsurgency forces, relying on helicopter support, were deployed in Pakistan's Baluchistan Province to combat another separatist rebellion. This operation, albeit small and limited, was of considerable concern to Iran, which had a large

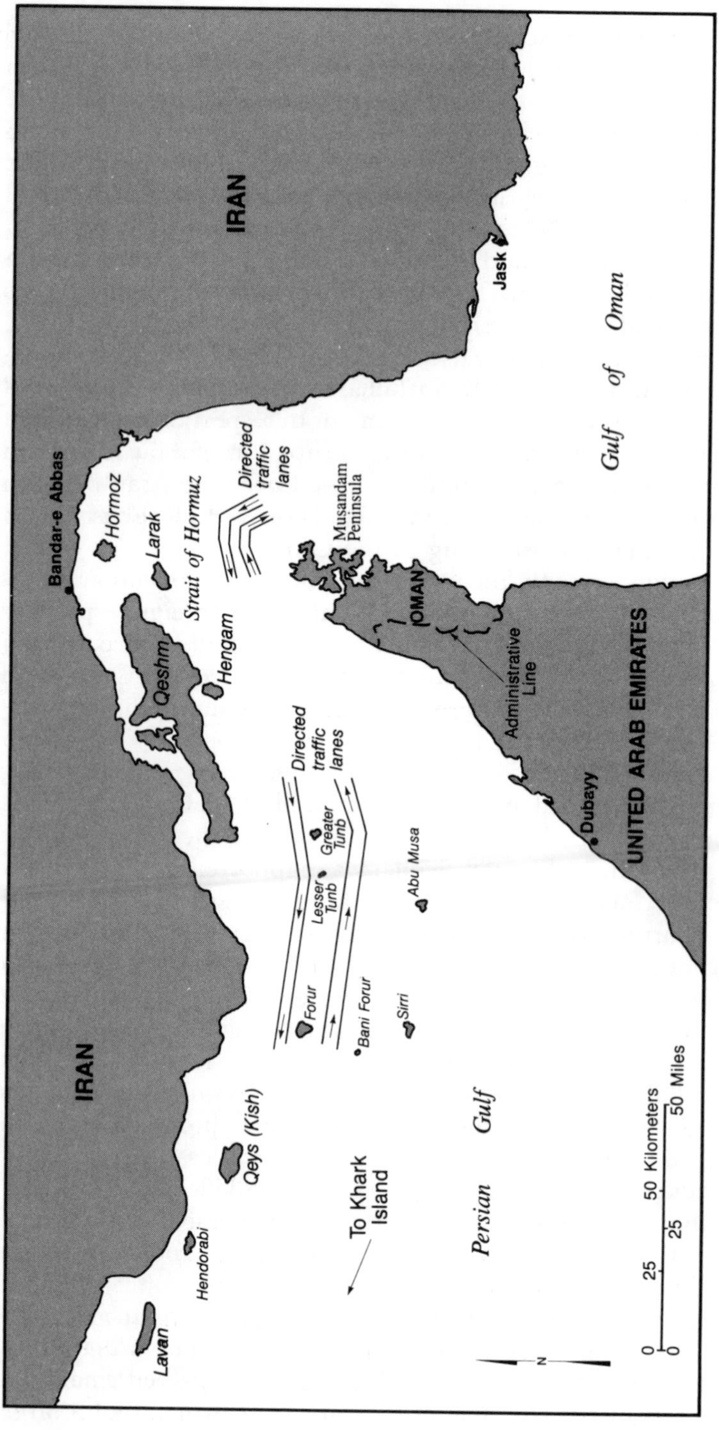

Figure 10. Strait of Hormuz and Vicinity

Baluch population of its own. The shah sought to buy insurance against a possible insurrection in Iran by helping Pakistan crush a Baluch uprising.

The shah continued to assist his allies in Oman and Pakistan after 1977. More important, Iran had served notice that it would engage its military to preserve the status quo in the Persian Gulf region, a status quo that was heavily tilted to its advantage. On more than one occasion, the shah stated that he would not refrain from maintaining the security of the Gulf, whether or not his troops were invited to intervene.

Iran had also come of age in the larger context of the Middle East. Between 1958 and 1978 Iran participated in war games conducted under the auspices of the Central Treaty Organization (CENTO), which grouped Turkey, Iran, Pakistan, and Britain (with the United States participating as an observer). Although CENTO declined in significance over the years, its military exercises, especially the yearly Midlink maritime maneuvers, provided useful training for the Iranian armed forces. The shah also participated in United Nations (UN) peacekeeping missions, sending a battalion to the UN buffer zone in the Golan Heights as part of the United Nations Disengagement Observer Force in 1977. The bulk of this force also served in southern Lebanon following the Israeli invasion of 1978. The Iranian contingent in the United Nations Interim Force in Lebanon was withdrawn in late 1978, however, following several desertions by Shia Muslim soldiers sympathetic to the local population.

On January 16, 1979, as the shah was preparing to leave Iran for the last time, he was still confident that his army could and would handle any internal disturbances. Still under the impression that the Soviet Union and Iraq were the greatest threats to his country, he left behind a United States-designed army prepared for external rather than domestic requirements.

The Revolutionary Period

Lack of leadership at the general staff level and below in the Imperial Iranian Armed Forces (IIAF) had literally frozen the military between December 1978 and February 1979. In the melee of the Revolution, mob scenes were frequent; on several occasions the army fired on demonstrators, killing and injuring many civilians, the most famous such encounter occurring at Jaleh Square in Tehran. In response to these incidents, army units of the IIAF, responsible for law and order in Tehran and other large cities, were attacked by mobs. Within days after the Revolution's success, several religious leaders, however, claimed that the armed forces had "joined the nation" or "returned to the nation" and cautioned against indiscriminate vengeance against the military.

The government took prompt steps to reconstitute the armed forces, weakened in both numbers and morale. Contrary to the general perception in 1979 and 1980, Khomeini did not seek the disintegration of the armed forces but rather wished to remold the shah's army into a loyal national Islamic force. Troops that had heeded Khomeini's appeal to disband were called back in March 1979. A new command group established in February 1979 was composed of nine officers with impeccable revolutionary credentials: they had all been imprisoned under the shah for different reasons. Khomeini relied on the advice of Colonel Nasrollah Tavakkoli, a retired Special Forces officer, to recruit ideologically compatible officers for the armed forces. General staff personnel were all called back to coordinate the nascent reorganization; division and brigade command positions were promptly filled by loyal and reliable officers. The Imperial Guard, the Javidan Guard, and the Military Household of the shah were the only organizations that were permanently disbanded.

The revolutionary government decided to formulate as clearly as possible the functions and roles of the armed forces, particularly in relation to internal security. In contrast to the shah's regime, it entrusted internal security functions to the newly established Pasdaran. Pasdaran clergy were also engaged to disseminate Islamic justice and were assigned to units of the armed forces to help communicate Khomeini's instructions and to provide religio-political indoctrination.

Much of this early cooperation was an extension of the military's existing support for the Revolution. For example, even though the head of the air force, General Amir Hosain Rabii, opposed the Revolution, many air force cadets and young *homafars* (skilled military technical personnel) supported it. Revolutionary groups that had played prominent roles in the seizure of power, however, were hostile to the military. These included the Mojahedin (Mojahedin-e Khalq, or People's Struggle), the Fadayan (Cherikha-ye Fadayan-e Khalq, or People's Guerrillas), and even the Tudeh, which called for a drastic purge of the military. The Mojahedin, especially, threatened the military's position because it had captured the Tehran arms factory and government arsenal depots and was thus armed. Moreover, the Mojahedin quickly organized into "councils" and recruited personnel in military posts throughout the country, seeing themselves as the military core of the new order. These councils were then turned into debating forums where conscripts could air past grievances against officers. The Tudeh, for its part, called on the government to return to active duty several hundred officers dismissed or imprisoned under the shah for their membership in the Tudeh.

The provisional government recognized the threat implicit in these demands. In the absence of a centralized command system, the military balance of power would eventually tilt toward the heavily armed guerrilla groups of the left. Hojjatoleslam Ali Khamenehi (who became president of Iran in 1981) and many of the leading ayatollahs were very suspicious of the leftist guerrillas. The members of the Revolutionary Council (a body formed by Khomeini in January 1979 to supervise the transition from monarchy to republic) would have preferred to balance the power of the leftist guerrillas with that of the Pasdaran, but the Pasdaran was in its formative stage and had neither the necessary strength nor the training.

The ultimate elimination of the Mojahedin, Fadayan, and Tudeh was a foregone conclusion in the ideological framework of an Islamic Iran. To this end, revolutionary leaders both defended and courted the military, hoping to maintain it as a countervailing force, loyal to themselves. In one of his frequent public pronouncements, Khomeini praised military service as "a sacred duty and worthy of great rewards before the Almighty" and solicited military support for his regime, declaring that "the great Iranian Revolution is more in need of defense and protection than at any other time." Prime Minister Mehdi Bazargan denounced guerrilla demands for a full-scale purge of the military.

In the end, the leadership decided in February 1979 that a purge of the armed forces would be undertaken, but on a limited scale, concentrating on "corrupt elements." The purge of the military started on February 15, 1979, when four general officers were executed. Two groups were purged, one consisting of those elements of the armed forces that had been closely identified with the shah and his repression of the revolutionary movement and the other including those that had committed actual crimes of violence, particularly murder and torture, against supporters of the Revolution. A total of 249 members of the armed forces, of whom 61 were SAVAK (Sazman-e Ettelaat va Amniyat-e Keshvar, the shah's internal security organization) agents, were tried, found guilty, and executed between February 19 and September 30, 1979. Significant as this figure is, it represented only a small percentage of military personnel.

Apart from the replacement of senior officers, various structural changes were introduced in the aftermath of the Revolution (see Command and Control; and Organization, Size, and Equipment, this ch.). But because of the lack of leadership at headquarters, command and control were at best tenuous. Local commanders exercised unprecedented autonomy, and integration of the regular armed forces with the Pasdaran was not even considered. Lack of coordination within the Pasdaran and between it and regular army personnel resulted in shortages for the Pasdaran of desperately needed supplies, ranging from daily rations to ammunition; such supplies usually found their way only to army depots.

In isolated areas, cooperation between the Pasdaran and the regular military eventually emerged. For example, in West Azarbaijan, prorevolutionary officers in the 64th Infantry Division in Urumiyeh (also cited as Urmia to which it has reverted after being known as Rezaiyeh under the Pahlavis) extended a helping hand to the Pasdaran in the latter's efforts to crush an uprising. The 64th Infantry Division's leading officers, including Colonel Qasem Ali Zahirnezhad and Colonel Ali Seyyed-Shirazi, were strong advocates of cooperation. They made proposals in which they argued that the Pasdaran and the regular military should be completely integrated at the operational level while maintaining separate administrations. They envisaged joint staffs at divisional and higher echelons, joint logistical systems, and joint procurement of equipment. By accepting logistical assistance from the military, the Pasdaran could become combat ready. From the regular armed forces' perspective, cooperation would turn members of the Pasdaran into professional soldiers. The process would also create a level of mutual dependence, thereby preventing antimilitary measures. Airings of proposals for similar cooperative measures received sympathy from some officers at the National Military Academy, where Commandant Colonel Musa Namju, expanding on Colonel Zahirnezhad's and Colonel Seyyed-Shirazi's earlier proposals, wrote several widely read documents. Little or no support came from Minister of Defense Mostofa Ali Chamran, who was more concerned with the impact that a full and rapid reorganization of the military might have on the Revolution.

Neglected for over a year, Iran's ground forces fared poorly during the first stages of the Iran-Iraq War (see The Iran-Iraq War, this ch.). Ironically, logistical shortcomings rather than desertions or combat defects were the problem. By the end of 1980, Iranian leaders finally recognized supply deficiencies and the more important command and control problems that were crippling the military. Colonel Namju resurrected the group proposals, and Chamran appointed Colonel Zahirnezhad and Colonel Seyyed-Shirazi to senior command and staff positions at the front.

In Tehran, President Abolhasan Bani Sadr attempted to gain control of the armed forces but failed for several reasons. Above all, Khomeini would not permit the Supreme Defense Council (SDC) to be dominated by any faction, and he was not prepared to make an exception for Bani Sadr. Prime Minister Mohammad Ali Rajai, Bazargan's successor, and his Islamic Republican Party (IRP) allies, concerned with the Revolution as much as the war, were adamant in their opposition to Bani Sadr's unilateral decisions. Bani Sadr was also weakened by his frequent interference in purely military affairs (in which his poor judgment in military matters became evident) as well as by competition with clergy members.

Despite the rift between Bani Sadr and the IRP, the SDC appointed him supreme commander over all regular and paramilitary units. His control of the military was tenuous, however, because by early 1981 IRP members were demanding representation at the senior levels of command. In addition, the front as an operational area was organized into subordinate field sectors and operational sectors, with little official liaison among the different service staffs. Moreover, the war effort was going poorly.

Bani Sadr's ouster from the presidency and Chamran's death at the front galvanized the Urumiyeh group to push for implementation of the reorganization proposals. Colonel Namju was the new defense minister, and reorganization of the command system received his full support. By September 1981, SDC approval was ensured and coordination with the Pasdaran initiated. Deputy Commander in Chief of the Pasdaran Kolahduz supervised the first operational integration of the regular military with the Pasdaran. Even the air force relented, and Brigadier General Javad Fakuri authorized additional close air support for ground forces. On September 24, 1981, a new command and control system was finalized at a Tehran meeting hosted by Pasdaran commander in chief Mohsen Rezai, who agreed to test the new proposals. An operation was launched to liberate Abadan and force the Iraqis to the west bank of the Karun River. Within four days, Iran's coordinated attack was successful, and the Iraqis retreated. For the first time since the outbreak of hostilities, a full-scale integration at the staff level produced positive results.

On September 29, 1981, several high-ranking military leaders, including Colonel Namju and Kolahduz, were killed in an airplane crash. Colonel Zahirnezhad, promoted to brigadier general, took over as chief of the Joint Staff of the armed forces, and Colonel Seyyed-Shirazi took Zahirnezhad's post as commander of armed forces. These appointments ensured the full implementation of the new command system.

Command and Control

According to Article 110 of the 1979 Constitution of the Islamic Republic of Iran, the *faqih* (see Glossary) is empowered to appoint and dismiss the chief of the Joint Staff, the commander in chief of the Pasdaran, two advisers to the SDC, and the commanders in chief of ground, naval, and air forces on the recommendation of the SDC. He is also authorized to supervise the activities of the SDC and to declare war and mobilize the armed forces on the recommendation of the SDC. As *faqih,* Khomeini, although maintaining the role of final arbiter, has delegated the post of commander in chief to the president of the Republic.

In addition to specifying the duties of the commander in chief, Article 110 establishes the composition of the SDC as follows: president of the country, prime minister, minister of defense, chief of the Joint Staff of the armed forces, commander in chief of the Pasdaran, and two advisers appointed by the *faqih.* Other senior officials may attend SDC meetings to deliberate national defense issues. In the past, the minister of foreign affairs, minister of interior, minister of the Pasdaran and his deputy, air force and navy commanders in chief, War Information Office director, and others have attended SDC meetings. The ground forces commander in chief, Colonel Seyyed-Shirazi, is a member of the SDC as a representative of the military arm for the *faqih,* whereas Majlis speaker Hojjatoleslam Ali Akbar Hashemi-Rafsanjani is representative of the political arm for the *faqih.*

Iran's strategic planning and the establishment of its military and defense policies are the responsibilities of the SDC, which has representatives at operational area and field headquarters to provide political and strategic guidance to field commanders. SDC representatives may also veto military decisions. But reports in 1987 indicated that SDC orders to regional representatives have been modified to limit the heavy casualty rates caused by their inappropriate advice. Inexperienced nonmilitary religious advisers have seen their interference in purely technical matters dramatically curtailed.

The Urumiyeh reorganization proposals recognized the administrative separation of the services as part of Iran's political reality. Consequently, as of 1987 there were two chains of command below the SDC, one administrative and the other operational. To some extent this dual chain of command existed because the revolutionary government had retained a modified version of the organizational structure of the IIAF, which was modeled on the United

States division of powers between the administrative functions of the service secretaries and the operational functions of the secretary of defense and chiefs of staff. In addition, the IRP leaders wanted to limit friction between the regular military and the Pasdaran. According to Speaker Hashemi-Rafsanjani, the service commanders in chief, the minister of defense, and the minister of the Pasdaran were removed from the operational chain to avoid further friction between the two groups.

In 1987 the Ministry of Defense continued to handle administrative matters for the regular armed forces. The chain of command flowed from senior unit commanders (division, wing, and fleet) to intermediate-echelon service commanders and to service commanders in chief and their staffs. Similarly, the Ministry of the Pasdaran handled the administrative affairs of the Pasdaran. The chain of command flowed from senior unit commanders (operational brigades in the case of combat units) to the ministry staff officers. In the case of internal security units, the chain of command went from local commanders to provincial commanders (who were colonels) and then to provincial general commanders (who were generals).

The Joint Staff of the armed forces, composed of officers assigned from the various services, the Pasdaran, the National Police, and the Gendarmerie, was responsible for all operational matters. Its primary tasks included military planning and coordination and operational control over the regular services, combat units of the Pasdaran, and units of the Gendarmerie and National Police assigned to the war front. Joint Staff members were also empowered to integrate fully the regular and paramilitary forces in operational planning. The components of the armed forces Joint Staff were modeled on the United States joint and combined staff system.

Staff members of J1—Personnel and Administration—conducted planning and liaison duties with their counterparts at the ministries of defense, interior, and the Pasdaran. They also supervised budgeting and financial accountability and the preparation of operational budgets for Majlis approval for all the armed services.

Personnel of J2—Intelligence and Security—carried out operational control for intelligence planning, intelligence operations, intelligence training, counterintelligence, and security for all elements of the armed forces. They also handled liaison with the *komitehs* (revolutionary committees) for internal security matters and with SAVAMA for foreign intelligence (see SAVAMA, this ch.).

Staff members of J3—Operations and Training—conducted training, operational planning, operations, and communications. The operational planning and operations sections were further divided into eleven subsections for planning and coordination of the services, including: the Iranian Islamic Ground Forces (IIGF), IIGF Aviation, IIGF Chemical Troops, IIGF Artillery Troops, IIGF Engineer Troops, Iranian Islamic Air Force (IIArF), Iranian Islamic Navy (IIN), IIN Aviation, the Pasdaran, the Gendarmerie, and the National Police.

Personnel of J4—Logistics and Support—coordinated and provided liaison for the services. Primary responsibility for logistics and supply rested with the services through the ministries of defense, interior, and the Pasdaran; collection and coordination of supplies and coordination of transportation to the war front, however, remained under the control of J4.

Staff members of J5—Liaison—handled liaison and coordination with nonmilitary organizations and with those military organizations not covered by Joint Staff-level arrangements. Organizations covered by J5 included the Ministry of Defense, Ministry of Interior, Ministry of the Pasdaran, Office of the Prime Minister, Council of Ministers' Secretariat, SDC, Majlis (particularly the Defense and Foreign Affairs Committee), the Foundation for Popular Mobilization, the Foundation for the Disinherited, the Foundation for Martyrs (Bonyad-e Shahid), the Foundation for War Victims, and the Crusade for Reconstruction (Jihad-e Sazandegi or Jihad).

The office of the staff judge advocate provided legal counsel to the Joint Staff and facilitated liaison with the revolutionary prosecutor general and the military tribunal system of the armed forces. The Political-Ideological Directorate (P-ID) staff members operated the political-ideological bureaus of the Joint Staff components and the political-ideological directorates and bureaus of the operational commands. This office also developed and disseminated political-ideological training materials, in close cooperation with the Foundation for the Propagation of Islam and the Islamic associations of the services. Finally, P-ID members conducted liaison duties between the Joint Staff and the Islamic Revolutionary Court of the Armed Forces.

Members of the Inspectorate General handled oversight functions over the staff components and liaison with the inspectors general of the operational commands. Special Office for Procurements staff members controlled and coordinated procurement of military equipment and supplies from foreign sources through the Ministry of Defense, the Ministry of the Pasdaran, the Ministry of Commerce and Foreign Trade, and the Central Bank of Iran.

In general, operational area commands were subordinate to the Joint Staff, and each armed force component was subordinate to

Members of the shah's Imperial Iranian Armed Forces

the operational area command in accordance with its own command structure. In 1987 there was only the Western Operational Area Command, which was responsible for the war with Iraq. Established to provide more effective control of wartime operations, this area may have been the precursor of the planned Northern, Southern, and Eastern Operational Area Commands.

The Western Operational Area Command was similar in structure to the armed forces Joint Staff except that it was also the lowest operational echelon at which naval forces were integrated into combined-services operations and planning. Although operational area command Joint Staff members exercised operational control over all troops within their area, they were subject to several constraints. Generally speaking, Pasdaran, Gendarmerie, and National Police units operating in an internal security mission, particularly against insurgents, were detached from the operational area command and subordinated to the senior Pasdaran commander in the province in which they were engaged. Air and naval units continued to be partially controlled by their service commanders and responded to the Western Operational Area Command Joint Staff through specialized liaison staffs. The commander of the operational area was further burdened by the presence at his headquarters of an SDC representative and a personal representative of Khomeini. Both of these influential individuals could effectively take any matter over the commander's head to higher authority. In 1987 the SDC representative in the Western Operational Area Command was also the Pasdaran commander for the operational area command, a situation that further complicated the command and control system.

Below the Operational Area Command were four field headquarters (FHQ), code-named FHQ Karbala, FHQ Hamzeh Seyyed ash Shohada, FHQ Ramadah, and FHQ An Najaf. The FHQs were organized on the model of the Western Operational Area Command except that they did not have naval integration. Subordinate to each FHQ were from three to eight operational sectors. Each operational sector did not necessarily have its own air support unit.

Additional echelons consisting of a commander and staff drawn from the Joint Staff of the participating FHQs could be created during major offensives. The purpose of these echelons was to overcome logistical shortcomings, concentrate and deploy forces as needed, and combine the services, particularly the naval forces, in offensive operations.

The reorganization of the command-and-control system could largely be attributed to the Urumiyeh proposals. The war with Iraq naturally increased the level of integration, particularly between regular military officers commanding Pasdaran units and Pasdaran officers commanding regular military units. Logistical problems also came under increasing scrutiny because of the war. The military's weak infrastructure required the centralization of logistics and supply. The sophisticated computer inventory and accounting systems of the ground, air, and naval logistical commands had been sabotaged during the Revolution, and the country lost valuable time while bringing these systems back into service.

Improvements in logistical support proved quite rewarding, revealing, for example, that Iran possessed twice as many critical spare parts for its aircraft as were previously believed to exist. Nevertheless, the Iranian armed forces faced a logistical dilemma in deploying supplies to troops at the front; lack of maintenance skills translated into a decreased repair and salvage capacity, creating serious bottlenecks. Vehicles in need of repair had to be transported to repair centers hundreds of kilometers from the front, along stretches of poorly maintained roads and railroads. Under such circumstances cannibalization of damaged equipment for spare parts, particularly for sophisticated equipment, became the norm. Without a solution in sight, Iranian authorities relied on the "down time" between major offensives to resupply units before resuming offensive operations. This practice further prolonged the war, because multiphased operations could not be launched and sustained.

Organization, Size, and Equipment

As *faqih,* Khomeini is constitutionally designated supreme commander of the armed forces. He has delegated his powers to the president, who may in turn delegate authority as required. Important decisions regarding defense policies are made by the SDC, which combines senior members of the armed services with senior members of the government.

Army

In 1979, the year of the shah's departure, the army experienced a 60-percent desertion from its ranks. By 1986 the regular army was estimated to have a strength of 305,000 troops (see table 8, Appendix). In the fervor of the Revolution and in the light of numerous changes affecting conscripts and reservists, the army underwent a structural reorganization. Under the shah, the army had been deployed in 6 divisions and 4 specialized combat regiments supported by more than 500 helicopters and 14 Hovercraft. An 85-percent readiness rate was usually credited to the force, although some outside observers doubted this claim. Following the Revolution the army was renamed the Islamic Iranian Ground Forces (IIGF) and in 1987 was organized as follows: three mechanized divisions, each with three brigades, each of which in turn was composed of three armored and six mechanized battalions; seven infantry divisions; one airborne brigade; one Special Forces division composed of four brigades; one Air Support Command; and some independent armored brigades including infantry and a "coastal force." There was also in reserve the Qods battalion, composed of ex-servicemen.

After the mid-1970s, military manpower was unevenly deployed. Nearly 80 percent of Iran's ground forces were deployed along the Iraqi border, although official sources maintained that the military was capable of rapid redeployment. Although air force transports were used extensively, redeployment was slow after the start of the war. The Mashhad division headquarters, in the eastern part of the country, has remained important because of Soviet military operations in Afghanistan and resulting Afghan migration into Iran (see Refugees, ch. 2).

In the past, Iran purchased army equipment from many countries, including the United States, Britain, France, the Federal Republic of Germany (West Germany), Italy, and the Soviet Union. By late 1987, Iran had diversified its acquisitions, obtaining arms from a number of suppliers. Among them were the Democratic People's Republic of Korea (North Korea), China, Brazil, and

Israel. The diversity of the weapons purchased from these countries greatly complicated training and supply procedures, but, faced with a war of attrition and a continuous shortage of armaments, Iran was willing to purchase from all available sources (see Foreign Influences in Weapons, Training, and Support Systems, this ch.).

The IIGF operated almost 1,000 medium tanks in 1986 (see table 9, Appendix). Although a large number were British-made Chieftains and American-made M–60s, an undetermined number of Soviet-made T–54 and T–55s, T–59s, T–62s, and T–72s were also part of the inventory, all captured from the Iraqis or acquired from North Korea and China. There was also a complement of fifty British-made Scorpion light tanks. Several hundred Urutu and Cascavel armored fighting vehicles from Brazil joined American-made M–113s and Soviet-made BTR–50s and BTR–60s. An undetermined number of Soviet-made Scud surface-to-surface missiles were acquired from a third country, believed to be Libya. And in November 1986, the United States revealed that it had supplied the Iranian military with Hawk surface-to-air missiles and TOW antitank missiles via Israel.

The army's aviation unit, whose main operational facilities were located at Esfahan, was largely equipped with United States aircraft, although some helicopters were of Italian manufacture. In 1986 army aviation operated some 65 light fixed-wing aircraft, but its strength lay in its estimated 320 combat helicopters, down from 720 in 1980.

Navy

The Iranian navy has always been the smallest of the three services, having about 14,500 personnel in 1986, down from 30,000 in 1979. Throughout the 1970s, the role of the navy had expanded as Iran recognized the need to defend the region's vital sea-lanes (see table 10, Appendix). In 1977 the bulk of the fleet was shifted from Khorramshahr to the newly completed base at Bandar-e Abbas, the new naval headquarters. Bushehr was the other main base; smaller facilities were located at Khorramshahr, Khark Island, and Bandar-e Khomeini (formerly known as Bandar-e Shahpur). Bandar-e Anzelli (formerly known as Bandar-e Pahlavi) was the major training base and home of the small Caspian fleet, which consisted of a few patrol boats and a minesweeper. The naval base at Bandar-e Beheshti (formerly known as Chah Bahar) on the Gulf of Oman had been under construction since the late 1970s and in late 1987 still was not completed. Smaller facilities were located near the Strait of Hormuz.

The Navy's airborne component, including an antisubmarine warfare (ASW) and minesweeping helicopter squadron and a transport battalion, continued to operate in 1986 despite wartime losses. Of six P-3F Orion antisubmarine aircraft, perhaps two remained operational, and of twenty SH-3D ASW helicopters, possibly only ten were airworthy. Despite overall losses, the navy increased the number of its marine battalions from two to three between 1979 and 1986.

Entirely of foreign origin, Iran's naval fleet has suffered major losses since the beginning of the war, when it was made up of American- and British-made destroyers and frigates, and some sixty smaller vessels and one of the largest Hovercraft fleets in the world. The Hovercraft had been expressly chosen to operate in the shallow waters of the Persian Gulf and proved useful in the 1971 occupation of Abu Musa and the Tunbs. After the cancellation of foreign orders in 1979, the rapid matériel advance of the navy was halted. For example, the shah's government had ordered six Spruance-class destroyers equipped for antiaircraft operations and three diesel-powered Tang-class submarines from the United States. Washington canceled the sale of these vessels, selling the submarines to Turkey and absorbing the destroyers into the United States Navy. In 1979 Khomeini also canceled an order for six type-209 submarines from West Germany.

What naval vessels remained in 1987 suffered from two major problems—lack of maintenance and lack of spare parts. After the departure of British-United States maintenance teams, the Iranian navy conducted only limited repairs, despite the availability of a completed Fleet Maintenance Unit at Bandar-e Abbas; consequently, several ships were laid up. Lack of spare parts also plagued the navy more than other services, because Western naval equipment was less widely available on world arms markets than other equipment.

Iran's ambitious plans for escort and patrol capabilities in the Persian Gulf and the Indian Ocean may not be realized until the Bandar-e Beheshti naval facility is completed. The country's interest in navigation through the Strait of Hormuz has not diminished, as the contemplated deployment of Chinese-made Silkworm HY-2 surface-to-surface missiles on Larak Island in 1987 clearly indicated. This development underscored Iran's interest in Gulf waters and the navy's role, along with that of Pasdaran units, in protecting them or in denying them to others.

Air Force

The shah's air force had more than 450 modern combat aircraft, including top-of-the-line F-14 Tomcat fighters and about 5,000 well-trained pilots. By 1979 the air force, numbering close to 100,000 personnel, was by far the most advanced of the three services and among the most impressive air forces in the developing world. Reliable information on the air force after the Revolution was difficult to obtain, but it seems that by 1987 a fairly large number of aircraft had been cannibalized for spare parts.

Before the Revolution, the air force was organized into fifteen squadrons with fighter and fighter-bomber capabilities and one reconnaissance squadron. In addition, one tanker squadron, and four medium and one light transport squadron provided impressive logistical backup. By 1986 desertions and depletions led to a reorganization of the air force into eight squadrons with fighter and fighter-bomber capabilities and one reconnaissance squadron. This reduced force was supported by two joint tanker-transport squadrons and five light transport squadrons. Some seventy-six helicopters and five surface-to-air missile (SAM) squadrons supplemented this capability.

Air force headquarters was located at Doshan Tapeh Air Base, near Tehran. Iran's largest air base, Mehrabad, outside Tehran, was also the country's major civil airport. Other major operational air bases were at Tabriz, Bandar-e Abbas, Hamadan (Shahroki Air Base), Dezful (Vahdati Air Base), Shiraz, and Bushehr. Since 1980 air bases at Ahvaz, Esfahan (Khatami Air Base), and Bandar-e Beheshti have also become operational.

Throughout the 1970s, Iran purchased sophisticated aircraft for the air force. The acquisition of 77 F-14A Tomcat fighters added to 166 F-5 fighters and 190 F-4 Phantom fighter-bombers, gave Iran a strong defensive and a potential offensive capability. Before the end of his reign, the shah placed orders for F-16 fighters and even contemplated the sharing of development costs for the United States Navy's new F-18 fighter. Both of these combat aircraft have been dropped from the revolutionary regime's military acquisitions list, however.

When the Iran-Iraq War started in 1980, Iran's F-14s, equipped with Phoenix missiles, capable of identifying and destroying six targets simultaneously from a range of eighty kilometers or more, inflicted heavy casualties on the Iraqi air force, which was forced to disperse its aircraft to Jordan and Oman. The capability of the F-14s and F-4s was enhanced by the earlier acquisition of a squadron of Boeing 707 tankers, thereby extending their combat radius to 2,500 kilometers with in-flight refueling.

By 1987, however, the air force faced an acute shortage of spare parts and replacement equipment. Perhaps 35 of the 190 Phantoms were serviceable in 1986 (see table 11, Appendix). One F-4 had been shot down by Saudi F-15s, and two pilots had defected to Iraq with their F-4s in 1984. The number of F-5s dwindled from 166 to perhaps 45, and the F-14 Tomcats from 77 to perhaps 10. The latter were hardest hit because maintenance posed special difficulties after the United States embargo on military sales.

China and North Korea with their "independent" policies on arms sales, were the only countries willing to sell Iran combat airplanes. Iran had acquired two Chinese-made Shenyang J-6 trainers in 1986. Unconfirmed reports in 1987 indicated that Iran was receiving Shenyang F-6s (Chinese-built MiG-19SFs), and that Iranian pilots were receiving training in North Korea. The reconnaissance squadron has also struggled to perform its duties with limited equipment. Once flying close to thirty-four aircraft, by late 1987 it may have been reduced to eight, having converted five Tomcats to serve in a noncombat role. It was not clear whether these five airplanes were in addition to the ten in the interceptor squadrons. Given the technical sophistication of reconnaissance aircraft, it was almost impossible to acquire from non-Western sources new ones capable of performing to Iranian standards. The only substantial acquisition was the purchase of forty-six Pilatus PC-7s from Switzerland. Iran requested three Kawasaki C-1 transports and a 3D air defense radar system from Japan, but this transaction did not appear to have materialized by 1987. Reports also indicated that Iran had placed with Argentina an order for thirty Hughes 500D helicopters.

From its inception, the air force also assumed responsibility for air defense. The existing early warning systems, built in the 1950s under the auspices of CENTO, were upgraded in the 1970s with a modern air defense radar network. To complement the ground radar component and provide a blanket coverage of the Gulf region, the United States agreed to sell Iran seven Boeing 707 airborne warning and control system (AWACS) aircraft in late 1977. Because of the Revolution, Washington canceled the AWACS sale, claiming that this sensitive equipment might be compromised. Finally, the air force's three SAM battalions and eight improved Hawk battalions were reorganized in the mid-1980s (in a project involving more than 1,800 missiles) into five squadrons that also contained Rapiers and Tigercats. Washington's sale of Hawk spare parts and missiles in 1985 and 1986 may have enhanced this capability.

The air force's primary maintenance facility was located at Mehrabad Air Base. The nearby Iran Aircraft Industries, in addition to providing main overhaul backup for the maintenance unit, has been active in manufacturing spare parts.

Source and Quality of Manpower

Armed forces manpower increased substantially throughout the 1970s as the shah implemented Iran's "guardian" role in the Gulf. Following the outbreak of the Revolution, there was a sharp drop in the number of military personnel, which in 1982 stood at 235,000, including the Pasdaran but excluding reserves. In contrast, total military personnel, including the Pasdaran but excluding reserves, stood at 704,500 in 1986. In addition to active-duty personnel, some 400,000 veterans, organized in reserve units after the outbreak of the war, were subject to recall to duty. Two-thirds of army personnel were conscripts; in the air force and navy, the majority were volunteers.

The National Military Academy was the largest single source of commissioned officers in the 1970s, but since 1980 a significant number of commissions have been awarded for wartime heroism and leadership at the front. Although air force and navy officers had attended military academies or participated in cadet programs in the United States, Britain, or Italy before 1979, few foreign contacts have been recorded since the Revolution. In the few instances in which contact was established, it was with Asian states, namely China and North Korea. Unlike the army, the air force and navy have experienced high attrition, and it must be assumed that operations have been streamlined to be effective with fewer personnel.

Class differences in the armed forces remained virtually undisturbed by the Revolution. Commissioned officers came from upper class families, career noncommissioned and warrant officers from the urban middle class, and conscripts from lower class backgrounds. By 1986, an increasing segment of the officer corps came from the educated middle class, and a significant number of lower middle-class personnel were commissioned by Khomeini for leadership on the battlefield.

Iran's 1986 population of approximately 48.2 million (including approximately 2.6 million refugees) gave the armed forces a large pool from which to fill its manpower needs, despite the existence of rival irregular forces. Of about 8 million males between the ages of eighteen and forty-five, nearly 6 million were considered physically and mentally fit for military service. Revolutionary leaders have repeatedly declared that Iran could establish an army of 20 million to defend the country against foreign aggression. Since the beginning of 1986, women have also been encouraged to receive military training, and women were actually serving in special Pasdaran units as of late 1987. The decision to encourage women to join in the military effort may indicate an increasing demand for personnel or an effort to gain increased popular support for the Revolution. It could also mean that conscription was not replacing war losses or retirements.

Compulsory conscription has been in effect since 1926, when Reza Shah's Military Service Act was passed by the Majlis. All males must register at age nineteen and begin their military service at age twenty-one; the law, however, is of limited significance in view of government pressures for volunteer enlistments in military units at an earlier age. According to the act, the total period of service is twenty-five years, divided as follows: two years of active military service, six years in standby military service for draftees, then eight years in first-stage reserve and nine years in second-stage reserve. In 1984 the Majlis passed the new Military Act. It amended conscription laws to reduce the high number of draft dodgers. Newspapers have carried reports of people caught trying to buy their way out of military service, at an unofficial figure of about US$8,000 for forged exemption documents. Under the prerevolutionary law, temporary or permanent exemptions were provided for the physically disabled, hardship cases, convicted felons, students, and certain professions. Draft evaders were subject to arrest, trial before a military court, and imprisonment for a maximum of two years *after* serving the required two years of active duty. Few draft dodgers, if any, were sent to jail; the normal procedure was to fine them the equivalent of US$75 (1986 exchange rate). Under the 1984 law, draft evaders were subject to restrictions for a period of up to ten years. They could be prevented from holding a driver's license, running for elective office, registering property ownership, being put on the government payroll, or receiving a passport, in addition to being forced to pay fines and/or receive jail sentences. Exemptions were given only to solve family problems. Moreover, all exemptions, except for physical disabilities, were only for five years. Those seeking relief for medical reasons had to serve but were not sent on combat duty. Under the amended law, men of draft age were subject to conscription, whether in war or peace, for a minimum period of two years and could be recalled as needed.

In the past, a consistent weakness of the armed forces had been the high illiteracy rate among conscripts and volunteers. This reflected the country-wide illiteracy rate, which stood at 60 percent in 1979. Compounding this dilemma, many conscripts came from those areas where Persian was not spoken. Thus, the military first had to teach the conscripts Persian by instituting extensive literacy training programs.

By 1986 the country's overall literacy rate was estimated at 50 percent, a dramatic improvement. This gain was also reflected in the regular armed forces. Of the three services, the air force fared best in this respect, as it had always done. Yet even the air force, which had developed training facilities for support personnel and *homafars,* was short of its real requirements. With the 1979 withdrawal of foreign military and civilian advisers, particularly from the United States and Pakistan, the operation, maintenance, and logistical functioning of armed forces' equipment was hampered by a critical shortage of skilled manpower. As purchases from non-Western countries increased, Iran came to rely on Chinese, Syrian, Bulgarian (unconfirmed), and North Korean instructors and those from the German Democratic Republic (East Germany), among others.

In 1987 the impressive progress of the regular armed forces was counterbalanced by manpower shortages. Without the support of large numbers of irregular forces and volunteers, it was difficult to foresee how this shortage might be overcome.

Foreign Influences in Weapons, Training, and Support Systems

Foreign influence on the regular armed forces has historically been massive, vital, and controversial. Around the turn of the century, before Reza Shah unified the military, officers from Sweden, Britain, and Russia commanded various Iranian units (see Historical Background, this ch.). These officers were unpopular because they were perceived as occupiers rather than as advisers, and the seeds of xenophobia were planted. Aware of these sentiments, Reza Shah tried to minimize direct foreign military influence, although an exception was made for Swedish officers serving with the Gendarmerie. Between the two world wars, a large number of Iranian officers attended military academies in France and Germany, where they received command and technical training. In a further effort to counter the influence of both Britain and Russia (by that time, the Soviet Union) in Iranian affairs, Reza Shah attempted to establish closer ties with Germany, a relationship that would be controversial during World War II. After 1945 the United States gradually became more influential and had a significant impact on the Pahlavi dynasty's leadership and the military.

With the establishment during World War II of a small United States military mission to the Gendarmerie (known as GENMISH) in 1943, Washington initiated a modest military advisory program. In 1947 the United States and Tehran reached a more comprehensive agreement that established the United States Army Mission Headquarters (ARMISH). Its purpose was to provide the

Ministry of War and the Iranian army with advisory and technical assistance to enhance their efficiency. As a result, the first Iranian officers began training in the United States, and they were followed by many more over the next three decades. The United States initiated its military assistance grant program to Iran in 1950 (the bilateral defense agreement between Iran and the United States was not concluded until 1959) and established a Military Assistance Advisory Group (MAAG) to administer the program. In 1962 the two missions were consolidated into a single military organization, ARMISH-MAAG, which remained active in Iran until the Islamic revolutionary regime came to power in 1979. Between 1973 and 1979, the United States also provided military support in the form of technical assistance field teams (TAFTs), through which civilian experts instructed Iranians on specific equipment on a short-term basis. Although the GENMISH program ended in 1973, United States military assistance to Iran rose rapidly in the six years before the Revolution.

United States military assistance to Iran between 1947 and 1969 exceeded US$1.4 billion, mostly in the form of grant aid before 1965 and of Foreign Military Sales credits during the late 1960s. The financial assistance programs were terminated after 1969, when it was determined that Iran, by then an important oil exporter, could assume its own military costs. Thereafter, Iran paid cash for its arms purchases and covered the expenses of United States military personnel serving in the ARMISH-MAAG and TAFT programs. Even so, in terms of personnel the United States military mission in Iran in 1978 was the largest in the world. Department of Defense personnel in Iran totaled over 1,500 in 1978, admittedly a small number compared with the 45,000 United States citizens, mostly military and civilian technicians and their dependents, living in Iran. Almost all of these individuals were evacuated by early 1979 as the ARMISH-MAAG program came to an abrupt end. Ended also was the International Military Education and Training (IMET) Program, under which over 11,000 Iranian military personnel had received specialized instruction in the United States.

Washington broke its diplomatic ties with Tehran in April 1980, closing an important chapter with a former CENTO ally whose security it had guaranteed since 1959. The relationship had evolved dramatically from the early 1950s, when Iran depended on the United States for security assistance, to the mid-1970s, when the government-to-government Foreign Military Sales program dominated other issues. Arms transfers increased significantly after the 1974 oil price rise, accelerating at a dizzying pace until 1979. From fiscal year (FY—see Glossary) 1950 through FY 1979, United States arms sales to Iran totaled approximately US$11.2 billion, of which US$10.7 billion were actually delivered.

The transfer of such large volumes of arms and the presence of thousands of United States advisers had an unmistakable influence on the Iranian armed forces. The preponderance of American weapons led to a dependence on the United States for support systems and for spare parts. Technical advisers were indispensable for weapons operations and maintenance.

After the Revolution, Iranians continued to buy arms from the United States using Israeli, European, and Latin American intermediaries to place orders, despite the official United States embargo. Israeli sales, for example, were recorded as early as 1979. On several occasions, attempted arms sales to Iran have been thwarted by law enforcement operations or broker-initiated leaks. One operation set up by the United States Department of Justice foiled the shipment of more than US$2 billion of United States weapons to Iran from Israel and other foreign countries. The matériel included 18 F-4 fighter-bombers, 46 Skyhawk fighter-bombers, and nearly 4,000 missiles. But while the Department of Justice was attempting to prevent arms sales to Iran, senior officials in the administration of President Ronald Reagan admitted that 2,008 TOW missiles and 235 parts kits for Hawk missiles had been sent to Iran via Israel. These were intended to be an incentive for the release of American hostages held by pro-Iranian militiamen in Lebanon. Unverified reports in 1987 indicated that Iranian officials claimed that throughout 1986 the Reagan administration had sold Iran ammunition and parts for F-4s, F-5s, and F-14s. In addition, Tehran reportedly purchased United States-made equipment from international arms dealers and captured United States weapons from Vietnam.

Despite official denials, it is believed that Israel has been a supplier of weapons and spare parts for Iran's American-made arsenal. Reports indicate that an initial order for 250 retread tires for F-4 Phantom jets was delivered in 1979 for about US$27 million. Since that time, unverified reports have alleged that Israel agreed to sell Iran Sidewinder air-to-air missiles, radar equipment, mortar and machine gun ammunition, field telephones, M-60 tank engines and artillery shells, and spare parts for C-130 transport planes.

By 1986 Iran's largest arms suppliers were reportedly China and North Korea. China, for example, is believed to have supplied Iran with military equipment in sales funneled through North Korea. According to an unconfirmed report in the *Washington Post,* one particular deal in the spring of 1983 netted Beijing close to US$1.3 billion for fighters, T-59 tanks, 130mm artillery, and light arms.

China also delivered a number of Silkworm HY-2 surface-to-surface missiles, presumably for use in defending the Strait of Hormuz. As of early 1987, China denied all reported sales, possibly to enhance its diminishing position in the Arab world. North Korea agreed to sell arms and medical supplies to Iran as early as the summer of 1980. Using military cargo versions of the Boeing 747, Tehran ferried ammunition, medical supplies, and other equipment that it purchased from the North Korean government. According to unverified estimates, total sales by 1986 may have reached US$3 billion.

Other countries directly or indirectly involved over the years in supplying weapons to Iran have included Syria (transferring some Soviet-made weapons), France, Italy, Libya (Scud missiles), Brazil, Algeria, Switzerland, Argentina, and the Soviet Union. Direct foreign influence, however, was minimal because most purchases were arranged in international arms markets. Moreover, the influence of the major arms suppliers was balanced by other international relationships. Many of the above-mentioned West European states in 1987 had arms embargoes against shipments to Iran, but nevertheless some matériel slipped through. Also, West European states often wished to keep communication channels open, no matter how difficult political relations might have become. For example, despite strong protests from the United States, the British government in 1985 transferred to Iran a fleet-refueling ship and two landing ships without their armament. The British also allowed the repair of two Iranian BH-7 Hovercraft. In 1982 Tehran began negotiations with Bonn for the sale of submarines. Iran also approached the Netherlands and, in 1985, purchased two landing craft, each sixty-five meters long and having a capacity exceeding 1,000 tons. The influence of the Asian arms-supplying countries was further minimized because purchases were made in cash upon delivery with no strings attached. Finally, foreign influence was less pronounced in 1987 than at any time since 1925 because a defiant Tehran espoused "independent" foreign and military policies, based on a strong sense of Islamic and nationalistic values.

Domestic Arms Production

In 1963 Iran placed all military factories under the Military Industries Organization (MIO) of the Ministry of War. Over the next fifteen years, military plants produced small arms ammunition, batteries, tires, copper products, explosives, and mortar rounds and fuses. They also produced rifles and machine guns under West German license. In addition, helicopters, jeeps, trucks, and trailers were assembled from imported kits. Iran was on its way to manufacturing rocket launchers, rockets, gun barrels, and grenades, when the Revolution halted all military activities. The MIO, plagued by the upheavals of the time, was unable to operate without foreign specialists and technicians; by 1981 it had lost much of its management ability and control over its industrial facilities.

The outbreak of hostilities with Iraq and the Western arms embargo served as catalysts for reorganizing, reinvigorating, and expanding defense industries. In late 1981, the revolutionary government brought together the country's military industrial units and placed them under the Defense Industries Organization (DIO), which would supervise production activities. In 1987 the DIO was governed by a mixed civilian-military board of directors and a managing director responsible for the actual management and planning activities. Although the DIO director was accountable to the deputy minister of defense for logistics, Iran's president, in his capacity as the chairman of the SDC, had ultimate responsibility for all DIO operations.

By 1986 a large number of infantry rifles, machine guns, and mortars and some small-arms ammunition were being manufactured locally. On several occasions, clerics delivering their Friday sermons in Tehran claimed that Iran was engaged in a full-scale military production program, and the Iranian press regularly reported the successful production of new items ranging from washers to helicopter fuselage parts. For example, the professional military displayed, at the Permanent Industrial Exhibition in Tehran, a collection of hermetic sealing cylinders for Chieftain tanks and artillery flame-deflectors with artillery pads. They also displayed Katyusha gauges, personnel carrier shafts, gears, gun pulleys, carriages for 50mm caliber guns, 155mm shells, bases for night-vision telescopic rifles, parts for G–3 rifles, various firing pins, and flash suppressors for 130mm guns.

In 1987 the military took pride in being able to repair various transmitters, receivers, and helicopter engines. A number of unverified reports also alluded to the repair of the testing equipment of F–14 hydraulic pressure transmitters and generators. Similarly, Iran claimed to have manufactured an undisclosed number of Oghab rockets, probably patterned on the Soviet-made Scud-B surface-to-surface missiles the Iranians received from Libya. In mid-1984 the navy claimed to have successfully repaired the gas turbines of several vessels in Bandar-e Abbas. Moreover, Pasdaran units reportedly repaired Soviet- and Polish-made T–54, T–55, T–62, and T–72 tanks, captured from the Iraqis in 1982, at their armor repair center.

Troops of the Pasdaran in Qasr-e Shirin
Copyright Lehtikuva/PHOTRI

The monopoly of the regular armed forces over domestic arms production and repair industries ended in 1983 when the SDC authorized the Pasdaran to establish its own military industries. This new policy was in line with the Pasdaran's growing political and military weight. Beginning in 1984, the first Pasdaran armaments factory manufactured 120mm mortars, antipersonnel grenades, various antichemical-warfare equipment, antitank rockets, and rocket-propelled grenades.

Special and Irregular Armed Forces

A primacy of state interest over revolutionary ideology was reflected in the Khomeini regime's treatment of the military. Reports to the contrary notwithstanding, the Khomeini regime never eliminated imperial Iran's regular armed forces. Certainly, key military personnel identified with the deposed shah were arrested, tried, and executed. But the purges were limited to high-profile military and political figures and had a clear purpose: to eliminate Pahlavi loyalists. As a means of countering the threat posed by either the leftist guerrillas or the officers suspected of continued loyalty to the shah, however, Khomeini created the Pasdaran, designated as the guardians of the Revolution. The Constitution of the new republic entrusts the defense of Iran's territorial integrity and political independence to the military, while it gives the Pasdaran the responsibility of preserving the Revolution itself.

Soon after Khomeini's return to Tehran, the Bazargan interim administration established the Pasdaran under a decree issued by Khomeini on May 5, 1979. The Pasdaran was intended to protect the Revolution and to assist the ruling clerics in the day-to-day enforcement of the new government's Islamic codes and morality. There were other, perhaps more important, reasons for establishing the Pasdaran. The Revolution needed to rely on a force of its own rather than borrowing the previous regime's tainted units. As one of the first revolutionary institutions, the Pasdaran helped legitimize the Revolution and gave the new regime an armed basis of support. Moreover, the establishment of the Pasdaran served notice to both the population and the regular armed forces that the Khomeini regime was quickly developing its own enforcement body. Thus, the Pasdaran, along with its political counterpart, Crusade for Reconstruction, brought a new order to Iran. In time, the Pasdaran would rival the police and the judiciary in terms of its functions. It would even challenge the performance of the regular armed forces on the battlefield.

Since 1979 the Pasdaran has undergone fundamental changes in mission and function. Some of these changes reflected the control of the IRP (until its abolition in 1987) over both the Pasdaran and the Crusade for Reconstruction. Others reflected the IRP's exclusive reliance on the Pasdaran to carry out certain sensitive missions. Still others reflected personal ambitions of Pasdaran leaders. The Pasdaran, with its own separate ministry, has evolved into one of the most powerful organizations in Iran. Not only did it function as an intelligence organization, both within and outside the country, but it also exerted considerable influence on government policies. In addition to its initial political strength, in the course of several years the Pasdaran also became a powerful military instrument for defending the Revolution and Islamic Iran.

Organization and Functions

According to a classified report captured and released by the students who occupied the United States embassy in Tehran, initially the Pasdaran was planned as an organization that would be directly subordinate to the ruling clerics of the Revolution. According to this report, the Revolutionary Council in 1979 was composed of 12 members and the Pasdaran of 30,000 members, divided as follows: Central Council of Saltanatabad, Tehran, 4,000 members; Provincial Command, 20,000; other commands for border checkpoints and key areas, 3,000; and a training center at Aliabad, 3,000.

The commander of the Pasdaran was Ayatollah Lahuti and its chiefs of staff were Hojjatoleslams Hashemi-Rafsanjani and Gholam Ali Afrouz.

From this modest beginning, the Pasdaran became a formidable force. According to the International Institute for Strategic Studies, in 1986 the Pasdaran consisted of 350,000 personnel organized in battalion-size units that operated either independently or with units of the regular armed forces. In 1986 the Pasdaran acquired small naval and air elements, and it has claimed responsibility for hit-and-run raids on shipping in the Persian Gulf. Darting out from bases on a chain of small islands in Swedish-built speedboats equipped with machine guns and rocket-propelled grenades, the Pasdaran has established a naval zone in northern Gulf waters. Hosain Alai, the Pasdaran naval commander, announced on April 27, 1987, that the Pasdaran was in "full control" of certain portions of Gulf waters and would continue to operate from Farsi Island, between Iran and Saudi Arabia, as well as from Sirri, Abu Musa, and Larak islands. At that time 200 Pasdaran pilots reportedly were in training in East Germany.

According to the Muslim Student Followers of the Iman's Line, the Pasdaran, under the guidance of such clerics as Lahuti and Hashemi-Rafsanjani, was also "to act as the eyes and ears of the Islamic Revolution" and "as a special task force of the Imam (see Glossary) Khomeini to crush any counterrevolutionary activities within the government or any political usurper against [the] Islamic Government." Over the years the IRP's leadership used the Pasdaran to eliminate opposition figures and to enhance its own position. Pasdaran units worked with and were subordinate to clergy leaders not just at the national level, but throughout the country as well.

Operations

An early operations commander of the Pasdaran was Abbas Zamani (Abu Sharif), a former teacher from Tehran. A graduate of the College of Education (Islamic Law Section), Zamani received guerrilla training in Lebanon. As early as 1970, when he first traveled to Beirut, he established contacts in Lebanon with the Palestine Liberation Organization (PLO) and various guerrilla groups there. Unverified reports have claimed that the Pasdaran has received organizational and training assistance from the PLO, but no Palestinians were known to have visited the Aliabad or other Pasdaran training grounds. Khomeini and his supporters in Iran, as well as many other Iranians, have continued to support the Palestinians, however. For example, PLO leader Yasir Arafat was one of the first world leaders to visit Tehran after the Revolution; he opened a diplomatic office in what formerly had been the Israeli mission.

The Pasdaran has been quite active in Lebanon. By the summer of 1982, shortly after the second Israeli invasion of Lebanon, the Pasdaran had nearly 1,000 personnel deployed in the predominantly Shia Biqa Valley. From its headquarters near Baalbek, the Pasdaran has provided consistent support to Islamic Amal, a breakaway faction of the mainstream Amal organization that contemplated the establishment of an Islamic state in Lebanon. The secular Baathist Syrian regime has found the Pasdaran presence in Lebanon alternately helpful and threatening. In 1987 the Pasdaran's alleged involvement in anti-American terrorism in Lebanon remained difficult to confirm.

By September 1980, the Pasdaran was capable of deploying forces at the front. Initially, the forces were sent to conduct operations against Kurdish rebels, but before long they were deployed alongside regular armed forces units to conduct conventional military operations. Despite differences, the Pasdaran and the regular armed forces have cooperated on military matters.

The Pasdaran was also given the mandate of organizing a large people's militia, the Basij, in 1980. In a 1985 Iranian News Agency report, Hojjatoleslam Rahmani, head of the Basij forces of the Pasdaran, was quoted as stating that there were close to 3 million volunteers in the paramilitary force receiving training in some 11,000 centers. It is from Basij ranks that volunteers have been drawn to launch "human wave" attacks against the Iraqis, particularly around Basra. More recently, the Pasdaran, on Khomeini's instructions, has initiated the training of women to serve the Revolution.

Role in National Security

From the beginning of the new Islamic regime, the Pasdaran functioned as a corps of the faithful. Its role in national security evolved from securing the regime and eliminating opposition forces to becoming a branch of the military establishment. The Pasdaran's most problematic role, however, has been in intelligence.

Although little is known about the Ministry of the Pasdaran, its intelligence-gathering operations, and its relationship with SAVAMA, several reports have speculated that the Pasdaran has maintained an intelligence branch to spy on the regime's adversaries and to participate in their arrests and trials (see SAVAMA, this ch.). Khomeini implied Pasdaran involvement in intelligence when he congratulated the Pasdaran on the arrest of Iranian communist Tudeh leaders. Observers also believed that the Pasdaran had contacts with underground movements in the Gulf region. Given their importance in domestic politics, it would have been possible for Pasdaran members to be assigned to Iranian diplomatic missions, where, in the course of routine intelligence activities, they could monitor dissidents. Observers believed that Pasdaran influence might be particularly important in Kuwait, Bahrain, and the United Arab Emirates.

Under the command of Mohsen Rezai, the Pasdaran became large enough to match the strength of the regular military. Its power base remained strong in 1987, with the continuing support of Khomeini and other religious authorities. Having eliminated armed leftist groups such as the Mojahedin and the Fadayan, the Pasdaran had fulfilled all IRP expectations. With the abolition of the IRP in 1987, however, observers were uncertain whether the Pasdaran would continue to enjoy unlimited support from high-ranking clerics. Staunchly religious, nationalistic, and battle-trained since 1980, the Pasdaran had emerged as a critical force in determining Iran's national security strategy. In a post-Khomeini era, the Pasdaran could wield enormous power to approve or disapprove governmental changes. In contrast to the Pasdaran, which had a primary responsibility for upholding the Revolution, the major concern of the Iranian military was the prosecution of the war with Iraq.

The Iran-Iraq War

As of June 1987, the major events of the war could generally be divided into six overlapping phases: the original Iraqi offensive, Iranian mobilization and resistance, the Iranian counteroffensive, the war of attrition, Iraqi internationalization of the war, and the surge in superpower involvement. In addition, there was the tanker war in the Persian Gulf, which extended over several of these phases.

The Original Iraqi Offensive

Baghdad originally planned a quick victory over Tehran. On September 22, 1980, Iraqi fighter aircraft attacked ten air bases in Iran. Their aim was to destroy the Iranian air force on the ground—a lesson learned from the Arab-Israeli June 1967 War. They succeeded in destroying runways and fuel and ammunition depots, but much of Iran's aircraft inventory was left intact. Simultaneously, six Iraqi army divisions entered Iran on three fronts in an initially successful surprise attack. On the northern front, an Iraqi mountain infantry division captured Qasr-e Shirin, a border town in Bakhtaran (formerly known as Kermanshahan) Province, and occupied territory thirty kilometers eastward to the base of the Zagros Mountains. This area was strategically significant because the main Baghdad-Tehran highway traversed it. On the central front, Iraqi forces captured Mehran, on the western plain of the Zagros Mountains in Ilam Province, and pushed eastward to the mountain base. Mehran occupied an important position on the major north-south road, close to the border on the Iranian side. The main thrust of the attack, however, was in the south. Iraqi armored units easily crossed the Shatt al Arab waterway and entered the Iranian province of Khuzestan. While some divisions headed toward Khorramshahr and Abadan, others moved toward Ahvaz, the provincial capital and site of an air base. Supported by heavy artillery fire, the troops made a rapid and significant advance—almost eighty kilometers in the first few days. In the battle for Dezful in Khuzestan, where a major air base is located, the local Iranian army commander requested air support in order to avoid a defeat. President Bani Sadr, therefore, authorized the release from jail of many pilots, some of whom were suspected of still being loyal to the shah. With the increased use of the Iranian air force, the Iraqi progress was somewhat curtailed (see fig. 11).

The last major Iraqi territorial gain took place in early November 1980. On November 3, Iraqi forces reached Abadan but were repulsed by a Pasdaran unit. Even though they surrounded Abadan on three sides and occupied a portion of the city, the Iraqis could not overcome the stiff resistance; sections of the city still under Iranian control were resupplied by boat at night. On November 10, Iraq captured Khorramshahr after a bloody house-to-house fight. The price of this victory was high for both sides, approximately 6,000 casualties for Iraq and even more for Iran.

Iranian Mobilization and Resistance

Iran may have prevented a quick Iraqi victory by a rapid mobilization of volunteers and deployment of loyal Pasdaran forces to the front. Besides enlisting the Iranian pilots, the new revolutionary regime also recalled veterans of the old imperial army, although many experienced officers, most of whom had been trained in the United States, had been purged. Furthermore, the Pasdaran and Basij (what Khomeini called the "Army of Twenty Million" or People's Militia) recruited at least 100,000 volunteers. Approximately 200,000 soldiers were sent to the front by the end of November 1980. They were ideologically committed troops (some members even carried their own shrouds to the front in the expectation of martyrdom) that fought bravely despite inadequate armor support. For example, on November 7 commando units played a significant role, with the navy and air force, in an assault on Iraqi oil export terminals at Mina al Bakr and Al Faw. Iran hoped to diminish Iraq's financial resources by reducing its oil revenues. Iran also attacked the northern pipeline in the early days of the war and successfully closed Basra's access to the Persian Gulf.

Iran's resistance at the outset of the Iraqi invasion was unexpectedly strong, but it was neither well organized nor equally successful on all fronts. Iraq easily advanced in the northern and central sections and crushed the Pasdaran's scattered resistance there. Iraqi troops, however, faced untiring resistance in Khuzestan. President Saddam Husayn of Iraq may have thought that the ethnic Arab minority of Khuzestan would join the Iraqis against Tehran. Instead, many allied with Iran's regular and irregular armed forces and fought in the battles at Dezful, Khorramshahr, and Abadan. Soon after capturing Khorramshahr, the Iraqi troops lost their initiative and began to dig in along their line of advance.

The Iranian Counteroffensive

Iran had created the SDC in 1980 to undertake what the Iranians called Jang-e Tahmili, or the imposed war. Iran launched a counteroffensive in January 1981. Both the volunteers and the regular armed forces were eager to fight, the latter seeing an opportunity to regain prestige lost because of their association with the shah's regime. Iran's first major counterattack failed, however, for political and military reasons. President Bani Sadr was engaged in a power struggle with key religious figures and eager to gain political support among the armed forces by direct involvement in military operations. Lacking military expertise, he initiated a premature attack by three regular armored regiments without the assistance of the Pasdaran units. He also failed to take into account that the ground near Susangerd, muddied by the preceding rainy season, would make resupply difficult. As a result of his tactical decision making, the Iranian forces were surrounded on three sides. In a long exchange of fire, many Iranian armored vehicles were destroyed or had to be abandoned because they were either stuck in the mud or needed minor repairs. Fortunately for Iran, however, the Iraqi forces failed to follow up with another attack.

After Bani Sadr was ousted as president and commander in chief, Iran gained its first major victory, when, as a result of Khomeini's initiative, the army and Pasdaran suppressed their rivalry and cooperated to force Baghdad to lift its long siege of Abadan in September 1981. Iranian forces also defeated Iraq in the Qasr-e Shirin area in December 1981 and January 1982. The Iraqi armed forces

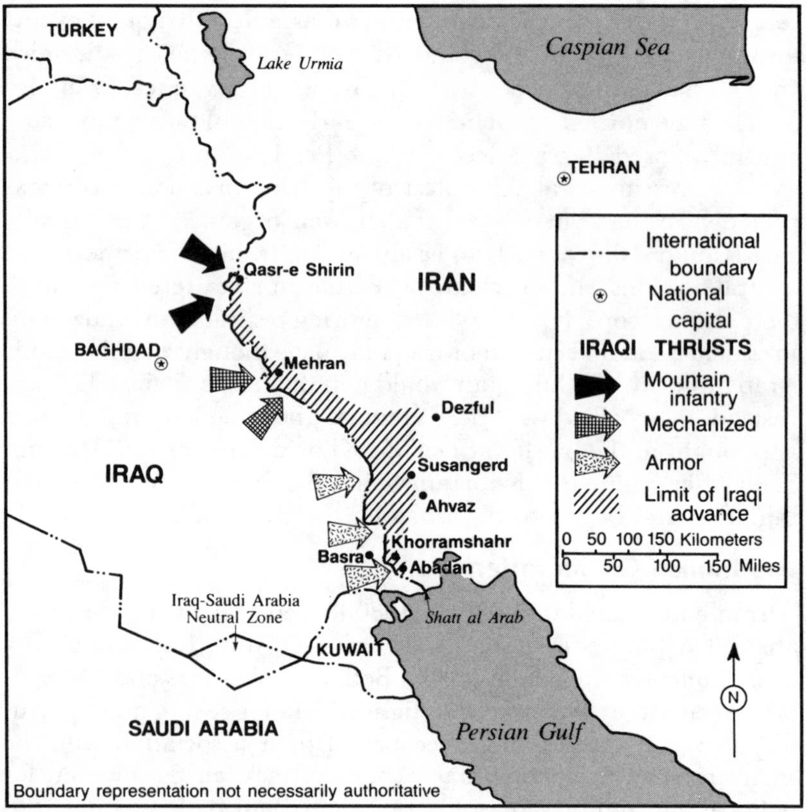

Figure 11. Initial Iraqi Attack on Iran, September–November 1980

were hampered by their unwillingness to sustain a high casualty rate and therefore refused to initiate a new offensive.

In March 1982, Tehran launched a major offensive called "Undeniable Victory." Its forces broke the Iraqi line near Susangerd, separating Iraqi units in northern and southern Khuzestan. Within a week, they succeeded in destroying a large part of three Iraqi divisions. This operation, another combined effort of the army, Pasdaran, and Basij, was a turning point in the war because the strategic initiative shifted from Iraq to Iran. In May 1982, Iranian units finally regained Khorramshahr, but with high casualties. After this victory, the Iranians maintained the pressure on the remaining Iraqi forces, and President Saddam Husayn announced that the Iraqi units would withdraw from Iranian territory.

The War of Attrition

The "war of attrition" began after the Iranian high command passed from regular military leaders to clergy in mid-1982. Although Basra was within range of Iranian artillery, the clergy used "human-wave" attacks by the Pasdaran and Basij against the city's defenses, apparently waiting for a coup to topple Saddam Husayn. All such assaults faced Iraqi artillery fire and received heavy casualties.

Throughout 1983 both sides demonstrated their ability to absorb and to inflict severe losses. Iraq, in particular, proved adroit at constructing defensive strong points and flooding lowland areas to stymie the Iranian thrusts, hampering the advance of mechanized units. Both sides also experienced difficulties in effectively utilizing their armor. Rather than maneuver their armor, they tended to dig in tanks and use them as artillery pieces. Furthermore, both sides failed to master tank gunsights and fire controls, making themselves vulnerable to antitank weapons.

Internationalization of the War

Beginning in 1984, Baghdad's inability to end the war on the ground led to new military and diplomatic strategies. Iraq tried to force Iran to the negotiating table by various means. First, President Saddam Husayn sought to increase the war's manpower and economic cost to Iran. For this purpose, Iraq purchased new weapons, mainly from the Soviet Union and France. Iraq also completed the construction of what came to be known as "killing zones" (which consisted primarily of artificially flooded areas near Basra) to stop Iranian units. In addition, according to *Jane's Defence Weekly* and other sources, Baghdad used chemical weapons against Iranian troop concentrations and launched attacks on many economic centers. Despite Iraqi determination to halt further Iranian progress, Iranian units in March 1984 captured parts of the Majnun Islands, whose oil fields had economic as well as strategic value.

Second, Iraq turned to diplomatic and political means. In April 1984, Saddam Husayn proposed to meet Khomeini personally in a neutral location to discuss peace negotiations. But Tehran rejected this offer and restated its refusal to negotiate with Saddam Husayn.

Third, Iraq sought to involve the superpowers as a means of ending the war. The Iraqis believed this objective could be achieved by attacking Iranian shipping. Initially, Baghdad used borrowed French Super Etendard aircraft armed with Exocets. In 1984 Iraq returned these airplanes to France and purchased approximately thirty Mirage F-1 fighters equipped with Exocet missiles. Iraq launched a new series of attacks on shipping on February 1, 1984 (see The Tanker War, this ch.)

Gradual Superpower Involvement

In early 1987, both superpowers indicated their interest in the security of the region. Soviet deputy foreign minister Vladimir Petrovsky made a Middle East tour expressing his country's concern over the effects of the Iran-Iraq War. In May 1987, United States assistant secretary of state Richard Murphy also toured the Gulf emphasizing to friendly Arab states the United States commitment in the region, a commitment which had become suspect as a result of Washington's transfer of arms to the Iranians, officially as an incentive for them to assist in freeing American hostages held in Lebanon. In another diplomatic effort, both superpowers supported the UN Security Council resolutions seeking an end to the war (see Foreign Policy, ch. 4).

The war appeared to be entering a new phase in which the superpowers were becoming more involved. For instance, the Soviet Union, which had ended military supplies to both Iran and Iraq in 1980, resumed large-scale arms shipments to Iraq in 1982 after Iran had launched its offensive into Iraqi territory. Subsequently, despite its professed neutrality, the Soviet Union became the major supplier of sophisticated arms to Iraq. In 1985 the United States began clandestine direct and indirect negotiations with Iranian officials that resulted in several arms shipments to Iran.

Iranian military gains inside Iraq after 1984 were a major reason for increased superpower involvement in the war. In February 1986, Iranian units captured the port of Al Faw, which had oil facilities and was one of Iraq's major oil-exporting ports before the war.

By late 1986, rumors of a final Iranian offensive against Basra proliferated. On January 8, Operation Karbala Five began, with Iranian units pushing westward between Fish Lake and the Shatt al Arab. They captured the town of Duayji and inflicted 20,000 casualties on Iraq, but at the cost of 65,000 Iranian casualties. In this intensive operation, Baghdad also lost forty-five airplanes. Attempting to capture Basra, Tehran launched several attacks, some of them well-disguised diversion assaults such as Operation Karbala Six and Operation Karbala Seven. Iran finally aborted Operation Karbala Five on February 26.

In late May 1987, just when the war seemed to have reached a complete stalemate on the southern front, reports from Iran indicated that the conflict was intensifying on Iraq's northern front.

This assault, Operation Karbala Ten, was a joint effort by Iranian units and Iraqi Kurdish rebels. They surrounded the garrison at Mawat, endangering Iraq's oil fields near Kirkuk and the northern oil pipeline to Turkey.

By late spring of 1987, the superpowers became more directly involved because they feared that the fall of Basra might lead to a pro-Iranian Islamic republic in largely Shia-populated southern Iraq. They were also concerned about the intensified tanker war. During the first four months of 1987, Iran attacked twenty ships and Iraq assaulted fifteen. Kuwaiti ships were favorite targets because Iran strongly objected to Kuwait's close relationship with the Baghdad regime. Kuwait turned to the superpowers, partly to protect oil exports but largely to seek an end to the war through superpower intervention. Moscow leased three tankers to Kuwait, and by June the United States had reflagged half of Kuwait's fleet of twenty-two tankers.

Finally, direct attacks on the superpowers' ships drew them into the conflict. On May 6, for the first time, a Soviet freighter was attacked in the southern Gulf region, hit by rockets from Iranian gunboats. Ten days later, a Soviet tanker was damaged by a mine allegedly placed by Iranians near the Kuwait coast. More shocking to the United States was the May 17 accidental Iraqi air attack on the U.S.S *Stark* in which thirty-seven sailors died. The attack highlighted the danger to international shipping in the Gulf.

The Tanker War

The tanker war seemed likely to precipitate a major international incident for two reasons. First, some 70 percent of Japanese, 50 percent of West European, and 7 percent of American oil imports came from the Persian Gulf in the early 1980s. Second, the assault on tankers involved neutral shipping as well as ships of the belligerent states.

The tanker war had two phases. The relatively obscure first phase began in 1981, and the well-publicized second phase began in 1984. As early as May 1981, Baghdad had unilaterally declared a war zone and had officially warned all ships heading to or returning from Iranian ports in the northern zone of the Gulf to stay away or, if they entered, to proceed at their own risk. The main targets in this phase were the ports of Bandar-e Khomeini and Bandar-e Mashur; very few ships were hit outside this zone. Despite the proximity of these ports to Iraq, the Iraqi navy did not play an important role in the operations. Instead, Baghdad used Super Frelon helicopters equipped with Exocet missiles or Mirage F-1s and MiG-23s to hit its targets.

In March 1984, the tanker war entered its second phase when an Iraqi Super Etendard fired an Exocet missile at a Greek tanker south of Khark Island. Until the March assault, Iran had not intentionally attacked civilian ships in the Gulf. The new wave of Iraqi assaults, however, led Iran to reciprocate. In April 1984, Tehran launched its first attack against civilian commercial shipping by shelling an Indian freighter. Most observers considered that Iraqi attacks, however, outnumbered Iranian assaults by three to one.

Iran's retaliatory attacks were largely ineffective because a limited number of aircraft equipped with long-range antiship missiles and ships with long-range surface-to-surface missiles were deployed. Moreover, despite repeated Iranian threats to close the Strait of Hormuz, Iran itself depended on the sea-lanes for vital oil exports. Nonetheless, by late 1987 Iran's mine-laying activities and attacks on ships had drawn a large fleet of Western naval vessels to the Gulf to ensure that the sea-lanes were kept open.

Role of the Air Force

Despite Iraqi success in causing major damage to exposed Iranian ammunition and fuel dumps in the early days of the war, the Iranian air force prevailed initially in the air war. One reason was that Iranian airplanes could carry two or three times more bombs or rockets than their Iraqi counterparts. Moreover, Iranian pilots demonstrated considerable expertise. For example, the Iranian air force attacked Baghdad and key Iraqi air bases as early as the first few weeks of the war, seeking to destroy supply and support systems. The attack on Iraq's oil field complex and air base at Al Walid, the base for T-22 and Il-28 bombers, was a well-coordinated assault. The targets were more than 800 kilometers from Iran's closest air base at Urumiyeh, so the F-4s had to refuel in midair for the mission.

Iran's air force relied on F-4s and F-5s for assaults and a few F-14s for reconnaissance. Although Iran used its Maverick missiles effectively against ground targets, lack of airplane spare parts forced Iran to substitute helicopters for close air support. Helicopters served not only as gunships and troop carriers but also as emergency supply transports. In the mountainous area near Mehran, helicopters proved advantageous in finding and destroying targets and maneuvering against antiaircraft guns or man-portable missiles. During Operation Karbala Five and Operation Karbala Six, the Iranians reportedly engaged in large-scale helicopter-borne operations on the southern and central fronts, respectively. Chinooks and smaller Bell helicopters, such as the Bell 214A, were escorted by Sea Cobra choppers.

In confronting the Iraqi air defense, Iran soon discovered that a low-flying group of two, three, or four F-4s could hit targets almost anywhere in Iraq. Iranian pilots overcame Iraqi SA-2 and SA-3 antiaircraft missiles, using American tactics developed in Vietnam; they were less successful against Iraqi SA-6s. Iran's Western-made air defense system seemed more effective than Iraq's Soviet-made counterpart. Nevertheless, Iran experienced difficulty in operating and maintaining Hawk, Rapier, and Tigercat missiles and instead used antiaircraft guns and man-portable missiles.

As the war continued, however, Iran was increasingly short of spare parts for damaged airplanes and had lost a large number of airplanes in combat. As a result, by late 1987 Iran had become less able to mount an effective defense against the resupplied Iraqi air force, let alone stage aerial counterattacks.

Role of the Navy

In late 1987, an accurate estimate of Iranian naval capability was difficult. In the November 1980 offensive against Iraqi ports and oil facilities, Iran lost at least two corvettes and two missile boats. Nevertheless, the Iranian navy was able to supply Abadan by night (with food and arms for the armed forces and the remaining civilians) until late 1981, when Iranian forces regained the city.

Lacking parts and qualified personnel, few Iranian ships were deployed outside limited coastal areas, where their main functions were patrol and search missions. The Iranian navy stopped and searched hundreds of ships suspected of carrying military equipment destined for Iraq. Beginning in 1984, some Iranian military elements such as the Pasdaran also assaulted ships in the Persian Gulf. In May 1987, reliable sources reported that a Soviet ship was assaulted by a Pasdaran unit speedboat; such Pasdaran raids were largely ineffective, however, because of the weapons used—machine guns and rocket-propelled grenades.

Armed Forces and Society

Status in National Life

Since 1979 Iran has witnessed political and military changes with long-lasting domestic repercussions. The shah relied on the country's considerable military strength to implement his policy goals. When his rule was replaced by a theocratic regime with a new domestic agenda, political power presumably rested in the hands of Khomeini and a group of cautious clerics bound by deeply conservative religious values. In the turmoil of the Revolution, the regular armed forces lost their preeminent position in society primarily because of their close identification with the shah.

The military was paralyzed by fast-moving events and incapable of effective action, and its downfall was accelerated when a number of key senior officers fled the country, fearing reprisals from the revolutionary regime. The public trials and executions of high-ranking military officers further tainted the military's image. On February 15, 1979, three days after the official declaration of the republic, a secret Islamic revolutionary court in Tehran handed down death sentences on four generals. Five days later the regime ordered the execution of four more generals. Other military officers were executed for the Islamic crimes of "causing corruption on earth" and "fighting Allah," according to an interpretation of *shariat* (see Glossary). The new regime considered these officers as Pahlavi holdovers, lacking proper Islamic credentials and therefore potential instigators of military coups. When protests were voiced about summary executions, Ayatollah Mohammad Reza Mahdavi-Kani, the cleric in charge of the *komitehs,* replied, "We must purify society in order to renew it." The resulting leadership vacuum in the military took several years to fill.

Mobilized to fight a foreign enemy, the armed forces by 1981 were gradually developing autonomy and an esprit de corps, despite their acrimonious infighting with the Pasdaran, whose independent military power acted as a check on any possible coup attempts by the armed forces. The Khomeini regime, aware of its dependence on the armed forces, adopted a new strategy aimed at assimilating the military into the Revolution by promoting loyal officers and propagating Islamic values. Leaders recognized that as long as the country was at war with Iraq and was experiencing internal political turmoil, they would need a loyal army on the battlefield as well as the loyal Pasdaran on the homefront. Despite the need for military support, however, the revolutionary regime continued to exercise tight control over the armed forces and to regard them with some suspicion.

Political rivalries notwithstanding, the regular armed forces' professionalism and impressive performance in the war stood as clear alternatives to the early "human-wave" tactics of the Pasdaran and Basij, which cost hundreds of thousands of lives and achieved little. The armed forces' respectable military performance also helped exonerate them from the role they had played during the Pahlavi period. Since September 1980, the military has demonstrated that it could and would defend the country and the legitimate government.

The Defense Burden

Military expenditures under the shah were high and unpopular. Even after the 1974 rise in the price of petroleum, a disproportionately high percentage of the government's annual budget was devoted to military expenditures. Iran's military establishment occupied a special place, and the civilian population, particularly in the rural areas, disapproved of its privileged status. Despite the nation-building activities in which the armed forces were engaged (especially in the area of education), Iranian society in general never fully shared the shah's commitment to a buildup that drained the treasury of scarce resources.

Since 1980 the armed forces' budget has been prepared by the Ministry of Defense (formerly the Ministry of War under the shah) in consultation with the SDC. The latter is also consulted by the Ministry of the Pasdaran in preparing its budget. In turn, the prime minister, who is also a member of the SDC, submits the completed package to the Majlis for debate, approval, and appropriation.

In the absence of official data, the precise levels of military expenditures are difficult to determine. Figures collected and analyzed by the Stockholm International Peace Research Institute for the 1976–83 period indicate a reduction in defense expenditures from the equivalent of US$14.6 billion in 1976 to US$5.2 billion in 1983. Not surprisingly, the sharpest decline occurred in 1979, when the revolutionary regime either canceled or postponed contracted purchases. The most notable cancellations were the navy's six Spruance-class destroyers and three Tang-class submarines. The air force also canceled big-ticket items, including 160 F–16 fighters and 7 Boeing E3A–AWACS aircraft. Admittedly, some cancellations were caused by economic difficulties during the shah's last years in power. With a reduction in Iran's oil revenues during the 1977–78 period, the shah reluctantly agreed to scale down ambitious construction projects, such as the naval facility at Chah Bahar (now Bandar-e Beheshti) on the Gulf of Oman and the military industrial complex at Esfahan.

Nevertheless, the revolutionary government abandoned many military projects, not only because most were contracted with American corporations such as Northrop and Boeing, but also because the new regime's priorities were different. The Khomeini government claimed to represent the oppressed masses and promised to provide for their needs. To this end the government chose to reallocate massive defense expenditures in other directions.

This trend was rapidly reversed, however, with the revolutionary government's first war budget in 1981. Because published figures are lacking, reliable estimates of Iran's defense expenditures are difficult to make. For example, according to the International Institute for Strategic Studies, defense expenditures in FY 1981-82 may have been somewhere between US$4.4 and US$13.3 billion; if so, the latter figure would represent 41.6 percent of Iran's total budget. By 1987 all defense expenditures, including those of the Pasdaran and Basij and payments to the families of war martyrs, may have totaled US$100 billion.

Iran's prerevolutionary defense budgets were high by the standards of developing countries, and large expenditures for its armed forces continued through the early 1980s. Despite the outbreak of the war, Iran's gross national product (GNP—see Glossary) climbed from an estimated US$107 billion in 1979 to US$158 billion in 1984. Military expenditures climbed similarly from an estimated US$8.8 billion in 1979 to US$11.3 billion in 1984. The United States Arms Control and Disarmament Agency's statistics indicated that military expenditures as a percentage of GNP increased from 6.6 percent to 7.2 percent between 1980 and 1984. More significantly, according to some estimates, military expenditures represented 19.7 percent of central government expenditures in 1980 and 29.9 percent in 1984. By all accounts, the impact of these large military expenditures on Iranian society has been considerable.

The World Bank (see Glossary) estimated that with almost one-third of the annual budget allocated to the war effort, other sectors of the economy, including education, health, and housing, experienced sharp declines. Iran's revolutionary government, however, rechanneled some of its military disbursements to the nonmilitary population. For example, veterans, disabled veterans, and widows continued to receive financial support from the government. In rural areas, ad hoc procurement mechanisms were rapidly put in place to feed and clothe the swelling volunteer ranks. These activities created employment opportunities that channeled government monies to the civilian population.

Ingenious as these steps were, the burden of defense expenditures left some of Tehran's revolutionary promises unfulfilled. Khomeini had criticized the shah's regime for squandering Iran's assets by pouring a large percentage of oil revenues into the military and denying basic services to the majority of the population, but in some cases Khomeini was obliged to do the same thing. It was true that after 1980, economic conditions improved proportionately faster for the lower classes than for any other group (see War Costs, ch. 3). Still, the revolutionary regime was exacting great sacrifices from those who could least afford it.

The Impact of Casualties on Society

Iran's population, based on the preliminary results of the October 1986 census, was slightly more than 48 million, including approximately 2.6 million refugees from Afghanistan and Iraq. The population was expected, according to United States Bureau of Census projections, to increase to nearly 56 million in 1990 and 76 million in the year 2000. In 1986 the 18 to 30-year-old and 31 to 45-year-old male populations stood at about 5.2 and 3.5 million, respectively. In the absence of reliable information on Iran's war casualties, the significance of these figures was difficult to assess. Estimates of war-related deaths ranged between 180,000 and 300,000. Loss of life was especially high among the 18- to 30-year-old male population; a generation of young and potentially productive citizens had been reduced significantly, and the survivors had been physically and mentally scarred by the war.

Casualties also affected Iran's attempts at industrial recovery. The campaign to resuscitate steel, petrochemical, and other plants faced critical manpower shortages, raising criticisms from the more conservative elements in the regime. The manpower shortages were exacerbated by the 1982 military campaigns that had mobilized up to 1 million volunteers on more than one occasion.

Coupled with the deteriorating economic situation, the high human cost of the abortive Iranian thrusts into Iraq in 1982 to 1984 generated war-weariness and discontent even among the regime's staunchest supporters, the urban and lower classes. The number of recruits dropped because of disenchantment stemming from political divisions, which sometimes produced conflicts that turned violent in the streets of major cities. The Khomeini regime, relying on the total devotion of the Pasdaran and the Basij, appealed to national and religious feelings to rekindle morale. In a series of rulings issued in the autumn of 1982, Khomeini declared that parental permission was unnecessary for those going to the front, that volunteering for military duty was a religious obligation, and that serving in the armed forces took priority over all other forms of work or study. The government mounted a simultaneous effort to quell demonstrations by political groups like the Mojahedin and the Tudeh (see Internal Security, this ch.). The demise of left-wing guerrilla organizations, however, did not reduce opposition to the war. New elements calling for a settlement of the conflict with Iraq emerged. Because of this opposition, former Prime Minister Bazargan urged a negotiated end to the war, realizing that Iran might fall victim to its own political rigidity. For the revolutionary regime, however, the war remained a legitimizing tool, despite its high cost.

Treatment of Veterans and Widows

In 1980 the Khomeini government established two special foundations to care for those affected by war. The Foundation for Martyrs and the Foundation for War Refugees (Bonyad-e Jangzadegan) provided welfare and services to veterans and survivors. It also established the Foundation for War Victims (veterans) and the Foundation for the Disinherited (Bonyad-e Mostazafin), which looked after orphans.

With more than 1 million people killed or maimed by the war, the cost of financing compensations and pensions mounted rapidly. War-related expenses included the costs of the Pasdaran and the Basij, compensations and pensions to the war disabled and the families of the dead, the funding of the Foundation for War Victims and the War Reconstruction Fund. Despite these mounting costs, the government was generous to the survivors of the dead. A regular soldier's family reportedly received compensation of US$24,000 and full salary as a pension; additionally, the equivalent of US$60 monthly was deposited in the bank account of each of his minor children until they reached eighteen. The government assisted the family in renting, buying, or building a house. Less generous amounts were paid to the families of the Pasdaran and the Basij who died on the front. Disabled soldiers reportedly received US$30 monthly, and the seriously injured were cared for in veterans' hospitals.

In an official Iranian publication, *Summary Report: An Estimate of the Economic Damages of the Imposed War of Iraq Against Iran,* the damages caused to the Iranian economy up to March 1983 were cited as equivalent to US$135.8 billion, including the loss of oil revenue (US$35 billion) and agricultural output (US$23 billion). A dozen cities and 1,200 villages were reported destroyed and another 19 cities partially damaged. The war had created no fewer than 1.5 million Iranian refugees by early 1983. In 1987 more recent documentation cited the war's costs at approximately US$300 billion.

Internal Security

The Islamic Revolution destroyed the structures on which the shah's internal security policies depended. Mohammad Reza Shah had not tolerated dissent, had reacted strongly when challenged, and had relied on an elaborate internal security police force to enforce his absolute authority. Over the years, Khomeini had vigorously condemned the shah's secret police operations and continually called on Iranians to rise against a perceived tyrannical ruler.

Iraqi forces severely damaged the port of Khorramshahr in October 1980
Copyright Lehtikuva/PHOTRI

By the late 1970s, the shah's internal security organizations were in disgrace because of their abuses. In early 1979, the revolutionary regime dismantled existing security organizations and called on loyal citizens to protect the Revolution. Yet, like the shah, the revolutionary regime faced clear opposition to its authority.

Internal Security in the 1970s

The Pahlavi regime identified the Fadayan, the Tudeh, and several ethnic groups as opponents to the shah's rule. To meet their rising challenge, the shah relied on security forces whose agents infiltrated many underground organizations. By early 1970, a sophisticated intelligence-gathering system was in place, reporting all currents of political dissent directly to the monarch.

In 1971 opposition forces took the initiative by launching a terrorist campaign against the regime. At the time, this was perceived as a nuisance and an embarrassment to the shah, because the monarchy was not "threatened." Nevertheless, opposition to the shah grew stronger when the monarch authorized unrelenting punishment of those accused of security violations. Hundreds of young Iranians were arrested, tried, and sentenced. Many were tortured and some executed for their unwavering opposition. In 1976 opposition forces clashed with the police in a series of gun battles that took place in the streets of Tehran. With heightened visibility, terrorist groups mounted successful attacks on police posts, further threatening the regime's hold on internal security. By 1978 organized opposition to the monarchy reached a high point with ideologically incompatible groups joining in efforts to overthrow the shah. Leftist guerrillas joined student and religious organizations in calling for political change.

The two most important leftist guerrilla groups operating in Iran in 1979 were the Mojahedin and the Fadayan (see Antiregime Opposition Groups, this ch.). After its initial formation in 1965 as a discussion group of religiously inspired university graduates, the Mojahedin had splintered several times. The graduates who composed the Mojahedin were thoroughly disillusioned with the shah's regime and advocated armed struggle. In the course of the 1970s the Mojahedin gradually gained notoriety. The Mojahedin and the Fadayan conducted a systematic assassination campaign from 1971 to 1976 against Iranian security officials and United States military and defense-related personnel stationed in Tehran. The shah was also a target, as evidenced by periodic uncoverings of assassination plots. This wave of violence was met by an equally strong and determined campaign of arrests and executions. Iranian students abroad also became part of a cycle of action and counteraction: in the United States and Western Europe, students who protested against the shah were kept under surveillance so that punitive action could later be taken against them. In addition, the Mojahedin and the Fadayan conducted a propaganda campaign in support of "the Iranian armed struggle" and against the shah, SAVAK, and what was termed "institutionalized repression in Iran" (see SAVAK, this ch.).

Within Iran's borders, stiff government security measures notwithstanding, organized opposition was never eliminated. Although the shah had declared illegal all opposition political parties, labor unions, peasant organizations, and university student groups, antigovernment sentiments remained high, especially among the clerical community. By late 1977, student demonstrations increased in frequency, with a vocal minority calling on Iranians to "raise their voices against absolute rule." These protests, timed to call President Jimmy Carter's attention to the human rights situation in Iran, resulted in the arrest of hundreds of demonstrators, many of whom were allegedly tortured by SAVAK forces.

In January 1978, conservative religious students demonstrated in the holy city of Qom to protest an article in the progovernment newspaper *Etalaat* that they considered slandered Ayatollah Khomeini, who was then living in exile in An Najaf in Iraq.

Religious leaders were also outraged at what they perceived to be the shah's violations of sacred Islamic laws in such areas as the role of women in society and the imposition of a secular legal system that usurped clerical authority. Attempts by the police to disperse demonstrators resulted in several deaths.

The religious leadership called for a general strike across the country for February 18, to highlight the forty-day mourning period for those killed in Qom. Far more serious disturbances erupted on that day in the city of Tabriz, precipitating the worst riots since 1963. After several days of widespread arson directed at banks, movie theaters, and hotels in Tabriz, the army moved in to restore order. Nonviolent protests occurred in Tehran and other major cities. According to the government 12 persons were killed in Tabriz and 250 persons arrested. In reality, the casualty figure was much higher and the arrests more numerous. Ironically, the deaths presented the next opportunity for confrontation. When demonstrators, commemorating the forty-day mourning period, defiantly marched through streets of many cities, the armed forces reacted as expected. To protect themselves and restore order, they opened fire, killing and injuring more civilians. The result was a sequence of events in which the opposition, led by influential clerics, conducted "religious commemorations," and the government interpreted them as challenges to law and order. With neither side relenting, the cycle of violence spread.

Observers of these tragic events pointed out that the reemergence of large-scale protest demonstrations was only made possible because of the shah's more liberal policies toward the nonviolent expression of dissent. Indeed, the shah confirmed on several occasions his commitment to more "liberal" political reforms, but at the same time he warned that the dissident movement was "completely illegal" and that he would "not let it get out of hand." Illegal or not, mass protest demonstrations did get out of control when the shah openly chastised the clerics for "destroying the country." The shah could not end these demonstrations, which gathered more support throughout 1978. Workers from the oil industry, heeding the call of the religious authorities, slowly paralyzed Iran's economic sector. It became only a matter of time before the shah lost control over Iran's internal security.

Law Enforcement Agencies

Intensely concerned with matters of internal security in the post-1953 environment, the shah authorized the development of one of the most extensive systems of law enforcement agencies in the developing world. The Gendarmerie—the rural police—and the National Police gained in numbers and responsibilities. The secret police organization, SAVAK, gained special notoriety for its excessive zeal in "maintaining" internal security. But as in the regular armed forces, the shah's management style virtually eliminated all coordination among these agencies. A favorite approach was to shuffle army personnel back and forth between their ordinary duties and temporary positions in internal security agencies, in order to minimize the possibility of any organized coups against the throne. Added to this list of institutional shortcomings was agencies' all-important public image, cloaked in mystery and fear. Iranians in and out of the country came to perceive these agencies as "arms" of the shah's absolute power and resented them deeply.

SAVAK

Formed under the guidance of United States and Israeli intelligence officers in 1957, SAVAK developed into an effective secret agency. General Teymur Bakhtiar was appointed its first director, only to be dismissed in 1961, allegedly for organizing a coup; he was assassinated in 1970 under mysterious circumstances, probably on the shah's direct order. His successor, General Hosain Pakravan, was dismissed in 1966, allegedly for having failed to crush the clerical opposition in the early 1960s. The shah turned to his childhood friend and classmate, General Nematollah Nassiri, to rebuild SAVAK and properly "serve" the monarch. Mansur Rafizadeh, the SAVAK director in the United States throughout the 1970s, claimed that General Nassiri's telephone was tapped by SAVAK agents reporting directly to the shah, an example of the level of mistrust pervading the government on the eve of the Revolution.

In 1987 accurate information concerning SAVAK remained publicly unavailable. A flurry of pamphlets issued by the revolutionary regime after 1979 indicated that SAVAK had been a full-scale intelligence agency with more than 15,000 full-time personnel and thousands of part-time informants. SAVAK was attached to the Office of the Prime Minister, and its director assumed the title of deputy to the prime minister for national security affairs. Although officially a civilian agency, SAVAK had close ties to the military; many of its officers served simultaneously in branches of the armed forces. Another childhood friend and close confidant of the shah, Major General Hosain Fardust, was deputy director of SAVAK until the early 1970s, when the shah promoted him to the directorship of the Special Intelligence Bureau, which operated inside Niavaran Palace, independently of SAVAK.

Founded to round up members of the outlawed Tudeh, SAVAK expanded its activities to include gathering intelligence and neutralizing the regime's opponents. An elaborate system was created to monitor all facets of political life. For example, a censorship office was established to monitor journalists, literary figures, and academics throughout the country; it took appropriate measures against those who fell out of line. Universities, labor unions, and peasant organizations, among others, were all subjected to intense surveillance by SAVAK agents and paid informants. The agency was also active abroad, especially in monitoring Iranian students who publicly opposed Pahlavi rule.

Over the years, SAVAK became a law unto itself, having legal authority to arrest and detain suspected persons indefinitely. SAVAK operated its own prisons in Tehran (the Komiteh and Evin facilities) and, many suspected, throughout the country as well. Many of these activities were carried out without any institutional checks. Thus, it came as no surprise when, in 1979, SAVAK was singled out as a primary target for reprisals, its headquarters overrun, and prominent leaders tried and executed by *komiteh* representatives. High-ranking SAVAK agents were purged between 1979 and 1981; there were 61 SAVAK officials among 248 military personnel executed between February and September 1979. The organization was officially dissolved by Khomeini shortly after he came to power in 1979.

SAVAMA

Little information existed in 1987 on SAVAK's successor agency, SAVAMA. According to General Robert E. Huyser, President Jimmy Carter's last special envoy to imperial Iran, SAVAMA's first director was Major General Fardust, who was arrested in December 1985 for being a "Soviet informer." But after this major arrest the revolutionary government's keen desire to gain an upper hand over leftist guerrilla organizations may have influenced certain IRP leaders to relax their previously unrelenting pursuit of military intelligence personnel. Key religious leaders, including Majlis speaker Hashemi-Rafsanjani, insisted on recalling former agents to help the regime eliminate domestic opposition. Consequently, some intelligence officers and low-ranking SAVAK and army intelligence officials were asked to return to government service because of their specialized knowledge of the Iranian left. Others had acquired in-depth knowledge of Iraq's Baath Party and proved to be invaluable in helping decision makers.

Although it is impossible to verify, in 1987 observers speculated that some of SAVAK's intelligence-gathering operations were turned over to SAVAMA. It remained to be determined whether these newly authorized operations proved effective and whether there was coordination with other branches of government, including the powerful Pasdaran.

Gendarmerie and National Police

The Gendarmerie, numbering nearly 74,000 in 1979, was subordinate to the Ministry of Interior. Its law enforcement responsibilities extended to all rural areas and to small towns and villages of fewer than 5,000 inhabitants. The International Institute for Strategic Studies estimated its manpower at 70,000 in 1986.

The National Police operated with approximately 200,000 men in 1979, a figure that has not fluctuated much since. Like the Gendarmerie, the National Police was under the Ministry of Interior, and its responsibilities included all cities with more than 5,000 in population—a total of 53 percent of the population. In addition, the National Police was responsible for passport and immigration procedures, issuance and control of citizens' identification cards, driver and vehicle licensing and registration, and railroad and airport policing. Some of these duties were absorbed into the Ministry of the Pasdaran during the early years of the Revolution, and cooperation between these two branches seemed extensive.

Since 1979 both these paramilitary organizations have undergone complete reorganizations. IRP leaders quickly appointed Gendarmerie and police officers loyal to the Revolution to revive and reorganize the two bodies under the Republic. Between 1979 and 1983, no fewer than seven officers were given top National Police portfolios. Colonel Khalil Samimi, appointed in 1983 by the influential Hojjatoleslam Nategh-e Nuri, then minister of interior, was credited with reorganizing the National Police according to the IRP's Islamic guidelines. The Gendarmerie followed a similar path. Seven appointments were made between 1979 and 1986, leading to a full reorganization. In addition to Brigadier General Ahmad Mohagheghi, the commander in the early republican period who was executed in late summer of 1980, five colonels were purged. Colonel Ali Kuchekzadeh played a major role in reorganizing and strengthening the Gendarmerie after its near collapse in the early revolutionary period. The commander in 1987, Colonel Mohammad Sohrabi, had served in that position since February 1985 and was the first top officer to have risen from the ranks.

As of 1987, the National Police and the Gendarmerie reflected the ideology of the state. Despite their valuable internal security operations, the roles of both bodies were restricted by the rising influence of the Pasdaran and the Basij.

Antiregime Opposition Groups

The Khomeini regime has faced severe challenges from several opposition groups, including royalists, National Front bureaucrats, intellectuals and professionals, communists, guerrilla organizations, Kurdish rebels, and distinguished *mujtahids* (Shia clerics whose demonstrated erudition in religious law has earned them the privilege to interpret law). Of these, the royalists and the National Front leaders have operated mainly from foreign bases or underground cells. The communists were purged in 1983 when the Tudeh's leadership was almost entirely arrested. The main guerrilla group, the Mojahedin, claimed to have made strides in organizing a war of attrition against the regime. But because it has operated since July 1986 primarily from Baghdad, thus giving the impression of collaboration with Iraq, the Mojahedin's effectiveness and credibility may have been lessened by the war. The Kurds have been fighting the regime since their 1979 rebellion, even though Tehran has kept them off balance by using Pasdaran forces. Finally, National Front politicians have openly displayed their differing views, mostly in West European capitals, although the group led by former Prime Minister Bazargan was the only domestic "opposition" party tolerated by the regime.

Mojahedin

In the early 1970s, founders of the Mojahedin movement decided to organize operations against the shah's government. Initial demands made by Mojahedin leaders, most of whom were executed between 1972 and 1975, covered such points as the cancellation of all security agreements with the United States; expropriation of multinational corporations; nationalization of agricultural and urban land, banks, and large industries; administration of the army and other institutions by people's councils; creation of a "people's army"; regional autonomy for Iran's ethnic minorities; and various measures to benefit workers and peasants. Unlike other anti-shah organizations, the Mojahedin channeled its efforts into gaining supporters and developing an effective party network. The members were ideologically inspired by a combination of Shia philosophy and Marxist sociology and attacked the shah and his perceived abuses. By 1979 the membership of the Mojahedin had reached a record high of 25,000, and it had hundreds of thousands of supporters. The movement frequently mobilized these masses against the shah.

The organization fell out of favor immediately after the Revolution, however, when its new leader, Masud Rajavi, boycotted the referendum on the new Constitution and advocated the total separation of the religious establishment and the state. Khomeini considered this a calculated and direct challenge to the IRP and the revolutionary regime. Rumors spread that the Mojahedin organization was a pawn of foreign powers, especially the United States. In response, the Mojahedin launched its own anti-Khomeini campaign by calling on the government to purify the Revolution.

President Bani Sadr supported the Mojahedin. When he lost the support of Khomeini, Bani Sadr sought refuge with Mojahedin leaders and was smuggled out of Iran, along with Rajavi and other senior representatives. In July 1981, the two leaders announced the formation of the National Council of Resistance (NCR) and launched a campaign to overthrow the Khomeini regime. From its headquarters in France, the NCR recruited additional support both within and outside Iran and welcomed ethnic minority leaders to its ranks. Its published charter was almost identical to the program of the Mojahedin. Partly to satisfy its diverse constituency and partly to distinguish itself from the Khomeini regime, the NCR offered a new agenda that reflected special concern for the interests of the lower middle class. In its attempt to gain the support of minor civil servants, shopkeepers, artisans, and small merchants, it adopted a slightly more moderate position than the one the Khomeini government had espoused concerning private property. The charter also promised to respect individual liberties, "except for persons identified with the shah's or Khomeini's regime," and guaranteed special rights for ethnic minorities, particularly the Kurds.

A score of other promises were made, including the return of land to farmers who would, however, be encouraged to consolidate their holdings in collective farms; the increase of available housing, education, and health services; the guarantee of equality for women; and the establishment of a "democratic army" in which the rank and file would be consulted on decisions and selections of officers. Yet, these promises could not be implemented because the NCR was not in power. The organization had to operate inside Iran, and the process strained the leadership's unity; disagreements over goals eventually led to the dissolution of the NCR. By March 1984, Bani Sadr and Kurdish leaders withdrew from the coalition. The French government asked Rajavi to leave France in July 1986. The Mojahedin set up their headquarters in Baghdad, whence they continued to launch military and propaganda offensives against the Khomeini regime.

In June 1987, Rajavi announced the formation of the Iranian National Army of Liberation, open to non-Mojahedin members,

A unit of the Iranian National Army of Liberation celebrates a victory over Iranian forces in Khuzestan Province
Courtesy Iran Liberation

that would escalate attacks. Subsequently, Mojahedin sources claimed to have set up military training camps near the war front and to have launched numerous attacks against Pasdaran outposts. The Mojahedin has also been active in Western Europe and the United States; it has organized numerous rallies, distributed anti-Khomeini literature, and recruited Iranians living abroad (see Opposition Political Parties in Exile, ch. 4).

Fadayan

Among the armed leftist guerrilla groups operating in Iran in 1987, the Fadayan was the most active. The Fadayan was established when smaller groups operating in Tabriz, Mashhad, and Tehran merged in 1970. Its founders were university students and graduates who saw violence as the only means to oppose the shah. As Iran's economic situation deteriorated in the mid-1970s, the Fadayan recruited workers from large manufacturing industries and the oil sector. Recruitment expanded to include such national and ethnic movements as those of Kurdish, Turkoman, Baluch, and Arab minorities. The Fadayan opposed both imperial and republican regimes but did participate fully in the Revolution, taking over various military barracks and police stations in Tehran, Tabriz, Hamadan, Abadan, and Shiraz in 1979.

In early June 1980, the Fadayan split into two factions: the Fadayan "Minority" and the Fadayan " Majority." The "Minority" faction, which was actually the larger of the two, has consistently opposed the Republic and considered Khomeini "reactionary." It vehemently condemned the Tudeh's cooperation with Khomeini prior to 1983. It also rejected the armed activities of the Mojahedin and advocated instead the expansion of underground cells. The "Minority" faction refused to join the NCR because of Bani Sadr's past association with the Khomeini regime. Subsequently, the "Minority" faction, along with a number of smaller leftist groups, established a new organization known as the Organization of Revolutionary Workers of Iran.

The Fadayan "Majority" faction moved closer to the views held by the Tudeh and supported Khomeini because of his anti-imperialist stance. This support of Khomeini changed in early 1983 when Khomeini turned against the Tudeh. In late 1987, the "Majority" faction was a satellite of the Tudeh (see Opposition Political Parties in Exile, ch. 4).

The falling out of the Fadayan with the Islamic government within the first year of the Revolution was attributed to the ideological rift that emerged between the Fadayan's leftist-secular agenda and the religious and ideological views of the clerical leadership. Khomeini's *velayat-e faqih* (see Glossary) was a powerful concept that swept aside all leftist arguments; the Khomeini view of the Revolution was appealing precisely because of its religious aspects, which were easily assimilated by the Iranian population.

Paykar

The Paykar (Struggle) Organization was formed in 1979 from a Mojahedin splinter group that advocated the total separation of the religious establishment and the state. It considered Khomeini's policies backward and damaging to Iran's long-term socioeconomic development. The Paykar, perceived by other leftist groups as a dogmatic movement, called for an end to the Iran-Iraq War, viewing it as a diversionary tactic "waged by two reactionary and unpopular regimes." In 1982, when several Paykar leaders were arrested, the organization ceased to function overtly, but in 1987 it was still suspected of operating underground cells in major Iranian cities.

The Role of Minorities in Internal Security

Ethnic cooperation has been a consistent national security problem for successive regimes throughout the twentieth century, and, after the 1979 Revolution, the Khomeini government faced one of its earliest challenges from Kurdish, Baluch, and Turkoman tribal members. The Turkoman and Baluch rebellions, which attempted to achieve greater autonomy, were quickly ended. The revolutionary regime went out of its way to accommodate opposition because it did not want any instability to develop on the border with neighboring Afghanistan. Tehran wanted at all costs to prevent foreign powers from exploiting ethnic discontent in southwestern Iran. By emphasizing shared religious and cultural values, the revolutionary government persuaded some tribal members to accept the central authority of Tehran, while it sought to co-opt others, such as the Turkomans and Baluchs, by providing special economic incentives.

A more pressing ethnic challenge to the regime came from Kurdish rebels in the northwest, who had long struggled for independence. In several 1979 meetings, Khomeini warned key Kurdish leaders that any attempts at dismantling Iran would be met with the harshest response, and he sent Pasdaran units to the north, underlining the seriousness of the government's intention. Despite these warnings, in the spring of 1979, seizing on the turmoil of the Revolution, the Kurdish Democratic Party of Iran, the Komala (Komala-ye Shureshgari-ye Zahmat Keshan-e Kordestan-e Iran, or Komala, or Committee of the Revolutionary Toilers of Iranian Kordestan) and the Kurdish branch of the Fadayan mounted a rebellion that the revolutionary regime crushed rather easily.

The confrontation between Tehran and the Kurds lessened sharply when the Iran-Iraq War broke out. Contrary to assumptions, Iraqi Kurds and their Iranian brothers did not cooperate to exploit weaknesses on both sides. Past divisions within the Kurdish communities effectively prevented joint pursuit of the long-cherished goal of an independent state. Not surprisingly, neither Baghdad nor Tehran was displeased by this outcome. Rather, both sides insisted on organizing special loyalist Kurdish military units to participate in the war and to demonstrate allegiance to their respective states.

In contrast to the Kurds, the Arab population of Khuzestan stood firmly behind the revolutionary government. Iranian Arabs rejected Saddam Husayn's call to "liberate Arabistan" from Persian rule and overwhelmingly opted to remain loyal to their country. Since 1980 Khuzestan has witnessed some of the bloodiest battles in the twentieth century, but its Arab inhabitants have not wavered in their allegiance.

Iran regards ethnic minority challenges with apprehension. It has taken every precaution, for example, to resist Iraqi- or Soviet-sponsored efforts to persuade the Kurdish minority to secede from

Iran. Much as the Pahlavi regime before it had done, the revolutionary government considered the unity of Iran vital to its national security. The commitment to defend the entire country, with all its ethnic groups, remained an uncompromised objective, and sensitive, pragmatic, and political steps have been taken since 1979 to strengthen national unity. Despite the commitment of the Khomeini regime to the revival of the Islamic community (*ummah*), it, no less than the shah's regime, sought to preserve Iran's territorial integrity as an aspect of national security.

Of all the issues facing revolutionary Iran since 1979, none was more serious than alleged human rights violations. Although the trend was toward greater adherence to constitutional guarantees, particularly after December 1982, when Khomeini issued several orders restricting arbitrary arrest and detention, Iran's human rights record showed serious abuses. Procedural safeguards were lacking for defendants tried in revolutionary courts, which handled virtually all political cases. In evaluating the hundreds of executions ordered each year, separating cases of executions for actual crimes from executions based purely on the defendant's beliefs, statements, or associations, was difficult, given the regime's practice of cloaking the latter category with trumped-up charges from the former category. Reliable statistics were not available in 1987 on the number killed for political or religious reasons under the Khomeini regime, but the number of persons executed each year for political reasons was high.

Amnesty International's 1986 annual report recorded an estimated 6,500 executions in Iran between February 1979 and the end of 1985; the report noted, however, that "Amnesty International believed the true figures were much higher, as former prisoners and relatives of prisoners consistently testified that large numbers of political prisoners were executed in secret." These killings were largely conducted by the government's own organizations, including the Pasdaran and the SAVAMA.

Political opposition to the revolutionary regime was punished in ways other than execution. Iranians listed as "killed while resisting arrest," but actually alive and in jail, were too numerous to count, according to Amnesty International. Torture in Iran's prisons was rampant and covered a wide range of inhuman practices, particularly in Tehran's notorious Evin Prison. Mock executions, along with blindfolding and solitary confinement, were favorite methods of torture, according to witness reports assembled by Amnesty International. Beatings of all kinds were common, and prisoners were regularly beaten on the soles of their feet until they could no longer walk. Individuals also suffered damaged kidneys as a result of being kicked and beaten.

The revolutionary prosecutors continued to revise Iran's civil code to conform more closely with their interpretation of Islamic law. In January 1985, for example, Tehran announced the inauguration of a new machine for surgical amputation of the hands of convicted thieves. As interpreted in Iran, this punishment consisted of amputation of the four fingers of the right hand. There were subsequent announcements of the occasional use of this device to administer justice. Death by stoning was allegedly reinstituted as a punishment for certain morality crimes, at least in remote areas of the country. There were many reports of floggings, both as a means of torture and as a formal punishment for sexual offenses.

Although the Constitution guarantees many basic human rights, including rights related to due process (e.g., the right to be informed in writing of charges immediately after arrest, the right to legal counsel, the right to trial by jury in political cases), the revolutionary court system ignored these provisions in practice for "security reasons." When there was a formal accusation, the charge was usually subversion, antiregime activities, or treason. Political arrests were made by members of the Pasdaran or, less commonly, by *komiteh* members. Members of the National Police and Gendarmerie were not normally involved in arrests made on political or moral charges. In political cases, warrants for arrests were seldom used. Consequently, there was no judicial determination of whether these detentions were in conformity with Iranian law. Detainees were frequently held for long periods without charge and in some cases were tortured. For political crimes, no access to a lawyer was permitted; such cases were heard, if at all, by the revolutionary judiciary, and bail was not permitted.

Religious opposition as well as political opposition has met with severe punishment. For example, Iran's largest non-Muslim minority, the Bahais, have suffered persecution. Charges against Bahais were vague, but penalties were severe. As of December 1986, 767 Bahais had been imprisoned and approximately 200 Bahais had been executed or had died following torture (see Non-Muslim Minorities, ch. 2).

Between 1979 and 1982, these abuses of human rights were all defended as necessary to safeguard the Revolution. Tehran launched a systematic attack on its opponents in order to protect its own interpretations of revolutionary norms. Since then, many revolutionary leaders have adopted a more relaxed mood without jeopardizing perceived internal security requirements. It remained to be seen in late 1987 whether the revolutionary regime would be able to maintain the internal security it felt it needed without returning to the drastic measures characteristic of the early period of the Revolution.

* * *

An early, albeit cursory, introduction to the Iranian armed forces after the 1979 Revolution is William F. Hickman's *Ravaged and Reborn.* Gregory F. Rose's "The Post-Revolutionary Purge of Iran's Armed Forces: A Revisionist Assessment" and "Soldiers of Islam: The Iranian Armed Forces since the Revolution" provide detailed information on the purges of the military and the ensuing reorganization. Nikola B. Schahgaldian's *The Iranian Military under the Islamic Republic* is the most complete source on the Pasdaran and Basij forces. The best source of current data on the size, budget, and equipment inventory of the armed forces is the annual *The Military Balance,* published by the International Institute for Strategic Studies. Historical background material is presented most completely in J.C. Hurewitz's *Middle East Politics.* On the postrevolutionary period, Dilip Hiro's *Iran under the Ayatollahs* and Ruhollah K. Ramazani's *Revolutionary Iran* are indispensable. For the Iran-Iraq War, Jasim M. Abdulghani's *Iraq and Iran* provides comprehensive coverage of events leading up to the war. The writings of Anthony H. Cordesman on the war itself are very valuable, as is the excellent account in Efraim Karsh's "The Iran-Iraq War: A Military Analysis." (For further information and complete citations, see Bibliography.)

Appendix

Table

Table 1. Metric Conversion Coefficients and Factors

When you know	Multiply by	To find
Millimeters	0.04	inches
Centimeters	0.39	inches
Meters	3.3	feet
Kilometers	0.62	miles
Hectares (10,000 m^2)	2.47	acres
Square kilometers	0.39	square miles
Cubic meters	35.3	cubic feet
Liters	0.26	gallons
Kilograms	2.2	pounds
Metric tons	0.98	long tons
	1.1	short tons
	2,204	pounds
Degrees Celsius (Centigrade)	9 divide by 5 and add 32	degrees Fahrenheit

Table 2. Major Cities, Census Years 1976 and 1986

City	1976	1986*
Tehran	4,496,000	6,022,000
Mashhad	670,000	1,419,000
Isfahan	671,000	928,000
Tabriz	598,000	808,000
Shiraz	416,000	800,000
Ahvaz	329,000	396,000
Kermanshah (Bakhtaran after 1979)	290,000	389,000
Qom	246,000	338,000
Rasht	187,000	259 000
Karaj	138,000	252,000
Abadan	296,000	250,000
Qazvin	139,000	244,000
Urumiyeh	163,000	219,000
Hamadan	155,000	207,000
Kerman	140,000	202,000

*Preliminary.

Table 3. Ethnic and Linguistic Groups, 1986
(exclusive of refugees)

Ethnic Group	Language	Population [1]	Percentage
Persians	Persian	23,100,000	51.0
Azarbaijanis	Turkic	11,500,000	25.2
Kurds	Kurdish	4,000,000	8.8
Gilakis and Mazandaranis	Persian dialects	3,450,000	7.5
Baluchis	Baluchi	600,000	1.3
Lurs	Luri	550,000	1.2
Arabs	Arabic	530,000	1.2
Fars Turks [2]	Turkic dialects	250,000	0.5
Qashqais	Turkish	250,000	0.5
Turkomans	-do-	250,000	0.5
Bakhtiaris	Luri	250,000	0.5
Armenians	Armenian	250,000	0.5
Assyrians	Assyrian	32,000	--[3]
Other	Persian and Turkic dialects, English, French, German, Georgian, Russian	600,000	1.3
TOTAL		45,612,000	100.0

[1] Estimated; rounded off to nearest 10,000.
[2] Includes Abivardis, Afshars, Baharlus, Inanlus, detribalized Qashqais, and other Turkic-speaking groups.
[3] 0.007 percent.

Source: Based on information from Patricia Higgins, "Minority-State Relations in Contemporary Iran," in Ali Banuazizi and Myron Weiner, eds., *The State, Religion, and Ethnic Politics,* Syracuse, 1986, 178.

Table 4. Non-Muslim Religious Minorities, 1986

Religious Minority	Language	Population*
Bahais	Persian, Turkish	350,000
Armenian Christians	Armenian	250,000
Jews	Persian, Kurdish	50,000
Assyrian Christians	Assyrian	32,000
Zoroastrians	Persian	32,000

*Estimated.

Table 5. Oil Production and Exports, 1980–85
(in millions of barrels per day)

	1980	1981	1982	1983	1984	1985
Production	1.47	1.32	2.39	2.44	2.03	2.19
Exports	0.80	0.71	1.62	1.72	1.52	1.57

Source: Based on information from George Jaffé and Keith McLachlan, *Iran and Iraq: The Next Five Years,* Special Report No. 1083, Economist Intelligence Unit, London, 1987, 12.

Table 6. Estimated Production of Major Crops 1981, 1982, and 1983
(in thousands of tons)

	1981–82	1982–83	1983–84
Barley	1,700	1,903	2,034
Cotton (lint)	275	358	300
Legumes	290	296	290
Oil Seeds*	105	138	188
Onions	675	965	736
Pistachios	122	95	84
Potatoes	1,540	1,814	1,740
Rice	1,624	1,605	1,215
Sugar beets	3,231	4,321	3,648
Sugar cane	1,677	1,810	2,053
Wheat	6,610	6,660	5,956

*Sunflower seeds and soybeans.

Source: Based on information from *The Middle East and North Africa, 1987,* London: Europa Publications, 1986, 416.

Table 7. Major Trading Partners, 1985
(in percentages)

Destination of exports from Iran		Sources of imports to Iran	
Japan	15.9	West Germany	16.3
Italy	9.4	Japan	13.4
Turkey	8.8	Britain	6.7
Singapore	7.1	Italy	6.0
Syria	6.5	Turkey	5.9
Spain	5.6	Soviet Union	4.5
Netherlands	5.5	Singapore	3.9
France	5.0	Spain	2.8
United States	4.8	Argentina	2.8
Romania	4.4	Netherlands	2.7
West Germany	4.0	Kuwait	2.0
Other	23.0	Other	33.0
TOTAL	100.0	TOTAL	100.0

Source: Based on information from Economist Intelligence Unit, *Iran: Country Report, 1987,* No. 1, London, 1987, 2.

Table 8. Armed Forces Manpower
Selected Years, 1977–86

Type and Description	1977	1979	1982	1984	1986
Armed forces					
Reserves	300,000	300,000	400,000	350,000	350,000
Army	220,000	285,000[1]	150,000[2]	250,000[2]	305,000[2]
Navy	22,000	30,000	10,000	20,000	14,500
Air force	100,000	100,000	35,000	35,000	35,500
Total armed forces	642,000	715,000	595,000	655,000	704,500
Paramilitary forces					
Gendarmerie	70,000	74,000	5,000	5,000	70,000
Pasdaran	–	30,000	40,000	250,000	350,000
Basij	–	n.a.	n.a.	2,500,000	3,000,000
Mojahedin	–	n.a.	30,000	n.a.	n.a.
Total paramilitary forces	70,000	104,000	75,000	2,755,000	3,420,000
Forces abroad					
Oman	1,000	5,000[3]	–	–	–
Syria (UNDOF)	383[4]	–	–	–	–
Lebanon	–	–	n.a.	650	1,000
Total forces abroad	1,383	5,000	–	650	1,000

n.a.—not available.

[1] Sixty percent of the army is reported to have deserted in 1979 after the Revolution began. Figures given are for prerevolutionary period.

[2] Conscripts made up 100,000 personnel for 1982 and 1984. The number was estimated at 200,000 for 1986.

[3] The Oman contingent had grown to 5,000 by 1979, when it was brought home.

[4] Some of the United Nations Disengagement Observer Force (UNDOF) soldiers also served in United Nations Interim Force in Lebancn, from which they were also withdrawn in 1979.

Table 9. Major Army Weapons, 1986

Type and Description	Number in Inventory
Tanks (medium)	
T-54,T-55, T-59, T-62, T-72, Chieftain Mk3/5, M-47/-48, M-60A1	1,000
Tanks (light)	
Scorpion	50
Armored vehicles	
EE-9 Cascavel	130
BMP-1	180
BTR-50/-60	500
M-113	250
EE-11 Urutu	300
Guns, howitzers (including self-propelled), mortars, and surface-to-surface missiles (SSM)	
105mm, 130mm, 155mm, 175mm, 203mm	600
81mm, 120mm	3,000
SSM: Scud	n.a.
Recoilless rifles	
57mm, 75mm, M-40A/C 106mm	n.a.
Antiaircraft guns (including self-propelled) and surface-to-air missiles (SAM)	
25mm, 57mm	1,500
SAM: Hawk/Improved Hawk, SA-7, RBS-70	n.a.
Antitank weapons	
ENTAC, SS-11/-12, M-47 Dragon, BGM-71A TOW	n.a.
Fixed-wing aircraft	
Cessna (185, 310, O-2A)	56
Fokker F-27	2
Rockwell Shrike Commander	5
Dassault Mystère-Falcon	2
Helicopters	
AH-1J Cobra (attack)	n.a.
Bell 214A	270
AB-205A	35
CH-47C Chinook	n.a.

n.a.—not available.

Source: Based on information from International Institute for Strategic Studies, *The Military Balance, 1986–1987,* London, 1986, 96.

Table 10. Major Naval Weapons, 1986

Type and Description	Number in Inventory
Destroyers	
With surface-to-air missiles (SAM)	1
US Sumner-class	2
Submarines, Type-1200	6*
Frigates, with surface-to-surface missiles (SSM) and SAM	4
Corvettes, US PF-103	2
Fast patrol boats	
Kaman (La Combattante II) with 7 Harpoon SSM	8
Patrol boats	7
Minesweepers (US MSC 292/268 coastal)	2
Landing ships and craft	8
Logistical support ships	4
Hovercraft, Wellington BH-7	2
Fixed-wing aircraft	
Orion P-3F	2
Shrike Commander	4
Fokker F-27	4
Dassault Mystère-Falcon 20	1
Helicopters	
Sikorsky SH-3D	10
Sikorsky RH-53D	2
AB-212	7

*On order; delivery pending end of Iran-Iraq War.

Source: Based on information from International Institute for Strategic Studies, *The Military Balance, 1986-1987,* London, 1986, 96-97.

Table 11. Air Force Weapons, 1986

Type and Description	Number in Inventory
Fighter-bombers, with air-to-air missiles (AAM) and air-to-surface missiles (ASM)	
F-4D/E Phantom	35
Fighters	
F-5E/F Tiger	45
Fighters-interceptors	
F-14A Tomcat	10
Reconnaissance	
RF-4E	3
F-14A	5
Tankers-transports	
Boeing 707	10
Boeing 747	7
Transports	
C-130E/H Hercules	26
Fokker F-27	9
Aero Commander 690	2
Dassault Mystère-Falcon 20	4
Trainers	
Bonanza F-33 A/C	26
Shooting Star T-33A	7
Pilatus PC-7	46
Shenyang J-6	2
Helicopters	
AB-206A Jet Ranger	10
AB-212	5
Bell 214C	39
CH-47 Chinook	10
Sikorsky S-55 (HH-34F)	10
Sikorsky S-61A4	2
Surface-to-air missiles	
Rapier	n.a.
Tigercat	25
Hawk (improved?)	1,000
Air-to-air missiles	
Phoenix	n.a.
AIM-9 Sidewinder	n.a.
AIM-7 Sparrow	n.a.
Air-to-surface missiles	
AS-12 Maverick	n.a.

Source: Based on information from International Institute for Strategic Studies, *The Military Balance, 1986–1987,* London, 1986, 97.

Bibliography

Chapter 1

Abrahamian, Ervand. *Iran Between Two Revolutions.* Princeton: Princeton University Press, 1982.

Afkhami, Gholam R. *The Iranian Revolution: Thanatos on a National Scale.* Washington: Middle East Institute, 1985.

Akhavi, Shahrough. *Religion and Politics in Contemporary Iran: Clergy-State Relations in the Pahlavi Period.* Albany: State University of New York Press, 1980.

Alexander, Yonah, and Allan Nanes (eds.). *The United States and Iran: A Documentary History.* Frederick, Maryland: University Publications of America, 1980.

Algar, Hamid. *Religion and State in Iran in 1785–1906: The Role of the Ulama in the Qajar Period.* Berkeley and Los Angeles: University of California Press, 1969.

Amirsadeghi, Hossein. *Twentieth Century Iran.* London: Heinemann, 1977.

Amnesty International. *Iran: Documents Sent by Amnesty International to the Government of the Islamic Republic of Iran.* London: 1987.

Arberry, A.J. *The Legacy of Persia.* Oxford: Oxford University Press, 1953.

Arfa, Hassan. *Under Five Shahs.* London: John Murray, 1964.

Arjomand, Said Amir (ed.). *From Nationalism to Revolutionary Islam: Essays on Social Movements in the Contemporary Near and Middle East.* Albany: State University of New York Press, 1984.

______. *The Shadow of God and the Hidden Imam.* Chicago: University of Chicago Press, 1984.

Avery, Peter. *Modern Iran.* New York: Praeger, 1965.

Bakhash, Shaul. *Iran: Monarchy, Bureaucracy, and Reform under the Qajars, 1858–1896.* London: Ithaca Press, 1978.

______. *The Reign of the Ayatollahs: Iran and the Islamic Revolution.* (2d ed.) New York: Basic Books, 1984.

Bakhtiar, Chapour. *Ma fidelité.* Paris: Albin Michel, 1982.

Bamdad, Badr ol-Muluk. *From Darkness into Light: Women's Emancipation in Iran.* (Ed. and trans., F.R.C. Bagley.) Hicksville, New York: Exposition Press, 1977.

Banani, Amin. *The Modernization of Iran, 1921–1941.* Stanford: Stanford University Press, 1961.

Bani-Sadr, Abol Hassan. *L'espérance trahie.* Paris: Papyrus, 1982.

Bartol'd, Vasilii Vladimirovich. *Turkestan down to the Mongol Invasion.* London: Luzac, 1968.

Bashiriyeh, Hossein. *The State and Revolution in Iran, 1962–1982.* New York: St. Martin's Press, 1984.

Bayat, Mangol. *Mysticism and Dissent: Socioreligious Thought in Qajar Iran.* Syracuse: Syracuse University Press, 1982.

Bayne, E.A. *Persian Kingship in Transition.* New York: American Universities Field Staff, 1968.

Beck, Lois. *The Qashqa'i of Iran.* New Haven: Yale University Press, 1986.

Bellan, L. L. *Chah Abbas I: sa vie, son histoire.* Paris: 1932.

Bharier, Julian. *Economic Development in Iran, 1900–1970.* New York: Oxford University Press, 1971.

Bill, James A. "Iran: Is the Shah Pushing It Too Fast?" *Christian Science Monitor,* November 9, 1977, 16–17.

______. *Iran: The Politics of Groups, Classes, and Modernization.* Columbus, Ohio: Merril, 1972.

Binder, Leonard. *Iran: Political Development in a Changing Society.* Berkeley and Los Angeles: University of California Press, 1962.

Bosworth, C.E. *The Ghaznavids: Their Empire in Afghanistan and Eastern Iran, 994–1040.* Edinburgh: Edinburgh University Press, 1963.

______. *The Medieval History of Iran, Afghanistan, and Central Asia.* London: Variorum Reprints, 1977.

Bosworth, C.E. (ed.). *Iran and Islam.* Edinburgh: Edinburgh University Press, 1971.

Bosworth, Edmund, and Carole Hillenbrand (eds.). *Qajar Iran: Political, Social, and Cultural Change, 1800–1925.* Edinburgh: Edinburgh University Press, 1983.

Browne, E.G. *A Literary History of Persia.* 4 vols. Cambridge: Cambridge University Press, 1925–28.

______. *The Persian Revolution of 1905–1909.* London: Cambridge University Press, 1910.

Burrell, R.M. "Iranian Foreign Policy During the Last Decade," *Asian Affairs* [London], 61, February 1974, 7–15.

Busse, Heribert (ed. and trans.). *History of Persia under Qajar Rule.* (Translated from the Persian of Hasan-e Fasai's Farsnameh-ye Naseri). New York: Columbia University Press, 1972.

The Cambridge History of Iran. 6 vols. Cambridge: Cambridge University Press, 1968–86.

Christopher, Warren (ed.). *American Hostages in Iran.* New Haven: Yale University Press, 1985.

Chubin, Shahram, and Sepehr Zabih. *The Foreign Relations of Iran: A Developing State in a Zone of Great-Power Conflict.* Berkeley and Los Angeles: University of California Press, 1974.

Cole, Juan R.I., and Nikki R. Keddie (eds.). *Shi'ism and Social Protest.* New Haven: Yale University Press, 1986.
Cottam, Richard W. *Nationalism in Iran.* Pittsburgh: University of Pittsburgh Press, 1964.
Curzon, George. *Persia and the Persian Question.* 2 vols. London: Frank Cass, 1966.
Eagleton, William. *The Kurdish Republic of 1946.* London: Oxford University Press, 1963.
Elgood, Cyril. *Safavid Medical Practice.* London: Luzac, 1970.
Elwell-Sutton, L.P. *Modern Iran.* New York: Gordon Press, 1976.
______. *Persian Oil: A Study in Power Politics.* London: Lawrence and Wishart, 1955.
Eskelund, Karl. *Behind the Peacock Throne.* New York: Alvin Redman, 1965.
Fesharaki, Fereidun. *Development of the Iranian Oil Industry: International and Domestic Aspects.* (Praeger Special Studies in International Economics and Developments.) New York: Praeger, 1976.
Fischer, Michael M.J. *Iran: From Religious Dispute to Revolution.* Cambridge: Harvard University Press, 1980.
Frye, Richard Nelson. *The Golden Age of Persia.* London: Weidenfeld and Nicolson, 1975.
______. *The Heritage of Persia.* London: Weidenfeld and Nicolson, 1962.
______. *Persia.* (3d ed.) London: Allen and Unwin, 1969.
Garthwaite, Gene. *Khans and Shahs: The Bakhtiyari in Iran.* Cambridge: Cambridge University Press, 1983.
Ghirshman, R. *Iran: From the Earliest Times to the Islamic Conquest.* London: Pelican, 1954.
Goodell, Grace. *The Elemental Structures of Political Life: Rural Development in Pahlavi Iran.* Oxford: Oxford University Press, 1986.
Graham, Robert. *Iran: The Illusion of Power.* London: Croom Helm, 1978.
Greaves, Louise Rose. *Persia and the Defence of India, 1884–1892.* London: University of London, Athalone Press, 1959.
Hairi, Abdul Hadi. *Shi'ism and Constitutionalism in Iran.* Leiden: E.J. Brill, 1977.
Halliday, Fred. *Iran: Dictatorship and Development.* Harmondsworth, New York: Penguin Books, 1979.
Heikal, Mohamed. *The Return of the Ayatollah.* London: André Deutsch, 1981.
Hodgson, Marshall G.S. *The Venture of Islam.* Chicago: University of Chicago Press, 1974.
Holod, Renata (ed.). *Studies on Isfahan: Proceedings of the Isfahan Colloquium.* (Iranian Studies, 7.) Boston: Society for Iranian Studies, 1974.

Hoveyda, Ferydoun. *The Fall of the Shah.* London: Weidenfeld and Nicolson, 1979.

Huot, Jean Louis. *Persia.* (2 Vols.) Cleveland: World Publishing, 1965–1967.

Huyser, Robert E. *Mission to Tehran.* New York: Harper and Row, 1986.

Ismael, Tareq Y. *Iraq and Iran: Roots of Conflict.* Syracuse: Syracuse University Press, 1982.

Issawi, Charles. *The Economic History of Iran, 1800–1914.* Chicago: University of Chicago Press, 1971.

Jacqz, J. (ed.). *Iran: Past, Present, and Future.* New York: Aspen Institute, 1976.

Katouzian, Homa. *The Political Economy of Modern Iran: Despotism and Pseudo-Modernism, 1926–1979.* New York: New York University Press, 1981.

Kazemi, Farhad. *Poverty and Revolution in Iran: The Migrant Poor, Urban Marginality, and Politics.* New York: New York University Press, 1980.

Kazemzadeh, Firuz. *Russia and Britain in Persia, 1864–1914.* New Haven: Yale University Press, 1968.

Keddie, Nikki R. *Iran: Religion, Politics, and Society.* London: Frank Cass, 1980.

______. *An Islamic Response to Imperialism: Political and Religious Writings of Sayyid Jamal ad-Din "al-Afghani."* Berkeley and Los Angeles: University of California Press, 1968.

______. *Religion and Politics in Iran: Shi'ism from Political Quietism to Revolution.* New Haven: Yale University Press, 1983.

______. *Religion and Rebellion in Iran: The Iranian Tobacco Protest of 1891–1892.* London: Frank Cass, 1966.

______. *Roots of Revolution: An Interpretive History of Modern Iran.* New Haven: Yale University Press, 1981.

______. *Sayyid Jamal ad-Din "al-Afghani": A Political Biography.* Berkeley and Los Angeles: University of California Press, 1972.

Kedouri, Elie, and Sylvia Haim (eds.). *Towards a Modern Iran: Studies in Thought, Politics, and Society.* London: Frank Cass, 1980.

Kelly, J.B. *Britain and the Persian Gulf.* Oxford: Oxford University Press, 1968.

Keyuani, M. "Artisans and Guild Life in the Later Safavid Period: Contributions to the Socio-Economic History of Persia," *Islamkundliche Untersuchungen* [Berlin], 65, 1982.

Khomeini, Ruhollah. *Islam and Revolution: Writings and Declarations of Imam Khomeini.* (Trans. and annotated by Hamid Algar.) Berkeley: Mizan Press, 1981.

Kuniholm, Bruce R. *The Origins of the Cold War in the Middle East: Great Power Conflict and Diplomacy in Iran, Turkey, and Greece.* Princeton: Princeton University Press, 1980.

Ladjevardi, Habib. *Labor Unions and Autocracy in Iran.* Syracuse: Syracuse University Press, 1985.

Laing, Margaret. *The Shah.* London: Sidwick and Jackson, 1977.

Lambton, Ann K.S. *Landlord and Peasant in Persia: A Study of Land Tenure and Land Revenue Administration.* London: Oxford University Press, 1969.

______. *State and Government in Medieval Islam: An Introduction to the Study of the Islamic Political Theory of the Jurists.* Oxford: Oxford University Press, 1981.

Ledeen, Michael, and William Lewis. *Debacle: The American Failure in Iran.* New York: Random House, 1981.

Lenczowski, George. *Russia and the West in Iran, 1918–48.* Ithaca: Cornell University Press, 1949.

Lenczowski, George (ed.). *Iran under the Pahlavis.* Stanford: Hoover Institution Press, 1978.

Lockhart, Laurence. *The Fall of the Safavid Dynasty and the Afghan Occupation of Persia.* Cambridge: Cambridge University Press, 1958.

______. *Nadir Shah: A Critical Study Based Mainly on Contemporary Sources.* London: Luzac, 1938.

McDaniel, R. *The Shuster Mission and the Persian Constitutional Revolution.* Minneapolis: Bibliotheca Islamica, 1974.

Malcolm, Sir John. *A History of Persia.* 2 vols. London: John Murray, 1815.

Mazzaoui, Michel. *The Origins of the Safavids: Shi'ism, Sufism, and the Gulat.* Wiesbaden, West Germany: F. Steiner, 1972.

Millspaugh, Arthur. *The American Task in Persia.* New York: Arno Press, 1973.

Minorsky, Vladimir. *The Turks, Iran, and the Caucasus in the Middle Ages.* London: Variorum Prints, 1978.

Minorsky, Vladimir (ed. and trans.). *Tadhkirat al-Muluk: A Manual of Safavid Administration.* London: Luzac, 1943.

Mottahedeh, Roy P. *Loyalty and Leadership in an Early Islamic Society.* Princeton: Princeton University Press, 1980.

______. *The Mantle of the Prophet: Religion and Politics in Iran.* New York: Simon and Schuster, 1985.

Munshi, Iskandar. *The History of Shah Abbas the Great.* 2 vols. (Trans., R.M. Savory.) Boulder, Colorado: Westview Press, 1978.

Nashat, Guity. *The Origins of Modern Reform in Iran, 1870–80.* Urbana: University of Illinois Press, 1982.

Oberling, Pierre. *The Qashqa'i: Nomads of Fars.* The Hague: Mouton, 1974.

Olmstead, A.T. *History of the Persian Empire: Achaemenid Period.* Chicago: University of Chicago Press, 1948.

Pahlavi, Ashraf. *Faces in a Mirror: Memoirs from Exile.* Englewood Cliffs, New Jersey: Prentice-Hall, 1980.

Pahlavi, Mohammad Reza Shah. *Answer to History.* New York: Stein and Day, 1980.

______. *Mission for My Country.* London: Hutchinson, 1961.

Parsons, Anthony. *The Pride and the Fall: Iran, 1974–1979.* London: Jonathan Cape, 1984.

Perry, John R. *Karim Khan Zand: A History of Iran, 1747–1779.* Chicago: University of Chicago Press, 1979.

Ramazani, Ruhollah K. *The Foreign Policy of Iran, 1500–1941: A Developing Nation in World Affairs.* Charlottesville: University Press of Virginia, 1966.

______. *Iran's Foreign Policy, 1941–1973: A Study of Foreign Policy in Modernizing Nations.* Charlottesville: University Press of Virginia, 1975.

______. *The Persian Gulf: Iran's Role.* Charlottesville: University Press of Virginia, 1972.

______. *Revolutionary Iran: Challenge and Response in the Middle East.* Baltimore: Johns Hopkins University Press, 1986.

Roosevelt, Kermit. *Countercoup: The Struggle for the Control of Iran.* New York: McGraw-Hill, 1979.

Rubin, Barry. *Paved with Good Intentions: The American Experience and Iran.* Oxford: Oxford University Press, 1982.

Sachednia, A.A. *The Idea of the Mahdi in Twelver Shi'ism.* Albany: State University of New York Press, 1981.

Saikal, Amin. *The Rise and Fall of the Shah.* Princeton: Princeton University Press, 1980.

Savory, Roger. *Iran under the Safavids.* Cambridge: Cambridge University Press, 1980.

Shuster, W. Morgan. *The Strangling of Persia.* New York: Century Company, 1912, Reprint Greenwood Press, 1968.

Sick, Gary. *All Fall Down: America's Tragic Encounter with Iran.* New York: Random House, 1985.

Spuler, Bertold. *Die Mongolen in Iran.* Leiden: E.J. Brill, 1985.

Stempel, John D. *Inside the Iranian Revolution.* Bloomington: Indiana University Press, 1981.

Upton, Joseph M. *The History of Modern Iran: An Interpretation.* Cambridge: Harvard University Press, 1960.

Wilber, Donald. *Iran: Past and Present.* (rev. ed.) Princeton: Princeton University Press, 1981.

______. *Riza Shah Pahlavi, 1878–1944.* Hicksville, New York: Exposition Press, 1975.

Wilson, Arnold. *The Persian Gulf.* London: Allen and Unwin, 1928.

Woods, John. *The Aqquyunlu: Clan, Confederation, Empire.* Minneapolis: Bibliotheca Islamica, 1976.

Wright, Denis. *The English Amongst the Persians.* London: Heinemann, 1977.

______. *The Persians Amongst the English.* London: I.B. Tauris, 1985.

Yeselson, Abraham. *United States-Persian Diplomatic Relations, 1883–1921.* New Brunswick, New Jersey: Rutgers University Press, 1956.

Zonis, Marvin. *The Political Elite of Iran.* Princeton: Princeton University Press, 1971.

Chapter 2

Abrahamian, Ervand. *Iran Between Two Revolutions.* Princeton: Princeton University Press, 1982.

Akhavi, Shahrough. *Religion and Politics in Contemporary Iran: Clergy-State Relations in the Pahlavi Period.* Albany: State University of New York Press, 1980.

Arasteh, Reza. *Education and Social Awakening in Iran.* Leiden: E.J. Brill, 1962.

Arjomand, Said, Eric Hooglund, and William Royce. *The Iranian Islamic Clergy: Governmental Politics and Theocracy.* Washington: Middle East Institute, 1984.

Ashraf, Ahmad. "Bazaar and Mosque in Iran's Revolution." Pages 16–18 in *MERIP Reports,* No. 113. Washington: Middle East Research and Information Project, March–April 1983.

Bakhash, Shaul. *The Reign of the Ayatollahs: Iran and the Islamic Revolution.* New York: Basic Books, 1984.

Bashiriyeh, Hossein. *The State and Revolution in Iran, 1962–1982.* London: Croom Helm, 1984.

Bayat, Assef. "Workers' Control after the Revolution." Pages 19–23 in *MERIP Reports,* No. 113. Washington: Middle East Research and Information Project, March–April 1983.

Beck, Lois. *The Qashqa'i of Iran.* New Haven: Yale University Press, 1986.

Chesnoff, Richard Z. "Paris: The Iranian Exiles," *New York Times Magazine,* February 12, 1984, 23.

Fassih, Ismail. *Sorraya in a Coma.* London: Zed Press, 1985.

Ferdows, Adele. "Shariati and Khomeini on Women." Pages 127–38 in Nikki R. Keddie and Eric Hooglund (eds.), *The Iranian*

Revolution and the Islamic Republic. Syracuse: Syracuse University Press, 1986.

Ferdows, Emad. "The Reconstruction Crusade and Class Conflict in Iran." Pages 11–15 in *MERIP Reports,* No. 113. Washington: Middle East Research and Information Project, March–April 1983.

Fischer, Michael M.J. *Iran: From Religious Dispute to Revolution.* Cambridge: Harvard University Press, 1980.

______. "Islam and the Revolt of the Petite Bourgeoisie," *Daedalus,* 111, No. 1, Winter 1982, 101–25.

Fisher, W.B. "Physical Geography." Pages 3–110 in W.B. Fisher (ed.), *The Cambridge History of Iran,* 1. Cambridge: Cambridge University Press, 1968.

Good, Mary-Jo Delvecchio. "The Changing Status and Composition of an Iranian Provincial Elite." Pages 269–88 in Michael Bonine and Nikki R. Keddie (eds.), *Modern Iran: The Dialectics of Continuity and Change.* Albany: State University of New York Press, 1981.

Haeri, Shahla. "Power of Ambiguity: Cultural Improvisations on the Theme of Temporary Marriage," *Iranian Studies,* 19, No. 2, Spring 1986, 123–54.

Halliday, Fred. *Iran: Dictatorship and Development.* New York: Penguin Books, 1979.

Higgins, Patricia. "Minority-State Relations in Contemporary Iran." Pages 167–97 in Ali Banuazizi and Myron Weiner (eds.), *The State, Religion, and Ethnic Politics: Afghanistan, Iran, and Pakistan.* Syracuse: Syracuse University Press, 1986.

Hiro, Dilip. *Iran under the Ayatollahs.* London: Routledge and Kegan Paul, 1985.

Hooglund, Eric. "Iran, 1980–1985: Political and Economic Trends." Pages 17–31 in Nikki R. Keddie and Eric Hooglund (eds.), *The Iranian Revolution and the Islamic Republic.* Syracuse: Syracuse University Press, 1986.

______. *Land and Revolution in Iran, 1960–1980.* Austin: University of Texas Press, 1982.

______. "Reza Shah Pahlavi." Pages 175–76 in Ainslie Embree (ed.), *Encyclopedia of Asian History,* III.

______. "Rural Participation in the Revolution." Pages 3–6 in *MERIP Reports,* No. 87. Washington: Middle East Research and Information Project, May 1980.

______. "The Search For Iran's 'Moderates'." Pages 5–6 in *MERIP Reports,* No. 144. Washington: Middle East Research and Information Project, January–February 1987.

______. "Social Origins of the Revolutionary Clergy." Pages 74–83 in Nikki R. Keddie and Eric Hooglund (eds.), *The Iranian Revolution and the Islamic Republic.* Syracuse: Syracuse University Press, 1986.

Iran. *Statistical Yearbook.* Tehran: Center for Statistical Studies, 1364 [1985–86].

Kazemi, Farhad. *Poverty and Revolution in Iran: The Migrant Poor, Urban Marginality, and Politics.* New York: New York University Press, 1980.

Keddie, Nikki R. "The Minorities Question in Iran." Pages 85–108 in Shirin Tahir-Kheli and Shaheen Ayubi (eds.), *The Iran-Iraq War: New Weapons, Old Conflicts.* New York: Praeger, 1983.

______. *Roots of Revolution: An Interpretive History of Modern Iran.* New Haven: Yale University Press, 1981.

Keddie, Nikki R., and Eric Hooglund (eds.). *The Iranian Revolution and the Islamic Republic.* Syracuse: Syracuse University Press, 1986.

Ladjevardi, Habib. *Labor Unions and Autocracy in Iran.* Syracuse: Syracuse University Press, 1985.

Loeffler, Reinhold. "Economic Changes in a Rural Area since 1979." Pages 93–108 in Nikki R. Keddie and Eric Hooglund (eds.), *The Iranian Revolution and the Islamic Republic.* Syracuse: Syracuse University Press, 1986.

______. "The National Integration of Boir Ahmad," *Iranian Studies,* 24, No. 4, 1982, 689–711.

Momen, Moojan. *An Introduction to Shi'i Islam.* New Haven: Yale University Press, 1985.

Najmabadi, Afsaneh. "Mystifications of the Past and Illusions of the Future." Pages 147–61 in Nikki R. Keddie and Eric Hooglund (eds.), *The Iranian Revolution and the Islamic Republic.* Syracuse: Syracuse University Press, 1986.

Smith, Terrence. "Iran: Five Years of Fanaticism," *New York Times Magazine,* February 12, 1984, 21–22.

Sunderland, E. "Pastoralism, Nomadism, and the Social Anthropology of Iran." Pages 611–83 in W.B. Fisher (ed.), *The Cambridge History of Iran,* I. Cambridge: Cambridge University Press, 1968.

(Various issues of the following publications were also used in the preparation of this chapter: Foreign Broadcast Information Service, *Daily Report: Middle East and Africa* and *Daily Report: Near East and South Asia;* and *Iran Times.*)

Chapter 3

Abrahamian, Ervand. *Iran Between Two Revolutions.* Princeton: Princeton University Press, 1982.

Alnasrawi, Abbas. "Dependency Status and Economic Development of Arab States," *Journal of Asian and African Studies,* 21, Nos. 1–2, 1986, 17–31.

______. "Economic Consequences of the Iran-Iraq War," *Third World Quarterly* [London], 1986, 869–95.

______. *OPEC in a Changing World Economy.* Baltimore: Johns Hopkins University Press, 1985.

Amuzegar, Jahangir. *Iran: An Economic Profile.* Washington: Middle East Institute, 1977.

Bakhash, Shaul. *The Reign of the Ayatollahs: Iran and the Islamic Revolution.* New York: Basic Books, 1984.

Bamberger, Robert, and Clyde Mark. *Distribution of Oil from the Persian Gulf: Near-Term US Vulnerability.* Washington: Library of Congress Congressional Research Service, October 1, 1986.

Behdad, Sohrab. *Foreign Exchange Gap, Structural Constraints, and the Political Economy of Exchange Rate Determination in Iran.* Granville, Ohio: Denison University, forthcoming.

Central Bank of the Islamic Republic of Iran. *Economic Report and Balance Sheet, 1362* [1984]. Tehran: 1984.

Clawson, Patrick. "Islamic Iran's Economic Policies and Prospects." (rev. ed.) (Paper presented to Council on Foreign Relations, November 1986.) Washington: February 1987.

Cottam, Richard. "The Iranian Revolution." Pages 55–87 in Juan R.I. Cole and Nikki R. Keddie (eds.), *Shi'ism and Social Protest.* New Haven: Yale University Press, 1986.

Economist Intelligence Unit. *Iran: Country Profile, 1986.* London: 1986

______. *Iran: Country Profile, 1987.* London: 1987.

______. *Iran: Country Report, 1986,* Nos. 1–4, London: 1986.

______. *Iran: Country Report, 1987,* No. 1, London: 1987.

Ferdows, Emad. "The Reconstruction Crusade and Class Conflict in Iran." Pages 11–15 in *MERIP Reports,* No. 113. Washington: Middle East Research and Information Project, March–April 1983.

Fisher, W.B. "Iran." Pages 404–30 in *The Middle East and North Africa, 1987.* (33d ed.) London: Europa, 1986.

Halliday, Fred. "Iranian Foreign Policy since 1979: Internationalism and Nationalism in the Islamic Revolution." Pages 88–107 in Juan R.I. Cole and Nikki R. Keddie (eds.), *Shi'ism and Social Protest.* New Haven: Yale University Press, 1986.

______. "Year IV of the Islamic Republic." Pages 3–8 in *MERIP Reports,* No. 113. Washington: Middle East Research and Information Project, March–April 1983.

Hooglund, Eric. *Land and Revolution in Iran, 1960–1980.* Austin: University of Texas Press, 1982.

Hooglund, Eric, and Nikki Keddie (eds.). *The Iranian Revolution and the Islamic Republic.* Syracuse: Syracuse University Press, 1986.

"An Initial Glance at the 1366 [1987–88] Budget Bill," *Iran Press Digest* [Tehran], March 17, 1987, 2–6.

International Road Federation. *World Road Statistics, 1981–85.* Geneva: 1986.

International Road Transport Unit. *World Transport Data.* Geneva: 1985.

Iran: A Special Report. London: Middle East Economic Digest, February 1977.

Jaffé, George and Keith McLachlan. *Iran and Iraq: The Next Five Years.* Economist Intelligence Unit Special Report No. 1083. London: 1987.

Jakubiak, Henry, and M. Taher Dajani. "Oil Income and Financial Policies in Iran and Saudi Arabia," *Finance and Development.* Washington: International Monetary Fund, 1986.

Johns, Richard, and Michael Field. "Oil in the Middle East and North Africa." Pages 96–142 in *The Middle East and North Africa, 1987.* (33d ed.) London: Europa, 1986.

Kazemi, Farhad. *Poverty and Revolution in Iran: The Migrant Poor, Urban Marginality, and Politics.* New York: New York University Press, 1980.

Keddie, Nikki R. "Oil Economic Policy and Social Conflict in Iran," *Race and Class,* 21, No. 1, 1979, 13–29.

Kielmas, Maria. "Iran Restores the Soviet Connection," *Middle East* [London], November 1986, 23.

Lautenschlager, Wolfgang. "The Effects of an Overvalued Exchange Rate on the Iranian Economy, 1979–1984," *International Journal of Middle East Studies,* 18, 1986, 31–52.

McCaslin, John C. (ed.). *International Petroleum Encyclopedia.* Tulsa: Penn Well, 1986.

The Middle East and North Africa, 1987. London: Europa, 1986.

Nyrop, Richard F. (ed.). *Iran: A Country Study.* Washington: GPO for The American University, 1978.

Rosen, Barry M. (ed.). *Iran since the Revolution: Internal Dynamics, Regional Conflict, and the Superpowers.* New York: Columbia University Press, 1985.

Sarkis, Nicolas (ed.). *Arab Oil and Gas Directory, 1982.* Paris: Arab Petroleum Research Center, 1982.

Sciolino, Elaine. "Iran Allows Pragmatism to Dictate Its Shopping List," *New York Times*, April 26, 1987, A3.

Tibi, Bassam. "The Iranian Revolution and the Arabs: The Quest for Islamic Identity and the Search for an Islamic System of Government," *Arab Studies Quarterly*, 8, No. 1, Winter 1986, 29–44.

———. "The Renewed Role of Islam in the Political and Social Development of the Middle East," *Middle East Journal*, 37, No. 1, Winter 1983, 3–13.

United Nations. Food and Agriculture Organization. *Yearbook of Fishery Statistics, 1984*. 58. Rome: 1984.

———. *Yearbook of Forest Products, 1973–1984*. Rome: 1986.

United States. Central Intelligence Agency. *Economic and Energy Indicators*. Washington: January 1986–March 1987.

———. *Handbook of Economic Statistics, 1986*. Washington: 1986.

United States. Department of Agriculture. *Middle East and North Africa: Situation and Outlook Report*. Washington: GPO, April 1986.

———. *World Indices of Agriculture and Food Production, 1976–85*, No. 744. Washington: GPO, July 1986.

United States. Department of the Interior. Bureau of Mines. *Mineral Industries of the Middle East*. Washington: April 1986.

Welt, Leo. "The Middle East's Changing Economy," *Management Review*, 76, February 1987, 63–65.

World Bank. *World Development Report, 1986*. Oxford: Oxford University Press, 1986.

———. *World Tables, 1986*. Baltimore: 1986.

(Various issues of the following publications were also used in the preparation of this chapter: British Broadcasting Corporation, *Summary of World Broadcasts* [Reading, United Kingdom]; *Christian Science Monitor; Daily News* [Tehran]; Economist Intelligence Unit, *Country Report: Iran* [London]; Foreign Broadcast Information Service, *Daily Report: Middle East and Africa; Foreign Report* [London]; International Monetary Fund, *Direction of Trade Statistics* and *International Financial Statistics; Iran Monitor* [Geneva, Switzerland]; *Iran Times;* Joint Publications Research Service, *Near East/South Asia Report; Middle East* [London]; *Middle East Economic Digest (MEED)* [London]; *Middle East Economic Survey* [Limassol, Cyprus]; *Middle East Research and Information Project (MERIP) Reports; MEMO* [Limassol, Cyprus]; *News Review on West Asia* [New Delhi]; *Oil and Gas Journal;* and *Taxes and Investment in the Middle East* [Amsterdam].

Chapter 4

Abdulghani, Jasim M. *Iraq and Iran: The Years of Crisis*. Baltimore: Johns Hopkins University Press, 1984.

Abrahamian, Ervand. *Iran Between Two Revolutions.* Princeton: Princeton University Press, 1982.

Akhavi, Shahrough. "Clerical Politics in Iran since 1979." Pages 57–73 in Nikki R. Keddie and Eric Hooglund (eds.), *The Iranian Revolution and the Islamic Republic.* Syracuse: Syracuse University Press, 1986.

______. "Elite Factionalism in the Islamic Republic of Iran," *Middle East Journal,* 41, No. 2, Spring 1987, 181–201.

Alaolmolki, Nozar. "The New Iranian Left," *Middle East Journal,* 41, No. 2, Spring 1987, 218–33.

Atkin, Muriel. "The Islamic Republic and the Soviet Union." Pages 191–208 in Nikki R. Keddie and Eric Hooglund (eds.), *The Iranian Revolution and the Islamic Republic.* Syracuse: Syracuse University Press, 1986.

Bakhash, Shaul. "Islam and Social Justice in Iran." Pages 95–115 in Martin Kramer (ed.), *Shi'ism, Resistance, and Revolution.* Boulder, Colorado: Westview Press, 1987.

______. *The Reign of the Ayatollahs: Iran and the Islamic Revolution.* New York: Basic Books, 1984.

Bashiriyeh, Hossein. *The State and Revolution in Iran, 1962–1982.* London: Croom Helm, 1984.

Benard, Cheryl, and Zalmay Khalilzad. *"The Government of God": Iran's Islamic Republic.* New York: Columbia University Press, 1984.

Bulliet, Richard. "Time, Perceptions, and Conflict Resolution." Pages 65–81 in Shirin Tahir-Kheli and Shaheen Ayubi (eds.), *The Iran-Iraq War: New Weapons, Old Conflicts.* New York: Praeger, 1983.

Chesnoff, Richard Z. "Paris: The Iranian Exiles," *New York Times Magazine,* February 12, 1984, 22–23.

Chubin, Shahram. "The Islamic Republic's Foreign Policy in the Gulf." Pages 159–71 in Martin Kramer (ed.), *Shi'ism, Resistance, and Revolution.* Boulder, Colorado: Westview Press, 1987.

Cobban, Helena. "The Growing Shi'i Power in Lebanon and Its Implications for the Future." Pages 137–55 in Juan Cole and Nikki R. Keddie (eds.), *Shi'ism and Social Protest.* New Haven: Yale University Press, 1986.

"Constitution of the Islamic Republic of Iran," *Middle East Journal,* 34, No. 2, Spring 1980, 184–204.

Cottam, Richard. "Iran and Soviet-American Relations." Pages 227–40 in Nikki R. Keddie and Eric Hooglund (eds.), *The Iranian Revolution and the Islamic Republic.* Syracuse: Syracuse University Press, 1986.

———. "Iran's Perception of the Superpowers." Pages 133-47 in Barry Rosen (ed.), *Iran since the Revolution: Internal Dynamics, Regional Conflicts, and the Superpowers*. New York: Columbia University Press for Brooklyn College, 1985.

Ferdows, Adele. "Shariati and Khomeini on Women." Pages 127-38 in Nikki R. Keddie and Eric Hooglund (eds.), *The Iranian Revolution and the Islamic Republic*. Syracuse: Syracuse University Press, 1986.

Halliday, Fred. "Year IV of the Islamic Republic." Pages 3-8 in *MERIP Reports,* No. 113. Washington: Middle East Research and Information Project, March-April 1983.

Hiro, Dilip. *Iran under the Ayatollahs*. London: Routledge and Kegan Paul, 1985.

Hooglund, Eric. "Iran and the Gulf War." Pages 12-18 in *MERIP Reports,* No. 148. Washington: Middle East Research and Information Project, September-October 1987.

———. "Iran, 1980-1985: Political and Economic Trends." Pages 17-31 in Nikki R. Keddie and Eric Hooglund (eds.), *The Iranian Revolution and the Islamic Republic*. Syracuse: Syracuse University Press, 1986.

———. "The Search for Iran's 'Moderates'." Pages 5-6 in *MERIP Reports,* No. 144. Washington: Middle East Research and Information Project, January-February 1987.

———. "Social Origins of the Revolutionary Clergy." Pages 74-83 in Nikki R. Keddie and Eric Hooglund (eds.), *The Iranian Revolution and the Islamic Republic*. Syracuse: Syracuse University Press, 1986.

Karimi, Setareh. "Economic Policies and Structural Changes since the Revolution." Pages 32-54 in Nikki R. Keddie and Eric Hooglund (eds.), *The Iranian Revolution and the Islamic Republic*. Syracuse: Syracuse University Press, 1986.

Khalilzad, Zalmay. "The Iranian Revolution and the Afghan Resistance." Pages 257-73 in Martin Kramer (ed.), *Shi'ism, Resistance, and Revolution*. Boulder, Colorado: Westview Press, 1987.

Kostiner, Joseph. "Shi'i Unrest in the Gulf." Pages 173-86 in Martin Kramer (ed.), *Shi'ism, Resistance, and Revolution*. Boulder, Colorado: Westview Press, 1987.

Loeffler, Reinhold. "Economic Changes in a Rural Area since 1979." Pages 93-108 in Nikki R. Keddie and Eric Hooglund (eds.), *The Iranian Revolution and the Islamic Republic*. Syracuse: Syracuse University Press, 1986.

Mottahedeh, Roy P. "Iran's Foreign Devils," *Foreign Policy,* No. 38, 1980, 19-34.

Norton, Augustus R. "The Origins and Resurgence of Amal." Pages 203–18 in Martin Kramer (ed.), *Shi'ism, Resistance, and Revolution.* Boulder, Colorado: Westview Press, 1987.

______. "Shi'ism and Social Protest in Lebanon." Pages 156–78 in Juan R.I. Cole and Nikkie R. Keddie (eds.), *Shi'ism and Social Protest.* New Haven: Yale University Press, 1986.

Ramazani, Ruhollah K. *Revolutionary Iran: Challenge and Response in the Middle East.* Baltimore: Johns Hopkins University Press, 1986.

Sick, Gary. *All Fall Down: America's Tragic Encounter with Iran.* New York: Random House, 1985.

______. "Iran's Quest for Superpower Status," *Foreign Affairs,* 65, No. 4, Spring 1987, 697–715.

(Various issues of the following publications were also used in the preparation of this chapter: Foreign Broadcast Information Service, *Daily Report: Middle East and Africa; Daily Report: Near East and South Asia; Iran Times; New York Times;* and *Washington Post.*)

Chapter 5

Abdulghani, Jasim M. *Iraq and Iran: The Years of Crisis.* Baltimore: Johns Hopkins University Press, 1984.

Afshar, Haleh. "The Army." Pages 175–98 in Haleh Afshar (ed.), *Iran: A Revolution in Turmoil.* Albany: State University of New York Press, 1985.

Akhavi, Shahrough. "Elite Factionalism in the Islamic Republic of Iran," *Middle East Journal,* 41, No. 2, Spring 1987, 181–201.

Alaolmolki, Nozar. "The New Iranian Left," *Middle East Journal,* 41, No. 2, Spring 1987, 218–33.

Amnesty International. *Amnesty International Report, 1986.* London: 1986.

Amnesty International. *Law and Human Rights in the Islamic Republic of Iran.* London: Amnesty International Secretariat, 1980.

Arjomand, Said Amir (ed.). *From Nationalism to Revolutionary Islam: Essays on Social Movements in the Contemporary Near and Middle East.* Albany: State University of New York Press, 1984.

El-Azhary, M.S. (ed.). *The Iran-Iraq War: An Historical, Economic, and Political Analysis.* New York: St. Martin's Press, 1984.

Bakhash, Shaul. *The Reign of the Ayatollahs: Iran and the Islamic Revolution.* New York: Basic Books, 1984.

Ball, George W. *Error and Betrayal in Lebanon.* Washington: Foundation for Middle East Peace, 1984.

Benard, Cheryl, and Zalmay Khalilzad. *"The Government of God": Iran's Islamic Republic.* New York: Columbia University Press, 1984.

Bill, James A. "Power and Religion in Revolutionary Iran," *Middle East Journal,* 36, No. 1, Winter 1982, 22–47.

Bradley, C. Paul. *Recent United States Policy in the Persian Gulf.* Grantham, New Hampshire: Thompson and Rutter, 1982.

Bussert, Jim. "Iran-Iraq War Turns Strategic," *Defense Electronics,* 16, September 1984, 136–46.

Canby, Steven L. "The Iranian Military: Political Symbolism Versus Military Usefulness." Pages 100–130 in Hossein Amirsadeghi (ed.), *The Security of the Persian Gulf.* New York: St. Martin's Press, 1981.

Chubin, Shahram. "Hedging in the Gulf: Soviets Arm Both Sides," *International Defense Review,* 20, No. 6, June 1987, 731–35.

______. "Leftist Forces in Iran," *Problems of Communism,* July–August 1980, 1–25.

Cordesman, Anthony H. *The Gulf and the Search for Strategic Stability: Saudi Arabia, the Military Balance in the Gulf, and Trends in the Arab-Israeli Military Balance.* Boulder, Colorado: Westview Press, 1984.

______. "The Iran-Iraq War in 1984: An Escalating Threat to the Gulf and the West," *Armed Forces Journal,* 121, March 1984, 22–24.

______. "The Iraq-Iran War: Attrition Now, Chaos Later," *Armed Forces Journal,* 120, May 1983, 36–43.

Daly, Thomas M. "The Enduring Gulf War," *United States Naval Institute Proceedings,* 111, No. 5, May 1985, 148–61.

Danziger, Raphael. "The Persian Gulf Tanker War," *United States Naval Institute Proceedings,* 111, No. 5, May 1985, 160–67.

Darius, Robert G., John W. Amos, and Ralph H. Magnus. *Gulf Security into the 1980s: Perceptual and Strategic Dimensions.* Stanford: Hoover Institution Press, 1984.

Dekmejian, R. Hrair. *Islam in Revolution.* Syracuse: Syracuse University Press, 1985.

Dowdy, William L., and Russell Troods (eds.). *The Indian Ocean: Perspectives on a Strategic Area.* Durham, North Carolina: Duke University Press, 1985.

Evans, David, and Richard Campany. "Iran-Iraq: Bloody Tomorrows," *United States Naval Institute Proceedings,* 111, No. 1, January 1985, 33–43.

Fischer, Michael M.J. *Iran: From Religious Dispute to Revolution.* Cambridge: Harvard University Press, 1980.

Hammond, Thomas T. *Red Flag over Afghanistan: The Communist Coup, the Soviet Invasion, and the Consequences.* Boulder, Colorado: Westview Press, 1984.

Heller, Mark (ed.). *The Middle East Military Balance, 1985.* Tel Aviv: Jaffee Center for Strategic Studies, Tel Aviv University, 1985.
Hickman, William F. *Ravaged and Reborn: The Iranian Army, 1982.* Washington: Brookings Institution, 1982.
Hiro, Dilip. *Iran under the Ayatollahs.* London: Routledge and Kegan Paul, 1985.
Hunter, Shireen. "After the Ayatollah," *Foreign Policy,* No. 66, Spring 1987, 77–97.
Hurewitz, J.C. *Middle East Politics: The Military Dimension.* New York: Praeger, 1969.
Huyser, Robert E. *Mission to Tehran.* New York: Harper and Row, 1986.
International Institute for Strategic Studies. *The Military Balance, 1978–1979.* London: 1978.
______. *The Military Balance, 1981–1982.* London: 1981.
______. *The Military Balance, 1982–1983.* London: 1982.
______. *The Military Balance, 1983–1984.* London: 1983.
______. *The Military Balance, 1984–1985.* London: 1984.
______. *The Military Balance, 1985–1986.* London: 1985.
______. *The Military Balance, 1986–1987.* London: 1986.
Iran. *Summary Report: An Estimate of the Economic Damages of the Imposed War of Iraq Against Iran.* Tehran: Islamic Republic of Iran, Ministry of Foreign Affairs, March 1983.
Ismael, Tareq Y. *Iraq and Iran: Roots of Conflict.* Syracuse: Syracuse University Press, 1982.
Karsh, Efraim. "The Iran-Iraq War: A Military Analysis," *Adelphi Papers,* No. 220, Spring 1987.
Keddie, Nikki R. *Roots of Revolution: An Interpretive History of Modern Iran.* New Haven: Yale University Press, 198l.
Khalilzad, Zalmay. "Islamic Iran: Soviet Dilemma," *Problems of Communism,* January–February 1984, 1–20.
Kurth, James R. "American Perceptions of the Israeli-Palestinian Conflict and the Iranian-Iraqi War," *Naval War College Review,* 38, No. 1, January–February 1985, 75–86.
Malik, Hafeez (ed.). *International Security in Southwest Asia.* New York: Praeger, 1984.
Martin, Douglas. *The Persecution of the Baha'is in Iran, 1844–1984.* Ottawa: Association for Baha'i Studies, 1984.
Martin, Lenore G. *The Unstable Gulf.* Lexington, Massachusetts: D.C. Heath, 1984.
Modarres, Morteza. *Tarikh-e Ravabet-e Iran va Iraq: Siyasi, Farhangi, Eghtesadi.* (Iran and Iraq: A History of Political, Cultural, and Economic Relations.) Tehran: Ketan Foroshi Foroghi, 1351 [1973].

Mottale, Morris Mehrdad. *The Arms Buildup in the Persian Gulf.* Lanham, Maryland: University Press of America, 1986.
O'Ballance, Edgar. "The Iraqi-Iranian War: The First Round," *Parameters,* 11, 54–59.
______. "The Kurdish Factor in the Gulf War," *Military Review,* 61, No. 6, June 1981, 13–20.
Olson, William J. (ed.). *US Strategic Interests in the Gulf Region.* Boulder, Colorado: Westview Press, 1987.
Perron, Ronald A. "The Iranian Islamic Revolutionary Guard Corps," *Middle East Insight,* 4, No. 21, June–July 1985, 35–39.
Rafizadeh, Mansur. *Witness: From the Shah to the Secret Arms Deal: An Insider's Account of U.S. Involvement in Iran.* New York: W. Morrow, 1987.
Rajaee, Farhang. *Islamic Values and World View: Khomeyni on Man, the State and International Politics.* Lanham, Maryland: University Press of America, 1983.
Ramazani, Ruhollah K. *The Foreign Policy of Iran, 1500–1941: A Developing Nation in World Affairs.* Charlottesville: University Press of Virginia, 1966.
______. "The Iran-Iraq War: Underlying Conflicts," *Middle East Insight,* 3, No. 5, July–August 1984, 8–11.
______. *Iran's Foreign Policy, 1941–1973: A Study of Foreign Policy in Modernizing Nations.* Charlottesville: University Press of Virginia, 1975.
______. "Iran's Islamic Revolution and the Persian Gulf," *Current History,* 84, January 1985, 5–8.
______. *The Persian Gulf and the Strait of Hormuz.* Alpen aan den Rijn, The Netherlands: Sijthoff and Noordhoff, 1979.
______. *The Persian Gulf: Iran's Role.* Charlottesville: University Press of Virginia, 1972.
______. *Revolutionary Iran: Challenge and Response in the Middle East.* Baltimore: Johns Hopkins University Press, 1986.
______. *The United States and Iran: The Patterns of Influence,* New York: Praeger, 1982.
Renfrew, Nita M. "Who Started the War?" *Foreign Policy,* No. 66, Spring 1987, 98–108.
Rose, Gregory F. "The Iranian Islamic Armed Forces: An Assessment." (Paper prepared for Office of Assistant Chief of Staff, G2/DSEC, 4th Infantry Division [Mechanized], Fort Carson, Colorado, September 1983.)
______. "The Post-Revolutionary Purge of Iran's Armed Forces: A Revisionist Assessment," *Iranian Studies,* 17, Nos. 2–3, Spring-Summer 1984, 153–94.

______. "Soldiers of Islam: The Iranian Armed Forces since the Revolution." (Paper prepared for Office of Assistant Chief of Staff, G2/DSEC, 4th Infantry Division [Mechanized], Fort Carson, Colorado, 1984.)

Rubinstein, Alvin Z. *The Great Game: Rivalry in the Persian Gulf and South Asia.* New York: Praeger, 1983.

______. "Perspectives on the Iran-Iraq War," *Orbis,* 29, No. 3, Fall 1985, 597–608.

Schahgaldian, Nikola B. *The Iranian Military under the Islamic Republic.* (R-3473-USDP.) Santa Monica: Rand, March 1987.

Sick, Gary. *All Fall Down: America's Tragic Encounter with Iran.* New York: Random House, 1985.

Sreberny-Mohammadi, Annabelle, and Ali Mohammadi. "Post-Revolutionary Iranian Exiles: A Study in Impotence," *Third World Quarterly,* 9, No. 1, January 1987, 108–29.

Stempel, John D. *Inside the Iranian Revolution.* Bloomington: Indiana University Press, 1981.

Taheri, Amir. *The Spirit of Allah: Khomeini and the Islamic Revolution.* Bethesda, Maryland: Adler and Adler, 1986.

Tahir-Kheli, Shirin, and Shaheen Ayubi (eds.). *The Iran-Iraq War: New Weapons, Old Conflicts.* New York: Praeger, 1983.

United States. Arms Control and Disarmament Agency. *World Military Expenditures and Arms Transfers, 1986.* Washington: GPO, April, 1987.

Vlahos, Michael. "Middle Eastern, North African, and South Asian Navies," *United States Naval Institute Proceedings,* 111, No. 3, March 1985, 52–57.

______. "Middle Eastern, North African, and South Asian Navies," *United States Naval Institute Proceedings,* 112, No. 3, March 1986, 53–58.

World Armaments and Disarmament: SIPRI Yearbook. Cambridge: MIT Press, for Stockholm International Peace Research Institute, 1976.

World Armaments and Disarmament: SIPRI Yearbook. Cambridge: MIT Press, for Stockholm International Peace Research Institute, 1977.

World Armaments and Disarmament: SIPRI Yearbook. Cambridge: MIT Press, for Stockholm International Peace Research Institute, 1978.

World Armaments and Disarmament: SIPRI Yearbook. Cambridge: MIT Press, for Stockholm International Peace Research Institute, 1979.

World Armaments and Disarmament: SIPRI Yearbook. Cambridge: MIT Press, for Stockholm International Peace Research Institute, 1980.

World Armaments and Disarmament: SIPRI Yearbook. Cambridge: MIT Press, for Stockholm International Peace Research Institute, 1981.

World Armaments and Disarmament: SIPRI Yearbook. Cambridge: MIT Press, for Stockholm International Peace Research Institute, 1982.

World Armaments and Disarmament: SIPRI Yearbook. Cambridge: MIT Press, for Stockholm International Peace Research Institute, 1983.

World Bank. *World Development Report, 1986.* Oxford: Oxford University Press, 1986.

Wright. Robin. *Sacred Rage: The Wrath of Militant Islam.* New York: Simon and Schuster, 1985.

Yodfat, Aryeh Y. *The Soviet Union and the Arabian Peninsula: Soviet Policy Towards the Persian Gulf and Arabia.* New York: St. Martin's Press, 1983.

(Various issues of the following publications were also used in the preparation of this chapter: *BBC Summary of World Broadcasts* [Reading, United Kingdom]; *Jane's Defence Weekly; Middle East* [London]; *Middle East Economic Digest (MEED)* [London]; *United Nations Chronicle;* and *Washington Post.*)

Glossary

barrels per day—Production of crude oil and petroleum products is frequently measured in barrels per day, often abbreviated bpd or bd. A barrel is a volume measure of forty-two United States gallons. Conversion of barrels to tons depends on the density of the specific product. About 7.3 barrels of average crude oil weigh one ton. Heavy crude would be about seven barrels per ton. Light products, such as gasoline and kerosene, average close to eight barrels per ton.

beg—A tribal leader; term is used by some Turkic-speaking tribes.

development plan—Iran's development plans have been of varying length and had various names. The plans and their dates under Mohammad Reza Shah were as follows: First Development Plan—September 21, 1948, to September 20, 1955; Second Development Plan—September 21, 1955, to September 20, 1962; Third Development Plan—September 21, 1962, to March 20, 1968; Fourth Development Plan—March 21, 1968, to March 20, 1973; and Fifth Development Plan—March 21, 1973, to March 20, 1978. The Sixth Development Plan, beginning March 21, 1978, was never completed because of the 1979 Revolution. The First Development Plan of the Islamic Republic ran from March 21, 1983, through March 20, 1988.

faqih—An expert in religious jurisprudence, specifically a Shia (*q.v.*) cleric whose mastery of the Quran, the traditions of the Prophet and the Twelve Imams, and the codices of Shia Islamic law permit him to render binding interpretations of religious laws and regulations.

fiscal year (FY)—Corresponds to the Iranian calendar year, which begins March 21 and ends March 20.

gross domestic product (GDP)—The total value of goods and services produced within a country's borders during a fixed period, usually one year. Obtained by adding the value contributed by each sector of the economy in the form of compensation of employees, profits, and depreciation (consumption of capital). Subsistence production is included and consists of the imputed value of production by the farm family for its own use and the imputed rental value of owner-occupied dwellings.

gross national product (GNP)—Gross domestic product (*q.v.*) plus the income received from abroad by residents, less payments remitted abroad to nonresidents.

hadith—Tradition based on the precedent of Muhammad's words that serves as one of the sources of Islamic Law (*shariat, q.v.*).

hejab—Modesty in attire; defined by the Shia clergy to mean that women and girls must cover all their hair and flesh except for hands and face when in public. It is not necessary to wear a *chador* (a cloth serving as a cloak) to conform with *hejab,* although the two terms often are equated.

hezbollahi—Literally, a follower of the party of God. *Hezbollahis* originally were followers of a particular religious figure who eventually came to constitute an unofficial political party. They were not an irregular or paramilitary group.

imam—Among Twelver Shias the principal meaning is a designation of one of the twelve legitimate successors of the Prophet Muhammad. Also used by both Shias (*q.v.*) and Sunnis (*q.v.*) to designate a congregational prayer leader or cleric.

International Monetary Fund (IMF)—Established along with the World Bank (*q.v.*) in 1945, the IMF is a specialized agency affiliated with the United Nations and is responsible for stabilizing international exchange rates and payments. The main business of the IMF is the provision of loans to its members (including industrialized and developing countries) when they experience balance of payments difficulties. These loans frequently carry conditions that require substantial internal economic adjustments by the recipients, most of which are developing countries.

Islamic clergy—The religious leaders of Shia (*q.v.*) Islam, which group includes numerous mullahs (*q.v.*), who in general possess only rudimentary religious education; *mujtahids,* a relatively small body of religious scholars, the majority of whom are accorded the title of *hojjatoleslam;* and a small number of the most learned and pious of the *mujtahids,* who are given the title of *ayatollah.*

jihad—The struggle to establish the law of God on earth, often interpreted to mean holy war.

kadkhuda—The village headman in rural Iran; also used as the title for leaders of some tribal clans.

madraseh—A religious college or seminary that trains men in Islamic jurisprudence.

mahriyeh—An agreed upon amount of money and/or property that a groom provides his bride as specified in the marriage contract.

Majlis—the term is used in two senses: the legislative body of imperial Iran, which included both a senate—composed of members appointed by the shah and elected members—and an elected lower house of representatives; and, the lower house alone. The Senate provided for in the constitution did not come into existence until 1950; the Senate was dissolved under Mossadeq but was revived later. Khomeini's revolutionary Constitution of 1979 eliminated the Senate, leaving only the lower house, or Majlis, in existence.

maktab—Primary school operated by Shia clergy.

mostazafin—Literally, the disinherited; originally a religious term for the poor, which has become popularized.

mullah—Generic term for a member of the Islamic clergy; usually refers to a preacher or other low-ranking cleric who has not earned the right to interpret religious laws.

muta—A temporary marriage, the duration of which is stipulated by contract. Only Twelver Shias (*q.v.*) recognize *muta* marriages.

Organization of Petroleum Exporting Countries (OPEC)—Coordinates petroleum policies of thirteen major producing countries. In early 1987 members included Algeria, Ecuador, Gabon, Indonesia, Iran, Iraq, Kuwait, Libya, Nigeria, Qatar, Saudi Arabia, the United Arab Emirates, and Venezuela.

rial—Iranian currency. Average official rate in 1987 was 71.46 rials to US$1. Official exchange rate, as of December 19, 1984, is determined daily based on Special Drawing Right (*q.v.*) rial rate and applies to all foreign exchange transactions. In practice, the unofficial black market rate is as much as ten times the official exchange rate.

shariat (sharia in Arabic)—Islamic canon law. Among Shias (*q.v.*) the *shariat* includes the Quran and the authenticated sayings of the Prophet (hadith) and the Twelve Imams.

shaykh—Leader or chief. Term is used by Iranian Arabs for tribal chiefs and by Lurs and Kurds for religious leaders.

Shia (or Shiite)—A member of the smaller of the two great divisions of Islam. The Shias supported the claims of Ali and his line to presumptive right to the caliphate and leadership of the world Muslim community, and on this issue they divided from the Sunnis (*q.v.*) in the first great schism of Islam. Later schisms have produced further divisions among the Shias.

Special Drawing Right (SDR)—A standardized monetary unit used by the International Monetary Fund (*q.v.*). It is standardized against all currencies using it instead of the home country's currency and is drawn from a pool of contributions by member countries.

Sunni—A member of the larger of the two great divisions of Islam. The Sunnis, who rejected the claim of Ali's line, believe that they are the true followers of the sunna, the guide to proper behavior composed of the Quran and the hadith (*q.v.*).

topping plant—A plant that removes only the lightest commodity from crude oil.

velayat-e faqih—The guardianship of the religious jurist. Concept elaborated by Ayatollah Khomeini to justify political rule by the clergy.

White Revolution—Term used by Mohammad Reza Shah Pahlavi to designate the program of economic and social reforms he initiated in 1963.

World Bank—Informal name used to designate a group of three affiliated international institutions: the International Bank for Reconstruction and Development (IBRD), the International Development Association (IDA), and the International Finance Corporation (IFC). The IBRD, established in 1945, has the primary purpose of providing loans to developing countries for productive projects. The IDA, a legally separate loan fund but administered by the staff of the IBRD, was set up in 1960 to furnish credits to the poorest developing countries on much easier terms than those of conventional IBRD loans. The IFC, founded in 1956, supplements the activities of the IBRD through loans and assistance specifically designed to encourage the growth of productive private enterprises in the less developed countries. The president and certain senior officers of the IBRD hold the same positions in the IFC. The three institutions are owned by the governments of the countries that subscribe their capital. To participate in the World Bank group, member states must first belong to the International Monetary Fund (IMF—*q.v.*).

Index

Published Country Studies

(Area Handbook Series)

550-156	Paraguay	550-89	Tunisia
550-185	Persian Gulf States	550-80	Turkey
550-42	Peru	550-74	Uganda
550-72	Philippines	550-97	Uruguay
550-162	Poland	550-71	Venezuela
550-181	Portugal	550-32	Vietnam
550-160	Romania	550-183	Yemens, The
550-51	Saudi Arabia	550-99	Yugloslavia
550-70	Senegal	550-67	Zaire
550-180	Sierra Leone	550-75	Zambia
550-184	Singapore	550-171	Zimbabwe
550-86	Somalia		
550-93	South Africa		
550-95	Soviet Union		
550-179	Spain		
500-96	Sri Lanka		
550-27	Sudan		
550-47	Syria		
550-62	Tanzania		
550-53	Thailand		

☆U.S. GOVERNMENT PRINTING OFFICE: 1989 242-444 00011

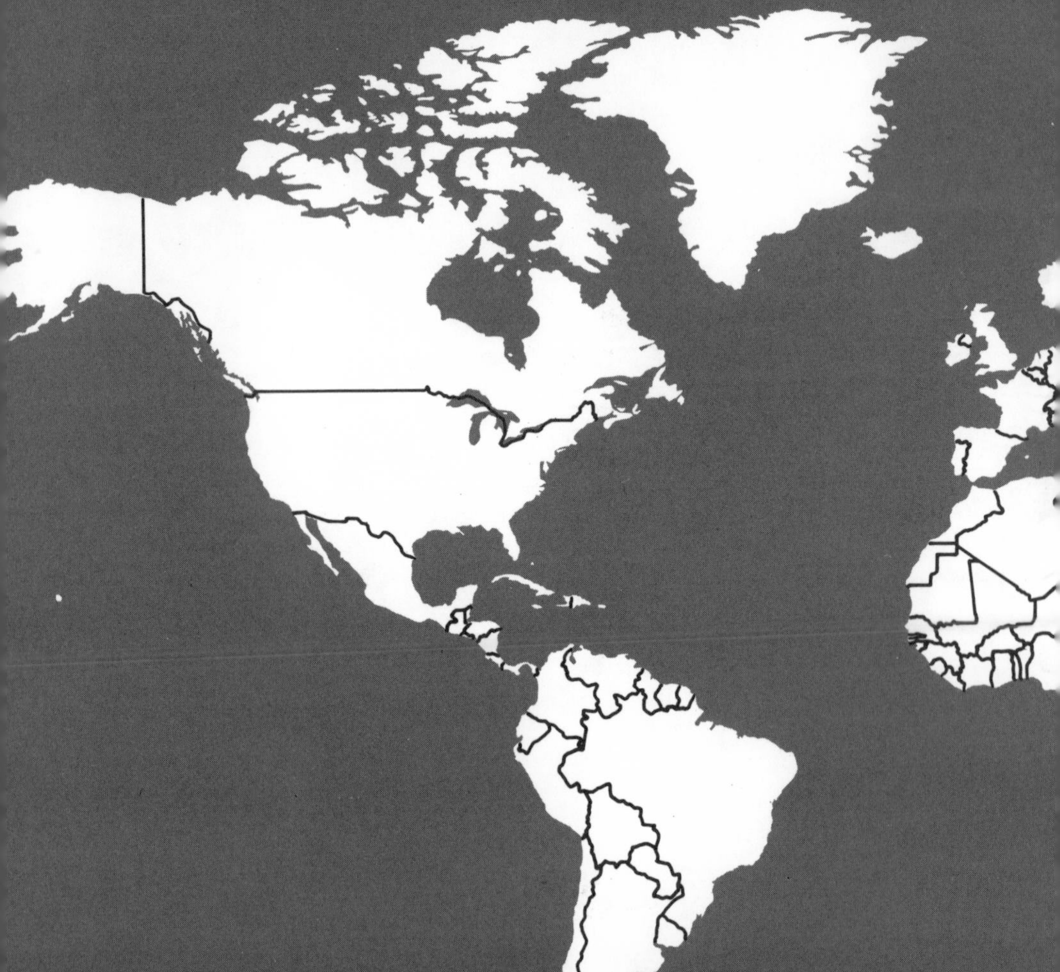